Th

EVENTS, DEAR BOY, EVENTS

'This collection is a delight from beginning to end. There's a gem on almost every page. Such a volume is a great idea, hugely enhanced by Ruth Winstone's brilliant eye.' *Peter Hennessy*

'Diaries are the most intimate historical source, and Ruth Winstone has brilliantly welded together the best of them into a compellingly seductive narrative. We learn of ambition and vanity, of folly and brilliance, of friendship and rivalry, of the law of unintended consequences, and the cumulative effect is like a great rolling novel. Political history has never been so palatable.' *David Kynaston*

'A vivid and vital chronicle of our recent political past, culled from the pages of Britain''s greatest twentieth-century diarists, who were there at the time and saw history happen. It is an enthralling read, full of old friends and new acquaintances, and there is no other book like it!' *David Cannadine*

'Ruth Winstone's edited volume of diary entries provides a fascinating and original series of insights into modern Britain, spanning the years from Lloyd George's coalition of 1918 to that of 2012. Its miscellany of vignettes, drawn from intellectuals and figures from the arts as well as politicians, vividly illuminates the pieces from which the mosaic of British twentieth-century history was constructed.' *Kenneth O. Morgan*

EVENTS, DEAR BOY, EVENTS

*A Political Diary of Britain
from Woolf to Campbell*

EDITED AND INTRODUCED BY
RUTH WINSTONE

PROFILE BOOKS

First published in Great Britain in 2012 by
PROFILE BOOKS LTD
3A Exmouth House
Pine Street
London EC1R 0JH
www.profilebooks.com

Printed and bound in Great Britain by
Clays, Bungay, Suffolk

A CIP catalogue record for this book is available from the British Library.

ISBN 978 1 84668 432 6
eISBN 978 1 84765 463 2

The paper this book is printed on is certified by the © 1996 Forest Stewardship
Council A.C. (FSC). It is ancient-forest friendly. The printer holds FSC chain of
custody SGS-COC-2061

FSC
Mixed Sources
Product group from well-managed
forests and other controlled sources
Cert no. SGS-COC-2061
www.fsc.org
© 1996 Forest Stewardship Council

Contents

Contents

For Joan Marigold

Introduction

On the eve of the millennium, two men confided their anxieties to their diaries. Chris Mullin wondered what kind of a world his (as yet unborn) grandchildren would inherit. Alec Guinness asked 'Oh Sceptre'd Isle set in the polluted sea, where are we heading?' They voiced a more general feeling of awe at the scale of change that had come about in Britain in the twentieth century and of what lay ahead (though they had no inkling of how close 9/11 was).

'Events, dear boy, events', the phrase attributed to Harold Macmillan, makes the point that the unexpected can ruin the best-laid plans. In Macmillan's own time, the abdication of Edward VIII, Dunkirk, the 1945 election, Suez, the Profumo scandal, all challenged expectations and sometimes derailed governments; thirty years later it was the poll tax riots, the Maastricht Treaty, the 9/11 attack, Iraq and the death of David Kelly, the credit crisis, MPs' expenses. There were many straws in the wind to warn of these events, but often straws are ignored until a crisis overtakes everything. Diaries, with no firm idea of what the significance or conclusion might be, record the unfolding events together with all the incidental observations and confidential thoughts of their authors.

The invitation to edit a 'political diary of Britain' was irresistible, not least because tweets and blogs and social networks may have put an end to diary-keeping. It coincided with an exhibition on Identity at the Wellcome Trust in which over a hundred volumes of diaries were on show and the Trust very generously allowed me access to the collection. It included the wartime diaries of General Alan Brooke, Joyce Grenfell and Noël Coward, the 'prison diaries' of both Jimmy Boyle and Lord Longford, *A Year with Swollen Appendices* by Brian Eno, the Alec Guinness volume, and a host of other treasures to augment my existing shelves of political diaries and memoirs which ranged from Harold Nicolson, Tony Benn and Violet Bonham Carter to Gyles Brandreth, Paddy Ashdown and Oona King. The definition of 'political' thus became more and more elastic as *Events, Dear Boy, Events* took shape. No one could appreciate the pressures facing Churchill without reading Brooke's masterfully edited account of the Second World War; or understand the evolution of the Labour Party without the diaries of Beatrice Webb, who had probably the greatest influence on the character of the Labour Party besides Ramsay MacDonald. I read all of these volumes of diaries, and produced a list of just over seventy diarists. Omissions included, regrettably, several whom a different editor of the same book might have considered essential – C. P. Scott, for example, James Lees-Milne and Anthony Powell.

Inevitably in a book of this nature, there are gaps and simplifications – the independence and break up of India, for example, which had long-term consequences still felt today; or Rhodesia's declaration of 'UDI' in 1965 which occupied so much of Harold Wilson's time. It is not a history – there are many fine historians who have interpreted the twentieth century in all its aspects. Nor is it intended to be a nostalgic account of Great Britain. It is an impressionist view of politically changing times – of two wars, loss of the empire, the rise and fall of socialism, devolution, a civil war, global migration, European integration – during which Britons and their institutions have been stolidly resilient. The monarchy, trade unions, love of animals, the BBC, the House of Lords, the established Church (just), horse-racing, shooting and fishing, all-pervasive class differences, the parliamentary and party system, have all survived. And the period began and ended with a coalition government.

It has been a much harder project than I imagined it could possibly be, but made huge fun by John Davey, who has guided me through the book from the start, and Andrew Franklin and the team at Profile Books. It could not have been done without the help of Tony Benn, James Goddard, Jen Laney, Jayne Bryant, Patricia Moberly, David Wedgwood Benn, Christina Weir, Roger Luxton-Jones, Laura Rhode, Tom Arno, Ken Edwards and my remarkable mother Joan Marigold. I am indebted to all those editors whose hard work on the original diaries I have plundered, and who are listed in an appendix (not Brian Eno's!). Readers should be aware that I have retained the style and idiosyncrasies of punctuation and spelling of my diarists, hence the inconsistencies from entry to entry; but I accept all blame for editorial errors.

Ruth Winstone
August 2012

Chapter One

1921–1931
The Internecine Years

After 1918 power ebbed away from the Liberal Party, from British imperialism (slowly) and from unearned wealth, and moved towards organised Labour (fleetingly), the United States of America, the new Soviet Union, and the mighty press proprietors. There was no shortage of diarists to record this fundamentally changing post-war world.

Beatrice Webb – intellectual, well connected and rich – embodied the new creed of socialist paternalism, from which the Labour Party has never escaped; Walter Citrine, an electrician who became a masterful trade union organiser, found himself at the head of the first 'general' strike of labour in 1926. Despite their diametrically opposite origins, their diaries show them united in concluding that the labour movement needed more authoritarian leadership in order to succeed.

For the MPs or future MPs who kept diaries, such as Leo Amery, Harold Nicolson, Henry 'Chips' Channon and Alfred Duff Cooper, it was clear that, personally, they felt their privileges and position under threat, and that politically the Great War and the Treaty of Versailles which followed it had resulted in discontent at home and trouble abroad, particularly in Europe, where even then some saw that the post-war settlement had already created the conditions for the next world war.

Others on the fringes of public life, or beginning their journeys into it, were well placed to observe the sublime and the ridiculous: Lt. Louis Mountbatten, Violet Bonham Carter (daughter of H. H. Asquith, the former prime minister), John Reith (future Director General of the BBC); George Riddell (Lloyd George's media man, an early cross between Rupert Murdoch and Alastair Campbell), Frances Stevenson (Lloyd George's mistress), Thomas Jones (senior civil servant), Robert Bruce Lockhart (diplomat, journalist and spy), the writer/publisher Virginia Woolf, and the novelists Evelyn Waugh and George Orwell.

The collapse of the Liberal Party arose in part from the events of December 1916. Herbert Asquith, whose eldest son had been killed three months earlier in France, was struggling to lead the country in what was a European war for imperial supremacy. Supported by *The Times* and *Daily Mail*,* David Lloyd George, Asquith's Liberal colleague in the Cabinet, replaced Asquith as Prime Minister (but not as Liberal Party leader) and emerged in 1918 as the political hero who had turned disaster into victory – a victory that had cost the lives of over a million British and Empire subjects.

In the General Election that followed, the 'Asquith Liberals' refused to join Lloyd George's new 'Lib–Con' coalition government, which lasted for four years.† By 1926, a number of senior Liberal MPs had transferred allegiance to the new Labour Party. The Asquith–Lloyd George split endured into the next decades, and the party almost died from its wounds. The 'women's war' which had indeed been waged along the lines of a military campaign, entered a 'truce' for the duration of the war and the procrastination and prevarication of the politicians over votes for women could not be sustained after 1918.

By 1922 the Labour Party, resting on the three pillars of socialism, trade unionism and Christianity, had become a political force under the organisational brilliance of its elected chairman and leader, James Ramsay MacDonald. An inconclusive result in the General Election in 1923 led to MacDonald becoming the first Labour Prime Minister of a minority administration. He was a lonely and unhappy figure at Number 10: widowed in 1911 with five children to bring up, he never remarried. This first ever Labour government lasted only a year, to be

---

* *The Times* and the *Daily Mail* were owned, with other papers, by Alfred Harmsworth, the 1st Lord Northcliffe, who was appointed Director of Propaganda by Lloyd George. His brother Harold Harmsworth (the 1st Lord Rothermere) owned the *Daily Record* and *Sunday Pictorial* and, after Northcliffe's death, acquired the *Mail*.

† The so-called 'coupon' election of 1918 returned an overwhelming majority for the Coalition Conservative and Liberal candidates who were officially endorsed by the receipt of the coupon (a letter of support from the Coalition government). Seventy-three Sinn Fein MPs were also elected, but did not take their seats in the Commons. The label 'Unionist' (referring to the supporters of Union with Ireland) was still attached to some candidates and Conservative MPs were often referred to as Unionist MPs.

replaced by the Conservatives who remained the dominant influence in British politics for the next two decades. When Labour returned briefly to government in 1929, interest in the policies and parties of National Socialism on the German and Italian models began to attract some leading politicians from the mainstream parties.

As the first chapter opens, Lloyd George is into the third year of his Coalition – a Liberal Prime Minister depending on Conservative support.

Sunday, 30 January 1921
10 Downing Street

The Prime Minister asked me to come round at 8 o'clock to have some dinner and to sing Welsh hymns.

Miss Stevenson joined us at dinner upstairs and the conversation somehow got quickly on to Victor Hugo. I confessed I had never read any of the novels and this set the PM going and with great eloquence he told us the story of Les Miserables – 'the greatest book ever written not excepting Holy Writ. I have read it twenty times ...'

Sometime during dinner the German indemnity was mentioned. The PM said they could pay the hundred millions a year easily enough. I suggested it was less than the capital of Lord Leverhulme's companies* and that he (the PM) could minimise it by speaking of it in that fashion.

We adjourned to the drawing room and for an hour Miss Stevenson played Welsh music.

Thomas Jones

Tuesday, 8 February 1921

The growing unemployment has added to the ferment of rebellious discontentment. The wonder is that there is not more outward sign of angry resentment. Perhaps it is due to the fact that for the first time some sort of weekly allowance is being received without the stigma of

---

* William Lever was founder and owner, with his brother, of Lever Brothers, soap manufacturers. He built up a business empire with palm oil plantations in the Belgian Congo. He became Lord Leverhulme in 1917.

pauperism ... The principle of deterrence is completely discarded: no one suggests that unemployment is to be punished.

The Labour Party alone has had its enquiry and report (into unemployment) – the Labour Party is more and more taking the position of the only alternative Government to Lloyd George.

Beatrice Webb

Friday, 15 April 1921
Richmond-on-Thames

At 10 tonight, unless something happens meanwhile, all trains, trams, buses, mines and perhaps electric light works come to an end. The servants have been to the Co-ops and brought back a weeks groceries. We have a bundle of candles. Our most serious lack is coal, as Nelly forgot to order any. We burn coke in the drawing room and cook on gas. Still heaven knows why, I don't believe the strike will happen.*

Virginia Woolf

Sunday, 17 April 1921

And I was perfectly right. The strike didn't happen. About 7 o'clock L[eonard] rang up Margaret and heard that the Triple Alliance had split: the railwaymen and transport workers refusing to go on with it, and leaving the miners by themselves. Nothing is yet accurately known. Presumably the miners will have to give in, and I shall get my hot bath, and bake home made bread again; yet it seems a pity somehow – if they're to be forced back and the mine owners triumphant. I think this is my genuine feeling, though not very profound.

Virginia Woolf

*The Triple Alliance between the Miners' Federation of Great Britain, the National Union of Railwaymen and the National Transport Workers' Federation had called a co-ordinated strike in response to threatened wage reductions following the return of the mining industry to private ownership.

Sunday, 24 April 1921

Coal. The opinion in general is that the owners ought never to have put forward such a big cut in wages and that some scheme for graduating the fall should have been devised ... This has been Churchill and Montagu's line and they are right.

Luckily for the Government, the miners confused the issue by flooding the mines and clamouring for a subsidy. The PM [Lloyd George] fastened on this and rode off on the back of the poor pit pony and pulled round ... Then came the collapse of the Triple Alliance and the Red Revolution was postponed once more. It was the most exciting day since the armistice – three Cabinet meetings and endless comings and goings, the PM in great form as the day went on in his favour. The Strike Committee very sick ... The Strike books had been issued ... the troops were steaming in ship and train from Ireland, from Malta, from Silesia to defend us from the men of Fife. The Duke of Northumberland was lecturing about Moscow and the Miners in the *Morning Post* ... I think we shall slide into at any rate a temporary settlement, the owners going without profits for 3 or 4 months, the men putting up with a reduction of from 2 to 3 shillings per day ...

Thomas Jones

Monday, 27 June 1921

Today the manual working class is descending rapidly into destitution: not far off, relatively to the standard they attained during the war, from the destitution they suffered in 1840–50 ... The universal lowering of the wages of the factory operative and the mechanic, and the sweeping away of the Agricultural Wages Board has completed the disillusionment; and the miners are now proved to have been right when they told the other trade unionists that if they were beaten it would be a rout for the whole working class.

Beatrice Webb

Thursday, 14 July 1921
10 Downing Street, Irish negotiations

De Valera has gone, after having been with D[avid Lloyd George] nearly 3 hours. I have never seen D so excited as he was before De Valera arrived, at 4.30. He kept walking in and out of my room and I could see he was working out the best way of dealing with DeV. As I told him afterwards, he was bringing up all his guns! He had a big map of the British empire hung up on the wall in the Cabinet room, with great blotches of red all over it. This was to impress DeV. In fact, D says that the aim of these talks is to impress upon DeV the greatness of the B.E. and to get him to recognise it, and the King. In the course of conversation today D said to DeV: 'The B.E. is a sister-hood of nations – the greatest in the world. Look at this table: There sits Africa – English and Boer; there sits Canada – French, Scotch and English; there sits Australia, representing many races – even Maoris; there sits India; there sit the representatives of England, Scotland and Wales; all we ask you to do is to take your place in this sisterhood of free nations. It is an invitation, Mr De Valera: we invite you here.'

D said he was very difficult to keep to the point – he kept going off at a tangent and talking formulas and refusing to face facts. And every time D seemed to be getting him and De Valera appeared to be warming, he suddenly drew back as if frightened and timid. D says he is the man with the most limited vocabulary he has ever met!

D turned to another tack and said, 'I shall be sorry if this confer-ence fails: terrible as events have been in Ireland, it is nothing to what they will be if we fail to come to an agreement ... I hesitate to think of the horror if war breaks out again in Ireland.'

'But,' said De Valera, getting very excited: 'This is a threat of force – of coercion.' 'No, Mr De Valera,' said D, 'I am simply forecasting what will inevitably happen if these conversations fail, and if you refuse our invitation to join us.'

Frances Stevenson

Monday, 29 August 1921
Scotland

With LG and Mrs LG to Blair Atholl where we remained until Wednesday, when we motored to Inverness. The Duke and Duchess most kind and hospitable. It was interesting to see the relics of the chieftain system – kilted pipers after dinner, kilted gamekeepers and servants – all most impressive.

The Duke says he has to pay 18s 7d in the £ in taxation and fears he will be unable to continue to live at Blair Atholl. As it is, for a part of the year he occupies a small house on the estate. The Duchess is a talented person and a hard worker. She is a brilliant pianist and has composed some excellent music.

George Riddell

Lord Louis Mountbatten accompanied David, the Prince of Wales (later Edward VIII) on a naval tour which took them to India and Japan – both of which countries were especially significant for the young sub-lieutenant.

Thursday, 17 November 1921

HMS *Renown*

We anchored in Bombay Harbour at 6.30 am. I dressed in white full dress at once, as there was a lot to do.

At 9.00 H. E. the naval C-in-C came on board. He left after ten minutes and then the Viceroy, accompanied by Lord Rawlinson (the military C-in-C) and 7 of the Ruling Princes attached to the staff, paid his official call. The Ruling Princes were dressed in their full state clothes and looked magnificent …

When this was all over the official procession started. This was done on a magnificent scale (rather too magnificent to be to David's liking, I fear) … The reception he got was really rather wonderful considering that Mr Mahatma Gandhi had arrived at 7 o'clock this morning and was putting all his forces in the field to boycott David.

Louis Mountbatten

Wednesday, 7 December 1921

The amazing skill with which Lloyd George has carried through the negotiations with his own Cabinet and with Sinn Fein has revolutionised the political situation. Whether or not it be true, few enlightened persons, even among the Liberals and Labour men, believe that any other man could have got this peace by understanding; no other leader could have whipped the Tories to heel and compelled them to recognise the inevitability of Irish independence.

Beatrice Webb

Tuesday, 7 February 1922

A question of conscience has been agitating my mind these days. I read those gruesome accounts of the Russian famine and wonder whether we are not brutes in failing to give all our available income, over and above the requirements for our own work, to the Russian Famine Fund? ... The always present doubt whether, by saving a Chinese or Russian child from dying this year, you will prevent it dying next year, together with the larger question of whether those races are desirable inhabitants, compared to other races, paralyses the charitable impulse. Have we not English children dying from lack of milk? Obviously one would not spend one's available income in saving a Central African negro from starving or dying from disease; I am not certain that I would deny myself to save a Frenchman.

Beatrice Webb

Wednesday, 12 April 1922

Japan

On looking out of the bathroom scuttle at 6.45 a.m. I was able to catch my first glimpse of the famous Fujiyama.

I came on deck in time to see the Japanese First Fleet fire their 21-gun salute. Next to our own service I have never seen such fine ships; any one of them could have taken us on, on equal terms ... I received the impression that here was a power to be reckoned with in a way in which no one who has not been here and seen for himself can possibly conceive ... As we entered the breakwater a flight of aeroplanes flew out to meet us. It is largely owing to General Woodroffe's efforts, when he was last out here, that our R.A.F. are teaching the Naval Air Service here, and most of our officers in the mission are ex-R.N.A.S. men ... Our own people say that the Japanese do not make good pilots.

Louis Mountbatten

Wednesday, 10 May 1922

It was still quite cool today. I think we are all sorry to be leaving such an interesting and picturesque place as Japan, but there can be no doubt about everyone's joy at the prospect of returning home, especially mine! The return voyage is expected to last exactly six weeks.

As regards Japan from the point of view of a world power – my visit has been an eye opener to me as regards her resources, her ships, her army. Their Navy is a crib of ours, their Army bears the unmistakable stamp of Prussia, their newspapers and police are revoltingly American and their ladies copy the latest Paris fashions. Nevertheless they are losing their old stoicism and unless considerable improvement in pay and conditions of living are granted to the services, they will have a mutiny. Japan is paying the penalty of taking civilisation upon her. Unrest is growing among the working classes. Strikes and May Day disturbances have already started. A war might save them, as the people are still ultra patriotic: this is the war I fear.

Louis Mountbatten

Thursday, 22 June 1922

Just heard the sad news about Henry Wilson* – Will the Irish troubles never end? D[avid Lloyd George] very upset as we all are. Whatever he has done lately, he was a most lovable person, and we were very near him during the war. Can scarcely believe the news. It will put the whole Irish question back into the melting pot again. D had been warned ... that there were dangerous Irishmen in London ... but we had been rather inclined to discount the warning at this juncture.

Frances Stevenson

Saturday, 22 July 1922

To Chequers where I remained until Monday morning.

Much talk about trade conditions. The PM most anxious for facts that would confirm his opinion that Germany is on the edge of bankruptcy. Not getting these from Mond or Geddes† he did not pursue the subject. Geddes said that the Dunlop Company, of which he is chairman, have a big bicycle tyre factory in Germany and that one of the best tests of a country's prosperity is the number of bicycle tyres required. Just now his factory cannot turn out enough, which leads

---

* Field Marshal Sir Henry Wilson was assassinated in London by IRA volunteers.
† Guests at Chequers: Alfred Mond was Minister for Health (and founder and first chairman of ICI); Sir Eric Campbell Geddes, a brilliant administrator brought into the war government by Lloyd George to run the military railways, was subsequently appointed First Lord of the Admiralty (despite having no parliamentary or naval experience).

him to think the German working classes, notwithstanding the fall of the mark, are not doing so badly. This was a shock to LG but on the other hand it may well be that the tyres are being exported. Who can tell?

George Riddell

Wednesday, 16 August 1922

I should be reading *Ulysses* and fabricating my case for and against. I have read 200 pages so far – not a third; and have been amused, stimulated, charmed, interested by the first 2 or 3 chapters – to the end of the Cemetery scene; and then puzzled, bored, irritated, and disillusioned as by a queasy undergraduate scratching his pimples. And Tom, great Tom [T. S. Eliot], thinks this on a par with *War and Peace*! An illiterate, underbred book it seems to me …

Virginia Woolf

The Coalition government of Conservatives and Liberals under Lloyd George ended in October 1922, and a General Election was held on 15 November.

Monday, 23 October–late November 1922
Scotland

I felt a very different atmosphere about [the election in] Paisley altogether this time. There were 5,000 unemployed out in the streets and great distress. Coming out of a schoolhouse meeting, a woman said to me 'Could you bring up your children on 15/- a week?' – I said, 'No, I couldn't.' She said, 'Well why should *you* have so much and I so little?' a question to which there is obviously no answer. I never hated anything more than this 'straight fight with Labour' and feeling that they regarded one as a sleek canting capitalist. One might criticise their rudeness – their unfairness – their inaccuracy – their lack of good humour and all of our sense of the courtesies of a fight – but yet emotionally we felt that in their shoes we wld have voted Labour every time. The tide of one's emotions was – however wrongly and unreasonably – with them.

Violet Bonham Carter

Wednesday, 13 December 1922

This morning I had the interview about the BBC. Sir William Noble*
came out to get me and he was smiling in a confidential sort of way.
Present were [representatives of the wireless manufacturers]. I put
it all before God last night. They didn't ask me many questions and
some they did I didn't know the meaning of. (The fact is I hadn't the
remotest idea as to what broadcasting was and I hadn't troubled to
find out. If I had tried I should probably have found difficulty in discovering anyone who knew.) I think they had more or less made up their
minds that I was the man before they saw me and that it was chiefly a
matter of confirmation.

They asked me what salary I wanted and I said £2,000.

John Reith

Thursday, 28 December 1922

I told Mother I wanted her to live to see me a knight anyhow. I feel
if this job succeeds and I am given grace to succeed in it, I might not
be far off this. I do want a title for dear Mother's sake and Muriel's
[Reith's wife] and other similar reasons. May I never forget dear
Mother's prayer. I must take Christ with me from the very beginning
and all through this difficult work. I cannot succeed otherwise. I can
do all things through Christ.

John Reith

Wednesday, 17 January 1923

I spent a couple of hours talking with LG. Labour is the only properly
organised party. Their organisation is about as good as it can be, while
that of the other parties is old-fashioned and inappropriate to present
conditions.

LG said that his difficulty was that if he organised his own party,
that would tend to intensify the differences between him on the one
hand and the Conservatives and Asquithian Liberals on the other. He
said he did not propose to go to the House of Commons much this
session, but intended to help the Government. The position of the

---

* Sir William Noble was Director of the British Broadcasting Company.

nation was far too dangerous for him to oppose rational measures. We required a united front.

George Riddell

Thursday, 1 March–Friday, 2 March 1923
Berlin

Up in the grey dawn of 5.30 and into a crowded train. Dirty plush carriages 3rds converted into 2nds – and 2nds into Firsts. We crawled off very slowly (coal being bad in quality and insufficient in quantity I was told) ... In my carriage was a nice Englishwoman – three intolerable and grotesque music hall Americans and a rather quiet German. The Americans made me very shy by joking all the time about the exchange – '5,000 marks – that's a nickel' – 'shall I give you a million marks or so – that's two American dollars' etc. We got out at the frontier ... I changed £2 for which I received 2,000,000 marks – great bundles of paper chase money which I could hardly carry.

Outwardly everything appears absolutely normal in Berlin.

Big luxury shops full of jewels, furs and flowers – just like the ones in Bond St or Rue de la Paix ... Under the surface, terrible quiet tragedies go on, mostly in respectable middle class homes. People who starve and are ashamed of starving poison themselves every day.

Violet Bonham Carter

Saturday, 28 July 1923
Durham

We have fought our war, we are victorious amid our peace and today there are more men under arms, more reasons for future war, more insecurity, more desire to fight and more standing armies in spite of the hundreds of acres of graveyards strewn over Central Europe ... the one security for peace and for national existence is disarmament.

Ramsay MacDonald

Tuesday, 21 August 1923

We are just about to bring off the connecting up of Savoy Hill [BBC HQ] to all the stations by telephone line at 6.00 pm each night. This is the beginning of SB (Simultaneous Broadcasting) and will bring wonderful results all over.

John Reith

Wednesday, 29 August 1923

I read the news bulletin at 7.00 pm – the first real SB. The switchboard is quite thrilling. Everything went successfully.

John Reith

Monday, 10 September 1923

Everything is now in shape for the BBC Magazine and from various alternatives I chose *Radio Times* for the title.

John Reith

Monday, 3 December 1923

Seaham, Durham – General Election

After an hour's address the other night I found myself being asked a series of questions which seemed to be about every department of foreign and home affairs – our present relations to Russia, the character of the Soviet Government, the capital levy, the Treaty of Versailles, the cure for unemployment, the possibility of protective tariffs, the state of education. I answered to the best of my ability – exactly as I should have done at the London School of Economics. I discovered afterwards that these were the questions with which they had been plying the unfortunate Tory candidate, who tried to evade them and ended by flatly refusing to answer. 'Even our candidate's *wife* can answer our questions – leave alone our candidate,' shouted one miner at the Tory candidate to the delight of the hostile audience.

Beatrice Webb

Wednesday, 12 December 1923

J. R. Macdonald is apparently not capable of personal intimacy: he never had 'loves' among his colleagues. What has happened to him in the blaze of success is that he has lost his hatreds. All men and women are to him just circumstances – an attitude in a leader which I can readily understand and do not altogether disapprove! It is not unlikely that J. R. M. and Sidney will end in a sort of intimacy based on the common task of discovering the great measure of administrative and political efficiency.

Beatrice Webb

Saturday, 5 January 1924
Sussex

A fine still morning and not too cold. The country was looking lovely in its austerest winter garb. The birds were fairly plentiful in the morning and I never shot better – nor indeed so well. Mason says he will probably give up the shoot next year. He can't afford it with a Labour Government in. This will be very sad. We had a capital lunch – Chambertin 1904 – and I was able to shoot three drives in the afternoon where there were not many birds.

Duff Cooper

Tuesday, 8 January 1924

In the evening I went to the Albert Hall to see what was called the Labour Victory demonstration. It was a very tame show. It struck no note of revolution but rather one of respectable middle-class noncon-formity. They sang hymns between the speeches which were all about God.

Duff Cooper

Friday, 18 January 1924

Sidney [Webb] came away feeling that the Cabinet would err on the side of respectability – too many outsiders and too many peers.

... The Inner Cabinet – J. R. MacDonald, Clynes, Snowden, Thomas, Webb, Henderson and Ben Spoor as Chief Whip – met this morning in J. R. M.'s room ... As Sidney expected the Cabinet, which J.R.M. had limited to 14, was now 20 – various important persons having refused to take office *unless in Cabinet*. S is to take Board of Trade on ground that he is to preside over unemployment; Tom Shaw is to be Labour; Wheatley Minister of Health* – both excellent appointments from trade union and left sections standpoints.

Beatrice Webb

Saturday, 26 January 1924

I gather that an unexpected difficulty has occurred regarding the recognition of Russia which MacDonald wishes to effect immediately. It appears that the King [George V] absolutely refused to receive a Soviet Ambassador as that would entail shaking hands with him. It was then suggested that a Minister should be received – but here again the King was adamant. He is an obstinate and outspoken little man.

Harold Nicolson

Monday, 3 March 1924

Mr Asquith, benign, beautiful and patriarchal, presided at the end of the long table and talked, in his clear bell-like Jacobean English, with a wealth of metaphor. Mrs Asquith, distraite, smoked and read the papers during luncheon, and occasionally said something startling like, a propos of spiritualism, 'I always knew the living talked rot, but it is nothing to the nonsense the dead talk.' She also said she could not help being sorry for ghosts – 'Their appearances are so against them.'

Henry 'Chips' Channon

Friday, 7 March 1924

Have a long talk with Ramsay MacDonald in the morning regarding Anglo-Italian relations. He sits there puffing at a pipe and very dour and sad and disillusioned. He waggles his leg with impatience, perplexity or despair, and yet he does not seem to wish to hurry the conversation, but goes slowly, slowly. Rather tentative are his remarks and very

---

*John Wheatley, Labour MP for Glasgow Shettleston, was best known for the 'Wheatley' Housing Act of 1924, which greatly expanded municipal housing.

Scotch in sound. He flares up at once at the thought of Mussolini. His eyes give a sudden flash: 'The greatest rascal in the world.'

Harold Nicolson

Saturday, 15 March 1924

What interests me as a student of the British Constitution is the unlimited autocracy of the British P.M. – if he chooses to be autocratic or slips into it through inertia or dislike of discussion. It was MacDonald who alone determined who should be in his Cabinet; it is MacDonald who alone is determining what the Parliamentary Labour Party shall stand for in the country. So far as I gather from S and other members of the Cabinet, they are not consulted about what shall be the attitude towards France; certainly no documents are circulated prior to despatch ... The PM alone determines what line he takes toward other countries.

MacDonald wants 8 million voters behind him and means to get them even if this entails shedding the Independent Labour Party, the idealistically revolutionary section who pushed him into power. That ladder will be kicked down!

Beatrice Webb

Saturday, 17 May 1924

I have had two miners' wives from the Seaham Division staying with me for the Women's Conference.

What interested me was the moral refinement and perfect manners of these two women who had never seen London before and never stayed in a house with servants. One of them was a delicate, excitable and intellectual woman – the other a phlegmatic Scot – they were attractively clothed and their talk was mostly about public affairs – the one emotionally stirred by the Socialist faith and familiar with all its shibboleths; the other shrewd, cautious and matter-of-fact ... They were completely at their ease and their attitude to their host and hostess was more towards a class teacher and a minister of religion than to social superiors.

Beatrice Webb

Saturday, 5 July 1924

Just back ... from Knole, where indeed I was invited to lunch alone with his Lordship.* His Lordship lives in the kernel of a vast nut. You perambulate miles of galleries; skip endless treasures – chairs that Shakespeare might have sat on – tapestries, pictures, floors made of the halves of oaks; and penetrate at length to a round shiny table with a cover laid for one. A dozen glasses form a circle, each with a red rose in it. What can one human being do to decorate itself in such a setting? One feels that one ought to be an elephant able to consume flocks and be hung about with whole blossoming trees – whereas one solitary peer sits lunching by himself in the centre, with his napkin folded into the shape of a lotus flower ...

It's the breeding of Vita's that I took away with me as an impression, carrying her and Knole in my eye as I travelled up with the lower middle classes, through slums. There is Knole, capable of housing all the desperate poor of Judd Street, and with only that one solitary earl in the kernel.

Virginia Woolf

Wednesday, 29 October 1924

Here ends the episode of a Labour Government and also of a Minority Government – an episode which Sidney thinks, on the whole, good for the education of the Party – and as far as he is concerned, a good joke, which like most good jokes, ought not to be repeated. J R MacDonald remains an enigma: we certainly did not expect and cannot now explain either the brilliant success of his handling of the Franco-German situation or the shocking fiasco of the last phase of his Premiership – culminating in the complete collapse of any Cabinet leadership during the General Election.

Beatrice Webb

---

*Lord Sackville (Lionel Sackville-West, 3rd Baron Sackville). Knole was the fifteenth-century family home of the Sackville-Wests, near Sevenoaks, Kent. Lord Sackville's only child, Vita, was Harold Nicolson's wife and Virginia Woolf's friend and lover. When Lord Sackville died, and the inheritance passed to a male relative, Vita was left without a home, which led to the Nicolsons' decision to buy Sissinghurst.

In the General Election of 29 October 1924, the Conservatives were returned with a 200-plus majority of MPs. For the Liberal Party, the results spelled the end, with only forty Liberals of all hues elected.

Sunday, 1 February 1925

We have suffered a severe blow from this government ... Actually behaving far worse to us at the Admiralty than the Labour Party. Of course it is all Winston as Chancellor. He has gone economy mad, and the result is that the Govt are not proposing to build any cruisers at all. Well, this obviously has to be fought, and if I have never done anything else of value for my country I must withstand this at all costs.

[Admiral] David Beatty

Thursday, 27 March 1925

Muriel and I dined at No. 10 with the PM and Mrs Baldwin; no one else was there. They were very friendly. I think I did some useful work for Broadcasting. Going to Savoy Hill (BBC Headquarters) there was a detective in the front of the car and the PM was very funny about him. He said it was one of the great perquisites of the office and that he thought he had obtained true eminence when his car drove down the wrong side of Piccadilly one day when he was in a hurry. I suggested that my ability to broadcast from my own study was also greatness in a form, to which he agreed. The PM said he would like to have a [broadcasting set-up] at Chequers, so I said we would supply him with one, or would he prefer to pay for it. He said he does not like sponging on anyone but quite frankly he would like to have it given to him, and that he was overdrawn at the bank. He said he used to be quite well to do but there was no money in his present job.

John Reith

Spring 1925
Miners' Conference

Arthur Cook,* excitable and fiery, hammered home his points vehemently, in contrast with Herbert Smith, the miners' president. I liked

---

* A. J. Cook, General Secretary of the Miners' Federation of Great Britain.

this old man. Smith was as straight as a die. I liked his calm way of looking at difficulties. Always cool and steady, he never got flustered. There he sat in his blue suit and soft collar, with his little moustache turning grey, and his high balding forehead, with his spectacles resting on the end of his nose.

Practically all of [the miners' delegates] with the exception of Cook and Noah Ablett, and I think two others, were past middle-age. There was old Straker of Northumberland, neatly dressed – boots well-polished, hair carefully parted at the side and his little goatee beard trimmed well, sitting quiet – more like a Sunday-school teacher than anything else, one of the most vigorous opponents of the new agreements. Then there was Tom Richards from South Wales, trembling of head and hand like a man with shell-shock. I don't know what is the matter with him but he is always the same – old and evidently not in very good health but with a perfectly clear mind – always to the point. Then old Finney of Staffordshire – brown eyes with a mild expression in them – more like a kindly grandfather than a vigorous, aggressive trade unionist. Yet these are the men who in a few weeks from now will be denounced as Bolshevists and extremists.

Old and young are marked with the bluish powder and coal dust of shot-firing, which identifies the miner at once.

Walter Citrine

Wednesday, 12 August 1925

For three months I have written nothing ...

During the summer I read a paper on Egypt to the Institute of International Affairs, spoke on the League of Nations at East Ham, addressed an assembly of teachers, went to Walsall for a Conservative fete, went twice to Oldham and spoke twice in the House.

I wanted to speak on the naval debate – against the construction of the cruisers – but I couldn't get in.

We had a heavenly Whitsuntide at the cottage in Bognor – one of the best weeks I have ever had. I saw Daisy and Dollie once or twice but had no other affairs.

Duff Cooper

Monday, 14 September 1925
Rodmell, Sussex

A disgraceful fact – I am writing this at 10 in the morning in bed in the little room looking into the garden, the sun beaming steady, the vine leaves transparent green ...

We have been in the throes of the usual servant crisis ... Nelly says Lottie wants to come back; we offer to have her; she denies it – to Karin ...

But we are on the laps of the Gods: we don't intend to raise a finger either way.

Virginia Woolf

Tuesday, 15 September 1925

After we had drunk some beer in a slum bar we went on to Mary's where we found some very odd painters quite drunk and rather naked. They were for the most part what Mary called 'Paris Queers'. The party was given in honour of a negro who is acting in a play called *Emperor Jones* but he had a fit in his dressing-room.

Evelyn Waugh

Thursday, 24 September 1925
Rodmell, Sussex

Sad to think a week only left of this partially wrecked summer ... Maynard and Lydia* came here yesterday – Maynard in Tolstoi's blouse and Russian cap of black astrachan – A fair sight both of them to meet on the high road! ... my heart, in this autumn of my age, slightly warms to him, whom I've known all these years, so truculently pugnaciously and unintimately. We had very brisk talk of Russia: such a hotch-potch, such a mad jumble, M says, of good and bad, and the most extreme things that he can make no composition of it – can't yet see how it goes. Briefly, spies everywhere, no liberty of speech, greed for money eradicated, people living in common, yet some, L[ydia]'s mother for instance with servants, peasants contented because they own land, no sign of revolution ...

But to tell the truth I am exacerbated this morning ... Lily is a

---

*Economist John Maynard Keynes and his Russian ballerina wife, Lydia Lopokova.

wide-eyed sheep dog girl who comes from Iford to 'do'; but can't scramble an egg or bake a potato, and is thus ill armed for life, so far as I can see.

Virginia Woolf

Saturday, 26 September 1925
Midland Hotel, Manchester

I spent the morning in my room reading and preparing a speech, and after a fortifying luncheon I proceeded in the train and the rain to Oldham where I stood on the step of the Town Hall while 2,500 boy scouts filed past. Thence I went to the Blue Coat School and then to a terrible tea which lasted from five to seven in Greenacres Hall. Then I had to make my speech to this enormous audience of small boys. I hadn't realised what it would be and had prepared quite the wrong sort of speech. It was a failure but I doubt it could have been a success. I knew I wasn't holding their attention – a terrible feeling which I have never had before. Afterwards I attended a small meeting of the chief members of my executive committee, whom I found very dissatisfied and critical of the [Conservative] Government. Their main grounds of criticism are: 1. The failure to deal with the political levy 2. The settlement of the French debt 3. The subsidy to the miners 4. The alleged weakness in dealing with the Reds. I did my best to satisfy them. The Hall porter this morning told me to back Seredella for the Newbury Cup.

Duff Cooper

Sunday, 18 April 1926

During the last few days I have been allowing people to arouse me to the fact that there is probably going to be a general coal strike at the end of the month and the hope that its consequences are incalculable. And I have begun to think whether perhaps April 1926 may not in time rank with 1914 for the staging of house parties in sociological novels. I suppose that the desire to merge one's individual destiny in forces outside oneself, which seems to me deeply rooted in most people and shows itself in social service and mysticism and in some manner debauchery, is really only a consciousness that this is already the real mechanism of life which requires so much concentration to perceive that one wishes to objectify it in more immediate (and themselves subordinate) forces. How badly I write when there is no audience to arrange my thoughts for.

Evelyn Waugh

Tuesday, 4 May 1926

Although the strike did not actually start until midnight, many of the workers had been coming out in anticipation. It appears that the article which should have appeared in the *Mail* denounced the TUC General Council and the trade union movement as enemies of the King. It is alleged that we were out to smash the constitution and starve the women and children. The men would not print it and it was sent round to the *Evening News*. The compositors there refused to set it and came out.

The movement spread, with the consequence that last evening, there was not a single newspaper in the city …

The strike is complete. The reports are simply marvellous. Everywhere the utmost solidarity and eagerness to respond to the Council's instructions.

There has been an attempt to print *The Times* and the police have drawn a cordon across the road to Printing House Square, and are constantly preventing the pickets getting near the place. I phoned the Superintendent in charge and he agreed to allow six pickets to pass, so that two could picket at each of the three doors of the building.

Walter Citrine

Wednesday, 5 May 1926

The emergency news service is getting under way. I am vetting every item of every bulletin.

Things are really badly muddled and Churchill [Chancellor of the Exchequer] wants to commandeer the BBC. I met [the Home Secretary] who broadcast an appeal for 5,000 special constables. I had a talk with him after about the BBC position and got him to agree to what I wanted.

John Reith

Saturday, 8 May 1926

This morning we had a telegram from the All-Union Central Council of Trade Unions of Russia and a cheque from their bank for £26,000. We decided we could not accept this and to return the money.

A heated discussion took place this morning at the General Council because of speeches by Cook and Herbert Smith, who insisted that the miners should be included in discussions that were taking place with Samuel.* Bromley, of the locomotive men, was very emphatic. 'By God we are all in this now and I want to say to the miners in a brotherly, comradely spirit, but straight – that this is not a miners' fight now. I am willing to fight right along with them and to suffer as a consequence, but I am not going to be strangled by my friends.'

Walter Citrine

Sunday, 9 May 1926

Baldwin broadcast last night: he rolls his *rs*; tries to put more than mortal strength into his words. 'Have faith in me. You elected me 18 months ago. What have I done to forfeit your confidence? Can you not trust me to see justice done between man and man?' ...

No I don't trust him: I don't trust any human being, however loud they bellow and roll their *rs*.

Virginia Woolf

Tuesday, 11 May 1926

On Wednesday reports of rioting had come in from all big towns and they have gone on ever since. Richard and I had gone down to Hammersmith to see what was going on but arrived too late, after the police had made a baton charge and recaptured six motor buses which the strikers had broken.

Evelyn Waugh

---

* Herbert Samuel, chairman of the 1925 Royal Commission into the Coal Industry. The recommendation of the Samuel Commission, including reorganisation of the industry and reductions in miners' wages, contributed to the General Strike.

Wednesday, 12 May 1926

We have had our General Strike. Imperfect as it has been, mechanically and in the evolution of policy, it has been the most magnificent effort of rank-and-file solidarity that the British movement has ever displayed. Never again will the Congress undertake the custodianship of any movement without the clear, specific and unalterable understanding that the General Council and the General Council alone shall have the free untrammelled right to determine policy.

How can we, with the millions of interests and considerations to review, allow our policy to be dominated entirely by considerations of one union only [the miners]?

Were we to continue the disruption and dismemberment of the railway and transport unions? To bleed white the organisations who had thrown their all into the melting pot? To sacrifice the individual members who, faced by heavy penalties for breach of contract, had responded with unparalleled loyalty to the call of the movement?

The outstanding lesson of the General Strike of 1926 is that authority must be vested exclusively and entirely in the directing body.

Walter Citrine

May 1926

For the British Trade Union Movement I see a day of terrible disillusionment. The failure of the General Strike of 1926 will be one of the most significant landmarks in the history of the British working class. Future historians will I think regard it as the death gasp of that pernicious doctrine of 'workers' control' of public affairs through the trade unions, and by the method of direct action. This absurd doctrine was introduced into British working class life by Tom Mann and the Guild Socialists* and preached insistently before the War, by the *Daily Herald* and George Lansbury. In Russia it was quickly repudiated by Lenin and the Soviets ...

On the whole I think it was a proletarian distemper which had to run its course and like other distempers it is well to have it over and done with at the cost of a lengthy convalescence.

Beatrice Webb

---

* Guild socialism advocated workers' democratic control of industry, mediated through trade-based associations and inspired by the medieval guild system.

Friday, 21 May 1926

Last night D[avid Lloyd George] dined with me. I left the office about 6.30 and he was to come on at 7.30. He was a little late, and came in very excitedly, so that I could see something had happened. 'I have been expelled from the Party.' ... The Asquith women are of course at the bottom of it. My chief concern last night was to get D into a calm frame of mind. It was a blow for him – rather a cruel one. It faced him with a crisis the like of which he had not quite experienced before. He has now before him a fight for his political life.*

Frances Stevenson

Friday, 16 July 1926

I do hope you won't make Mummy nervous by being too wild. Of course men must work, and women must weep, but all the same I do hope that you will remember that Mummy is a frightful coward and does fuss dreadfully about you. It is a good rule always to ask before you do anything awfully dangerous. Thus if you say, 'Mummy, may I try and walk on the roof of the green-house on my stilts?', she will probably say 'Of course darling', since she is not in any way a narrow-minded woman. And if you say, 'Mummy, may I light a fire in my bed?', she will again say, 'Certainly, Niggs.' It is only that she likes being told about these things beforehand.

Harold Nicolson to Nigel (aged nine)

Wednesday, 10 November 1926

The poor [Liberal] Party seems faced with two alternatives – to starve or be bought. I believe that without LlG and his corrupting fund in the background,† it could have saved itself by its own efforts and lived as the Labour Party does – more cheaply – but on democratic finance –

---

*That fight led to Lloyd George becoming the Leader of the Liberal Party for the first time, replacing Asquith who had been leader since 1908. As a result, a number of Liberal MPs left and joined the Labour Party.
† A reference to the 'cash for honours' scandal that engulfed Lloyd George in the mid-1920s. The scandal led to the passing of the Honours (Prevention of Abuses) Act 1925.

but with doles and bribes, fantastic salaries and champagne lunches flung in all directions it cannot possibly do so.

It is so different from the feeling one had in 1918. The Party was clean – we had no Jonah on board.

Violet Bonham Carter

Monday, 7 February 1927
Passfield Corner

Ellen Wilkinson reached here on Friday for lunch, in a state of collapse from over-speaking at great mass meetings mainly about China.

The daughter of a Lancashire cotton-spinner of rebellious temper and religious outlook she passed from the elementary school to the pupil-teacher centre from thence on a scholarship into Manchester University where she took a good degree ... and finally landed herself in the House of Commons in 1924 as MP for Middlesbrough.

She believes the present trend of trade unionism is towards *one big Union*! She believes it because it is the catchword of today – just as 'workers control' was the catchword of yesterday. Certainly one big union is inconsistent with workers' control; but that does not trouble her.

If the Labour Movement fails to provide the right environment for the development of statesmanship, the government of the country will remain during long periods in the hands of the present governing class who have both brains and leisure; with short futile intervals of Labour Cabinets, tossed in and out of power by conflicting waves of rebellious doctrine, each successive term ending in apathy or disillusionment and party disintegration.

Beatrice Webb

Sunday, 14 August 1927

Dined with 'Tommy' [Lady Rosslyn], Hamish ... and Twiston. After dinner, talked to the two boys who made my hair curl with stories about immorality and drinking at Eton and Oxford. The modern youth seems to grow up much more quickly than in my day.

Robert Bruce Lockhart

Tuesday, 20 September 1927

[Sidney and I] have started an investigation into the present administration of outdoor relief to the able-bodied up and down the country.

Can we discover the new issues and gauge the new proportions of the problems involved e.g. chronic unemployment? And is there any practicable solution, should this unemployment prove not only to be chronic but also progressive? If such a disaster is imminent will any change in administration, policy and procedure avail to alter the result? Might it not be a question of muddling through, curbing and checking the present Poor Law administration until a lowered birth rate, emigration and even a higher death-rate brought about a new equilibrium of population with national resources?

Beatrice Webb

Friday, 13 April 1928

Winston Churchill asked me to go and see him at the Treasury this afternoon. I was there for about an hour, he giving me tea. Churchill was anxious to know what we were going to do about the Budget. I said we were ready to broadcast from the House of Commons direct, but that it had been turned down. He asked me to have another try for this with the PM and added that I had a great influence with him. I told him what we were going to do otherwise, and he said he would like to come to the studio and speak for 15 minutes the next night, factual and uncontroversial. Much discussion about the handling of political controversy. He asked if the rumours of my leaving the BBC were true and said he was very thankful they were not. He said he thought I had about the biggest job in the country.

John Reith

Wednesday, 2 May 1928

There has been an event lurking in the background of our life – intensely interesting but unimportant to us personally – the break-up of the Christian church in Great Britain. The rejection of the revised Prayer Book by Parliament and the consequent unseemly controversy which has raged among the ecclesiastics – the revelation of an indifferent and almost scornful public opinion – has awakened the English public to the fact that the English are no longer Christians in any real sense of the word. No one troubles to assert this fact, and no one denies it. What is becoming something near a public scandal is the paucity of candidates alike for the Anglican priesthood and for the Free Church ministry. Meanwhile Dean Inge openly advises in the pages of a profane journal, that no candidate for order now believes in the supernatural element in the Christian faith ... How long this queer state of mind, the Church, with its creed and its rites, its pomps and its ceremonies, can continue part of the British Constitution is difficult to foretell!

Beatrice Webb

Sunday, 23 September 1928
Evening Standard, London

Had a long talk with Lord Beaverbrook this morning about foreign politics. He is very anti-League (of Nations), thinks that war in Europe is inevitable and that, if we stay out, a European war might be just as advantageous to us as the last war was to America. Therefore we must pull out of the League. I think he is wrong. The way to get war is to say it is coming, and I doubt if we could keep out of a big European war.

Robert Bruce Lockhart

Sunday, 7 October 1928

The Labour Party is doing well in the country: J R MacDonald and Henderson and the Evolutionists have swept Communism and left-wingism out of the way, Maxton and Cook have fizzled out and Liberalism shows little signs of being a powerful rival for progressive support. All's well for electoral purposes. Whether it is equally well for the business of government, if or when the LP gets into power is another question! It depends on the young men of the party and the persistency of the British working-class and the self-devotion of the brain-working adherents to Socialist principles.

Beatrice Webb

Friday, 19 October 1928

Lloyd George's day. Great speech in morning on tactics of party and great speech at night on foreign policy. Latter was very dramatic. He came down to hall, armed with a copy of the treaty of Versailles, said we ourselves went to war for a scrap of paper, and now we had not kept our own word with Germany.

LG is still the greatest dynamic force in British politics.

Robert Bruce Lockhart

Thursday, 6 December 1928

*Letter to the Prince of Wales from his younger brother**

My dear old David

Since writing to you this evening I have seen Dawson.† Papa's temperature has gone up again tonight which is a worry but has not altered papa's condition very materially ...

There is a lovely story going about which emanated from the East End that the reason of your rushing home is that in the event of anything happening to Papa I am going to bag the throne in your absence!!!! Just like the Middle Ages ...

Ever yours

Bertie

The General Election of 30 May 1929 returned 288 Labour MPs – its best result since its formation – but without an overall majority, the Liberals (relatively united) holding the balance. During the short-lived Labour government, negotiations were held in London to agree self-imposed limits on the world's greatest naval powers: Great Britain, the USA, Japan, France and Italy. Britain and the USA were to retain supremacy in numbers of ships and tonnage. There were also talks aimed at finding a compromise on Indian self-rule.

Lord Beaverbrook (Max Aitken), ally of Lloyd George in the First World War, and of Churchill in the Second, campaigned through his newspapers for a policy of 'imperial preference' in trade during the inter-war years, though the Conservative Party was not entirely in favour. Harold Nicolson found himself working for Beaverbrook's papers, the Evening Standard *and* Daily Express. *Leo Amery, a minister in Conservative governments in the 1920s, turned to business in the 1930s, and was also*

---

*Letter quoted from *A King's Story: the Memoir of HRH the Duke of Windsor* (Cassell, 1951).
†The King's doctor, Bertrand Dawson.

an early proponent of Zionism in the Conservative Party.

Friday, 31 May 1929

London

The oculist said to me this afternoon 'Perhaps you're not as young as you were.' This is the first time that has been said to me: and it seemed to me an astonishing statement. It means that one now seems to a stranger not a woman, but an elderly woman. Yet even so, though I felt wrinkled and aged for an hour, and put on a manner of great wisdom and toleration ... even so I forgot it soon; and am 'a woman' again.

Coming up Southampton Row, a man snapped me and then said stop; and made me pay 6d for a silly little damp film, which I did not want ... my face marked me for his victim.

'We are winning' Nelly [a servant] said at tea. I was shocked to think that *we both* desire the Labour Party to win – why? Partly that I don't want to be ruled by Nelly. I think to be ruled by Nelly and Lottie would be a disaster.

Virginia Woolf

Thursday, 27 June 1929

Talk with Neville Chamberlain the first I have had with any of my late colleagues about the situation. He told me that Lloyd George is very anxious to bring about the fall of the present (Labour) Government at the earliest possible moment, his fear being that if they continue for two or three years and behave moderately half the Liberal party will join them. His notion is to get us in some way to cooperate on some committee dealing with electoral reform. I hoped that we would have no truck with any such scheme both because of my general objection to coalitionism and because I felt sure that the only immediate result would be indignation among the working classes that even a moderate Labour government had been ejected by capitalist intrigue.

Leo Amery

Tuesday, 16 July 1929

A good talk with Chancellor (after lunch). He [Philip Snowden] was rather anxious at the extent to which the Zionists are letting in a Communist type of Jew as well as by the growing restlessness of the Arabs and thinks some sort of nominated council will have to be created.

Leo Amery

Tuesday, 22 October 1929

I meet First Lord of the Admiralty [A. V. Alexander], in Whitehall. The Admirals, I fear, have got a firm grip on him.

He has been to sea with the Battle Fleet, and believes that there is a new gun which will shoot down aeroplanes from the sky. 'I could fire it myself,' he says, 'and write my name in the sky in letters of smoke. No aeroplane could live under such fire.' He denounces the Air Force. They are very dangerous. They have the ear of the Cabinet, of every Cabinet.

Hugh Dalton

Wednesday, 4 December 1929

[William] Wedgwood Benn and Phil [Noel-Baker] to lunch to talk Five Power Conference and battleships in particular. Wedgwood Benn is to be our fourth principal delegate ... I think Wedgwood Benn will be on the side of the Angels. He says truly that the leaders of our Party have talked so long, without having the power to act, that now they are excessively timid in action.

Phil and I press on him the need to cut down battleships, thus making a Peace gesture and saving money. We must never lay down a battleship again. We haven't done so since 1922 and it would be intolerable to start again in 1931, even the smaller, cheaper kind which our Admiralty propose.

Hugh Dalton

Thursday, 23 January 1930

I was summoned by Lord Beaverbrook ... (found him) alone writing a cross letter to his son about bills. In a few minutes Winston Churchill slouched in. Very changed from when I last saw him. A great round face like a blister. Incredibly aged ... His spirits also have declined and he sighs that he has lost his old fighting power.

They talked the whole time about Empire free trade. Winston says that he has abandoned all his convictions and clings to the conviction of free trade as the only one which is left to him. But he is clearly disturbed at the effect on the country of Beaverbrook's propaganda. He feels too old to fight it. 'Thirty years ago,' he said, 'I should have welcomed such a combat: now I dread it.' He seems to think Baldwin absolutely hopeless ...

Beaverbrook uses every wile to secure if not his support then at least his agreement not to oppose. I must say he is rather impressive. Young and nervous he walks about the room piling argument on argument and statistic on statistic. There is no question but that he is passionately sincere and has really studied his subject.

Harold Nicolson

Wednesday, 26 March 1930

On to the *Daily Express* office ... I see an intolerable man who treats me and literature as if they were both dirt.

To make it worse I am sent out to represent the *Standard* at the Knights of the Round Table dinner. There is no seat for me and I creep away in dismay and humiliation. I never foresaw that writing for the Press would actually be so degrading.

Harold Nicolson

Wednesday, 21 May 1930

Mosley resigns [from Government over unemployment policy]. If the Government survives this summer it will be by the tacit connivance of the other two parties who are not ready for an election. Also public opinion is against it on the ground that Great Britain mustn't show division of opinion now it is confronted with revolution in India.

Beatrice Webb

Thursday, 29 May 1930

Has MacDonald found his superseder in Oswald Mosley? MacDonald owes his pre-eminence largely to the fact that he's the only artist, the only aristocrat by temperament and talent in a party of plebeians and plain men. Hitherto he has had no competitor in personal charm and good looks, delightful voice and the gift of oratory. But Mosley has all these, with the élan of youth, wealth and social position added to them. Like MacDonald Mosley began as a Utopian but today he is a disillusioned Utopian, while Mosley has still a young man's zeal and is, I think, able to use other men's brains.

Beatrice Webb

Wednesday, 9 July 1930

Lady Astor had been tittle-tattling all round the lobbies about MacDonald and Lady Londonderry. And Virginia Woolf – with whom we dined on 11th July – supported this: MacDonald and Lady L. had withdrawn after dinner into a half-darkened room and sat together – the common herd being herded into another, more brightly lit chamber.

What easy prey some of our people are! And how they are laughed at behind their backs, and ignored when they are out of office!

Virginia Woolf quoted Beatrice Webb to her, 'Marriage is the waste-paper basket of the emotions.'

Hugh Dalton

Saturday, 23 August 1930
At the Sitwells' home

Went to Renishaw. The household was very full of plots. Almost everything was a secret and most of the conversations deliberately engineered in prosecution of some private joke. Ginger, for instance, was told that Ankaret's two subjects were arctic exploration and ecclesiastical instruments; also that Alastair played the violin. Sachie liked talking about sex. Osbert was very shy. Edith wholly ignorant ...

The servants very curious. They live on terms of feudal familiarity, e.g. a message brought by footman to assembled family that her ladyship wanted to see Miss Edith upstairs. 'I can't go, I've been with her all day, Osbert, you go.' 'Georgia, you go' etc. Footman: 'Well, come on. One of you's got to go.'

Evelyn Waugh

Tuesday, 9 September 1930

Baldwin must wish to hurry on a General Election before he is dismissed by Beaverbrook and Rothermere. The Labour Party will be decisively beaten at the polls and I think JRM will cease to be leader and Arthur Henderson will succeed him. Great Britain will become protectionist under Neville Chamberlain's premiership ...

With two million unemployed there is as yet not the remotest sign of *urgent discontent,* no soup kitchens, no newspaper agitation, no frantic appeals for money, no growth in the Communist Party ... have large bodies of men become reconciled to an idle life on a *secure* but low level of consumption?

Beatrice Webb

Saturday, 4 October 1930
Passfield Corner

A spate of high-class social functions this week – I avoid two dinners and receptions at Lancaster House but got through two lunches and an afternoon gathering in a little over 24 hours, and a Buckingham Palace state dinner on Friday, returning here for the middle of the week to rest and write letters.

Beatrice Webb

Sunday, 5 October 1930

We start off at 10 to motor to Chequers. On passing through Bromley we half-see a poster blown by the wind which looks like 'Airship destroyed.' We stop later and buy a paper. We find that the R.101 has crashed near Beauvais and that [the Air Secretary, Lord] Thomson with 43 other people have been burnt alive.

When we arrive we find that the PM is up in London. Ishbel (his daughter) says he will be in a dreadful state. He arrives about 1.30. He looks very ill and worn. Bennett, the Prime Minister of Canada is there. Ramsay begins to introduce him to Vita but forgets his name.

He makes a hopeless gesture – his hand upon his white hair – 'My brain is going', he says, 'my brain is going.' It is all rather embarrassing. He then tells us that the bell beside his bed had rung that morning ... he dashed up to London in 55 minutes.

The King was in a dreadful state. Ramsay seemed more worried about the King's dismay than about anything else.

The PM pours out to Vita the miseries of his soul: he cannot sleep: two hours a night is all he gets: he can do no work: 'the moment I disentangle my foot from one strand of barbed wire it becomes entangled in another. If God were to come to me and say "Ramsay, would you rather be a country gentleman than Prime Minister?" I should reply, "Please God, a country gentleman."' He is a tired, exhausted man. Bless him.

Harold Nicolson

Monday, 22 December 1930

Bertram Mills gives a luncheon for 1,100 people at Olympia. I am about to enter when I hear a voice behind me. It is Ramsay MacDonald. He says, 'Well this is my one holiday in the year, I love circuses.' At that moment they hand him a telegram. He opens it. He hands it to me with the words, 'Keep this, my dear Harold, and read it if ever you think you wish to be Prime Minister.' It is a telegram from some crank society abusing him for attending a luncheon in honour of a circus proprietor – since performing animals are cruel. He is disgusted and his pleasure spoiled.

Harold Nicolson

Wednesday, 25 February 1931

An amazing act of arrogance, Oswald Mosley's melodramatic defection from the Labour Party, slamming the door with a bang to resound throughout the political world. His one remaining chance is to become the He-man of the Newspaper Lords in their campaign against Baldwin's leadership of the Conservative Party. But Mosley's egotism would presently clash with Beaverbrook's and they would part company. As an orator – as a platform performer in a political circus – he would be pre-eminent. A foreign journalist at the Labour Party Conference nicknamed him the 'English Hitler'. But the British electorate would not stand a Hitler. Mosley has bad health, a slight intelligence and an unstable character – I doubt whether he has the tenacity of a Hitler. He also lacks genuine fanaticism. Deep down in his heart he is a cynic. He will be beaten and retire. In the chaos of our political life today there will still be many meteors passing through the firmament. There is still Winston Churchill to be accounted for. Have there ever been so many political personages on the loose?

Beatrice Webb

Wednesday, 29 April 1931

I drove back with Margot* who, as usual, is very bitter about everything. She is furious with me for joining [Mosley's] New Party and tries to imply that this is a personal disloyalty to the memory of old Asquith. When I said that it would be equally disloyal to my affection for that old man, to have joined Lloyd George, she merely pinched me very hard with a long, claw-like hand and tells me not to become tiresome ...

Dined with Clive Bell and Keynes. Keynes is very helpful about the economics of the New Party. He says that he would, without question, vote for it. The attitude of the Labour Party on the Sunday Cinema Bill ... has disgusted him. He feels that our Party may really do an immense amount of good and that our Programme is more sound and certainly more daring than that which any other party can advance.

Harold Nicolson

Tuesday, 30 June 1931

One of the reasons given for the alleged decline of Great Britain and her approaching doom is that the Englishman has lost his love of money. Now it so happens that the Russians, whether rich or poor, were before the revolution one of the most dishonest and dishonourable of peoples. Hence the terrific discipline enforced by the Communist party – the summary shooting of officials who defraud or steal. Communism represents a frantic effort to make the Russian people honest and disinterested, punctual and assiduous in the service of the community – on these issues it is intensely and fanatically puritan. In this devotion to a State, Communist Russia is exactly opposite to the USA with

---

* Margot née Tennant, the second wife of the former Prime Minister, H. H. Asquith.

its amazing laxness and tolerance of fraud and self interest in public officials ... the *millionaire* gangsters have become popular heroes.

Beatrice Webb

Thursday, 23 July 1931

I am working at the *Evening Standard* office when at about 11 a.m., Tom [Oswald Mosley] rings me up and says will I come round at once. He had, at that moment received letters from John Strachey and Allan Young* resigning from the Party. I go round at 12.30 and find the Council gathered together in gloom. We try to get hold of our two delinquents but they are out and will not return till 6.0 ... We adjourn for luncheon.

Back at the office, I begin drafting statements to the Press in order to meet John's impending announcement. While thus engaged a letter comes in containing that announcement. It says they have resigned because Tom, on such subjects as the Youth Movement, Unemployment Insurance, India and Russia, was adopting a fascist tendency. On all these points, except Russia (where John's memo was idiotic) they have had their way.

At 5.30 we at last find they have returned ... Tremulous and uncouth, John Strachey sits down ... He then begins, quivering with emotion to indicate some of the directions in which Tom has of late abandoned the sacred cause of the worker. He says that ... [Tom] is acquiring a Tory mind ... [that Tom] considers socialism a 'pathological condition'. John much dislikes being pathological. His great hirsute hands twitch neurotically as he explained to us, with trembling voice, how unpathological he really was.

Undoubtedly the defection of John ... will do enormous electoral harm to the Party. Politically, however, it will place Tom in a position where, with greater ease, he can adhere to Lloyd George and Winston.

Harold Nicolson

---

* Allan Young had been a candidate in the Ashton-under-Lyme by-election of April 1931, the first election contested by Mosley's recently formed New Party. He came a poor third to the Conservative and Labour candidates.

Saturday, 25 July 1931

Today we have the great outstanding contradiction that while there is capacity in the country and throughout the world to turn out wealth at a greater rate than mankind has ever known, every great capitalist country is slowly but surely having its wheels of industry brought to a standstill.

The great capitalist powers have just met* to try to save one of their number from bankruptcy, not because of any special love they have for that one country but because of their sure and certain knowledge that if the country's economic system crashes, the others would topple over with it.

James Maxton

Saturday, 15 August 1931

Harold [Nicolson] is starting a new paper *Action* on Oct 1st; costing 2d. Cold, wet, lights at luncheon. The cat kittened in the coalhole; the valuable spaniel bitch died in childbed next door. A wet wild August; the coldest for 14 years; and the farmers here burning their hay. Meanwhile the country is in the throes of a crisis. Great events are brewing. Maynard visits Downing Street and spreads sensational rumours. Are we living then through a crisis; and am I fiddling? And will future ages, as they say, behold our predicament (financial) with horror? Sometimes I feel the world desperate; then walk among the Downs.

Virginia Woolf

Monday, 24 August 1931
Warsaw

From a newspaper which someone else was reading I gathered there was something by way of a political crisis at home, so when I got to the hotel I put through a call ... A little later a wire which Miss Nash had sent informed me that the Labour Government had resigned, that

---

*Representatives of Britain, France, USA and Germany met to try to avert a banking collapse in Germany.

MacDonald was Prime Minister of a National government, and giving the names of the Cabinet.

John Reith

Wednesday, 26 August 1931

Pay a round of visits ... to the [Foreign Office] and say goodbye to officials ...

Shall I, one day, return as Secretary of State? It is not impossible, but politics are a queer uncertain business. The prospects of all of us 'younger' men are, however, much improved by the defections and the clearance at the top ...

Rumour later confirmed, puts Lord Reading* at the Foreign Office. Precedents are indeed being broken. First a Secretary of State who has had no university education. Now one who has no foreskin.

Hugh Dalton

Thursday, 27 August 1931

I don't believe that Mac[Donald] deliberately led the Cabinet into a trap: *tried* to get them into agreeing to economies in the process of bargaining with the USA financiers, all the time intending to throw his colleagues over and form a National Government – but *he drifted into doing it* – largely because he is secretive – he never *can* be frank – yet he will let the cat out of the bag in a moment of queer indiscretions to someone who is a comparative stranger ... or even an enemy like Lansbury. I trust the Labour Party is quit of him, finally and completely, and I wish him well among the Duke and Duchesses.

Beatrice Webb

Sunday, 30 August 1931
Kent

We went on through Sevenoaks to Seal and a man we met advised us to try for a job at Mitchell's farm about three miles further on. We went there but the farmer told us he could not give us a job as he had nowhere where we could live and the Government inspectors had

---

*Rufus Isaacs, 1st Marquess of Reading.

41

been snouting round to see that all hop-pickers had 'proper accommodation.' (These inspectors, by the way, managed to prevent some hundreds of unemployed from getting jobs in the hop fields this year. Not having 'proper accommodation' to offer to pickers, the farmers could only employ local people who lived in their own houses.)

George Orwell

Wednesday, 2 September – Saturday, 19 September 1931

Most of the people who go down hopping have done it every year since they were children and they pick like lightning. And know all the tricks such as shaking the hops up to make them lie loose in the bin etc. The most successful pickers are families who have two or three adults to strip the vines, and a couple of children to pick up the fallen hops and clear the odd strands. The laws about child labour are disregarded utterly and some of the people drive their children pretty hard. The woman in the next bin to us, a regular old-fashioned East Ender, kept her grandchildren at it like slaves. – 'Go on, Rose, you lazy little cat, pick the 'ops up. I'll warm your arse if I get up to you' etc until the children, aged from 6 to 10, used to drop and fall asleep on the ground. But they liked the work and I don't suppose it did them more harm than school.

George Orwell

Tuesday, 22 September 1931

Party meeting at 11.30. We discuss *fascism* … The worst of it is that the communists will collar our imaginative appeal to youth, novelty and excitement. We decide to call the Youth Movement the Volts (Vigour-Order-Loyalty-Triumph).

Harold Nicolson

Monday, 26 October 1931

I have passed an announcement to be made in all news bulletins today pointing out the duty of people to vote and that the future prosperity etc. of the country depends on them. I have no doubt that this will be regarded as tendentious by the Labour party.

John Reith

In the recriminations that followed the end of the 1929–31 Labour government, Ramsay MacDonald was held to blame for the 'betrayal' of the Labour Party. His reputation never recovered. In the election that followed, on 27 October 1931, thirteen 'National Labour' MPs were elected, remaining with MacDonald to serve in the newly constituted National Government, and were expelled from the Labour Party. Only fifty-two 'real' Labour MPs were elected – a massacre for the party; and Oswald Mosley's New Party put up twenty-four candidates (including Mosley) though none was elected.

Chapter Two

1932–1940
Belling the Cat

The political situation in the seven or eight years before the Second World War was complex and confused. Fear of another war was one sentiment which united most of the diarists – from the pacifist Vera Brittain, the Foreign Office senior civil servant Alexander Cadogan, the socialist playwright and novelist J. B. Priestley, and the young composer and at that time communist sympathiser Benjamin Britten.

The diaries of Hugh Dalton, an academic economist turned Labour MP, display an insidious but (so far as I have found) rare note of anti-Semitism, while Blanche 'Baffy' Dugdale, a well-connected and passionate British Zionist, was principally concerned with prosely-tising the Zionist case to the British government. The Conservative MPs Duff Cooper and Chips Channon took opposite positions on the 'appeasement' question in their diaries: Channon, susceptible to those with wealth and power, consistently favoured Chamberlain's tempor-ising approach, while Duff Cooper, the more substantial politician, stood strongly against it.

In 1932 Malcolm Muggeridge, at that time an iconoclastic, anarchic young journalist based in Moscow, encountered an earnest young Christian, Harold Macmillan, when he was visiting Russia, and noted that he was 'hopeless about British politics'.

Ramsay MacDonald continued as Prime Minister of a National Government until 1935. The remnants of the real Labour Party were led by Arthur Henderson and George Lansbury, while the remaining Liberals were led by Herbert Samuel. Lloyd George led a small group of Independent Liberals between 1931 and 1935. After the election of 1935 the Conservative Prime Ministers Stanley Baldwin and Neville Chamberlain were successively in charge until 1940.

War solved the problem of unemployment, reducing the jobless from over two million in 1939 to less than 100,000 by 1944. It also marked the end of the conspicuous excesses of the very rich that, until his abdication as Edward VIII, had been exemplified in London society by the Prince of Wales and his set. The official photographer at the beginning of the war was Cecil Beaton, with access to anyone and everyone: his photographs captured the romantic heroism of the young men in the services, but the pen portraits he wrote describing the men's boredom, comradeship and fear of the war are just as vivid.

Wednesday, 6 January 1932

Rome

Spend most of the day reading *fascisti* pamphlets. They certainly have turned the whole country into an army. From cradle to grave one is cast in the mould of fascismo and there can be no escape. I am much impressed by the efficiency of all this on paper. Yet I wonder how it works in individual lives and shall not feel certain about it until I have lived some time in Italy. It is certainly a socialist experiment in that it destroys individuality. It destroys liberty. Once a person insists on how you are to think he immediately begins to insist on how you are to behave. I admit that under this system you can attain a degree of energy and efficiency not reached in our own island.

Harold Nicolson

Tuesday, 19 April 1932

I go to the New Party meeting in Great George Street. Tom (Mosley) says that he has been asked ... to join the Tory Party, and that he has been asked to lead the Labour Party. He will do neither of these things. He wished to coordinate all the fascist groups with Nupa [New Party] and thus form a central fascist body under his own leadership. I say that I think this is a mistake. He says that it would be impossible for him to re-enter the 'machine' of one of the older parties. That by doing so he would again have to place himself in a strait-waistcoat. That he has no desire for power on those terms. That he is convinced that we are entering a phase of abnormality and that he does not wish to be tarred with the brush of the old regime. That he thinks, as leader of the fascists, he could accomplish more than as a party back-bencher, and that in fact he is prepared to run the risk of further failure, ridicule and assault, than to allow the active forces in this country to fall into other hands. I again say that I do not believe this country will ever stand for violence, and that by resorting to violence he will make himself detested by a few and ridiculed by many. He says that may be so but that he is prepared to take the risk. I say that on such paths I cannot follow him. We decide to think it over.

The argument, though painful, is perfectly amicable ... Yet I hated it all, and with battered nerves returned to Cannon Street and took the train home.

Harold Nicolson

Saturday, 14 May 1932

Our journey [to the USSR] put off for one week owing to ice in the Gulf of Finland – thus prolonging the worry of our elaborate preparations – alike in bodily comforts and the tutoring of our minds. Continuously revolving and discussing hypothetical conclusions about Russia and forecasting our book. What amazes me is the originality and completeness of the constitution imposed, in the course of little more than a decade, on 160 millions, made up of different races, with different religions and languages, scattered over one-third of the habitable globe, by a group of émigrés without experience, carrying out the theories of a German Jew. Soviet Russia, in its political and economic constitution, differs from that of any other state, past or present.

The salient and distinctive feature of Soviet Russia is ... the establishment of a Spiritual Power over and above the ostensible government, dominating all other elements, central and local. The Communist Party welds, in one united body, all the constitutions, races, creeds, languages, cultures, included in the New Russia ... it has its Holy Writ, its prophets and its canonised saints; it has its Pope, yesterday Lenin and today Stalin; it has its code of conduct and its discipline; it has its creeds and its inquisition. And yet it has no rites or modes of worship ...

Today there is the fact that this new social order is not only promising work and wages to its subjects, but alone among states is increasing the material resources and improving the health and education of its people.*

Beatrice Webb

Friday, 10 June 1932

Long discussion after supper until quite late about sex and sex experience, my reaction to matrimony and theirs to virginity. We all seemed to imagine we were highly sexed, but this is certainly only true of Winifred (Holtby). Phyllis (Bentley) repeated that ... she had never been anyone's mistress, but had always wished for sex experience and still did.†

Vera Brittain

Friday, 17 June 1932

When Winifred had gone to sleep, I went down for my bath. I heard strange noises in the basement and went down to find ... (Dorothy) in the kitchen sitting in the dark crying after a quarrel with her young man (who had no business to be here anyway). I told D that as I wasn't always spying in the kitchen she really might try to show she could be trusted, and she said perhaps she'd better give me notice, but I told her it was after midnight and she wasn't to be so silly. She was so upset I really couldn't be very angry.

And afterwards I thought a good deal about the various forms of unhappiness and how strange it was that within the same day I should have under my roof the successful and extremely intelligent woman novelist of 37 crying bitterly because (it amounts to that) she hadn't had a man, and at the other end of the intellectual scale the little

---

* At this time, parts of the USSR were in the grip of a famine caused or exacerbated by the collectivisation of farms policy and the First Five Year Plan (1928–32) of the Communist Party under its General Secretary, Joseph Stalin. Between 6 and 8 million citizens died of hunger.
† Winifred Holtby and Phyllis Bentley were both novelists, best known for *South Riding* and *Inheritance* respectively. Holtby and Vera Brittain were lifelong friends and Holtby shared a home with Vera and her husband for many years.

housemaid of 20 crying just as bitterly because she had. I decided that on the whole it was probably far more bearable to be Dorothy ...

Vera Brittain

Monday, 27 June 1932

Warren Fisher [head of the Civil Service] rang up to ask if I could see him at 4.15. He told me without any introductory warning as to secrecy that on this Friday in the House of Commons Neville Chamberlain would announce the conversion of the whole two thousand million [First] War Loan from 5 per cent to 3 and a half per cent. I really felt rather dazed to be in possession of such a secret which was not even to be communicated to the Cabinet until 9.00pm on Thursday. This of course is a first class scoop for us.

John Reith

Saturday, 3 September 1932

en route from England to Russia on SS Cooperazia

Instead of being well on our way to Leningrad we are still in Hamburg. Most of yesterday was spent unloading a cargo, chiefly of hides; and then they began to take on a very large amount of stuff, steel bars, billets, machinery of all kinds. This loading will probably go on till tonight, when we hope to leave for Russia.

It annoys me to see this immense purchase of iron, steel and machinery from Germany. Germany is giving Russia the longer credits which we refuse. But Germany is doing it out of the immense loans which our bankers have made to her of English money, and which (since the standstill agreement of August 1931) she refuses to repay. Hence, we are in fact financing Russia and risking our money indirectly on all this cargo which is being loaded today – only instead of it being at least manufactured in Middlesbrough or Stockton, it is coming from Stuttgart and Essen.

Harold Macmillan to his mother, Helen Macmillan

Friday, 16 September 1932

Today I arrived in Moscow. Already I have made up my mind to call this the *Diary of Journalist* and not the *Diary of a Communist*. Moscow is an exquisite city. All the time I alternate between complete despair and wild hope.

Malcolm Muggeridge

Tuesday, 20 September 1932

Moscow

Our [Russian] teacher, it appears, works at the university. She used, she said, to enjoy her work until she fell under the suspicion of 'indeterminate idealism'. She has an icon in her room and is very religious; amiable in that curious, and not altogether pleasing, Christian way.

Malcolm Muggeridge

Monday, 26 September 1932

Moscow

We went to the opera house. Stalin and most of the leading members of the Government were on the platform ... I have never seen a man in the full employment of power so little outwardly conscious of it.

In our box was a man called Macmillan, a Conservative Member of Parliament belonging to the Young Men's Christian Association group. He knew my father. He seemed pretty hopeless about British politics and had all sorts of good views about national planning and what not.

Malcolm Muggeridge

Wednesday, 28 September 1932

Leningrad

In all the splendid rooms of the Catherine Palace there are reminders of how the peasantry were starved and bullied amid all this splendour. In one room, where there are set out a lot of robes etc., there is a great announcement saying that these ridiculous dressings-up still go on in Capitalist countries; then there is a picture of the King opening Parliament (taken from the *Illustrated London News*) and also a photograph of George V at the Coronation. I was looking at this with a little amusement when my eye was suddenly attracted by a familiar physiognomy – it was a drawing ... of the Duke [of Devonshire] in his robes (I suppose at the Coronation) and holding the Queen's crown on a cushion. I don't know how it got into Bolshevik hands, but above was this delightful inscription 'Typical Boyar of the old regime in Capitalist countries, living on the exploitation of the working classes.'

Harold Macmillan to his mother, Helen Macmillan

Sunday, 2 October 1932

London. Yes I will allow myself a new nib. Odd how coming back here upsets my writing mood. Odder still how possessed I am with the feeling that now, aged 50, I'm just poised to shoot forth quite free and straight and undeflected my bolts ... I don't believe in ageing. I believe in forever altering one's aspect to the sun.

I am reading DHL* with the usual sense of frustration ... To me Lawrence is airless, confined.

Government hoofing him out, like a toad; and banning his book; the brutality of a civilised society to this panting agonised man; and how futile it was.

Virginia Woolf

Tuesday, 4 October 1932

Moscow

For Stalin to feel himself bound in a short space of time to make Russia industrialised (economic Empire-building) may have very serious consequences indeed; and if his project quite fails to come off may be more awful than plagues and famines as far as the population is concerned.

Malcolm Muggeridge

Saturday, 8 October 1932

For nearly eight months I have given this diary a rest.

The Parliamentary Party is a poor little affair, isolated from the N.E.[North-East] whose only MP is Lansbury. Attlee is deputy leader ... a 'purely accidental position' as someone puts it – and he and

---

* Virginia Woolf was reading *The Letters of D. H. Lawrence*, edited by Aldous Huxley, which was published in September 1932. The banned book may have referred to *The Rainbow*.

Cripps ... sit in Lansbury's room at the House all day and all night and continually influence the old man.

Vera Brittain

Monday, 24 October 1932

Found Amy [Burnett, housekeeper] in tears this morning; reason being that now, owing to new tariffs, cheap meat, eggs and vegetables are unobtainable and her family have to live chiefly on bread and margarine. *Voici* one of the results of Ottawa? I talked to Amy for some time about tariffs and how the only way to have the cheaper commodities accessible once more was to turn the Conservatives out at the next election.

Winifred [Holtby] and I went down to Sidmouth for a week; as we drove over Westminster Bridge and passed County Hall (where the riot over the Means Test took place last week) we saw dozens of police assembling, for fear of another riot ...

Vera Brittain

Friday, 25 November 1932

This is a low period in my life. Also insofar as I was really enthusiastic about Communism, I feel now completely disillusioned. It's easy, of course, to say that its failure in Russia is neither here nor there. But the type of person who's been put into a position of power in Russia is just the type who'd be put into a position of power anywhere. Besides, when all is said and done, the world, at the moment, is exceedingly melancholy ...

The newspapers are a record of the decay of European civilisation. We belong to the decay. We are the decay.

Now the snow has come. It makes the streets of Moscow lovely, particularly at night.

Malcolm Muggeridge

Wednesday, 30 November 1932
Yorkshire

Phyllis took me out for a long walk along what she calls 'the Rocks' – a road above a deep rocky valley filled with mill chimneys, tall, slender and tragically smokeless; indeed the whole atmosphere seemed much cleaner and clearer than I had expected because so few mills are working. It was just before sunset; as we walked a thick mist rose from the valley enveloping the mills and chimneys and nothing more was visible but a long brilliant snake of lights moving away towards Lancashire.

Vera Brittain

Thursday, 5 January 1933
Moscow

I have been reading Cobbett's *Rural Rides* again. It is peculiarly apposite to the situation in Russia. 'How long will it be ere the ruffians, the base hirelings, the infamous traders who own and conduct the press; how long ere one of them, or all of them together, shall cause a cottager to smile; shall add one ounce to the meal of the labouring man!' This I think sometimes as I read *Pravda* and *Isvestia*.

Malcolm Muggeridge

Saturday, 18 February 1933
Nottingham

On the Saturday, I went with two Nottingham friends to see an association football match, for it was the local 'Derby Day', Notts Forest *versus* Notts County ... the day was hung about with a cold mist that soon melted into a drizzle; but that did not prevent the supporters of Notts Forest and Notts County, two distinct groups of partisans (though on what principle they elect themselves I cannot imagine) from filling the ground to the palings.

The huge crowd would roar like maniacs but then in the silence that followed you would hear [one woman] gently remonstrate with a player: 'Nay, Bob, you ought to let 'Erbert 'ave it.'

Nearly everything possible has been done to spoil this game: the heavy financial interests; the absurd transfer and player-selling system; the lack of any birth or residential qualifications for the players; the betting and coupon competitions; the absurd publicity given to every feature of it by the press ... but the fact remains that it is not yet spoilt and it has gone out and conquered the world.

J. B. Priestley

Saturday, 29 April 1933

Bruno Walter. He is a swarthy, fattish man; not at all smart. Not at all the 'great conductor'. He is a little Slav, a little semitic. He is very nearly mad; 'You must not think of the Jews' he kept on saying 'You must think of this awful reign of intolerance. You must think of the whole state of the world. It is terrible – terrible. That this meanness, that this pettiness, should be possible! ... We are now a disgrace.'

[He says] all the time soldiers ... marching. They never stop marching. And on the wireless, between the turns, they play military music. Horrible horrible! He hopes for the monarchy as the only hope. He will never go back there ... we must make them [the Germans] feel themselves outcasts – not by fighting them; by ignoring them. Then he swept off to the music ...

Virginia Woolf

Friday, 12 May 1933

Citrine to lunch ... Citrine is a sensible fellow, with a wider range of interests than many. He says that in Germany, the collapse of the socialist and T.U. movements is the more inexplicable, because there were said to be plans fully worked out, though known only to half a dozen inside people, for a General Strike and for destroying power stations, etc, if a Fascist dictatorship was attempted. Local comrades, enquiring what to do, were told that everything had been thought out and that, at the right moment, the call would be issued ... And then something went wrong.

Perhaps the Reichstag fire forestalled and frightened them. Anyhow, as Ruth [Dalton's wife] says, it's like a steamroller going over a worm.

Hugh Dalton

Tuesday, 27 June 1933

[Lord] Scone, who has just been to Denmark, told me in the House in the afternoon that the Danes are breeding their pigs for length so successfully that they look like gigantic dachshunds. The next step no doubt will be for someone to breed a pair of middle legs to sustain the weight.

Leo Amery

Friday, 4 August 1933

Wystan Auden reads us some of his new poem[s] in the evening. I follow Auden in his derision of patriotism, class distinctions, comfort, and all the ineptitudes of the middle classes. But when he also derides the other soft little harmless things which make my life comfortable I feel a chill autumn wind. I feel that were I a communist, the type of person I should most wish to attack would not be the millionaire or the imperialists, but the soft, reasonable, tolerant, secure, self-satisfied intellectual like Vita and myself. A man like Auden with the fierce repudiation of half-way houses and his gentle integrity makes one feel terribly discontented with one's own smug successfulness. I go to bed feeling terribly Edwardian and back-number, and yet, thank God, delighted that people like Wystan Auden should actually exist.

Harold Nicolson

Thursday, 5 October 1933
Labour Party Conference, Hastings

On Tuesday we went to Hastings; a queer experience always, that conference: a door opened into a buzzing bursting humming perfectly self-dependent other world ... But they were all marking time owing to a compromise. There are details I never get clear. When one of the tub thumpers was up, we went and sat on the balcony. The Hall is a very gay frivolous seaside hall, adapted for musical concerts and dances and so on.

... we could only stand very little of Hugh Dalton; and so we went out, got into the car, and drove home.

Virginia Woolf

Wednesday, 11 October 1933

Go to see Tom Mosley at Ebury Street.

He says he is making great progress in town and country alike. He gets very little money from the capitalists but relies on canteens and subscriptions. His aim is to build up from below gradually, and not to impose construction from above as we did in New Party days.*

Harold Nicolson

Autumn 1933

The Southampton coach

This was the first motor coach I had ever travelled in, and I was astonished at its speed and comfort. I never wish to go any faster. And as for comfort, I doubt if even the most expensive private motors – those gigantic three thousand pound machines – are as determinedly and ruthlessly comfortable as these new motor coaches ... They offer luxury to all but the most poverty-stricken. They have annihilated the class-distinction between rich and poor travellers. No longer can the wealthy go splashing past in their private conveyances, driving the humble pedestrian against the wall, leaving him to shake his fist and curse the proud pampered crew. The children of these fist shakers go thundering by in their own huge coaches and loll in velvet as they go. Perhaps it is significant that you get the same over-done comfort, the same sinking away into a deep seat of plush, in the vast new picture theatres. If the proletariat has money in its pocket now, it can lead the life of a satrap. And it does. It is the landed folk with their rattling old cars, their draughty country houses, their antique bathrooms and cold tubs, who are the Spartans of our time.

J. B. Priestley

Thursday, 30 November 1933

Dined with Stafford Cripps before his contribution to the political series [on radio]. He had some extraordinary opinions but I think I got him to agree that the Post Office should be de-nationalised to the BBC type of constitution ... We argued about the state of the electorate

* In October 1932 Mosley, influenced by Mussolini in Italy, had recast the New Party as the British Union of Fascists; Nicolson left the New Party at that point.

in regard to responsibility and intelligence. It is odd that I should be almost entirely socialist in my outlook in regard to the point on which the socialists put so much importance, namely the nationalisation of public services.

John Reith

Tuesday, 19 December 1933
Germany

Arrived in Berlin in time for a bath and breakfast before going to the Kirsch Kopfer* board meeting ... After the Board I drove out with Wasserman to the works. He spoke very frankly about the situation, and though a Jew himself and distressed about the fate of his own people, more particularly the younger educated men, was very fair minded and even generous about Hitler whom [he] thinks a great man in some ways ... in his efforts to get rid of German particularism, to unite the Protestant churches and to find agreement with France. He also thinks that apart from an improvement in the internal industrial situation there is a much better general feeling between capital and labour, partly due to the positive preaching of the Nazi gospel, partly to the suppression of Communist grousing. His colleague, also of the Deutsche Bank was strongly of the view that Hitler had saved the country from the Communist danger. A number of us lunched at the Works and then went round. Everything was much busier than in January, and the actual output is fully 40% up, most of it internal trade.

Leo Amery

Monday, 15 January 1934

Lord Rothermere came out in open support of Tom Mosley and in favour of British Fascism both in the *Mail* and in the *News*. Roosevelt announces his dollar revaluation scheme. As far as I can see, it will not affect the present exchange value of the dollar very much.

Robert Bruce Lockhart

---

*Kirsch Kopfer was a German company of which Leo Amery was a board member.

Sunday, 18 February 1934
Churt, Surrey

D[avid Lloyd George] and I sitting and smoking ... after Sunday breakfast when the Press Association rang up to know whether we had heard of the death of the King of the Belgians [killed in a mountaineering accident]. Greatly shocked and distressed. Gave D's appreciation of the King over the telephone.

We talked of Kings, D saying that now there was no King of outstanding strength in Europe with the possible exception of the King of Serbia. I suggested our own [George V], but D said: 'Quite frankly, he is not a man of strength. He is admirable and reliable, but has never interfered in any emergency, and would not be capable of doing so should any emergency arise. If he had someone strong behind him to act he would carry out orderly, faithfully and with courage. But nothing more ...' There were just two or three pillars one regarded as being bulwarks against trouble – Mussolini and the King of the Belgians amongst them (and incidentally he is not a Belgian, said D). D regards Hitler as a very great man.

In the evening [Gerald Seely] came to supper ... S told us of Hitler's amusement at a letter he had received from Dr Temple, the Archbishop of York, in which the latter said that before recommending one of his congregation to go to Oberammergau, he would like Hitler's assurance that the performance did not contain any anti-Semitic propaganda! Seely swears this is true and that Hitler himself told him, with a twinkle in his eye!

Frances Stevenson

1934
Blackburn

I met a most pleasant youngster who had a job in a firm that makes automatic looms. They sell these in Lancashire, and immediately put a few more weavers out of work. They have been selling them for years all over the world, and every time one is loaded on to a ship at Liverpool, a good piece is snipped off Lancashire's trade. And then there began to appear, at places like Blackburn's Technical College, which is of course kept going with public money, certain quiet, industrious, smiling young men from the East, most anxious to learn all that Lancashire could teach them about the processes of calico manufacture. They sat through their courses, missed nothing, smiled at their instructors for the last time and disappeared into the blue … there also disappeared into the blue a good deal of Lancashire's trade with the East.

I do not know what will happen to the cotton industry. Possibly this is only the worst of its periodic collapses. I suspect, however, that all the reorganisation and rationalisation and trade agreements and quotas and tariffs and embargoes in the world will not bring back to Lancashire what Lancashire has lost. The trade grew like Jack's beanstalk and it has lately been dwindling in the same magical fashion.

'Lancashire must have a big plan.' … Since when did Lancashire cease to be a part of England? Under what flag are little Joyce and Muriel and their parents in that Blackburn back street?

No man can walk about these towns, the Cinderellas in the baronial household of Victorian England, towns meant to work in and not to live in, and now even robbed of their work, without feeling that there is a terrible lack of direction and leadership in our affairs.

J. B. Priestley

Wednesday, 21 March 1934

Went up last night to accompany D[avid Lloyd George] on his 'Whither Britain' broadcast …

We dined before the broadcast with John Reith – he is a curious character – a cross between a canny Scot and a medieval saint – but more of the fanatic in him than the academic. He firmly believes in the mission of the B.B.C. to purify the life of the nation.

Beaverbrook has been running a campaign against the B.B.C. and Reith says it is a purely personal one against him, and that B is out to bust the B.B.C.

Frances Stevenson

Wednesday, 28 March 1934

Saw Vansittart* at the Foreign Office and had an interesting talk. He thinks affairs in the Far East have quietened down and that neither

---

* Robert Vansittart was Permanent Under-Secretary at the Foreign Office from 1930 until 1938, when he was replaced by his Deputy, Alexander Cadogan. Vansittart was made 'Chief Diplomatic Adviser', creating a very uneasy relationship between the two 'mandarins'.

Russia nor Japan, however much they hate each other, is prepared for war in the near future. He thought Germany is a real menace. He was very much in favour of a clear enunciation of policy on the part of the British Government, and said he had tried to bring this about. The indecision and indefiniteness of 1914 was a salutary example in this respect. An inevitable sequence would, however, be a considerable increase of armaments.

John Reith

Wednesday, 18 April 1934

A curious little fact.

Instead of smoking 6 or 7 cigarettes as I write of a morning, I now, for 3 mornings, make myself smoke only one. And rather enjoy doing without.

Virginia Woolf

Tuesday, 8 May 1934

Took to the road in the wet and cold and drove in a downpour through Wales, through Shrewsbury (disappointing) through Much Wenlock (good) and much green and prosperous country till we reached Worcester and took up lodging for the last time at the Star. L[eonard] told me not to stare so at the other tea drinkers, but I find it difficult not to gaze at these real English, these dwellers in the very heart of the land, who talk of horses all the time and meet their men friends in the lounge, and sit drinking and laughing and bandying county gossip under pictures of famous race horses. Horses rule England.

Virginia Woolf

Monday, 6 August 1934

I believe that in the last thirty years the age of development is much later than it used to be. Colin Maclean, who is at ——'s at Harrow, tells [my wife] that the bigger boys use powder, put scent behind their ears, read *Vogue* and wear frightfully nancy clothes. Jean asked why the other boys did not laugh them out of it. Colin's answer was that these were the 'big shots' and the best boys at games.

Robert Bruce Lockhart

Tuesday, 25 September 1934

Churt, Surrey

Macmillan came down yesterday, seeking D[avid]'s advice. The young Conservatives are worried (1) about the present political situation which they do not like for reasons connected with Policy (White Paper, Unemployment etc) and (2) because they think that the most progressive of them are bound to lose their seats at the next election, the Govt being too secure and Ramsay having no intention of going. Moreover he is not anxious to be drawn back into politics at this moment and he told Macmillan that nothing on earth would induce him to take office with the present Govt ...

What D has at the back of his mind is the consolidation of a small block of progressive opinion behind him after the election in the hope that the Gov majority will be so small that a block of votes of even 20 or 30 would influence things one way or another. Then D, with his little party, would be all powerful and could dictate policy, which is just what he would like.

Frances Stevenson

Monday, 1 October 1934

Senghennyd, Caerphilly

Dear Sir,

Please accept enclosed P.O. 15/- towards your relief fund for the dependants of the Gresford Colliery Explosion.

We are a family who have not forgotten the horrors of October 14th, 1913 when we lost our dear son and brother at a very tender age (14).*

Our deepest sympathy goes out to the bereaved families, we know alas! too well, the suffering they endure.

Yours with deepest sympathy

---

* An explosion in October 1913 at the Universal Colliery, Glamorgan, was the worst mining disaster in the UK with the loss of 439 miners. At Gresford, Wrexham, twenty-one years later, on 22 September 1934, 266 men died.

Tuesday, 11 December–Wednesday, 12 December 1934

[The private secretary to the PM] phoned to me from No 10 in the evening to say that the PM was anxious to see me next morning. As I had seen him so lately and he had talked about the BBC I thought this might be something interesting. However it was only that the Cabinet wanted him to broadcast a New Year's message. He said the National government was misrepresented so much in the newspapers that the Cabinet thought they had better tell the public their point of view over the wireless. I said that of course they were able to do this by order, but I did not think it would be very advisable.

John Reith

Wednesday, 23 January 1935

Lunched with Emerald [Maud Cunard] to meet Mrs Simpson ... She is a nice, quiet, well-bred mouse of a woman with large startled eyes and a huge mole. I think she is surprised and rather conscience-stricken by her present position and the limelight which consequently falls upon her. Emerald dominated the conversation with her brilliance, her mots and epigrams, some mild, some penetrating, dart like flashes from a crystal girandole. She had that morning rung up Kingsley Wood, the Postmaster General himself, about her telephone being out of order.

Henry 'Chips' Channon

Tuesday, 19 February 1935
Lowestoft

Mum has Mrs Owls and Mrs Woodger to tea. After which I spend one and a half hours knocking at people's front doors up this road – delivering Peace Ballot papers.* A foul job – but it may do a little good, and make a few people use their brains. But of course it would be my luck to get allotted a road just packed with die-hards – Indian colonels, army widows, typical old spinsters etc!

Benjamin Britten

---

*The 1934–35 Peace Ballot, though not an official referendum, was a nationwide questionnaire designed to gauge support for the League of Nations and international disarmament (organised by the League of Nations Union).

Thursday, 21 February 1935

In the evening I went to Lady Astor's ball: though the house was literally lined with lilac, there was little – if anything – to drink. The Duchess of York was in pink and very charming to me. She danced with Anthony Eden who is really becoming very handsome and important.

The War killed or ruined millions; it must have made a few people, a few young men, like Anthony Eden, who would not be where he is except that there are so few; it certainly made me ...

The belle of the ball was Isobel Manners; they are angels, those Manners girls.

Henry 'Chips' Channon

Saturday, 20 April 1935

In the public world there are emphatic scares ... One of these days they may come true.

There is a dutiful perfunctory stir about the Jubilee. We have subscribed £3 towards buns and a bus shelter in Rodmell.

And there are incessant conversations – Mussolini, Hitler, MacDonald. All these people incessantly arriving at Croydon, arriving at Berlin, Moscow, Rome; and flying off again – while Stephen [Spender] and I think how to improve the world.

Virginia Woolf

Sunday, 5 May 1935

Jubilee Sunday. King's Road Chelsea one vast patriotic shriek like the rest of London. Cinema and Town Hall fronted with red geraniums and white daisies; red, white and blue bunting. All the flags sold out at Woolworth's.

W[inifred] and I went to Hyde Park at 3.30 for the Labour May Day demonstration ... Usual British crowd which is the despair of Continental countries – good-humoured, tolerant, long-suffering, nobody out at elbows yet nobody smart; air of patience and respectability rather than rebellion or daring. Usual facility for turning everything into a picnic (as for a long time it did the War) and refusing to be tragic about it ...

What the crowd did reveal was exactly why we have had 25 years of an unshaken King and Queen during precisely the period when the monarchs of half the countries in the world have been flying for their lives. We are far too tolerant, agreeable, good-humoured and accommodating to do anything so drastic and cruel as to overthrow a throne.

Vera Brittain

Friday, 31 May 1935

Charles Brook [Labour candidate] this morning said that Attlee came to speak at Smethwick last week, when they expected an important announcement on current issues. And he talked about – the 'Sino-Jap dispute'! ... Infinitely remote from the audience both in time and space. Little man, little head, little speech, little essay!

Hugh Dalton

Monday, 3 June 1935

Speak with Maisky [Soviet Ambassador]. He is worried by Labour Party attitude in Parliament on rearmament. He says 'By all means, talk with Hitler, and come to agreements and compromises. But talk to him with a rifle in your hand, or he will pay no regard to your wishes' ... He suggests that Labour Party should agree to let votes for larger armaments go through, on condition Government makes non-aggression pact with Soviet Union. A little too simple!

Hugh Dalton

Whitsuntide, June 1935

Much gossip about the Prince of Wales' alleged nazi leanings; he is alleged to have been influenced by Emerald (who is rather eprise with Herr Ribbentrop) through Mrs Simpson.

He has just made an extraordinary speech to the British Legion advocating friendship with Germany. It is only a gesture, but a gesture that may be taken seriously in Germany and elsewhere. If only the chancelleries of Europe knew that his speech was the result of Emerald Cunard's intrigues, themselves inspired by Herr Ribbentrop's dimple!

Henry 'Chips' Channon

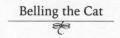

Tuesday, 30 July 1935

I am bored by this Italian-Abyssinian dispute and really I fail to see why we should interfere. Though of course the League of Nations will stand or fall by it. But I am a little uneasy that the destinies of countless millions should be in the exquisite hands of Anthony Eden, for whom I have affection even admiration – but no blind respect. Why should England fight Italy over Abyssinia, when most of *our* far flung empire has been won by conquest?

Henry 'Chips' Channon

Thursday, 5 September 1935

John and I go to prom in the evening (ticket from BBC) – vile, the only interesting things being Busoni's Rondo Arleschinesco – which was very exciting and of course Rimsky Korsakov's Cap. Espagnol which was pure gold after the exaggerated sentimentality and nobilmenti of Elgar's 1st symphony, I swear that only in Imperialist England would such a work be tolerated. – tho' of course it is well done – which is more than could possibly be said of Vaughan Williams Viola Suite – bad in work and idea.

Benjamin Britten

Wednesday, 2 October 1935

Yesterday we went to the Labour Party meeting at Brighton.

It was very dramatic, Bevin's attack on Lansbury. Tears came to my eyes as Lansbury spoke. And yet he was posing I felt – acting, unconsciously, the battered Christian man. Then Bevin too acted I suppose. He sank his head in his vast shoulders till he looked like a tortoise. Told L[ansbury] not to go hawking his conscience round ... The women delegates were very thin-voiced and insubstantial. On Monday one said, It is time we gave up washing up ... Too much rhetoric, and what a partial view: altering the structure of society: yes, but when it's altered? Do I trust Bevin to produce a good world, when he has his equal rights? ... These are some of the minnows that go round my head and distract me from what is, after all, my work.

Virginia Woolf

Thursday, 3 October 1935

War. The Italians have bombed Adowa, killing 1,700, including nurses, women and children. Their first victim being Red Cross Hospital. All day news has drifted in, much of it, no doubt, false and exaggerated. Where shall we be in a fortnight's time? Winston has made a stirring speech in Bournemouth demanding increases in our defences.

Henry 'Chips' Channon

Wednesday, 30 October 1935

Went to Peace Conference, by way of a joke, yesterday and saw several baboon faced intellectuals; also some yearning, sad, green dressed negroes and negresses, looking like chimpanzees brought out of their cocoanut groves to try to make sense of our pale white platitudes.

Virginia Woolf

Friday, 1 November–Friday, 8 November 1935

The political talks [on radio] go on; hopeless, and there is very little interest in the election. Snowden's performance was awful ... Arthur Greenwood's political talk was really disgusting. I felt it was a prostitution of broadcasting. MacDonald began well but deteriorated.

Stanley Baldwin gave the final political talk. Very earnest, impressive and emphatic, but he didn't tell people to vote, as he should have done.

John Reith

Thursday, 14 November 1935
Sunderland

Polling Day.

Afternoon, spent most of time in damp and dark east end canvassing in houses with pitch-dark stairs worn and broken in many places; tin baths and buckets on landing; walls felt shiny and damp to touch. Habitations more fit for monkeys than human beings; wondered how many bugs I was picking up. Taken round by very intelligent little boy of 13.

All of us very depressed as return of polling cards didn't indicate a very favourable prospect for us and first results on wireless showed that, though a few old Labour strongholds were won back, the great towns in the North, such as Newcastle, were still voting National Govt with large majorities.

Vera Brittain

Wednesday, 4 December 1935

House of Commons

There is something very strange about Stanley Baldwin. At first sight he is a solid English gentleman, but then one observes odd nervous tricks. He has an extraordinarily unpleasant habit of smelling at his notes and licking the edges slightly as if they were a flap on an envelope. He scratches himself continuously. There are russet patches across his head and face. And a strange movement of the head, with half-closed eyes, like some tortoise half-awake smelling the air – blinking, snuffy, neurotic.

I went to the smoking-room, which was an unwise thing to have done. I wanted to see if I could find Ralph Glyn with whom I was supposed to be lunching today. But the smoking-room was full of old boys sitting round tables and drinking whisky. It is not in the least like the smoking-room at the Travellers Club. It is far more like the bar of a pub. Shouts and laughter and an almost complete absence of decorum.

Harold Nicolson to Vita Sackville-West

Tuesday, 10 December 1935

After luncheon I went round to the Privy Council Office for a meeting of our National Labour Party. It is a lovely room with a huge sculp-tured fireplace and many Queen Anne inkstands. Ramsay sat there in front and we others sat on either side. We discussed the future organisation and policy of our Party. It was a ridiculous and rather painful discussion. It boiled down to the question of Party funds. We had so much in hand which would enable us to keep on for such and such a time. How were we to get more money? Ramsay dismissed that question as secondary. 'One can always get money,' he said, 'for great political purposes.' Kenneth Lindsay, who is an impatient and able man, suggested that we might discuss what those purposes were. We all winced at that. 'We shall,' said Ramsay, 'be neither red, white nor blue. We stand for Labour within the Baldwin organisation. We shall further the aims of the organisation but we shall remain OURSELVES.' Having said that, he struck the arm of his chair with a clenched fist and gazed upwards to where, above the mantelpiece, God was most likely to be found. 'OURSELVES,' he repeated fervently, like a Covenanter dedicating his sword and buckler. We did not even like to look at each other so awkward were our feelings. It was by then 3.30 p.m., and in acute embarrassment we broke up.

Harold Nicolson to Vita Sackville-West

Thursday, 12 December 1935

I lunched with Lady Bridgeman and we talked about Baldwin (with whom she is to spend next weekend) and politics. I said I would like to be minister of defence. I said she could tell SB that I could do some odd job.

John Reith

Thursday, 19 December 1935

My second speech in the House ... two [MPs] thought I went too far in calling Mussolini a lunatic ...

We have been having days of drama – for poor old Westminster. Hoare resigning. Baldwin much shaken personally. An amazing bag of letters protesting against the proposed 'exchange of half an Empire for a corridor of camels.'* Very exciting while it lasted.

Hugh Dalton

Monday, 23 December 1935

Anthony Eden has been appointed Foreign Secretary by Mr Baldwin. His appointment is a victory for 'The Left', for the pro-Leaguers. He has had a meteoric rise, young Anthony. I knew him well at Oxford,

---

* A reference to the Hoare–Laval Pact, a proposal by the British Foreign Secretary Samuel Hoare and French Prime Minister Pierre Laval to end the Second Italo-Abyssinian War. Italy would be given control of southern Abyssinia (now Ethiopia), whilst Abyssinia would retain access to the sea via the port of Assab, a so-called 'corridor for camels'. The proposal collapsed, causing Hoare to resign.

where he was mild, aesthetic, handsome, cultivated and interested in the East – now at thirty-eight he is Foreign Secretary. There is hardly a parallel in our history. I wish him luck; I like him; but I have never had an exaggerated opinion of his brilliance, although his appearance is magnificent.

Henry 'Chips' Channon

Tuesday, 31 December 1935

New Year's Eve, London

After dinner G* and I went to St Paul's where a watch-night service was being held both inside and out, to see the new year in. So thankful to get rid of 1935 that we wanted to do something to mark its passing.

Couldn't hear a word of the service or the community singing of war songs and 'Abide with Me' for the shouting and yelling of the mob and their constant performance on squeakers.

We walked back from Ludgate Hill to Piccadilly ... In Strand, outside Strand Palace, a few ladies somewhat drunk, in evening dress.

Picked up a taxi in Piccadilly; got home about 1.30 and to bed about 2.30. Goodbye to 1935, the worst, cruellest and saddest year since the War.

Vera Brittain

Saturday, 11 January 1936

Was glad I had hair, eyebrows, nails done as gathering [at Bedford College] was even more ghastly exhibition than usual of sartorial monstrosities – dating from the days when intellect in a woman was supposed to annihilate any pretensions to personal attractiveness and any obligations to improve one's appearance. Chief exception Dorothy Sayers who while grown enormous and deliberately eccentric is at least not dowdy.

Vera Brittain

* George Gordon Catlin (known as Gordon), Vera Brittain's husband and Shirley Williams's father.

Monday, 13 January 1936

Tonight at eight-thirty

Meet Sibyl Colefax at the Aperitif, then on to the Phoenix Theatre for the first night of Noël Coward's play. Sibyl breaks to me the fact that the other two members of our party are the Prince of Wales and Mrs Simpson.

Mrs Simpson is bejewelled, eyebrow-plucked, virtuous and wise. I had already been impressed by the fact that she had forbidden the Prince to smoke during the entr'acte in the theatre itself. She is clearly out to help him. Our supper party at the Savoy Grill goes right enough, but I find the Prince gazing at my tie and soft collar in a mood of critical abstraction – the eye of Windsor blue surrounded by jaundice. Nobody pays any attention to him, and what is odd is that the waiters do not fuss unduly. The Prince is extremely talkative and charming. I have a sense that he prefers our sort of society either to the aristocrats or to the professed highbrows or politicians. Sibyl imagines that she is getting him into touch with Young England. I have an uneasy feeling that Mrs Simpson, for all her good intentions, is getting him out of touch with the type of person with whom he ought to frequent.

Go home pondering on all these things and a trifle sad … Because I think Mrs Simpson is a nice woman who is flaunted suddenly into this absurd position. Because I think the P. of W. is in a mess. And because I do not feel at ease in such company.

Harold Nicolson

Friday, 17 January 1936

Very cold. Kipling critically ill at Middlesex Hospital. Rumours that the King is seriously ill again.

Vera Brittain

Monday, 20 January 1936

To Blackheath all day until 6.0 when I eat out and come back here to work for the evening …

Very dramatic announcement from BBC at 9.38 – 'King dying.' All stations close down except for an impromptu service – Psalm 23, a colossal prayer. Further announcement at 9.45 – when bulletin is repeated – Stuart Hibbert getting more awed and quavery than ever

– ditto at 10.0 – 10.15 – 10.30 – 10.45 (feelings are now working off a bit) – 11.0 – 11.15 (definitely cool now, tho' Hibbert still emotional) – 11.30 – 11.45 – 12.0 (really this King <u>won't</u> die) so I switch off and continue my work till 1.45 (finishing score, thank God!).

Benjamin Britten

January 1936

On the 25th I lunched with the Athlones. They had invited me before the King's death and I thought the luncheon would be put off but telephoned to make sure and found that it wasn't. The point of it was to meet the Duke of Coburg.* It was a gloomy little party – so like a small bourgeois household. It reminded me of the days when I was learning German in Hanover. I was tactfully left alone with the Duke of Coburg after luncheon in order that he might explain to me the present situation in Germany and assure me of Hitler's pacific intentions. In the middle of our conversation His Duchess reappeared carrying some hideous samples of ribbon in order to consult him as to how the wreath they were sending to the funeral should be tied. He dismissed her with a volley of muttered German curses and was afterwards quite unable to pick up the thread of his argument.

Duff Cooper

Wednesday, 29 January 1936

Wigram phoned. Asked how long notice we needed of a talk by the King [Edward VIII] as they were going ahead with that now, though he added he hadn't seen the King all day. He hoped that Queen Mary would stay on at Buckingham Palace and take her part as of old. Also that the King would live there which he didn't seem to want to do.

He said the Queen had gone to Communion on Sunday – which led me to say how deplorable it was that the King hadn't gone to church last Sunday. He quite agreed and said that it was even worse that he hadn't gone the Sunday before.

John Reith

---

*The Duke of Saxe-Coburg and Gotha was brother to Princess Alice, Countess of Athlone. Both were Victoria's grandchildren.

Saturday, 1 February 1936

I took Shirley to cinema to see pictures of King's funeral procession and two Mickey Mouse films – preceded by the lurid Tallulah Bankhead picture called *Between the Devil and the Deep Blue Sea* [the film was *Devil and the Deep*].

Vera Brittain

Tuesday, 11 February 1936

Last night to Co-Op Hall with various people from the NUWM to hear Wal Hannington speak.* A poor speaker, using all the padding and clichés of the Socialist orator and with the wrong kind of cockney accent (once again, though a Communist, entirely bourgeois), but he got the people well worked up. Was surprised by the amount of Communist feeling here. Loud cheers when Hannington announced that if England and USSR went to war USSR would win. Audience very rough and all obviously unemployed (about one in ten of them women) but very attentive. After the address, a collection taken for expenses – hire of hall and H's train fare from London. £1–6–0 raised – not bad from about 200 unemployed people.

You can always tell a miner by the blue tattooing of coal dust on the bridge of his nose. Some of the older men have foreheads veined with it like Roquefort cheese.

George Orwell

Monday, 24 February 1936

The day was devoted in the House of Commons to a discussion of foreign relations. People in this country are coming round to the folly of our pro-Geneva, anti-Mussolini policy. It took the expense of it to do that: English idealism, especially when false, falls like a punctured balloon when the question of expense crops up. The £7 million spent on our fleet in the Mediterranean has brought home to many people our extravagant misguided folly. Today for the first time, although we always said it must soon happen, regrets were expressed that Samuel Hoare's proposals [for Abyssinia] were not put into operation.

---

* Wal Hannington was National Organiser of the National Unemployed Workers' Movement, and a founder member of the Communist Party of Great Britain.

These late nights in the foetid atmosphere of the House of Commons nearly kill me, though Mr Baldwin was quite amiable to me in the lobby today, while Lady Astor rushed about like a decapitated hen ...

Henry 'Chips' Channon

Monday, 24 February 1936

Took midday train to Manchester for Farnworth ...

How often now I seem to have been on railway journeys through industrial Lancashire and Yorkshire. Lectured to a parish church Mutual Improvement Society (12 guineas). Good audience in long schoolroom but two front rows of quite juvenile children rather putting off, especially as the subject was 'Youth Morals Today and Yesterday' and I had to leave out one or two of my best stories.

Vera Brittain

Sunday, 1 March 1936

Suffolk

Beth [sister] and I go for a long walk along beach to Little Holland ... In afternoon – gramophone and wireless. The King (Edward now) makes a speech to the 'Empire'. I had hope[d] that he would at least say something interesting – feeling that he is more of a personality than his father – something about the foreign situation or the League of Nations – but I was very disappointed. Listen to a show of Walton's Symphony ... dull is not the word for the last movement.

Benjamin Britten

Saturday, 7 March 1936

The international situation is ludicrously complicated – Germany now discards Locarno and Versailles and occupies Rhine territory – Italian successes on Abyssinian front continue in spite of financial difficulties – Japan owing to the shooting of her statesmen in last week's revolt*

---

* On 26 February, in a short-lived insurrection in Tokyo, some 1,500 troops and young officers of the Japanese Imperial Army had attempted to overthrow the government. Several politicians, including the finance minister, were killed.

is more militaristic than ever – and Russia is pressed on the other side as well by Germany and Poland. Central Europe is a hotbed of intrigue – and our rearmament plans mount up and up – etc etc!!!!

Benjamin Britten

Tuesday, 10 March 1936

London

After lunch shopped, saw Mr Watt, then went up to Zionist Office and had tea with Chaim [Weizmann], just back from Palestine and arranging interviews with politicians of all sorts. He said time is come when HMG must make up its mind whether it intends actively to assist the National Home, or just go on holding the balance. The Jews must know where they are – and on the answer will depend much of their loyalty to us, and perhaps the peace and defence of Palestine.

Blanche 'Baffy' Dugdale

Friday, 13 March 1936

Aldous refuses to sign the latest manifesto* because it approves sanctions. He's a pacifist. As usual, I think Oh this will blow over. But its odd, how near the guns have got to our private life again, I can quite distinctly see them and hear a roar, even though I go on, like a doomed mouse, nibbling at my daily page.

A very concentrated laborious spring this is: with perhaps 2 fine days: crocuses out; then bitter black and cold. It all seems in keeping: my drudgery, our unsociability; the crisis; meetings; dark – and what it all means no one knows.

Virginia Woolf

Monday, 16 March 1936

G and I went to American Consulate after lunch to find out how the children and I could go to America with him on a non-quota immigrant visa in case of a War which we could not endorse. Procedure far more complicated than it used to be but can be done ...

Colossal correspondence this morning; answered it but still can't

---

* A reference to Aldous Huxley and further League of Nations sanctions against Italy.

get on with novel. I fear War more than Fascism; anyhow I am sure that you can't use Satan to cast out Satan; that Fascism which sprang from colossal injustice will only grow stronger if the injustice is rammed home; that the only way to kill it is to ostracise it as we have the Mosley movement. The Press and all the people I meet seem to be divided into 1) those who hate murder in Germany but don't mind it in Russia; 2) those who hate murder in Russia but don't mind it in Germany; 3) a few minoritarians like myself who hate it anyway ... 'What shadows we are and what shadows we pursue!'

Vera Brittain

Wednesday, 18 March 1936

The Barnsley public baths are very bad. Old-fashioned bathtubs, none too clean, and not nearly enough of them. I judged by the appearance of the place there were at most 50 baths – this in a town of 70–80 thousand inhabitants, largely miners, not one of whom has a bath in his own house, except in the new Corporation houses.

George Orwell

Friday, 20 March 1936
Bloomsbury, London

Theres a tap on the window. I thought it was my little dressmakers apprentice come with my dress. But it was oh dear – a girl fainting. Can I have a drop of water? She was hardly able to walk. Sat on the area steps while I got one. Then I took her in: got L[eonard]: hotted soup. But it was a horrible thing. Shed been walking all day to get work, had neuritis – ... had had a cup of tea for breakfast, lived in one room alone in Bethnal Green ...

We gave her tongue, 2 eggs and 5/-. Never saw unhappiness, poverty so tangible. And felt its our fault. And *she* apologised.

Virginia Woolf

Tuesday, 28 April 1936

Luncheon alone with Robert Vansittart [of the Foreign Office] at his house. Van was extremely pleasant and friendly. His view is that a German hegemony in Europe means the end of the British Empire and that we have no right to buy Germany off for a generation by offering her a free hand against the Slav countries. Once she has established herself in an unassailable position she will turn round upon us and we shall be too weak to resist her. I think he is right in theory but in practice it would be quite impossible for us to get the British people to fight Germany for the sake of the Czechs.

Harold Nicolson to Vita Sackville-West

Tuesday, 19 May 1936

I have been reflecting a great deal on the hopelessness of trying to hold out for right in these days – moral issues or anything. There is no support from quarters whence one should have it. Most everything goes by default or by a combination of default on the part of those who should care, and of active hostility and propaganda from the other side. Look at what we have in the King. This is bound to have an effect on all grades.

John Reith

Wednesday, 10 June 1936

London

Went to Zionist Office for a Conference ... Chaim put forward a proposal ... to offer to suspend immigration (into Palestine) for a period in order to help Government.* The idea was so passionately turned down by all except myself that it is obviously impracticable. Ben-Gurion's opposition was the most important, for as Chaim himself said, the unity of Jewry is our chief asset and he would never do anything to split it ... B-G says it would not only rend the Zionist movement in twain, but would instantly start civil war in Palestine, for nothing has kept the Jews from retaliating all these seven weeks except the determination to do nothing to stop immigration.

Blanche 'Baffy' Dugdale

---

*The 1936 Arab Revolt was a nationalist uprising by Palestinian Arabs against the British colonial mandate of Palestine and mass Jewish immigration into the territory. The outbreak led to the establishment of the Palestine Royal Commission. The Commission ultimately recommended partition of Palestine between Arabs and Jews, a proposal initially endorsed by the British government, but later rejected as unworkable.

Wednesday, 1 July 1936

Lunch with Rudolph Holzmann* – who is being driven out of the country because of his nationality. He is going to Italy now because that is the only country which will accept German currency now, and he is forbidden to make money here. It is a bloody shame as he is a fine musician, to say nothing of being a delightful person.

Benjamin Britten

Monday, 13 July 1936

See Ramsay MacDonald. He is busy already with papers regarding the Coronation ... This brings him to the problem of the King's appalling obstinacy and to the unfortunate Court Circulars in which Mrs Simpson's name figures as a guest. He says this is making a bad effect in the country. 'The people,' he says, 'do not mind fornication, but they loathe adultery.' The only person who can remedy this situation is Mrs Simpson herself, but there is always the possibility that her head (which as a head is not exceptional) may become turned.

Harold Nicolson

Wednesday, 22 July 1936

News makes me sick from Spain. The rebel Fascists seem to be doing better and according to the definitely pro-fascist *Daily Telegraph* – practically all N. Spain, Morocco and alot of South is in their hands – including Barcelona!

After dinner read alot more Marx. Hard going though edifying.

Benjamin Britten

Monday, 27 July 1936

Austen Chamberlain, the doyen of the House of Common donkeys, made a really stupid speech in which he attacked Germany with unreasoning violence. He is ossified, tedious and hopelessly out of date.

The situation in Spain, where civil war has been waging, is very serious. The army of the Right elements, revolted by the appalling Left

---

* Rudolph Holzmann (1910–92), a German composer who went to Lima in 1938 where he became known as an ethnomusicologist.

government, have tried a coup de main to seize power. For a few days we had hoped that they would win, though tonight it seems as if the Red Government, alas, will triumph.

Henry 'Chips' Channon

Thursday, 13 August 1936
Berlin

I don't know how to describe this dazzling crowded function. We drove to the Ministereum in the centre of Berlin and found its great gardens lit up and 700 or 800 guests gaping at the display and splendour. Goering, wreathed in smiles and orders and decorations, received us gaily, his wife at his side ... a table was reserved for us, with the Brunswick clan, Ernest August in a green uniform and the daughter Princess Frederika, typically royal of another age with a marabou boa, and the Hamilton boys. Towards the end of dinner a corps de ballet danced in the moonlight: it was the loveliest coup d'oeil imaginable, and there were murmurs of delighted surprise from all the guests who agreed that Goering had indeed eclipsed Ribbentrop which indeed we had been told was his ambition. The end of the garden was in darkness and suddenly with no warning, it was flood-lit and a procession of white horses, donkeys and peasants appeared from nowhere ...

The music roared, the astonished guests wandered about. 'There has never been anything like this since the days of Louis Quatorze', someone remarked, 'Not since Nero,' I retorted but actually it was more like the fetes of Claudius but with the cruelty left out ...

There is something un-Christian about Goering, a strong pagan streak, a touch of the arena, though perhaps like many who are libidinous-minded like myself, he actually does very little. People say that he can be very hard and ruthless, as are all Nazis when occasion demands, but outwardly he seems all vanity and childish love of display.

Henry 'Chips' Channon

Thursday, 5 November 1936

I meet Phil Green (a jazz-merchant who is writing the jazz for *Love from a Stranger*) at Baker St at 10.0 and together we depart for Denham. Arrive after a tortuous journey – four changes, everlasting waits, snail-like travelling in antique trains when we <u>do</u> eventually move – at

12.15!! These English suburban railway systems. Spend the whole day on the set.

Madrid bombed by air for umpteenth time. No. of children killed not specified. 70 were killed in one go the other day.

Benjamin Britten

Tuesday, 10 November 1936

I walked to the House of Commons as we had been warned not to bring cars. The lobbies were full of the hunger marchers come to protest against the new unemployment regulations, the so-called Means Test.

During questions, someone asked, innocuously, about the coming Coronation. McGovern* jumped up and shouted 'Why bother, in view of the gambling at Lloyds that there *will not be one?*' There were roars of 'Shame! Shame!' and he called out, 'Yes ... Mrs Simpson.' This was the first time her name had been used in the House of Commons, although the smoking room and lobbies have long buzzed with it. I was shocked, but the truth is that the monarchy has lost ground in a frightening manner. Prince Charming charms his people no more ...

Later I went out into the lobby and found it full to suffocation with marchers, who were being incited by Communists. Many of them wore red shirts and ties. At the door was a queue singing the Red Flag. It really seemed as if trouble must break out. But it didn't and about 8.30 I took the last look at these unfortunate people who have been goaded and misguided by their leaders into walking from Lancashire and South Wales.

On my way home I passed the Abbey, which looked beautiful and calm and flood-lit because it is Armistice eve. Many people, mostly women, were planting little crosses tied to poppies on the lawn surrounding the Abbey and in the cool light they looked holy, sad and peaceful. As I watched the silent scene, the grey, middle-aged women, thinking of their lost sons, I thought of my warm, gold and pink boy waiting for me at home.[†]

Henry 'Chips' Channon

---

*John McGovern was one of five Independent Labour MPs elected in 1931. Independent-minded throughout his political career, he died in 1968.
† Paul Channon, who himself became a Conservative MP. He died in 2007.

Tuesday, 17 November 1936

Lord Cecil to tea … Bright merry eyes … [Cecil says] I'm convinced by Winston. An alliance of France England and Russia. B[ertrand] Russell – insane! Complete insanity! To tell us we are to submit to Hitler! Do what Hitler tells us! What do you think, Sally? Caresses Sally [dog] with his long pointed fingers. Had been speaking in Manchester … The L Mayor of M. said to him We want Dalton as leader. Attlee's not a colourful man …

Very nice of him to come of course. I was flattered. And it was raining and he went home in the Tube. Very poor he said. Has sacrificed 5 or 6,000 a year when he gave up the Bar. Cdn't afford a car. I wanted to ask him to call me Virginia but refrained.

Virginia Woolf

Thursday, 26 November 1936

On Crewe Station I saw Winston Churchill, pale-looking, I thought and unsure of himself. He bought a copy of *Truth*. In the carriage going to Stockport were three middle-aged men, one of whom said he knew I'd been on the *Manchester Guardian*, because he'd often seen me in the Thatched House, where he used to go for drinks. Being reminded of the *Guardian*, coming back into this smoky, misty North, stirred me.

Malcolm Muggeridge

Saturday, 28 November 1936

The Battle for the Throne has begun. On Wednesday evening … Mr Baldwin spent one hour and forty minutes at Buckingham Palace with the King and gave him the ultimatum that the Government would resign, and that the press could no longer be restrained from attacking the King, if he did not abandon all idea of marrying Mrs Simpson. Mr Baldwin had hoped, and thought to frighten the monarch, but found him obstinate, in love and rather more than a little mad; he refused point blank and asked for time to consult his friends. 'Who are they?' M Baldwin demanded. The audience was not acrimonious, but polite, sad and even affectionate, I am told. 'Lord Beaverbrook,' the King retorted. The Prime Minister gasped and departed …The King saw

Beaverbrook yesterday and last night Beaverbrook went to see Wallis, and thus our dinner party 'chez elle' was postponed.

Henry 'Chips' Channon

Sunday, 29 November 1936

I reflect sometimes on 'politics'. The whole horrid technique should be abolished. Government of a country is a matter of proper policy and proper administration, in other words efficiency. It need not be different in nature from the government of a business – only in degree. And the policy should be set according to the Christian ethic. I wonder if I shall be called to this. I do not wish to be a dictator, but I should appreciate this chance of magnifying Christ – but of course I am not fit for this.

John Reith

Friday, 4 December–Tuesday, 8 December 1936

The Simpson crisis has been a great delight to everyone. At Maidie's nursing home they report a pronounced turn for the better in all adult patients. There can seldom have been an event that has caused so much general delight and so little pain.

Evelyn Waugh

Wednesday, 9 December 1936

My train … left an hour late. Clear day by the time we got to Preston. Country beautiful outside Carlisle – olive green fields and brown woods lightly powdered with snow; sun shining from clear pale-blue sky.

Met by Rev. Mr Cairns at Dunfermline. He told me rumour all over Dunfermline, said King had abdicated but Duke of York wd not take Crown. We hurried over high tea to listen in to 6 o'clock news but it only said that Baldwin wd make statement tomorrow. Opinion here very hard on King – purely in view of Mrs S's 'morals'. My suggestion – that if Mrs S had been a foreign princess with whose country we had

desired an alliance her past wd not have been so adversely scrutinised
– received in silence.

Vera Brittain

Thursday, 10 December 1936

The House is crowded and rather nervous and noisy. I am glad to
have got my front row of the stalls so early. The Prime Minister
[Stanley Baldwin] comes in, pushing past the encumbered knees of
his colleagues, and finds his place. He has a box with him, and on
sitting down, at once discovers that he has lost the key. He probes
and rummages for a bit and then finds the key. He unlocks the box,
extracts some sheets of paper with the royal monogram in red, and
with it some flimsy notes of his own, more squalid than a young
Labour candidate would dare to produce at a Wapping by-election.
He collects them hurriedly and the next minute seizes the red-
monographed sheets, walks firmly to the Bar, turns round, bows, and
advances to the Chair. He stops and bows again. 'A message from the
King,' he shouts, 'signed by his Majesty's own hand.' He then hands
the papers to the Speaker.

The latter rises and reads out the message of Abdication in a
quavering voice. The feeling that at any moment he may break down
from emotion increases our own emotion. I have never known in any
assemblage such accumulation of pity and terror.

The Prime Minister then rises. He tells the whole story. His papers
are in a confused state. He confuses dates and turns to Simon, 'It
was a Monday, was it not, the 27th?' The artifice of such asides is so
effective that one imagines it to be deliberate. There is no moment
when he overstates emotion or indulges in oratory. The tragic force of
its simplicity. It was Sophoclean and almost unbearable.

On leaving the library, I bumped straight into Baldwin in the
corridor. It was impossible not to say something. I murmured a few
kind words. He took me by the arm.

'You are very kind,' he said, 'but what do you really think about it?'
I detected in him that intoxication which comes to a man, even a tired
man, after a triumphant success. 'It was almost wholly unprepared. I
had a success, my dear Nicolson, at the moment I most needed it. *Now
is the time to go.*' I made no answer.

'You see,' he went on – still holding me by the arm, 'the man
is mad. *MAD*. He could see nothing but that woman. He did not

realise that any other considerations avail. He lacks religion. I told his mother so. I said to her "Ma'am, the King has no religious sense." ... *He* doesn't realise that there is anything beyond. I told his mother so. The Duke of York has always been bothered about it. I love the man. But he must go.'

No man has dominated the House as Baldwin dominated it tonight, and he knows it.

Harold Nicolson

Friday, 11 December 1936

Papers expressed general sympathy with D of York for the awkward circumstances of his accession. I cannot believe that stiff, shy, slow-brained man and his snobbish, limited little Duchess will do anything to increase the prestige of the monarchy, but Baldwin and the Archbps will doubtless be delighted at replacing the high-spirited and determined Edward with a wooden figurehead exuding all the domestic and family virtues so dear to the older generation.

Vera Brittain

Wednesday, 23 December 1936

The Archbishop of Canterbury must be losing his enfeebled mind. He has given a press lunch and is about to launch a 'Back to God campaign' and has roused other Bishops to support him. A more efficient way of making the Church of England ridiculous, I don't know. He has misread the feeling in the country, for whatever people may have thought about the King/Simpson situation, no-one wanted religious recrimination afterwards and the Church of England have certainly not gained adherents by its un-Christian attitude. Indeed it has lost much support, and has now become ridiculous.

Everyone agrees that 'finis' should now be written to the tragedy of Punchinello and Columbine.

Henry 'Chips' Channon

Tuesday, 5 January 1937

Captain Philip Mumford came to tea to talk to me about pacifism and the Peace Pledge Union. What really made me join and promise to speak, however, was not his conversation (though he is a decent, agreeable and clear-headed person) but Bertrand Russell's *Which Way to Peace?*

Vera Brittain

Friday, 8 January 1937

Hurriedly do some more parts ... before meeting Wystan Auden at Tottenham Court Road. He goes off to Spain (to drive an ambulance) tomorrow. It is terribly sad and I feel ghastly about it, tho' I feel it perhaps the logical thing for him to do – being such a direct person. Anyhow it's phenomenally brave. Spend a glorious morning with him – at Lyons Corner House, coffee-drinking. Talk over everything and he gives me two grand poems – a lullaby, and a big simple folky Farewell – that is overwhelmingly tragic and moving.

At 3.42 meet Mum and Aunt Julianne from Frinton ...

Benjamin Britten

Wednesday, 13 January 1937
Entebbe, Uganda

After dinner last night we discussed the capacity of the African brain. Kauntze [the Director of Medical Services] said that it had been proved by Windt that the cells of the African brain were undeveloped. What he wanted to find out was whether these cells developed in the educated African. So we must cut up a student and see.

Harold Nicolson

Thursday, 21 January–Friday, 22 January 1937

The Webbs came along on Sunday morning. I hadn't seen them since 1932, before I went to Russia. They were just the same and rather self-consciously affable, as though insisting 'Of course we know you'll attack us and the Soviet regime, but we're people who don't mind in the least being disagreed with. That's your point of view, and this is ours.' We only showed our fangs once or twice, and that only momentarily, as when Beatrice said if Russia and Germany went to war

Germany would be 'soundly whipped.' The children came up to see them and shook hands with Webb as though he'd been some strange sea monster.

Malcolm Muggeridge

Sunday, 28 February 1937

Bitter day, colder than any this winter …

After lunch we went off to Hyde Park to speak in Dick Sheppard's Peace Protest against the Govt rearmament programme …

As I stood on the cart the wind literally thumped my back and the sleet lashed my face, but I couldn't complain when so many 'crocks' had bravely turned up. Dick Sheppard began 'I'm afraid you won't be able to hear me in this gale, I'm an asthmatic.' Laurence Housman said 'I hope you won't mind if I keep my hat on but I'm over seventy.' Canon Morris said: 'I'm keeping my hat on too, as I've only just recovered from scarlet fever'! How the audience – 200 or 300 at least – endured as they did for over an hour is beyond my comprehension, but the English are incredible.

Vera Brittain

Tuesday, 4 May 1937

To the Palace at 5.30. With Hardinge [private secretary to King George VI] for a while. Logue, the King's stutterer curer came in. He is much more in charge than anyone else. King in very good form. We got a desk fitted up so that he could talk standing.

The two princesses came charging down the passage followed by a little brown dog and then by a stout nurse. They came into the room where we were, said they had heard the talk in the news room and generally played about. The King paid no attention to them.

John Reith

Sunday, 9 May 1937

Wet and filthy day. In afternoon with Peter Pears to the Left Book [Club] meeting – musicians circle … Some very good and some

equally boring speeches. The secret is I suppose that while the issue*
is most terribly serious and urgent, the means are most terribly dull
and unsympathetic. Anyway it makes us depressed as purgatory and it
takes all the wonders of Lyons' cream 'gateaux' to cheer us up!

Benjamin Britten

Thursday, 24 June 1937
Embassy of the Soviet Union, London

Saw Maisky at his Embassy at 7.

I saw Maisky alone, as I generally do, but I daresay there was an
unseen listener to our conversation. I began by saying, 'It is some time
since we met and a lot of things have been happening in your country
which have disturbed us a good deal. I should like you to give me some
information about them. I hope they have not seriously weakened the
Red Army.' He replied, 'Let us put that down as No 2 on our agenda.
I should like first to speak about Spain …'

We then passed on to Item 2 on the agenda. He gave a long explanation largely on familiar lines, of the recent trials and executions. He
said that the Generals … were definitely pro-German, anti-French and
anti-British … There was no doubt that they were plotting a military
dictatorship in Russia, close friendship with Russia, the elimination in
some measure of Capitalism in Russia and the cession to Germany of
part of the Ukraine including Odessa, in return for the re-absorption
of the Baltic States into the Soviet Union. They were willing, on these
terms, to let Germany have a free hand in the West. I said that I found
the story about ceding even part of the Ukraine almost incredible …

He said that I must remember the immense area of the Soviet
Union. I might think that the analogy was for this country to cede
Scotland to Germany. In fact, the analogy was rather to cede Trinidad.

As I was going away … I said '… I have made suggestions to you
before on other questions, for instance that you should ask Mr Dmitrov
[Secretary of the Communist International in Moscow] that he should
take steps to liquidate the Communist Party in this country and let its
members join the Labour Party as individuals. This would get rid of
many difficulties and would improve relations between your country
and the Labour Movement. I am sure that you have already passed on

---

* It is not clear which issue Britten was referring to, but it might be the German
bombing of the Spanish town of Guernica.

that suggestion of mine.' He laughed a little uncomfortably; perhaps at this point he was more acutely conscious of the unseen listener ...

Hugh Dalton

Friday, 25 June 1937

To the Albert Hall meeting last night ...

Basque children singing on the gramophone. Robeson sang: a sympathetic malleable nigger, expressive, uninhibited, all warmth and the hot vapours of African forests.

Virginia Woolf

Sunday, 27 June 1937

The Foreign Affairs Committee is addressed by Anthony Eden. He gives a general review of the problems from Tokyo to Washington.

He admits that Non-Intervention [in Spain] has largely failed ... He makes a great point of the fact that whereas the difficulties of the dictator states are hidden behind a steel curtain, all our own cards are on the table. We must never bluff. But in fact the position is better than formerly since both Germany and Italy are abating their former truculent attitude. The foundations of peace, he says, are firmer than we suppose, and our diplomatic position with the neutral countries in the Eastern Mediterranean and in the United States is stronger than ever before.

Harold Nicolson

Tuesday, 27 July 1937

Snape

Back for tennis at club with Peter Pears, Teddy Rogers and Archdale. Quite good fun – play for once quite well on form.

They both (PP and TR) come back for a meal.

Result number x of the appalling British foreign policy is now starting:- just as she before raped Manchuria, as Italy raped Abyssinia, as Fascism in general is raping Spain, Japan is now getting her filthy military clutches onto Pekin.

Benjamin Britten

Thursday, 2 September 1937

London

Edgar and I dined with HG Wells – Moura* was there and the Weizmanns. We talked, among other things, of 'greatness'. HGW doubted its existence. I said 'What about Shakespeare?' He branched off to say that there was a great affinity between Shakespeare and Defoe, Dickens and Charlie Chaplin! These three latter he thought must be Jewish. He was sure about Defoe [and] suspected it of Dickens whose art was very like Chaplin's in its use of pathos. He talked a good deal of nonsense – but he has the art to conceal a good deal of his self-conceit. Sometimes he says interesting things – amid a lot of rot – as for instance that a man seldom produces good art if he has lived always in his own class and circle.

Moura was charming – she is the perfect type of cultivated European.

Blanche 'Baffy' Dugdale

Monday, 27 September 1937

Ramsay MacDonald in my room for three-quarters of an hour this morning. Very ga-ga, poor man.

John Reith

Sunday, 24 October 1937

Chicago and St Louis

On train read par. in *Chicago Tribune* that Dick Sheppard had won the Rectorial Election at Glasgow University by a big majority, beating Winston Churchill and JBS Haldane. A pacifist Rector where once Lord Birkenhead, as Rector, made his speech about glittering swords! It shows there are times when the powers of self-interest and materialism can be conquered by the spiritual forces of the world.

Vera Brittain

---

*Moura Zakrevskaya (later Baroness Budberg) was a mistress of H. G. Wells and suspected of being a Russian double-agent. Her half-sister was the great-grandmother of Nick Clegg, leader of the Liberal Democratic Party since 2007.

Monday, 10 January 1938

Palestine

This very night we heard of the murder of Mr Starkey, a British archae-
ologist, on the Hebron Road.

Tea – and I gave them a sketch of how things have been going in
London. Ben-Gurion asseverates that 75 per cent of the Yishuv [the
Jewish community in Palestine] are pro-Partition. I told him the time
is come when that must be publicly proved. He wants Chaim to go to
USA in February and organise a big pro-Jewish state demonstration
there.

This may be a good plan – but I think Ben-Gurion over-estimates
importance of USA opinion on HMG.

Blanche 'Baffy' Dugdale

*In January 1938, President Roosevelt secretly proposed a conference of
Britain, France, Germany and Italy in Washington to reduce European
tensions. Relations between the US and Britain were themselves poor, and
Prime Minister Neville Chamberlain rebuffed this initiative in favour of his
conciliatory policy towards Italy and Germany.*

*Anthony Eden considered that close Anglo-American cooperation
could avert war (but was away from London when Chamberlain replied to
Roosevelt) and Chamberlain's reply precipitated his resignation as Foreign
Secretary in February 1938.*

*It was a critical event in the build up to the war. Eden was replaced by
Lord Halifax. (Eden returned to government as Foreign Secretary in 1940.)*

Tuesday, 18 January 1938

All these days busy discussing with A[nthony Eden] this question of
Roosevelt's initiative. Whatever else may be decided, *we must not turn
him down.*

Alexander Cadogan

Tuesday, 25 January 1938

2.30 meeting of Foreign Policy Committee ... P.M. explained his idea of a reshuffle of central Africa. Quite good, as *presentation*, but it won't satisfy the Germans. However A, quite rightly, didn't criticise. Only made one point – accepted by P.M. – that if we make colonial concession it is *only* as part of a *general* settlement.

Alexander Cadogan

Thursday, 27 January 1938

Usual talks with Montagu Norman [Governor of the Bank of England]. Tonight I told him of my ultimate despairing hope of an appeal to Christ for the country and I found him definitely sympathetic. He is so against piling up armaments. He says that is his main problem – where the money is to come from to pay for it all. I hope if I were PM I would have the strength to stake all on Christ.

John Reith

Monday, 21 February 1938

Foul day again. Went to see Halifax about 11. [He is] in 'temporary charge'. Tells me he hasn't been offered the post. I told him of dangers if he accepted. Talked to him about policy. Brave words butter no parsnips ... Dined at home. Everything is very hateful. A[nthony Eden] came in to FO this morning to say goodbye. I think that on the facts, an ordinary man ought to have stayed. A., being what he is, was right to go.

Alexander Cadogan

Tuesday, 8 March 1938

I work away with Richard Law. He is a great friend of Eden's. He said that the P.M. had of late been definitely rude to Eden and that the latter had derived the impression that he was wanting to drive him out. The P.M. had returned a snubbing message to President Roosevelt. Eden had much resented this since it ruined his policy of close relations with

America. The P.M. is bitterly anti-Russian and also anti-America. The soul of the ironmonger is not one which will save England.

Harold Nicolson

Friday, 11 March 1938

An unbelievable day in which two things occurred. Hitler took Vienna and I fell in love with the Prime Minister.*

The morning was calm, the PM enchanting. I am in and out of his room constantly now.

Early on there were messages announcing mysterious movements of troops in Bavaria, with the usual denials from Berlin. Then there was a grand luncheon party at 10 Downing Street at which the Chamberlains entertained the Ribbentrops,† the Halifaxes, the Winston Churchills etc. By then the news had reached the FO that the Germans had invaded Austria and from 5 to 7pm reports poured in. I was in Halifax's room at 7.30 when the telephone rang. 'The Germans are in Vienna' and five minutes later, 'The skies are black with Nazi planes' ... All night messages flowed in; by midnight Austria was a German province.

It is certainly a set-back for the Chamberlain government. Will my adorable Austria become Nazi-fied?

Henry 'Chips' Channon

Sunday, 13 March 1938

Leicester West constituency‡

A perfect spring day which shows Leicester at her ugliest. Round to the Newfoundpool Working Men's Club. They are all anti-Chamberlain, saying 'Eden has been proved right.' My own stock has gone up greatly over my speech. My broadcast also pleased them. It is amazing how many of them listen in to serious debates. It really encourages one. I

---

* Austria was invaded by Germany in March 1938 and incorporated into the German 'Greater Reich'. Chips Channon, a Chamberlainite, had been appointed Parliamentary Private Secretary to Rab Butler, number two at the Foreign Office since February 1938 when Lord Halifax replaced Eden as Foreign Secretary.

† Joachim von Ribbentrop, Foreign Minister in Germany, 1938–45.

‡ In the General Election of 1935 Harold Nicolson was elected for Leicester West as a 'National' Labour MP (i.e. a 'follower of Ramsay MacDonald') with Conservative support. He was never comfortable in the role.

go away feeling how far better in mind these men are than the Tories. I wish I did not hate the Conservatives quite so much.

Harold Nicolson

Monday, 14 March 1938

Chamberlain makes a dry statement threatening a double rearmament effort but giving little indication of real policy. The Opposition behave beautifully and do not hoot or scream. There is a sense of real national crisis. Winston makes the speech of his life in favour of the League. I deliberately refrain.

Harold Nicolson

Monday, 14 March 1938

L.N.U., Labour Party and all the so-called peace-lovers (except the P.P.U.)* are shouting war! For 20 years they have been propaganding in favour of negotiation rather than war. But in this, the acid test, they are back again preferring war to negotiation.

Vera Brittain

Wednesday, 16 March 1938

We *must* not precipitate a conflict now – we shall be smashed. It *may* not be better later, but anything may happen (I recognise the Micawber strain) ...

Rearm, above *all* in the Air. That is the policy of the line of least resistance, which the Cabinet will probably take. But I am convinced it is the lesser evil ... But can the Government weather the next few months on a policy of apparent inactivity? There are all sorts of intrigues afoot (Winston, SB [Stanley Baldwin] &c.) God knows: it's an awful situation, and God help us all.

Alexander Cadogan

*LNU: League of Nations Union; PPU: Peace Pledge Union.

Saturday, 26 March 1938

Go to Cliveden about 5.30. Huge party – ordinary sort of crowd, plus the PM and Mrs Chamberlain ... Sat between Lady Ravensdale and Mrs Fitzroy at dinner. Musical chairs after – won by PM!

Alexander Cadogan

Friday, 8 April 1938

Lunched with Kingsley Martin [editor of the *New Statesman*] at the Savile Club ... He said that Chamberlain had at last got a coherent foreign policy whether right or wrong. He took the view that this country was so weak in arms, and London so indefensible, and France so weak, that we could not afford to antagonise in any degree a German-Italian combination.

Martin spoke at some length of the state of mind of politicians and public after Hitler's march on Vienna. The idea of a new coalition government was very much in the air. Churchill was to be Prime Minister and Eden Foreign Secretary. The Labour Party and Liberal Party would be strongly represented in the Cabinet. It was said that Bevin would be willing, if offered the Ministry of Labour. It was said that five Cabinet ministers ... were prepared to resign from the present Government and join a new one. Martin had been very active in running as go-between at this time ... Attlee, at the beginning had not been unfavourable ... Such a government would have sought allies everywhere and made a definite commitment to Czechoslovakia. It would have actively explored the possibility of bringing the Russians right into a scheme of mutual guarantees. But the idea died away within a few days. By the following Monday there was nothing left of it.

Hugh Dalton

Monday, 11 April 1938

I talked to Attlee who had very bad accounts of aircraft production. He heard that aeroplanes had been exported to Finland complete with all the latest gadgets which we could not get ourselves. Cripps had arrived with a story that workmen at Bristol were being told to paint swastikas on newly completed fighting aeroplanes for export to Germany ...

If it were true we should raise public hell about it.

Hugh Dalton

Monday, 25 April 1938

My room has been repainted: beautiful new sandy carpet laid: precious blue leather chairs, new fire-irons &c. – and smell of paint.

Not too much work ...

Wrote minute ... stressing the parrot-cry of 'Rearmament' is mere confession of failure of foreign policy. We *must* reach a modus vivendi with Germany.

Alexander Cadogan

April 1938

Paris

Every afternoon while I was there except two I paid a visit to a brothel. On one of the days excepted I had tea with Nadege de Ganay which from one point of view amounted to the same thing although combined with a good deal of gossip. She is an intimate friend of [Albert] Sarraut who is once more Minister of the Interior and who tells her everything.

Duff Cooper

Sunday, 1 May 1938

On board HMS Enchantress. *At sea*

I have had a busy week preparing a paper for the Cabinet on the future of the Navy. In it I suggest that we should abandon the absurd new system of rationing the defence departments. I suggest that the sensible plan must be to ascertain your needs for defence first and then enquire as to your means of meeting them. If it is really the case that they cannot be met, then there must be some fundamental change of policy either foreign, imperial or domestic. I sent advance copies of my paper to the PM, the Chancellor and Inskip* on Thursday. There is however a danger that he and the PM may decide to withhold it.

Duff Cooper

*Thomas Inskip, Minister for the Coordination of Defence, 1936–9.

Monday, 6 June 1938

Chamberlain (who has the mind and manner of a clothes-brush) aims only at assuring temporary peace at the price of ultimate defeat. He would like to give Germany all she wants at the moment, and cannot see that if we make this surrender we shall be unable to resist other demands. If we assuage the German alligator with fish from other ponds, she will wax so fat that she will demand fish from our own ponds. And we shall not by then be powerful enough to resist.

Yet if we provoke Germany now (when our defences are in a pitiable state), she will or may destroy us utterly. We all know that at the moment Germany is not prepared for a European War. But if we really oppose her, she may drive us into it. And if we do not oppose her she will become so strong that we cannot face it ...

The Italians are already distrusting Mussolini, and after our Czechoslovak success the Germans are distrusting Hitler. The spell may have been broken, and I know that it is little more than a spell. But what happens if the Japanese involve America in an Asiatic war, involve Russia as well, detach some of our ships – then Germany can strike in Europe.

We have lost our will-power, since our will-power is divided. People of the governing classes think only of their own fortunes, which means hatred of the Reds. This creates a perfectly artificial but at present most effective secret bond between ourselves and Hitler. Our class interests, on both sides, cut across our national interests. I go to bed in gloom.

Harold Nicolson

Friday, 17 June 1938

I met an Austrian yesterday who had just got away from Vienna, and what he said made me ill. There is a devilish sort of humour in their cruelty. For instance, they rounded up the people walking in the Prater on Sunday last, and separated the Jews from the rest. They made the Jewish gentlemen take off all their clothes and walk on all fours on the grass. They made the old Jewish ladies get up in to the trees by ladders and sit there. They then told them to chirp like birds. The Russians never committed atrocities like that. You may take a man's life; but to destroy all his dignity is bestial. This man told me that with his own eyes he had seen Princess Starhemberg washing out the urinals at the Vienna railway-station. The suicides have been appalling. A great cloud of misery hangs over the town.

Harold Nicolson

Sunday, 10 July 1938

The main subject of discussion at the Cabinet on Wednesday was whether we should now give financial assistance to China. The sum was £20,000,000 ... that would enable them to continue the war [against Japan] for another year.

The suggested loan to China would be direct intervention in the Far Eastern War. Was this the moment to do it when the Czechoslovak question was still unsettled, when our relations with Italy were passing through a period of deterioration and when the new Government in Japan was definitely more moderate than its predecessor and was endeavouring to improve Anglo-Japanese relations?

Duff Cooper

Thursday, 28 July 1938

McGowan [head of Imperial Chemicals] came at 12. Wants to sell 100,000,000 cartridges to Chinese but not good enough security. Wanted Government to help. We discussed means of juggling it up with some of his Government contracts but came to the conclusion it couldn't be worked.

Forgot to say Ford car delivered at 10. I drove it on Embankment. It seems very nice. Bless its career.

Alexander Cadogan

Wednesday, 14 September 1938

The Prime Minister opened proceedings and spoke for 50 minutes, gradually revealing to us his intention of paying a personal visit to Hitler. We were being told, not consulted, for the telegrams had already gone off. Approval was unanimous and enthusiastic. I said that the danger I foresaw was that we might strengthen the case of the Germans, if they accepted the plan that we proposed and the Czechs didn't, and we might be represented as having betrayed and deserted the Czechs.

Duff Cooper

Sunday, 18 September 1938

At Attlee's request I made a pilgrimage to his little Victorian villa at Stanmore, which I have never been inside before, to meet Necas, Czech Minister of Social Welfare, who is paying a flying visit to London, and Kosina who came to interpret ... Necas is a tall man, finely built, and full of courage, very Slav looking, with a small beard.

He began by laying out the familiar Czech case with aid of maps and statistics. We know all this by heart, but it would have been unkind to cut it short. He said 'We would sooner die and be drowned in our own blood than become Hitler's slaves. Every man in our country knows what is coming, every woman, even every child. We shall be massacred, but we shall fight to the last rather than give in.' Kosina said 'People in this country don't understand Hitler is like a shark. When he tastes blood he wants more. The more he eats, the greater his appetite becomes.' The circle of mountains round Bohemia has stood as the frontier for nearly 1,000 years. Once that frontier is given up, all the defensive strength of Czechoslovakia disappears ...

Hugh Dalton

Wednesday, 21 September 1938
London

Zionist Office this morning. Chaim reported on his talk with Malcolm* on Monday night, expressed his opinion that the Partition policy had been abandoned by HMG (as he believes) at the bidding of Hitler and Mussolini. He spoke solemnly of the need for the Jews to return to their traditional policy of relying on themselves alone – not on Babylon – not on Assyria – not on Egypt – and now not on the British Empire. Though to him, Chaim, reliance on Britain had hitherto been as the 'Rock of Gibraltar.' But now his policy would be uncompromising

---

* Malcolm MacDonald (son of Ramsay) was a National Labour MP who served in the National government of 1935–40. He was then Secretary of State for the Colonies and was moved to the Dominion Office, charged by Neville Chamberlain with resolving tensions in Palestine between Jews and Arabs.

hostility to Britain – to work, silently at first, toward arming and preparation, which in time (he knew not how long) would enable Jewry to pursue its own policy in the Middle East.

Blanche 'Baffy' Dugdale

Saturday, 24 September 1938

Meeting of 'Inner Cabinet' at 3.30 pm and PM made his report to us. I was completely horrified – he was quite calm for total surrender. More horrified still to find that Hitler had evidently hypnotised him to a point. Still more horrified to find PM has hypnotised H[alifax] who capitulates totally … there was practically no discussion. John Simon – seeing which way the cat was jumping – said that after all it was a question of 'modalities' whether the Germans went in now or later! Ye Gods! …

If we have to capitulate, let's be honest. Let's say we're caught napping: that we can't fight now, but that we remain true to our principles, put ourselves straight into war conditions and *rearm. Don't* – above all – let us pretend we think Hitler's plan is a *good* one! I've never had such a shattering day, or been so depressed and dispirited. I can only hope for a revolt in the Cabinet and Parliament.

Alexander Cadogan

Wednesday, 28 September 1938

I walk down to the House at 2.15 p.m. passing through Trafalgar Square and down Whitehall. The pigeons are clustered round the fountains and children are feeding them. My companion says to me 'Those children ought to be evacuated at once, and so should the pigeons.' As we get near the House of Commons there is a large shuffling, shambling crowd and there are people putting fresh flowers at the base of the Cenotaph. The crowd is very silent and anxious. They stare at us with dumb, inquisitive eyes.

Harold Nicolson

Wednesday, 28 September 1938

11.30 PM sent telephone messages to Hitler and Musso saying he ready to go to Germany again … [The British Ambassador] Henderson rang me to say Hitler invited PM Musso (accepted) and Daladier to Munich tomorrow. Dictated message and ran with it to the House ... PM used it as peroration – with tremendous effect and House adjourned – thank God!

Alexander Cadogan

The signatories to the Munich agreement in the small hours of 30 September 1938 were Daladier for France, Hitler, Chamberlain and Mussolini for Italy. The terms of the Agreement were that the Sudeten territory of Czechoslovakia was ceded to Germany, a Commission was charged with 'ascertaining the remaining territory of predominantly German character'. Britain and France agreed to guarantee the new frontiers and Germany and Italy would join the guarantee once the 'question of the Polish and Hungarian minorities in Czechoslovakia' had been settled. The four heads of government would meet again in three months if the minorities question had not been settled.

Historian John Wheeler-Bennett wrote of Munich: 'Hitler had gained everything. He had said that his troops would enter the Sudetenland on 1 October 1938 – and they would do so, the only difference being that now they would not have to fight their way in and would complete the occupation in ten days without resistance ... The division [of opinion in Britain] was not on party lines for though the greater part of the "anti-Munich" forces were to be found among the Socialists and Liberals, and the Conservatives constituted the main support for the Government, there were sizeable minorities in both camps. In the country as a whole, families were divided and friendships sundered ... In West End clubs and East End public houses; in railway trains and in suburban parlours; wherever men and women met together the subject was debated with heat and acrimony.'*

Thursday, 29 September 1938

To Middlesex Territorial Force Offices to be interviewed. Really very funny. They were most civil. Left it that I might accept a battalion command (searchlight).

John Reith

---

* *Munich: Prologue to Tragedy* by John W. Wheeler-Bennett (London, 1948)

Friday, 30 September 1938

Marvels of organisation recited on the BBC last night. All who wish to leave London [are] to go to certain tube stations, with a thick coat and enough food for the day: children to bring no glass bottles; parents not to come. Public will then be taken free of charge to towns and villages 50 miles out of London. Each will be given a stamped card on which to write to friends. No choice of destination. &c.

Virginia Woolf

Sunday, 2 October 1938

War broken out already L[eonard] thought. Then the BBC statement that all poisonous snakes at the Zoo would be killed, and dangerous animals shot – vision of London ravaged by cobras and tigers ... Duff Cooper has resigned.

Virginia Woolf

Monday, 3 October 1938

Keynes to tea yesterday. All a put up job between Chamberlain and Hitler, Maynard said. Never had been any chance of war.

Rain. Wind. Apples falling ... dear old M. so sanguine, so powerful, somehow lovable too, and Lord how Brilliant.

Virginia Woolf

Thursday, 6 October 1938

Our group decide that it is better for us all to abstain, than for some of us to abstain and some to vote against. We therefore sit in our seats, which must enrage the Government, since it is not our numbers that matter but our reputation. Among those who abstained were Eden, Duff Cooper, Winston, Amery, Cranborne, Wolmer, Roger Keyes, Sidney Herbert, Louis Spears, Harold Macmillan, Richard Law, Bob Boothby, Jim Thomas, Duncan Sandys, Ronald Cartland, Anthony Crossley, Brendan Bracken and Emrys-Evans. That looks none too well in any list. The House knows that most of the above people know far more about the real issue than they do.

It was clear that the Government were rattled by this. In the first place, the P.M. gave a pledge that there would be no General Election. In the second place he made the astounding admission that his phrase about 'peace in our time' was made under the stress of emotion. The House breaks up with the Tories yelling to keep their spirits up. But they well know that Chamberlain has put us in a ghastly position and that we ought to have been prepared to go to war and smash Hitler. Next time he will be far too strong for us.

Harold Nicolson

Thursday, 15 December 1938

Ivone Kirkpatrick [First Secretary at British Embassy] turned up from Berlin. He has been told … that Hitler will bomb London in March! … I then saw H[alifax] and told him the K story. He saw PM at 7 and latter summoned a meeting of the Ministers concerned for 10 am tomorrow. Glad he takes it seriously …

Alexander Cadogan

Monday, 9 January 1939

Irritating day as secretary didn't turn up owing to fact that her children's nurse was given a week-end holiday and simply did not come back last night. Gave no notice or anything. Married women's work in this country is difficult owing to no lack of ability or organising power in themselves, but to deplorable domestic system of individual household management. Strongest possible argument for state-supplied crèches, nursery schools, communal kitchens, etc as in Russia. Half the population's intellectual power running to waste from avoidable thraldom to domesticity. Absolutely no reason why a woman shouldn't have the best of both worlds as a man always has had.

Vera Brittain

Tuesday, 10 January 1939
en route London to Rome

Calm crossing. Lunched on train with PM, Halifax and Dunglass [Alec Douglas-Home]. Paris 5.45 … Desultory [talks] – no proper secretariat or interpreter, and we just sat in chairs. PM and H tried to talk French. That sort of talk always ineffective.

Alexander Cadogan

Thursday, 12 January 1939

Rome

Lunch. Musso very pleasant and we talked nearly the whole time. I reminded him of a former meeting (1924) and he told me of his visit in 1922. I flattered him and drew him about Rome. He told me of what he had done and was doing and of reclaiming the marshes, Ostia etc. We talked about Americans … He affected to take not much account of them. He admitted there wasn't such a thing as an Aryan race – only an Aryan language. Said only 20% of Germans were fair haired. Rest were Dinarios, Alpinos &c.

After lunch walked around the Palace and I had another talk with Musso. He lectured me on Etruscan and early Roman history …Talked to me also about their youth training, beginning at the age of 6, and ending at 55! I said there was quite a bit of that that we might copy in England. We talked French the whole time.

Alexander Cadogan

Thursday, 19 January 1939

In Tube this morning saw a poster with pictures of Stalin, Hitler and other dictators above a Madame Tussauds advt. 'The only place in the world where they all live together at peace.'

Vera Brittain

Saturday, 4 February 1939

Vita and I go round to the Beales' [farm at Sissinghurst] where there is a television set lent by a local radio-merchant. We see a Mickey Mouse, a play and a Gaumont British film. I had always been told that the television could not be received above 25 miles from Alexandra Palace. But the reception was every bit as good as at Selfridge's. Compared with a film, it is a bleary, flickering, dim, unfocused, interruptible thing, the size of a quarto sheet of paper such as this on which I am typing.

But as an invention it is tremendous and may alter the whole basis of democracy.

Harold Nicolson

Thursday, 23 February 1939

Lunched at the University Women's Club with Mrs Corbett Ashby to meet two Arab women – wives of Arab delegates to the present Palestinian conference ... Oh! That University Women's Club – full of grim-looking desiccated spinsters in appalling tweeds. Heaven preserve Shirley from an academic career!

It was refreshing to hear the Arab view of the Jews, who apparently behave to the Arabs in Palestine exactly as people in other countries behave to *them*!

Vera Brittain

Monday, 27 February 1939

Meeting to launch the renunciation of war by the joint pacifist group from the Christian churches.

I found the meeting – which was as much a service as a meeting – really most moving. We sang 'God moves in a mysterious way' which I hadn't heard since it made me weep during the War, the Oxford version of Luther's 'Ein Feste Burg' and 'Jesus shall reign where'er the sun'. Canon Raven and Donald Soper were the other speakers beside myself.* I felt a little strange among so many clerics, but spoke as a lay person representing the other lay people there who were looking to the pacifist message from the Christian churches to give us a lead and become more widespread. I *do* like Canon Raven.

Vera Brittain

Monday, 20 March 1939

These are awful days. The crisis is worse, really, than last Sept., but the public don't know it. It's more critical and more imminent and

---

*Canon Charles Raven was Regius Professor of Divinity at Cambridge University; Dr Donald Soper was a Methodist minister, President of the Methodist Conference, 1953–4.

more acute. And I'm afraid we have reached the cross-roads. I have always said that, as long as Hitler could pretend he was incorporating Germans into the Reich, we could pretend that he had a case. If he proceeded to gobble up other nationalities, that would be the time to call 'Halt!' That time has come, and I must stick to my principle, because on the whole, I think it right. I don't believe that he can gobble up all Europe or at least I don't believe that, if he does, it will do him much good. But we must have a moral position, and we shall lose it if we don't *do* something now. PM's speech was all right on sentiments, but the country – and other countries – are asking 'What are you going to do?' If we say plainly, we risk goading Hitler into attacking us. But that is a risk that must be taken. This country has taken risks before. But of course we are *not* ready (nor ever shall be).

Alexander Cadogan

Friday, 31 March 1939

Back at FO at 2.45 and as there wasn't anything frightful or urgent, went out and walked round lake in the Park. Saw scyllas in bloom. I was feeling pretty awful by now, but sight of flowers and mowing machines and domestic couples of ducks, restored my balance.

By the way, in the Park … I met Raczynski [the Polish ambassador] coming back from the House, seemingly pleased.* The die is now cast and Hitler may bomb us. But I think we've done right.

Alexander Cadogan

Monday, 17 April 1939

Saw Maisky, who is leaving tomorrow for Moscow for consultation. He says that Romania is thought in Moscow to be more crucial than Poland (1) because she is militarily weaker, (2) because she is internally more divided, containing some pro-German elements, (3) because Hitler on the Black Sea would be only thirty miles from Odessa, and (4) because

---

* On 31 March, the British and French governments announced a guarantee of Polish independence in the event of military invasion by Germany. This marked the official abandonment of appeasement by Chamberlain. This was followed in April by an Anglo-French guarantee to support Greece and Romania. On 15 April, 'a period of fantastically complicated transactions' between London, Paris and Moscow began for some sort of an agreement with the Soviet Union.

Germany would then have her oil. Also Romania is more willing than Poland to accept Soviet aid ...

Hugh Dalton

Thursday, 20 April 1939

Lovely spring day. Hitler's birthday!! I had arranged that HM should not wish him 'happy returns' (as we don't want any of them!) but only congratulations on his 50th birthday – blast him! Picked up Halifax at 9.45.

PM has agreed to conscription! Hopes to announce it on Tuesday.

Alexander Cadogan

Saturday, 20 May 1939

I dictated paper for Cabinet on Russia. Rather delicate, weighing up the pros and cons. In his present mood PM says he will resign rather than sign alliance with Soviet. So have to go warily. I am, on balance, in favour of it. So I think is H[alifax].

Alexander Cadogan

Wednesday, 24 May 1939

[A Member] engages me in conversation on the Terrace and asks whether I have ever considered becoming a Mason. I say no. He then explains how useful this association is and tells me that there is a lodge at the House of Commons, called the New Welcome Lodge, to which a number of Labour MPs belong.

He assured me there was no politics in Free Masonry but there was a wonderful sense of fellowship etc. I thanked him [but declined and] added, 'There is a good deal of talk going round about this Lodge.' 'There ought not to be,' said he, slightly embarrassed I thought.

Hugh Dalton

Friday, 26 May–Friday, 2 June 1939
Labour Party Conference, Southport

In private session things were said both by Bevin and Francis Williams*
concerning the weakness of Attlee's leadership. He, poor little man, has
been ill and is going into a Nursing Home for an operation (prostate
gland). I hear that the view is now taken both by Citrine and Bevin
that a change in leadership must be made ... To shift anybody from
anywhere in this sheepishly loyal movement of ours is a Herculean
task ...

Ellen Wilkinson has an indiscreet article, not under her signature,
in *Time and Tide*.

Hugh Dalton

Wednesday, 14 June 1939

Party meeting at which a vote of sympathy with Attlee in his illness,
and of personal confidence in him, is passed nem con. (Attlee is due
to have his second operation for prostate within ten days of the first
... It is by no means sure that he will come through.)

Party to meet Nash (New Zealand Minister of Finance) at the
Savoy.

Among those present was Kirkpatrick, whom I had known at the
Foreign Office and who came back from Berlin at the end of last year
... I asked Kirkpatrick whether he thought that speedy agreement of
the Anglo-Soviet Pact would halt Hitler or hasten his next offensive.
Kirkpatrick thought that it would probably halt him, though it was
impossible to be sure. On the Anglo-Russian negotiations, he said,
evidently critical of the way in which they had been conducted from
this end, 'At the beginning our Government thought they were inviting
the Russians to join the Turf Club and that they would fall over themselves with delight. The Russians on the other hand, felt that they had
a valuable oriental carpet to sell and were dissatisfied with the price
offered.'

Hugh Dalton

* Francis Williams was editor of the Labour paper, the *Daily Herald*. He would later
serve as Controller of Press Censorship and News at the Ministry of Information.

Wednesday, 21 June 1939

Gladwyn [thinks] … a general war would certainly mean the early collapse of the regime in Italy. Musso … has now been furnished with a phlegmatic German blonde, partly to symbolise the Axis and partly because the very exciting dark Italian lady whose place she has taken was thought to be exciting him too much.

Van[sittart], Gladwyn and Kirkpatrick* all take an optimistic view of the Russian negotiations …

Hugh Dalton

Tuesday, 27 June 1939

America

My dear Enid

Thank you very, very much for sending the photos. If they were sent to make me homesick they certainly succeeded! The trees were heavenly – and the small car did the oddest things to my heart!

As you see we are on the way to New York (by train) – a reason for the pencil and the wobbley writing … I'm looking forward to New York. But also feeling a bit nervous about it – with all its sophistication and 'New Yorker' brightness. I can't do that sort of thing very well!

No plans for the autumn yet – even as far as one can possibly plan these days. Things of course look very black to us out here – but I'm hoping that as usual, actually on the spot you find them less frightening. Here, I'm afraid, one is inclined to speak of Europe in the past tense.

Benjamin

Letter from Benjamin Britten to Enid Slater

Wednesday, 28 June 1939

Citrine, Morrison and I appointed by the National Council of Labour to … an interview with the P.M. on the international situation. P.M. has with him Halifax.

---

* Robert Vansittart, Chief Diplomatic Adviser; Gladwyn Jebb, Private Secretary to Cadogan; and Ivone Kirkpatrick, who had returned to London from the British Embassy in Berlin.

Citrine says we are much disturbed at long delay in getting Pact [with Russia] ...

I gathered two impressions, first that the P.M. makes more of the difficulties than Halifax, who once intervened to correct him regarding the Baltic States, but, second, that none the less, the P.M. realises that now a failure of the negotiations would be very damaging to him and to the Government ... He told us a long story about how difficult it was to deal with the Russians. This was particularly so with Molotov. 'He has never been out of Russia in his life. He sits up on a higher chair than the rest when negotiations take place, and this does not create a very friendly atmosphere ...'

The P.M. also told us that Molotov had proposed, as an alternative to a more elaborate agreement, the conclusion of a simple Triple Pact of mutual assistance against direct aggression. I asked 'Would not this be excellent and a good beginning?' The P.M. said no, because it was so drafted by the Soviets as to exclude Soviet assistance to us if we became involved in war with Germany by reason of a German aggression against Poland, Romania or any other guaranteed State.

Hugh Dalton

Friday, 14 July 1939
Wallington

Warm, but rainy. Took nets off strawberries and began weeding, which is almost impossible owing to the growth of the bindweed. Phloxes (perennial) beginning to flower.

12 eggs.

Manchester Guardian Weekly considers pro-Churchill move inside the Conservative party has been checkmated.

George Orwell

Monday, 17 July 1939

Very small newt tadpoles put into aquarium seem to disappear. Fear the large ones may be eating them, but if so this must only occur at night.

George Orwell

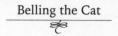

Wednesday, 9 August 1939

Took completed typescript of 'Testament of Friendship' up to Harold Macmillan in London. Long talk with him. We discussed the possibility of war and both felt it might still be avoided.

Vera Brittain

Sunday, 13 August 1939
Bath

Lunched at the Pump Room and drove to Corsham where Alec [brother] was playing cricket against the Sappers in charge of the dump. Six thousand civilians were at work storing explosives in fifteen miles of subterranean trench under the ground.

Alec made a good score and took some wickets.

Evelyn Waugh

Tuesday, 22 August 1939
Wallington

One of the newts is now mature. Its gill formations are gone and it lies on top of the water with its head in the air much of the time. The water-snail was yesterday sucking at the piece of raw meat we put in for the newts.

Officially stated in Berlin that Ribbentrop flies to Moscow tomorrow to sign non-aggression pact with USSR.

Illegal radio ... has been broadcasting anti-conscription propaganda ... PO engineers state that they have tracked down location of radio within a few houses and will soon run it to earth. Indication is that it takes at least some days to locate an illegal radio.

George Orwell

Tuesday, 22 August 1939
Mar, *Plymouth*

I have a feeling that I shall not have much more of my beloved yacht. At six I listen to the News. The Germans and the Russians have announced that they propose to sign a non-aggression pact and that Ribbentrop is on his way to Moscow for the purpose. This smashes our peace-front and makes our guarantees to Poland, Rumania and Greece very questionable. How Ribbentrop must chuckle. I feel rather stunned by this news and sit on the deck in bewilderment with the fishing smacks around me. I fear that it means that we are humbled to the dust.

Harold Nicolson

Monday, 28 August 1939

Last night Halifax and Nevile Henderson [the British Ambassador to Germany] rigged up some instructions to Henderson for guidance in his talk with Hitler. At NH's suggestion, they included offer of Non-Aggression Pact with Germany! I managed to kill this with PM and Halifax.

Alexander Cadogan

Wednesday, 30 August–Thursday, 31 August 1939

Virtually no news. Communications are passing to and fro but the Cabinet are revealing nothing. Parliament adjourned for a week.

Hot, yesterday and today fairly heavy rain. Finches beginning to flock. Very heavy mists in the early mornings.

George Orwell

On 1 September 1939, a combination of German armoured forces and war planes crossed the Polish border, destroyed the railway system and the Polish air force. A week later Warsaw, 150 miles away, was attacked. On 3 September, Prime Minister Neville Chamberlain announced that Britain was at war with Germany. On 17 September, the Soviet Union also invaded Poland, and by the end of the month the country was divided between the two powers.

Sunday, 3 September 1939

At 1.50 I motor down with Victor Cazalet to Sissinghurst. There are many army lorries along the road and a few pathetic trucks evacuating East End refugees. In one of those there is an elderly woman who shakes her fist at us and shouts that it is all the fault of the rich. The

Labour Party will be hard put to it to prevent this war degenerating into class warfare.

When I reach Sissinghurst I find that the flag has been pulled down.

Harold Nicolson

Monday, 4 September 1939

The King broadcast a speech last night which was badly spoken enough, I should have thought, to finish the royal family in this country. He should never be allowed to say more than twenty words.

Later there were Greenwood and Sinclair.* They talked about gallant Poland, our liberties, democracy etc in a way which raised very grave doubts in my mind ... Personally I prefer Chamberlain's line to all this sanctimoniousness, which is that he has done his best to give Hitler everything but feels now that he can give nothing more.

Stephen Spender

Thursday, 28 September 1939
Wallington

Decided after all not to get rid of the older hens. [In the spring] we might also go in for rabbits and bees. Rabbits are not to be rationed. The butcher says that people will not as a rule buy tame rabbits for eating but their ideas change when meat gets short. Titley says he made a lot of money out of rabbits at the end of the last war.

4 eggs.

George Orwell

Thursday, 19 October 1939
New York

My darlingest Beth
Please don't think I've forgotten you! Why I don't write every day is because Air-mail is so beastly expensive – and it is the only mail that gets to places in reasonable time.

---

* Arthur Greenwood, acting Leader of the Labour Party (Attlee was ill), and Archibald Sinclair, leader of the Liberal Party.

I try to write to you and Barbara [Britten's sisters] every week alternately – and please tell the other all the news – that sort of thing.

Thinking of you all day and wondering what is happening now. The papers are hysterical here – you complain that you're not told enough – well we're told too much. And half of it is false rumours. I nearly died when I heard that the length of the East Coast had been raided, but it turned out that it was only a scare.

You heard the grand news about the first performance of the Violin Concerto in New York by the Philharmonic? So I shouldn't be too bad tempered – but if only you were here … you could come over and keep house for Peter and me!

xxxxooooxxxx BEN

Letter to Beth Welford from Benjamin Britten

Sunday, 3 December 1939

Blackout material is now tacked to the orange and yellow striped curtains, one of the wall-lights flickered on the blink and then went out. Since Graham, the manservant, got a job in the Air Ministry, and with Mrs Graham, her cat in her arms, has bidden us farewell, there is no one to mend it. The front door bell is also broken.

We try to get used to restrictions, shortages and irritations, but it is being a long, hard winter.

Cecil Beaton

Monday, 1 January 1940

The breakfast supplied by Mrs Chamberlain* is really hardly edible, and so after sleeping at No 10 I went across to the Travellers to feed well and in comfort. It is the Prime Ministerial coffee which is at fault: it tastes of strong burnt chicory and is, curiously enough, a source of pride to the Chamberlains and their staff who believe it to be unique in its excellence.

The Cabinet, instigated by Winston [at the Admiralty], are considering a daring offensive scheme in Northern Scandinavia, which they think might bring Germany to her knees but which also to my mind

---

*The diarist John Colville was at this point Assistant Private Secretary to the Prime Minister, Neville Chamberlain.

is dangerously reminiscent of the Gallipoli plan. Briefly, they have decided that if Germany could be denied her Scandinavian supplies of iron ore she would have to give up the struggle.

John Colville

March 1940

To amuse the troops on (Salisbury) Plain, as well as keep up our own spirits, some friends and neighbours organised a pantomime. Success greeted *Heil, Cinderella* but not before much suffering.

The excitement of the theatre keeps one warm under ordinary conditions; but to change one's woollen clothes, in a below-zero Nissen hut, for cotton motley was as great an effort as to plunge into an ice bath. Small wonder that, the prevalent flu epidemic apart, most of us were struck low with every throat and chest malady. At each performance some new piece of bad news greeted us. 'Margaret's off tonight.' (Prince Charming). 'Maggie Hyde's feeling terrible.' (The pianist). 'David's ricked his back.' (Buttons). However, undeterred we planned an elaborate tour. We went to south coast towns, through ice and snow and at last reached our goal in London – to hand over quite a large sum to the 'Cigarettes for the Troops' fund.

Cecil Beaton

April 1940
New York

The country scenery (or what I've seen of it) can be very striking, but it's not like England as it hasn't been <u>lived in</u> – it's dead and colourless ... America in general is reactionary – particularly at the moment – to be a liberal is dangerous – to be a communist is fatal ... The present Bertrand Russell case has shocked us all – because of his ideas of Marriage, he was removed from his Higher Maths lecturing position at N. York University. America is nationalist and chauvinistic – her interest in Europe is patronising – full of advice but refusing to take the consequences. When I saw the way things were going in Europe I used to think that the only hope was America – now I'm sadly disillusioned.

Benjamin Britten

Friday, 10 May 1940

I was still asleep, recovering from the emotions of the past days, when my private telephone tinkled and it was Harold ringing from the Air Ministry to say that Belgium and Holland have been invaded; bombs are falling on Brussels and parachutists on the Hague. Another of Hitler's brilliantly conceived coups, and of course he seized on the psychological moment when England is politically divided, and the ruling caste riddled with dissension and anger ...

At the FO all was in confusion and the Mandarins, some of them, seemed more downhearted that the invasion of the Low Countries has probably saved Chamberlain, than cast down by the invasion itself ...

During the afternoon a message came from the Labour people that they would join a Government, but refused to serve under Chamberlain. Action had to be taken immediately. Neville hesitated for half an hour, and meanwhile Dunglass rang me – could not Rab persuade Halifax to take it on?* Rab was doubtful as he had already this morning had conversations with [Halifax] who was firm – he would not be Prime Minister. I don't understand why, since a more ambitious man never lived, nor one with, in a way, a higher sense of duty and 'noblesse oblige.' Nevertheless I persuaded Rab to go along to Halifax's room for one last final try; he found Halifax had slipped out to the dentist's ... we rang No. 10 but Alec Dunglass said that already the die had been cast.

At 6.30 I rang up No. 10 and the loyal Miss Watson told me that the PM would broadcast at 9.00 pm and her voice breaking, hung up the receiver. Shortly afterwards Alec Dunglass and Jock Colville arrived and told us that the PM had just come back from the Palace, Winston had kissed hands and was now Premier ... We were all sad, angry and felt outwitted.

I opened a bottle of champagne and we four loyal adherents of Mr Chamberlain drank 'To the King over the water.'

Henry 'Chips' Channon

---

*Alec Dunglass (Alec Douglas-Home, later Lord Home) was Principal Private Secretary to the Prime Minister, Neville Chamberlain; this was a last attempt to persuade Lord Halifax, via his junior minister at the Foreign Office, R. A. 'Rab' Butler, to take on the premiership. Three days earlier, on 7 May, the House heard Leo Amery, a leading opponent of Chamberlain's policy, denounce him in the 'Norway debate' (on Britain's unsuccessful invasion of Norway) with the famous words, 'In the name of God, go!' Churchill was First Lord of the Admiralty from September 1939 until 10 May.

Friday, 17 May 1940

One of the strangest incidents in Monday's memorable debate in the House of Commons was the reception accorded to Mr Neville Chamberlain. Mr Churchill, on entering, had been greeted from all parts of the House with what can correctly be described as 'sympathetic' cheers, since there was not a member who did not desire to demonstrate the sympathy felt for a man shouldering so great a burden at so sad a time. But when Mr Chamberlain stalked in from behind the Speaker's chair he was greeted with an ovation verging on a demonstration. He seemed startled for a moment by the virulent enthusiasm of his friends; he hesitated, smiled, and made a stiff and bashful indication of the head. The friends continued to roar applause; one of the stoutest of his supporters, Mr Walter Liddall, the Scunthorpe stalwart, actually yelled ...

The Prime Minister himself appeared totally unaware of these currents of feeling. There is a certain naïveté about Mr Churchill as about all truly great men. He sat there, hunched like a surly bulldog, with Mr Attlee peeping out behind his left shoulder. He is a great-spirited man and therefore generous, nor has he ever allowed rancour to infect his lavish zest or to check the rush and thunder of his adventure.

Harold Nicolson

Chapter Three

1940–1945
'Even to the End'

In May 1940, Britain had no effective allies* in Northern Europe, and a vast distant empire at risk. The evacuation of Dunkirk was imminent; the Battle of Britain a few months ahead. A force had been sent to (neutral) Iceland in an attempt to keep control of the North Atlantic, to be replaced later by American troops; during 1940 the United States also supplied Britain with large quantities of arms and with destroyers – but the United States was not to enter the war formally until December 1941.

The war years were well served by diarists at home and abroad of whom a few have been quoted to give a partial impression of an extraordinary story. Leo Amery, from 1940 to 1945 the Secretary of State for India in the wartime Coalition government, unsurprisingly called his diaries *The Empire at Bay*. Hugh Dalton was by then Minister for Economic Warfare; Harold Nicolson and Duff Cooper were, in the early days, at the Ministry of Information. Of the military diarists, Admiral Louis Mountbatten was a controversial appointment – as his personal diary demonstrates – as Supreme Allied Commander, South

---

*The Allies became a collective term for France, the USA, Russia (after 1941), China, Australia, Canada, New Zealand, South Africa, India, Malaya, the British West Indies, the colonies, mandates and protectorates. There were two and a half million Indians and 300-plus West Indians in Allied uniforms, with a Caribbean Regiment formed, very late in the day, in 1944. The main countries of the Axis were Germany and Austria, Italy, Japan, Hungary, Bulgaria, Romania and Thailand.

East Asia, 1943–6; General Sir Alan Brooke, Commander of Home Forces and from 1941 Chief of Imperial General Staff, somehow also managed to write a masterful series of letters and diaries through the war. A young Tony Benn,* was sent to Rhodesia to learn to fly, while a Wren officer, Audrey Deacon, was on cypher duties in Plymouth.

Nella Last (a Mass Observation volunteer known as 'Housewife, 49') kept a personal account during the war and the post-war peace of her life in the shipyard town of Barrow-in-Furness; Malcolm Muggeridge 'found himself' learning Portuguese in Lisbon as a member of the Secret Intelligence Service.

Harold Macmillan, representing the British government in Algiers, with de facto responsibility for North Africa, chronicled the campaign against the German army in the Italian colony of Libya. Joyce Grenfell also found herself in Algiers, entertaining injured British servicemen during a whirlwind tour which took her to Palestine and India. Noël Coward gave workplace concerts all over England, not always happily, as his diary records.

Throughout the war Vera Brittain describes her continuing campaign in the cause of pacifism, while Baffy Dugdale kept her focus on Palestine and a Jewish state. John Colville and Charles Wilson (later Lord Moran), as Churchill's Private Secretary and personal doctor respectively, were two of the closest witnesses to the 'struggle for survival' – but whereas Moran was concerned with the impact of Churchill's health on the war, it was, wrote Colville subsequently, President Roosevelt 'whose powers were failing'.

Friday, 24 May 1940

Winston Churchill is 65. He has just been appointed Prime Minister and I have become his doctor, not because he wanted one, but because certain members of the Cabinet, who realised how essential he has become, decided that somebody ought to keep an eye on his health.

It was in these rather ambiguous circumstances that I made my way this morning to Admiralty House, wondering how he would receive me.† Though it was noon I found him in bed reading a document. He

---

* Anthony Wedgwood Benn was known to his family when young as 'James', and to friends and colleagues as Tony or Wedgie. In 1941 his father was made a Viscount and Tony's older brother Michael became heir to the peerage.
† As First Lord of the Admiralty Churchill lived at the Admiralty building, which he continued to occupy for several weeks. Chamberlain remained in the Cabinet.

went on reading while I stood by the bedside. After what seemed quite a long time, he put down his papers and said impatiently, 'I don't know why they are making such a fuss. There's nothing wrong with me.'

He picked up the papers and resumed his reading. At last he pushed his bed-rest away and, throwing back the bed-clothes, said abruptly, 'I suffer from dyspepsia and this is the treatment.'

With that he proceeded to demonstrate to me some breathing exercises. His big white belly was moving up and down when there was a knock at the door, and the PM grabbed at the sheet as Mrs Hill came into the room.

Soon after I took my leave. I do not like the job and I do not think the arrangement can last.

Charles Wilson (Lord Moran)

Thursday, 30 May 1940
Off the French coast

I can hardly believe that I have succeeded in pulling the four divisions out of the mess we were in, with allies giving way on all flanks. Now remains the task of embarking which will be a difficult one. Went to see how embarkation was proceeding and found the whole thing at a standstill due to lack of boats!! Went to see Gort* and got little satisfaction …

Went down to beach at 7.15 pm and was carried out to open boat, and with Ronnie Stanyforth and Barney Charlesworth† we paddled out to destroyer and got aboard …We have been waiting till 10pm before starting, rather nerve wracking as the Germans are continually flying round and being shot at, and after seeing the ease with which a few bombs can sink a destroyer, it is an unpleasant feeling.

Later: We never started until 12.15 am, at 3 am we were brought up short with a crash. I felt certain that we had hit a mine or been torpedoed. But she remained on an even keel and after some shuffling about proceeded on slowly. I heard later from the commander that he had 3 routes to select from, one was under gun fire from the coast, one had a submarine and mines reported in it, and the other was very

---

*Field Marshal John Gort, Commander-in-Chief of the British Expeditionary Force in France (BEF).

†Both were aides-de-camp to General Brooke. Barney Charlesworth was killed in an air crash in February 1945. Brooke described it as one of the worst personal blows of the war.

shallow at low water. He chose the latter and hit the bottom, damaging a propeller slightly. Finally arrived at Dover at 7.15 am. Wonderful feeling of peace after the last 3 weeks!

General Alan Brooke

Friday, 31 May 1940

Tens of thousands from BEF [British Expeditionary Force] getting back across the Channel hungry, tired, half-clad, and in any kind of boat that will take them, bombed all the time.

Unprofitable morning, then went to the Peace Pledge Union and worked on Pacifist ambulance scheme ... after tea at the Euston Hotel [I] walked in Regent's Park amid shaded mauve pansies and lupins in many delicate colours. Desertedness of everything gave impression of Sunday. Since most of the iron railings had gone for conversion into armaments, the Park looked like a vast green field, very fresh and vivid. A few elderly people were sitting in chairs, a few young people sailing in boats with striped sails. Such an illusion of peace. I felt as though I were watching the funeral of civilisation elegantly conducted. So the Roman Empire must have appeared just before the barbarians marched in.

Vera Brittain

Friday, 31 May 1940

Everybody elated by the progress of the Evacuation. One of the world's greatest defeats is being redeemed by an outstanding achievement of organisation and gallantry. The BEF rearguards, though decimated, are standing firm against fearful odds; the RAF activity over Dunkirk is ceaseless; the Navy has attempted and achieved the incredible. Two hundred and twenty-two men-of-war have been used in the evacuation and 665 other vessels. The sailors are so tired that they are working automatically, but they are apparently quite undaunted.

The PM flew to Paris this morning with Attlee and the CIGS* but

---

*Clement Attlee, leader of the Labour Party, was Lord Privy Seal in the Coalition government, Deputy Prime Minister, 1942–45; the Chief of the Imperial General Staff (CIGS) was Field Marshal Sir John Dill.

alas without taking a Private Secretary. As a result I had very little to do but gossip with Brendan Bracken.

John Colville

Saturday, 1 June 1940

Barrow-in-Furness

Today in town there seemed such an anxious feeling and women asked each other eagerly if sons or husbands had 'arrived in England' yet. I heard of telegrams received and, still more anxiously waited for. One big party of soldiers came off the train to march to the Fort on Walney. They looked hot and tired and the wave of sweat and the queer acrid smell of damp khaki made one wonder at the plight of the retreating army.*

Nella Last (Housewife 49)

Saturday, 15 June 1940

Cabinet at 10. French army seems to have disintegrated. After Neville [Chamberlain] brought up proposal ... for fusion of British and French Governments – I had meanwhile drafted telegram to Bordeaux [to where the French Government had fled from Paris] suggesting French Government should come here. That is the most practical step.

I broke away at lunchtime – I've had ten weeks non-stop and it's too much almost – even for me!

... Went out in a deluge of rain and picked peas and dug potatoes for our dinner, which was excellent. Did some writing after, but won't look at work. Everything awful, but 'Come the three corners of the world and we will shock them.' We'll all fight like cats – or die rather than submit to Hitler. US look pretty useless. Well, we must die without them.

Alexander Cadogan

---

*After the Dunkirk evacuation, the remaining British and Allied troops in France were withdrawn at Alan Brooke's insistence.

Friday, 16 August 1940

Only a few minutes after the 5 o'clock to Salisbury had left Waterloo the air raid sirens sounded. Then the guard, a little man of over fifty years, came along the corridor crying 'All blinds down.' Above the noise of the train we heard thumps and bangs. We went on with our reading or minding our own business with lowered eyelids. The English behave impassively even in the face of disaster. Imagine this carriage filled with Latins! The screams! The hysterics!

When later we were on our way to Salisbury again, the damage all along the line was already being cleared up and the craters in the open fields were quickly filled before cows could fall in and break their legs. The guard in our train became emotional when the crisis was over. Waving victoriously out of the windows at the women and children clustered together, rejoicing in their safety, he ad libbed: 'Those women have had a lot to put up with ... It's a hell of a strain for them with the responsibility of all their children to look after ...'

On the somewhat halting journey (because of delayed action bombs, our train was diverted to Southampton, where another raid was in progress) miscellaneous snippets of information were picked up. Nine people had been killed at Basingstoke. Overton had got it badly.

Cecil Beaton

Saturday, 31 August 1940

Sir H Dowding and Sir C Portal came to dinner.* Dowding is splendid: he stands up to the PM, refuses to be particularly unpleasant about the Germans, and is the very antithesis of the complacency with which so many Englishmen are afflicted. He told me that he could not understand why the Germans kept on coming in waves instead of concentrating on one mass raid a day which could not be effectively parried. Ismay [General Hastings 'Pug' Ismay, Churchill's chief military assistant] suggested that they might be short of planes and have to use bombers *twice* daily. There was a great discussion about the ethics of shooting down enemy pilots landing by parachute: Dowding

---

*This was at the height of the Battle of Britain: Air Chief Marshal Hugh Dowding was Commander-in-Chief, Fighter Command (retired in November 1940) and Air Marshal Charles Portal, Commander-in-Chief, Bomber Command (Air Chief Marshal from October 1940).

maintaining that it should be done and the PM saying that an escaping pilot was like a drowning sailor.

John Colville

Saturday, 21 September 1940
Barrow-in-Furness

Aunt Sarah proudly showed me her work of the last two days – packing her bits of treasures in 'lots and lots of newspaper' and covering them with rugs and carpets – to keep them safe from bombs! Poor old lamb ...

The countryside was a painted glory of crimson and gold and green, so heartbreakingly lovely, and it was impossible to believe that in the South – our South – there was death and destruction. I wonder if everyone has the queer disbelief that I have so often. And will it keep until bombs come and wreak havoc on Barrow, and I've seen death and destruction for myself? I feel as if between me and the poor London people there is a thick fog, and it's only at intervals that I can believe it is our own people – not Spaniards or French or Dutch.

Nella Last

October 1940
Official war photographer

In the infernos of the Underground the poor wretches take up their positions for the night's sleep at 4 o'clock in the afternoon. The winter must surely bring epidemics of flu, even typhoid. The prospect is not cheering ... Nothing can really dash the spirits of the English people, who love to grumble and who, in spite of their complaints, are deeply confident of victory.

Churchill, still with cigar in mouth, looked so lonely and alone in this large room. This would make an aptly symbolic picture. From my distant vantage point, I clicked my Rolleiflex, and Haupt let off a flash. This surprised the Prime Minister. Although his sentences were not perfectly formed, I would hazard that the following would be an interpretation of the barks, wheezes and grunts that turned my blood cold: 'Hey damn you, young fellow, what the hell are you up to with your monkey tricks? Stop all this nonsense! I hate candid camera photographs! Wait till I'm prepared: the glass of port taken away, my spectacles so – this box shut, the papers put away thus – now then – I'm ready, but don't try any cleverness on me!'

The PM settled himself and stared into my camera like a bulldog guarding its kennel. Click!

Cecil Beaton

Sunday, 20 October 1940
My twenty-first birthday, Plymouth

Terry sent me a lovely Swedish vase. I was also given Andre Maurois's *The Battle of France*. It is strange to read of the state of things in France at this time last year ... So much has happened since then that we could not have thought possible if anyone foretold it: Norway, Denmark, Holland, Belgium and France. Poland had already been overrun. A Pole on the wireless the other day talked about the siege of Warsaw. There were no anti-aircraft defences and the ammunition ran out, while the city was bombarded from the ground as well as the air. It was terrible. Looking back it seems almost worse than at the time.

Audrey Deacon

Tuesday, 12 November 1940

Chamberlain is dead: and if we hold on till March we have broken the back (or whatever the phrase is). These two facts sum up the papers. I could add about Greece ... Hitler's speech ... no: time goes so heavy and slow that nothing marks the days. A bomb fell at lunch yesterday. There is nothing new. Eastbourne bombed.

Virginia Woolf*

Saturday, 16 November 1940
Barrow-in-Furness

Barrow is plunged in gloom over the terrible Coventry bombings for it's a town that many Barrow people have moved to in times of bad trade. I have many friends and old neighbours there, and also a cousin and his wife, and no word as to their safety or otherwise

---

* Virginia Woolf drowned herself on 28 March 1941.

has yet come through. At Spark Bridge there was the same feeling of unease, for several people had sons and daughters who had gone to work in Coventry. One woman was very upset, for she had refused to let her daughter come home to have her second baby. There was some trouble when she came home to have her first baby: the mother said she was tired of being put on ... The poor woman was distraught as she remembered her daughter's words about the flat she occupied 'in the shadow of the cathedral.'

Nella Last

Friday, 13 December 1940

Barrow-in-Furness

Isa Hunter came tonight to tell me her 'guests' had gone. It's rather frightening to think, if one invites a soldier, one can have an experience like Isa has had. The two soldiers – Welsh boys – were very nice in every way the first time; the second time they asked for three helpings of everything, and after dinner was finished started again on the trifle that was left in the dish, were rude to the maid, ate every chocolate and apple and nut on the sideboard, smoked every cigarette in the cedar box Isa has, and asked for 'smokes for the road' on their departure. On the third visit the married one brought his wife back from leave and asked if she could be put up for the night.

A huge pile of luggage was taken upstairs and Isa's bedroom was criticised and rearranged ... [The wife] unpacked a clock, make-up box and various oddments and talked of arrangements for the future – presumably at Isa's house – and seemed surprised when told that arrangements were only for one night.

Nella Last

Wednesday, 1 January 1941

I stayed on duty late, until the PM in the early hours ascended to the roof to look at the stars and the new moon. Eden and Kingsley Wood spent much of the evening here discussing the question of financial assistance from America. I sat in the room while the PM drafted a forceful telegram to Roosevelt, not hiding from him the dangerous drain on our resources. Sombre though the telegram was, with its warning that only by American financial help could Hitlerism be 'extirpated' from

Europe, Africa and Asia, the PM seemed to enjoy drafting it … But he obviously fears that the Americans' love of doing good business may lead them to denude us of all our realisable resources before they show any inclination to the Good Samaritan.

John Colville

January 1941

Scotland

On the return journey [from a visit by Churchill to Scapa, Orkney] Tom Johnston dined us at the Station Hotel at Glasgow, and I sat next to Harry Hopkins, an unkempt figure.* After a time Hopkins got up and, turning to the PM said:

'I suppose you wish to know what I am going to say to President Roosevelt on my return. Well I'm going to quote you one verse from that Book of Books in the truth of which Mr Johnston's mother and my own Scottish mother were brought up: "Whither thou goest, I will go; and where thou lodgest I will lodge: thy people shall be my people, and thy God my God."' Then he added very quietly: 'Even to the end.'

I was surprised to find the PM in tears. He knew what it meant. Even to us the words seemed like a rope thrown to a drowning man.

Charles Wilson

Wednesday, 22 January 1941

Plymouth

The Communist newspapers, the *Daily Worker* and *The Week*, have been suppressed. Though this may seem necessary I am inclined to think it unwise. It will drive the movement underground and give it a legitimate grievance.

Audrey Deacon

---

*Tom Johnston was Secretary of State for Scotland during the war; Harry Hopkins was President Roosevelt's special adviser, who passed most of January 1941 in the UK on a reconnaissance trip, spending much time with Churchill negotiating Lend-Lease. The Lend-Lease Bill passed through US Congress in March 1941 and authorised the President to sell or lease material to any anti-Axis country in return for any kind of direct or indirect payment. It gave the President huge discretionary powers: by September 1946 the British Empire Lend-Lease value was over $30 billion.

Thursday, 30 January 1941

The Lease and Lend Bill, which proposes to lend material to this country, repayable in kind after the war, has passed the US Foreign Affairs Committee.

This morning in a fit of energy I stripped the dining room windows of their anti-blast cellophane and paper strapping, which were going mouldy, and replaced them with net (ex-curtains) stuck to the glass. It is an improvement.

Audrey Deacon

Wednesday, 19 March 1941
St Ives, Cornwall

News of a heavy raid on Hull.

Also casualties of Clydeside and Merseyside raids last week given as very heavy: 500 deaths in Clydeside, 500 in Merseyside; 500 injured in Merseyside, 800 in Clydeside. (The usual '500' which I now realise from visits to blitzed areas represents the 'official' figure for a big Blitz. Actual casualties are obviously far more.)

Had hair washed at Preed's little shop in the town; done by new assistant who told me she has just come here from Birkenhead and was in the Blitz there last Wednesday. She said … 10,000 homeless people were now sleeping in stations and shelters. Local authorities hope-lessly Conservative. According to her, 3 miles of docks were virtually obliterated and 50 landmines fell last Wednesday in the area.

Vera Brittain

Sunday, 6 April 1941
Barrow-in-Furness

I wonder if we are so used to dreadful shocks that we are hardening. Today when we heard news on the wireless of Germany declaring war on Yugoslavia and Greece, there was none of that sick shock we had when we heard of Holland and Belgium being overrun. I wonder too if the fact of Greece being so far away helped to soften the blow. Soon it looks as if the whole world will be alight, and the prophesied

Armageddon upon us all. It seemed to dim the sunshine and when snow showers started to fall, that seemed more fitting.

Nella Last

Sunday, 13 April 1941
Ministry of Information

From the propaganda point of view, all that the country really wants is some assurance of how victory is to be achieved. They are bored by talks about the righteousness of our cause and our eventual triumph. What they want are facts indicating how we are to beat the Germans. I have no idea at all how we are to give them those facts. Fundamentally ... the British people have lost confidence in the power of the sea. Norway was a nasty knock. [And] 'How,' they ask 'was Germany able to land four divisions in Libya?'

Harold Nicolson

Tuesday, 29 April 1941
Plymouth

War Zone Courts have been constituted. They will not function in any area until it has been declared a war zone, when they will operate with wide powers.

Two planes were brought down in each of two raids on Plymouth and another four last night ... Plymouth is now to be an evacuation area. For the past fifteen months the C-in-C and the Lord Mayor have been trying to get it scheduled. It is now said to be one of the worst blitzed places in the country.

Audrey Deacon

Tuesday, 27 May 1941

I woke up this morning after a strenuous and very thrilling night watch and heard that the *Bismark* had been sunk (by *Dorsetshire*) some hundred miles west of Brest ...

More than 100 ships were in the chase ... for a time *Bismark* was lost; but was picked up again by Coastal Command aircraft. She was alone.

Admiral Lutjens sent a signal to Hitler saying that though incapable of manoeuvre, he would fight to the last shell; and went down with colours flying ...

Audrey Deacon

June 1941

The work of Coastal Command and Fleet Air Arm, concerned as it is with our seas and shores (and those occupied by the enemy) is the least spectacular if perhaps the most strenuous, and even dangerous. Coastal Command is relied upon to be the eyes and ears of the RAF and is an air force within the air force with its own land planes, bombers, fighters and flying-boats to ward off attack from the air ...

A jovial red-cheeked officer with a ginger, lavatory-brush moustache, completes his conscientious report of yet another monotonous daily sortie. He scratches his sandy head and asks 'How many g's in Skagerrak?' The pink and perky flight orderly who comes in with a wicker cage of carrier pigeons does not know. The use of homing pigeons to carry messages is as old as Solomon: the early Persians trained these birds for the ancient Greeks to dispatch the results of Olympic races. Today, when modern methods have failed, they are considered the most reliable means of communication, and many men have been saved by these birds flying as quickly as forty miles an hour back to their home loft. The last act the navigator performs when his wireless fades out is to release the two pigeons carrying messages giving the position of the aircraft.

The fighter pilot is never away for more than two hours, but Coastal Command pilots, on their long flights hundreds of miles out over the Atlantic, must exercise enormous patience ... Some of the feats of endurance do not bear contemplation. Gunners are clamped in the medieval vices of the narrow fuselages where they have bled to death. Sometimes they fly in temperatures so low that a thermos of tea becomes frozen the moment the cap is unscrewed.

Cecil Beaton

Tuesday, 1 July 1941

Walked and met A [Anthony Eden]. He had spent from 11 pm till 2 am with PM. But I gather nothing emerges. We are not prepared to take advantage of this Heaven-sent (and short) opportunity of the Germans being heavily engaged in Russia.* We shall look awful fools! But there it is.

Alexander Cadogan

Thursday, 10 July–Friday, 11 July 1941

Caught 10.30 train for Plymouth. Drove to Grand Hotel through terrible devastation.

Michael Redgrave arrived at 5.30. Extremely healthy and happy. What a magic the Navy does to people. Having left a luxurious film star life to be an ordinary seaman, he is obviously having a wonderful time. We dined and I drove him back to HMS *Raleigh*.

Friday: Spent morning with Lady Astor [the Conservative MP for Plymouth Sutton] walking round the devastated town. A strange experience.

The whole town a pitiful sight. Houses that held sailor families since the time of Drake spread across the road in rubble and twisted wood. Lady A. delivered a tirade against Winston.

Watched the people of Plymouth dancing on the Hoe. A large dance floor, white-coated, several hundred girls gaily dressed, dancing very well with sailors, soldiers, marines etc in the strong evening sunlight. A sight so infinitely touching, not that it was consciously brave, but because it was so ordinary and unexhibitionist.

Noël Coward

October 1941

By the end of the war much will be in ruins, ideas as well as buildings. The power of the bankers must lie buried in the debris of the City of London, the ghosts of vested interest must stalk disconsolate through the gutted warehouses, the abuses of the big monopolies must have been washed down the sewers by our jets. The old capitalist system, like the captive Samson, must perish in the ruins which it has pulled down on itself.

---

* On 22 June 1941, Germany had, without declaring war, invaded Russia, despite the German–Soviet non-aggression pact.

The people alone will survive – the tough invincible working people … When peace comes we will build a Brave New World.

Peter Pain*

Wednesday, 10 December 1941

Arrived at WO to be informed that both the *Prince of Wales* and the *Repulse* had been sunk by the Japs! This on top of the tragedy of Honolulu puts us in a very serious position for the prosecution of the war. It means that for Africa eastwards to America through the Indian Ocean and the Pacific, we have lost command of the sea.[†]

Chiefs of Staff conference moved to 10 Downing Street at 12 noon when we discussed the naval situation with the PM. He had stood shock well.

Spent afternoon in office with series of visits. Starting with Sir Keith Murdoch who controls Australian group of newspapers.

General Alan Brooke

Saturday, 20 December 1941

On board the Duke of York *to visit President Roosevelt*

Since we left the protection of the Clyde we have been battened down for eight days listening to the dull pounding of the great seas on the ship's ribs.

To say that the PM does not seem any the worse for wear from the tedious days below deck is an understatement. He is a different man since America came into the war. The Winston I knew in London frightened me. I used to watch him as he went to his room with swift paces, the head thrust forward, scowling at the ground, the sombre countenance clouded, the features set and resolute, the jowl clamped down as if he had something between his teeth and did not mean to let go. I could see that he was carrying the weight of the world and wondered how long he could go on like that and what could be done

---

* Peter Pain was the barrister for the Fire Brigades Union and an auxiliary fireman.
† The reference to Honolulu is to the Japanese assault on the US Pacific Fleet and airfields at Pearl Harbor, on the Pacific island of Oahu, on 7 December 1941, which put the entire American battleship force out of action. In a separate engagement, during an attempt by the Royal Navy to intercept a Japanese invasion fleet off Malaya, on 10 December, the Japanese Navy used bombers to sink two Royal Navy vessels.

about it. And now – in a night it seems – a younger man has taken his place ... the tired dull look has gone from his eye; his face lights up as you enter his cabin ...

Charles Wilson

Monday, 22 December 1941
Flight to Washington

After nine days' racket I cannot get the sound of the great seas out of my head.

Our Lockheed was over the lights of Washington in three quarters of an hour ... On landing I let the PM have a start before I got out. Looking round I noticed a man propped up against a big car, a little way off. The PM called me and introduced me. It was President Roosevelt. Even in the half light I was struck by the size of his head. I suppose that is why Winston thinks of him as majestic and statuesque, for he has no legs to speak of since his paralysis. He said warmly that he was very glad to welcome me ... he began immediately to speak of the casualties at Pearl Harbour, many of them with very bad burns. He made me feel that I had known him for a long time. Halifax [British Ambassador] took me in his car to the Mayflower Hotel, while Max (Beaverbrook) went with the PM to the White House.

Charles Wilson

Sunday, 15 February 1942

It is the fact that, even now, we still seem to be muddling and unprepared, that has, after a dark winter and long periods of snow, ice and dirty skies, given so many people at home a feeling of cynical desperation or what's worse – sheer apathy. I believe that for the first time the English now do seem to realise the possibility of defeat.

We hear that Singapore, to which we have been sending reinforcements, and which was defended by 80,000 men, has surrendered. This is one of the most shattering blows.

The gloom is all pervading ... the cold, the untidiness, the ugliness of people in London, a lack of smartness in our army and, above all, the off-handedness and apathetic laziness of the people, have become a slight obsession with me.

Cecil Beaton

Thursday, 19 March 1942

Portugal

Here in Lisbon is the last vestige in Europe of our old way of life now precariously existing.* It is like the owner of some ancestral mansion moving when ruined into the lodge with one or two of his pictures, a piece of plate or so, one aged servant in threadbare livery. Here are cafes, neon signs, money haggling, petit dejeuner with fat pats of butter brought in on a tray, jangling trams and taxi cabs and newspapers of all the nations. One deep and significant change may, however, be noted, the pound sterling has lost its magical qualities; rub, rub at the lamp and no all-powerful djinn appears, at best only a reluctant slut who must be coaxed for any service at all.

Malcolm Muggeridge

March 1942

Official war photographer in Libya

The general hospital at Tobruk† has suffered remarkably little from the bombing. At this time one of the senior surgeons, named Simpson Smith, with the rank of Colonel, a fair good-looking sportsman, was bemoaning the fact that most of his cases were accidental. 'It worries me that there's this terrible continuous waste. The other day we had seventy four cases all in at once: burns – very bad.'

The doctor's enthusiasm for me to photograph his various exhibits is sometimes hard to face. He rubs his hands. 'Splendid, Beaton. There's a great deal to show you – burns all the colours of the rainbow. But best of all we've got in a field case. You are lucky! We've just received a South African, who was driving in a truck when a mine went off ...'

Cecil Beaton

Monday, 30 March 1942

I considered with much quiet mirth, Sir Stafford Cripps, the British Government's Special Envoy to India, and Gandhi closeted together;

---

*Malcolm Muggeridge spent a few months learning Portuguese, before going on to Mozambique.

† From April to November 1941 Tobruk had been under siege by German and Italian forces, defended for most of the time by an Australian division. The port was vital to the Axis for supplies into North Africa.

sympathy entirely with, and money on, Gandhi. He knows the game; after Halifax as Viceroy, Cripps will be easy money. The British raj then [in 1931] was still powerful enough to induce Gandhi to visit Halifax. Now Cripps visits Gandhi.

Malcolm Muggeridge

Monday, 13 April 1942
Plymouth

I've now got my second stripe [promotion to Second Officer in the Wrens, in charge of the Watch].

One night watch, I lost the sapphire from my engagement ring. We swept the office and looked everywhere but couldn't find it. When I took the ring back to Bowdens, they sent it back to the makers, who of course replaced the stone free of charge. Which was very lucky though of course it should never have come out. I then proceeded to lose my fountain pen.

We recently had a 'Warship Week' here in competition with Portsmouth (who we beat); we raised £140,000 odd, having aimed at £12,000 ... I went out selling savings certificates in an ambulance one afternoon.

Audrey Deacon

Sunday, 19 April 1942
Barnes, London SW13

It was so wonderful to have your two dear letters – Ben and I collected them when we went up to Boosey and Hawkes the day after we arrived.

We had a prolonged and rather boring journey. We sat in New York for several days and again in other places on the way up the coast – and the actual Atlantic crossing took only twelve days – but they were spent in the most desolate company – callow, foul mouthed witless recruits. How we missed you and William.

Coming back here has been the most odd and mixed experience. The countryside looking dazzlingly green – uniforms everywhere – destruction so cleared up that it looks like peacetime planning – the starchy food that fills but does not nourish – no fruit or cream at all – little butter – three eggs a month – and so on – but one's friends are very glad to see one and couldn't be more welcoming.

Our plans are of course vague. We have to register as pacifists which will take a little time. I hope very much that I will be able to work with the Quakers – I think I shall join them. If only I were a better person!

Last night there was the enclosed cutting in the paper. I'm dreadfully afraid it means Roger has gone.*

Always your Peter

Letter from Peter Pears to Elizabeth Mayer in New York

Wednesday, 24 June 1942
Nairobi

Staying now at Government House, servants, car with flag, black soldiers who present arms, etc. Governor a small Pickwickian figure, kindly, shrewd, remarked that indication of our lack of belief in ourselves and our civilisation was that we no longer attempted to make the blacks like us but insisted they were better as they were. Sad place, Nairobi, like India, twilight of Empire, all over and done with. Young secretary attempts to suggest that, on the contrary, wonderful new possibilities opening up, Empire based not on fear but on genuine collaboration, etc. Governor, wife and I listen politely.

Malcolm Muggeridge

Sunday, 5 July 1942
Lagos

Radio latest: The desert battle has raged for five days:† we are still holding the enemy. Dimbleby said, 'There is no cause yet for optimism, but we need not be pessimistic,' which seems a fair statement of the case.

Denton, the Information Officer, told me that the women journalists visiting the Middle East have made themselves pretty unpopular. One who is known as the WOV (World's Oldest Virgin) boasted that she acquired most of her information in bed. [Another] was by far the most popular, and she was a beautiful, smiling woman until she transformed herself into a journalist; then her mouth became contorted and

---

*Peter Pears's friend, Roger Burney, was British Liaison Officer on the Free French submarine *Surcouf* which in February 1942 went down with all hands somewhere in the Bermuda Triangle in circumstances that remain mysterious.
† The first battle of El Alamein.

turned down at the corners, her eyes popped and she barked: 'How many aeroplanes are passing through here a week? I must have hard facts and figures for the American public.'

Cecil Beaton

Friday, 6 November 1942

Began day with two concerts in the Speke aircraft factory. Three thousand seven hundred at each performance.

There can be no doubt about it, I have no real rapport with the 'workers', in fact I actively detest them en masse. They grumble and strike and behave abominably while their very existence is made possible by sailors and merchant seamen who get a quarter or less than a quarter what they do. In addition to this they are obtuse and slow-witted and most outrageously spoilt.

Noël Coward

Wednesday, 2 December 1942
Barrow-in-Furness

Never since I first listened to a speaker on the air have I felt as interested as I was tonight by Sir William Beveridge. I'll feel a bit more hopeful about the 'brave new world' now and begin to feel a real effort will be made to grasp the different angles of the many problems. His scheme will appeal more to women than to men for it is they who bear the real burden of unemployment, sickness, child-bearing and rearing – and the ones who, up to now have come off worst.

I sat on the edge of the tiled curb [sic] to bake my shoulder and get the ache out and stuffed another wee rabbit as I listened ... Trouble with menfolk of my generation, they looked on women 'to be cared for' – and did not realise how hard we worked, how small an allowance we had to bring up our families on and, when, as in our case, sickness and an operation had to be met and paid for, what a bitter struggle things could be.

Nella Last

Thursday, 17 December 1942

I passed the table where Mrs Hockey sits. I've thought sometimes, 'Poor darling, how brave she is, she can still smile,' but today I noticed the smile was as forced as that of a painted clown. She caught my overall as I passed and I bent down while she whispered in a flat tone, 'I got Michael's Christmas greeting card today, Mrs Last. He said "Who knows where I'll be at Christmas, Mom."' No tears were in her eyes; the light seemed to have faded. I felt pity burn like a flame in me – but I could only hold her hand tightly for a second, and get on with my work.

Nella Last

Saturday, 30 January 1943
Oxford

Not much happened today except an invasion exercise ... In one of the main streets loudspeakers were broadcasting the noise of an air raid – machine guns, whistling bombs, flak, aircraft, explosions.

I returned to the College and was about to get down to some work when there was a knock at the door. In walked a Fellow of the College.

'Excuse me,' he said 'but I must ask you to vacate your room and become a casualty. I am about to light an incendiary bomb outside your door. You will have to go to the first aid post.'

'Would you be so very kind as to give me some superficial wound, sir,' I said. 'I am very busy.' 'I think we can manage that,' he said as he fixed a label on me bearing the words 'slight burns.'

The Fellow lit a bomb of tar and straw at the bottom of the stairs ... After nearly a quarter of an hour five or six gas-masked figures arrived and tripped over the stirrup pump. Luckily for them they just got the pump working before the fire went out!

All the best Mike

Your affectionate and admiring bro

Letter to Michael Benn from Tony Benn

Friday, 12 February 1943

Germans still retreating in Russia. All newspapers filled with Churchill's speech in the House yesterday about the Casablanca conference* and making the enemy 'bleed and burn.' Wonder how many years it will take this country to recover from having Al Capone at its head.

Vera Brittain

Tuesday, 23 February 1943

Papers this morning full of resounding tributes to Red Army on 25th anniversary; Russian victories still going on,† and Stalin seems likely now to be the chief victor of the war.

Vera Brittain

Monday, 17 May 1943

A [Anthony Eden] didn't arrive (with a cold!) until lunch-time. Really it's impossible to work like this.

4.30 saw A. for a few moments about a number of things. 5.30 Cabinet. V good Lancaster attacks on German dams!‡ Sinkings much better. 15 U-boats this month so far. (We want to keep up that rate.) Discussion on Thanksgiving Service on Wednesday [for the victory in North Africa] ...

Alexander Cadogan

Wednesday, 19 May 1943

German fighter-bombers have been making these nights in London rather noisy – we have 2 or 3 alerts and an amount of gunfire which interferes with sleep – a bore. And we don't shoot down quite enough of them.

We had good seats (for the Thanksgiving Service at St Paul's), next to the Aisle. (But it was damned cold.) A dignified service and luckily

---

* Churchill and Roosevelt and their respective Chiefs of Staff met to consider, among other things, the future of the war in the Mediterranean and the High Command in North Africa.
† Presumably a reference to the end of the battle of Stalingrad earlier in the month.
‡ The night-time 'Dambusters' operation on the River Ruhr which resulted in the flooding of the German cities Dortmund and Kassel.

Hitler didn't bomb King, Lords, Commons and everything else. What a target!

Alexander Cadogan

Thursday, 20 May 1943

Victory Parade, Tunis

Left Algiers at 7 am … arrived at Tunis aerodrome about 10 am. On arriving at the aerodrome we found all the notabilities of North Africa having just arrived or arriving by plane.*

About 30,000 troops took part in the parade which lasted over two hours. In addition of course there were troops lining the streets. The audience consisted of all the civil population (including Italians) … First came the French – Zouaves, Tirailleurs, Moroccan and Algerian native troops, Foreign Legion. The procession was led by a detachment of Spahis, making a brave show with their white horses, red cloaks, red leather saddles and drawn swords. As they passed the saluting base they rose in their saddles.

The great majority of French were of course natives. The men are splendid – many with great beards and whiskers. But their equipment and clothing were pitiful – antiquated rifles, torn cloaks, slippers or bare feet. They had a tremendous reception from our own troops in the audience …

Two American regiments [were] led by a fine brass band. In contrast to the French, the American equipment and clothing are almost indecently rich. Every private soldier has a pair of lovely brown leather shoes with rubber soles.

He also has a pair of leather gloves which would cost me a fiver in England; he has a wonderful kind of golfing jacket, a splendid helmet, lots of gadgets hung round, and is altogether a very expensive fellow who has cost his treasury a lot of money.

The British decided to put on a show … the First Army – which in November 1942 came to North Africa an inexperienced body of troops, most of whom had never seen a shot fired – determined to show us that it was worthy of being linked with the Eighth Army in

---

*In North Africa, the allied success of the second battle of El Alamein was followed by the surrender of German and Italian forces in mid-May 1943. The victory celebrations were attended by General Eisenhower.

a splendid partnership which under Alexander's magnificent general-ship, had achieved one of the greatest victories in British history.

Appearing from apparently nowhere a faint sound of pipes. Soon came into view the massed pipers of Scots Guards, Irish Guards and all the Highland Regiments available ... They marched in slow time, passed the saluting platform and neighbouring stands – the tune was 'Flowers of the Forest.' Then they countermarched ... and as they passed a point on the return, broke into quick time and marched away into the distance. The effect was really very dramatic and made a splendid prologue. Then began the long march of our men in splendid procession.

Unlike the French and Americans, the British were in drill, not battle, order – shorts, stocking and boots, no helmets ([just] forage caps and berets) ... With the forage cap or beret you can see his face – his jolly, honest, sunburnt, smiling, English, Scottish or Irish face – relaxed now, not worn or harassed as men look in battle – and confident and proud.

I really like the modern generals, in shorts and shirts instead of boots and spurs – looking so young – some of the generals and colonels are really boys.

Harold Macmillan

Thursday, 24 June–Friday, 25 June 1943

I went by the 0830 bus to Barnstaple to see Terry [husband] who had a free day. After lunch we baked in the sun by the river in our shirt sleeves. I had to leave again by the 1742 bus (the last?) from Bideford, so Terry went back with me as far as Bideford Quay. In spite of going straight after night watch (one hour's sleep) I didn't feel very tired.

The RAF has been bombing the Ruhr very heavily; the Germans no longer attempt to make light of the raids. It is a ghastly business.

Audrey Deacon

Sunday, 4 July 1943

At twelve o'clock the prime ministerial car fetched me and drove me to Chequers. Found Mrs Churchill alone and played a little croquet with her ... an hour closeted with the PM during which we played six-pack (bezique) and I took ten shillings off him. At dinner he was very gay and sang old-world Cockney songs with teddy bear gestures. In the course of the day he said he had been mistaken over the abdication. Mrs Churchill added later that his mistake had proved providential because it had kept him out of office at a moment when it would have been compromising.

After dinner we saw a news-reel and I played the piano for hours and then left.

Noël Coward

Monday, 2 August 1943

Sissinghurst

We go to the village fete at Sissinghurst Place. All the village children dress up and there is one little boy who impersonates Montgomery riding in a tank. There are many side-shows. One of them is a darts contest in which people are invited to throw darts at large cartoons of Hitler, Tojo and Mussolini. The Mussolini target does no business at all. Hitler and Tojo attract great crowds but people do not want to throw darts at Mussolini as they say he is 'down and out.' Really, the English are an amazing race.

Harold Nicolson

Friday, 27 August 1943

Stayed at the Avon Hotel (Amesbury) ... Terry had had a hectic week, with 60 miles marching since Monday; his feet were covered in blisters. He gave me a lovely book: the Phaidon Press Rembrandt.

The Quebec Conferences are finished. Roosevelt has gone back to the States and Churchill is having a short holiday in Canada. Louis Mountbatten, Chief of Combined Operations, has been appointed to the command of Allied forces in South-East Asia. It is a supreme command like that of Eisenhower.

Audrey Deacon

Tuesday, 16 November 1943

Barrow-in-Furness

[My husband] said he would wash up while I got ready to go to the canteen committee meeting.

I felt it such a waste of time – nothing is ever done ... Same old thing: we all complained of badly apportioned stores, the filthy lavatory, no toilet for the girls, no disinfectants for the lav or smelly sink, no supervision of the slap-happy char who did only the bits that showed, no basin or dishes to mix things in, no kettles – only pans – to boil water for tea. When I get going I'm bad to stop and I'd the thirteen other members of the canteen behind me, agreeing and egging me on. [But] nothing will be done when it's carried to the general meeting.

Tiger Tim was well discussed, poor smelly animal ... I stuck up for him, he is a nice wee beast. I said 'Will one more smell make any difference to the general odour of mice, mouldy bread, a room with practically no ventilation, gas stoves, dirty sinks and lavatory? Don't blame it all on poor little Tiger Tim and don't talk so lightly of sending him off to be slept away.'

Nella Last

Sunday, 14 November–Tuesday, 23 November 1943

Much talk of aerial bombardment, and rockets that will half demolish London. It will be unpleasant, and there is no doubt that the Germans are 'up' to something.

There is serious unrest among the Conservatives at the growing influence and power of Beaverbrook; it is said the new triumvirate of Bracken, Cherwell and Beaverbrook rule the country when the PM is abroad, and dominate and fascinate him when he is at home.

Tuesday: The last day of the dying session was largely given up to argument about Mosley's inopportune release (from prison), which has caused considerable excitement in the country, largely whipped up by Communists and Jewish elements. I walked to the House and saw nothing unusual though I was told that an angry crowd had surrounded the St Stephen's entrance [of the House of Commons] and policemen had had to use batons: then the public lobby was crowded with young factory workers indignantly protesting at his release. I rather enjoyed the ironical scene of the Labour Party so enraged by the release of one of their ex-Ministers by a Labour Home Secretary! Their indignation seemed great. Morrison made an excellent case for his [release] order; he is an able parliamentarian and he put it over with skill and persuasion, explaining that Mosley had been examined by five eminent physicians who reported unanimously that his [poor] health demanded his release from Holloway ... he is an unscrupulous but not unattractive fellow.

Henry 'Chips' Channon

While the House of Commons was exercised about the release of Mosley from detention, Winston Churchill was in Persia to meet the leaders of the United States and the USSR (at the Teheran Conference) to discuss the next moves against Germany and to start to plan a post-war settlement, once the Axis powers were defeated. It was the first time Roosevelt and Stalin had met, and Churchill found himself isolated. Stalin was concerned to reduce the military action in the Mediterranean and Italy, and to see British troops transferred to southern France. Much of the discussion was about the details of Operation Overlord (the invasion of France), with Stalin attempting to dictate the terms of the operation. Churchill was accompanied by, among others, his doctor and the Chief of Imperial General Staff, General Brooke, who concluded that Stalin's 'political and military requirements could now be best met by the greatest squandering of British and American lives in the French theatre'.

The Teheran Conference, and the Yalta Conference in the Crimea in February 1945, effectively settled the post-war incorporation of Eastern Europe into the USSR.

Sunday, 28 November–Monday, 29 November 1943
Soviet Embassy, Teheran

The PM loves to be on the move once more; the thrust and parry of these conferences are much to his liking; he feels he is getting on with the war. But as he flew over the dark, jagged crags which guarded the approach to Teheran, his mind was full of misgivings ...

The PM cannot get Anthony's warning out of his head. He said that when the Foreign Ministers met at Moscow last month, Stalin appeared so anxious for a second front that our people began to wonder if all was well with the Red Army. Stalin, Eden reported, could talk of nothing else.

Roosevelt cannot understand why both men take this question of a second front so much to heart.

Anyway he has come to Teheran determined, if I can trust Harry (Hopkins),* to come to terms with Stalin and he is not going to allow anything to interfere with that purpose. The mathematics of this is two to one, and before the first day was spent (Alan) Brooke said to me: 'This Conference is over when it has only just begun. Stalin has got the President in his pocket.'

About midnight I went to the Legation to the PM's room to see if he needed anything. I found Clark Kerr [British ambassador to Moscow] and Anthony Eden with him, glasses of whisky in their hands. The PM was talking in a tired, slow voice, with his eyes closed.

'There might be more bloody war. I shall not be there. I shall be asleep. I want to sleep for billions of years. But you will be there.' He stopped. 'Charles hasn't a drink – When I consider the vast issues,' he went on, 'I realise how inadequate we are.'

'You mean a war with Russia?'

I do not think he heard. Then he appeared to make a great effort to cast off the black depression that had settled on him.

Charles Wilson

Monday, 29 November 1943

Soviet Embassy, Teheran

We ... sat down at 4 pm to another long 3 hour conference! Bad from beginning to end. Winston was not good, and Roosevelt even worse. Stalin meticulous with only two arguments. Cross Channel operation (Overlord) on May 1st and also offensive in Southern France! Americans supported this view quite unaware of the fact that it is already an impossibility. Finally decided that Americans and ourselves should have another meeting tomorrow with a view to arriving at some form of solution for our final plenary meeting at 4 pm.

I have little hope of any form of agreement in discussions. After listening to the arguments put forward in the last 2 days I feel more like entering a lunatic asylum or a nursing home than continuing with my present job. I am absolutely disgusted with the politicians' method of waging a war!! ... It is lamentable to listen to them. May God help

---

*The President's adviser and Charles Wilson were on confidential terms and Hopkins, who was present at the negotiations, reported back to Wilson.

us in the future prosecution of this war, we have every hope of making an unholy mess of it and being defeated yet!

General Alan Brooke

Tuesday, 30 November 1943

Teheran

All day Stalin has been as amiable as he can be and it was in this mood that he came to the dinner party at the Legation, to celebrate Winston's sixty ninth birthday. The atmosphere was genial; things seemed to go smoothly from the outset. It is true there was one discordant note. The President made a speech proposing the health of Brooke. Just as he was ending his speech, Stalin rose and said he would finish the toast. Looking across the table at the CIGS, Stalin said:

'General Brooke has not been very friendly to the Red Army and has been critical of us. Let him come to Moscow, and I'll show him that Russians aren't bad chaps. It will pay him to be friends.'

While Stalin was saying this CIGS sat very quiet and grim ... he does not pretend to like Stalin; he is indeed repelled by the man's bloody record.

Charles Wilson

Sunday, 12 December 1943

South East Asia Command HQ, New Delhi*

Troubles never come singly. The Commanders-in-Chief (led, I am sorry to say, by James Somerville) had staged a communal protest about the organisation of our respective Planning Staffs and so I had them all down to an informal meeting at Faridkot House this morning. I pointed out that this was not a British set-up, but an Anglo-American one and that we had to accept some of the Americans' ideas on planning. They wanted the right to hold separate meetings without me, so I asked Giffard:

'Did you ever have meetings of your Corps Commanders in the 14th army?'

---

* At the age of forty-three, Mountbatten was appointed Supreme Commander of the allied forces in South East Asia, over the heads of older and more senior colleagues, including the Commanders-in-Chief in the South East Asia Command, Admiral James Somerville, General George Giffard and Air Marshal Richard Peirse.

'Yes,' he replied, 'from time to time, when I wanted their views.'

'What would you have said if they held meetings without you and sent you joint resolutions signed by each of them?'

Giffard unhesitatingly replied: 'I should never have allowed that. That would be mutiny.'

I finished up with: 'Thank you for pointing out so clearly what you three Commanders in Chief are doing to me.'

The real trouble is that the various Commanders in Chief and the Americans were having a very happy time without anyone to integrate their efforts; each going their own way, and they very naturally resent a Supreme Commander being put over them, and naturally resist efforts at integration and unification; and unless I am firm, I might as well throw up the job.

Louis Mountbatten

Saturday, 25 December 1943

Christmas Day, Barrow-in-Furness

I said 'Happy Christmas' to my husband. He scowled and muttered. Looked at him. I thought 'Over thirty two years of slavery, patience beyond belief, your house kept a home, whatever happens your meals ready always, perfectly cooked, and served – yet I'm treated with less consideration than the average man would dare to treat a servant. Not a flower, a card – or a sweet although you had the sweet coupons in your pocket thereby preventing me from getting any myself.' I felt as if a little flickering flame burned even lower.

Nella Last

Thursday, 27 January 1944

The Hotel Victoria, Algiers

We have a room on the third floor, number 26, with two very comfy beds, stone floors, three windows and two balconies and running water, cold only. It seems that is universal in Algiers. No hot water bottle shook me a little, but a pair of golf socks and my fur coat on the bed got me off to sleep and I awoke much too hot.

Needless to say ENSA has done the minimum of advance work and no one was expecting us.

Joyce Grenfell

Tuesday, 1 February 1944
Algiers

We went to Hospital Number 95. In the first ward there were two of the illest men I have ever seen, I think. Just skulls with living, wide, very clear eyes. It was a huge ward and difficult to know where to put the piano. We put it in the centre in the end which meant that I had to keep spinning round as I sang. I tried a monologue, but it was no good in there – too big, too decentralised. While I was walking around, talking before we began, I said to the illest of the two very ill ones that I hoped he'd excuse my back when I had to turn it on him and he said he would if I'd excuse him for not being shaved. Oh, gosh.

Joyce Grenfell

Thursday, 3 February 1944
Algiers

One of the very ill men in the first ward we did ... died that night. I wish I could tell his family how he smiled and even sang with us.

The final concert ... was in a much smaller square whitewashed ward with about sixteen beds in it. Lovely for sound. Lots of eye patients, including a completely blinded boy who was being taken care of by a couple of pals with all the tenderness of mothers. When I sang a funny song or did a monologue their eyes were on him to see if he was amused. They were happy when he was, and exchanged looks. He was shy and completely unadjusted still to this new blank in his life ... But he sang with us and he cried a little. It was the gentleness of his two friends and their concern and solicitude that moved me so much.

An ex-jockey from the north told me his pal was a good singer and we got the pal to perform. He gave us a truly heavenly song called 'Blaydon Races', verse after verse, in a true horn of a voice, full of rough rhythm and vitality.

Joyce Grenfell

Friday, 18 February 1944

Jaipur, India

The Maharajah had arranged a shoot for us. In my simplicity I had imagined a certain amount of personal risk was involved; but not on this occasion at any rate.

We drove into the mountains where the preparations had begun last night, when a tethered goat was provided for the dinner of a female leopard … We sportsmen retired behind the foliage-covered windows of a small concrete building to watch the misery of the bait.

As the mountain landscape faded into darkness, plaintive bleats rang through the canyons. The lonely chained animal strutted in circles round its stake. Suddenly, in panic, its blunt rock-like profile darted this way and that. Then its front legs collapsed, and the animal lay quite still. Why was I allowing myself to be party to something I considered so ignominious? It was awful to watch an animal suffering the mental torments that, mercifully, most of us leave behind in the night nursery.

The goat continued to emit pathetic, grating croaks, like whimpers of despair, then, exhausted by misery, lay down to sleep. After one and a half hour's sleep no leopard came and the colonel who was organizing the shoot said that it was useless to remain. The anticlimax was crushing, but the joy of the goat when we came out of hiding to unleash it was heavenly to see. The goat, at any rate, had one more day to live.

Cecil Beaton

Tuesday, 28 March 1944

Westminster

An historic and altogether unexpected day. I walked to the House where the Education Bill was being discussed in the committee stage and soon realised that the House was in an odd, restless, and insubordinate mood. At about 4.45 Thelma Keir, nice but tactless, like all Cazalets, moved the amendment to the Education Bill for equal pay for men and women teachers. The House was crowded, and it was obvious that a storm was brewing. Rab for the first time held firm and was resolute. The principal of equal pay had nothing to do with him and he ought not to be placed in that position … after further parley and rising heat the House divided and the result was announced of

117 against the Government and only 11 for it. The first defeat Mr Churchill has sustained. The House gasped, as it began to realise the implications and I was appalled at the Government's defeat on the very eve of the Second Front. This will cause jubilation in Germany. The young Tory reformers, led by Quintin Hogg ... are to blame.

Henry 'Chips' Channon

Monday, 5 June 1944

I slept in an empty ward – or rather stayed awake most of the time. Soon after six I was brought a cup of tea, and then Sister came in and said he (Terry) was worse, especially during the past hour. I went down and saw him ... For a few minutes I felt faint but afterwards found Sister and got her to ask the Resident Surgical Officer to see him again. He told me that Terry's condition was very grave. I went back and dressed. Soon after I was told Warwick had arrived. We waited a little and then Sister told us to go to the ward. Then she said: 'I'm afraid he has just died.'

I just don't know how to start again. I had looked to Terry for support and comfort for so long; absolutely everything was bound up with him.

I am very glad we were married: we had long enough together to know how wonderful it was.*

Audrey Deacon

Tuesday, 6 June 1944
Southern Rhodesia

I went up for over an hour and half during which time I finished spins and started on my final and crucial task – finding out whether I will ever be able to land an aircraft. It was not until breakfast time that I heard the great news ... Flying Officer Freeman told me the real 'gen.' He had heard General Eisenhower's broadcast announcement to the world of an Allied invasion of the French coast and containing the gist of issued orders to the underground movement ... It appears that paratroopers have been dropped inland to capture aerodromes and that the beach landings were effected after an armada of 4,000 big ships and

---

*Just over a year. Terry Deacon had been hit in the neck by a splinter during a practice shoot at Tidworth.

many thousand little ones, escorted by detachments of the RN, had crossed the Channel ...*

When the work station gathered at midday, with clerks and fitters, the officers, the instructors and the pupils, and the air was quiet from lack of planes, we sang 'Onward Christian Soldiers' and 'Fight the Good Fight.'

I thought at once of Mike and ... the skill and courage which distinguished him from the ordinary run of pilots.

Tony Benn

Tuesday, 27 June 1944

Telegram to Tony Benn ('James')

DARLING JAMES OUR PRECIOUS MICHAEL GAVE HIS LIFE JUNE 23RD AFTER OPERATIONAL ACCIDENT DAVE AND I REACHED HIM DON'T GRIEVE DEAREST HE SUFFERED NO PAIN IS SAVED COMPLETE PARALYSIS FAMILY HOLDS TOGETHER FOR ALWAYS DEAREST LOVE MA

Thursday, 6 July 1944

At 10 pm we had a frightful meeting with Winston which lasted till 2 am!! It was quite the worst we have had with him. He was very tired as a result of his speech in the House concerning the flying bombs, he had tried to recuperate with drink. As a result he was in a maudlin, bad-tempered drunken mood, ready to take offence at anything, suspicious of everybody, and in a highly vindictive mood against the Americans. In fact so vindictive that his whole outlook on strategy was warped.

I began by having a bad row with him. He began to abuse Monty because operations were not going faster, and apparently Eisenhower had said that he was over-cautious. I flared up and asked him if he could not trust his generals for five minutes instead of continuously abusing them and belittling them. He said that he never did such a thing. I then reminded him that during two whole Monday cabinets in front of a large gathering of ministers he had torn Alexander to shreds for his lack of imagination and leadership in continually attacking at

---

* Operation Overlord, which involved 6,500 vessels landing over 130,000 Allied forces on five Normandy beaches; 12,000 aircraft provided cover and bombed German targets. It became known as D-Day.

Cassino. He was furious with me but I hope it may do some good in future.

Field Marshal Alan Brooke

Friday, 14 July–Friday, 21 July 1944

God what a week! And how many more of them are we to have? After a lull, when we had hours at a stretch without flying-bombs and we began to feel we had got the measure of them and that they were dying down, on Tuesday night we lay and listened to an almost continuous stream being poured over us – all night long the sky was filled with the drone of the approaching, passing, stopping engine of a flying-bomb; and so it has more or less gone on through the week.

On Wednesday morning I got to the Bank station and as [I] walked up Princes Street heard the danger overhead warnings from the Bank. I didn't know there was an alert on even, but quickened my pace [to the Northern Insurance Company] … A deafening roar and a sickening thud, followed by our huge eight foot windows crashing in, frame and all, plaster and glass careering down the lift shafts.

By a miracle we had no bad casualties.

Vivienne Hall

September 1944

The flying bombs and those beastly V2s, exploding from out of nowhere, have created havoc in London since I left for the Far East nearly a year ago. After travelling home via the States and enjoying for a spell the glitter of New York life, I was stunned to see such wreckage to poor inoffensive streets which contain no more important a target than the pub at the crossroads. Miles of pathetic little dwellings have become nothing but black windowless facades. Old, torn posters hang from scabrous walls, the leaves on trees have changed to tallow under a thick coating of cement powder.

After celebrating the liberation of Paris, in New York, I thought that things might be looking up a bit everywhere. But no. War in England is more total than ever, hardships always increasing.

Yet, in spite of all the horror and squalor, London has added beauty. In its unaccustomed isolation above the wastes of rubble, St Paul's is seen standing to supreme advantage, particularly splendid at full moon.

The moon, in the blackout, with no other light but the stars to vie with, makes an eighteenth century engraving of our streets. St James's Park without its Victorian railings, has become positively sylvan ... There are pigs sleeping peacefully in improvised styes in the craters ...

Cecil Beaton

Monday, 2 October 1944

Gaza

Wynne Rushton who was ENSA billeting officer in Cairo last time, has coped well and remembered my plea to get us to the really out of the way places. ENSA has laid on a large Naafi bus capable of seating eighteen people, but having removed some of the benches, it now holds our piano – quite a good one too. Viola is delighted. We plan to hang all our dresses from the rod at the back of the bus and that will save continual packing and unpacking which is the part of this job that kills one, particularly as we are doing mostly one night stands.

The breeze doesn't rise in the evening here as it does in Cairo. I must say I will always have a very special feeling for C, but I don't think Samson missed much by being eyeless in Gaza.

Joyce Grenfell

Tuesday, 31 October 1944

Today the PM was gay, enjoying himself, and seemed in such high spirits that no-one doubts but that he will lead the Conservative Party triumphantly to victory at the Polls: though he wisely dispelled any hope of an early dissolution, and it now looks as if we shall have another year of this wondrous Parliament ...

Henry 'Chips' Channon

Sunday, 5 November 1944

Dreadful news that Lord Moyne (the Colonial Secretary) has been murdered in Cairo ... if this murder is really committed by the Stern Gang, the Yishuv (Jewish community) must now take action against them, which may well plunge the country in civil war. Also there is the risk to Chaim's life. It is a dreadful tragedy.

Blanche 'Baffy' Dugdale

Saturday, 11 November 1944

Paris

Churchill and De Gaulle are to lay a wreath on the Unknown Warrior's grave and watch the march past of France's war effort – including the Moroccans, Algerians, Fire Services, Post Office men, etc.

The crowds, red-nosed with cold and crying, were quiet in their gratitude ... When the leaders passed the crowd shouted in unison 'Chour-cheel!'

It was remarkable that this great mass of humanity should gather within a few miles of an enemy that was now in retreat, but until only a short while ago, all-conquering.

Mrs Churchill told of the effort it had been to make conversation with De Gaulle at yesterday's banquet. While sitting on the General's right, and seeking desperately for conversational gambits, she reflected to herself on the difficulties of the lot of Madame de Gaulle. Suddenly the General broke the silence by remarking: 'I have often thought it must be very difficult for you being the wife of Winston Churchill.'

Cecil Beaton

Wednesday, 6 December 1944

Dined with Beaverbrook at the Savoy – a party of 21.

Max was jovial, presided genially, and mixed the cocktails. Speeches. I over-ate and drank, and came home by Underground, where I was shocked to see the stations full of people sleeping in bunks, miserable heaps of dirty humanity.

Henry 'Chips' Channon

Monday, 25 December 1944

Christmas Day, Secunderabad

When I woke up at 8 I counted back the hours and found it was about half past midnight in England and I wondered if Aunt N. was in the little room behind the boudoir as she always used to be on Christmas Eve. It won't be much of a day with both Jakie and Michael away; David too, perhaps? I count myself lucky to be away really. It's a sad moment somehow with the war getting longer instead of finishing as we hoped and the news being generally disquieting. I wonder if Reggie is at Oxford. And Ma and Tommy? And how my Pa is. Apart from these little anxieties ... it's good to be miles off in isolation with a job to do that involves a certain amount of self-immolation. Viola is a heavenly companion and we have reached that comfortable state of sympathy when silences are often more articulate than speech.

The last show of the day was in the penicillin ward. Many bed patients, mostly feeling pretty low, for I gather that penicillin isn't much fun; it hurts and the treatment includes injections every three hours.

I was asked for 'Just a Song at Twilight' which ordinarily I avoid because it's so sad but the asker was the illest man in the ward, a creature of bone in a cast, so we did it and they roared it in a comforting sort of way.

I had a couple of rather bad come overs and nearly blacked out which was alarming but I didn't quite and it passed.

Joyce Grenfell

Wednesday, 28 February 1945

The Prime Minister and Anthony Eden's abortive attempts to explain away, to justify, our ignominious surrender to Stalin, whilst they pleased some section of the Left have deeply shocked public opinion.* People, gentlemen not easily excited like Alec Dunglass [Douglas-Home] and James Willoughby D'Eresby made eloquent pleas for Poland, and the unfortunate and pathetic and charming Polish Ambassador, Count Raczinski, was in the Gallery.

I am horrified by the inconsistency of some Members of Parliament, members of society, who went about abusing Mr Chamberlain

---

*The perception was that at the Yalta Conference, 4–11 February 1945, the second meeting of Roosevelt, Stalin and Churchill, Stalin was the victor, achieving the continued occupation of Eastern Poland, the extension of Soviet influence in Eastern Europe and the division of Germany and Berlin.

about appeasement in 1938 and 1939 and now meekly accept this
surrender to Soviet Russia.

Henry 'Chips' Channon

Friday, 13 April 1945
Alexandria

We heard on the news today that President Roosevelt was dead.* We
were all gathered round the Sergeants' mess when the eight o'clock
news was read and the first, long item concerned his sudden collapse
and death. Everyone was absolutely hushed for some minutes, a more
marked silence than is ever accorded to great items of war news.

Without a doubt everyone was as shocked and as sad as if Churchill
himself had died.

Service life – particularly in air crew – gets you accustomed to
death of friends and colleagues. It was rather strange and impressive
to be there.

Tony Benn

Friday, 13 April 1945

At the Zionist office we figured out that although an unmitigated
disaster for Britain, the death of FDR may have some compensations
for the Jews. He was a friend, but an ignorant and rather wobbly one ...
The Jewish vote in the USA lost importance after his Election ... Spent
morning drafting condolence telegrams from Chaim [Weizmann] and
Jewish Agency.

Blanche 'Baffy' Dugdale

Sunday, 29 April–Monday, 30 April 1945
Whatlington

The war has virtually ended and I'm back at Whatlington, just as I was
five and a half years ago, in my same room, looking out at the same
window, turning over the same books; only five and a half years have
gone by. During these five and a half years I've been here and there,

---

*Roosevelt died on 12 April 1945 and was replaced by Vice-President Harry Truman,
who took his place at the ensuing post-war negotiations.

and committed many follies, and sometimes I suppose I shall write an account of them. The last six months I've been in Paris. Now I have to begin another life, the Nazis having been defeated. The Nazis were supposed to destroy my life, along with much else, but they've failed, and I'm left with it on my hands – a rather battered, shabby affair now.

Malcolm Muggeridge

Saturday, 28 April–Tuesday, 1 May 1945
Gaza

The American–Russian link-up is broadening and Germany is rife with rumour ... The end cannot be far off now. I wonder if I shall be in Jerusalem to celebrate it – what an appropriate place it would be. In the evening we saw *The Lamp Still Burns Brightly* with Rosamund John and Stewart Granger, produced by Leslie Howard. It was a fine tribute to nursing, and also pointed out some necessary reforms in a fine profession.

[1 May] I woke up early – it was cold. The train was steaming through the Sinai desert and by the light of the full moon I could discern an expanse of silver sand.

We got up and washed before the train pulled into Gaza. Here we had breakfast at the NAAFI and afterwards we wandered up and down the platform and were attracted by the quantity of lavatories. There was one for British officers, one for nursing sisters, one for women officers and one for Indian officers, and separate ones again for women other ranks, British other ranks and South African other ranks.

Tony Benn

Tuesday, 1 May 1945

In the middle of dinner I brought in the sensational announcement, broadcast by the Nazi wireless, that Hitler had been killed today at his post at the Reichs chancery in Berlin and that Admiral Doenitz was taking his place. Probably H has in fact been dead several days but the 1st May is a symbolic date in the Nazi calendar and no doubt the circumstances ('fighting with his last breath against Bolshevism') were carefully invented with an eye to the future Hitler Myth and Legend. The P.M.'s comment over dinner was: 'Well I must say I think he was perfectly right to die like that.' Lord B[eaverbrook]'s reply was that he obviously did not.*

John Colville

Thursday, 3 May 1945

Fall of Berlin to the Russians yesterday afternoon on last night's midnight news. News, and also of surrender in Italy, confirmed in morning papers. Went into Southampton with Amy (amid pouring rain) to see news in cinema giving the atrocity pictures of the concentration camps. Saw also Roosevelt's burial. Pictures of camps (as horrible as I expected, largely pictures of living skeletons and disintegrating bodies) accompanied by a hate-arousing talk which omits to point out that half victims in camps (and all before 1939) were Germans; and that camps, and Gestapo, wouldn't have existed if opposition to Hitler had not been tremendous.

Vera Brittain

Tuesday, 8 May 1945

Today is the official celebration of the end of the war. I walked up the hill to get some cigarettes, and saw each cottage decorated with little flags.

We went to Church. The parson said: 'Let us pray for a new world.' What a foolish prayer! Better the old prayer for that peace which the world cannot give, for the granting of petitions as may be most expedient. 'Lead kindly light amid the encircling gloom,' we sang after we had prayed for a new world; an exquisite line which made me think again of Newman.

Malcolm Muggeridge

---

*Fearing capture by the encroaching Soviet Red Army, Hitler had in fact committed suicide on 30 April 1945, shooting himself with a revolver. His wife Eva (née Braun) also committed suicide with him by ingesting cyanide.

Saturday, 19 May 1945

Chequers

A lovely hot day. Went for a long walk and did my best to put the great array of papers in the box, most of which have been unlooked at for many days, in order.

Harold Macmillan, summoned from Italy ... arrived at tea-time with Robert Cecil, who is acting as his A.D.C. The P.M. was still loitering with his geese and goldfish ponds (recently plundered of their, to him, precious occupants by a thief or an otter – it was long before anyone dare break the news) at Chartwell ... I don't like the would-be ingratiating way in which Macmillan bares his teeth.

The P.M. arrived for a late dinner and after it we saw a film ... a good deal of aimless discourse took place.

John Colville

Thursday, 24 May 1945

The P.M. devoted the day to the formation of what the press calls a 'Caretaker Government'.

With politicians coming and going – glints in all their eyes – and the Chief Whip in constant attendance, no work was done, even in regard to a telegram from Stalin demanding a third of the German Navy and merchant fleet (all of which have surrendered to us).

I was interested by some of the bombing figures showing our and the American share of the bombing of Germany:

RAF 678,500 tons
U.S. Army Air Force 684,700 tons $\Big\}$ on Germany only
Total for both forces everywhere in Europe: 2,170,000 tons
Losses in Europe: RAF 10,801 aircraft; USAAF 8,274 aircraft

John Colville

Thursday, 24 May 1945

The election [is to be] in July. The thought of possibly being governed by Attlee, Morrison, Bevin and Co is too horrible to contemplate. I hope above all that Winston is returned with a vast majority. He may have his faults but he is the only big man we have got. The Labour boys are a shoddy lot of careerists.

Noël Coward

Monday, 18 June 1945

Over all Europe hangs the cloud of insufficient supplies, disjointed distribution, lack of coal and a superfluity of destitute and displaced persons. The situation is no easier, nor are the prospects apparently brighter, than before the first shot was fired.

At home the first intoxication of victory is passing. The parties are creating bitterness, largely artificial, in their vote-catching hysteria ...Without Winston's personal prestige the Tories would not have a chance. Even with him I am not sanguine of their prospects, though most of their leaders are confident of a good majority. I think the service vote will be Left and the housing shortage has left many people disgruntled. The main Conservative argument is the prevailing good humour of the people and the accepted point that Attlee would be a sorry successor to Winston at the meeting of the Big Three and in the counsels of the Nations.

John Colville

The General Election was held on 5 July 1945, but the full results were not known (a large number of votes being cast by members of the Armed Forces still abroad) until 26 July.

Wednesday, 11 July 1945
South of France*

The PM disclosed during luncheon that he had had reassuring reports ... which confirmed (an) earlier estimate of a majority of a hundred. I said Max (Beaverbrook) had set his heart on winning this election. The PM turned to me and said: 'Do you think his support is a liability or an asset?' He described him as a remarkable man. 'There is no one like him. He has made several Governments in my lifetime. It's better

---

* Churchill took a holiday from 7 to 15 July 1945, accompanied by, among others, his Private Secretary John (Jock) Colville and his doctor Charles Wilson (by now ennobled as Lord Moran).

to have his support than his opposition. The *Express* has a circulation of between three and four millions.'

I hummed something out of the *Mikado*; the PM's eyes brightened, he began to sing refrain after refrain from that opera. He sang, with great gusto, 'A wandering minstrel I.' He loved the words and the tunes. And Mary in her eager way joined in. Then I asked him about some game they had played at Chartwell and soon we were saying, 'I had a cat,' to be asked by one's neighbour 'What kind of cat?' Whereupon one had to find adjectives beginning with the letter chosen, a tame cat, a timid cat, a troublesome cat, a tabby cat and so on until no more adjectives would come into your head and you were counted out, and only those with a full vocabulary were left in. Winston searched his store-house of words as earnestly as if he were writing for posterity. This went on until ten minutes to four, when the PM went off to the Nairns to paint.

Charles Wilson (Lord Moran)

Monday, 23 July 1945
Potsdam Conference, Occupied Germany

When I went into the PM's room this morning he was breakfasting. I found Sawyers mopping the table by the bed; the PM had upset his pineapple juice. Sawyers took a long time and the PM got impatient.

'That will do Sawyers; you can do that later.' But Sawyers went on mopping.

'Oh leave it Sawyers, leave it. Come back later.'

Immediately Sawyers had left the room the PM turned to me with great solemnity.

'I am going to tell you something you must not tell to any human being. We have split the atom. The report of the great experiment has just come in. A bomb was let off in some wild spot in New Mexico. It was only a thirteen-pound bomb but it made a crater half a mile across. People ten miles away lay with their feet towards the bomb; when it went off they rolled over and tried to look at the sky. But even with the darkest glasses it was impossible. It was the middle of the night but it was as if seven suns had lit the earth; two hundred miles away the light could be seen. The bomb sent up smoke to the stratosphere.'

'It is H. G. Wells stuff,' I put in.

'Exactly,' the PM agreed. 'It is the Second Coming. The secret has been wrested from nature. The Americans spent £400 million on it ... It is to be used on Japan, on cities, not on armies. We thought it would be indecent to use it on Japan without telling the Russians so they are to be told today. It has just come in time to save the world.'

I own I was deeply shocked by this ruthless decision ... I went out and wandered through empty rooms. I once slept in a house where there had been a murder. I feel like that here.

Lord Moran

Thursday, 26 July 1945

Plymouth

This morning before I got up a telegram arrived to say that I am to report pm 31st to HMS *Fledgling* ...

The election results were announced today – Labour has a majority of 152 (I think). Personally I voted Conservative – more because I thought Churchill and Eden were two good men to carry on in their present jobs than for any other reason – but I'm not really surprised that Labour has won. After all the Conservatives had been in since 1935, and before the war, at least, weren't particularly bright. But nobody was then, really.

Churchill had come back specially from the Potsdam conference to learn the result. The Conference (between the 'Big Three' – Churchill, Stalin and Truman) had not ended.

Audrey Deacon

Thursday, 26 July 1945

London

Winston asked me to go and see him at the No 10 Annexe at 4 pm. [I had been told that] his intention was to do nothing until after Sunday, have a Cabinet on Monday and then resign. This we all felt was wrong, for obviously Truman and Stalin won't wait at Potsdam indefinitely, and, as Winston says nothing will induce him to go back there himself, somebody from this country must take his place.

Then I was called into his room where he was sitting in his siren suit, with the usual banana-sized cigar, taking counsel of David

Margesson.* He did not look depressed, nor did he talk so. He attributed his defeat to the people's reaction from their sufferings of the past five years – they have endured all the horrors and discomforts of war, and, automatically, they have vented it on the government that has been in power throughout the period of their discontent.

He had changed his mind about his course of action – perhaps David and I helped him to make it up afresh. Anyhow, he decided to resign tonight, and in our presence dictated a new letter to Attlee, tearing up the draft of a previous one. This was the final version:

> My dear Attlee
> In consequence of the electoral decision recorded today, I
> propose to tender my resignation to the King at seven o'clock
> this evening on personal grounds. I wish you all success in the
> heavy burden you are about to assume.
> Yours v sincerely
> W.S.C.

... As to Potsdam Winston felt that Attlee ought to get the name of his Foreign Secretary approved at once and take him to Potsdam.

Alan Lascelles[†]

Saturday, 28 July 1945

I went to White's at about 11. Results were already coming in on the tape, and in an hour and a half it was plainly an overwhelming defeat. Practically all my friends are out ... 10,000 votes against Winston in his own constituency for an obvious lunatic.

To the Rothermeres' party – a large, despondent crowd joined later by a handful of the defeated candidates.

Evelyn Waugh

Tuesday, 7 August 1945

I had a long and somewhat dreary day. First of all a Chiefs of Staff meeting with Mountbatten and Lloyd of the Australian Army. The latter

---

* David Margesson was a former Conservative Chief Whip and Secretary of State for War who was made a scapegoat for the fall of Singapore in 1942.
† Alan Lascelles, Private Secretary to King George VI.

was quite excellent and clear headed. The former was as usual quite impossible and wasted a lot of our time. Always fastening onto the irrelevant points, repeating himself, failing to recognise the vital points etc etc. Seldom has a Supreme Commander been more deficient of the main attributes of a Supreme Commander than Dickie Mountbatten.

Then our first [Labour] Cabinet meeting. We were asked to deal with the strategic situation! I had to start, and go all round the world starting with the occupied zone etc. I was asked many questions by Bevan, Miss Wilkinson etc, all of them mainly influenced by political as opposed to military motives. A wonderful transformation of the Cabinet with a lot of new faces, however some of the old ones are still there such as Attlee, Bevin, Stafford Cripps, Morrison, Alexander.*

Field Marshal Alan Brooke

Friday, 10 August 1945

The Stock Market has recovered and is actually soaring. Evidently it does not fear the Socialist Government, now that the first shock has worn off.

Terry [Terence Rattigan] came to lunch at about 12.55. He said (he is a wireless addict) 'Turn on the news'; and we did, as we sipped our pre-prandial cocktails. The wireless announced that Japan had asked for peace, but insists on the rights of the Emperor.† They want to save the *Mikado*.

The streets were crowded with people singing and littered with torn paper. People tear telephone books to bits and throw them into the streets.

Henry 'Chips' Channon

Wednesday, 22 August 1945

Barrow-in-Furness

The dusk fell quickly tonight and there were no stars in the overcast sky. It's grand to think that this winter will have no blackout, that bright

---

*Clement Attlee, Prime Minister; Ernest Bevin, Foreign Secretary; Stafford Cripps, President of the Board of Trade; Herbert Morrison, Lord President of the Council; and A. V. Alexander, First Lord of the Admiralty.

†Atomic bombs had been dropped on Hiroshima and Nagasaki on 6 and 9 August 1945.

lights will be in the streets and from lightly curtained windows. How remote the last six years are becoming. I pray so deeply for real peace – for ordinary people who ask so little of life beyond simple needs, food and shelter for their families and a little for small enjoyments.

Tonight I thought of the dreadful new bomb – we will always live in the shadow of fear now ... I feel again this world of ours has blundered into a beam of wickedness and unrest ... it's some evil force that affects us all.

Nella Last

Chapter Four

1945–1951
'A Beam of Wickedness and Unrest'

The war had ended with a victory for Britain and her allies, but the future for foreign affairs for Britain looked bleak. The 'dreadful new bomb' had been made and used and could not be unmade. Germany and Berlin were physically divided between the Allies. The Soviet Union and the United States attempted to control Eastern and Western Europe – the former militarily, the latter economically through the Marshall plan. A new war involving Britain brewed in Korea. The British mandate in Palestine was abandoned in the face of increased determination, post-Holocaust, by the Zionists to establish a Jewish state. By the end of the war, the abrupt ending of Lend-Lease and the cost of the war meant the UK had the largest external debt in history, culminating in a financial crisis in 1947.

Domestically, post-war politics were dictated by the new Labour government's election manifesto. Its modest title, 'Let Us Face the Future', belied an ambitious programme of public ownership of coal, electricity, gas, transport, iron and steel; and a National Health Service – all carried out against a backdrop of shortages, rationing and controls: rationing of meat did not end until 1954.

The 1945–51 Labour government has been described as one of a tortoise and four hares. The hares racing the Prime Minister, Clement Attlee, were Ernest Bevin, Stafford Cripps, Hugh Dalton and Herbert

Morrison.* Another hare racing up behind was Hugh Gaitskell, the MP for Leeds South, who might have become Prime Minister (by 1950 he was Chancellor of the Exchequer) had he lived. His diaries and those of Dalton, and the not-yet-elected Tony Benn, record the spirit of the times. Conservative diarist, Harold Macmillan, representing a depressed industrial constituency, and an advocate of Keynesianism and economic planning, would have been quite at home in the post-war Labour government. The Liberal Party had returned twelve MPs to parliament – and Violet Bonham Carter, by now the mother-in-law of future Liberal leader, Jo Grimond, strived hard with her family to keep the Asquith Liberal legacy alive. Alan 'Tommy' Lascelles had returned to royal service with King George VI in 1935: he had resigned from serving the king's brother in 1928, reporting much later in his diary that he had, to put it mildly, found it difficult to work with him.

Nella Last, 'Housewife 49', whose diary ended 1945 on such a pessimistic note, continued to write for Mass Observation from Barrow-in-Furness, well into the 1950s and 1960s.

Tuesday, 21 August 1945

The United States has announced the end of Lend-Lease – which makes the financial outlook for this country pretty grim. The announcement was made without consulting the British Government; and a mission is being sent to try and make some arrangement.

Last week the routine release-signal came for me. I am not volunteering for postponement of release. I think the best thing is to get out and set about finding a job. It is estimated that more than a million men and women will have been released by the end of the year.

Audrey Deacon

Tuesday, 4 September–Monday, 10 September 1945
Leeds South constituency

On the Saturday night after Working Men's Club, a meeting with the doctors of Leeds and the Health Service. I was rather impressed with

---

* *The Tortoise and the Hares* (2008) is the title of a book by Giles Radice (later an MP and diarist): Stafford Cripps and Hugh Dalton were successive Chancellors of the Exchequer; Ernest Bevin was Foreign Secretary and Herbert Morrison, Lord President of the Council.

them and they, as I subsequently heard, with me. The most remarkable thing was that they all agreed that a doctor should either be 100% in the Service or completely outside it. This is one of the main points on which the Party have insisted. Their chief worry is that of being put under stupid local authority committees or officials and they produced some evidence to show that in the case of voluntary hospitals there was a good deal more self-government.

Curiously little interest appears to be taken by the civilian population in demobilisation, though it is the outstanding political question of the moment. Up to now South Leeds electors have been very moderate in corresponding with their Member.

Hugh Gaitskell

Thursday, 20 September 1945

It's dreadful to read of the food and fuel shortage and the winter coming on. Poor gay Vienna again facing famine, and all the Balkan states, which are only a name in the paper to us. Greeks, French, Dutch – all the same – hungry and cold. I've had to pinch and scrape at times, economise the rest, to make things go round, but have always managed to serve a tempting meal if it had only been baked potatoes and herrings, when the boys rushed in 'simply starving'. There has been always a fire to welcome them home ...

When I think of those poor women who suffer twice – once for their families and then for themselves – my heart aches. Mrs Woods ... said that half of Europe should die out including the treacherous French who had 'let us down and didn't deserve help in any way'.

Nella Last

Wednesday, 17 October 1945

Following the breakdown of the Foreign Ministers' Conference* Bevin told me this ... that, just as he himself was going – and this would have

---

* The Council of Foreign Ministers comprised the Foreign Ministers of the USA, Soviet Union, Great Britain, China and France, and had been established by the Potsdam Conference in the summer of 1945 following the surrender of Germany. It was charged with responsibility for administering peace treaties with the various Axis powers and for settling territorial disputes following the end of the war. The first meeting took place in London, but was marred by disagreements between the USA and the Soviet Union on the subject of the occupation of Japan.

been perhaps three quarters of an hour after I had left – he was in the outer hall with Molotov, Gusev [Russian ambassador] and Madame Gusev. Molotov was 'drinking all his toasts as usual' and, Bevin thought, had by now drunk rather too much even for him. Molotov then said 'Here's to the Atom Bomb!' And then he added, 'We've got it.' Gusev at this point put his hand on Molotov's shoulder and hurried him away.

Hugh Dalton

Wednesday, 24 October 1945

Committee on Palestine at 3 – ... Decided partition was dead and best procedure to call Arabs and Jews into Conference in London ?Jan.

Alexander Cadogan

Wednesday, 31 October 1945

Aneurin Bevan to see HM. I rather like him, and his ideas on housing. He has a respect for the countryside and the amenities generally. He advocates sky-scrapers (ten or twelve storeys) on the outskirts of country towns, rather than sprawling settlements; the former, he says, need not be a blot on the landscape any more than a church steeple, and they would save acres of green fields covered by the latter.

Alan Lascelles

Tuesday, 6 November 1945

[My wife] Kitty's brother, Bill, staying with us, described his experiences as a prisoner-of-war in the Far East.

He had to march from Singapore to Siam and all along the road local villagers arranged heaps of bananas and limes for them to take as they went past. Innumerable such acts of kindness took place – e.g. rickshaw coolie who carried his stuff and would not take money – all of which show that the over-simplifications of revolutionaries and patriots – natives hating white oppressors ... are as ever rubbish.

'So little trouble do men take in the search after truth; so readily do they accept whatever comes first to hand' – Thucydides.

Malcolm Muggeridge

Monday, 12 November 1945

Barrow-in-Furness

I'd like to … listen to clever competent people talking about this loan from America. I feel America has not acted like a good neighbour at all.

The New Year is going to be a shock for people. Things will be tight and on the whole more difficult than in the war years, for there will be so many more civilians and so many less things to buy. I feel America is laying the foundations of resentment which will recoil on her, whereas she could have laid those of real comradeship, and in life there are no rewards and no revenge – only consequences. I feel it's the fact that we have a Labour Government, that if Churchill had still led, things would have been a lot different.

Nella Last

Thursday, 6 December 1945

[Sir Frederick] Burrows, Governor Designate of Bengal, came to luncheon and got a GCIE (Knight Grand Commander of the Order of the Indian Empire). He started life as a railway porter at Ross-on-Wye, and has been head of the National Union of Railwaymen. A nice, square-shouldered, straight-eyed man, who may do the job very well. Mrs B is a nice old cup of tea, with the figure of a cottage loaf. She will not bring much glamour to Government House, Calcutta; but she will certainly do less mischief than Lady Ronaldshay did.

After luncheon, E. Bevin, who reluctantly, and having been rushed into it … has agreed to go to Moscow next week, and try and coax Molotov back from the tent in which he has been sulking since September.

Alan Lascelles

Friday, 7 December 1945

Winston is becoming rather a pathetic spectacle. The barber's shop downstairs at the House was all through the war decorated with pictures of Churchill in every possible pose. When the new Parliament assembled all this had been taken down and, the day after my Budget Statement, the old boy went in to get his hair cut. The barber, so I am informed by one who was present, said to him 'Sir, why don't you go right away? That would be much better than hanging about this place like you're doing.'

Hugh Dalton

Friday, 4 January 1946
Zionist Office, London

A little warmer, and a little less bronchitic. At Zionist Office, Gershon Hirsch, just back from Central Europe, began a most interesting account of the Jewish conditions and a heart-rending description of the utter poverty and starvation in Hungary, but everywhere the indomitable Zionist spirit prevailing. General Morgan speaks of a 'conspiracy' (though I don't believe he meant this ill-chosen phrase in an anti-Semitic way). But there certainly is a highly organised Jewish migration away from Poland all along the routes which will lead them eventually to Palestine. We are only beginning to get glimpses of it here, but it is epic in size and quality.

Blanche 'Baffy' Dugdale

Friday, 11 January 1946
Barrow-in-Furness

Three of our Polish friends came into the Canteen to say goodbye. Such nice lads. They could not speak very much English when they came and one had such a poor smashed face, which has gradually been repaired and quite a good matching eye put on. The first time I saw him I nearly fainted. I felt a frantic prayer to keep smiling at him and I must have done for he stayed to talk at the counter. It made Mrs Fletcher and Mrs Howson ill so I always served him, poor dear. They brought in each a bunch of violets and shook hands as they said goodbye. I said to Gregory, the boy with the damaged face, 'My blessing and good wishes go with you my dear and may you find your mother and sister very soon.' He bent and kissed me and said 'I thank you little mother' and suddenly I could have howled, thinking that soon all our Canteen friends would go and not need us any more …

Nella Last

Sunday, 3 February 1946

Windsor

What a good thing that the King persuaded Attlee to put Bevin, and not Greasy Dalton, into the Foreign Office and what a good thing Bevin is our spokesman at this juncture rather than Eden, or any other Tory. If Eden, or even Winston, had made this slashing attack on Communism, the foreigners would only have shrugged their shoulders and said, 'What else can one expect from a British capitalist and aristocrat?' They can't say that of Ernie.

Alan Lascelles

Friday, 8 March 1946

Sometimes (but not very often, thank God) I think, as well as talk, about politics. Thinking is better because, in thought, it's unnecessary to take up a position ... In thought I feel certain that Europe will be conquered by the Bolsheviks where the Nazis failed. Their triumph is coming and is comprehensible, but still disagreeable for us and for England. Perhaps it is necessary. Even, however, if I admit to its necessity or inevitability, I will not therefore falsify my own reactions and approve of it. That is real sycophancy, the instinct to attach oneself to success, to power, quite apart from the implications, personal and social ... I belong to what is decaying and I will go downhill with it, not despairing because it doesn't matter. Everything decays, and in its decay fertilises new life. Autumn is only absurd if it tries to be spring, and evergreens are sad and disappointing foliage.

Malcolm Muggeridge

Monday, 11 March 1946

I lunch at the Beefsteak and sit next to Barrington-Ward [Editor of *The Times*]. His view is that our working people will not work, not because they are temperamentally lazy, not because they dislike income tax but because they have nothing to buy with what they earn. Once there are things in the shops they will work well enough. I do not believe this. I believe that our lower classes are for some curious reason congenitally indolent; and that only the pressure of gain or destitution makes them work. When their profits are taken for income tax and they are insured against destitution their natural indolence comes to the surface.

Harold Nicolson

Monday, 8 April 1946

Dalton came, to expound the Budget to the King. He seemed very bobbish and confident that the next financial year would be an easier one. He told me he was going to restore some of the earned income allowance, and reduce excess profits tax, and purchase tax, but said nothing about income or surtax. The deficit will be £70 millions instead of £1,000, as was expected. Also said that the American loan had gone through; the Pope had helped in this, by telling the Irish Catholics in USA to stop opposing it.

Dalton is a very unlikeable man. When he was Minister of Economic Warfare, he was so unpopular with all his subordinates that they formed an 'Apple Club', each member being obliged to buy an apple in rotation, and place it on the doorstep, 'to keep the Doctor away'.

Alan Lascelles

Wednesday, 15 May 1946

Crossman thinks that HMG's reaction to the Palestine report was very bad and that it is absurd to talk of disarming the Hagana, which is only a Jewish Home Guard and quite distinct from the Terror Gangs.* He complains of the presence of so many anti-Semites in HMG and the Colonial Office. He says we have nothing to fear from the Arabs, who have no arms.

Hugh Dalton

---

*The Hagana were a Zionist paramilitary organisation which, along with other groups, such as Irgun and Lehi, fought for the defence of the 'Jewish homeland' and the protection of Jewish immigrants on Palestinian land, which was still under the control of the British Mandate. To their critics they were terrorist organisations perpetrating killings and land grabs against the Arab population.

Friday, 21 June 1946

Puff* came round to fetch me at quarter to 9 to see him get the *Daily Mail* award for the best film of the year – *The Way to the Stars*. Nearly 600,000 people voted. We drove to the Dorchester where there was a vast mob waiting to see the 'stars' arrive. They rushed round the cars like hungry animals ... we were hardly able to get out. But a most typical English policeman of the wisest sort said to them firmly but soothingly, 'Now this is only an *ordinary* man and an *ordinary* woman so please let them get out.'

Puff introduced me to Stanley Holloway, a delightful man – as delightful off, as on, the screen. The arrival of Margaret Lockwood (the female prize winner) was just what the crowd was waiting for. She looked quite *absurd!* But just what a film-star should look like. A vast orchid – a white fur coat – a white dress covered with tinsel stars ... Rosamund John looked better.

I was introduced to J Arthur Rank – a very queer looking cove.

Violet Bonham Carter

Wednesday, 14 August 1946

Barrow-in-Furness

There was great excitement at North Scale – squatters were moving into the RAF huts. I feel shocked at the good Army and RAF huts that are going to waste while people are wanting homes so badly. Nissen huts could be made as comfortable as the hideous prefabs, I'm perfectly sure.

I felt, 'Jolly good luck to all the squatters. In these days when we are anchored down with ration books and restrictions and growing into a nation of yes men, it's good to find someone yet with pluck and spirit.'

Nella Last

---

*Anthony Asquith, film director/producer and brother of Violet Bonham Carter.

Monday, 23 November 1946

The French called the occupying German army 'the grey lice'. That is precisely how I regard the occupying army of English socialist government.

Evelyn Waugh

Friday, 20 December 1946

There is a steady run of varied trouble about food, and the constant prospect of a shortage of fuel. 'Starve with Strachey and shiver with Shinwell' is one of the Tory slogans which is going around.* On the other hand, one has, I hope, an occasional feeling that in twelve or eighteen months' time we should be through the worst of most of these shortages. But, as I constantly tell my colleagues, we shall be on the rocks in two years' time if we have exhausted the Canadian and US Loans, unless we have severely cut down our overseas expenditure (military and other) and built up our exports ...

We are inviting (Burmese) leaders to come to London to discuss how to quicken up the process of Burmese independence either inside or outside the Empire.

It is quite clear that we can't go on holding people down against their will, however incompetent they are to govern themselves, for the whole pace, as determined in the East, has quickened in the war years and it would be a waste both of British men and money to try to hold down any of this crowd against their will. They must be allowed to find their own way, even through blood with corruption and incompetence of all kinds, to what they regard as 'freedom'.

Hugh Dalton

Wednesday, 1 January 1947
Barrow-in-Furness

Gradually a feeling of pity, rather than let-them-suffer, towards POWs seems to be creeping into people's attitude. Mrs Whittam is very kind to those at a nearby camp. They made rope slippers very skilfully and asked three packets of cigarettes for them, and Mrs Whittam gave

---

* A mocking reference, during the harsh winter of 1946–7, to John Strachey, Labour Minister for Food, and Emanuel Shinwell, Minister of Fuel and Power.

everyone a pair for Xmas so that those poor lads could feel they were capable of earning something if it was only cigs!

What interests me is – nobody has a good word for the Poles and I never see anyone talking to them. Yet any I've had speak to me are quite nice friendly boys or men ... They walk about like shadows, rarely conversing, and the look in their eyes, sometimes of far horizons, grieves me sorely.

Nella Last

January 1947

Sir Alexander Korda on the telephone.

'How are you, Saisille, old boy? When shall I see you?' drawled the Hungarian voice.

When after battling through the snow I arrived at his office in his landering, great Piccadilly house Sir Alex was pacing up and down the large room trying to keep warm. He was wearing his overcoat: there were no lights on. We were enjoying a peak of the Shinwell winter season and the gas and coal supply had given out.

'Hullo old boy!' He peered at me through the gloom. 'Well, I've got two pieces of news for you. One good – one bad.'

'Tell me the bad first.' ...

'No, I'll tell the good first. You've always tried to bully me into making *Ideal Husband* as a film. Well, we're going to do it. That's the good news. Now for the bad: we start shooting in three weeks' time.'

'But that's also good news,' I said with genuine enthusiasm.

'I want you behind the camera with me – and of course to do the costumes and all sorts of odd jobs. Start right away. We'll do it entirely in the period of when the play was written – 1895.'

Out in the snow again I took up my position at the end of a long bus queue. The nineties seemed to me so much longer ago than a mere fifty years: in comparison with today's life in England under a Labour government it could have been as remote as ancient Rome. What a self-indulgent era it had been! The blessings of equality were unknown, neither had the virtues of austerity been recognised. With altogether too much pleasure and leisure most people over-ate and drank too much and wasted hours in conversation.

One bus after another, filled to the ceiling with steaming, wet humanity, went by without stopping ... Snow and mud from roaring streamlined cars and motorbike traffic spattered the still motionless queue.

At last a bus hove in sight in which I was able to find an inch of space on its running board.

Cecil Beaton

Friday, 7 March 1947

Barrow-in-Furness

The blizzard reached us last night and we woke to find all snowed up. While my husband dug a way out, I rose in my dressing gown and hurriedly packed soup in a jar for him to heat at the shop, and made beef roll sandwiches for him. I opened the door and passed out the milk bottle to put on the window sill 'in hopes.' Shan We [the cat] seemed to lose his head – he took a header into the deep snow and disappeared except for the tip of his brown tail. I leaned forward and heaved, and we both fell backward into the hall, bringing in a pile of snow. The cross-eyed look of reproach he gave me and the anxious look he gave his tail, as if surprised to find it still on, nearly sent me into hysterics of laughter ...

Snow ploughs kept the bus routes open, but two cars were stranded in our short road. I was surprised when the Co-op lorry came, but the driver asked to phone for a motorised lorry to come as it was too much for the horse ...

I offered the kitchenette matting to cover his neck and head a little and Mrs Atkinson and I fed him bread and apples. He was a nice old spoiled horse – he raised his shaggy hoof to shake hands. I made tea for the driver and boy and Mrs Atkinson and I had ours, and later the lorry driver.

Nella Last

Thursday, 13 March 1947

I go to see Mummy. She takes my having joined the Labour Party as a cruel blow. 'I never thought,' she said, 'that I should see the day when one of my own sons betrayed his country.' Freddy [Nicolson's brother] is equally indignant. 'I suppose,' he says, 'you will now resign from all your clubs.' They live such a sheltered life poor people, that they see things out of proportion. But I hate hurting Mummy.

Harold Nicolson

Tuesday, 18 March 1947

A good day's rehearsal [of *Present Laughter*]. Farewell cocktail party to Dickie and Edwina (Mountbatten), who are going off to be Viceroy and Vicereine of India. I wonder if they will come back alive.

Noël Coward

Tuesday, 29 April 1947

Attended a meeting of our United Europe committee in Duncan Sandys charming house in Vincent Square. Present, Duncan Sandys, self, Victor Gollancz and Oliver Stanley.* Victor Gollancz rather put the cat among the pigeons by suggesting that he was going to say that the only hope for a United Europe lay in a United Socialist Europe. I pointed out that if we all said something of the kind in our own political idiom it would not 'go' very well.

He eventually said he might temper it down to something like 'social democracy'.

Violet Bonham Carter

Friday, 18 July 1947

The formal ending of British imperial dominion in India. This took place a little after 12.30 o'clock in the King's Robing Room under the Victoria Tower, which has, since the bombing of the House, acted as the Lords' chamber.

Churchill was not there, nor were Simon, Salisbury, Halifax, Wavell, Templewood ... This was a sad way to treat a fine and states-manlike piece of liberating legislation. What worried them no doubt was a short sentence from sub-section 2 of Clause 7 – 'the assent of the Parliament of the United Kingdom is hereby given to the omission

---

* An unlikely combination – Duncan Sandys and Oliver Stanley, Conservative MPs (Sandys was chairman of the international executive of the European Movement 1947–50); Victor Gollancz, left-wing publisher; and Liberal grandee, Violet Bonham Carter.

from the Royal style and titles of the words *Indiae imperator* and the words *Emperor of India.*'

Tony Benn

Friday, 25 July 1947
Barrow-in-Furness

Mrs Howson came in. She hindered my work but the rest was welcome. She asked me if I'd seen last night's *North Western News* and if I'd seen Eric's death in it. Poor creature – he had gassed himself. He was one of life's misfits and I bitterly opposed him coming to the Canteen as a cook. He had the reputation of being a 'kinkie' and certainly kept strange company. Yet at Canteen he worked well and would do anything for anyone who gave him a kind word. He was always a grand help to me when we gave the Canteen parties [and] would see to the fires and get the cups out and help wash up.

Nella Last

Friday, 25 July–Saturday, 26 July 1947
Durham Miners' Gala

At Durham this evening Bevin and I had a short talk. He is all for 'fighting it out' and can't believe that the miners won't work harder and produce more coal. He will make a great appeal to them tomorrow ...

Bevin made a magnificent address, speaking to the miners as only he can and appealing to them, in effect, to work an extra half hour.

I have arranged to drive back to London with Bevin, who never goes by train if he can help it. I am alone in the same car with him and Bob Dixon and some policemen in a second car. We have another detective sitting in front of us beside the driver. These Jews have made all this fuss necessary.* Bevin is very long-winded and very vain.

---

*Three members of the Zionist paramilitary group Irgun were arrested by the British authorities, charged with terrorist activities and sentenced to death. In response, Irgun captured two British Army sergeants (not three as Dugdale reports). When the Irgun militants were executed, Irgun hanged their British hostages. The following day they suspended their bodies from a tree and placed mines below. The incident, which led to anti-Jewish riots in England, was described by the Anglo-Jewish Association as 'a barbarous act of a kind peculiarly repugnant to civilised man'.

Near the end of the journey I return to the earlier question. I urge him not to put out of his mind the possibility of becoming P.M. and so we part.

It is a very hot night and I go to bed reflecting on these two major possibilities; the replacement of Attlee by Bevin and the possibility of my own resignation …

Hugh Dalton

Sunday, 3 August 1947

The weekend news is all bad. As regards Palestine the hanging by Irgun of the three sergeants blackens the whole picture, and no wonder. As regards everything else the economic crisis is upon us, and looks like being worse even than was anticipated. Michael says we shall look back on 1947 as our last year of luxury!

Blanche 'Baffy' Dugdale

Saturday, 20 September 1947

Cabinet this morning on Palestine. Decided that (we) shall say at UN that we will, as recommended, give up Mandate; that we will implement any plan on which Arabs and Jews agree; but that we won't impose on either any plan to which the other objects.

Three Service Ministers and Chiefs of Staff were waiting outside, but on my suggestion weren't asked in.

Phil Noel-Baker [Secretary of State for Air] walked in himself about five minutes later … He said the Air Staff wanted to stay in Palestine but he thought they were wrong. Bevin said, 'Tell them that if they want to stay, they'll 'ave to stay up in 'elicopters.' This if we stick to it is a historic decision.*

Hugh Dalton

---

*The British Mandate for Palestine had existed since 1920. In 1947 the UN proposed a partition plan to replace the British Mandate with 'Independent Arab and Jewish States', which the Arabs rejected. The British went ahead and ended their Mandate in April 1948 and the State of Israel was declared by the Jewish provisional government.

Wednesday, 1 October 1947
Barrow-in-Furness

My husband came rushing in excitedly and said 'How would you like a fridge for your birthday?' and said a shop had four in and the proprietor, an electrician who often works on big jobs with my husband, has promised him one for a long time.

I feel a bit indifferent as I think if I'd been let have one and paid for it myself by instalments when the boys were home, it would not have cost so much – £29 10s – and I would have had it when most needed. I've done so long without it, I could have gone on doing so.

Nella Last

Monday, 13 October 1947

Spent the whole day at work except for a break at luncheon when I went down to the House of Commons to see Frank Byers [Liberal Chief whip]. We lunched together in a quite empty dining room on potted shrimps and roast beef. I spoke to him very frankly about the Party position and the choice which seemed to face us. We must face the possibility of being completely wiped out at the next Election as a parliamentary force ... The alternative would be a deal over seats with the Tories with PR as a condition and an agreed programme. I shouldn't like it and it might split the party and give the left wing to Labour. I see all the rocks and shoals very clearly but I fear complete parliamentary extinction.

Violet Bonham Carter

Wednesday, 15 October 1947
Barrow-in-Furness

Mrs Whittam and I sat and talked. She has had a wonderful lot of things sent from America lately – it cost her nearly £6 for duty! Her daughter has sent shoes and a dress, stockings and rubber overshoes, and stacks of food – dried fruits and chocolate, meat, milk and jam. She is wisely putting some on the shelf. We had a real good grizzle as we conjectured about the austerity ahead, wondering how long it would last. She had backed Firemaster and it came in second – she never seems to back a loser in a big race.

Nella Last

Friday, 30 January 1948

Looking ahead to further sources of gloom, one has only to turn to the Middle East. Upon this rather large neck of land between the Black Sea, Mediterranean and the Persian Gulf is centred by far the most important source of oil in the world. Should Russia over-run this area there would not merely be insufficient oil for Britain but for a large part of the rest of the world. And even without Russia, it is difficult enough. The Arab states are making difficulties about the pipe line because of the Palestine question … How precarious it will all be even when the output is doubled, as we plan for the next four to five years.

Coal, however, is a bright spot, not merely because output is getting up but because consumption is extraordinarily low. It is an amazing contrast with only six months ago.

It is not unlikely that the habit of economy which we have [at] last engendered, combined with high prices, will hold back consumption within the expansion of demand. Well it is all to the good if we can export more. This should be possible. But there are anxieties. What will the Americans do? … What if the Marshall Plan itself contains provision for the continuance of large exports of coal to Europe, which in effect will be free. Where then are our markets? …

I cannot believe the Americans would do this.*

Hugh Gaitskell

Tuesday, 24 February 1948

Visit to Heinemann. Discussed Graham Greene's new novel, *The Heart of the Matter*.

Greene's previous novel *The Power and the Glory* I consider to be one of the best contemporary novels, and this is in the same genre. Greene, we agreed, is a Jekyll and Hyde character, who has not succeeded in fusing the two sides of himself into any kind of harmony. There is a conflict within him, and therefore he is liable to pursue conflict without.

---

*They did.

I remember him saying to me once that he had to have a row with someone or other because rows were almost a physical necessity to him.

Our lives have always run in a curiously parallel way. He succeeded me at the Ministry of Information; when he was in West Africa, in SIS, I was in East Africa, and we used to communicate in cipher. Then he went to Eyre and Spottiswoode and became my publisher and I went to Heinemann's and became his. I always say to him that the great quest of his life has not been virtue but sin, and that this quest has been completely fruitless. He is a sinner manqué. In the Blitz ... I remember the longing he had for a bomb to fall on him, but of course it didn't, and I told him it wouldn't.

Malcolm Muggeridge

Wednesday, 25 February 1948
North Croydon by-election

Yesterday I had a horrible day. I had to go round [as Labour candidate] with the *Daily Herald* photographer for feature pictures. Well the first thing they wanted me to do was to visit an old Trades Unionist of 89 years of age. We drove up to his horrid little house. The old man was very ill in bed. He insisted upon getting up. He sat on the bed while the photographer dressed him. He panted terribly and I thought he was going to die. Then we sat him down in his arm chair and I posed beside him. Suddenly he remembered that he had not brushed his hair and he struggled up again and poured a little oil into a tin and then dabbed the brush in it. Thereafter the photograph was taken.

Then I was dragged into a grocer's shop ... The photographer in the excitement of the chase made me climb up a ladder of an unfinished house and interview the workmen doing the roof ... Not my sort of thing at all.

Letter to Vita Sackville-West from Harold Nicolson

Wednesday, 25 February 1948

At 9 on the news we heard that Benes* had capitulated ...

---

* President Edvard Beneš of Czechoslovakia, elected in 1946, was under pressure of a coup from the pro-Soviet Czechoslovakian Communist Party; he remained in power but resigned in June 1948 after refusing to sign a new constitution for a Communist state.

How can they? They will just be prisoners of the communists. Free press has already been forbidden and all the frontiers closed so that no one can get out. The trap has closed on another country. The Czech bastion has fallen for the 2nd time – but this time not by an assault from without but 'betrayed by what is false within.'

Violet Bonham Carter

Thursday, 1 April 1948

All is not well with the Abbey Division of Westminster Labour Party. The growth of the organisation has produced cliques and endless bickering. Wilf Messer is a wonderfully reliable and steady chap. Jack Jones, the chairman, is the best type of trade unionist. But there is an ambitious, bitter and intriguing group. The measure of the tragedy is that it has reached the point where Mrs Hammond, a splendid woman, is resigning and if we can't keep a woman like that in the Party, what hope is there of increasing our membership?

Tony Benn

Thursday, 8 April 1948

My chartered accountant seems to think that I shall not be completely ruined by the wicked Capital Levy [in the Labour Government's budget].

Henry 'Chips' Channon

Tuesday, 20 April 1948

To the pictures … Last time I saw *Mrs Miniver* was in wartime, when we had worry and fear, but high hopes and courage – hopes of all the good we could do, the feeling that we could do as much for peace as for war, never realising the queer frustration – frustrating everything – everybody would find when the ceasefire sounded in Europe and certainly never thinking of the flare-up in Palestine, or that Stalin would replace Hitler in his bid to rule the world. I loved every minute of the picture, wondering again just why futile silly pictures are made, crime and sex glorified, slime and mud flaunted, when a simple picture of such nice people packs the cinema, as I'd not seen for a long time – first house at that!

Nella Last

Friday, 23 April 1948

We dined with the Prime Minister to meet Princess Elizabeth and the Duke of Edinburgh last week. It was a small intimate party, the others being the two Attlee girls, the McNeils, Harold Wilson and Christopher Mayhew. Nevertheless there was a good deal of etiquette. We all had to arrive well before the Royal pair and be lined up in the Drawing-room to greet them; the PM and Mrs Attlee bringing them upstairs. While waiting we all became very frivolous. We had been talking about capital punishment. Harold reminded us that it was still a capital offence to rape a Royal Princess! Then they came in and we were introduced ... After dinner each of the males was brought up to the Princess and shoved down beside her on a sofa for a quarter of an hour's conversation. She had a very pretty voice and quite an easy manner but is not, I think very interested in politics or affairs generally. We talked a little about fuel economy and she said that Queen Mary's house [Marlborough House] was the coldest she knew; she hardly ever had a fire anywhere. I asked if this was because she was Spartan or because of the house, but she said 'No' – it was because of her national duty.

Hugh Gaitskell

Thursday, 10 June–Saturday, 12 June 1948

I took my god-son to the Zoo. Rather enjoyed the aquarium. Fishes have always seemed to me the most fantastic variant of life. I remembered reading a famous Portuguese sermon addressed to the fishes, on the grounds that they must have been particularly favoured of God since, when, at the time of the Flood, all the animals perished except those in the Ark, the fishes multiplied. It was a good time for them.

Noted that quite a number of the cages are now empty at the Zoo, but the crowd stared as interestedly at the empty cages as at the others. In other words, the Zoo, like so much else, has only a kind of symbolic existence. It is the idea of seeing rather than actually seeing the animals which matters, and if there were no animals at all, but only a lot of empty and carefully labelled cages and pools, probably as many people would go.

Malcolm Muggeridge

Sunday, 27 June–Monday, 28 June 1948

Tony and Violet [Powell] came in to listen to Attlee's radio appeal to the public and to the dockers.* It was a commonplace and uninspiring performance. He has that curious trait I have always noticed with social workers of adopting a different sort of voice when addressing poor people, a kind of version of their slang, a feeble attempt to be salty and emphatic. The poor little man seemed very nervous, and incapable of rising to his responsibilities. At the same time one should be grateful that he is a decent little man and took the line he did.

Malcolm Muggeridge

Monday, 12 July 1948
Kent

We went to Chislet Colliery and down to the pit bottom where there is fluorescent lighting; a really impressive set of underground offices and even underground lavatories – pretty well unknown elsewhere. In the evening the National Coal Board gave a supper party; good speeches and a happy atmosphere. There is no doubt there are advantages in having men from the Services in these jobs for the simple reason that doing something for its own sake and because it is their job comes naturally. They have been brought up to believe in service and so, as it were, take to nationalisation. [The Chairman, Rear Admiral] Woodhouse blurted out in the middle of his speech – 'I have no hesitation in saying nationalisation is already a success.'

Peggy Ashcroft came to tea on Sunday ... This was all for [my daughter] Julia's sake who has now made up her mind to go on stage. But Peggy was not very encouraging.

Hugh Gaitskell

---

* Anthony Powell, novelist and close friend of Muggeridge. Unofficial dock strikes in London and Liverpool had led the Labour government to declare the first national state of emergency since 1926.

Friday, 16 July 1948

Two distressing things have happened. The Americans are sending squadrons of Flying Fortresses to land in East Anglia.* And the Russians have stated that they will be carrying out the training of their fighter aeroplanes across our corridors to Berlin. This is very dangerous ... The City is getting panicky. Yet I cannot seriously believe that war is possible. It is so different from previous wars and rumours of wars. It seems to be the final conflict for the mastery of the world. The prizes are so enormous; the losses so terrible ... as always these things are governed not by mistakes or intentions, but by the dreadful chain of circumstance.

Harold Nicolson

Thursday, 12 August 1948

Winston and Clemmie sent the car for me at 7 and I found them in their lovely new house in Hyde Park gate ... W. looked well – very calm. We had some champagne and sandwiches and then left in a car for the film. There were large crowds in Leicester Square and he got a great reception outside the theatre.

I sat between W. and Clemmie and Norman Collins, the author of the film, beyond. It was not a very good film, *London Belongs to Me* – well acted by Fay Compton, Richard Attenborough etc. Winston watched it like a child – arguing with the story 'But it wasn't murder – he didn't murder her.' Then we drove back to the Savoy where we had supper.

[W] thinks that the Russians fear the Atom Bomb too much to face war – and that even if she overran Europe her communications could be cut by air and her armies would rapidly become helpless.

Violet Bonham Carter

Friday, 15 October 1948

Had an hour at Foreign Office with Bevin at his invitation. He thinks we may reach a balance with Russia which will last a long time.

---

* As Cold War tensions mounted after the war, particularly after the Soviet blockade of Berlin in the summer of 1948, the US Air Force increased the number of its Boeing B-17 'Flying Fortress' bombers at various air bases in East Anglia.

He is trying 'to organise the middle of the planet' – W Europe, the Mediterranean, the Middle East, the Commonwealth.

If only we pushed on and developed Africa, we could have U.S. dependent on us and eating out of our hand in four or five years. Two great mountains of manganese are in Sierra Leone etc. U.S. is very barren of essential minerals, and in Africa we have them all.

Hugh Dalton

Wednesday, 9 March–Thursday, 10 March 1949

Devon

Went to Exeter to stay with the Dean, my former tutor S C [Spencer Cecil] Carpenter, arriving there in the evening.

On Thursday morning, we wandered round the Cathedral – very beautiful. Much admired the manner in which the blitzed part is being restored. A certain local builder, named Reed, the day after the bomb fell on the cathedral, began to collect together the shattered pews, screens, etc. People thought he was mad at the time but, as it turns out, he has been able to reconstruct a large part of the interior. Similarly, builders are perfectly restoring the shattered part of the structure. I found it touching and rather inspiring to see them all at work.

Carpenter rather disconcerted to learn from a letter he opened at breakfast that the *Daily Telegraph* did not want him to contribute any more of his Saturday articles. He told me that the money from these was what he had hoped to live on after his retirement, as his pension as a dean would only be £200 a year.

Malcolm Muggeridge

Monday, 14 March–Tuesday, 15 March 1949

I looked at George Orwell's new novel about the future, *1984*, which I found rather repugnant. It is in the Aldous Huxley genre, imagining life in a totalitarian state. These horrors in 'futures' are really as silly as their converse – the early Wells utopias … I was made to think of this by reading a slab of Wells' autobiography, particularly his journey to Russia to persuade Gorky and other Russians to join the PEN Club and allow freedom of expression – surely the most Quixotic-like enterprise ever undertaken by man.

Malcolm Muggeridge

Sunday, 17 April 1949

Cranham Sanatorium, Gloucestershire

Curious effect, here in the sanatorium, on Easter Sunday, when the people in this (the most expensive) block of chalets mostly have visitors, of hearing large numbers of upper-class English voices. I have been almost out of the sound of them for two years, hearing them at most one or two at a time, my ears growing more and more used to working-class or lower-middle-class Scottish voices.

It is as though I were hearing these voices for the first time. And what voices! A sort of over-fedness, a fatuous self-confidence, a constant bah-bahing of laughter about nothing, above all a sort of heaviness and richness combined with a fundamental ill-will – people who, one instinctively feels, without even being able to see them, are the enemies of anything intelligent or sensitive or beautiful. No wonder everyone hates us so.

George Orwell

Friday, 17 June 1949

I start writing the first chapter of my book on George V. I begin

> 'Prince George was born at Marlborough House, London, at 1.30 am on the morning of June 3, 1865.'

I gaze at the sentence in wonder, realising what a long journey I have to go before I reach his death. It is like starting in a taxi on the way to Vladivostock.

Harold Nicolson

Tuesday, 21 June 1949

Much amused by Tony Powell's account of how his sister-in-law, Julia Mount, now got new lease of life because she earns 16/- a day showing people round house of Marquis of Bath, a friend. She said she usually got two bob or half-a-crown when she was tipped 'because she was a lady.' Tony said that her being a lady would lead him to give her a smaller rather than larger tip. About 400 people came daily to house – Longleat; and Bath and his friends all greatly uplifted thereby. Good commentary, I thought, on present situation that aristocracy find new purpose in life, as well as income, by showing visitors round their houses.

Malcolm Muggeridge

Tuesday, 28 June 1949

It never rains but it pours! Right in the middle of the dollar crisis comes the news that the railwaymen have decided to adopt Go-slow tactics next Monday. If this threat matures I am afraid we shall have the pits stopping before long ... But there can be no doubt that the National Union of Railwaymen by their attitude are going to do an immense amount of harm to the Government, and indeed to the whole cause of nationalisation. I must say the technique of modern Government becomes almost intolerably difficult. On the one hand, the key Ministers are hopelessly overworked. Stafford [Cripps, Chancellor of the Exchequer] spends his time dashing between Paris, Brussels and London, thinking out and arguing out the most frightfully complicated questions of international trade and payments, and somehow or other all this has got to be explained to the general public sometime. The P.M. is perhaps so successful because he is content to let others do the work. I noticed that he was at Lords on Saturday morning and Wimbledon on Saturday afternoon. Poor Stafford spent most of *his* weekend in bed ... in a state of complete exhaustion.

Hugh Gaitskell

Wednesday, 17 August 1949

I fear I am getting rather down on George V just now. He is all right as a gay young midshipman. He may be all right as a wise old king. But the intervening period when he was Duke of York, just shooting at Sandringham, is hard to manage or swallow. For seventeen years in fact he did nothing at all but kill animals and stick in stamps.

Letter to Vita Sackville-West from Harold Nicolson

Saturday, 15 October 1949

On board the Queen Mary *bound for Southampton*

Sat on promenade deck and wrote thanking letters to USA ... I find there is constantly something to be done onboard ship. Lifeboat drill or filling in a form or something for one's passport. I tried to cash a £2 Traveller's Cheque at the Midland Bank and they began by refusing to do it – saying that they weren't allowed to give any change. I said, 'But then what is the good of a Traveller's Cheque?' They said it must be paid as a unit. I objected that I couldn't afford to pay £2 for a stamp – which I happened to want at the moment! They could not explain their reason except that Stewards might sell pound notes on the black market. I pointed out that it would be a very unprofitable occupation at this moment.* Finally I said that on the *Empress of Canada* coming out they had all changed our cheques without the slightest difficulty – 'Ah but you see, Madam, there wasn't a *bank* on that ship'!! Alice in Wonderland!

No wonder the world finds it difficult to do business with us ...

Violet Bonham Carter

Wednesday, 28 December 1949

It has ... been a good year financially and I seem to have spent £2,000 less than I've made, despite the loss of £500 at Deauville. Even so it is rather alarming to find that I have spent over £4,000. I have no idea how much Diana has spent. She keeps no accounts – but she seems to have plenty. We have paid practically no taxation. How long can that go on?

Duff Cooper

Saturday, 31 December 1949

We gave a party ... mostly to local Hampstead friends, many of them in the Government. It was an enormous success. I missed the highlight of the evening when Eva Robens† after drinking in the New Year and getting more and more restive because of what she regarded as the

---

* Weeks earlier there had been a dramatic devaluation of the pound from $4.03 to $2.80.
† Eva Robens, wife of Alfred Robens, a junior minister under Gaitskell at the Ministry of Fuel and Power. Harold Wilson at this time was President of the Board of Trade.

phlegmatic behaviour of those present, looked hard at Harold Wilson and said 'You come from north of the Trent, don't you? Surely you know how to behave!' and then proceeded to fling her arms around him and kiss him passionately, to his great embarrassment. As he had previously been giving a lecture on why the ladies could not obtain nylons – which was full of statistics and all very sober – this incident gave great pleasure.

Hugh Gaitskell

Friday, 24 February 1950
Orkney

It is all over – at least not quite all – for there are still about 150 seats to come in.*

On Thursday – polling day – we awoke in Laura's arctic cottage at Merbister – Dounby – romantically placed on the edge of a lake but unservanted, unheated and unlit by anything but Aladdin lamps and guttering candles.

We awoke with horror to a very cold day and the news that there was snow in Shetland – and that it was lying. This is sinister – because in Shetland the polling booths are sometimes 7 and even 12 miles away – and the poor Lib crofters are very old …

We hardly saw a car except once or twice one of our own. We went back to lunch at the Kirkwall Hotel – then Laura went on duty at the Polling Station (she had been sworn in) to help 'illiterate' voters. We were told a charming story about one man who could neither read nor write but who turned up with a photograph of Jo and said *'That's* the man I want to vote for' …

We climbed up to bed with our guttering candles in our hands and our hearts in our boots, and I lay like a sausage hugging my hot water bottles and not daring to move a limb because of the icy sheets.

Violet Bonham Carter

*The General Election of 23 February 1950. Violet Bonham Carter was in the Shetland Isles canvassing for her son-in-law, Jo Grimond (married to Laura Bonham Carter), who was the Liberal candidate for Orkney and Shetland. The result for the islands took four days to collect and count. The Liberal Party fared badly nationally, but Jo Grimond was elected.

Tuesday, 28 February 1950

I get a message to go at once to No 10. Attlee says that he has come to the conclusion that to take Housing out of Health at present would be too big a surgical operation. He therefore would like me to take the Colonies. I at once refuse. 'That is not my kingdom,' I say. 'I have never studied Colonial questions. I would much prefer the home front.' (I had a horrid vision of pullulating, poverty stricken, diseased nigger communities, for whom one can do nothing in the short run and who, the more one tries to help them, are querulous and ungrateful; of Malaya and a futile military campaign; of white settlers, reactionary and troublesome in their own way as the niggers ... of all the silliness and emotion about a black man who married a white typist* ... of Parliamentary questions by pro-native cranks and anti-native capitalists – all this in a rush of a few seconds.) P.M. was a bit surprised and taken aback. Then he said 'Of course, you could be Minister for Town and Country Planning right away and perhaps we could bring Housing in later.' I said I would much prefer this provided my place in the Hierarchy was maintained, and made clear.

Hugh Dalton

Tuesday, 28 March 1950

To tea with A J Cummings [political editor of the *News Chronicle*] and talk about the (Liberal) Party which he thinks is finished. He agrees with me that pressure groups are no good. He also agrees that Electoral Reform might give us one last chance. He is however very pessimistic about Winston being able to get it thro' his party. He says there was a meeting of the 22 Club – a quite important Tory Club – and that W.

---

* 'A black man who married a white typist': Seretse Khama married Ruth Williams in 1948. Seretse was a member of a royal tribe of Bechuanaland, at that time a British Protectorate. He had met Ruth Williams, a clerk at Lloyd's of London, whilst training to be a barrister in England. The marriage proved controversial on both sides. On his return to Bechuanaland, his family demanded an annulment of the marriage, but he refused, while pressure from the apartheid government in neighbouring South Africa, where interracial marriage was illegal, persuaded the British government to exile Khama and Williams from Bechuanaland. The couple would later return, and in 1966 Khama was elected the first President of the newly independent (and renamed) Botswana.

met and spoke to them and they were very hostile ... Here they felt was a chance of wiping the Liberal Party off the block once and for all.

Violet Bonham Carter

Thursday, 15 June 1950

I am horrified by the Labour manifesto [refusing to join the European Community]. It will do immense harm abroad and shake any authority which we have left. It is a truly deplorable document.

I am deeply distressed by it. How I wish I had not been such an impulsive fool as to join the Labour Party. It was certainly the cardinal error of my life. But I cannot redeem it now.

Harold Nicolson

Wednesday, 12 July 1950

Dined with William Deedes, now an MP, and a character named Enoch Powell, Member of Parliament for one of the Wolverhampton divisions. He made a great impression when we ran into each other on an Army intelligence course in May, 1940 – Mongolian features, very bright eyes, receding forehead, sprouting moustache. In the war he determined to get into the Operations Branch, and did, becoming a Brigadier. Then, he told me, he went to India, became mad on the place, learned Hindustani, etc, decided that British Raj was the most wonderful thing in history and that to participate in it, London was the place. On being demobilised therefore, made for London; looked up Conservative in the telephone directory, went along to Conservative Party Central Office, worked there; was adopted for not very hopeful constituency, lived there for eight months concentrating on his candidature and to everyone's amazement got elected by 600 votes.

If things get tough quite likely will hear of him.

Malcolm Muggeridge

Wednesday, 2 August 1950

Tea with W[inston] at 5.15. [He] arrived hot from Attlee (if one can be such a thing) looking pink and well and without the bulging, lowering look of doom about his forehead which I thought the world situation warranted ...

I asked him whether he thought Attlee was feeling the *Atlas* weight of his responsibility. 'Yes,' he said, 'his hand shook as I was talking to him today.'

'My hand doesn't shake – look at it – it's quite steady.' And it was.

'If a man in the street,' he said, pointing out of the window, 'was threatening us two with a Howitzer shouldn't we be right to shoot him before he pulled the trigger?'

'Yes – but how could we ever prove he was going to pull the trigger – to the satisfaction of our own consciences – and other people's?' There is the snag of the Preventive War.

He sent me back across the Park in his car. I arrived just in time to set out for another intoxicating evening at *Top Hat* ... the second night running!

I don't know which gives me the greatest kick – Winston or Fred Astaire.

Violet Bonham Carter

Wednesday, 2 August 1950

Dined with WSC [Churchill, and others]. Long discussion. WSC very gloomy about the defence situation; he was much depressed by his interview ... with Attlee. It seems that to scrape together 3,000 men and their equipment for Korea will take two months! Even then, the anti-aircraft guns can only be obtained by taking some of those now in Lincolnshire defending the American 'atomic' bombers. What have they done with the war equipment? It would appear that they have thrown it into the sea.

Harold Macmillan

Tuesday, 21 November 1950
Council of Europe, Strasbourg

We began by an address from the French Foreign Minister, Robert Schuman. This strange melancholy, quixotic figure, half politician, half priest, gave a characteristic address, well phrased, philosophic, and rather impractical.* The [proposed] European army is clearly not so

---

* Robert Schuman, Prime Minister of France for two brief periods in 1947–8; his war experience led him to become one of the proponents of a supranational European union, of which the Council of Europe and European Coal and Steel Community were the beginnings.

much to fight the Russians as ... to unite Germans and Frenchmen. It is to be accompanied by all the paraphernalia of the Coal and Steel Plan; committees of ministers, parliamentary bodies and all the other 'organs' which the French love so much ...

Harold Macmillan

Friday, 24 November 1950
Council of Europe, Strasbourg

The debate was on Duncan Sandys' motion for a European Army. The official Germans wouldn't support it unless it was a Federal Army.

Reynaud spoke well – then Harold Macmillan. His stuff is always excellent – but he cannot appear spontaneous and thus any attempt at emotion always rings false. Passionate speech by Guy Mollet against rearming Germany – frankly admitting that he still mistrusted her and could not forget the past.*

Violet Bonham Carter

Monday, 27 November–Tuesday, 28 November 1950

It is said that Iraq means to follow Egypt in repudiating her treaty with Britain. This may be followed by Persia becoming troublesome. The Russians might then be tempted to start a drive in the Middle East where the prize is a really great one – the greatest source of oil supply in the Old World.

Meanwhile, with typically British escapism, the House of Commons is ... discussing whether or not the Festival of Britain amusement park should or should not be open on Sunday afternoons.

Harold Macmillan

Wednesday, 13 December 1950

Lunched with Coote, Johnstone† and Hugh Gaitskell, Chancellor of the Exchequer. Gaitskell rather soft-looking, large face which always

---

*Duncan Sandys, Conservative MP and chairman of the international executive of the European Movement 1947–50; Paul Reynaud, French premier in 1940, imprisoned by Germans during war; Guy Mollet, French Socialist leader, Prime Minister 1956–7.
†J. C. Johnstone and Sir Colin Coote, *Daily Telegraph* journalists. Coote was editor 1950–64.

looks slightly unshaven; amiable and in his way, intelligent, rather like a certain type of High Church clergyman with a slum parish. He talked about the ending of Marshall Aid which he was going to announce in Parliament that day; quite clear from what he said that we hadn't chosen to relinquish it, but had been told by the Americans that we couldn't have any more. Much amused when Gaitskell said that at the London School of Economics they had a machine which demonstrated the economic system electrically, by lighting up buttons in different colours so that, if for instance inflationary pressure was increased other things happened. Gaitskell was dead serious about this, couldn't understand why it made me laugh so much.

Malcolm Muggeridge

Wednesday, 13 December 1950

Whatever might be the technical advantages of not 'getting bogged down' (as the phrase goes) in Korea I am sure that a moral defeat would mean the end of the white man's position in the East and that the moral collapse might spread to the West.

If Indo China goes, Siam follows. Then Malay falls. Hong Kong is of course indefensible in such circumstances. Burma goes next, and Communism may easily seize India. Churchill has put too much emphasis on the purely military needs of Europe. Europe's supremacy in the world largely depends on her position in Africa and Asia.

Harold Macmillan

Thursday, 14 December 1950

Winston was 'booed' in the House by hundreds of enraged, roaring Socialists who will live to be ashamed of themselves – if Stalin spares them; but he carried on undaunted, unflinching and rather relishing the scene. My impression was that he deliberately created it; in veiled but vigorous language, he told the country that there could be no question of a Coalition* unless the government abandoned their mad steel nationalisation project.

Henry 'Chips' Channon

---

* At the end of 1950 the Labour government had a majority of only five and Winston Churchill, leader of the Conservatives, raised the prospect of a coalition at the next election. In the event, in 1951 the Conservatives won an outright majority.

Christmas 1950

[The King's Private Secretary, Lascelles] said that HM was much incensed by the theft of the Coronation Stone from Westminster Abbey. Lascelles managed to keep the news from him until after the Christmas broadcast was safely over. He wanted to go back on the air to appeal for its return!

It seems that silly 'practical jokers' or (more likely) 'Scottish Nationalists' carried out the exploit on Christmas Day (early in the morning). It was brought to London by Edward I in 1296. It should have been returned by the English after some treaty or other early in the 14th century, but this clause was not carried out. Lascelles seemed quite incensed at the 'theft' and still more at the Duke of Montrose's approval. I hazarded the opinion that if it were found in Scotland, it would not in fact go back to Westminster.* What a strange and delightful interlude in the great world tragedy – a sort of Scottish harlequinade.

Harold Macmillan

Wednesday, 10 January 1951

The international outlook gets gloomier and gloomier. If we can stabilise the position in Korea then it is still possible I think that some kind of negotiated settlement may be reached between the Americans and Chinese. But so long as the Chinese are advancing they are not likely to be ready to talk, and if we are actually thrown out of Korea pressure in America for some retaliatory action on China will be very, very strong ...

If we desert [America] obviously it may have very serious consequences in their participating in European defence.

It is not surprising that in these circumstances there is now developing something like a panic about our Defence programme.

Hugh Gaitskell

---

*The Stone had been stolen by four Scottish students and was eventually recovered and returned to Westminster in the spring of 1951. In 1996 the Stone was returned permanently to Scotland when not needed for coronations.

Monday, 29 January 1951

I am a very new Member of Parliament* and it is still exciting to bump into Winston in the Members' lavatory, as I did the other day. It is still pleasant to be called by my Christian name by Aneurin Bevan and to call him Nye ... Still feeling like a very new boy.

After Questions, the Prime Minister made a long-awaited statement on the new Defence plans, involving rearmament costing £4,700,000,000 over the next three years and the call-up of 235,000 reservists this summer. It was received in glum silence on our side of the House. Some Labour MPs asked hostile questions and this was used by the Tories as fresh evidence of a Labour split. I went away wanting to discuss it with my colleagues but I don't really know them well enough and this frustrated me.

Tony Benn

Sunday, 11 February 1951

To Bristol for my first visit since the by-election. We got up to find it in the middle of a full-scale atomic bomb exercise. What a sign of the times. The centre of the city, laid flat by the air raids in the last war, was full of military and police searching for 'radio-activity'. However, traditional British imperturbability was well demonstrated by the fact that all the high-ups lunched in comfort at the Grand Hotel where we were staying.

Tony Benn

Monday, 12 February 1951

Winston sent for me to 'consult' me about the latest phase of his controversy with Attlee about the 'atomic' agreement made in the war between himself and Roosevelt. As was admitted in ... the House the other day, this agreement (which was very favourable to us) was allowed to come to an end a year or two ago. It was in fact abrogated by the McMahon Act [of 1946] which Congress passed on the advice, no doubt, of the administration. The Churchill–Roosevelt Agreement was secret. It has not been published since. Presumably Congress

---

*Benn had been elected an MP at the Bristol South East by-election on 30 November 1950, replacing Sir Stafford Cripps, who resigned his seat due to ill-health.

was not informed of its existence. It was not a binding treaty but it was a 'gentleman's agreement.' A treaty could not have been made in 1943 without disclosing the secret to Congress. But of course our position, now, is much injured. We have not now the right to equal share in discoveries and developments ... Moreover we no longer have the protection of the original agreement, by which neither we nor the Americans have the right to use the atom bomb without the agreement of the other. With the American bombers on the East coast [of England], armed with the atom bomb, this is an important point ...

Harold Macmillan

Wednesday, 14 March 1951

I made a joke in the House in the small hours when Florence Horsburgh – dried up old spinster – was making a speech on sausages. 'What do we do with a sausage?' I said, 'The same as they do with bananas at Girton.' She only caught 'bananas' and said that unfortunately we had not got any now ...

Hugh Dalton

Monday, 19 March 1951

On Thursday, a slip of paper was being circulated round the House

GALA SMOKING CONCERT
IN THE SMOKING ROOM
THE HOUSE OF COMMONS MALE VOICE CHOIR
under its conductor
JIM*
NO PAIRS NO PACK DRILL

About 10 o'clock the Smoking Room began filling up. There must have been 80 Labour MPs in there ... Whenever a Tory came in they all sang: 'Why were you born so beautiful, why were you born at all.' When any Labour MP went to the bar they sang 'My drink is water bright, water bright fresh from the crystal stream.'

Then, they started to sing a parody of John Brown's body: 'We'll make Winston Churchill smoke a Woodbine every day, We'll make

*James Callaghan.

Winston Churchill smoke a Woodbine every day, We'll make Winston Churchill smoke a Woodbine every day, When the red revolution comes. Solidarity for ever ...' etc

It was great fun and we had certainly captured the Smoking Room from the Tories if nothing more.

Tony Benn

Thursday, 22 March 1951

Great row in Cabinet today over Hugh [Gaitskell]'s proposal, backed by Health Ministers and Edith Summerskill, to charge something for false teeth and spectacles; to put a ceiling on Health Expenditure and to make a series of increases in Old Age Pensions.

Summerskill [said that] people would care much more about increased pensions than a bit on teeth and glasses.

Nye as expected made heavy weather. We were giving up a great principle of the Welfare State. We could no longer speak of a 'free health service.' American press would give banner headlines to our retreat ... His own position would be rendered impossible: his prestige would be undermined as Minister of Labour ... The truth was this was the cost of rearmament. Why not cut £23 million off the arms estimates.

Only Harold Wilson, rather ineffectively, backed Nye.

Hugh Dalton

Tuesday, 10 April 1951

Budget Day

Suspense and a brooding atmosphere at the House, when Gaitskell, rather nattily if unsuitably dressed and wearing a red carnation, began to address the crowded and attentive benches.

Winston who had seemed so boyish recently suddenly seemed sleepy and old. Perhaps he had had too rich a lunch ... Mrs Chamberlain and Mrs Atlee were in the Speaker's Gallery. Bevin, on the front bench, looked thin and had the parchment pallor one associates with death ... Doom has now struck.

Gaitskell has a Wykehamist voice and manner and a 13th century face. He began in moderate fashion and at once put the House in a receptive mood by his clear enunciation and courteous manner; he was lucid, clear and coherent and there was a commendable absence of Daltonian sneers or bleak Crippsian platitudes. A breath of fresh air ... Eventually Gaitskell announced a rise in petrol and 6d on the income tax, and a heavy increase on distributed profits – that was all. Once again we have been let off revolutionary legislation, or confiscatory political contrivances.

Henry 'Chips' Channon

Monday, 16 April 1951

Mr Bevin died on Saturday.

Bevin was in many respects a very bad Foreign Secretary. His Palestine policy was absurd, for he succeeded in the most impossible result of becoming equally odious to Jew and Arab. His attitude to united Europe was petty. But he has done one immense service to Britain and to the world. He has imposed upon an unwilling and hesitant party a policy of resistance to Soviet Russia and Communism. A Tory Foreign Secretary (in the immediate post-war years) could not have done this.

Harold Macmillan

Saturday, 21 April 1951

Visit to Anthony Eden – little shabby-smart house in Mayfair, Chesterton Street, off Curzon Street; seated with him talking and drinking rather stingily concocted martinis ... Habit of getting up and straightening a picture, then standing back. Weak face, with protruding teeth, mark of vanity. He said he couldn't make up his mind whether he ought to go to the Foreign Office or be Leader of the House (assuming, of course, that the Conservatives get into power) and I said he should try and do both, with good deputies. This pleased him enormously. About Winston, he said gravely that his health was not as good as people thought, and that he could speak of this with an easy conscience because, as far as his own private inclinations were concerned, he'd vastly rather be Foreign Secretary than Prime Minister.* The only funny remark was when he said, in answer to my question as to whether the Attlee

---

*Following the Conservative victory in the October 1951 General Election, Eden was appointed Foreign Secretary and Deputy Prime Minister.

Government was likely to fall soon: 'I don't think Winston can hold them together much longer.'

Malcolm Muggeridge

Monday, 23 April 1951

The resignation of Nye was announced this morning.* Harold Wilson's position was uncertain though it was announced later today that he too intended to go. I arrived at the Commons at two and went up into the Members' Gallery. With the sunlight pouring in through the windows opposite, the Chamber was suffused in a warm glow of light. Jennie Lee [Bevan's wife, a Labour MP] came in at about ten past three and sat, flushed and nervous, on the very back bench, below the gangway. At twenty past three Nye walked in briskly and jauntily and went straight to his seat three rows back. He looked pale and kept shifting his position and rubbing his hands. The front benches on both sides were very full – Churchill, Eden and the Tories sat quietly.

The Government Front Bench looked sicker and sicker as the speech went on and the violence of the attack intensified. Jennie Lee behind him sat forward and became more and more flushed. Every now and again he pushed back the lock of his iron-grey hair. He swung on his feet, facing this way and that and his outstretched arm sawed the air. He abused the Government, threw in a few anti-American remarks for good measure. He attacked the Treasury, economists, and the unhappy combination of an economist at the Treasury. Gaitskell showed clearly the contempt he felt [for Nye].

The fact is that though there was substance in what he said, Nye overplayed his hand. His jokes were in bad taste. I felt slightly sick ... It has to be said he has written the Tory Party's best pamphlet yet.

Tony Benn

Tuesday, 18 September 1951
Birch Grove, Sussex

Went out before dinner and shot a duck. An excellent dinner with venison from Langwell. I was so tired after dinner that I treated myself to my favourite vice – I read *Rob Roy*.

---

* Nye Bevan resigned as Minister of Labour in protest at NHS prescription charges brought in by Gaitskell's Budget announcement two weeks earlier.

In Persia it is clear that there will be a test between bankruptcy (on which HMG are relying) and a more or less revolutionary position by Dr Mossadeq and his supporters.*

Pre-election fever is growing in intensity. Attlee is lying low, like Brer Rabbit, and sayin' nuffin'.

Harold Macmillan

Tuesday, 2 October 1951

Correct proofs etc of my election address.† Most candidates put too much into the address and make the type too small. They forget that 80 years of full and compulsory education have produced an electorate that is practically illiterate and cannot understand any but the simplest words ...

The evacuation of Abadan is now to take place immediately and in the most humiliating manner imaginable. The Persians refuse to allow the British cruiser to come alongside the pier (which is British property) so that the last 350 odd employees may go aboard.

Harold Macmillan

Tuesday, 16 October 1951
Bristol

At 7, Caroline and I went over to the Central Hall for the great rally which the Prime Minister was to address. There were nearly 3,000 people there.

Every Labour candidate in Bristol spoke and as I stood up to speak I felt sick with emotion. Mastery of an audience that size is a strong task, but what an intoxicating experience it is.

Clem and Vi could be seen on the way to the platform ... [the chairman] introduced 'Comrade Clem Attlee' and pushed him forward. But the bouquet had been forgotten and Alderman Mrs Keel gave Vi the flowers with a moving little speech.

---

* Mohammad Mossadeq was Prime Minister of Iran from 1951 to 1953. During his administration he nationalised the Iranian oil fields that had previously been owned by the Anglo-Iranian Oil Company (later British Petroleum or BP). This led later to the overthrow of Mossadeq with the complicity of the CIA.

† The second General Election in twenty-one months was called for 25 October 1951.

Clem quietly and sensibly reviewed the work of the Government abroad and at home, linking each to the work of two famous West-countrymen, Ernest Bevin and Stafford Cripps. 'They have both left us now,' he said, 'but other young ones have come to take their place. Christopher Mayhew one of the most brilliant young men, to replace Ernie Bevin, and Tony Wedgwood Benn, another brilliant man, to replace Stafford Cripps.'

When he sat down Tony Crosland moved his vote of thanks, and paid tribute somewhat backhandedly by saying there has never been an anti-Clem faction in the party (which was both patently untrue and damning with faint praise). We ended with the first verse of the Red Flag.

Tony Benn

Chapter Five

1951–1962
The Baby Boomers

Winston Churchill returned unexpectedly as Prime Minister in the General Election of October 1951. From almost the start of the 1951–5 government, the Conservative and Labour parties were preoccupied with who should succeed their leaders. Churchill was unwell, as Lord Moran's diaries show, but hung on until the last possible minute against the heir-apparent, Anthony Eden. There was dissatisfaction with Clement Attlee, but following the death of Ernest Bevin there was no obvious MP to replace him, except possibly the brilliant but volatile Welshman, Aneurin Bevan.

The division of Germany and Berlin persisted and continued to cause tensions. In 1949 the victorious People's Liberation Army had added China to the Communist 'bloc' and the Cold War spread to Asia. Stephen Spender wrote of 'the tragedy of Europe' as politicians planned a united revitalised continent in the form of a common market, a federal state or a defence community. Harold Macmillan describes his protégé Edward Heath's enthusiasm for the European project. Differences of opinion on Britain's future place in Europe become evident within both the left and right of politics.

One of Macmillan's responsibilities in the 1951–5 government was housing: both he and Richard Crossman (in the 1960s) for Labour were enthusiastic proponents of large-scale house-building under public control and of 'slum clearance', policies with unforeseen and sometimes disastrous results. Both kept diaries at this period and into the 1960s.

Disentangling Britain's African empire produced seemingly endless and insoluble problems in the 1950s, much to Macmillan's despair as Prime Minister (only the tip of the iceberg is visible in this chapter): but for Tony Benn the anti-colonial campaigns and the Suez Canal crisis in 1956 were welcome signs of African nationalism. Closer to home, another disaster unfolded at the same time as the Suez crisis, when the forces of the Soviet Union crushed the first uprising in its European empire, in Hungary. 'Sublime courage against hopeless odds,' wrote Violet Bonham Carter as the tanks rolled into Budapest. Frances Partridge, last of the 'Bloomsburys', noted approvingly that the nuclear disarmament campaign was growing.

Future Conservative MP Gyles Brandreth, and the leader of the Fire Brigades Union, John Horner, make fleeting appearances as the 'swinging sixties' begin.

Sunday, 28 October 1951
Chartwell, Kent

Message from Churchill to come out to Chartwell. I expected this. On arrival at 3 pm found him in a most pleasant and rather tearful mood. He asked me to 'build the houses for the people.' What an assignment! I know nothing whatever about these matters, having spent 6 years now either on defence or foreign affairs. I had of course hoped to be Minister of Defence and said this frankly to Churchill. But he is determined to keep it in his own hands. I gather the reason is the frightful muddle in which defence has been allowed to fall.

I asked Churchill what was the present housing 'set-up.' He said he hadn't any idea. But the boys would know. So the boys (Sir Edward Bridges, Head of the Home Civil Service and Sir Norman Brook, Cabinet Secretary) were sent for – also some whisky.

Churchill says it is a gamble – make or mar my political career. But every humble home will bless my name, if I succeed.

On the whole it seems impossible to refuse – but, oh dear, it is not my cup of tea ... I really haven't a clue how to set about the job.

Harold Macmillan

End of October 1951

If Clem dies soon, or if Vi persuades him to retire, there'll be a problem. Under Herbert it won't be a happy ship, nor a Socialist ship either. Nye can hardly hope to gather support in Parliamentary party for some time ... but memories and moods are short. Hugh has a long way to go.*

Winston is feeling the burden ... he's seventy seven now and I don't believe he can stick it.

Dick Crossman and I had a row in Smoke Room on first day. I attacked him for making a speech ... saying that 'Bevanism' would within twelve months cease to be a heresy and become policy of party. Only 'Bevanites' had been honest. I said what is 'Bevanism'? All this posturising and egoising!

Hugh Dalton

Thursday, 1 November 1951

To the school gym class ... The gym instructor, in his white clothes, gave instructions. Matthew, age six and a half, was in the second row and I noticed that he never heard any orders. He just guessed, or copied what the other boys were doing. 'Hands on hips!' roared the instructor. Mathew put his on his head. Then they had to climb up a kind of gate of six bars, passing through the gap between the top two bars, and coming down the other side ... One of the boys got stuck trying to crawl between the two top bars. He waited half way through shaking and trembling. All the other boys started laughing at him, until they were stopped by the instructor.

And on the way home in the bus where I sat with Matthew, one of his little friends who was seated directly in front of us suddenly turned and said, 'Spender, is that old white-haired gentleman with spectacles your daddy?' 'No' said Matthew with perfect self-possession. When we got off the bus and were at a safe distance from his little friend I asked Matthew why he had said I was not his father. 'Because you aren't', he exclaimed passionately. 'You aren't like what he said you were.'

Stephen Spender

* After the election, Clement Attlee stayed on as Leader of the Labour Party, with Herbert Morrison as his deputy; Aneurin Bevan was unofficial leader of the Labour left; Hugh Gaitskell, future leader of the Labour Party.

Monday, 5 November–Friday, 9 November 1951

I have seen representatives of the building unions (Coppock and Fawcett*) [who] were very pleasant. I told them I knew little or nothing about the problem [of housing shortage]. They were much amused by this. 'The last ministers knew everything. It was no good trying to talk to them. They talked at us.' This referred to Dalton and Bevan. The union leaders support the Labour Party. But they have little affection for the political leaders. I gave Coppock and Fawcett tea in the House of Commons. F (who is a fine hearty fellow, weighing 15 to 16 stone, I should say) consumed buns at a prodigious rate ...

We have that 300,000 'target' (often, I fear, turned into a 'promise') round our necks. Timber and steel are the bottlenecks and, with the economic crisis and rearmament, will get worse.

Harold Macmillan

Tuesday, 6 November 1951

At the Parliamentary Party meeting this morning Attlee opened the discussion on the King's Speech, like a schoolmasterly bird snapping up the morsels. What is significant is the cheerfulness and morale of the Party, compared with its state of semi-disintegration just before the election. What a difference it makes not to be scared of losing your seat! They are even almost friendly to the Bevanites, out of sheer general sense of well-being. Personally I am inclined to regard this sort of optimism as extremely complacent. We are in opposition, without any idea of a constructive Socialist policy and it may be a great deal more difficult to unseat the Conservatives than many of my colleagues imagine.

In the King's Speech debate itself Winston followed [Attlee] ... with a supreme peace appeal.

The election has had a real result on both parties. It has made them realise that the people of this country really do want peace and I fancy Winston and Eden have a better chance than Attlee and Morrison. The latter had to lean over backwards in being pro-American for fear of being accused of appeasing Communism. Winston and Eden have to lean over backwards trying to get peace with Stalin in order to

---

* Richard Coppock was General Secretary of the National Federation of Building Trades' Employers and President of the Building Industries' National Council. Luke Fawcett was General Secretary of the Amalgamated Union of Building Trade Workers and a member of the Federation's Executive.

rebut the charge of war-mongering. But how far is the Old Man really prepared to go? Is he prepared to persuade Truman to give up the rearmament of Western Germany ... for an agreement with the Kremlin about a unified disarmed Germany?

Richard Crossman

Friday, 16 November 1951

The meetings [in the October General Election] varied from extremely rowdy at Lewisham (on Persia) to very stolid in Yorkshire. The difference between Yorkshire and the rest of the country is quite extraordinary. It is almost a convention that when one goes to speak in support of another candidate to say something nice about the candidate, and this normally evokes enthusiastic cheers from the audience. It never failed to work everywhere until I got to Leeds where my first meeting was in West Leeds for Charlie Pannell. He is a good Member of Parliament and popular in his constituency. But my extremely nice remarks about him were apparently ignored by the audience who did not make a sound. They listened very carefully to everything I said about Persia, which was the first part of my speech, and then when I stepped back for a moment they burst into applause.

I then resumed my speech about the cost of living and they applauded at the end. On leaving the meeting I was talking to the constituency chairman about the rock-like immobility of the audience, and he said 'Yes, you were very clever to step back at that point. They thought you had finished the speech – that's why they clapped.'

Hugh Gaitskell

Monday, 3 December 1951

After dinner on Sunday Ben, the son of Harold Nicolson ... told an interesting story about the ten days he spent at Windsor Castle as Deputy Keeper of the King's Pictures ...

Parlour games were played after dinner and the Queen chose her favourite game. The master of ceremonies took all the male guests outside and provided them with brass pokers, shovels etc. After ten minutes practice they were then made to goose step down the long drawing room past the King, the Queen and the Princesses, who found it exquisite fun seeing Sir Stafford Cripps, Lord Ismay and Anthony Eden doing 'eyes right.'

Richard Crossman

February 1952

On February 5th there began a debate [on Korea] in the House. I heard Anthony Eden make a somewhat insipid speech and then the Opposition put down a vote of censure on the PM personally. He prepared to answer it on the following day by a fighting speech revealing the dramatic fact that the Labour government had gone further in committing us to bomb China in certain circumstances than anyone supposed and that he had entered into no new commitments.

On the morning of February 6th I arrived at No 10 early and asked the Private Secretary on duty for the text of the speech. He said that there was no need to think of it further: Edward Ford had just been round from Buckingham Palace to announce that the King was dead.

When I went to the Prime Minister's bedroom he was sitting alone with tears in his eyes, looking straight in front of him and reading neither his official papers nor the newspapers ... I tried to cheer him up by saying how well he would get on with the new Queen, but all he could say was that he did not know her and that she was only a child.

John Colville

Thursday, 21 February 1952

Lord Moran's home

This evening, when I was about to go down to dinner, the telephone rang; it was Winston's voice. Usually the secretary calls me to the telephone before he comes.

'Where are you Charles? I'd like to see you.'

When I got to No. 10 I found him sitting on his bed in his boiler suit. He looked at me intently as if he were interested in me and wanted to know what I was thinking – so different from his usual detached and almost absent-minded greeting.

'I am glad you have come. I took up the telephone when I woke an hour ago and I couldn't think of the words I wanted. Wrong words seemed to come into my head, but I was quite clear what was happening and did not say them. This went on for about three or four minutes. Then the operator asked, "Do you want the Private Office?" What does it mean Charles? Am I going to have a stroke?' ... 'My pulse was alright,' he said putting his finger on his radial artery. 'Take it now, Charles ... Tell me, Charles what happened? Why couldn't I find the words I wanted?'

I explained that some of the small vessels in his head had gone into a state of spasm, contracting so that the circulation to the speech centre was diminished.

He offered to send me home in his car but I thanked him and said I would walk some of the way. I wanted to do a little hard thinking. In the past I have taken great risks when I let him carry on at Washington after the heart attack, and again at Monte Carlo, two and a half years ago, when he had a stroke.

Ought he to resign or could we do anything to patch him up for a little ...?

I knew that he had set his heart on seeing the young Queen crowned before he gave up office. That it was a bad time for Anthony [Eden] to take over was clear to him; he would be held responsible for the unpopular austerity measures ... I was beginning to see that it was not the moment for him to go.

Lord Moran

February 1952

During the next weeks much happened ... there was trouble over the name of the Royal House ...

This had all arisen because Queen Mary sent for me on February 18th to say that Prince Ernst August of Hanover had come back from Broadlands and informed her that Lord Mountbatten had said to an assembled house party of royal guests that the House of Mountbatten now reigned.

John Colville

Sunday, 2 March 1952
Birch Grove, Sussex

Church in the morning ... A large congregation of boy scouts; girl guides; brownies, cubs etc. We had the hymn 'All things bright and beautiful', but in deference to modern political thought the third verse was omitted (viz. 'The rich man in his castle/The poor man at his gate/ God made them high or lowly/And ordered their estate'). What rot!

Harold Macmillan

Tuesday, 25 March 1952

To a joint meeting of the defence and foreign affairs group [of the Labour opposition]. This meeting opened with a rambling speech by Shinwell and then there came quite a sensible discussion centring on the Russian proposal for a Four-Power conference to consider an independent, armed Germany.

This meeting showed the extraordinary situation prevailing in the parliamentary Labour Party. Seventy people were there and seventy people, in a general debate, without any preliminary preparation, cannot achieve a policy decision. The Russian Note was delivered eighteen days ago. In the sixteen days between its delivery and the publication of the Western Powers' reply, no one, either at Transport House or in Westminster was competent to work out the Labour Party's reaction or put forward our suggestions as to what the Three Power reply should be ...

There is no machinery for making the Labour Opposition a real fighting opposition with a policy.

Richard Crossman

Thursday, 27 March 1952

This week has been curiously flat. The controversy over the sensational Bevanite split has all petered out, as all controversies do, and what is clearer than ever is that the parliamentary opposition is almost entirely leaderless and without drive or energy.

Richard Crossman

Thursday, 1 May 1952

I went yesterday to the 'New Town' of Basildon – in Essex. This struck me as pure *Martin Chuzzlewit*. It was 'Little Eden' again.

What a mad venture – without any of the facilities. No water; no sewerage; no river to pollute (except the Crouch, which cannot be polluted because of its oyster bed), no industry – and jolly few houses.

Harold Macmillan

Thursday, 15 May 1952

Tonight the PM and Mrs C gave a farewell dinner for the Eisenhowers at No 10, on the eve of his departure from SHAPE* to become a candidate in the Presidential Election. There were thirty two to dinner, including most of the war-time chiefs and the present Service ministers – Alexanders, Tedders, Alanbrookes, Portals, Jumbo Wilson, Attlees, etc ...

When Ike left he said that if he were elected he would pay just one visit outside the USA – to the UK – in order to show our special relationship. The atmosphere could not have been more cordial – though things almost started badly with neither the PM nor Mrs C knowing that it was white tie and decorations.

John Colville

Friday, 16 May 1952
Chartwell, Kent

Alone with the PM who is low ... he spoke of coalition. The country needed it he said, and it must come. He would retire in order to make it possible; he might even make the demand for it an excuse for retiring. Four-fifths of the people of this country were agreed on four-fifths of the things to be done.

John Colville

Tuesday, 20 May 1952

For nearly a fortnight I have been in Manor House Hospital, having my appendix out ... I took with me an enormous load of books and, as usual, read very few of them apart from the *History of the Times* dealing with the years from 1912 to 1939. What struck me was the enormous power of the press in politics before 1918 and its steady decline since then. Northcliffe could really make and unmake Cabinet ministers ...

---

*Supreme Headquarters Allied Powers Europe in Paris, the administrative centre of the forerunner of the North Atlantic Treaty Organisation (NATO).

Of course the main influence of *The Times* in its day was in foreign affairs, where its leading articles were really studied as semi-official statements of British policy.

[The decline is due to] the rise to power of the Labour Party, which tends to write off nearly all newspapers as capitalist. A Labour Cabinet, for that reason, is not nearly as open to newspaper influence as a Conservative Cabinet. But the basic reason is the extension of the franchise in 1918 and the coming into being of a real thing called democratic public opinion, whereas in the old days, political decisions really were taken by an oligarchy and a newspaper proprietor operated as a member of an oligarchy with a particularly loud voice.

Richard Crossman

Wednesday, 21 May 1952

I cannot help feeling it is both wrong and foolish to denationalise transport and steel, however doctrinaire may have been the motives of the late Government in nationalising them. When the Labour Government get back they will be renationalised.

John Colville

Friday, 30 May 1952

It is difficult to see how our economic ills can be cured and at the moment nothing that is done seems to be more than a short-term palliative. The remedy for 50 million people living in an island which can maintain 30 million and no longer leads the world in industrial exports or in capital assets invested abroad is hard to find. Harold Macmillan said to me at the Turf yesterday that he thought development of the Empire into an economic unit as powerful as the USA and the USSR was the only possibility ...

Mrs Churchill does not think [Winston] will last long as Prime Minister.

John Colville

Tuesday, 3 June 1952

As I read Hansard [on the debate on the introduction of commercial television] I was conscious of the long shadow of that gaunt old covenanter, Lord Reith, across its pages. I could see him as he rose in his place like another John Knox to scourge the infidel. 'I am slow of speech,' he began, 'reluctant to waste your lordships' time and my own.' He claimed no credit at all for what had been done when he was Director General of the BBC during the first sixteen years of its existence. He tried to do as he had been taught in the Manse ... Of the worth and consequence of British broadcasting, its flower and essence, he spoke with pride: today it commanded the respect and admiration of the whole world. 'What grounds are there,' he cried, 'for jeopardizing that heritage and tradition?' It was a betrayal and a surrender.

'Need we be ashamed of moral values or of intellectual and ethical objectives? It is these that are here and now at stake.'

Those who had spoken in the debate – the men who count in the deliberations of the House – were not concerned with making debating points. They were preoccupied with the effect of television over the years upon the minds and lives of their fellow citizens, the importance, to borrow Lord Kirkwood's words, of somehow educating our people to understand the meaning of the vital problems which come before them.

Lord Moran

Monday, 30 June 1952

To Tony's [Crosland] flat to meet Callaghan, Jenkins and Jay.

Frank talk. I told them Germans were murderers, individuals excepted. They'd killed all my friends in First War, etc. *Deutschland uber alles* was their song and they meant it. You couldn't tie them with snips of paper like the European Defence Community ... The order to advance will be given in German, and we should be expected to obey.

Roy, Tony and Jim all excused themselves from dining.

I am very angry and worked up about it all. I see Europe going by default. Free economy Germany will be forging ahead; with all their gifts of efficiency displayed to the full. And we, in our mismanaged, mixed-economy, over-populated little island, shall become a second-rate power, with no influence and continuing 'crises.'

Hugh Dalton

Saturday, 19 July–Wednesday, 23 July 1952

Westminster Hospital

I spent [the last thee days] partly sitting with Zita [Crossman] and partly on the terrace outside the Casualty Ward overlooking Horse-ferry Road, where there is a nice tree in the garden.

The two memories I have of those three days are, first, the warmth of friendship from all sorts of unexpected people, and secondly the odious problems of the Health Service.

I was a bit puzzled why, about every six hours, I was asked whether Zita should go to a private ward ... When I mentioned it to [our doctor, Harris] on Sunday after Zita had died, he said to me that of course she had only been got into Westminster Hospital because he had said to [the consultant] Meadows that, if he could get her into the Casualty ward, I would agree to her being a private patient. I said, 'But why couldn't she have got in as a National Health patient?' And he said, 'I haven't got one of my patients into the Westminster, ever.'

So much for the theory that we have removed the money element from sickness. It wasn't the fault of anybody in the hospital. It's just the system of having, within one building, the public wards and the private wards.

Richard Crossman

July 1952

Aren't we All? Haymarket Theatre, London

The seats around Haymarket were lined with people held back by a concourse of policemen. The audience had to be seated half an hour before 'the Royals' arrived. It sat cheerfully talking. The Royal Box was decorated with hideous small, bronze and yellow chrysanthemums.

Throughout the performance the Regal Box was being surreptitiously watched by half the audience, so that the play received scant attention; but the general atmosphere was uncritical and good-natured, the display of manners and loyalty impressive. It was very interesting to note how the Royal Family seem to have acquired a communal manner of behaviour. They have developed an instinctive self-protection so that they should not bump into each other or stumble down a step. They move in slow motion with care and a fluid grace: their technique is so perfected that it appears entirely natural. No doubt but that much of this charm and grace is very special to the Queen Mother. The reigning Queen has developed independently but her charm and interested wonder is inherited from her mother's genius.

If the Queen Mother were anyone other than she is (ridiculous supposition) would one come so readily under her spell? Would one admire quite so much those old fashioned dainty movements? The sweetly pretty smile with tongue continually moistening the lower lip? Yes – whoever she were she could not be faulted.

Cecil Beaton

Monday, 11 August 1952

Winston took Meg and me to see *The Innocents*, a stage version of Henry James' *The Turn of the Screw*. He got a great welcome but embarrassed us by being unable to hear and asking questions in a loud voice ... Anthony Eden and Clarissa Churchill* are engaged. Clarissa, who was at Chartwell for the weekend, is very beautiful but she is still strange and bewildering, cold if sometimes witty, arrogant at times and understanding at others. Perhaps marriage will change her and will also calm the vain and occasionally hysterical Eden.

John Colville

Monday, 18 August–Tuesday,19 August 1952
North Devon

Arrived at Barnstaple at 6.45 and drove to Lord Fortescue's house, where I spent the night. Lord F is Lord Lieutenant and seems very competent and sensible.

We left at 8.45 and drove to Lynton with short stops at two villages on the way, which had also been injured. The urban district consists of two separate towns – one, Lynton, on the hill; the other, Lynmouth, on the shore. The damage was to Lynmouth, and caused by the tremendous flood forcing the river out of its bed, so that what was the High Street is now the river. The immense quantity of boulders (said to be 40,000 tons) destroyed the bridges. The problems of reconstruction are very considerable; the major cost will be in roads and bridges. I met all the local councillors, the County Council authorities, the heads of

---

*Winston Churchill's niece; Eden was twenty-three years her senior.

the Army, Police and of the voluntary services (Red Cross, WVS etc.) at a conference in the little Town Hall after the tour of the town.

One of the problems is to look after all the people evacuated from Lynmouth (about 1,000) without altogether destroying the economic life of Lynton as well. So it was agreed not to take over the remaining hotels, but to encourage visitors ...

Drove to Dulverton, stopping at one or two villages (such as Exford) on the way where a good deal of damage has been done.

Harold Macmillan

Friday, 22 August–Monday, 25 August 1952

W[inston] has persuaded Truman to join with him in sending a message, signed by them both, to Mossadeq about the Persian oil question. W himself did it and the FO oil people agreed. It is the first time since 1945 that the Americans have joined with us in taking overt joint action against a third power ...

Eden, completing his honeymoon in Lisbon, is furious ... the stealing by Winston of his personal thunder.

John Colville

Sunday, 31 August 1952
Birch Grove, Sussex

A week's shooting is a wonderful rest. All thought of politics, business, family troubles and all the rest is put aside, and for some 8 hours a day everything is concentrated on the vastly exciting and infinitely serious problems of trying to kill grouse.

I shot fairly well on the whole; at some drives very badly, at others almost brilliantly ... I shot the highest and fastest I have ever killed.

Harold Macmillan

Friday, 26 September–Monday, 29 September 1952
Labour Party Conference, Morecambe

When I got on the train at Euston I found Tom O'Brien and Geoffrey Bing in the first-class restaurant car and we travelled down together. Tom O'Brien, who is next year's TUC chairman and an Irish rogue of the highest quality, entertained us to the biggest meal that I have ever had in a restaurant car. It lasted from five o'clock till a quarter to eleven and included endless rounds of drinks, two bottles of white wine, two bottles of red wine and then liqueurs – as well as all the courses the Railway had to offer. 'Some of my delegates,' Tom said after dinner, 'have the insolence to challenge me on my expense account!'

I woke up [on Saturday] to a morning of sunshine, rainclouds and a superb view across the mud to the mountains of the Lake District. There is nothing whatsoever to be said for Morecambe except this view, which appeared at thirty-hour intervals for a minute or two throughout the week. It's a minor Blackpool, dumped down on mud flats, with a four-mile long promenade, with the Grosvenor at one end, the Winter Gardens in the middle and the other big hotel at the other end, so that life was spent in going from one to the other in a blustering, driving wind. By the end of the Conference everybody had streaming colds, as well as heartache.

[On Monday, I was] in time to hear the chairman read out the obituary notice, which included Stafford Cripps and [George] Tomlinson. At this point the chairman turned to Attlee and asked him whether he wanted to say anything. Attlee doodled and shook his head. It was the first indication of the astonishing lack of leadership which he displayed throughout.

Richard Crossman

Saturday, 27 September 1952

There is a general feeling that the Tories have recovered a good deal of ground in the last few months. Certainly ministers have settled down.

The Trade Union leaders, frightened of communism and not on very good terms with their colleagues in the political wing of the party, are anxious to 'play ball' with us.

All the same, there is a distrust and even fear of the Tories, which is based on the suspicion and jealousy of the 'proletariat', now come into its own, and determined to maintain its standard of *'panem et circenses'* at all costs.* If *panem* is rather scarce, *circenses* are all the more vital. 2/- or 3/- on the rent to keep the house from falling down will

---

* 'Bread and circuses' – a political policy of Roman origin to distract and appease the populace through the satisfying of basic wants and banal, shallow spectacles.

be bitterly resented and probably fought to the end. But 12/6 a week on the 'never, never' system to buy the television set is a necessity.

... All the inflationary wages of the people are spent on the few available luxuries or pleasures. Roughly, these are tobacco, alcohol and (for the war) books. (Now television, cinemas, dancing etc. are taking the place of books).

Perhaps the most noticeable, and painful, difference between our position now and when we were last in office (1945) is our relationship to the US. Then we were on an equal footing – a respected ally. Then it was the Churchill–Roosevelt combination (or its aftermath). Now we are treated by the Americans with a mixture of patronising pity and contempt ... They are really a strange people. Perhaps the mistake we make is to continue to regard them as an Anglo-Saxon people. That blood is very much watered down now; they are a Latin-Slav mixture with a fair amount of German and Irish.

Harold Macmillan

Monday, 24 November 1952

People are prattling of the Coronation already, of whom will and will not be summoned, of their robes and places and arrangements. The Dowager Peeresses are nervous lest they are not invited. Members of Parliament too are in a ticklish position. In fact conversation has taken on a Gilbert and Sullivan quality. Coaches and robes, tiaras and decorations. Winnie Portarlington announced at luncheon that she has harness but no coach; Circe Londonderry has a coach but no horses; Mollie Buccleuch has no postillions – but five tiaras. People are obsessed by their Coronation prerogatives.

Henry 'Chips' Channon

Thursday, 27 November 1952

Steel Bill was resumed this afternoon. [John] Freeman (a Bevanite socialist) opened with a very able speech ... The debate dragged on in a desultory way till 9 pm when [Jack] Jones (Socialist) wound up in a glorious platform, tub-thumping, emotional speech, tears in his eyes – but all, or nearly all, fake emotion. The contrast between the icy precision of Freeman (scholar; intellectual; gentleman) and Jones (steel workers' union) was very interesting. On the whole I prefer

Jones. I wound up for the Government ... part boisterous and racy ... [part] a serious and philosophic argument – a restatement of The Middle Way and a plea for the view that Government 'supervision' of a great industry could be better done without 'ownership'.

Harold Macmillan

Thursday, 1 January 1953
Queen Mary

A quiet day on board ...

[Winston] said that if I lived my normal span I should assuredly see Eastern Europe free of Communism ...* He lamented that owing to Eisenhower winning the presidency [in November 1952] he must cut much out of Volume VI of his War History and could not tell the story of how the United States gave away, to please Russia, vast tracts of Europe they had occupied and how suspicious they were of his pleas for caution. The British general election in July 1945 had occupied so much of his attention which should have been directed to stemming this fatal tide.

John Colville

Thursday, 8 January 1953
Washington, Farewell dinner for President Truman

After dinner Truman played the piano. Nobody would listen because they were all busy with post-mortems on a diatribe in favour of Zionism and against Egypt which Winston had delivered at dinner (to the disagreement of practically all the Americans present, though they admitted that the large Jewish vote would prevent them disagreeing publicly). However, on W's instructions I gathered all to the piano and we had a quarter of an hour's presidential piano playing before Truman left. He played with quite a nice touch and, as he said himself, could probably have made a living on the stage of the lesser music-halls.

The Americans, apart from Truman and Marshall, stayed till 1.00 am. I had an uneasy feeling that the PM's remarks – about Israel, the European Defence Community, and Egypt – though made to the

---

*John (Jock) Colville died in 1987. General (Ike) Eisenhower, who had been in Supreme Command of the Allied Forces in Europe during the war and later Supreme Commander of NATO, replaced Harry Truman as President.

members of an outgoing administration, had better have been left unsaid in the presence of the three, Bradly, Bedell Smith and Matthews, who are staying on with Ike and the Republicans.

John Colville

Sunday, 11 January–Monday, 12 January 1953

It seems that in *The Listener* my discussion with Bertrand Russell on television is highly praised. Can't but think of him as vainglorious, ape-like. The true destroyer of Christendom isn't Stalin or Hitler or even the Dean of Canterbury and his like, but Liberalism.

Malcolm Muggeridge

Friday, 16 January–Saturday, 17 January 1953

Anthony Eden and his new wife Clarissa came to stay for a night ... He is much less nervous and much less easily offended (or frightened) than he used to be. I think he notices that we all want him to succeed to the Throne and that no one is intriguing to supplant him.

But when will Churchill go?

Eden agreed that in the last few months – or weeks – the political situation had changed. A Socialist victory at the next general election was no longer inevitable. All this made it more important to get the change in the Premiership before any radical alteration in the atmosphere.

Harold Macmillan

Sunday, 1 February–Thursday, 5 February 1953
East coast of England

We got back late on Saturday night from a Bromley Young Conservatives 'do.' The wind and rain were terrific.

It was hard to make out just what was the extent of the Great Flood. But it was clear it was a terrible calamity ranging from Yorkshire to Kent ...

[On 3 February] we flew first to Manly airfield and managed to get a car to take us to Mablethorpe and Sutton. The sea had burst through the sea defences (the sand dunes etc.) and flooded both these resorts and a good deal of agricultural land. About 6,000 people had been evacuated – their houses being uninhabitable. The water was not very deep (as it was low tide) but would rise again with the tide to 3 or 4 feet.

We went about in a 'Duck' and saw everything. The chairman, town clerk, surveyor and other officials seemed to have done well. All the people had gone to Louth, or villages in the county. From Manly we flew to Sculthorpe (now being used by the American Air Force). There was a fine array of Generals, Eagle colonels etc. and great kindness. The first car broke; so it was decided to 'motivate alternative transportation.' We drove to Hunstanton ... and saw similar damage there. Unfortunately the loss of life was high, owing to the sea having broken through the sea wall and swept away a number of little bungalows. These were largely occupied by officers and non-commissioned officers of the American Air Force. About 26 or so were drowned ...

At Hunstanton I got a telephone call (the telephone had just been repaired) about a row in the House of Commons in my absence ... the Socialists are still trying to make capital out of the disaster, of course.

It is really remarkable how kindly neighbours have been. In Whitstable about 6,000 are homeless yet only 50 are in the 'rest centres'. All the rest have found a home in Kentish towns and villages.

Harold Macmillan

Saturday, 7 February 1953
Cincinnati, USA

I am torn by the tragedy of Europe. Everything points to it and has always pointed to it and I wonder whether we have not known about it far longer than we think ... longer than my own lifetime. Just as Baudelaire in 1850 writes of the horror of the world being Americanised (which we think of as quite a recent idea) so perhaps we were born in the shadow of the decline of Europe ...

The grotesque idea occurs to me that the kindness of Americans to us is like the kindness of people to invalids.

Stephen Spender

Monday, 2 March 1953

Went to the 'press' preview of the Ideal Home Exhibition at Olympia. We have an extremely good Ministry of Housing exhibit ... We show two 'people's houses' (one three bedroom, one 2 bedroom). One of these is the new 'open' design which will I think be popular in the South and with young people. It gives them a large sitting room and dining room and 'lounge' all in one room, from which the stairs go up. (This is in place of the old front parlour where no one ever sat and which was reserved for the 'corpse'.)

Harold Macmillan

Friday, 6 March 1953

Stalin's death is officially announced by the Kremlin. All through yesterday, the strangest bulletins, with an extraordinary wealth of detail, both as to the illness and its treatment, were published to Russia and to the world. It appeared as if all the doctors were heavily insuring themselves against accusations of incompetence or treachery.

There is no indication yet of where power will now reside. Will it be a committee of public safety? Will it be an individual? Will it be Molotov, Malenkov, Beria … ?

Harold Macmillan

Saturday, 28 March 1953

Poor Queen Mary died on Tuesday night. She would have loved to see the Coronation, but I feel it is better for her to die now rather than just before or just after it.

We are all dreadfully sad about poor Vivien. She is in a mental home and has been asleep for a week. She had apparently really gone over the edge, poor darling. Larry,* wisely, has gone away to Italy. It is a tragic story and my heart aches for both of them.

Noël Coward

Monday, 30 March 1953

This evening I went to see a C.B.S. show illustrating their weekly television news programme, edited by Ed Murrow, which goes on at three o'clock on Sunday afternoons. It is really superb. As the lights went up I heard Nye behind me saying 'Infantile, the whole thing is completely

---

* Vivien Leigh and Laurence Olivier, whose volatile marriage ended in 1960.

infantile.' The conclusion from this is that Nye does not think he was a great success on a television show which he himself did last week. He is like Churchill in this way. They are both babies where their own fame is concerned. On the way home I saw Westminster Hall still open and I thought I would look in on Queen Mary's lying-in-state. It was just midnight but there was only a very thin trickle of people going through. Indeed, this lying-in-state has been a popular flop ... You really can't have the preparations for a coronation going on and at the same time enjoy a good funeral.

Richard Crossman

Wednesday, 15 April 1953
Lunch at 10 Downing Street

The Iain Macleods were there and Mary and Christopher Soames.*

They are polling today in South Africa and we talked a little of that and other Africa problems. He [Winston] was, I thought, rather on the defensive about them and said how easy it was for people who did not live in multi-racial communities to lay down laws for those who did. I agreed but said that those Whites must come to some terms with the Blacks they had chosen to live amongst – and that Malan's terms[†] were impossible and that he was sowing the seeds of doom for himself and all Europeans in South Africa.

He became very puckish and schoolboyish and said 'Do you know why Black people don't wish to pray with White ones? Because they don't like their smell.'

I had no talk with Iain Macleod tho' I should have liked to. W suddenly said how increasingly he loved animals – particularly cats and goldfish.

Violet Bonham Carter

Thursday, 21 May 1953

At Cabinet this morning the P.M. was in a mood of almost schoolboy excitement. He has been invited (with the French Prime Minister) to

---

* Iain Macleod, Minister of Health; Mary and Christopher Soames, daughter and son-in-law of the Churchills.
† Dr D. F. Malan, leader of the Nationalist Party in South Africa, was a leading proponent of apartheid and Prime Minister of South Africa from 1948 to 1954.

meet President Eisenhower. The meeting is to be in Bermuda. This is much better than Washington. The P.M. is immensely pleased at this turn of events. He announced it this afternoon to the House of Commons ... but it has not saved M. [René] Mayer, the P.M. of France. He was voted out by the Assembly today.

Harold Macmillan

Wednesday, 27 May 1953

Today's banquet for the Queen in Westminster Hall really was quite an affair. The top table ran along the platform where Charles I was tried and behind it were magnificent banks of flowers.

The food was cold and not very good – rather fat New Zealand lamb cutlets and Empire wines. The speeches were commendably brief and I've never heard Churchill speak better. Despite the solemnity of the occasion he made a light-hearted parliamentary oration ... at one point he referred to the Americans and said that we have to be very careful these days when we talked about the American constitution, and then added 'I will therefore content myself with the observation that no constitution was written in better English.' Everybody was convulsed with laughter ...

Afterwards the Queen came down past us and stood just beside us while we sang 'God Save the Queen.' She had togged herself up in a singularly sober outfit and looked, close to, a rather dull, ordinary girl. Then Churchill strolled down and three or four of us shook him by the hand and congratulated him upon his speech whereupon, as usual, he nearly burst into tears with joy.

Richard Crossman

Wednesday, 17 June 1953

[Television] fills the whole political world. There are violent opinions, for and against. The BBC and *The Times* newspaper (now edited by William Haley, former head of the BBC) are putting up a tremendous fight to defend their monopoly. They have got Lords Halifax, Waverley and Brand – and of course the Bishops – to form a society for their support. The alleged American 'vulgarity' and especially their handling of the Coronation* has been whipped up into a great cry against sponsoring.

After all the tedious economic problems which no one can understand or solve, this is one issue on which everyone can have an opinion.

Harold Macmillan

Friday, 26 June 1953

Chartwell, Kent

'Look, my hand is clumsy,' the PM said as I entered his room. Transferring his cigar to his left hand, he made a wavering attempt to put it to his lips.

'It is so feeble. Hold out your hand Charles.'

And with that he tried to touch the tips of my fingers with the corresponding fingers of his own hand.

'I'm not afraid of death but it would be very inconvenient to a lot of people. Rab is very efficient up to a point, but he is narrow and doesn't see beyond his nose … '

When he had done I examined his left hand and arm. There was some loss of power in the left grip – and this had developed since yesterday, three days after the onset of the trouble. I do not like this, the thrombosis is obviously spreading.

Lord Moran

Saturday, 4 July 1953

This has been a most extraordinary week – full of drama.

Monday morning the Cabinet was summoned for 12 noon. Butler took the chair … He told us of the visit which he and Salisbury had paid to Chartwell on Friday, where they found the PM in poor health, but very gallant. With the greatest tact and the lightest of touches, he revealed to us (what we did not know) the nature of Churchill's illness. 'The speech was not very clear; the movements were not too easy.' (In fact he had had a 'stroke' – the left leg and arm were paralysed, and the left side of his face.)

---

* NBC, ABC and CBS all broadcast the ceremony, CBS after the event. Eighty-five million Americans watched it, though the proceedings were interrupted with advertisements at critical moments.

It was a terrible shock to us all, although revealed so discreetly. Many of us were in tears, or found it difficult to restrain them ...

Lunched with Lady Pamela Berry ... [who] is a devoted friend of Anthony Eden. She fears that Churchill will not be able to hold on till Eden is ready.* This (she thinks) cannot be till October. But can the PM last so long and can the truth be concealed so long? On July 2nd ... at 7 pm I left by car for Chartwell for dinner.

The Churchills are using the 'flat' upstairs.

PM was wheeled in and, as he entered the room, he cried out, 'I must congratulate you on a magnificent Parliamentary triumph. It was a masterpiece.' I sat down beside his chair, and he began to talk with great animation about the debate [the previous Wednesday]. He spoke without any difficulty and without any particular slurring of words (more than his usual lisp) ...

At dinner he talked so much at the beginning that he slobbered over his soup. He poured out some champagne with a steady hand and cried out 'you see, I don't spill precious liquor.' The atmosphere was not oppressive ... but positively gay. It was a kind of conspiracy we were all in – and it was rather fun to have such respectable people as Salisbury, Butler and co as fellow-conspirators ...

There were certainly times, at and after dinner, when I thought he was putting on an act – but it was a jolly brave one, anyhow. I was, at many times in the evening, nearer to tears than he. We discussed the possibility of a dissolution; death and Dr Johnson's fear of it; Buddhism and Christianity; Pol Roger – a wine, a woman and a horse ... But he talked most of Germany and Europe.

The situation is really fascinating. Butler is, of course, playing a winning game.

Harold Macmillan

Thursday, 16 July 1953

During the last week a journalistic orgy has been taking place over poor Princess Margaret and Peter Townsend. He has been posted to Brussels and she is in South Africa with the Queen Mother. She is returning tomorrow poor child, to face the *Daily Mirror* poll which is to decide, in the readers' opinion, whether she is to marry a divorced man

---

*On 12 April 1953 Eden had had an operation to remove gallstones during which his bile duct was damaged, leading to heath problems for the rest of his life.

or not! It is all so incredibly vulgar and, to me, it is inconceivable that nothing could be done to stop these tasteless, illiterate minds from smearing our Royal Family with their sanctimonious rubbish.

Larry and Vivien came to do *The Apple Cart* last week and supped here afterwards … no sign of there ever having been a mental breakdown.

Noël Coward

Thursday, 6 August 1953

Chequers

I drove down to Chequers through the green countryside, steeling myself inwardly. How should I find Winston? How much or little impaired?

I found Clemmie in the rose garden.

Clemmie said she felt sure he ought to retire in the autumn and begged me not to urge him to stay on if he asked my advice. She said, truly, that the Conference with the Russians, which he longed for, would not be just one Conference. It would be the start of a long struggle which might last for years.

He was just getting up and came into the big hall when we went in – dressed in his siren suit, walking with a stick but not too badly, his face quite normal – pink and no distortion.

At moments he became suddenly and unreasonably angry – like a violent child. He blazed forth against the BBC. 'I hate the BBC. It kept me off the air for 11 years. It is run by reds –.' Abuse of Reith followed – who could not be described as a 'red'.

After luncheon we went out into the garden, after numerous little houris had been summoned with papers etc., and a nurse brought shoes and zipped them on. It was sunny and after a little pacing on the grass we sat down on a seat and discussed his future. It was terribly poignant for he longs to keep his hold on the levers of power – and where would he be without them? 'Othello's occupation gone!'

I drove back feeling an unutterable sense of tragedy – at watching this last – great – ultimately losing fight against mortality.

Violet Bonham Carter

Sunday, 9 August 1953

The very success of the Housing drive brings new problems. Bricks and cement are still insufficient; we must curtail the programme. We *cannot* restrict New Towns; or special houses for miners; or other Govt needs. So any restriction must fall on the Local Authority schemes – and they don't like it. I hope that if we go on with the great slum clearance and Operation Rescue scheme in the autumn, LAs will be ready to begin to switch their activities. But there must be a gap – perhaps a year – to make new plans. If we could only get enough cement we could get through. Will there ever come an end to pouring cement into the ground for American bombers?

Harold Macmillan

Friday, 21 August 1953

Walked in woods with Blake (keeper) from 11–2 … We saw a good many wild birds on the Buttocks Bank side. I fear there are very few at the top end (garden etc.). The foxes have had them all; when we are rearing it's almost impossible to protect the wild birds from vermin. Perhaps next year we won't rear any tame pheasants and really have a go at vermin of all kinds – human included! But I never think the human poachers (unless really organised ones like some of the Wiltshire gangs) do as much harm as animal ones.

After supper worked till rather late. There seems to be a large number of difficult Compulsory Purchase Orders.

Harold Macmillan

Wednesday, 16 September 1953

Coventry constituency

Saturday was spent in the Stratford-on-Avon constituency where Tom Locksley, a young Coventry schoolmaster, is the candidate. We motored vast distances through rural Warwickshire to meetings attended by a score of people and, in one instance, by none.

At each of the Warwickshire villages I met the handful of people who are struggling to build a party, the majority of them being school-masters and schoolmistresses, and one got an astonishingly vivid picture of the problems involved. The schoolmasters in particular really are the salt of the earth.

Richard Crossman

Wednesday, 23 September 1953

Scotland

Left Nairn at noon and motored to Comrie. We came by Loch Tay and Loch Earn – a really lovely drive, in beautiful weather, sun and cloud and an occasional storm. At Blair Atholl we drove up to the Castle, now – like all the houses of the grandees – abandoned to the tourists, more or less ...

A pouch arrived, containing a very gloomy letter from Julian [Amery] from Strasbourg. He fears Germany more than Russia, and above all fears the European Defence Community and handing the leadership of Europe to Germany on a platter.

This balance of fears is a most difficult problem to decide ... It may be that Germany is no longer the potential master of Europe and that we are right in thinking only of the Russian menace. But – if we are wrong – there will be a heavy price to pay.

Harold Macmillan

Monday, 28 September 1953

The Americans, after three years of negotiation, have come to an agreement with Franco whereby they obtain naval bases in Spain. They are also obliging the Greeks to get rid of our naval mission and to have an American one instead. Gradually they are ousting us out of all world authority. I mind this as I feel it humiliating and insidious. But I also mind it since it gives grounds for anti-American feeling, which is I am sure a dangerous and quite useless state of mind. They are decent folk in every way, but they tread on traditions in a way that hurts.

Harold Nicolson

Thursday, 1 October–Friday, 2 October 1953

Labour Party Conference, Margate

This year's conference did not want to fight. Most delegates are sick of abuse and threats and splits. Herbert Morrison's withdrawal from the treasurership was a fine start.

The right wing of the Party won almost every vote of importance. Land nationalisation and other more extreme proposals were all defeated by big votes. A great deal of the friction between the trade unions and the constituencies arises from differences in the feelings between 'unpractical' people and the unions, with their huge roles ...

We can look forward to a good year in Parliament now and victory in a General Election.

David Butler, who stayed on a day further, tells me that Gaitskell made a good speech on education ('abolish the fees in public schools') and was attacked by Jennie Lee ('he still wants an educated elite learning Latin verse').*

Tony Benn

Sunday, 22 November 1953

Chatsworth, Derbyshire: family home of the Dukes of Devonshire

Drove in the afternoon over some of the High Peak country – most of the estate will alas be sold. I had a long talk this evening with Andrew about the Death Duties. To hand over four-fifths of a property is not easy when its character is so varied, ranging from shares, town property, rural estates, houses, woods, quarries and the like, to statues, pictures and books ...

It takes 400 years to save and build such a property. It disappeared on a winter afternoon at Eastbourne ... when my brother in law, the 10th Duke, died suddenly in the garden.†

Harold Macmillan

---

* David Butler, a political analyst, author of the indispensable series *British Political Facts* (10th edn, 2011); a close friend of Tony Benn.
† Edward Cavendish, the 10th Duke of Devonshire, died in mysterious circumstances in 1950; his death resulted in 80 per cent death duties on the estate. His son Andrew was heir to the dukedom. Harold Macmillan was married to Dorothy, sister of Edward.

Saturday, 5 December 1953
Bermuda

The PM is less sure about things today. It appears that when he pleaded with Ike that Russia was changed, Ike spoke of her as a whore, who might have changed her dress but who should be chased from the streets. Russia, according to Ike, was out to destroy the civilised world.

'Of course,' said the PM, pacing up and down the room, 'anyone could say the Russians are evil minded and mean to destroy the free countries. Well, if we really feel like that, perhaps we ought to take action before they get as many atomic bombs as America has. I made that point to Ike who said, perhaps logically, that it ought to be considered. But,' said Winston resuming his seat, 'if one did not believe that such a large fraction of the world was evil it could do no harm to try and be friendly as long as we did not relax our defensive preparations.'

I asked him what the French thought about all this. The PM, shortly: 'I take no account of them. They are harmless.'

A message came later from the French Prime Minister. He did not feel well; he had pain when he coughed and his temperature was nearly 105. I doubt whether he will take any more part in the conference.

Lord Moran

Thursday, 10 December–Saturday, 12 December 1953
Yorkshire

Left on night train for Leeds. A useful morning going round the Leeds 'slums' and housing estates. The special problem of the back to back houses is very acute in Leeds, as in some other Yorkshire towns. There are over 30,000 of them in Leeds – some very old and some of quite recent date ...

A tour round Sheffield [on the 12th]. The architect seemed very good. Some new flats (on the hill) should be very good.

Drove from Sheffield to Bradford. Here I had a political meeting in the St George's Hall. This was not quite (but very nearly) full. As it holds about 2,500 this was not bad for a political meeting nowadays, esp on a Saturday evening.

Harold Macmillan

Thursday, 4 February 1954

I went straight from the station at King's Cross to No 10 where I found Winston playing bezique with Clemmie ...

'I don't think I've been so well, Charles, the last two days. I must go without lunch, or be content with something light about noon.' He paced up and down the room a little unsteadily. Then he collapsed into his chair with a deep sigh.

[Then he] rose, went over to the table and opening *Punch*, handed it to me.

'They have been attacking me. It isn't really a proper cartoon. Have you seen it? Yes, there's malice in it. The *Mirror* has had nothing so hostile. Look at my hands – I have beautiful hands.'

It was true. Those podgy shapeless hands peering out from a great expanse of white cuff, were not his. I was shocked by this vicious cartoon; there was something un-English in this savage attack on his failing powers. The eyes were dull and lifeless. There was no tone in the flaccid muscles; the jowl sagged. It was the expressionless mask of extreme old age.*

So it had come to this. Winston was hurt.

Lord Moran

Wednesday, 3 March 1954

It is difficult to describe how low political morale was when Parliament resumed [in January] ... in four by-elections the Government proportion of the vote went up substantially and ours dropped. We couldn't even keep the Bevanite group together. Nye failed to turn up on Tuesdays, asked for our lunch to be changed to Thursdays and then didn't turn up on two successive Thursdays.

At this time he was also taking the view that the issue of German rearmament was not of great importance in the new atomic age. Sooner or later there would be German divisions, so why worry much?

Richard Crossman

---

*The cartoon by Leslie Illingworth in *Punch* and an accompanying article by *Punch*'s new editor Malcolm Muggeridge was the first public indication of Churchill's poor health.

Monday, 5 April 1954

Cabinet at 12 noon

PM gave us ... the text of the Churchill–Roosevelt agreement of 1943, on [the] Atom bomb, by which we definitely retained a veto on its use. This was removed by the McMahon Act, apparently without any protest, certainly any effective or public protest, from HMG. By 1948 we had to make a new agreement, formally abandoning all that Churchill had secured in 1943.

The *Daily Mirror* and the *Daily Herald* have come out with the most violent attacks on Churchill 'powerless to deal with the USA' and all that.

Harold Macmillan

Friday, 21 May 1954

Yesterday, Winston admitted, was a rough day ... He grinned broadly and I waited for what was to come.

'I was determined that the (1922) Committee should agree to a free vote in the House on Members' pay ...'

He became serious.

'It is all wrong when Members go about scratching a meal here and a meal there. Do you know Charles that a large number, perhaps as many as a hundred and twenty of the Members of the House, have less to live on than a coal-miner? Some of them, poor devils, are not sure of a square meal. When I think of the power and grandeur of their situation, I am certain that it is most dangerous to keep them in poverty; it is just asking for trouble ... One of the Committee rose and proposed the motion that there should be no increase in the payment of Members until Old Age Pensions were put on a satisfactory basis. I said, "What clap-trap." As if the two questions had anything in common.'

Montague Browne, when I saw him, put the matter rather differently. The meeting of the 1922 Committee had not gone very well ... 'You know, Lord Moran, he will play bezique, instead of mugging up whatever is coming up. Yesterday for example, he knew the Chancellor was going to the Committee, and he ought to have talked it over with him, but he gets absorbed in cards.'

Lord Moran

Friday, 21 May 1954

Cumberland

We started at 10 am with visits to Housing estates; slum clearance schemes; chemical factories; and so forth. Then we went out to Ennerdale Lake – a splendid luncheon with lake trout, chips, apple tart, cheese and beer at the charming little Anglers Hotel …

(The Whitehaven 'fathers' plan to destroy the charming little inn; build a large and vulgar hotel; turn the lake into a lido, and generally 'improve' the landscape. This will I trust be prevented by the National Park people and myself and my successors.)

Harold Macmillan

Friday, 4 June 1954

Nye Bevan, following his resignation [three years ago] … has lost much ground in the House. There is a bad split in Bevanite leadership. Crossman and Wilson both against him. He said that he would regard Wilson taking his place on the Parliamentary Committee as 'a gross act of personal disloyalty to myself.' Crossman said, 'Then you think Harold is expendable?' Bevan replied, 'Yes and so are you.'

New Statesman the next week declared that neither Morrison nor Bevan could now ever lead the party.

I said to someone that I was charged with sitting on the fence, but 'I'd sooner sit on the fence than lie down in the shit on either side of it.' Tony [Crosland] when I quoted this to him, replied, 'That is a civilian's answer. In war you have to lie in the shit.'

Hugh Dalton

Thursday, 24 June 1954

en route to Washington

The PM always agrees that Anthony [Eden] and he agree on most things in the field of foreign affairs, though it is not often very noticeable; they don't seem, for instance, to have much in common about Suez, or China, or their approach to the Americans. It is true that Winston has appointed Anthony as his heir – after all, someone has to follow him – but he still regards him as a young man, and he is not much influenced by his views.

Besides, when Winston's mind is set on something he can think of little else. He has always felt that the future of the world is bound up with the union of the English-speaking races. Now, at the end of a long day, nothing else seems to matter. He is going to America – he thinks it may be his last visit to his mother's native land – to see if anything can be done to narrow the rift about Moscow that is opening up between the two countries, and here was the Foreign Secretary bleating about what was wrong with the Americans.

Lord Moran

Tuesday, 24 August 1954
Chartwell, Kent

PM was in bed – so I had to wait 20 minutes till he had got up and put on his 'rompers' …

Luncheon lasted till nearly 4 pm. After a certain amount of desultory discussion about Soviet policy, EDC, NATO, Adenauer's position, the French confusion and the like, we got to the real point. Churchill feels better; he has good reports from his doctors; he means to stay as Prime Minister just as long as he can. In favour of this plan he adduced a number of arguments. First he (and he alone in the world) might be able to steer through the complications of foreign policy and international problems. He had a unique position. He could talk to anybody, on either side of the iron curtain, either by personal message or face to face.

It would be better for Eden if he (Churchill) were to go on till the Election. Or perhaps it might be wise to let Eden become PM just *before* the election. That could be decided later.

Thirdly he was PM and nothing could drive him out of his office, so long as he could form and control a Govt and have the confidence of the House. This continual chatter in the lobbies and the press about his resignation was intolerable. Naturally, like any man of nearly 80, who had had *two* strokes, he might die at any moment. But he could not undertake to die at any particular moment!

Harold Macmillan

Thursday, 2 September 1954

Chartwell, Kent

When, about four o'clock, Winston woke from an hour's sleep he could not stop yawning.

'The world,' he began, 'is in a terrible condition. The throwing out of the European Defence Community is a great score for the Russians.'

Then, waking up, his voice rose.

'The French have behaved in an unspeakable way, execrable. No thought at all for others, ingratitude, conceit,' he spat them out with intense distaste. 'I cannot feel the same about them in the future.'

I asked him if he had been surprised by the majority in the French chamber against EDC.

'No,' he answered.

He struggled into his zip-suit with Kirkwood's help.

He paused at the pond and rapped his stick against the stone pavement, when golden carp darted out of the shadows to gobble the maggots.

'They are twenty years old and will see me out; probably they will see you out too.'

Lord Moran

Tuesday, 14 September 1954

Summons to luncheon with PM. Since No 10 is really shut up, we went to Buck's Club. I must say I love the old man, altho' he is so selfish and so difficult. But he certainly has courage and panache. The great car, flying the standard of the Warden of the Cinque Ports; the bows and smiles to the crowd; the hat, cigar, stick – superb showman.

A dozen oysters; cream soup; chicken pie, vanilla and strawberry ice. Moselle and brandy washed this down.

Harold Macmillan

Friday, 1 October 1954

The PM's fear that America might withdraw from Europe and 'go it alone' was not without reason. When the Nine-Power conference met on Wednesday Mr [John Foster] Dulles spoke of a great wave of disillusionment which had swept over America after EDC had been rejected; there was a feeling, he said, that 'the situation in Europe is pretty hopeless.' It was in this bleak atmosphere that the delegates were asked to find some means of rearming Germany that would be accepted by a majority of the French Assembly. Round the table they sat doodling, mumbling, despairing.

Then Mr Eden rose and told the representatives of the Nine Powers that if the conference was successful Britain would undertake to keep on the Continent the forces now stationed there; that she would not withdraw them without the consent of the majority of the Brussels Treaty Powers, including West Germany and Italy, as well as France and the Low Countries.

Everyone felt that the situation had been transformed and that Mr Eden's pledge saved the conference when it seemed bound to end in a fiasco.

It was accordingly with a light heart that I entered the PM's bedroom this morning, as Kirkwood backed out with the breakfast tray. But somehow the PM did not seem particularly elated; indeed he seemed to take more interest in the result of the East Croydon by-election, and what the papers said about it, than in the conference.

Lord Moran

Thursday, 14 October 1954
Lake District

I spent the weekend ... in a hotel with the grammar school headmasters of Lancashire and Cheshire. The purpose of this was principally to discuss the Labour Party's proposals for education, and in particular the comprehensive school.

The headmasters began in a somewhat truculent mood and I was rather astonished to hear them say, one after another, that the Labour Party was against the grammar schools, that it had attacked them, that it was trying to destroy them etc.

Eric James [headmaster of Manchester Grammar School], in what was obviously a deliberately provocative speech, said that our policy was based on 'ignorance, frivolity and enmity.' He made however, some telling points, the most important of which I thought ... was the fact that in some areas to start a comprehensive school, instead of the present division between secondary modern and grammar schools, would in fact lead to more not less class division. You would get a residential area on the one side, where there was a comprehensive school and all the people there would be drawn from the middle or lower middle classes. On the other hand, you would have a working class area, and equally there all of the children would come from working class parents. This would be in contrast with the present situation whereby in the grammar school itself, owing to the fact that the places were free and that entry was on merit, there was now a complete mixing up.

The other main argument was, of course, the fear that in the comprehensive school the bright, clever children would be at a disadvantage.

I think that by the end of the weekend we had begun to understand each other's point of view better.

Hugh Gaitskell

Sunday, 26 December 1954

My own mind has been increasingly dominated by my thoughts about the effect of the H-bomb on our whole strategy and policy. How mad all this German rearmament is in view of the H-bomb and how much I sympathise with the French assembly which on Christmas Eve voted against German rearmament. I am more and more convinced that this whole idea of the West's containment of communism is the sheerest nonsense. My observation describing us as a Byzantium which would be lucky to survive the century of totalitarian man, is much nearer the truth than I like to think.

Richard Crossman

Thursday, 20 January 1955

We had a report from Kenya. It is too early to say whether there will be any response from the Mau-Mau to the surrender offer.*

More discussions about the West Indian immigrants. A Bill is being drafted – but it's not an easy problem. PM thinks 'Keep England White' a good slogan!

Harold Macmillan

---

*The Mau Mau was an anti-colonial group comprising mainly the Kikuyu, the largest ethnic group in Kenya. They led a rebellion against British rule from 1952 until 1960.

Wednesday, 26 January 1955

Churchill asked me to go round to No 10, which I did (about 9.30) I found him in bed, with a little green budgerigar (is that the spelling?) sitting on his head! ... He had the cage on the bed (from which the bird had come out) and a cigar in his hand. A whisky and soda was by his side – of this the little bird took sips, later on. Miss Portal sat by the bed – he was dictating. Really he is a unique, dear man with all his qualities and faults ...

He had just got a letter from the President about the atomic and hydrogen bombs ...

The bird flew about the room; perched on my shoulder and pecked (or kissed) my neck; flew to Miss Portal's arm; back to the PM's head, while all the time sonorous 'Gibbonesque' sentences were rolling out of the maestro's mouth.

Harold Macmillan

Tuesday, 8 March 1955

By some mischance I had to go through the sleet to Epsom, to find twenty-eight shivering Labour Party members waiting in a Co-op Hall, bewildered – utterly bewildered – and disheartened by the latest row [in the Party] because they really couldn't understand who was standing for what and why anybody was on any side. I explained about the H-bomb and in particular about the deterrent, spelling it out for them rather brutally, and no one raised a whisper of objection. I'm afraid the real fact is that it is now the dispute itself and not the issues that people are worrying about.

Richard Crossman

Friday, 25 March 1955

When he asked me to rejoin him, in October 1951, Winston said it would probably be only for a year. He did not intend to remain long in office but wished to initiate the recovery of the country under a Conservative Government. However, although many people ... predicted that Winston would make way for Anthony Eden after the Coronation he never had any intention of so doing ... but, of course, in the winter of 1953–54 Eden's 'hungry eyes' as Winston called them, became more beseeching and more impatient.

During the spring of 1954 ... [Eden] had extracted what he thought was a promise – and what almost certainly was a half promise – that W would go at the end of the session ...

Under pressure Winston next said that he would go on September 20th 1954 ... But in August 1954 the Prime Minister again changed his mind. Why should he resign? He wrote to Anthony, who was on holiday in Austria, a masterly letter which went through about six drafts ...

So he finally decided to go at the beginning of the 1955 Easter recess and, after he had ruminated on this for some weeks, he told A.E. and Rab Butler. He also invited the Queen to dine on April 4th 1955, on the eve of his resignation ...

The ensuing days were painful. W began to form a cold hatred of Eden who, he repeatedly said, had done more to thwart him and prevent him pursuing the policy he thought right than anybody else. But he also admitted to me on several occasions that the prospect of giving up after nearly sixty years in public life, was a terrible wrench. He saw no reason why he should go: he was only doing it for Anthony. He sought to persuade his intimate friends, and himself, that he was being hounded from office.

The truth was this. He could still make a great speech, as was proved in the defence debate on March 1st. Indeed none could rival his oratory or his ability to inspire. But he was ageing month by month and was reluctant to read any papers except the newspapers or to give his mind to anything that he did not find diverting. More and more time was given to bezique and ever less to public business ...

Was he the man to negotiate with the Russians and moderate the Americans? The Foreign Office thought not; the British public would, I am sure, have said yes. And I, who have been as intimate with him as anybody during these last years, simply do not know.

John Colville

Written shortly afterwards, but not dated.

On April 4th the Queen and Prince Philip dined at No 10. It was a splendid occasion. The party consisted partly of the senior Cabinet Ministers, partly of grandees like the Norfolks and partly of officials and family friends.

When they had all gone, I went up with Winston to his bedroom.

He sat on his bed, still wearing his Garter, Order of Merit and knee-breeches. For several minutes he did not speak and I, imagining that he was sadly contemplating that this was his last night at Downing Street, was silent. Then suddenly he stared at me with vehemence: 'I don't believe Anthony can do it.'

The next evening Winston put on his top hat and frock coat, which he always wore for audiences, and went to Buckingham Palace to resign.

John Colville

Friday, 1 April 1955

[At Bob Boothby's* house] ... Gossip freely. Eden, they say, is accepted but without enthusiasm. Eden, Butler and Macmillan are 'not a triumvirate but a trinity.' No friendship at the top here. But no present challenge from outside the three. Physically, Eden, though he was three times cut up, has made a wonderful recovery. He can still play tennis, and his movements at the box are much freer than either of the others. Butler is very tired ... and felt the loss of his wife very much. And Macmillan shuffles along like an old man. He had a gallbladder operation not long ago.

Boothby and I had remarked earlier to one another that these Wykehamists showed their hatred of one another too openly; we Etonians managed our relations, even when lethal, much more smoothly.

Hugh Dalton

Tuesday, 26 April 1955

Nye is going to spend most of the time travelling. He was perfectly amiable and as always when Elections come, quite conventionally loyal to the Party. Barbara and Ian Mikardo† are still convinced that 'Ban the H-bomb' is enough to win the Election on and they got some evidence for this view from an analysis which the *Daily Herald* made today of a questionnaire ... Out of forty eight items, the H-bomb and the cost of living easily came first, but I still think that, on peace, the H-bomb and all that, it is unlikely that we shall make much impact on trying

---

* Bob Boothby, later Lord Boothby, had been Conservative MP for East Aberdeenshire since 1924.
† Barbara Castle, MP for Blackburn; Ian Mikardo, MP for Reading.

to overbid the Tories. We are far more likely to do well on practical bread-and-butter issues.

Richard Crossman

The Conservative Party increased its seats in the General Election of 26 May 1955; the Labour Party lost eighteen; and the Liberals won six, the same as in 1951. Anthony Eden was, at last, Prime Minister; Clem Attlee and Clement Davies were still leaders of the Labour and Liberal parties respectively.

June 1955

Why did we lose the election? What do we do next?

The right will blame Bevan. The Bevanites will interpret it as the price paid for the right-wing policies and leaders.

But since 1951 the Tories have had good luck with the economic climate, people are generally better off and ... rationing [has] ended on everything but coal. There has been no unemployment. A family in a council house with a TV set and a car or motorcycle-combination on hire purchase had few reasons for a change of government.

Tony Benn

Friday, 3 June 1955

Poole, Dorset

Was fetched at 2 o'clock by a BBC car and driven down in pouring rain to an *Any Questions* programme.

We went after dinner to a wonderful modern engineering factory – brand new (not a brick in it or so we were assured) holding about 300 to 400 – all factory hands and their wives.

We had a lively programme getting the [railway workers'] strike, as I had foreseen – as the 2nd question – i.e. 'Should workers in nationalised industries be allowed to strike? Ought they not to be like the police.' Here we had a terrific slanging match between James Callaghan and Gerald Nabarro [Conservative MP for Kidderminster] on the merits and demerits of nationalisation – which was really out of order.

I ... pointed out the obvious difference between the old heroic strike of starving work people against tyrannical and 'skin flint' employers

(to use a favourite adjective of Callaghan's!) and the present inter-
union strikes of which the victims [are] not bosses but the public and
fellow-workers ...

Violet Bonham Carter

July 1955

The invitations did not suggest it was to be a 'Goodbye to No 10' party,
although all friends knew that this, in fact, was the chief reason for
forgathering. The cards informed us that 'Sir Winston was "At Home"
to celebrate the anniversary of Lady Churchill's birthday.'

Lady Churchill was dressed in black lace with orchids at the waist,
and her eyes were focused to other distances. Nevertheless she could
still throw out a few *mondanités* and answered some stupidity of mine
by saying that it was not surprising that they had made the rooms look
'lived-in' considering that this had been their home now for so long. It
was said that Lady Churchill was suffering agonies from phlebitis; but
there is still fire and dash in the consort of the old warrior.

Churchill's doctor was among the favoured; but none of his professional allies were invited ... Ghosts of former Governments abounded:
reminders of Asquith in Lady Violet Bonham Carter, with Etruscan
profile and scared donkey's eyes, tonight surprisingly *decolletée* in
bright pink satin – surprising because, with her great intelligence, and
intellectual interests, she has seldom shown an interest in chiffons ...
Still recognizable as having been a great Edwardian beauty was old
Pamela Lytton, curved and bent, but pink and white in black lace. It is
said that the young Churchill admired her above others and there was
a question of an engagement.

Tonight I peered at Churchill at the end of his long and glorious
career. His pale eyelashes were blinking, his thin wisps of delicate
white hair were combed neatly back, and I noticed the very peculiar
flat end to his bulbous nose which appeared as if cut off straight with
a knife. He sat hunched up, his shirt-front rose in a high big roll and
his waistcoat seemed almost 'Empire' in cut. He sucked on the end
of a cigar without pretence of smoking it. He made a few jokes that
showed that the old spirit had not deserted him and our laughter was
a little exaggerated with relief ... Churchill, aged eighty one, looked
fit – a very, very healthy baby – but he was somewhat deaf and hated

being shouted at by kind friends who were gallantly doing their best to amuse him.

Cecil Beaton

Tuesday, 19 July 1955

Geneva Peace Conference

The Russians came to dinner at the PM's villa. It was a purely Anglo-Russian affair [the USA and France were also represented at the Conference].

Khrushchev is an obscene figure; very fat, with a great paunch; eats and drinks greedily; interrupts boisterously and rudely; but did not hold the entire conversation in his hands, as he had done at the dinner with the Americans. Molotov was a bad colour; talked very little; and behaved more like a civil servant than a political chief. Marshal Zhukov was a good, soldierly and agreeable figure. He told me about his daughters – both of whom married the sons of marshals – regular Aldershot talk ...

Eden conducted the whole affair brilliantly. He exerted all his charm both at and after dinner. I got certain impressions as follows: (a) they are very relaxed after the removal of the tyrant, Stalin. (They said with glee that, since 1953, they worked a normal day, instead of all night!) (b) they don't want another Stalin – a bloody and uncertain tyrant (c) K is the boss, but not another Stalin. He controls the party and thus, in a country where there is no Parliament, he controls the Govt. (d) they are unable to accept the reunification of Germany in NATO and will fight it as long as they can ... the Germans treated them horribly and they hate them, (e) they do not fear war; they don't really believe the Americans are going to attack them, (f) they are anxious about China ...

I think they might prefer a weak nationalist or capitalist China which they could plunder, to a Communist China which they have to assist.

With all this bonhomie, it is sometimes hard to remember what ruthless and merciless men they are.

Harold Macmillan

Tuesday, 26 July 1955

PM gave the Cabinet an account of all we had done, said and heard at Geneva.

The last item on the agenda was an FO item – the vast and complicated problem of Arab/Israel relations – the Anglo-American plan on which we had long been working (known as Alpha) ... However, the item before was the suggested road changes at Hyde Park Corner. So we never got as far as Egypt or Palestine.

Harold Macmillan

Friday, 19 August 1955

Went to the opening night of *Titus Andronicus*. Peter Brook had done a stupendously good production, really most impressive and extremely clever in avoiding pitfalls. Larry was wonderful although, at moments, a little funny. Vivien was frankly not very good. She looked lovely throughout regardless of ravishment and her tongue being cut out and her hands cut off. Her clothes and hair-do were impeccable and her face remained untouched by tragedy. It is a very, very silly play with some good moments.

Personally I think if Larry had turned sharply on Vivien years ago and given her a clip in the chops, he would have been spared a mint of trouble.

Noël Coward

Friday, 7 October 1955

Yesterday evening I went down to Bournemouth to get a glimpse of the Tory Conference and found George Brown* on the train ... In the evening we had a tremendous dinner on the *Mirror* with 'Cassandra' [William Connor], Vicky [the cartoonist], and others ...

George Brown, warmed with wine, really revealed his trade union philosophy, which culminates in the argument that 'it's our Party, not yours.' When challenged by Bill as to why it belonged to George Brown and not to Dick Crossman, he said 'Well, just think what each of us was doing before the war. I was working for the Party. And what was he doing? Writing!' The word 'Writing' was said with such exquisite

---

* George Brown was Labour MP for Belper and a member of the Shadow Cabinet.

loathing that Cassandra intervened. 'When he hears the word "writing" he reaches for his revolver.' 'That's not far from it,' said George Brown. 'That's how we feel about these intellectuals ...'

Richard Crossman

Monday, 31 October 1955

Rushed home, changed and was called for by Puff [Anthony Asquith, brother of Violet] at 7.15 to go to Royal Command performance at the Odeon in Leicester Square.

The film of the evening – a very bad and slow Hitchcock about a Cat Burglar, *To Catch a Thief*. We went back to the Savoy for supper with a nice young man in Ranks ...

We were very late and didn't come out of supper till well after one. Puff overheard someone saying something about Princess Margaret which sounded like 'off.' He went back and bought two early morning editions. They had banner headlines 'Princess Margaret decides not to marry Group Captain Townsend.' Underneath was a most poignant statement – perfectly expressed – basing their decision on the Church's teaching of the indissolubility of marriage and her duty to the Commonwealth. It is a historic decision – and rends one's heart.*

Violet Bonham Carter

Wednesday, 2 November 1955
Paris – NATO meeting

At 8.30 we went to a dinner given by the Russians for the British.†
It was rather a painful affair, with the usual rather heavy jokes and bonhomie. The food (except for the caviare) was uneatable.

In the course of conversation, Molotov asked me what I was going back to England for. I said 'a debate in the House of Commons.' He said 'What about?' I said 'On a subject where you can really help me, if you would do so, on Maclean and Burgess. Can you tell me where

---

* Peter Townsend, a Battle of Britain pilot and an equerry to the Queen, had been divorced in 1952.
† From April to December 1955 Harold Macmillan was Foreign Secretary. In December he became Chancellor of the Exchequer.

they are?' He said, with real or assumed seriousness 'That is a matter which would require investigation.'

Harold Macmillan

Friday, 2 December 1955

Throughout the past fortnight the vague speculation about Attlee's future continued and in this morning's press there is another rumour that he is being pressed to make up his mind before Christmas. I have seen him a good deal recently ... but I have no idea what is going on in that inscrutable little head. I should guess that, during November, Hugh Gaitskell lost a little ground, mainly because our trade union MPs and some of the trade union leaders outside parliament are getting scared of the bright young men taking over the machine.

There is a strange new alignment growing up in the Party. On one side are the Socialist intellectuals, who want to prepare blueprints on the municipalisation of rented houses, National Superannuation etc., and on the other side are the trade unionists who are suspicious of this kind of Socialist planning. More and more the trade unionists feel that Nye belongs to them and will be able to express their views for them.

When Hugh Gaitskell expresses a Socialist sentiment, he sounds artificial and demagogic but I suppose he will settle down.

Richard Crossman

Thursday, 2 February 1956

The Deputy Leadership vote was announced this evening. Jim Griffiths 141, Nye Bevan 111 ...

Griffiths made a perfect little short speech. He had lived all his life in the Movement. He would cooperate loyally with our new Leader [Hugh Gaitskell] etc. Bevan, who was sitting on the platform with a most ugly, controlled, angry face, when asked by Hugh whether he would like to say anything, made a contemptuous, scowling gesture of refusal, seen by all, and remained seated. (There'll soon be more trouble, I thought ...)

I feel like a Creator who rested and beheld his handiwork after much hard labour and saw that it was good ... Hugh Gaitskell Leader, Jim Griffiths, wonderfully loyal Deputy and other younger people

in the Shadow Cabinet of which the average age is now fifty-two –
younger than that of the Tory Cabinet.

Hugh Dalton

Friday, 3 February 1956

The Afghan Minister came to see me yesterday. He is a rather small,
pale, pleasant-looking man, who speaks in a soft voice. It was therefore
difficult to follow what he said but broadly speaking it amounted
to this: that there were a fair number of people of Afghan stock in
Pakistan, occupying about half the North West frontier province. They
were in a state of more or less continual dispute or revolt against
the Pakistan Government, and there was great sympathy for them in
Afghanistan. His country did not want to alter the frontiers which he
admitted were those of British India, but they wanted to see some
form of semi-independent state created – Pathoonistan. Unfortunately
Pakistan would not even discuss the problem with them. The result
was that they might be driven more and more to look to Russia ... they
had recently had a loan of 100 million dollars without any strings.

Hugh Gaitskell

Thursday, 9 February 1956

Cabinet at 4 in the PM's room at HofC. PM looked very fit on his
return [from Washington] and has obviously enjoyed himself. Selwyn
Lloyd (For. Sec) looked rather exhausted.

The real success of the visit was on the atomic and hydrogen front.
The President has made decisions to give us (a) information and (b)
aid, which will save us millions and millions of pounds! ... Foreign Sec
added that he was impressed by the toughness which [John Foster]
Dulles was prepared to show about Israel, even in the Presidential
election year. PM said the only real difficulty was about atom *tests*. The
Americans were absolutely convinced now (contrary to their original
ideas) that if the bomb was exploded high up in the air, the ill effects
were negligible. PM thought this might be a nuisance politically, but
– as we have more than a year to go before our first test – an ultimate
advantage ...

Harold Macmillan

Tuesday, 28 February 1956

On Saturday I went with [my younger daughter] Cressida to the HMV place in Oxford Street to buy records, and the following amusing incident occurred:-

It was terribly crowded and we had great difficulty in getting anybody to attend to us. However, eventually I managed to get some records to try – jazz records – and we found a young girl – she can't have been more than 17 – to shepherd us to a cubicle where one could play the records. She left me there to play [them] while Cressida went off in search of other ones. As I was listening to the jazz, more or less dancing up and down to the rhythm who should put her head in but Elaine Burton, the Labour Member of Parliament for Coventry. Slightly embarrassed at being caught dancing on my own, I welcomed her. She said, 'I must tell you what the girl has just said to us. "Do you know, I believe the Chancellor of the Exchequer is next door."' This is not the first time that, so long [five years] after I held the office, people have still regarded me as Chancellor.

Hugh Gaitskell

Monday, 5 March 1956

The TUC meeting (intended to be the first of two; we are to see them again after we have seen the employers) went off in a strangely subdued atmosphere. They all behaved beautifully and were so respectable, in their dark blue suits and bowlers, that they looked like a lot of undertakers.

Harold Macmillan

Monday, 12 March 1956

I dined ... on 12th March with a body called the British [Socialist] Agricultural Society. They consisted of a mixture of wealthy farmers who are, of course members of the Party, and most of whom were Bevanites, and poor small-holder type of farmers, who seemed to be a good deal further to the Right. It was nevertheless quite a pleasant occasion. They were very outspoken and almost all agreed that the present policy was out of date; that the 1947 Agriculture Act was really now finished, or at any rate not adequate as a future policy, and that we should have to start afresh. Most of them I think, did not want to have the present system of subsidies, with threats of eviction against farmers who refused to play, and wanted to have some kind of different system in which efficiency was rewarded more directly and inefficiency penalised by the more obvious consequences, i.e. financial failure.

Hugh Gaitskell

Tuesday, 13 March 1956

A long Cabinet ... Cyprus; Malta; Transport Charges; and Nationalised Industries Finance; Farm Price Reviews; Aircraft for India etc. etc. The last raised a difficult point. Nehru wants us to make special efforts to supply him with Canberra bombers and the latest devices at a low price. But he also is said to be getting Russian bombers!

Then the paradox of Malta, which wants to join UK, while Cyprus wants to join Greece!

I was rather annoyed that the Farm Prices question was reopened.

But I stuck to my guns and won the support of the Cabinet on the real issue – nothing more on pigs, eggs, or milk. I agreed something on the calf subsidy ... So I hope it is settled at last at £25.2m.

Harold Macmillan

Thursday, 5 April 1956

Last night ... we had a very private dinner with the Trade Union leaders. There were present Tom Williamson, Frank Cousins, Jim Campbell, Bill Webber, Charlie Geddes, Harry Douglass and Ernest Jones; almost all the key people in the TUC ... and Alf Robens, George Brown and myself.

It took place in a private room at the Cafe Royal. During dinner itself there were some extremely interesting conversation[s] ... most of the Union leaders took the view that the new Soviet line* was certain to be reflected in the demands from the left wing in the unions for united fronts with the Communists of one kind or another.

---

* Following Stalin's death in 1953, a period of 'de-Stalinisation' took place in the Soviet Union. In a 'secret speech' delivered to the 20th Communist Party Congress in February 1956, Khrushchev had denounced Stalin and his purges, ushering in a period of liberalising internal reforms and a foreign policy of peaceful coexistence with the West that became known as the Khrushchev Thaw. Khrushchev's reforms were controversial amongst hardliners in the Soviet Union and divided the international Communist movement.

As to wages policy the discussion was lively though rather confused ... Frank Cousins, the latest arrival in the TUC but also the General Secretary or General Secretary elect of the most powerful union, the Transport Workers, was inclined to take the view that they could not make any kind of agreement or have any kind of understanding with the Government, and that there was nothing to be said for restraint of any kind. The others, on the other hand, said that in the interests of a future Labour Government, a policy of no restraint at all was dangerous even if this was carried out under the Tories ... it was an extremely successful evening.

Hugh Gaitskell

Sunday, 8 April 1956

I think the alternatives are now becoming clear. Alternative A or *Press Button A* – a hard Budget, calculated to give a shock to everyone, and to make foreigners feel we are in earnest. The 'Savings Package' (£20m) to be balanced by Tobacco, and 6d on standard rate of Income tax ... This would give us another £100m net for the surplus. Alternative B, or *Press Button B** – the 'Savings Package' to be paid for by Tobacco and Bread (less another 3/- on family allowance) giving a margin of £13m for surplus. £30m on profits tax to sweeten it ...

If I could really get ministers to face the full implications of Button B – real economies, with a realistic attitude to defence and some determination to trim at least the grosser extravagances of the Welfare State – it would be much better than raising still more taxation from a people who are already grossly overtaxed.

Today as a relaxation, I have read *Bleak House* ... They say nobody reads Dickens nowadays. More's the pity. He is a giant with all his faults and imperfections.

Harold Macmillan

Wednesday, 25 April 1956

My Labour friends told me that the dinner given by the Labour Executive to Bulganin and Khrushchev was a ghastly failure. Khrushchev made a

---

* A reference to the red telephone boxes – in which the caller paid 4d (four old pennies), and either pressed button A to connect, or B to get a refund. (Children learned very quickly how to empty the box of its coppers.)

speech saying that it was Russia alone who defeated Germany. George Brown, a Labour front-bench hearty, exclaimed, 'May God forgive you.'* Khrushchev broke off and asked the interpreter what he had said. It was translated. Khrushchev then banged the table and said 'What I say is true!' George Brown is not the mild type of Socialist. He replied, 'We lost half a million men while you were Hitler's allies!' *Silence penible* [painful silence].

And at the Speaker's luncheon yesterday George Brown went up with an outstretched hand to apologise but Khrushchev put his hand behind his back and said sharply, 'NIET.'

Letter to Vita Sackville-West from Harold Nicolson

Monday, 4 June 1956

[On Wednesday, 2 May] I went to the Royal Academy Banquet – always a tiresome occasion … The only interesting event which happened to me was a conversation with Sir Gerald Templer, the Chief of the Imperial General Staff; just as we were going away he came up to me and said that he wanted to tell me about his experience with Khrushchev.

He had had to look after Khrushchev at the Greenwich dinner, when the Russians had been entertained in the famous Painted Hall built in the time of William and Mary. Khrushchev had said to him, 'I understand that you are the head of the British Army.' Templer replied 'Well, so I am; anyway, I try to be.' 'Well then,' said Khrushchev, 'What do you think of the prospects of thermo-nuclear warheads on guided missiles?' Templer professed himself to be deeply shocked by this, that he said 'We really did not come down here, to this beautiful place, to talk about that kind of thing.' He afterwards said that he found Khrushchev quite unbearable and even added, 'I have never wanted to kill a man with my own hands so much.'

Hugh Gaitskell

Sunday, 1 July 1956
Returning from Glyndebourne

There has been a tragic uprising in Poland at Poznan, where the World Fair is being held. Hundreds of workers marched in a peaceful

---

* Hugh Gaitskell's diaries suggest that George Brown said 'God forgive him (Stalin)' but was mistranslated.

procession asking for 'Bread.' Their wages and living standards are desperate. They were fired on by the security police and desperate fighting ensued. Some of the soldiers handed over rifles and tanks to them. There has been heavy fighting and casualties – no one knows how many. The ice is breaking – but there is blood beneath it.

Violet Bonham Carter

Saturday, 21 July 1956

The BMC* strike is due to start on Monday. Iain Macleod [Minister of Labour] assures me that he does not intend to interfere. It seems that this is the advice of the Trade Union leaders (given in private). From the broader point of view, if we are to have friction – and I don't see how we can have the great readjustments we want without some friction – it's best to have it in the motor industry, where stocks are good and orders are not too good.

However the loyalty of the men is very great and ... cars will be declared 'black' and the railways and docks prevented from handling them.

Eden gives no real leadership in the House (for he is not a House of Commons man – he never enters the Smoking Room) altho' he is popular and respected in the country as a whole.

I had a talk on the telephone with the Lord Chancellor – about the hanging Bill. It wd. be very dangerous for the Govt to try to go back on the HofCommons 'free vote' or seem to yield to the pressure of the Party Conference.

The Archbishop of Canterbury (who is a silly, weak, vain and muddle-headed man) wants to have degrees of premeditation [as] the test. This is quite wrong. The test should be ... what exceptions are required in order to preserve the broad structure of a peaceful society. For instance Highway robbery and murder may not be so wicked – certainly not so repulsive – as a long prepared poisoning. But – in the 18th century – Highwaymen were more dangerous and troublesome to the guardians of the law and order than poisoners.

Harold Macmillan

---

*The British Motor Corporation, the predecessor to British Leyland. The strike was prompted by an attempt to remove one in eight of the workforce without any redundancy compensation.

Thursday, 26 July 1956

During the past fortnight or so the King of Iraq has been here and there have been various functions: one at Buckingham Palace, another at the Iraq Embassy and a third this evening at No 10 Downing Street. The king, who is a boy of 21, brought with him the Crown Prince, his uncle, and also Nuri as-Said, the old Statesman, now aged 67 … [This evening] was a men-only affair.

At about 10.45 I was sitting next to the King talking to him in one of the apartments, with the Lord Chancellor [Lord Kilmuir] sitting near. We had been talking away for some time about this and that, when Eden came up and said 'I want you to know – and I think the Opposition should know as well – what Nasser has done tonight. He has made a speech announcing that he is going ahead with the Aswan Dam,* that they cannot get any foreign money, but that, nevertheless, they are going ahead, and in order to finance it, they are taking over the Suez Canal Company and will collect the dues which the Company receives from ships using the Canal.'

Eden said that he understood that the Egyptian police had taken over the offices and the buildings of the Company already.

I asked him what he was going to do. He said he was getting hold of the American Ambassador immediately. He thought perhaps they ought to take it to the Security Council, and we then had a few moments conversation about the consequences, Selwyn Lloyd the Foreign Secretary standing near.

I said, 'Supposing Nasser doesn't take any notice?' Whereupon Selwyn said, 'Well I suppose in that case the old-fashioned ultimatum will be necessary.' I said that I thought they ought to act quickly, whatever they did, and that as far as Great Britain was concerned, public opinion would almost certainly be behind them. But I also added that they must get America into line. This should not be difficult, since after all, the Americans had themselves precipitated this by their decision to withdraw all financial assistance from the Aswan Dam.

In a half-joking way, I said, since the King and Crown Prince were both standing there, 'What do you think about it?' The Crown Prince rather wittily replied, after a bit, 'We had better send for our Prime

---

* The construction of a new dam on the Nile was considered a vital part of Nasser's industrial policy in order to regulate the annual flooding of the Nile and harness the water for agriculture and hydro-electric power.

Minister too – that's the constitutional position.' Whereupon there was general laughter.

Hugh Gaitskell

Thursday, 2 August 1956

Nasser has not, as far as I can see, violated any International treaty. What the treaties provide is that the Suez Canal should be open in time of peace and war, not who should own the Canal. It is highly inconvenient that a man like Nasser should have control of the Canal and be able to blackmail us by threats. It is also most unpleasant that his seizure may encourage other Arab countries to do the same. But we cannot persuade the Americans that the situation justifies the use of force, and I am not absolutely sure myself whether we should use or threaten it.

Harold Nicolson

Thursday, 2 August and Friday, 3 August 1956

I also had a talk with the so-called Foreign Affairs Steering Committee partly in order to smooth them down and make them feel that they had been consulted. John Hynd, Warbey, Tony Benn, as well as Denis Healey, Kenneth Younger and Alf Robens turned up. I was not much impressed with what the three first had to say. It is extraordinary how they rush to the defence of any eastern country and how completely they ignore the fact that Nasser is a dictator.

Tony Benn ... although talented in many ways, a good speaker and a man of ideas, has extraordinarily poor judgement.

Now we go away I hope for a fortnight to Pembrokeshire leaving the Government to cope with the situation. Eden told me that he hoped to get the Conference [of Suez Canal users] meeting within a fortnight.

Hugh Gaitskell

Wednesday, 8 August 1956

What all this Egypt thing is going to cost, one can't guess ...

PM did a broadcast and TV at 10 pm about the Suez crisis. *This could not have been better done.* It was fair, moderate, convincing and firm. I'm sure it will have a splendid effect, at home and abroad – esp in US. The Liberal and Socialist press here is beginning to get pretty flabby. 'No force, whatever happens' and 'Refer to United Nations' and so on. I have no doubt that the weekend intellectuals (*Economist, New Statesman, Observer* etc.) will be just as bad. Curiously enough, the 'gutter' press (*Mirror* and *Sketch*) have been pretty good. It's the Liberal intellectual who is always against his country.

Harold Macmillan

Thursday, 6 September 1956
TUC Conference, Brighton

Frank Cousins was very violent. He attacked me rather savagely; he attacked the Tory Government; he attacked the Tory Party, and declared that they [trade unions] would have nothing whatever to do with any form of pay restraint. It should be 'free for all.' ... Whether it will please the TU leaders as a whole remains to be seen. I think many of them already dislike Cousins.

Harold Macmillan

Thursday, 4 October 1956

The Suez situation is beginning to slip out of our hands ...

I try not to think that we have 'missed the bus' – if we have it is really due to the long time it has taken to get military arrangement into shape. But we must, by one means or another, win this struggle. Nasser may well try to preach Holy War in the Middle East and (even to their own loss) the mob and the demagogues may create a ruinous position for us. *Without oil and without the profits from oil*, neither UK nor western Europe can survive.

Harold Macmillan

Monday, 22 October 1956

The Government are in a terrible mess and they have lost confidence in Eden. The specific problems that confront them are Suez, the muddle over defence, the economic crisis and the awful bloodshed in Cyprus.*

* Riots erupted in Cyprus in response to the British government's deportation of the

The Labour Party on the other hand is in better shape than it has been since I have been an MP. Hugh Gaitskell has done very well as Leader despite the serious error he made at the start of the Suez crisis. Nye Bevan is Treasurer and has a real chance to make his contribution to the unity of the Party.

Tony Benn

Sunday, 28 October 1956
South Wales

To the [Bedwellty] miners' welfare institute where there was a crowded room of serious-minded people.

I sat listening to the miners talking of the bad old days – the soup kitchens, the struggles with the police, the terrible hunt for work … it was very moving and more than history – for in the crowded, smoky club room were many men gasping for breath from silicosis or limping from some industrial injury.

Today's news is mainly of the Hungarian crisis reaching its climax. The spontaneous rebellion against the Communist Government has virtually succeeded. The Iron Curtain has risen and people are moving freely in and out of Hungary with supplies and relief … the red white and green have reappeared to replace the hated scarlet banner of the Communist Government. Everyone in the world is breathless with hope that this may lead to a rebirth of freedom throughout the whole of Eastern Europe.

Tony Benn

Saturday, 3 November 1956

House of Commons meets at noon, for three hours and adjourns in uproar. Loud booing, and gestures at Eden, cries of 'Resign', 'Go' and 'Get Out.'

Thus ends a tumultuous week. It began on Monday with Israel crossing into Egypt and [was] followed by swift and complete Israeli victory in Sinai, rout of Egyptian Army and capture of large quantities of arms recently supplied by Russians and Czechs.

head of the island's Greek Orthodox Church, Archbishop Makarios. The Archbishop was accused of 'fostering terrorism' by supporting a campaign to unite Cyprus with Greece.

The myth of Egypt as a military power and a 'leader' of the Arab world is smashed for ever. All this is wonderful! Israel will now be more secure than at any time since 1948. And of the other Arab states, none moved against Israel in spite of all their Arab Leagues and Alliances.

Hugh Dalton

Saturday, 3 November 1956

Hugh Gaitskell rang me up this morning, said he was going to broadcast tomorrow night and told me to make all the necessary arrangements ... I therefore rang up Harman Grisewood, the Director of Sound Broadcasting at the BBC.

Grisewood was extremely short and sharp. He wanted to know what broadcast I meant. I explained that the Prime Minister was to broadcast tonight and that Gaitskell would want to reply tomorrow. He said this was an unwarrantable assumption as the PM was doing a ministerial broadcast. I said it would be controversial and we demanded to reply. He told me to do it through the usual channels and to make no announcement or assumption of any kind. I warned him that ... we would appeal for a BBC decision late tonight. 'That is quite impossible,' he replied, 'we shall all be in bed.' I told him this was an intolerable situation and that he must make arrangements for the BBC to receive our request and give a reply that night. At this he became a little chastened and said that he would ask Sir Alexander Cadogan, the Chairman of the BBC, to stand by.

Two footnotes to the day. Fighting between Members of Parliament is now almost inevitable. I saw Ernie Popplewell [Labour, Newcastle upon Tyne West] almost come to blows with Sir John Crowder [Conservative, Finchley] ... The situation has transformed Gaitskell from a 'desiccated calculating machine' into a man of unusual fire and passion.

Tony Benn

Sunday, 4 November 1956

The Russians have sent seven divisions into Hungary and are closing in on Budapest with 1,000 tanks. But we have no right to speak a word of criticism.

Harold Nicolson

Sunday, 4 November 1956

All through the day B* and I listened to the most agonizing broadcasts from Hungary – now being crushed by Soviet forces – tanks are moving in everywhere and a massacre is going on. All youth is rising and being mowed down. Children are hurling grenades at tanks. It is an extraordinary example of sublime courage against hopeless odds. Heart-rending. One feels guilty at one's impotence – and our *folly* has distracted the attention of the world from this tragedy. I cannot forgive it.

Violet Bonham Carter

Thursday, 22 November 1956

[Anthony Eden] is leaving for Jamaica without even a Private Secretary. William Clark, his PR adviser, said this was because all his staff were united by an intense loathing for the man but that is not the whole story. He has deliberately not made Rab Butler acting Prime Minister but only charged him ... with 'presiding over the Cabinet.' As one Conservative Member put it to me, 'You all underrate Rab. When the smoke has cleared you'll find him there on top of a mound of corpses with his knife dripping with blood and an inscrutable smile on his face.'[†]

Tony Benn

Thursday, 10 January 1957

I feel – who couldn't? – the tragic poignancy of Anthony's exit. To be PM was his life's aim ... he will have no chance of redeeming his reputation in the eyes of the present or of posterity. It is a Greek tragedy.

Violet Bonham Carter

---

* Sir Maurice Bonham Carter, Violet's husband, known as Bongie.
† Anthony Eden went on holiday to Jamaica in order to rest and recuperate, after the Suez Crisis had provoked another bout of ill-health. Various colleagues plotted his removal from office during his absence and he resigned on 9 January 1957. Despite the Conservative MP's prediction about Rab Butler, it was Harold Macmillan who succeeded Eden.

Sunday, 3 February 1957

The forming of the whole administration took about 10 days. On the whole it has been well received ...Without the help of Edward Heath (Chief Whip) who was quite admirable, we couldn't have done it.

It has meant seeing nearly a hundred people and trying to say the right thing to each. In the circumstances many considerations had to be borne in mind – the right, centre and left of the party; the extreme 'Suez' group; the extreme opposition to Suez; the loyal centre – and last but not least, U and non-U (to use the jargon that Nancy Mitford has popularised) that is, Eton, Winchester etc. on the one hand; Board School and grammar school on the other.

I have read a good deal in recent weeks – some Trollope, some Henry James, three volumes of Cobbett's *Rural Rides* ...

Harold Macmillan

Sunday, 17 February 1957

I have just read *Look Back in Anger* by John Osborne and it is so full of talent and fairly well constructed but I wish I knew why the hero is so dreadfully cross and what about? I should also like to know who, where and why he and his friend run a sweet-stall and if, considering the hero's unparalleled capacity for invective, they ever manage to sell any sweets? I expect my bewilderment is because I am very old indeed and cannot understand why the younger generation, instead of knocking at the door, should bash the fuck out of it. In this decade there is obviously less and less time for comedy as far as the intelligentsia is concerned.

Noël Coward

Thursday, 14 March 1957
10 Downing Street

I called a Cabinet for 10 am to settle the Farm Review question* ... Really we have so much trouble coming to us that we must try to have some friends and preserve the firm agricultural base of the party, in the House and the country.

---

*The agriculture review inquired into prices, markets and subsidies within the farming industry, and resulted in the 1957 Agriculture Act.

Minister of Labour's industrial report was gloomy. Shipbuilding seems pretty bad; general engineering almost as hopeless; railways very bad too. Sir John Forster will only reward the railwaymen 3% which they will certainly refuse.

Harold Macmillan

Sunday, 12 May 1957

Went over to Sidney Bernstein for luncheon. He's got just the house you'd expect – neatly converted farmhouse, very hygienic, neat American wife rather like Claire Bloom, time and labour saving devices. Bernstein looks rather benevolent and cheerful nowadays – tall, grey, a lean Ben-Gurion. His TV, he says, is now beginning to pay. Appears that he inherited music-hall from his father and that he and his brother built up present Granada business on this foundation.* Sidney is very left-wing, attends Labour Party conferences. What does he want? He doesn't know.

Malcolm Muggeridge

Saturday, 13 July 1957

The Anglo-Scandinavian Labour Youth Rally was held in Hyde Park this afternoon. I suppose between 1,000 and 2,000 people were there.

For some reason the thing absolutely lacked zip. Great drops of rain soaked the duplicating paper on which Harold Wilson's speech was written. It began to disintegrate as he hurried through it. The loudspeaker van was behind the platform so we could hear our own voices. It's absolutely infuriating and completely wrecks any chance of making a good speech.

Tony Benn

Monday, 12 August 1957
AWRE, Aldermaston, Berkshire

All day at Aldermaston – the Atomic Weapons (Research) Establishment. It is a remarkable place – 6,000 people employed – £20m a year.

---

*Sidney and Cecil Bernstein, cinema and television entrepreneurs who started Granada TV in Manchester.

It's worth it if it helps to prevent wars. Sir W Penney* is a splendid character, and – as at Harwell – I was struck by the keen and buoyant atmosphere of the place ... Of course the tragedy is that, in defence of the same cause, the American and British effort has to be duplicated, instead of shared.

Harold Macmillan

Tuesday, 5 November 1957

It's tempting to connect the present sudden storms and freak gales with the news that on Sunday the Russians launched a second satellite much bigger than the first, with a live dog inside it! This and its attendant circumstances, such as the frenzy among dog-lovers, deputations clamouring on the steps of the Russian Embassy, or the word satellite heard from Mrs Hoare's lips, has made everything seem like a novel from H G Wells instead of the humdrum world we've been living in so long.

Frances Partridge

Thursday, 21 November 1957

Meeting ... to consider our recommendations for future Labour Party broadcasts. It was most unsatisfactory in every way.

Nye Bevan was the cause of all the trouble and his whole attitude to TV is absolutely heart-breaking. He is frightened of it himself and completely anti-professional in his outlook. Probably the stupidest thing was his boast that he had *turned down* two invitations by BBC and ITA to go on the air to describe his recent visit to America. He thought that was very wise so that the public wouldn't see too much of him.

Tony Benn

---

* William Penney was a British mathematician who had worked on the Manhattan Project. He was appointed Director of the British nuclear weapons programme based at RAF Aldermaston in Berkshire.

Tuesday, 31 December 1957

What a dark and confused picture the curtain of the New Year goes up on. A definite Russian lead in Nuclear Power – with which we may not draw level for at least three years. Eisenhower an invalid, Dulles a calamity, France still a hopeless casualty ... A vacuum of leadership in Europe – meanwhile a kind of defeatism, neutralism, pacifism growing here – sometimes in the name of morality, sometimes of national independence and anti-Americanism ... Last year beginning with Suez and ending with Sputnik was a bad one. I pray that this one may be better.

Violet Bonham Carter

Sunday, 19 January 1958

Tour of the Commonwealth

To go from India (especially from New Delhi) to Pakistan is like going from Hampstead or North Oxford to the Border country or the Highlands. Iskander Mirza, the robust President of Pakistan and his wife (a Persian lady) are *grands seigneurs* – very charming hosts, not too intellectual, and good food and wine. (Nehru's food was uneatable. It was European, but like a bad boarding house.)

Pakistan is poor; politically unstable; in a state of religious turmoil (the mullahs have large tho' rather uncertain power) without a 'political class' – without so large an Indian Civil Service tradition as India, and practising corruption on the grand scale.

The one stable element in this situation is the Army – the Navy and the Air Force are also reliable.

Harold Macmillan

Wednesday, 12 March 1958

Warmly welcomed back by Mrs Hoare and Wilde.

How little we thought about politics or the world when we were in Spain! Now – a new feature of life – American bombers cruise overhead all the time, carrying the Bomb. The people of Newbury are made deeply anxious by this activity, as we see from the local paper and also by some alarming accident that occurred at the airfield only a week ago. Nor were they reassured by the frantic haste with which the personnel scrambled over the eight-foot walls for safety, before doing anything to warn the neighbourhood. There is, it seems quite a movement of a pacifist sort afoot.

Ralph remarked that by taking a stand against the Bomb one would find oneself in the company of cranks, emotionalists and Communists – considerations which don't affect me in the least.

Frances Partridge

Friday, 28 March–Saturday, 29 March 1958
Torrington by-election, Bideford, North Devon*

At about twenty to two a recount was formally announced by the Sheriff. The Conservatives had (quite rightly) demanded it. It was about twenty to three when he rose on the platform and announced the figures ... Liberal majority 219. It was a narrow shave – but we were *in*. Mark had wiped out a Govt majority of 9,000 odd ...

M R Bonham Carter (Liberal) 13,408
A F H Royle (Conservative) 13,189
L Lamb (Labour) 8,697

We then went down into the tumult of the crowd. Mark was carried shoulder high (and managed to retain quite an effective position), Leslie and I followed with the help of friendly policemen (all the police and postmen were on our side throughout!) Our hands were grasped and wrung as we struggled towards the Rose of Torridge – a nice Labour man almost ground my knuckles to dust saying, 'I'm a Socialist but I'm glad you've won.' (Lamb said much the same to me inside. One of the nice things about this country is that Labour recognise and remember the old Lib–Lab alliance and feel that we are nearer to them than the Tories.)

Violet Bonham Carter

Tuesday, 13 May 1958

Two MPs, Reg Sorensen and John Dugdale, have just returned from a visit to the Yemen where they were the guests of the Government and

---

* Mark Bonham Carter, elder son of Violet Bonham Carter (and married to Leslie), failed to hold the constituency in the October 1959 General Election. The constituency then called Torrington included the port of Bideford, where the count was held.

met everyone. Reg ... gave his impressions of the present absolute theocratic monarchy which came from a fairytale book. Public executions, slavery, and mutilation as a punishment for theft still survive. Reg recommended that Britain face the fact that the [British] Protectorate may want to join the Yemen.*

John Dugdale attached more importance to the Russian and Chinese missions. Particularly the Russian aid of $60 million and the technicians to build the port.

Nye ... began his characteristic philosophical waffling, full of phrases like 'in the problem of succession of power we are the contemporary culprits from an evolving imperialist transmutation ...'

He then launched an attack on me for my support of Arab nationalism: 'It is a sham and an eruption of hysteria against Zionism and the West. The Arabs are incapable of running anything with Islam round their necks. We should give this stretch of desert to Nasser, even if only to prove what a failure he is.'

Tony Benn

Thursday, 29 May 1958

10 am. Meeting of ministers.

The purpose was to discuss the position on nuclear weapons and tests. Our last test (a few weeks ago) was successful. Nevertheless it is absolutely vital for us to complete this series in Sept. If all goes well, we shall need only 2 explosions; but if (as is very possible) we have a failure in the new and very special system which we want to test, we shall need 2 more.† We should complete everything by October 31st (at latest) and prob before. Can we hold on against a) the public and political pressure now, b) the extension of this pressure which is likely to follow UN report on medical effects?

Harold Macmillan

---

* Britain controlled the southern part of Yemen as a Protectorate centred on the strategically useful port of Aden. British rule of the Aden Protectorate ended in 1967 and in 1990 southern Yemen united with the north to form the Republic of Yemen.
† There were ultimately four more nuclear tests at Christmas Island between August and September 1958.

Saturday, 23 August 1958

The first of our Christmas Island tests was done today – a small kiloton 'trigger' explosion. The megaton test is timed for Sept 8th or so. The question now arises about going on with it. In principle we can rely on the latest American understanding. In practice, it might be as well to have the knowledge which we shall get from this test.

The Greek Govt are in great difficulties, and there are gloomy telegrams from our ambassador in Athens. The Greeks, he says, will threaten – and perhaps be compelled – to leave NATO.

Harold Macmillan

Tuesday, 2 September 1958

The trouble [Notting Hill riots] continued on an even bigger scale last night. I toured the area before breakfast and saw the debris and corrugated iron up behind the windows of the prefabs where the coloured families live. The use of petrol bombs and iron bars and razors is appalling. There is a large area where it is not safe for people to be out.

The Labour Party really must say something about it.

Tony Benn

Saturday, 18 October 1958
Bristol South East constituency

Went to Barton House – the new 14-storey skyscraper of modern flats – this morning. It was a perfect autumn day with the sky blue and a shimmer of sunshine on the whole of Bristol. We went right to the roof and visited various flats. To see the bright airy rooms with the superb view and to contrast them with the poky slum dwellings of Barton Hill below was to get all the reward one wants from politics. For this grand conception of planning is what it is all about.

Tony Benn

Friday, 6 February 1959

Read a novel *No Love for Johnnie* by a Labour MP called Wilfred Fienburgh – now dead (in motor accident). If he hadn't died the other Labour MPs must have killed him. It proves what I have often said,

'The Labour movement began as a Crusade. It has now become a racket.' This book is reasonably well written and is a terrible picture of Labour MPs in the House, and their life and intrigues.

Harold Macmillan

Wednesday, 4 March 1959

Russian trip

We got back yesterday at about 6.15pm from our Russian journey … We left for Moscow on February 21st. The journey took about four hours (in a Comet). It was not, unfortunately, possible for me to take the diary – too risky in view of the continuous and highly skilled espionage to which we were subjected …

The consumption of food and drink is tremendous. The food (except for caviar, smoked salmon and similar pre dinner delicacies) is not good. The drink other than vodka (wh is very good) is bad – with the exception of some quite nice white wine from the Caucasus. Soviet brandy is just poison … how nice and how friendly all the people are. I spoke to many – crowds in the streets, in the factories, outside the places where we dined and outside the 'residences' put at our disposal. These gatherings – which grew in size as the visit proceeded and my speaking to them in this way got known – were uniformly good-mannered and attractive.

Some of the crowds were clearly anxious about Peace and War. The propaganda was terrifying. Everyone in Russia seems genuinely persuaded that the Americans, and probably British, have decided on a surprise attack – a 'bolt from the blue.' Everyone asks anxiously if we are going to keep the Peace. They are kept absolutely ignorant of all the provocations of Soviet policy all over the world.

Harold Macmillan

Friday, 24 April–Saturday, 25 April 1959

Visit to Lancashire

The Opposition have committed themselves – thro' Gaitskell and H Wilson – to a bitter attack on the Cotton scheme.* This is both foolish and dishonest.

---

*The Cotton Industry Act provided for grants for new machinery costs in return for

A very long day – 9 am to midnight … 6 or 7 speeches – impromptu – we covered many Lancashire towns, including Oldham, Rochdale, Bury, Stockport, Manchester. D[orothy] was with me. It was really a most heartening experience. With the masses of people whom we saw – they waited in large numbers in the streets – there was scarcely a 'boo'.

The more I think of the visit … the more pleased I am. Of course, I don't mean that the people who were so polite and friendly will all vote Tory. But I cannot believe that such courtesy and so little bitterness are not good signs. It is very different to the mood of 1945 or even 1950.

Harold Macmillan

Tuesday, 5 May 1959

I went to *A Taste of Honey*, a squalid little piece about squalid and unattractive people. It has been written by an angry young lady of nineteen [Shelagh Delaney] and is a great success.

Noël Coward

Saturday, 27 June 1959

Bristol South East constituency

To Bristol for the most dejected, depressing, inadequate, badly run, deadbeat Sale of Work that I have ever attended. If that is the Labour Party's image then something is wrong.

Tony Benn

Friday, 7 August 1959

Lunch at the Garrick and am told that it is announced that the Queen is to have a baby in January or February. What a sentimental hold the monarchy has over the middle classes! All the solicitors, actors and publishers at the Garrick were beaming as if they had acquired some personal benefit.

Harold Nicolson

---

redundancies and destruction of obsolete machinery in the Lancashire cotton mills.

Thursday, 8 October 1959
General Election day

I felt reasonably hopeful, as Ruth [Dalton] and I settled down in the flat ...

From the start, the results went wrong. Billericay, containing the New Town of Basildon ... Surely a Labour gain. But no, held by Tories with a 4,000 majority. True we held the two Salford seats but then came a stream of disappointments. Battersea South and Watford, both held by Tories, and a Tory gain from Labour at Acton. And so on and so on.

Hugh conceded the election about 1 a.m.

Denis Howell was out by 20 votes, after two recounts. This loss grieved me more than any other result. He was very much one of my Poodles, very shrewd (rarest of qualities in Labour Party nowadays.) Very loyal ...

And Jim Callaghan was in, but by less than 1,000.

Hugh Dalton

Thursday, 8 October–Monday, 12 October 1959
Washington

We arrived at the White House at 1930.

[President Eisenhower] had just flown back from California and had brought back some specially succulent steaks which he insisted on cooking himself for dinner and which were indeed very delicious.

The President was in absolutely wonderful spirits the whole evening. After dinner there was a film, *It Started with a Kiss*. The President gave us all the choice of whether we went to the film or stayed and gossiped. The ladies went to the film and the men stayed and gossiped.

This was election day in the UK and every half hour the President was on the telephone getting the latest news ... [he] could not conceal his pleasure when Gaitskell conceded the election ... what pleased him most was being able to work once more with his old friend Harold Macmillan, and that he thought that his re-election would be a notable contribution to summit negotiations and world peace.

Ike, Al [Gruenther] and I gossiped over old times and I heard an account of the President's visit to Europe and of Khrushchev's visit to the US.

The President told us that he considered Khrushchev the brightest man he had ever met, with the greatest detailed knowledge of any subject, and that the displays of temper were all carefully calculated to produce effect.

I was taken to all the activities in the [Hunter Army Airfield] Base and fully briefed on all that they do. Sixty operational B47 bombers and forty-three KC 97 refuellers are always ready within twenty-four hours ...

Perhaps the most terrifying aspect is that when these aircraft take off they actually carry one or two H bombs apiece. The conviction that the whole of Strategic Air Command have, that at a moment's notice they could blot out Russia, is really quite frightening, whereas the Americans, of course, only feel safe because of it.

Louis Mountbatten

Sunday, 11 October 1959

To the Gaitskells. Hugh was tired but mellow and said he wanted a holiday, which he deserved.

He [also] said several times, 'I'm not prepared to lose another Election for the sake of nationalisation.' He laid great stress on the disadvantages of the name Labour, particularly on new housing estates, and said, 'Of course, Douglas Jay is going to urge us to adopt a new one.' I reminded him that the prune had been resuscitated without a change of name by clever selling.

He also thought we must review our relations with the trade unions.

Tony Benn

Friday, 30 October 1959

A great flurry – Foreign Office, Commonwealth Relations Office, Colonial Office. A grave dilemma is presented to us. The Moroccans have put down a resolution in United Nations Assembly calling on the French to abandon the Bomb Test (atomic we think) which they have planned to set off in the Sahara. The Nigerians, Ghana and other Africans are terribly upset. It is an emotional reaction, for it is very unlikely that the Test will do any harm – certainly no more in Africa than elsewhere. They even talk about 'leaving the Commonwealth' if we do not vote for the resolution.

Harold Macmillan

Tuesday, 29 December 1959

We had Robert* to ourselves for supper last night, a perfect companion. After going over Christmas with a fine comb … we got on to psycho-analysis, both in theory and practice. It was fascinating to hear about it from someone as realistic and averse to mumbo-jumbo as he is. One thing he came up with was that the infant's pleasure in suckling was fully sexual. But if so wouldn't there be extreme differences in the psychological patterns of the breast-fed and bottle-fed? Robert also finds it interesting that some states of adult rage are speechless – because they refer back to the pre-speech period of infancy. I was rather struck by that.

Frances Partridge

Sunday, 24 January 1960
Port Elizabeth, South Africa

I cannot describe to you the horrors of Apartheid. I asked an Englishman how one pronounced the word and he said 'Apart' and then 'hate', and my God! Hate it is.

I was shocked when first landing at Durban to observe that all the seats along the esplanade (all of them, literally) were marked 'For whites only' … In the vast Post Office at Cape Town there were counters for whites and separate counters for the niggers. In fury at this, I queued up behind three niggers, but when my turn came the clerk said to me, 'Sorry, sir, you are at the wrong desk.'

You know how I hate niggers and how Tory Vita is. But I do hate injustice more than I hate niggers … truly you have no conception how shocking it all is. The pure police state. How happy we are with our freedom and our Parliamentary questions.

Harold Nicolson to Nigel Nicolson

---

*Robert Kee, writer, broadcaster and campaigner.

Wednesday, 2 March 1960

Spoke this morning at the Conference of American Women's Activities in the UK attended by 300 or more wives of American Air Force personnel. It was amazing to hear them introduced as 'Maxine Taylor, wife of General Taylor, Commander of East Anglia' etc. etc. Here is an army that has divided the UK up into its areas and commands. We know nothing about it.

Hugh Carleton Greene, new Director-General of the BBC, spoke to the public information group ... He was terribly unimaginative and cautious ... It was Auntie BBC at its best and worst.

But as a public service man he wasn't just on the make like the vulgar thrusting profit-rich ITV tycoons.

Tony Benn

Sunday, 13 March 1960

Return from visit to General and Madame de Gaulle

I felt tired from the strain of talking nothing but French (he refused to have anyone present) and trying not to fall into any major error of judgement.

He does not want political integration. He accepted the economic integration implied in the Treaty of Rome with regret. But it was signed, and he could not go back on it. But it has had a useful effect in making French industry more competitive. Politically it keeps Germany looking to the West. He does *not* want a united Germany; nor does he fear Germany for at least twenty five years.

Harold Macmillan

Tuesday, 22 March 1960

Terrible news of a massacre in South Africa – 65 Africans killed and 156 wounded are the latest figures. There were also minor riots in Cape Town.* Africans demonstrated at Pass Laws ... asking to be arrested, having left their passes at home. They threw stones (and fruit!) They

---

* At Sharpeville, outside Johannesburg, sixty-nine people were killed and another nineteen died at Langa, near Cape Town.

were of course unarmed. They were shot down by the police with Sten guns.

Violet Bonham Carter

Wednesday, 23 March 1960

With the exception of the *Daily Sketch* and the *Herald** the rest of the press seems conscious of the dangers to the Commonwealth of any foolish or rash reaction of HMG. Unfortunately the Canadians and the Indians – with somewhat different degrees of indignation – have condemned South Africa. So has the USA.

Harold Macmillan

Sunday, 27 March 1960

On Thursday I went with Binkie to see *The Dumb Waiter* and *The Room* at the Royal Court, two *soi-disant* plays by Mr Harold Pinter. They were completely incomprehensible and insultingly boring, although fairly well acted. It is the surrealist school of non-playwriting. Apparently they received some fine notices.

Noël Coward

Friday, 10 June 1960

This afternoon the Ford Motor Company put on a demonstration of the Levacar, a rail vehicle held above the rails by magnetic repulsion. I had fixed all this up so that Labour MPs could see it. Only one turned up. The BBC TV filmed it and the British Transport Commission sent some engineers but they were so incredibly negative and stick-in-the-mud. Of course there are tremendous difficulties and the whole idea is in its earliest stages but instead of concentrating on the development

---

*The *Daily Sketch*, a right-leaning tabloid, was owned by Associated Newspapers, who in 1971 merged it with its sister paper, the *Daily Mail*. The TUC still held a substantial stake in the *Daily Herald*, which in the 1920s had been its official organ. It supported Labour. In 1969 the paper was sold to News International who relaunched it as *The Sun*.

possibilities, they were chattering about the snags and difficulties and technical problems until one could have throttled them all.

Tony Benn

Sunday, 19 June 1960

The Labour row [over nuclear weapons] seems to grow in bitterness and intensity. One begins to wonder whether Gaitskell will be able to survive and ride the storm. I shd be sorry if he went, for he has ability without charm. He does not appeal to the electorate but he has a sense of patriotism and moderation. However I can't see either Wilson or Brown as better equipped.

Harold Macmillan

June 1960

Fire Brigades Union, Rothesay

We assume that in the next decade there will be no war. Quite clearly, if that assumption proves to be false, there will not be a fire service in the sixties because there will be nothing to serve in the next decade. The second assumption is that there is no major economic recession … In this 'affluent society' one should not forget the large number of people who are now defined as the 'casualties of the welfare state'. Old people, the sick, the injured, the underpaid. This so-called affluent society for Britain is basically the result of the fact that over the last few years the terms of world trade have been slightly in our favour. The terms of world trade, if they turned against Great Britain in its present precarious situation, could bring about a state of society which would hardly be called affluent, except for a number of people who, because it remains a capitalist society, would be able to safeguard themselves against the economic ills of any recession.

With rational planning of our resources, sound political action, a progressive trading policy, particularly with the swelling of the new socialist countries, full employment can be guaranteed and a rising standard of living maintained.

John Horner

Tuesday, 12 July 1960

This evening to the dance at the American embassy. There were 700 people there and we danced until dawn was breaking.

There were artificial trees with real fruit wired on to them ... four artificial swimming pools had been created in the garden which had been filled by the London Fire Brigade. Between and around them were gigantic candelabra wired for gas; from these tremendous candles burned continuous jets of flame.

We danced round beside the Armstrong-Joneses and saw the Queen Mother and Bob Boothby gazing at each other rather balefully across the champagne bottles.

Though we enjoyed every minute of it, we felt a bit like the Roman Senators must have felt the night before the Huns and Goths arrived to sack Rome. Such splendid extravagance carries with it an inevitable taste of decadence.

Tony Benn

Wednesday, 13 July 1960

Today Hugh [Gaitskell] ... gave up the ghost on [trying to remove] Clause 4. It will remain unchanged in the Party Constitution.

Of course the press will naturally and logically describe this as a great defeat and rebuff for Hugh ...

But neither he (Hugh) nor I realised the massive boneheadedness in all sections of the Party ... It has been a staggering and almost unbelievable experience.

Memorial service for Nye in Westminster Abbey on July 26th. Of course I shan't go. Utterly unreal and inappropriate! He was an 'unbeliever' and never pretended, as so many do, to be anything [else].

Hugh Dalton

Saturday, 6 August 1960

I have just read very carefully, *Waiting for Godot,* and in my considered opinion it is pretentious gibberish, without any claim to importance whatsoever. I know that it received great critical acclaim and I also know that it's silly to go on saying how stupid the critics are, but this really enrages me. It is nothing but phoney surrealism with occasional references to Christ and mankind. It has no form, no basic philosophy and absolutely no lucidity.

It's just a waste of everybody's time and it made me ashamed to think that such balls could be taken seriously for a moment.

To continue in this carping vein, I have also read *The Charioteer* by Miss Mary Renault. Oh dear, I do wish well-intentioned ladies would not write books about homosexuality.

I'm sure the poor woman meant well but I wish she'd stick to recreating the glory that was Greece and not fuck about with dear old modern homos.

Noël Coward

Thursday, 8 September 1960
Leningrad

At 12.30 we went to the Cazana Cathedral which is now run by the Academy of Sciences. It is a museum of the history of religion. Our guide, Nina, aged about 25, was an atheist theological student, writing a thesis on the reform movement in the Russian Orthodox Church. One section of the museum was on the history of the origins of Christianity and we were assured we could ask questions.

Q. Do you accept the historical fact of the man Jesus Christ living and dying, aside from his claims?

A. No. He never lived. There is no evidence of his life. He was fabricated later by others and the story of his birth, life, teaching and death is without foundation.

Q. Have you any exhibits showing the persecution of the Christians in Rome?

A. No. They were greatly exaggerated and were touched off by the incredible wealth of the Christians in Rome who offended the Emperor.

Attended a farewell dinner at the Restaurant Metropole. Everyone was so warm and friendly and they drove us to the dock and put us on board the *Estonia*. The wind was blowing and the rain bucketing down and we felt that winter was closing in on Leningrad and would hold it tight until the spring came to melt the ice … then warm and comfortable in our cabin, in this lovely new ship, we edged out into the sea, our Russian trip over.

Tony Benn

There are no more diary entries by Tony Benn until 1963; his father, Lord Stansgate, died in November 1960 and Benn inherited the peerage which he did not want. Benn went to America to lecture, and also became involved in a lengthy constitutional battle. This was eventually resolved by the passing of the Peerage Act 1963 which enabled hereditary peers to renounce their titles. Benn and several others did just that and he returned to the Commons after a by-election.

Friday, 30 September 1960
Kenya

At ten o'clock Patricia* and I rode to one of the African villages where four hundred children were called out of school to be introduced to us on our horses and listen to a speech by the District Commissioner.

The speech in reply by the headmaster said how happy the children were to be given this opportunity by the British to educate themselves. I had thought of asking for them to be given a half day holiday, but the District Commissioner explained that the usual form of *punishment* in an African school is to deprive a child of one day's attendance at school. I then suggested we might give them an *extra* half day's work on Sunday as a gesture, but he did not think that would be popular with the master!

Louis Mountbatten

Thursday, 6 October 1960

Thoughts about the Bomb have come to the fore because of the vote for Unilateralism at the Labour Conference last week. Robert [Kee] has been reporting all the political conferences. He told me on the telephone that he is now a Unilateralist, in spite of the fact that the speeches in favour were rotten and Gaitskell's (on the other side) excellent, because he thought it showed new life and genuine feeling in the Labour Party, something also that was gaining strength.

But how unreal such huge possibilities as atomic war and occupation by Russia seem as I write them down!

Frances Partridge

---

*The older of the Mountbattens's two daughters, the younger being Pamela.

Friday, 11 November 1960

Kennedy's election to the Presidency (which was announced on Wednesday afternoon) now seems to have been an extraordinarily small majority of votes – about half a percent.

I sent him a short congratulatory letter. I have for some weeks been trying to work out a method of influencing him and working with him. With Eisenhower there was the link of memories and a long friendship. I will have to base myself now on trying to win him by ideas. I have started working on a memorandum which I might send him – giving a broad survey of the problems which face us in the world.

Harold Macmillan

Tuesday, 6 December 1960

Dressed like lightning and went to the Atlantic European dinner for Edward Heath* – a private one to talk about the Common Market.

He spoke conversationally, sitting. He obviously wants to make a 'go' of it – and that as soon as possible – but thinks it important to choose the psychological moment. He thinks that Italy want us in unreservedly, that Germany is friendly and welcoming (and says that the Germans and we are working out solutions to outstanding practical difficulties). France is the obstacle ... We have no cards in our economic pack to play as inducements.

I like Heath – he is unpretentious, friendly, pink, 'bon coucheur', but as for being in the running for PM-ship – the idea is *absurd*!

Violet Bonham Carter

Monday, 12 December 1960

After all our efforts the three chief African leaders (Banda, Kaunda and Nkomo) have 'done the dirty' on us. Without any intimation of their intention, they ' walked out' of the Federation Conference at the end of this afternoon's meeting – this time, as they said in their respective Press Conferences and TV interviews 'for good'. After talking over the situation with the two Secretaries of State, I agreed to put out a

---

* Edward Heath was Lord Privy Seal, and in charge of Britain's negotiations to join the Common Market.

statement from HMG 'postponing' the territorial conferences until the situation is clearer.*

The real trouble is that Africans are vain and childish. Like children they easily get excited. Also the Press and TV do infinite harm in flattering their vanity.

Harold Macmillan

Tuesday, 17 January 1961

A difficult Cabinet at 11 am. We are to put up (on April 1st) the new Pensions Stamp (£120m). We have decided on a new Health Stamp (£48m). We accepted 2/- instead of 1/- prescription charge (£12m). We accepted the abolition of the subsidy on welfare orange juice and cod liver oil (£1.5 million). We accepted increased charges for spectacles and teeth (£2.5m). But I tried to steer them off abolishing the subsidy on welfare milk. I think this will be resented both by those who care about children's health, etc. *and* by the farmers ...

Harold Macmillan

Saturday, 25 February 1961

I would not have missed my Edinburgh experience for anything† and was more than ever impressed by Jo's public performance. His personality puts that of all other political leaders in the shade. To begin with – his very rare good looks – which hit one in the eye – his combination of almost schoolboy casualness and informality about clothes etc. with real dignity. He looks the part of a young 'great man'. Then the impact of his voice, delivery and gesture – the originality of thought and gesture, never falling into the almost inevitable trap of cliché. He has the goods and can deliver them matchlessly.

Would that he could be given by Fate a better armoury of material

---

*A conference in London called to discuss the future of the Central African Federation, set up by the British government in the 1950s to join together Southern Rhodesia, Northern Rhodesia and Nyasaland. Africans had not been consulted and Joshua Nkomo in Southern Rhodesia, Kenneth Kaunda in Northern Rhodesia and Hastings Banda in Nyasaland led African nationalist opinion against the Federation.
† Jo Grimond, Violet Bonham Carter's son-in-law, and Leader of the Liberal Party, was inaugurated as Rector of Edinburgh University on 24 February 1961.

weapons, in the way of money and organisation – and above all a group of able followers and henchmen approaching his own stature.

Violet Bonham Carter

Thursday, 13 April 1961

On television news, Professor Bernard Lovell said that getting a man into space was the greatest achievement of human history. By comparison with what? – presumably, Christianity, Shakespeare's plays, Chartres Cathedral, etc. Considered his observation probably the most fatuous I'd ever heard. One line of Blake is greater than getting to the moon. Believing so, I felt rather lonely, with everyone else, seemingly, taking Lovell's view. Feat presented to the world like woman's magazine fiction – handsome cosmonaut, suburban love, wife and two children, factory worker etc.

Malcolm Muggeridge

Saturday, 27 May 1961

Spent the day dog-alone and went by myself to the brilliant revue of the 'Angry Young Men' called *Beyond the Fringe* at the small Fortune theatre near Drury Lane. I had a good corner seat in the stalls which gave me an even greater sense of isolation. Laughing alone has always seemed to me an unnatural act – making one feel uncomfortable … But I sat and shook and writhed and shrieked and shouted with amusement for two hours by the clock. It was really brilliant … The targets were Macmillan, the Church, philosophers, and there were very good musical parodies … a terribly funny one of some pansies with plucking gestures, dressing in Sou'Westers to do a terrifically virile hearty TV advertisement for something like Lifebuoy Soap …

Violet Bonham Carter

Wednesday, 7 June 1961
Hamburg

Dropped into a teenage rock-and-roll joint. Ageless children, sexes indistinguishable, tight-trousered, stamping about, only the smell of sweat intimating animality. The band were English, from Liverpool, and recognised me. Long-haired, weird feminine sounds; bashing their instruments and emitting nerveless sounds into microphones. In conversation rather touching in a way, their faces like Renaissance carvings of saints or blessed virgins. One of them asked me 'Is it true you're a communist?' No, I said; just in opposition. He nodded understandingly; in opposition himself in a way. 'You make money out of it?' he went on. I admitted that this was so. He, too, made money. He hoped to take back £200 to Liverpool.*

Malcolm Muggeridge

Tuesday, 11 July 1961

[Watched] Gagarin's arrival on TV.† He has, I must say, got a most charming personality – natural, friendly, modest and always smiling and happy. He came down the steps from the aeroplane clapping the crowd which applauded him – a very nice habit.

If only his native country were like he is, we should be living in a far easier world.

Violet Bonham Carter

Friday, 25 August 1961

I suppose the newspapers will criticise us for being on holiday during the Berlin crisis, but actually this is nonsense. The situation has got considerably worse, however, during the week. The Russian and East German pressure on Berlin is growing apace. East Berliners are literally 'sealed off' and the crossing places are few and well guarded. There is, actually, nothing illegal in the East Germans stopping the flow of refugees and putting themselves behind a still more rigid iron curtain. It certainly is not a very good advertisement for the benefits of Communism – but it is not (I believe) a breach of any of our agreements.

Harold Macmillan

---

*This was probably John Lennon.
† Yuri Gagarin, Soviet cosmonaut, was the first man to travel to outer space, orbiting the earth in *Vostok 1*. He died in 1968 in a plane crash.

Monday, 18 September 1961

I've not said that while I was with the Cecils, the chief nuclear disarmament supporters including eighty-nine year old Bertie Russell, were put in jail because they refused to be bound over not to meet and 'sit down' in Trafalgar Square.*

Nicky, Harriet Hill and Henrietta Garnett ... described their grim experience – how rough the police had been, hauling them along the ground by their arms, throwing a young man on top of them when they lay there; how an inspector had kicked [Anne]; how the police had called them 'stupid cows' and asked each other 'What shall we do? Shit on them?'

How it had been almost a relief to get in the Black Maria but the journey rattling along in cells had horrified them; how no-one had given them anything to eat until they were brought up at Clerkenwell Court and fined £1 each at lunchtime next day; how they were crowded into an airless cell with a lavatory in it which everyone had to use; how some were wet and shivering from being thrown in the fountains.

Frances Partridge

Saturday, 25 November–Wednesday, 29 November 1961
Visit of General de Gaulle to Birch Grove, Sussex

The house is looking lovely and the servants are reinforced by three Government 'butlers'.

All sorts of other women, old or returned servants etc., seem to have appeared. Every room in the house is full ... We have taken five rooms at the Roebuck, for his doctors etc. Blood plasma is in a special refrigerator in the Coach House. Outside the gates the press swarm. The Red Lion is selling beer in hogsheads. Police (with and without alsatian dogs) are in the garden and the woods (one alsatian happily bit the *Daily Mail* man in the behind). Altogether a most enjoyable show.

De Gaulle now hears nothing and listens to nothing ...

The tragedy of it all is that we agree with de G on almost everything. We like the political Europe (union de patries or union d'Etats) that de G likes. We are anti-federalists; so is he. We fear a German

---

*The philosopher Bertrand Russell was amongst those imprisoned for failing to agree to an order not to take part in a non-violent 'sit-in' at Trafalgar Square.

revival and have no desire to see a reunited Germany. These are de G's thoughts too. We agree; but his pride, his inherited hatred of England, (since Joan of Arc), his bitter memories of the last war; above all his intense 'vanity' for France – she must dominate – make him half welcome, half repel us, with a strange 'love–hate' complex. Sometimes when I am with him, I feel I have overcome it. But he goes back to his distrust and dislike, like a dog to his vomit. I still feel that he has not absolutely decided about our admission [to] the Economic Community. I am inclined to think he will be more likely to yield to pressure than persuasion.

Harold Macmillan

Thursday, 18 January 1962

Cabinet at 11. Railway wages. Then the great question of Nuclear Tests. I showed the Cabinet my latest correspondence with President Kennedy and we agreed (after much helpful discussion) a final reply. We agreed to make Christmas Island available for tests; he agrees to my new initiative to try to bring them to an end.

Harold Macmillan

March 1962

Katsina, Northern Nigeria

The Emir of Katsina is holding the *Salla*, which celebrates the appearance of the new moon and the breaking of the thirty days fast of Ramadan.

For all those who live under the stress of modern civilisation, with its onslaught of noise, smells, commercialism, ever-increasing speed and refinements of killing, and for all those conscious of the Damoclean sword of nuclear war, a visit to Katsina is in the nature of a return to sanity. This is something that the human mind can comprehend. Katsina has always been noted for its learning and culture, and has attracted people of all nations since 1100, when it became the centre for the caravan trade with the Mediterranean ports. Today life seems easy. There are no signs of painful poverty. Prayers are said in thankfulness for continuing peace.

Cecil Beaton

Thursday, 8 March 1962

The doctors have come out with a tremendous report on the dangers of smoking – esp cigarettes. This puts us in rather a fix. For how are we to get £800m indirect revenue from any other source?

Harold Macmillan

Saturday, 7 April 1962

Pre-Budget Cabinet meeting

The increase (of tax) on clothing and furniture from 5% to 10% will be very unpopular and people will forget the many items, from motor cars to cosmetics, which come down by 5%. There is to be a Tax on Sweets – 15%, and soft drinks, which will bring in £40m.

Harold Macmillan

Monday, 9 April 1962

Hotel Berlin

Lunch didn't end till 3.30 so our tour of West Berlin was rather mercifully confined to what we really wished to see – i.e. the Wall. At first sight it is very much lower than one had imagined – tho' covered with barbed wire, broken glass etc. It runs for 30 miles, cutting across streets, churchyards – so that one sees pathetic withering wreaths hung on walls by people cut off from the graves of their dead.

In one street on the border line, where the houses front on the East and back on the West, we saw a green wreath tied with red ribbons lying on the pavement. I was told that this was where a woman had leapt from a 3rd storey window to her death …

Forty escapees have been shot dead by their own fellow-countrymen – the East German police. This is what shocks one most deeply. It is *so* easy to miss. Many of course *have* missed *and* helped – actively or passively – and some have deserted. It is impossible to telephone to the East now, even via Frankfurt, and letters and parcels are opened.

Violet Bonham Carter

Saturday, 14 July 1962

Morning drenched in pouring rain – a cruel day for Laura's fete at Kew … Newspapers announce the most dramatic and sweeping Government purge – for that is what it is. Gaitskell describes it truly as a 'massacre.' The chief sacrificial victim is Selwyn Lloyd! He leaves the Exchequer (with a Companion of Honour) and is succeeded by Maudling. The 'image' seems to me to remain the same because although seven 'old familiar faces' are gone the rest remain and meanwhile Supermac's image of unflappability and implacable loyalty to colleagues is tarnished by this 'night of the long knives.'* It is also a curious repudiation of Cabinet responsibility. They *all* approved the Pay Pause policy, defended it root and branch – Mac first and foremost – and are now using poor old Celluloid [Selwyn Lloyd] as a scapegoat. I think they will find they have miscalculated and that their transformation scene will have little effect …

Violet Bonham Carter

Wednesday, 3 October 1962

The 'one day' Railway strike is on.†

Altho' there is a certain lull we are in a great tangle in every part of the world. The Russians are clearly using Cuba as a counter-irritant to Berlin. The President is angry with us for not being willing to join a boycott or blockade. He is either unwilling or unable to understand that we cannot give orders to British shipping, esp ships on charter, to avoid going to Cuba without legislation. (In war of course, it's different, but we are *not* at war with Cuba.)

Things in Congo are no better, and here again the Americans are angry with us for not being willing to join in boycotting Congolese copper. (We cannot help remarking that the Americans own most of the rest of the world copper supplies and the market is dull.)

---

*The seven were Lord Kilmuir, Selwyn Lloyd (Chancellor of the Exchequer), David Eccles, Harold Watkinson and Lord Mills, all Conservatives; and John Scott Maclay and Charles Hill, who were 'National Liberals' in the Conservative government.
†Some railway workshops (e.g. Bromsgrove, Caerphilly, Darlington, Earlstown, Gorton and Lancing) were to close within three years; others merged or ceased certain functions.

Finally, we have now found out that they have lied to us over the Israel missiles and are still lying to us.*

Harold Macmillan

Wednesday, 24 October 1962
Bedales School, Hampshire

News:

1. I have got the part of Herald in *Murder in the Cathedral;* only 32 lines but an unprecedented achievement in the history of Bedales school plays. Becket will be played by Ben Powell (18), First Knight Robert Booth (18), First Priest Julian Langinger (18).

2. The end of the world is nigh! President Kennedy says that Russia has missile sites on Cuba and has imposed an arms blockade, there could be a nuclear war! Everyone here is taking it VERY seriously, especially Mr Gillingham and all the CND crowd. (At Bedales that's virtually everybody!) I say that it is because we have nuclear weapons that we are safe but nobody's listening to me! All over school people are working out where to hide in the event that the Bomb gets dropped – in cupboards, under the oak dining-room tables, etc ... but I am not very worried. We have a nuclear deterrent. It will deter!

3. Went to Pefe (Petersfield). Haircut. Woolworths. Watch.

4. Sent epistle to Jackie.

Gyles Brandreth

Thursday, 1 November 1962

On Monday morning the Crisis abated with the news that Russia was prepared to withdraw the Cuban bases. Straight from the unconscious rises my death-wish, left without immediate hope of fulfilment. I see that I'm really disappointed at not being atomised, although deeply relieved that Burgo, Henrietta, Shirley Penrose, Georgie and Rose are not.

Frances Partridge

---

*President Kennedy had reversed the former US policy and approved the selling of Hawk missiles to Israel in August 1962.

Chapter Six

1963–1972
Sexual Politics

This decade began with a sex scandal and finished with a sex revolution.* The end of three successive Conservative governments was confidently predicted in 1963. In the event the Labour Party scraped in with a majority of four seats. In March 1966 a second general election increased that to nearly 100. The diaries of Labour MPs Barbara Castle, Tony Benn and Richard Crossman evoke the spirit of the socialist sixties, while the tensions between the nation's politics and its culture can be seen in the diaries of Joe Orton (a young iconoclast with no time for the liberalising tendency), Kenneth Tynan (the first to use the f-word on television), Roy Strong (newly appointed director of the Victoria and Albert Museum), Michael Palin (a Python in embryo), and Peter Hall (future director of the new National Theatre).

The post-war governments of Churchill, Eden and Macmillan had been bedevilled by problems overseas, and had ended with De Gaulle's humiliating veto of his War ally's application to join the Common Market ('the Six'). The Labour governments of 1964–70 and 1974–9 were relatively free from foreign policy problems but, ironically, beset by conflict with trade unions. There is a glimpse of the tortuous progress of Barbara Castle's proposals (*In Place of Strife*, 1969), which she believed would bring about better industrial relations; when they were rejected there were profound consequences in the 1970s and lessons for a Conservative government some fifteen years later.

---

*Exemplified by the publication, in 1970, of *The Female Eunuch* by Germaine Greer and *Sexual Politics* by Kate Millett.

The first significant mention of immigration as a political issue came during 1968; from then on, as diaries of the later twentieth century reveal, it was the elephant in the room that successive governments dimly acknowledged but hoped would go away.

Edward Heath used his unexpected premiership in 1970 to achieve what as a Minister he had failed to do in 1963 – join Britain to the Common Market. In succeeding he introduced a permanent and destructive incubus into the left and right of the British body politic.

Heath's challenge to the miners – 'who rules Britain?'- was as yet irrelevant to a young lad called Jim Wilson minding pit ponies in the Glebe Colliery. The first intimations of the national miners' strike come at the start of 1972, in the unpublished diary of Peter Clarney, one of the Yorkshire 'flying pickets'.

The diaries of two future Conservative MPs make their appearance, those of Gyles Brandreth, an unlikely member of Lord Longford's Commission on Pornography, and of Alan Clark, who was hoping for a safe seat in Plymouth.

Friday, 18 January 1963

Hugh Gaitskell died today after a terrific fight for his life over the last week or so. Nobody realised how serious it was and it has dominated the press and television in an astonishing way. It is a terrible personal tragedy for him as he was closer to Downing Street than at any time in his life.

The odious thing about the obituaries is the way the Tories are building his death up with half an eye to suggesting that there is no possible successor. Macmillan's tribute was revolting, since he and Gaitskell hated each other.

For me Hugh's death produced mixed reactions. I have worked closely with him for twelve years and when he was at his nicest he could be very kind indeed. After the 1959 election he put me on the front bench as Shadow Minister of Transport.

On the other hand he was a divisive leader of the Party. He had a real civil servant's mind – very little imagination and hardly any understanding of how people worked ... it looks as if George Brown will succeed him and for a number of reasons he is totally unsuited to be Leader of the Party.

Tony Benn

Monday, 28 January 1963
Chequers

The weather is still cold; the last fortnight has been a nightmare on this account alone. The snow and ice have dislocated all our life – there has been nothing like it since 1947. In my view, the authorities, of all kinds, have done remarkably well. The streets and roads have been cleared and in spite of delays, trains and buses have kept running pretty well.

(On Friday night we had a breakdown from midnight till 4 pm Saturday, owing to the peculiar effect of frost and fog on insulators, which upset the grid from Birmingham to Buckinghamshire. However except for baths and central heating, it was not bad – we cook on coal at Chequers and there are good fires in the rooms.)

On the Brussels front everything has been reduced to chaos by the extraordinary behaviour of de Gaulle. He gave a 'press conference' (with all the Corps Diplomatique present) to denounce Britain and oppose – on principle – her entry into the Common Market.

The reasons given for de G's sudden decision ... are so diverse as to be ridiculous ...

De G is trying to dominate Europe. His idea is not a partnership but a Napoleonic or a Louis XIV hegemony.

It is, I fear, very hard on Ted Heath (Ld Privy Seal) who has been a wonderful ambassador and negotiator throughout.

Harold Macmillan

Friday, 8 February 1963

[In the summer of 1961] I had an ever increasing feeling that Labour politics was becoming unbearable ... I could not see that, even if we did win an election, and Gaitskell became Prime Minister, he would be heading the kind of Labour Government that I believed in or would give me the kind of scope I needed to do a job.

Then quite suddenly this Christmas came Gaitskell's illness and death. The whole situation inside the Party was transformed and overnight I was chucked into a battle to elect Harold Wilson.

From the day Hugh died, it seemed to me ... in view of Harold's reputation for shiftiness and manoeuvring his best campaign was to have no campaign at all and to be seen studiously doing nothing with closed eyes, while leaving the Party to make up its mind.

I went into the House and into an empty chamber. I ran into Michael Foot. He, too, has this wonderful sense that the incredible has happened and that all kinds of things which had been impossible before Gaitskell's illness are now possible again.

Richard Crossman

Friday, 15 March 1963

A silly story excited the House of Commons last night and the Press this morning.* Even papers like the *Yorkshire Post* gave front page headlines and long leading article to the nonsense.

After this episode I was forced to spend a great deal of today over a silly scrape (women this time, thank God, not boys) into which one of the ministers has got himself. It's Jack Profumo – Secretary of State [for] War. It would not matter so much if it was just an affair of morality. But unfortunately among the frequenters of this raffish and disreputable set which centres around Lord Astor (Bill Astor) was the Russian military attaché!

Anyway the Russian officer has been recalled as a security risk, no doubt, from *their* angle ...

I have been for some time meditating a direct approach to President Kennedy about the Nuclear Test Ban negotiation which has got hopelessly bogged down at Geneva.

Harold Macmillan

Monday, 25 March 1963

This evening I had fifty minutes with Harold [Wilson] in his room. It was a delight to find him so relaxed and easy. Gaitskell used to be so tense and tired and often signed letters while I presented my points to him.

---

* A reference to the case of William Vassall, a civil servant, who had been blackmailed to spy for the Soviet Union when they threatened to reveal his homosexuality.

[We] talked about how he was going to run the election.

He said 'I'm not going to sit in my hotel room putting shillings in the gas and writing articles for the *Sunday Times* in my pyjamas as Hugh used to. If I have to do articles I'll have J. B. Priestley travelling with me, writing them for me.'

Tony Benn

Wednesday, 27 March 1963

At 5 a difficult discussion with ministers and officials about Government offices. The Foreign Office ought to be pulled down and rebuilt. But in what style? Conventional (and bad) or modern (and risk – perhaps bad, perhaps v good). I want a glass tower; but no one agrees.

After the adjournment of the House a long meeting in my room [about Nigeria] …What sufferings we go through to try to keep the Commonwealth together.

Harold Macmillan

Tuesday, 16 April 1963

Ernest Marples, Minister of Transport, came at 3 and stayed till 5. He is really a remarkable figure and I only wish I had more ministers with his imagination and thoroughness. We talked about Railways, Roads, Ports and Docks, and whole plans for transport in the future. In ten years we have gone from 2 million to 6 million motor cars. In another ten years we may [go] to twelve and eventually to 18 million cars! What must we do *now* to prepare not so much for the roads between the towns but the towns themselves to prepare for these developments.

Harold Macmillan

Monday, 13 May 1963
St Mary-le-Bow Church, Cheapside, London

This evening … to a meeting of the Christian Agnostics to hear the Bishop of Woolwich, John Robinson, talking about his book *Honest to God* which we had gathered to discuss.* The Reverend Joseph

---

* The publication of the book caused controversy due to its existential interpretation

McCulloch had organised this group, justifying its name by reference to the line from Oranges and Lemons 'I do not know, says the great bell of Bow.'

Woolwich summed up briefly. He really is an academic with guts but he is coming under such heavy fire now that I wonder if he can stand up to the pressure.

Honest to God is certainly the most helpful Christian theology that I've ever come across and I'm sure millions of others feel the same.

Tony Benn

Tuesday, 14 May 1963

Meeting with President Kennedy, Washington DC

A large procession of tourists or aboriginals were forming up to be shown over the White House. We gave our names, which were checked by telephone, and I was taken to Arthur Schlesinger's room.* He left me with the Secretary and at about 12.05 the President strode in to fetch me ...

[He] took me into his own room – sat me on a sofa next to himself in his rocking chair and fired away. He has great simplicity, spontaneity, naturalness and charm – no 'high hat' or 'high horse', one feels immediately at ease as though one had known him all one's life.

He started off by asking if I'd enjoyed my visit here. I told him every moment of it both last year and this – and what an enormous difference I had felt last year in the atmosphere since his regime started ... This year I find it electric, as tho' the pulse of the world were beating here – as indeed it is. He went on to ask what relation I was to Raymond Asquith. I said he was my elder brother. He said he had read about him in John Buchan's *Memory Hold the Door* and also in Winston's *Great Contemporaries* and quoted the sentence about his 'striding into the crash and thunder of the Somme.' I was amazed at his verbatim memory.

He asked me if I liked H. Macmillan. I said I both liked and admired him in the Thirties. We were politically intimate – tho' not personally intimate (I didn't know anyone with whom he, Macmillan, could

and the proposal of a 'secular theology' in which God could be known through secular and cultural acts, not simply by traditional religious observance and church-going.
* Arthur Schlesinger, Jr (1917–2007), the historian, served as a special assistant to President John F. Kennedy from 1961 to 1963.

be said to be personally intimate.) ... He had long walrus moustachios, and high stiff collar, a limp, damp handshake and pince-nez – no political sex appeal and certainly no other kind either.

[President Kennedy] went on to describe how [de Gaulle] was now blocking all progress in Europe – in defence, economics etc. I asked him how he thought this road-block could be broken. He said, 'The root of the matter is that not only you in Britain but we in the USA have now become debtors and not, as we always used to be, creditors. The gold reserve has ebbed at the following rate (he then gave the figures for the last few years). Europe is economically for the moment in a stronger position than we are ...'

My impression was of a man well over life-size with power in reserve – who carried the world on his shoulders with buoyancy, and gaiety and without a trace of self-importance or swollen head.

Violet Bonham Carter

Sunday, 2 June–Sunday, 9 June 1963

I should think that the whole account in yesterday's papers of the trial of [Christine] Keeler and her negro friends must have been the biggest shock to public morality which has been known in this century.* I can't think of a more humiliating and discrediting story than that of the Secretary of State for War's being involved with people of this kind. It has social seediness and some fairly scabrous security background concerning Ivanov, the lying, the collusion and, the fact that Royalty and the Establishment back Profumo. Now the Queen will see him next week when he hands over his seals of office.

I would say that ... this will in fact enormously undermine the Government and so assist in creating the conditions for a Labour Party victory at the next Election.

Richard Crossman

---

*Keeler had had a relationship with John Profumo, Secretary of State for War, and also Yevgeny Ivanov, a naval attaché at the Soviet embassy. The affair emerged during a trial involving an altercation between two men with whom Keeler had also been involved, Antiguan Johnny Edgecombe and Jamaican musician Aloysius 'Lucky' Gordon. The security implications raised by Profumo's affair, and the fact that he lied about the relationship in a statement to the House of Commons severely damaged Harold Macmillan's Conservative government.

Friday, 14 June 1963

We had a party this evening [with] Robin Day, Val and Mark Arnold-Forster, Liz and Peter Shore, Michael and Claudie Flanders, Simon Watson-Taylor with Carmen Manley and another girl, David Hockney, Shirley Fisher ...

Obviously the main topic of conversation was the Profumo business which produces new sensations every few hours. Apparently the two main contenders now for the succession (to Macmillan) are Butler and Hailsham – with Hailsham edging ahead since his television broadcast last night when he lashed out at the decline in public morals and attacked *The Times*, the Bishop of Woolwich, the Labour Party and the Welfare State which encouraged people to believe they could get something for nothing.

Tony Benn

Saturday, 27 July 1963

Woke early, but after a good night. I feel a strange reaction. We have worked so hard and so long for the Test Ban and it has (until a few weeks ago) seemed hopeless, that I can hardly yet realise what has happened. When the President gave me (on the telephone) the news, which we had not yet got, I had to go out of the room. I went to tell D[orothy] and burst into tears. I have prayed hard too for this, night after night ...

Harold Macmillan

Thursday, 5 September 1963

I had rather an amusing luncheon party at Chequers today, which has caught the public imagination and come out very well on T.V. The captains of the English and West Indian elevens, who have just concluded a very interesting and sometimes exciting series of Test matches. W.I. won. The English captain (Mr Dexter) is a very nice young chap, and is Conservative candidate for Cardiff East. The W. Indian (Mr Worrell) is charming – quiet and good manners. I had as guests – Sir Learie Constantine (High Commissioner of Jamaica) who [is] a most charming and genial character. He was a great Test match cricketer.

Christopher Soames at 3.* He talked about new agricultural plan, which requires careful negotiation with countries involved. We also had a talk on the general political situation. He wants me to go on but realises that it is not likely we can win again. If I cannot go on (which Soames thinks a lot to ask, since it is not really in my interest) he is either for Butler or Hailsham.

Harold Macmillan

Friday, 18 October 1963

Macmillan resigned this morning and Home was asked to form a government. It is incredible that such a thing should have happened.[†]

Tony Benn

Friday, 22 November 1963

I had been out by myself to see the trade union film by the Boulting Brothers *I'm All Right Jack* – which I had missed in its heyday …

I came back by bus – sat lost in thought and passed the Park West stop by about a mile and a half. Walked back arriving late for dinner and found Cressida[‡] in the dining room having hers. I was about to explain my muddle and expatiate on the brilliance of *I'm All Right Jack* – when she stopped me and said 'Kennedy has been shot – he was killed.' My heart stopped. (Only yesterday I sent him my Romanes lecture.) I felt a personal stab of shock and horror more strongly than I could have thought possible … and with it a sense of terror for the world of which he was the Atlas – the only leader above life-size. His stature, power, courage and judgement gone – the extraordinary hold he had established over Khrushchev by his blend of strength and conciliation … his fight for all the right things – above all else Human Rights for Negroes.

---

*Soames was Minister for Agriculture, Fisheries and Food, and the son-in-law of Winston Churchill.

†On 8 October 1963, Macmillan wrote in his diaries that he had decided to stay on as Prime Minister to fight the next General Election, but on the same day he was taken to King Edward's Hospital for Officers, for emergency prostate surgery, and resigned on grounds of ill-health on 18 October. Lord Home (Sir Alec Douglas-Home) was able to renounce his hereditary earldom (and therefore be eligible to sit in the Commons as Prime Minister) under legislation passed earlier in 1963. This legislation also enabled Tony Benn, who had fought to get rid of the Stansgate peerage inherited from his father, to continue to be an MP.

‡Cressida was Violet Bonham Carter's elder daughter.

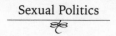

The West is orphaned. The world is orphaned.

Violet Bonham Carter

Saturday, 23 November 1963

In the last years your music has come to mean more and more to me – it shines out as a beacon (how banal I'm becoming!) in, to me at least, a chaotic and barren musical world and I am sure it does for thousands of others as well ... The War Requiem is worth hundreds of Lord Russells and Aldermaston marches and it will surely have the effect which you, possibly subconsciously, have striven for, for you have made articulate the wishes of numberless inarticulate masses.

Letter to Benjamin Britten from William Walton

Saturday, 30 November 1963

It is wonderful not to read the newspapers – except a rapid glance through *The Times*. It makes such a difference. One feels better, mentally and morally, not to be absorbing unconsciously, all that steady stream of falsehood, innuendo, poison which makes up the Press today, apart from purely informative sections. 'Gossip' in one form or another, is the main theme and mainstay of modern journalism. Altho' there are nowadays no servants, we are all regarded as making up a vast 'servants' hall' ...

Harold Macmillan

December 1963
Hampstead Road, London

Visited D Bryce Smith's artists' materials shop, a haunt of my extreme youth. This Euston neighbourhood, once flourishing, in a small Dickensian way, is now in the throes of a huge reconstruction; there are to be overpasses, underpasses, garages and skyscrapers. Meanwhile, little derelict shops are to be pulled down. My old Aladdin's Cave of hot-pressed and rice-paper notebooks still survives, with a lease of ten years to go, but all around is decay.

Cecil Beaton

Friday, 17 January 1964

Kingswood Youth Club, Bristol

About sixty youngsters were there and I don't think most of them wanted to listen to me at all, but the vicar had invited me and they sat there while I talked. As soon as I had finished and the questions had stopped, they leapt up and got on with their dancing and I was sorry I had accepted. I sometimes wonder if it is true that young people are supporting us. They were so defeatist about Britain and thought nothing could be done to improve things.

Tony Benn

Sunday, 9 February 1964

A pub crawl of the East End, a dozen of us in three cars; Chinese restaurant; only faintly amusing décor in the pubs; amazing to see the prosperity of the dockers, all well dressed, wearing starched collars and blue suits.

A pity I see so little of this part of London which has a historical grandeur completely lacking in the bourgeois prettiness of Kensington.

Cecil Beaton

Sunday, 1 March 1964

I follow up the news in rather a detached and desultory way. Everything is held up by the British and American elections, and till these things have taken place, there can be no real negotiation with Russia. Africa is having growing pains everywhere as was to be expected. S. Rhodesia is a problem because I fear Field will want to bring the independence issue to a crisis before the British election. Cyprus is insoluble and the Archbishop weak and crooked.*

Harold Macmillan

*Winston Field was Prime Minister of Southern Rhodesia from 1962 to 1964. Archbishop Makarios was the first President of the Republic of Cyprus following independence from Britain in 1960.

Thursday, 25 June 1964

Les Avants, Switzerland

Feeling an urge for a slightly heavier and grander car than the dear Triumph Herald, I've bought myself a perfectly beautiful Mercedes Benz – only 38,000 francs (£3,000) second-hand and in perfect condition. The price of a new one is £5,300. I'm collecting this treasure tomorrow ...

Now that I am a bona fide Swiss resident, all moneys earned by me will be paid to me here into Credit Suisse on which I shall pay 7.4 per cent tax. At the moment I am paying 50 per cent company tax in England.

Noël Coward

Sunday, 13 September 1964

I have read the Labour manifesto. It is rather cleverly directed to a) the young b) the moderate vote. There is very little 'Socialism' in it. If Baldwin were alive he would be gratified to see how both parties have moved to the Centre. But I suspect Wilson. He covers up a lot of dangerous proposals with smooth ambiguities. Our manifesto comes out this week ...

Harold Macmillan

Monday, 19 October 1964

Following the General Election

Up early and still waiting for the phone and still hearing of other people going to Downing Street. I had completely given up hope again. Then at 10.55 am the phone rang and I was summoned.

There was a huge crowd of photographers outside Number 10. I shook Harold by the hand and we had a chat about the situation and then he said 'By the way I want you to take the Post Office ... in about eighteen months I shall be reshuffling the Government and you will be in the Cabinet.'

I went to a call box and phoned Mother, came home and after lunch telephoned the Post Office and asked for the Postmaster General's office. 'What's your name,' asked a gruff voice. I gave it and a few minutes later came a different and oily voice: 'Good afternoon, PMG.

I think the DG wants to speak to you.' A minute later the Director-General came on the phone, said he had a lunch appointment and would come to see me at 3 o'clock.

I said I would like a car to take me there immediately.

Tony Benn

Tuesday, 27 October 1964

The new Government measures have been announced. It is not stop and go, we are told. But it amounts to 15% on all imported goods, excluding Food. (What a curious reflection on the great Free Trade and Protection controversies of the past.) This is supposed to damp down imports and must do so to some extent.

Wilson presents all this with great skill, like Kennedy, whom he is trying to imitate. Govt announcements on TV (not in Parl), 'the fireside chat' etc.

Harold Macmillan

Saturday, 5 December 1964

The telephone answering machine is an absolute God-send. I sit in the office and hear the thing ringing and ringing and then the machine answers and the telephone stops ... it gives me exactly the privacy I need.

Tony Benn

1965 (undated)

How different the youth of today (to my Edwardian childhood). David Hockney arrived (to be painted) on his way from Bristol. He turned up in his car wearing the thinnest of synthetic windbreakers over a T-shirt. 'Noh, I'm not corld. Is it corld outside? I get into my car and the heat's automatically on and I get out at the plaice I arrive at. You may think my cappe is a bit daft but I bought ert at Arrods because I wasn't looking whaire I was gohin and I knocked over all the hat stall and I put the mun to so mooch trooble I thought ah moost buy sommut!'

It staggers me how this young man can be so at home in the world.

When *I* first went to America I was too scared to ask a policeman which was up or down town.

Cecil Beaton

Monday, 4 January 1965

Defence, colour television, Concorde, rocket development – these are all issues raising economic considerations that reveal this country's basic inability to stay in the big league. We just can't afford it. The real choice is – do we go in with Europe or do we become an American satellite? Without a conscious decision being taken the latter course is being followed everywhere.

In reality the choice lies between Britain as an island and US protectorate, or Britain as a full member of the Six, followed by a wider European federation. I was always against the Common Market but the reality of our isolation is being borne in on me all the time.

Tony Benn

Sunday, 24 January 1965

Altho' the end has been inevitable since the stroke a fortnight ago, yet the shock is great. England without Winston! It seems impossible. Not even the oldest of us can remember England without him as a considerable figure. Church at 11. I read Ecclesiasticus [*sic*] and Corinthians instead of the regular lesson.

Harold Macmillan

Tuesday, 26 January 1965

A crucial Cabinet, the first after the Leyton by-election result. The only official item on the agenda was Sir Winston Churchill – the discussion about his funeral arrangements was soon dealt with. And then for the first time since we became a Government, Sir Burke Trend and the other Cabinet secretaries were asked to leave the room.

It was a council of war. Harold was relaxed as usual but he did suggest that we must consider our whole strategy in the light of Leyton and Nuneaton.*

---

*The Labour candidate at the Leyton (East London) by-election was Patrick

I suggested that the trouble was that we had not been able to get a clear message across. What was it we were trying to say to the people? Were we offering them blood, sweat and tears? With hope for better things in, say, two years' time? If this was so this didn't tally with our policy on [increasing] MPs' salaries or Cabinet ones either. You couldn't make that kind of appeal while making things more comfortable for yourself.

George Brown jumped in with a now typically pragmatic and fighting speech. He said vigorously that we had been guilty of too much morality and not enough politics. (Lord Longford nearly swooned at this. He said limply that he hoped he had misheard the First Secretary, but George waved him airily aside.) Here we were with a majority of three which could be undermined at any moment by one of our Members falling under a bus.

Barbara Castle

Wednesday, 27 January 1965

I took all the children to see the lying-in-state. They were much impressed, except for Joshua, aged seven, who thought we were going to 'Lyon's Steak' which he believed to be a restaurant. He was delighted as he is very fond of steak.

When he saw Westminster Hall he couldn't understand and said he knew there was a coffin under the flag, but he clearly didn't know what a coffin was or what it contained. The thing that made the biggest impression on him was the sight of the television cameras.

Tony Benn

Monday, 22 February 1965

Harold opened [Cabinet] with a very solemn statement about Tony Howard's article in the *Sunday Times*. He said the paper had thrown down a challenge to the Government by the creation of a 'Whitehall correspondent'. 'We can't recognise any such Whitehall animal. I have

Gordon-Walker, who had lost his Smethwick seat at the General Election of 1964 (where immigration and race played a large part). Gordon-Walker then lost Leyton (a safe Labour seat) to the Conservatives. The by-election in Nuneaton had been created for Frank Cousins, the General Secretary of the TGWU, who held it but with a much reduced majority.

instructed Ministers not to see this journalist. In spite of this, two Ministers at least did ... This is a very dangerous man doing a very dangerous job.'

Barbara Castle

Thursday, 4 March 1965

We managed to spend three-quarters of an hour discussing the creation of the new premises at Chelsea for the National Army Museum. I doodled through the endless discussion. Tony Crosland complained to me: 'There are twenty ministers debating this. If only there had been as much heat generated over Vietnam.' I retorted acidly, 'The Parkinson's Law of words operates in this Cabinet. Words expand to fill the time available for them. The length of these meetings is purely dictated by the PM's engagements.' He grinned agreement.

Barbara Castle

Wednesday, 24 March 1965

The Americans have been dropping 'gas' (really a form of tear-gas) bombs in Vietnam. This has upset the Government benches – at least below the Gangway ... Wilson and the Foreign Secretary [Michael Stewart] are giving the Americans 'unswerving support.' Do they remember Suez? Happily the United Nations is now prevented from any action because of the great dispute about 'subscriptions', and voting.*

Harold Macmillan

Wednesday 26 May 1965
Lunch at 10 Downing Street

In a little dining room where an Irish maid slammed down in front of me a plate with a piece of steak, two veg and a bit of cold salad. On the table were two tins of Skol beer, which I don't like. Harold saw this and while he took water, he gave me a glass of claret. After lunch we

---

*Countries in arrears on their UN subscriptions were not allowed to vote in the General Assembly. There were so many in arrears at this time that the General Assembly was ineffective.

went along to his little sitting-room and there he offered me a glass of brandy which he likes very much. I refused the brandy and accepted a second glass of claret.

Nothing could be more deeply petit bourgeois than the way he lives in those crowded little servants' quarters up there. But the fact that he doesn't, unlike Sir Alec Douglas-Home, use the state rooms for sitting in after dinner is only a proof that he is not corrupted by his new station in life ...

He had got me there to tell me his plans about housing. He has decided that all other social services must be cut back in order to have a magnificent housing drive and bring the annual production of houses up to 500,000 by 1970.

'We'll make housing the most popular single thing this government does ... We won't build another single mile of road if a cut-back is necessary in order to get that half-million houses a year. That's what I believe in,' he said.

Richard Crossman

Tuesday, 15 June 1965

Went to Cabinet determined to have a showdown about Vietnam. Opinion is mounting against the Americans as Johnson puts in thousands more ground troops and abandons all pretence that the Americans are there merely to 'advise.'

Over coffee at the 'Welsh' table I sounded out the boys about the Beatles' MBEs. The reaction was wholly unfavourable, the word 'gimmick' being prominent. This ploy of Harold's seems to have boomeranged ... He seems to have a streak of vulgarity which is also part of his strength.

Barbara Castle

Monday, 2 August 1965

I went up early to London and after an hour or so at the office, arrived at [Church House] Hall at 11.50. When I went in, just after Alec, they all stood up and clapped as in old days. The business was rather long – an hour – but very dignified. There were tributes to Alec, moved by Lord Carrington and seconded and supported. The motion of confidence in

Heath was again moved by Carrington and seconded (in an excellent speech) by Maudling.

The economic situation gets worse. A loss of gold last month,* which the authorities put at £50m and everyone believes (apart from juggling with figures) to be £150m ...

Harold Macmillan

Friday, 1 October 1965

To the Chinese Embassy to celebrate the anniversary of the liberation of China by the Communist regime. It was a splendid party and clearly the Chinese are moving more and more into the diplomatic world. I talked to the Labour candidate from Luton, who told me that he had been in China and was much impressed by the genuine participation of top people in the life of the community. He thought the rule that top management had to spend one day a week doing manual labour was a good one and I wish I could introduce it into the Post Office. But somehow I don't see myself as a cleaner or a postman without the thing becoming a huge press gimmick.

Tony Benn

Thursday, 23 December–Wednesday, 29 December 1965

Paper full of pictures of me. My appointment the sensation. The fact that I couldn't drive had almost, as Harold predicted when I tried to use this as an argument against appointing me, turned out to be an asset. Ted and I drove back to London so that I could kiss hands. Then into the Overseas Development Ministry with Tony Greenwood to introduce him and say my last farewells. I could hardly tear myself away from my beloved desk.

Back to London to the press mobs waiting for me outside the Ministry of Transport ... The place seemed intimidatingly masculine, the liftmen a bit gruff, and I noted there was no welcoming [Permanent Secretary] waiting at the door to greet me as Andrew had done when I

---

* Britain was at this time a member of the Gold Pool with the United States and six other European nations. The intention of the Pool was to allow sales of gold reserves amongst the member states in order to regulate the international gold price and maintain the stable exchange rates, as agreed at Bretton Woods in 1944. The Pool collapsed in 1968.

first went to ODM. But undeterred I smiled at everyone and was told afterwards that I was the first Minister of Transport ever to be seen smiling in the place.

Barbara Castle

Sunday, 9 January 1966

I have spent 3 days – Weds, Thurs, and Friday – preparing a TV talk or interview, which is to be released in time of publication of my first volume [of autobiography].

A vast quantity of engineers, 'technicians', secretaries, producers etc. arrived ... they all left on Friday about tea-time and I retired to bed, absolutely exhausted. With their technique, picture and words are on the same film or reel. Out of all this, 50 minutes or so are selected. I have received a modest fee for all this, but have really submitted to it in order to help my publishers ...

Harold Macmillan

Sunday, 6 February 1966
Chequers, Buckinghamshire

Peter Shore came to collect me to drive me down.

The place was crowded with the whole Cabinet and National Executive – about sixty in all.

Jim Callaghan said that the debt problem was not insoluble but he did not expect that the growth rate could be up to 4 per cent before 1968/9. He asked us not to be impatient and said we would have to have priorities within the public sector. He warned us that public expenditure was going up by 9 per cent this year ... He predicted that tax rates might have to go up and said that personal taxation was already too high.

After lunch Dick Crossman made a most effective speech about the need for a policy covering the whole physical environment and the need to share social furniture between different groups. He thought it was ludicrous to have a large playing field for a school and then find the local authority wanted more open space for general recreation etc.

Barbara then made a speech about transport in which she said that we must democratise car ownership and extend it more widely, spend more on the roads and get the physical integration of freight traffic on rail and road.

Crosland said a word about school building and how difficult it was to provide new schools to replace old ones with his present budget. He broadened it out to say that we needed to have a poverty programme covering housing, social services and education under a separate agency – rather taking a leaf out of President Johnson's book.

Tony Benn

Wednesday, 30 March 1966
Birch Grove, Sussex

Both Heath and Wilson made good final broadcasts – at least so people say. I have not looked at any TV. Happily we have not got the instrument at Birch Grove (except in the Servants' Hall). I fear a landslide to Labour.

Harold Macmillan

Macmillan's fears were confirmed at the General Election of 31 March 1966, when the Labour Party's overall majority in the Commons went up to 96, having been 4 at the Election eighteen months earlier.

Friday, 29 April 1966

I had a phone call from a man in Devon. He said that he had been unable to buy any 3d stamps the previous night, so instead bought 6d stamps and cut them in half with scissors and would I (as Postmaster General) authorise them to go through the post. I was helpful but said that I had no authority to do this and that he should have put the 6d stamps on and then written to me for a refund. Later I discovered that in fact he was a stamp dealer and actually sent out 600 of these half-stamps which he now claims are worth £15 a piece. I think he ought to be prosecuted.

Tony Benn

Tuesday, 3 May 1966

Lunch with Beeching* in his very elegant man-servanted house in Smith Square. (Nothing simple or suburban here.) An excellent lunch of scampi, lamb and strawberries accompanied by really superb wines. We talked transport policy all the time, Beeching laying down the law with an arrogance that comes, I suspect, from a clear mind that sees a logical answer to a situation and cannot tolerate any modification of it to meet human frailty. Though intellectually impressed by him I am glad now we didn't put him in charge of drawing up an 'integrated' transport policy as once mooted. It was typical of Beeching that, having contradicted everything I said during the meal, he then said abruptly, 'But don't think I am against everything you have done. I think you have done well to strengthen the economic side of the Ministry and are quite right to refuse to reconstitute the British Transport Commission,' and offered to help me in any way he could as he showed me the door.

Barbara Castle

Tuesday, 24 May 1966

I met all three rail unions at British Railways' headquarters.

My heart was in my mouth because I knew that [my policy] meant the closure of 3,000 more miles of lines, although the outcome would be a network of 11,000 route miles, instead of the 8,000 proposed in the second Beeching Report.

I told them I had got my colleagues' agreement to the survey into railway finances and stressed this meant a subsidy – open and overt – to the railways, something we had refused to other nationalised industries like coal. I then asked for questions. There was a long silence while I waited, hardly daring to breathe. At last Sid [Greene, National Union of Railwaymen Secretary] said slowly, 'I am very pleased with what we have heard. Clearly there is going to be a very good future for the men who are left in the system. Our trouble is , as I expect you know, with the men who will not have a place in it ... nonetheless I

---

* Dr Richard Beeching was Chairman of British Rail. His name was synonymous with the drastic reduction in railways lines and services across the country in favour of road transport. The policy was introduced under earlier Conservative governments, but Barbara Castle, then Labour's Minister of Transport, partly continued the policy.

am pleased with what we have heard and not least for the fact that we have had it all explained to us so fully in this way ...'

Barbara Castle

Wednesday, 29 June 1966

I spent the day at Peterborough clearing up another of the New Town entanglements Dame Evelyn [Sharp, the senior civil servant at Housing] left behind.

As we motored back to London I switched on the wireless and heard that the [seamen's] strike had been called off. So Harold has won yet another of his 'extra' victories. It was good enough to get the strike settled without giving anything away; it was even better to get it called off on the day after having denounced the communists in the union and challenged them to do their worst.

In the evening I dined with John Silkin in the House ... but despite Harold's tremendous victory Silkin and I found a sense of discomfort in the Members' dining room. The PM's operation had been too McCarthyite for the taste of our new backbenchers; the naming of names had been gratuitous and unnecessary.

Richard Crossman

Wednesday, 29 June 1966

To the Commons where Harold Wilson dissociated the Government from the American bombing of Haiphong and Hanoi. Heath criticised him for it and the left was less than generous. Very few people realised the immense significance of this act of dissociation.

Tony Benn

Thursday, 30 June 1966

[At Cabinet] I asked about press reports to the effect that we were hell bent on getting into the Common Market and it was now only a question of a few details. Harold said *The Times* report was wrong.

We turned to Concorde – a classic example of Tory incompetence. The cost of our share has risen to £250m. Nobody knew whether the sonic bang would affect sales; it might do so disastrously whereas we were relying on selling 150 of the planes. The Attorney General reported that we had no legal let-out; the treaty left us no loophole. So we might face compensation claims as expensive as staying in.

What the hell could we do? The only hope was that the French were as worried as we were about rising costs. It was agreed that Harold should sound them out during Pompidou's visit.

Barbara Castle

Sunday, 24 July 1966

Another week behind us and certainly the crisis has deepened. We have had during this week the destruction of the Wilson myth in the public eye and, even more, in my own private eye.

I try and reflect on why all this hit us. Harold, of course, is anxious to say that the seamen's strike was the cause of the trouble, and it is true that the strike was a great blow. But one has got to go right back to the SET budget which was the first absolutely fatal mistake.* Instead of doing what we expected him to do and imposing the austerity budget we are now getting in July, he and Callaghan avoided unpopularity (and helped to win the municipal elections) by introducing the gimmickry of the SET. The fact that the new tax would only operate as a deflater from September left five months of the year in which the price and wage inflation could run wild.

Richard Crossman

Thursday, 8 September 1966

Coventry East constituency

I spent the morning in Coventry at a meeting with the directors of the Standard Motor Works that I'd arranged many months before. I wondered whether to keep this engagement but am glad I did. The directors told me that they are going to put a lot of their men on short time but that they are confident that business is expanding and that all

---

*The reference to the National Union of Seamen's strike is the disruption caused and a state of emergency called during May–June 1966. Wilson alleged that the dispute was provoked by Communist elements in the union determined to bring down the government. The other 'fatal mistake' Crossman refers to is the imposition of Selective Employment Tax on the service sector but not on manufacturing, with a view to encouraging investment in the latter.

the men will be back at work in the spring and this is why they aren't bothering with any redundancy payments.*

Richard Crossman

Thursday, 22 September–Friday, 23 September 1966
Middlesex Hospital

To the hospital to see Law† ... A charming young female Dr got up from a table where she was writing and took me into her room. She told me that Law's temp was 101. She had had antibiotics but could she fight this infection which had congested one part of her lung, with her meagre reserves of strength? ...

I took her hand and tried vainly to get through to her ... I left her with an aching heart – only thankful that she was not suffering. That night when I was sitting in the drawing-room the telephone rang and the Sister told me she had 'passed peacefully away' at 11 o'clock. It was the end – of a life of selfless and devoted help and service to me and mine. For the last 44 years she has given herself to us – to me. Was I worthy of it?

Friday: Strange stunned night and all day today I have been expecting to see dear Law run into the room and ask 'Can I do anything for you?'

Violet Bonham Carter

Sunday, 23 October 1966

I'll just wind up my account of Chequers ... I suppose we clarified the difference between the Europeans (in Cabinet), who are really committed to getting in as soon as they can, and the much less united antis ... I think I managed to get across, that withdrawal from our East of Suez commitments is essential whether we enter the Market or not. It is an illusion that we could remain Great Britain by becoming a member of the EEC.

---

*Standard Motor Company was at this time a subsidiary of Leyland Motors Ltd, based at Canley in Coventry. By the end of 1966 they were to declare 12,500 car workers redundant and other car firms were to introduce short-time working.
† Rose Law, Violet Bonham Carter's long-serving maid. Violet had planned to go to visit her daughter and son-in-law, Jo Grimond, in Orkney and did not attend the funeral.

There's one other very important thing I must add about the Chequers weekend. It was interrupted by more than one big external event. As well as the escape of George Blake from Wormwood Scrubs* on Friday night there was the disaster at Aberfan, the Welsh valley where a huge coal tip broke away and ran over a school killing hundreds of children. Harold Wilson had gone straight down there by helicopter … I feel the whole thing has been emotionally exploited by the BBC in the most terrible and extravagant way. But I have no doubt that Harold Wilson was profoundly moved. The tragedy gave a macabre background to the weekend.

Richard Crossman

Monday, 14 November 1966

The Guildhall dinner. Harold had passed round the word that Ministers should only wear black tie – a gesture that the City didn't appreciate. Harold's speech was received with only perfunctory applause, despite his warm words about the Common Market.

By the end of the meal I was nauseated by all the lavishness: gold microphones among the gold plate; Dr Ramsey, the Archbishop of Canterbury proving himself a sycophantic servant of the Establishment in moving the toast to the Late Lord Mayor. Gerald Gardiner wasn't much better: 'A lot of things need modernizing or improving in Britain today. The one institution which is quite incapable of improvement is the Lord Mayor's banquet.' I suddenly wondered what we were all doing there among our enemies.

Barbara Castle

Thursday, 22 December 1966

At Cabinet I saved the Harrier vertical take-off jet, one of the most brilliant aeronautical innovations, which Denis Healey always tries to cancel on every possible occasion.

The Rootes–Chrysler deal[†] was approved by the Cabinet with

---

*George Blake was a British double-agent, who spied for the Soviet Union. After escaping from prison, he fled to Moscow where he was received as a national hero and retired on a KGB pension.
† The takeover of the British motor company, Rootes, by the American company, Chrysler.

general commendation. I tried to promote the idea of a special concession on electrical cars by taking off the tax and purchase tax so as to
encourage their development.

In the evening I did a long and – given my limited knowledge of
French – painful broadcast for the BBC French Service.

Tony Benn

Thursday, 19 January 1967

A very brief Cabinet. Harold and George [Brown] reported on their
visit to Italy on their Common Market tour. George said the talks
about our joining the EEC had gone as well as could be expected and
indeed rather better.

I reported what I had been told in Germany ... namely that de
Gaulle was determined not to have us in and that the Five* would not
be willing to risk disrupting the Common Market by defying him. In
other words we were wasting our time as long as de Gaulle was there.
There was a moment's hostile silence, then Harold said 'Well, Paris
will show.'

Barbara Castle

Thursday, 26 January 1967

Spent a quiet day before my Israeli dinner, at which I am the Guest of
Honour ... I was amazed by the emphasis on Jewish Nationalism – a
note struck again and again in the speeches. Had they been non-Jewish
English speakers I should have described them as extreme Jingoes. My
turn finally came and I spoke for about ten minutes stressing *Internationalism* (that after all was the object of the dinner).

Violet Bonham Carter

Wednesday, 15 February 1967

Went for a walk this morning. Weather cold, bright. A wind blew grit
about. Spent most of the time wiping running eyes with my handker-
chief. Kenneth [Orton's lover] went to have his passport photograph

---

*The Common Market (EEC) in 1967 comprised France, Germany, Italy, Belgium,
Luxembourg and the Netherlands.

taken. He had it done by polaroid camera. It cost 7s 6d for two. No negatives. I'd like a Polaroid camera. Most useful for taking porno-graphic pictures, I should say. We went to the record shop to enquire whether the new Beatles' single is out. It won't be on sale till Friday.

Watched a programme called *Three After Six* on television. It's just three middle-class people discussing 'problems' posed in the newspa-pers. Words like 'psychological aspects' and 'social workers' and 'the social and legal aspects of the case' and 'this poses great problems for the sociologist' abound in the programme. They discussed the proposed amendments to the abortion laws. Kept saying what is best for the 'mother' and 'of course, for the unborn child.' As though anyone in their right minds would consider the unborn child. Any more than one would consider the feeling of a tumour or cancer. How I hate the liberal-minded, smooth, middle-class, 'broad-minded', 'with-it' woman.

Joe Orton

Friday, 3 March 1967

A deliriously happy – as well as interesting – day. I did my oft-postponed helicopter tour of the Tilbury dock development. The Port of London Authority boys were delighted with my open terminals success, and the Director General told me the decision had come just in time. They could now go ahead with the freightliner terminal they are going to build inside the docks ready for the opening of the United States Line container dock next summer.

Barbara Castle

Wednesday, 10 May 1967

In the evening went to the state banquet at the Royal Naval College, Greenwich, for King Faisal of Saudi Arabia.

Had to hurry back to vote in the Common Market debate in the House and there was a massive vote in favour of application. Almost all the Tories and the majority of Labour MPs were in favour.

Tony Benn

Thursday, 22 June 1967

At Cabinet Harold reported on his visit to de Gaulle. He said de Gaulle was 'terribly terribly depressed and terribly terribly friendly.' He had talked in an apocalyptic way about his belief that we were heading for a third world war: there was no possibility of a middle east settlement without a Vietnam settlement. All in all de Gaulle had seemed more bored than hostile, and Harold was now more optimistic about our chances of getting into the Six.

Barbara Castle

June 1967

Reddish House, Wiltshire

Monday morning my breakfast is brought in – tea, charcoal biscuits, yogourt and the papers. I am looking out of the window at the green scene when I hear that war has started in the Middle East. Israel and Egypt are each saying the other was the first to be the aggressor.

The awful sinking dread surged through the nape of the neck to the solar plexus. At once one thinks, not of the suffering, the pain, the killings in the far land but, selfishly, of home and one-self. If the war spreads we are likely to become involved, even if only remotely, by, say, the rationing of fuel. It seems such a little time ago that we were doing all we could to scrounge an extra can of petrol. But the continual dread … the encroaching anxiety.

Cecil Beaton

Monday, 3 July 1967

This evening at ten prompt we started the all-night sitting on the report stage of the Bill* … The Chief (Whip) and I spent the night going round the lobbies and encouraging the troops.

Walking back to Vincent Square with Tam Dalyell† on a lovely clear morning we discussed the effect of getting the 'Buggers' Bill' through.

---

*The Sexual Offences Act 1967, under which homosexual acts in private between two men over the age of twenty-one ceased to be a crime in England and Wales. It remained a crime in Scotland until 1980.
†Tam Dalyell served as Labour MP for West Lothian from 1962 to 1983 (then as MP for Linlithgow until 2005). He was Richard Crossman's Parliamentary Private Secretary and shared a house in London.

Frankly it's an extremely unpleasant bill and I myself didn't like it. It may well be twenty years ahead of public opinion; certainly working class people in the north jeer at their Members at the weekend and ask them why they're looking after the buggers at Westminster instead of looking after the unemployed at home. It has gone down very badly that the Labour Party should be associated with such a bill. On the other hand we agreed that this had a boomerang effect in creating a positive demand for the Abortion Bill and it's clearer and clearer that this will [be] a pretty popular measure, especially among working-class women.

Richard Crossman

Tuesday, 18 July 1967

After ten o'clock we had an all-night sitting on the Coal Industry Order, specially arranged for the miners' group of MPs ... By the end of the night there were only two or three Tories present and miners' MPs were able to have the whole House of Commons to themselves for the protest which they wanted to make before accepting their fate.

It was a cosy occasion but pathetic because it was clear that provided they could make their protest these miners felt that they were bound to support the Government in an action which really meant the destruction of the mining industry. What these miners' MPs showed was a not very edifying loyalty, because people should not be as loyal as that to a Government which is causing the total ruin of their industry.

Richard Crossman

Tuesday, 18 July 1967

Enjoyed myself in the transport debate and my speech delighted the troops. My 'shadow' Peter Walker did me a good turn by presenting me as the nationalising bogey. Slipped out during the debate to see Frank Cousins and Tonge, chairman of the port employers, about the problem of redundancy that faces the industry as a result of containerisation. I asked Tonge point-blank what he thought about nationalisation of the docks. He hesitated, then said, 'God help me if this ever gets out, but I believe it is essential. Containerisation will make the industry capital intensive instead of labour intensive and this calls for central decisions which only Government can make.'

I wrote this down and handed it to Stephen [Swingler, junior minister for Transport] for his winding up speech (without of course mentioning Tonge).

As Stephen faithfully read out Tonge's exact words, the Tories shouted 'Rubbish!' What a pity we couldn't tell them where the remarks came from!

Barbara Castle

Tuesday, 10 October 1967

Balmoral

Martin Charteris (the Queen's Assistant Secretary) was at the front of the house waiting to take us round to the equerry's entrance at the side ... he told us what he'd laid on for the afternoon and showed us the geography of the house before taking us out for a little walk in the garden to see the autumn flowers. We learnt that there are twelve London policemen up there as well as a whole section of the London Post Office.

This week the Queen is alone, since the children are at school and the Duke is away on business. Apparently she enjoys this since what she really enjoys is riding. Indeed she was out riding when we arrived and we saw her return by the back entrance.

[After the Privy Council] we moved into the next room for drinks and here she explained (she didn't of course apologise) why she was twelve minutes late for the Council. When she was furthest from the house her horse had got a stone in its foot. 'One always carries one of those penknives, doesn't one, as an instrument for taking out stones, but today was the one day I didn't have it.' Then she mentioned that the horse she was riding was a Russian horse which Bulganin gave her on his visit. 'These Russian horses,' she said, 'are very obstinate. Some weeks ago Margaret took this horse out and had gone over six bridges and at the seventh bridge it had refused, although it was exactly like the others. It just wouldn't budge. Hours later the rest of the family had gone out and found Margaret and the horse standing by the bridge with the horse still mutinous.'

Over lunch I started to discuss the Philby story, which had

dominated all the Sunday papers, and asked whether she has read it. She said 'No, she didn't read that kind of thing.'*

Richard Crossman

Thursday, 12 October–Friday, 13 October 1967

A mad rush to get my train to the North West. James Drake, the new head of the Road Construction Unit (RCU) had come up to London in order to travel with me. He is a gloriously unpolished Northerner of blunt speech in a broad Lancashire accent, obsessed with roads and a real go-getter.

A most successful tour. It was a great moment to get out into the Pennines along the route of the M62 and to see, up in the hills, a Yorkshire RCU crane on the skyline …

This, the first east–west motorway, will revolutionise east–west links. I intend that there shall be more of these cross routes, instead of the endless radial routes into London. After a day talking to Drake I can really begin to see how I can get better planning and priorities into the roads programme.

A scare about a bomb in my sleeper.† The Preston CID were at the station to see me safely aboard. I slept well.

Barbara Castle

Monday, 23 October 1967

One of the biggest blows in the [forthcoming Leicester South West] by-election‡ has been the introduction of Barbara's breathalyser.

It is regarded as an extremely unpleasant attack on working-class drinkers. We are in danger of becoming known as the government which stops what the working classes really want. The Government which introduces the breathalyser is as unpopular with motor-car drivers as the Government which stops pirate radio stations is with the younger generation who listen to pop music. Today they had another

---

* *My Silent War*, the autobiography of Kim Philby, a British double-agent spying for the Russians, had featured in many papers, including a lead article in the *Sunday Times* on 8 October 1967.
† See entry for 23 October 1967 below.
‡ Polls presumably showed a preference for Conservatives who won the seat from Labour; a factor was considered to be the introduction of Barbara Castle's new drink-driving breathalyser test over which she was subjected to several bomb threats.

grouse about the Government – the announcement that we were going to stop coupons in cigarette cartons.

Richard Crossman

Saturday, 4 November 1967
Israel

My last day – alas! ... We started off on our last Refugee expedition to a place called Kalandia [a refugee camp near Ramallah]. It was in a way the most repaying of all. I did see families of real 'refugees' – who had been driven by the war from their homes 35 kilometres off and had walked the whole way with their small children. One very young looking mother had a baby in arms and several 'toddlers' with sweet faces and large brown eyes – very beautiful and expressive ...

I was wrung by their plight and asked the head of the Camp – a nice Arab – to tell the young mother with the baby how deeply I sympathised with her – and how beautiful I thought her children were. She very touchingly took my hand and kissed it – then placed it on her forehead. I felt helpless in the face of human tragedy.

No two peoples could have less mutual understanding or compatibility than the Arabs and the Jews.

Violet Bonham Carter

Saturday, 18 November 1967

Devaluation from $2.80 to $2.40 announced. A great moment of defeat for the Government.

The following day Wilson did his absurd broadcast on television saying 'The pound in your pocket won't be devalued.'

Tony Benn

Thursday, 23 November 1967

The rumours are already circulating about a takeover bid for Harold's job by Jim [Callaghan]. This is given weight by an astonishing article in *The Times* business news by Peter Jay, its economic editor, the most distorted account of the past three years I have ever read. Its theme is that Harold was an opponent of devaluation all along and even suppressed reports by his advisers in order to prevent the Cabinet discussing it.

Well this does not agree with my memory of the facts. And of course Peter Jay is married to Jim's daughter. There is no doubt that Jim sees himself at the very least as the Crown-Prince again.

Barbara Castle

Monday, 11 December 1967

To Paris in the HS125.* Collected Sir Patrick Reilly, the Ambassador, in Paris and went to Toulouse for the roll-out of the 002 Concorde. It was icy cold.

I didn't speak in French but I did say that as a tribute to this occasion we would now in future have a British Concord which would be spelt with an 'e.' There was great cheering. I said, 'That is "e" for excellence, "E" for England and "e" for *entente cordiale.'* This went down very well.

In fact there was a hell of a row about this ... I realised that this wasn't taken as a joke. I had an angry letter from a man who said 'I live in Scotland and you talk about "E" for England but part of Concorde is made in Scotland.' I wrote back and said that it was also 'E' for Ecosse – and I might have added 'e' for extravagance and 'e' for escalation as well!

I then discovered that the British Concorde had always been spelt with an 'e' but after the French vetoed British entry into the Common Market in the early sixties, the Government gave an order that Concorde was to drop the 'e.' So I had only reinstated the original spelling.

It was nice to see Concorde out of the hangar.

Tony Benn

Friday, 5 January 1968
Reddish House, Wiltshire

The building alterations were considered to be of a minor character until the men started to hack down an inside wall. Then one thing led to another.

The cisterns in the attic were about to burst and had to be replaced.

* A corporate jet produced by Hawker Siddeley. In 1977 the company became part of the nationalised British Aerospace.

When the faulty ones were brought down they were found to be filled with the bones of rats, birds, cats, and other animals, and with horror, we realised that for years we had been drinking the water in which these bodies had been decomposing.

Now, we are told that the roof above the garage may fall in any day, that certain walls are being pushed out too far, and that a perilously leaning chimney stack must be dismantled, brick by brick and put back again.

All this is a very boring way of spending a lot of money at a time when the country has been brought to economic chaos, and we are all fearful of what the new Labour Chancellor* may introduce in the way of taxes, squeezes and restrictions.

Cecil Beaton

Friday, 16 February 1968
Blackburn constituency

I positively enjoy my visits to Blackburn, despite the physical strain. I come down to earth with such a healthy bump. Indeed as I get out at Blackburn to walk across to the White Bull I wonder what reception I will get from the ordinary man and woman who are not at this moment exactly enamoured of the government.

Interestingly there are two topics which dominate all these conversations: my drink-and-driving Bill, and 'colour.' Four times during the day people (most of them Labour) said to me, 'I've no colour prejudice myself but …'

Barbara Castle

Monday, 4 March 1968

I went on … to George Weidenfeld's dinner.

I found myself engaged in a furious discussion about immigration. On this issue the whole of the London intelligentsia – well-educated public opinion, people who read the weeklies, the *Guardian* and *The Times*, every virtuous person and of course the Churches – are united in

---

* Roy Jenkins had taken over following Jim Callaghan's resignation in November 1967. A sharp rise in international oil prices and the UK dock strike had exacerbated economic woes and led to the devaluation of the pound.

denouncing the Immigration Act* as the most shameful and disgraceful Act of any government. I know it's nothing of the kind. I feel deeply what Perry Worsthorne said in the *Sunday Telegraph* – namely that we were right to push the Act through Parliament. We may have done it clumsily but we had to do this job and there is no public opposition to it. On the contrary there is overwhelming public approval and the intellectuals who were denouncing it this evening are a small minority.

Richard Crossman

Friday, 15 March 1968

Just before I went to bed I heard that George Brown had resigned and that Michael Stewart had been put in his place. So that is the end of Brown's tenure at the Foreign Office. It began with a threatened resignation because we didn't devalue and ended with a real resignation arising out of the consequences of devaluation.[†]

He is a person of extraordinary intellect, courage and ability but his instability is such that it is impossible to have him in a government. His resignation also raises the question of his deputy leadership of the party.

Tony Benn

Friday, 22 March 1968
Birmingham

A brilliantly sunny morning. At one viaduct which I was due to inspect a demonstration of road hauliers and drivers was waiting for me, banners aloft, with the slogan 'HANDS OFF ROAD TRANPORT'. I, of course, was whisked on to the road works by the officials accompanying me but [my team] got together, arranged for a site office to be made available for me and invited the demonstrators to depute ten men to talk to me.

Men, banners, photographers, reporters and I crowded into the small shed. One of the hauliers offered me a cigarette, another hoisted

---

*The Act imposed restrictions on the granting of British citizenship to 'Kenyan Asians', i.e. people from the Indian subcontinent who had settled in Kenya (and who on Kenyan Independence were given the right to choose UK citizenship – about 100,000 in February 1968). In early 1968 the Kenyan government started to give job and business priority to Kenyan citizens.
† The closing of the gold market.

me on to the table where I sat showing my knees. They crowded eagerly around me to pose for a photograph and with that instinct of mine I whisked one arm round the neck of the chief road haulier and the other round the neck of the lorry driver. The employer leaned his cheek against mine and cooed happily 'My wife will divorce me when she sees this.' I then turned out the photographers, lit my cigarette and got down to talking with the men in the friendliest possible way, reporters listening, trying to alleviate their fears about the reduction in drivers' hours.

Barbara Castle

April 1968

Lunch with the Queen Mother

The other guests arrived: Roy Strong in a psychedelic tie; Kirsty Hesketh, hatless and dressed by Courreges like a child's idea of a primrose; Leo d'Erlanger, mundane in a black coat and wearing a hat which he subsequently forgot; Jakie Astor; Irene Worth, just right in non-colours, and Diana Cooper, casual, as beautiful as ever, with her habitual basket occupied by Doggie, the chihuahua.

The Queen Mother's huge limousine arrived and out stepped the smiling, delightful, familiar figure. She was dressed in brilliant puce and magenta.

Cecil Beaton

Thursday, 4 April 1968

I got on to my night sleeper for Blackburn at 11.15 pm. I had just got into bed with my hot water bottle and warm milk when there was a tap at the door. The stationmaster held out a bit of paper. Would I please ring Whitehall 4433. I tucked my nightie into my knickers, pulled over a skirt and my coat and went out onto the cold platform with bare legs. They opened the Reservation office for me and got me No 10. It was Harold just to tell me he had decided that I should be Secretary of State of Employment and Productivity ...

Barbara Castle

Friday, 5 April 1968

Well, I am in the thick of it now, for better or for worse – probably worse. I am under no illusions that I may be committing political suicide. I have at last moved from the periphery of the whirlwind into its very heart. I hate the thought of leaving the Ministry of Transport. If I had stayed I think I could have made a really dramatic and mounting impact on road accidents, to say nothing of carrying through my transport plan.

If I go down in the disaster as well I may, at least I shall have become an adult before I die.

Barbara Castle

Saturday, 6 April–Sunday, 7 April 1968

The most appalling tragedy in the USA has shadowed all these days and blotted out all else. Martin Luther King has been murdered – a saint – the one voice raised and listened to by many for non-violence.

The funeral service was attended by 100,000 people of both races – [Robert] Kennedy, McCarthy, Nixon and Jacqueline Kennedy walked in the procession. There was a most moving transmission on TV. Our Race Relations Bill is just printed and about to be introduced. I said to Mark, 'Surely this tragedy will help it on its way. Even the blindest will see what we want to prevent.' He replied (and alas he may be right!) 'By some it will be used as an argument against letting any more coloured immigrants into this country.' One can think of little else.

Violet Bonham Carter

Saturday, 21 April 1968

The news today is dominated by Enoch Powell's speech in which he raised the racial issue by saying that he thought this country had gone mad to admit so many immigrants and that it was like adding a match to a pile of gunpowder. Enoch is of working class origins; he got a scholarship to a grammar school, did very well academically, became a professor at twenty-four, a brigadier at twenty-nine. But he has never been accepted in the Tory Party.

Tony Benn

Monday, 6 May 1968

One of my discoveries in my new job is that the Minister of Labour has always been furnished with security reports on the trade unions. The first one on my desk was about the inner Communist clique in the engineering unions. Says Security, of the fifty two members of the Amalgamated Engineering Federation's National Committee, ten are Communist Party members and nine more are sympathisers. They have been holding secret meetings under the chairmanship of Bert Ramelson, the Communist Party's chief industrial organiser. All very James Bond but I gather that Denis Barnes doesn't take these Security boys very seriously.

Barbara Castle

Saturday, 18 May 1968

I rose early and caught the 9.15a.m. train to Northampton, where I was picked up by Desmond Fitz-Gerald. Our tour began at Althorp where we were ticked off at length by the portly and extremely tetchy Lord Spencer.* Loathed by the county, as we were to learn at our other ports of call, his lordship has never recovered from not being made a KG. The house was freezing cold and we hung on to our coats as we were soldiered past the serried ranks of ancestors culminating in a grand gallery of Lelys and Van Dycks. We ended up in the lived-in part of the house where a decanter of sherry and two glasses stood on a silver salver in the middle of an oak table. Made to feel like servants we drank the ritual glass which betokened aristocratic hospitality before moving on to Brockhall, which turned out to be an entrancing, somewhat tumbledown small Jacobean house with a surprising interior in the Gothic mode ...

Our last port of call was Drayton, a quite wonderful house with an approach as though to a castle in *The Faerie Queen*. Here was a huge contrast to what had gone before and we were in a sense back where we had started at Althorp, only more so, a freezing interior with crumbling walls and disintegrating décor. The owners, one felt, were feeling the struggle to be an unequal one. Colonel Stopford-Sackville, a large jolly military gent, and his husky-voiced wife poured us out gin by the tumbler load. Drayton was filled with treasures and I longed to linger ...

* Grandfather of Diana Spencer, Princess of Wales; Althorp is the Spencer family home.

But the owners' real pride was their new kitchen. With all their problems I was hardly surprised.

Roy Strong

June 1968
Down the Glebe Pit, Co. Durham

As I was travelling out one of the lads asked me to take his pony as well as mine (Hawk) because it was too small to ride. So off I galloped on Hawk (bareback) holding onto his pony by a rope, but halfway out the rope slipped from my fingers. I stopped, got off Hawk and went back for the little one. I was just about to get back on Hawk when he galloped off. I was in a panic. He could go anywhere and get hurt, he was completely in the dark, he couldn't see where he was going … I flew outbye [i.e. away from the coalface] looking for him, dragging the poor little pony behind me. I was in such a state. When I went to the stables to tell the horse-keeper what happened, there was Hawk standing in his stall, none the worse for his adventure. I was lathered but at that moment over the moon to see him. He just looked as if to say 'What kept you?'

Jim Wilson

Wednesday, 12 June 1968

A much publicised 'revolt' against Jeremy Thorpe's leadership is taking place in his absence on his honeymoon. The young Liberals are at loggerheads with him for having alluded to them as 'Marxists' (where and when I don't know) and for saying that 'all capitalists are not callous'. (Capitalist is of course a dirty word in leftist circles.) I don't think Young Liberals matter much as they talk great nonsense and are best ignored, though they are an undoubted nonsense at Party Conferences.

Violet Bonham Carter

Wednesday, 26 June 1968

Tommy Balogh threw a party to precede his introduction in the House of Lords.

I must say this is incredible mumbo jumbo for grown-up men

to take part in but they really do enjoy dressing up even more than women and have an insatiable appetite for time-hallowed pantomime.

Then into the Commons to resume the exhausting marathon of the Prices and Incomes Bill.

Barbara Castle

Thursday, 11 July 1968

Another dreary three hours ... on the wretched public expenditure exercise. Cutting out £300 million is a miserable process. Wedgie, for instance, was nearly in tears at the suggestion that he should sacrifice £3 million of his expenditure. His cut would mean slashing the work he was doing on computers, machine tools, micro-electronics, all of which were beginning to yield results. Denis Healey has volunteered another £13m cut in defence so long as it is carried through with no publicity. He is always full of his own virtue in cutting the defence programme ... but somehow I never trust his claims and have a sinking and perhaps unjustified feeling that a lot of his so-called cuts are totally unreal.

Barbara Castle

Monday, 29 July 1968

Transport and Town and Country Planning [Bill] in committee. How little they seem to have to do with the issues which absorb and haunt and agonise, like Biafra and Czechoslovakia. One feels daily and hourly the humiliation of utter helplessness. We are selling arms for the destruction of a people which is starving to death.* Czechoslovakia is putting up an inspired fight for mental freedom – the freedom of the human spirit. Dubcek† has issued a classic statement of aims. Meanwhile vast armies are surrounding her –

Violet Bonham Carter

---

*Britain supplied arms to the Nigerian government to help crush the rebellion which was attempting to form an independent Republic of Biafra.
† Alexander Dubček, leader of Czechoslovakia, had attempted to liberalise the country through a series of reforms that became known as the Prague Spring, stating that he wished to create 'socialism with a human face'. The Soviet Union invaded Czechoslovakia in August 1968 to halt the reforms.

Wednesday, 31 July 1968

Rather thoughtlessly the Prime Minister had set up a new Cabinet Committee on the finances of the BBC [which Crossman had to chair] and it had its first meeting this afternoon. I asked straight away whether anyone there thought we still had a chance to go for advertising on the BBC. John Stonehouse who's the new Postmaster General and Roy Mason, the old one, both said they were against it. But I told them if nobody wanted advertising what this Committee had better do would be to try to improve the system of licensing. That's what we agreed and so under my chairmanship a major Cabinet controversy finally spluttered out.

Richard Crossman

Wednesday, 21 August 1968

A day that will not be forgotten. It was Stephen's birthday. That was the first thought in our minds when we woke up and then we heard the news that the Russians and the Warsaw Pact countries had invaded Czechoslovakia. My spirits sank because, although we had half expected this might happen in the summer we thought it had all been patched up: this really takes you right back to Hungary in 1956.

The rest of the day was devoted to Stephen's birthday and it being his seventeenth, he was able to drive on the highways.

Cabinet has been called tomorrow on the Czechoslovakian situation.

Tony Benn

Wednesday, 18 September 1968

The Society of Motor Manufacturers and Traders turned up in force for the meeting they had requested. They were clearly desperate men – saying that they had hardly had a strike-free day in the past few months, and the vast majority of them wild-cat strikes. The unions, they said, had lost control completely over their shop stewards and their rank and file and they didn't think the situation could be improved until collective bargains were made legally enforceable.

I can see my only hope is to force the trade unions to face up to their responsibilities publicly.

Barbara Castle

Tuesday, 21 January 1969

Terrible things happening in Czechoslovakia. A young student has poured petrol over himself and burnt to death as a protest. As may be imagined it has had an explosive effect on an already explosive situation. Crowds assemble in the Wenceslas Square and elsewhere in tears of grief and despair. Czechoslovakia is a nightmare – a Russian crime.

Violet Bonham Carter

Wednesday, 29 January 1969

Number 17 Powis Terrace is one of those late-Victorian stucco terraces in Notting Hill Gate with a vast columned portico and every sign that gentility had long since fled. The houses were now tatty tenements and I climbed up what can only be described as a squalid staircase-well to be met by David. Original is the only word one could ever apply to him with his bleached blond hair and owl spectacles. But I couldn't help loving him and admiring his quick logic and unique perception. He's rather large and square, getting fat in fact, and somehow terribly conscious of it. The whole time I was there he kept feeling beneath his shirt as though checking up on the expansion of the wodges. We sat down in his kitchen together with his slim blond American boyfriend, Peter Schlesinger, and lunched off consommé, toast and pate washed down with red wine … He agreed to draw Fred Ashton for me …

Every surface was white. In the sitting-room stood a Mackintosh chair, a rococo sledge, a divan bed with some cushions scattered across it and some coloured cut-out trees like those in a child's toy theatre. In the studio I noticed a frame containing a collage of newspaper cuttings of the Rolling Stones.

Roy Strong

Wednesday, 15 January 1969

Into the office for final polishing [of *In Place of Strife*]. First I called in George Woodcock [head of the TUC] to arrange about his announcement. I spilt a great yarn to him about how he could transform the whole atmosphere by what he said. 'You know George I really am not out to clobber the unions.'

'Of course you're not. No one could say that – or perhaps I should say they can't believe it even if they do.'

I do want to make Dick [Crossman] and Judith [Hart] eat dirt. Their assumption of superior concern for rank and file people has been almost more than I could bear. I have a hunch that I can carry people with me on this and I only hope that proves true. Of course I am swept with doubt from time to time as to whether I have entirely misjudged reactions. If I have I shall have mortally damaged my political career.

Barbara Castle

Monday, 3 February 1969

I took Melissa and Joshua with me this morning to meet Colonel Frank Borman, the American spaceman, who's come to Britain on the first stop of a European goodwill tour. I met him at the front of Millbank Tower [the Ministry of Technology building] and he presented me with a miniature of the module which is going to land on the moon this summer, and then I took him up. I had the little ones waiting in the lift and he was awfully sweet with them. We had a most interesting discussion.

He said as far as spin-offs from the moon programme were concerned the really valuable spin-off was management. Here was a programme that cost $40,000 million and involved 400,000 people. There were four million moving parts in the rocket spacecraft and they had got round the moon and splashed down within a few seconds of the computer predictions.

One thousand million people had heard him read from the Book of Genesis on the other side of the moon on Christmas Eve – about one in four of the world's population.

Tony Benn

Tuesday, 25 February 1969

President Nixon, who arrived yesterday on an official visit, made all the right noises at the airport. He even talked about the special relationship!

We all took up our usual places in the Cabinet room. There was a positively festive air about the whole proceedings with Harold [Wilson] making a few cracks, before inviting Nixon to tell us what he would like us to talk about. Nixon rose valiantly to this unusual setting and atmosphere and responded by making some rather discursive remarks about general social problems in particular the problem of youth and student revolt now manifesting itself everywhere, even Germany. What did we think it was all about? Harold made a few rather coarse jibes at Marcuse which irritated me as his lapses into philistinism always do, and I was delighted when Judith put him in his place, saying that as the mother of teenage sons she had decided to make a study of Marcuse and that we all ought to take him seriously because, as an apostle of violence, he was having a huge effect on young people. Wedgie gave us one of his scintillatingly pat little homilies on what technology was doing to internationalise the relationships of young people, to which Denis [Healey] vigorously retorted 'Rot.'

Richard delivered a brilliant cameo of a speech, culminating with the words 'They are looking for a religion and we can't give it to them because it doesn't exist.'

Barbara Castle

Sunday, 9 March 1969

Prescote Manor Farm, Banbury

Here at Prescote I am reflecting on the week. It's been dominated by the Ford strike. The Company [by] seeking an injunction to stop the unions breaking the contract caused an almost universal strike, then the Company lost its case and now the situation is worse than ever. Do Jones and Scanlon* want to smash the Company and get a huge pay rise without promising any productivity or accepting any discipline? ...

I have already described ... what a mess we got into with Barbara's White Paper *In Place of Strife* because of Roy Jenkins's extraordinarily lackadaisical agreement to rush through her package. By agreeing to

*Jack Jones, General Secretary of the Transport and General Workers Union, and Hugh Scanlon, President of the Amalgamated Engineering Union.

this, Roy [Chancellor of the Exchequer] has lost his incomes policy legislation; that is obvious now. The Government is not going to have another Prices and Incomes Bill and Callaghan has won de facto. We always assumed we would have Barbara's trade union reforms as our main policy and we thought this was a more constructive, more suitable electoral theme ...

Richard Crossman

Friday, 18 April 1969

Linwood, Renfrewshire

By helicopter in brilliant sunshine, to the Rootes factory at Linwood.

When the helicopter landed in its enclosed space I saw phalanxes of workers lining the wires. (It was their lunch break.) The managing director tried to wave me to a waiting car away from the wire, but I turned and walked towards the cheerful crowd – an old electoral instinct. They waved and I waved back and one of them called out 'Come in at the workers' gate, Barbara,' so I wheeled round, and so did the bosses, and we all walked through the workers' gate to a cheer.

A young apprentice leaning over the wire called out 'Give us a kiss, Barbara.' 'Of course,' I replied and held up my face. A great roar of delight went up and I prayed that the cameras had been around. They had!

And so it went on all day ... no hostile demonstrations only a young lad jumping down from the car assembly line with 'Think again, Barbara' spelt out on his white jumper, clutching my hand earnestly, while he said 'Think again. We are your friends.' I held on to his hand, asking *him* to think again because I was *his* friend, as my *In Place of Strife* showed.*

Barbara Castle

Thursday, 19 June 1969

A relaxed morning. Douglas suggested that I might at least retrieve some peace from the wreckage (of *In Place of Strife*) so I went and had

---

* *In Place of Strife* was never implemented, thwarted in Cabinet in the main by the Home Secretary, James Callaghan, with trade union support. Castle wrote in September 1968 of the 'industrial anarchy we faced' due to demarcation disputes between unions in one workplace, particularly the *motor* industry.

my hair done. Then into the office party where I thanked them all, high and low, for the work they had done, toasting them in champagne. 'I have spent the last few months delivering sermons up and down the country. You built the pulpit for me and it is not your fault that it has turned into a scaffold.'

Barbara Castle

Monday, 21 July 1969
Reddish House, Wiltshire

Unbelievable thrill of watching on television, like six hundred million others, man's first journey to the moon. We could not believe that we were actually watching men up on that bright crescent that could be seen in the sky from the garden on this marvellous summer's night.

Irene Worth, Elizabeth Cavendish and James Pope-Hennessy were staying and we sat glued with pulses throbbing and fears that [there] might be some last minute unforeseen disaster. The terror continued.

The heroes used poetic and imaginative phrases. Instead of the expected 'say brother, you should see these colours!' Armstrong said 'That's one small step for man, but one giant leap for mankind.'

Before they returned to earth they left an olive branch and medals in homage to the astronauts who had died in earlier unsuccessful attempts to reach this fantastic goal.

The household was up at 6 am to watch the splash-down, all but James, suffering terribly from DTs – what a tragedy!

Cecil Beaton

Tuesday, 19 August 1969

There were jokes in Cabinet about my new beard. We then settled down to discuss the Ulster situation.

The Stormont Government say it is the IRA who are the cause of the trouble, but this does not conform to British intelligence.

The meeting was quiet and Jim Callaghan I thought did very well. Harold was alright except that, as usual, he was much too tactical and there was too little thinking about the future. Denis was realistic in seeing that he might find himself in a position of sending in the troops against all the Protestants.* I wonder whether people understood how serious the situation was – whether in fact this was not the beginning of ten more years of Irish politics at Westminster which would be very unpleasant. None of us had thought it out very carefully.

Tony Benn

August 1969
Ireland

No one was around at the border, and the deserted roads were only inhabited by animals. We had a complete demonstration of nature as we drove through families of magpies and many more rabbits than one would see in England. Squirrels, mice, rats, hares and cats strayed across our path.

At Bogside the barricades of burnt-out lorries, trash of all sorts and barbed wire seemed merely fatuous and childish, but I suppose during the recent fighting they were of importance. Now the whole mess merely highlights the stupidity of the Irish fighting one another with the result that all are poorer even than they were before, and life in Ireland today is abysmally meagre. But the Irish love to fight …

Let us hope that [the IRA] will not be vicious enough to resort to their old tricks of destroying beautiful old houses and setting fire to stables without letting out the horses.

Cecil Beaton

Thursday, 23 October 1969

I was asked to one of the Archbishop of Canterbury's press lunches. The faded architectural pomp of the palace is bizarrely at variance with the lower-middle-class lifestyle lived within it. Sherry and orange juice were followed by a utilitarian lunch of stew, apple pie and cream, and cheese.

Archbishop Ramsey is a huge man with no neck, a sweet face and smile and marvellous eyes, all of it arising from a mound of pink and purple. After we'd eaten he held forth, rather apologetically I thought,

---

* Violence in Northern Ireland between Protestant and Catholic/Unionist and Nationalist communities led to soldiers being sent to 'restore order' on 14 August 1969. The Cabinet met to discuss the situation. James Callaghan was Home Secretary, Denis Healey was Defence Secretary and Harold Wilson was Prime Minister.

predicting a further decline of the Church of England, the saving grace being that Christian attitudes were still important in society even if they were no longer connected to belief. This sounded a pretty grim scenario to me.

Roy Strong

Wednesday, 5 November 1969

I only had one bit of business at home tonight. I have been trying to put my oar in to be sure that the British don't join in the American underground tests of nuclear weapons without, at least, a meeting of Ministers to discuss it. Denis Healey has been determined to get British nuclear weapons tested underground in the US and since I put my foot down, he has been trying to get at me. In the end I decided to ring Number 10 and I put the points to a private secretary to pass on to the Prime Minister. I said I would abide by his decision but I don't know whether Harold cares one way or the other.

Tony Benn

Wednesday, 19 November 1969

The Apollo 12 landed this morning and there was another moon walk, which, unfortunately, we weren't able to see because the television set had broken down.

Tony Benn

Wednesday, 10 December 1969

Long discussion on the future of Concorde. Everyone, including Wedgie, now agrees that for the first time we have a choice as to whether we continue the project or not, because the costs are escalating beyond all reason and give us a good case legally. Everyone is convinced that Concorde will be an economic flop.

Wedgie, chastened as he was, and admitting the scheme ought never to have been started, couldn't agree to [a confrontation with the French]. Eventually we agreed that we should review the project in June.

Barbara Castle

January 1970

San Francisco

It was a drizzly day outside and we decided this would be a good occasion to 'take our trip', my friend on mescalin, me on LSD. Having taken our pills, we hurried out to do provision shopping at the Safeway market. Suddenly everything became more brilliantly coloured; the package of food became incandescent, the fruits tremendously red, the vegetables electric green, and the cabbages purple. We were in splendid spirits and arrived home to a glowing kitchen. The little sitting-room was a dark cavern.

Now things began to happen! Reality was only there in fits and starts; all was changing and glowing and moving. There was a moment of terror. My companion was unrecognisable, his beard made into a square loaf of bread. The fuzz was horrible. I dare not look at myself.

My eyes were incredibly blue and my skin all dappled pinks. I felt a bit quavery and shook like a dog coming out of water, and I sweated. But I gave into the pleasure of it ... My friend's complexion had turned dark red, blotched with green-yellow; his eyes dark puce, his tongue almost black.

No ill-effects (next day). We were relaxed and content. My friend took me to the Methodist Chapel for Sunday morning service. It was a kind of revivalist meeting. The congregation was made up of clean laundered hippies, and negroes, mostly young people who came for a pleasant 'work-out' and a 'get-together' in a Christian frame of mind ...

Jesus Christ was referred to as our Director, songs by Dylan and from *Hair* were sung. The volume of noise became unbearable. For one and a half hours a condition of euphoria was sustained. We all linked arms and swayed from side to side in a state of jazzed-up emotion; a new religion?

Cecil Beaton

Tuesday, 3 February 1970

The main discussion in Cabinet was the Europe White Paper. Despite the modifications that have been made in the document, the cost of entry (to the Common Market) stands out in all its stark unpleasantness. And what interested me were the shocked reactions of some of the most devoted adherents of going in.

Denis Healey stressed that the argument of [British economic] growth was the key to the question, yet table 14 showed that membership was not necessarily synonymous with growth: some EFTA* countries had done better outside the Market than those inside. And he urged that we shouldn't exaggerate the political benefits. But the biggest surprise was Roy Mason (President of the Board of Trade). I am a pro-European, he said in effect, yet this document would cause me to pause.

Barbara Castle

Tuesday, 10 March 1970

I first met Jennifer Jenkins at Ann Fleming's. She struck me as an intelligent, Barbara Castle type of socialist lady, but her great project was to redecorate the staircase of Number 11 with portraits of all of her husband's predecessors as Chancellor. The lunch was of the type I'm worst at, totally political, with people who eat and drink nothing but politics morning, noon and night. I'd also lost my voice, which didn't help. Jo Grimond came out of it best as having more than a degree of wit and warmth, but Lady Gaitskell really is a bore of the first order, followed closely by Michael Astor, who is at least clever. He brought his latest wife ... And what, I wondered, was Roy Jenkins actually like or about?

Roy Strong

Tuesday, 21 April 1970

Supporting Labour is just another painless way of appeasing my social conscience. But it's not much, I cannot see how anyone with a social conscience could vote Conservative. The film which I was doing today has been written by John Cleese, who is now what you might call a committed Labour celebrity – and I mean that in a good sense – someone who is prepared to do something to keep the Conservatives out. At present Labour is increasingly successful in the polls.

Michael Palin

---

*European Free Trade Area, founded in 1960 by those countries unwilling or unable to join the European Economic Community (the Common Market). It was often referred to as the 'outer seven', as opposed to the 'inner six' nations of the EEC. Britain was a founder member but ceased to be a member on joining the EEC in 1973.

Tuesday, 12 May 1970

The papers this morning featured the new little plasticine figures of Tory politicians, called 'Yesterday's Men', which were designed by Alan Aldridge for use on Labour posters.

In the afternoon I had an impressive deputation of trade union officials and local MPs from Jarrow and Newcastle, pleading with me to try to save the yard.

Tony Benn

Thursday, 28 May 1970

Brief Cabinet

Harold said he thought there was too much complacency about and that we should all think of ways in which we could make our departmental policies more concrete for electioneering purposes – e.g. I had got my department to do me a detailed paper on how the Tory industrial relations policies would have affected the Pilkington strike. Their finding: it would not have stopped the strike and might well have made matters worse. Could we have from Treasury some concrete examples of the effects of the Tory tax proposals compared with our measures in the Budget?

'We can get all this through Transport House,'* said Crosland irritably. But I am appalled at our lack of good material with 'bite' as we go into the campaign. I've never felt less well-equipped for an Election but the others (Harold apart) seem so lackadaisical. Off to Blackburn to start my campaign.

Barbara Castle

Thursday, 28 May 1970

To Bristol, where the major problem at the moment is that the envelopes for the Election addresses, which were ordered a week ago from the regional organiser, have got lost on their way down from Newcastle.

Tony Benn

---

*Then Labour Party headquarters in Smith Square, Westminster, shared with the Transport and General Workers' Union and the TUC.

Thursday, 18 June 1970

Ideal polling weather, dry with warm sunshine. Every public opinion poll in the last two months had put Labour clearly ahead – the only possible shadow on the horizon was a one and a half per cent swing to the Tories in the latest opinion poll – taken after the publication of the worst trade figures for over a year and Britain's exit from the World Cup last Sunday. Nevertheless everything looked rosy for Labour ...

Edward Heath, perhaps more consistently written-off than any opposition leader since the war, consistently way behind Wilson in popularity, is the new Prime Minister.

The Labour government was courageous and humane in abolishing hanging, legalising abortion, reforming the laws against homosexuals, making the legal process of divorce less unpleasant, and banning the sale of arms to South Africa. I am very sad they are out of power, especially as I fear that it is on this record of progressive reform that they have been ousted.

Michael Palin

Friday, 19 June 1970

Elizabeth, the Queen Mother, has been very kind and is lending Royal Lodge for selected members of the family for the birthday party tonight, because she and Margaret and her staff are in fact living in Windsor Castle because it is Ascot Week.

Poor Lilibet had to go off very late to see the outgoing Prime Minister, Harold Wilson, at about 1800 and then to ask the new Prime Minister, Ted Heath, to form a Government at 1830.

Ted amused her by asking whether he might still come to the party to which he had been invited. She replied she would be delighted and, in fact, he did turn up later on that evening. He came straight up to me and said 'I have come to congratulate you on your seventieth birthday', and I replied, 'I hope you have come to receive congratulations on your victory.'

I then took the chance of telling him that he must do something about saving the aircraft carriers *Ark Royal* and *Eagle* right away, so as to be able to send at least one mobile flexible task force to the Middle East and Far East when necessary. He agreed he would have it looked into as a matter of urgency. To be honest this was my main reason for wanting the Conservatives to win this time.

Louis Mountbatten

Friday, 19 June 1970

The whole BBC circus was extraordinary – the chaotic comings and goings and the sense of bewilderment/hysteria that the result was not what they had expected or planned for. They were all set for a Labour victory and, suddenly, had to change tack. Interesting to note how well the politicians got on with one another (regardless of party), how wary they were of the BBC people, and how pleased with himself Robin Day is. It really is Mr Toad in a bow tie.*

Gyles Brandreth

Tuesday, 21 July 1970

A preview of Kenneth Tynan's *O! Calcutta!* at the Round House in Chalk Farm turned out to be an occasion notable for the boredom of it all. I have never been so aware how anti-erotic nudity could be or, when it came to the nude pas de deux, of the accuracy of Fred Ashton's observations that there were some parts of the anatomy over whose movements the choreographer had no control. There it was, a vast pile-up of sketches on wife-swapping, masturbation, knickers, lesbianism et al. Joe Orton's sketch on country house perversions was the only jewel in this tarnished crown, but even that needed cutting.

Roy Strong

Wednesday, 11 November 1970

My letter to my constituents 'Britain and the Common Market – the Case for a Referendum' was to come before the Shadow Cabinet today. But as Harold was at De Gaulle's funeral it was just noted and there was no comment. The only person who understood its significance

---

* Gyles Brandreth and Jack Straw (President of the National Union of Students) were representing 'British youth' on the BBC election results programme.

was Jim Callaghan, who said 'Tony may be launching a little rubber life-raft which we will all be glad of in a year's time.'

Tony Benn

Sunday, 24 January 1971

Morality and its intrusion into professional life in Britain: when Bobby Moore, the English football captain, drinks a beer in a night club at 1.30 a.m. before a game, he is not just fined ... he is reviled for immorality. Partly of course because he is not upper class and because his fame makes him 'an example to youth.' But the headmasterly tones of the editorials on this subject would be impossible anywhere else on earth – 'Moore on the carpet – 'Moore gets the stick' – one line school phrases are inevitable and sadly revealing. Few Englishmen ever leave school: they spend their lives in thrall not to their own approval but to the headmaster's.

Kenneth Tynan

Monday, 15 February 1971

Decimal day. Today, not only our old currency, but a small portion of our everyday language, dies for ever and is replaced. In looking back, this day will perhaps appear as just another step away from the archaic obstinacies that set Britain apart from other countries of the world, and a step which should have been taken much earlier.

Funnily enough I find myself resenting the new decimal coinage far less than the postal codes (which I fear will one day replace towns with numbers – and after towns, streets, and after streets ...?) or the all-figure telephone numbers which dealt one mighty blow to local feeling in London ...

For some inexplicable reason a number of smaller shops are still working in pounds, shillings and pence.

Michael Palin

Tuesday, 2 March 1971

Elizabeth Longford asked me to a small drinks party for Prince Charles. There were about a dozen of us. Antonia was there, pretty beyond belief, back from the Bahamas, with Hugh. Frank Longford,

Jack Plumb, Martin and Gay Charteris, the odd deb girl and the writer Marina Warner in appliqué hot-pants beneath a coat which went down to her ankles. All Marina could think of was that HRH was twenty-two and had he been to bed with anyone? He's a pleasant young man, earnest, with a boyish grin and a non-sophisticated sense of humour, prankish, thoughtful, kind and shy. He dresses in a very middle-aged way with narrow lapels and tiny shirt collars and narrow ties. I couldn't help being impressed by his sheer 'niceness.' We talked mostly about the National Portrait Gallery and Charles I.

Roy Strong

Tuesday, 20 April 1971

Rally for George Jackson and the Soledad Brothers – blacks imprisoned for racist reasons in a Californian jail – at the Central Hall. The star speaker is James Baldwin who says, 'if their children and my children have no future, nobody in this hall has any future.' He takes a straight socialist line, equating the suffering of the Soledad blacks with that of oppressed people everywhere. I recall arguing with him twelve years ago when he was battling for integration and equal opportunity: I begged him to find the answers in Marxism rather than racism … and asked him why he did not make the point that it was economic exploitation that kept the Negro down. 'If I said that,' he replied, 'they would call me a Communist. Christianity is safer.'

Kenneth Tynan

Thursday, 13 May 1971

Telephone call from Lord Longford. He is setting up an independent commission of inquiry to look at the whole question of pornography. Is there a problem? If there is, what can be done about it? 'It's a high-powered group. We've got two bishops, an archbishop, a High Court judge and Malcolm Muggeridge. But we need some young blood. I thought of you and Cliff Richard. What do you say?' I said yes.

Gyles Brandreth

Tuesday, 8 June 1971

First gathering of the Porn Commission TV Sub-Committee. I put on my new flared turquoise trousers, but sure enough, Cliff quite outdazzles me in a sumptuous plum velvet outfit, complete with medallions and silver and gold chains. His skin is pretty peachy too. The meeting is chaired by Malcolm Muggeridge, broadcaster and sage. Looking like a dandified turtle, he gets away with not knowing who anybody is by calling everybody 'Dear boy'. He introduces me to Peregrine Worsthorne: 'Dear boy, you must meet this dear boy.' I get the impression from Perry that, once upon a time, Malcolm was a bit of a goer, a proper red-blooded ladies' man, but now that his libido has collapsed he's discovered the joys of chastity and vegetarianism ...

We all agreed that, sadly, things ain't what they used to be – and Cliff declared that some of the dancing on *Top of the Pops* is undoubtedly designed to titillate – but, hand on heart, we couldn't say there was anything approaching what you'd call pornography to be seen on British TV. 'Mark my words,' said Malcolm, narrowing his eyes and smacking his lips, 'the rot's set in. If we don't do something now, within a generation nudity and profanity on the box will be commonplace, and rampant homosexuality will be offered us by way of entertainment.'

Gyles Brandreth

Wednesday, 9 June 1971

As the Common Market gets hotter, here are my feelings. If we want a Europe permanently divided along East–West lines; a mutual protection society for western capitalism; the death of all hopes for socialism (as opposed to Willy Brandt's Social Democracy) in Europe; if, in short, we want to resurrect Hitler's 1,000 year Reich – a Western European bloc dominated by Germany, implacably opposed to the socialist world, and even including countries like Spain which Hitler failed to incorporate – then we must make haste into the Common Market. If on the other hand we want true internationalism (instead of the parochial variety) we must stay out.

The Tory attitude: the EEC is a challenge for British industry. There will be unemployment and higher prices and small businesses will go to the wall: but this is all presented as if it were somehow an inevitable and character-building ordeal, like the prospect of execution which concentrated the mind of the Major in Pepys* so wonderfully.

Kenneth Tynan

Monday, 14 June 1971

Upper Clyde Shipbuilders are in difficulty. Looked through my old files and came across a confidential memorandum written by Nicholas Ridley for Heath in 1969 about how to cut up UCS.

I received it from Eric Varley† – I don't know where he got it from and I hadn't used it before because I was a bit worried about revealing a document which had been pirated in some way, picked up from a wastepaper basket or whatever. But with the possibility of UCS being knifed today – indeed the near certainty – I decided to let it come out.

I drafted a statement on UCS, calling for public ownership and workers' control in the yard itself, and went into the House of Commons. I had a filthy cold and felt terrible.

Tony Benn

Wednesday, 1 September 1971
Classiebawn, County Sligo, Ireland

This is the last day of the family holiday. I had six of my Security Guard in for drinks and small farewell presentations at 4 pm. They have been most discreet; I have had a total of four uniformed police and eight Special Branch Detectives of which three have been on round-the-clock duty in the house, besides two police cars for escort duties. I think the Irish Government were afraid the IRA might try to kidnap me and offer me in exchange for some of their leaders who are now in internment in Northern Ireland. However we had no trouble at all and it has been a very pleasant stay without any undue police activity.

Louis Mountbatten

---

*Samuel Pepys gave an eyewitness account of the execution of Major General Thomas Harrison in his diaries.
†Eric Varley was Labour MP for Chesterfield and chairman of the Trade Union Group of MPs. He was Parliamentary Private Secretary to Harold Wilson in the previous Labour government.

Saturday, 25 September 1971

The anti-porn campaigners took Trafalgar Square for a 'Festival of Light' this afternoon. The same faces one saw at Billy Graham's crusades at Harringay Arena fifteen years ago – mostly plain or downright ugly people whom life (due to the insanely high valuation put by capitalism on physical attractiveness) had never invited to its party, but who found themselves bidden by the Rev. Billy to an eternal party in heaven.

Kenneth Tynan

Wednesday, 12 January–Friday, 21 January 1972
Yorkshire

The lads on our housing scheme set off at 6.30 am, halfway to our destination two police vans passed us full of constables and there were no doubt in our minds where they were going, 'they must have some bloody good informers' someone said.

We had a good morning – we convinced some of the drivers [of coal wagons], quite a few turned back ...We had a rough afternoon – majority of wagons were getting through with no respect for anyone and the police were letting them. When the police were told about this they said they could do nothing as it was a private road.

There were two pressmen who nearly got run over ... There was a hostile feeling towards the pressmen due to adverse publicity the pickets had been getting in both national and local dailies.

On Saturday morning I went to the local Branch meeting where we were informed that the Barnsley area NUM had been allocated the 'East Anglia Area' to picket and a strike centre was to be set up in Norwich. Names were taken for a bus to travel down immediately we were required and to be prepared to go at short notice.

[On Monday] I went ... to the Social Security to put my claim in for my dependants. The idea to me of the SS was to pay you as little as possible and try and starve the miners back to work. Late that evening there was a knock on the door to tell me to be ready and to be prepared for a week away. We had to meet at 7 am at Strike Centre. The wife helped me pack my case with plenty of warm clothes as we had to be prepared for all kinds of weather.

Wednesday Due to constant surveillance of the coastline a collier was spotted off the coast and contacts ... said it was bound for

1. Alan Lascelles (left), private secretary to successive monarchs, did not reveal his contempt for the Prince of Wales (Edward VIII, here with arms crossed), for many years.

2. Beatrice Webb could have married Joseph Chamberlain instead of Sidney Webb – with interesting consequences for the Labour Party.

3. 'Tom, great Tom, thinks [*Ulysses*] on a par with *War and Peace*! An illiterate, underbred book it seems to me.' Virginia Woolf had a higher opinion of T. S. Eliot, left, than of James Joyce.

4. Frances Stevenson (far left) charted the long relationship with David Lloyd George (in civvies). The child is Jennifer, their daughter, in the early 1930s.

5. Trade union leader and diarist, Walter Citrine (top right, in scarf) with George Lansbury on the National Demonstration on Unemployment, Hyde Park, London, 1933.

6. Shirley and John Catlin on holiday, 1932, with their mother, Vera Brittain.

7. The first general manager and director general of the BBC, John Reith, (top left) personally supervised many broadcasts in the pre-war years.

8. At the crease in the actresses *v* authors cricket match, 1938, a relaxed J. B. Priestley.

9. Cecil Beaton, himself captured on film, just before he began his work as a Second World War photographer.

10. Before the war, Benjamin Britten moved to the US with Peter Pears, but returned disillusioned. 'To be a liberal is dangerous – to be a communist is fatal.'

11. Private secretary, trustee and executor to Winston Churchill, John 'Jock' Colville is pictured with Clemmie Churchill at Chequers.

12. A passionate campaigner for Zionism, Blanche 'Baffy' Dugdale, the niece of Balfour, is photographed visiting Jerusalem 1944.

13. 'Housewife, 49' was revealed to be Nella Last, a resident of the shipyard town, Barrow-in-Furness, pictured here with one of her sons, Cliff.

14. 'I do not like the job and I do not think the arrangement can last,' wrote Charles Wilson (later Lord Moran), on being appointed Churchill's doctor in May 1940.

15. Joyce Grenfell enchanted servicemen across the globe (pictured here in London 1944) when she and pianist Viola Tunnard joined the Entertainments National Service Association for the war.

16. Malcolm Muggeridge in Moscow in 1959, twenty-seven years after he first visited the Soviet Union and found the scales falling from his eyes.

17. Cricket bats: Ted Dexter (left), captain of England, and Frank Worrell (right), captain of the West Indies, flanking Harold Macmillan at Chequers, September 1963: Macmillan was to resign shortly after (due to events, not cricket).

18/19/20.
Iconoclasts
of post-war
liberalism:
Kenneth Tynan,
(top); Joe Orton,
(bottom left);
Jimmy Boyle
(bottom right),
sculptor, diarist,
writer, reformed
criminal.

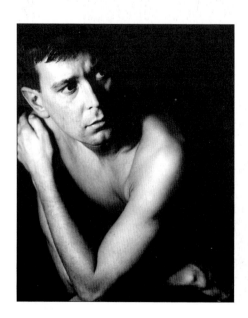

21. Violet Bonham Carter, keeper of the Liberal flame in the Thirties and Forties with her son-in-law, Jo Grimond, the MP for Orkney and Shetland. Grimond led the Liberals 1956–67.

22. Barbara Castle, in typical hands-on approach to politics (with a little help from the skipper), on board *Royal Daffodil II*, 1967.

23. 'Lilibet' and dogs with Louis Mountbatten, at Royal Windsor Horse Show, May 1973.

24. Tony Benn (right), joked that the 'e' in Concorde stood for England, Ecosse, excellence and extravagance.

25. Peter Hall taking over from Sir Laurence Olivier, at the newly-built National Theatre, on the south bank of the Thames, 1973.

26. Horse racing and journalism brought together the flamboyant Woodrow Wyatt, once a Labour MP, with royalty, politicians and the Murdoch family.

27. Jane and Alan Clark being taken walkies by their Rottweilers, two of the many pets they owned, Saltwood, 1994.

28. Another Labour horse-racing enthusiast – Foreign Secretary Robin Cook – looking up the form with John McCririck of Channel 4.

29. Deborah Bull, principal ballerina for The Royal Ballet – making it look so easy.

30. Sunderland South, always the first constituency to declare on Election night, with its MP from 1987 to 2010, Chris Mullin.

31. Oona King, Labour MP for Bethnal Green and Bow, campaigning at Columbia Road Flower market for the last time in 2005.

Rowhedge up river from Felixstowe ... The crane which was there to unload the vessel only managed a couple of grabfulls when his window was smashed.

The captain of the vessel was in and out of the bridge pleading for permission to unload but getting no satisfaction. As the tide was on the ebb he had no headway regarding unloading the vessel. The vessel had the hatches put back and secured ... the ship left for Rotterdam on the next tide.

Friday Was very quiet. The wife got the first Giro £9.80 that is for her 2 children and to pay the rent. I went with some mates and got some logs as to make the coal spin out what I had left.

Peter Clarney

Monday, 31 January 1972

There was a statement on the Bogside massacre yesterday in which thirteen catholics were killed by troops, following the illegal march which had been undertaken by the Civil Rights people against a ban. I think it is the largest number of people killed in the United Kingdom by British troops for 200 years or more. Bernadette Devlin (MP for Mid-Ulster) was not called by the Speaker [and so] at one point, she stamped down the gangway and went over and attacked the Home Secretary, Reggie Maudling, physically, an extraordinary sight. She smacked him and pulled his hair. People took her away and she was fighting with them.

Tony Benn

Saturday, 5 February–Monday, 7 February 1972

After a [Claimants Union] meeting we met Mr A Scargill by now known as Head of the Barnsley Flying Squad who told us he had been lecturing up and down the country and the support from people from outside the industry was tremendous.

More pickets arrived from Wales and Midlands. TGWU sent 600 hot pies, their fruit section sent boxes of apples, someone else sent cigs.

Peter Clarney

Saturday, 19 February 1972

The coal strike is over.

The picketing was called off at 1 pm this morning, and the miners, after a ballot next week, should be back at work at the weekend. They will have been out for eight weeks – and the country, we are constantly told, is losing millions of pounds due to industrial power-cuts ... the government, faced with either admitting that their incomes policy was unjust, or trying to break the miners, as they did the electricity workers last year, chose to try and break the miners. In the end the miners won – and the weeks of reduced pay and unemployment which they had added to their already unpleasant working conditions, were made worthwhile. I regard my £50 (donation) as well spent!

Michael Palin

Sunday, 12 March 1972

Keith and Susan Kyle gave a party in their house on Primrose Hill. This is living NW1 style which has no respect for a period house. At the bottom of the stairs a gate had been fixed to cage in the child, the walls vanished beneath swathes of paperbacks, the kitchen cum dining-room was scrubbed pine, the drawing room lined with a partic- ularly hideous gold-striped wallpaper. Everything was very NW1 including the dress of the guests. There was Peregrine Worsthorne in cuddly woollies buttoned down the front and baggy trousers. A J Ayer in a tatty suit desperately in need of an expedition to the dry cleaners with [his wife] Dee Wells, all cleavage, like a vampire on her night off. Vanessa Lawson was like a nymph gone mad in a dress of black nothing while Nigel, thicker than of yore, frustrated and clever, told me he had a constituency waiting for him in the coming election. The food matched the ambience: piles of cold meats, salad and cheese, washed down with rivers of cheap wine.

Roy Strong

Friday, 7 April 1972

Went to see Rupert Murdoch about [the campaign for] a referendum on the Common Market. He was with Larry Lamb, editor of the *Sun*, and with the editor of the *News of the World*. Murdoch is just a bit younger than me. He is a bright newspaper man who had made a humdinger of a success of the *Sun*, which nobody else was able to do anything about, and the *News of the World* although it has been declining in circulation, is now fairly stable. He was opposed to the referendum, because he was in favour of entering Europe, so his two editors were opposed to it as well. But I used all the arguments I could and they asked if I would write something about it.

Then I went to the Reform Club to see Alastair Hetherington (the *Guardian* editor) to try to persuade him to change his opinion.*

Tony Benn

Friday, 12 May 1972
Duke of Cornwall Hotel, Plymouth

I sit at a table in the bay window of a comfortable room in this old-fashioned hotel. Tomorrow I have a preliminary interview for the 'safest' of the three Plymouth sets. This afternoon I have been in reconnaissance.

I first visited Plymouth ten years ago when I collected Jane and new-born Andrew from the maternity ward at Freedom Fields hospital whither she had been rushed by ambulance [from our home in West Devon] in the bitter winter of 1962. There are some fine buildings in a hard grey stone, almost granite ... Also tracts of rubble-covered wasteland where the planners have not yet built over the bomb damage.

Hard to understand this, as it is more than thirty years since the great Luftwaffe raids of April 1941 when the whole population would, at nightfall, trek out on the Yelverton road and camp on Dartmoor. My father, who sometimes comes up with strange but usually accurate pieces of useless information told me quite some time ago that Plymouth was 'the most corrupt city in Britain' – which may explain it.

Alan Clark

Monday, 5 June 1972
Duke of Windsor's funeral

When Wallis arrived she looked very sad and somewhat embarrassed, so I went up and took her by the arm and escorted her round to every

---

*The Labour Shadow Cabinet had voted in March 1972 for a policy of holding a referendum on Britain's proposed membership of the Common Market. Roy Jenkins, George Thomson and Harold Lever resigned in protest. The referendum was eventually held in 1975, to withdraw from the Common Market.

member of the family, explaining who everybody was. Many she knew, but not all. Then Lilibet, Philip, Charles and Anne and also Elizabeth arrived, and they went up and were very sweet to Wallis. The ladies were then taken to their seats and the men formed a procession and walked behind the coffin as it was carried from the Albert Memorial Chapel round to the bottom of the nave and up between the congregation into the choir where it was placed on the trestles facing the altar.

Looking back I feel that on the whole everything went as well as could be hoped. The great thing was that Lilibet, Philip and Charles were able to go and see David during their State Visit to Paris, while he was still well enough to be able to get dressed and see them upstairs in his bedroom. Wallis told me what very great pleasure this had given to him, and obviously to her too. Then the friendly reception which Wallis had from the family healed the breach.

Louis Mountbatten

Tuesday, 18 July 1972

Reginald Maudling, the Home Secretary, has resigned, caught up in the Poulson bankruptcy and corruption scandal.* Gyles Brandreth, would-be Home Secretary, has had lunch with Barbie Buss, editor of *Woman* magazine, plus entourage, at The Ivy. They feted me royally. I am their new 'star'. I'm getting £65 a week. I have to give up writing for anyone else – *Woman's Own, Daily Mail, Observer*, etc.

Gyles Brandreth

Saturday, 26 August 1972

We went to visit Benjamin Britten to try to get him to write the music for *Akenfield*. Then three Suffolk men – author, composer and director – would do the film …

Britten has now taken a secret cottage in the middle of the cornfields where he is composing his next opera, *Death in Venice*. It is the only way to get peace. He told me he used to enjoy living in Aldeburgh until so many people stood on the garden wall to take pictures of him.

---

* Gyles Brandreth's footnote reads: 'Reginald Maudling (1917–79) Conservative MP, Chancellor of the Exchequer and Home Secretary. He had been a non-executive director of one of the companies of John Poulson, an architect who routinely used bribery to secure local government contracts.'

Then he moved inland. But now, even there, the noise of American bombers is disturbing. So among the cornfields he writes his operas.

Peter Hall

Wednesday, 6 September 1972

There was an awful massacre yesterday at the Munich Olympic Games – an appalling thing to have happened. Eleven Israeli athletes were killed by Arab terrorists from the Black September organisation.

Tony Benn

Monday, 9 October 1972

One major difference between the London theatre today and twenty years ago is the relative paucity of queers. In the heyday of Noel C and John G, a high proportion of the best young actors, directors and playwrights was queer. Nowadays: it's hard to think of more than a handful – Ian McKellen, Robin Phillips, Alec McCowan, the late Joe Orton. If true, what does this indicate? That permissiveness, bringing wider sexual opportunities to adolescents, has allowed many 'don't knows' to opt for heterosexuality instead of homosexuality. That social change has swelled the upper ranks of West End actors with alumni of state schools, where queers are relatively uncommon, instead of boys from public schools, where homosexuality flourishes?

Kenneth Tynan

Friday, 22 December 1972
Westminster School

The term is ending at last, a week after boys and masters have departed. News of Oxbridge candidates continues to give pleasure and cause surprise.

On the whole Westminster boys do well and the final results will show that we have had a successful year. How important is this? One very able scholar has missed an award and is quite content with a place; he has little respect for the scholarship stakes. His attitude is more mature than that of his peers and of those of us who watch the

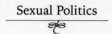

mounting total of awards on the list in the common room like party managers on election night.

John Rae

Chapter Seven

1973–1982
Who Governs Britain?

Prime Minister Edward Heath signed the Treaty of Rome in January 1973: Britain was now a member of the Common Market. Significant numbers in the Conservative and Labour Parties opposed membership. Only the Liberals appeared united in favour. No referendum had been held on entry, and a campaign soon began to persuade any future Labour government to hold a Referendum on whether Britain should *withdraw*. The diaries of Giles Radice, newly elected Labour MP and Euro-enthusiast, follow the trials and tribulations of the Europe issue over three decades. Roy Jenkins, the most passionately pro-European Labour MP, became President of the Commission in Brussels in 1976: his diary hints at the turmoil in the Labour Party which reached its height in 1981 when the 'gang of four' (including Jenkins) left the Party. Lord Longford, who had fortuitously decided to keep a diary for that year, observed that the Labour Party was at war with itself.

The 1971 Industrial Relations Act was the Heath government's attempt to 'control' union power and inflation. Efforts to dampen public service wage settlements were met with resistance. Successive sectors went on strike, and on 9 February 1972 a declaration of emergency imposed power cuts and rationing of energy – leading to 'the three-day week'. But the miners won a 25 per cent increase. When a second miners' strike began in February 1974, Ted Heath called a general election over the issue of 'who governs Britain?' – a gamble he expected to win (but didn't). The diaries of Peter Hall at the newly built National Theatre and Roy Strong at the Victoria and Albert Museum reveal the frustrations of creative leaders in the 1970s climate.

This was also, and tragically, the decade in which Ireland came back with a vengeance on to the political scene after fifty years, and terrorism in Britain became a frightening fact of life.

The diaries of the radically minded headmaster of Westminster School, John Rae, show the contrast between the lives of his public schoolboys and those on the council estates within a stone's throw of the school. Jimmy Boyle, in prison for the whole of the 1970s, works in an 'experimental' unit as a sculptor. Another artist, David Hockney, complains to Stephen Spender in Paris that 'no one in London protests' ...

Having persuaded the Plymouth Sutton Conservative Association to adopt him as their candidate, Alan Clark begins, in February 1974, his long love–hate relationship with Parliament.

As aide first to Harold Wilson and then James Callaghan, Bernard Donoughue has ringside access to prime ministerial life in all its glory and pettiness, with Marcia Williams, Joe Haines (Wilson's political and press secretaries), and Donoughue himself competing for Wilson's ear.

Wednesday, 3 January 1973

After a day's filming on *The Homecoming*, a quick change into the ridiculous panoply of the past: tails, white tie and my dangling CBE. It is the sheer discomfort of starch and stud which distresses me, quite apart from the unwilling feeling that I am now part of the Establishment and don't want to be.

The grand occasion was the Gala at Covent Garden to mark Britain's entry into the EEC. It was a Fanfare for Europe.

The Establishment – political, artistic and commercial – were out in force. On one side of the Queen's box, the Archbishop of Canterbury, on the other Lord Goodman.

Outside the Opera House noisy protestors jeered and jostled, surrounded by the largest collection of policemen I have ever seen in London. An effigy of Edward Heath was hanging at the gallows and the crowd chanted 'traitors, traitors, traitors' as we all disembarked in our finery.

Peter Hall

Thursday, 8 March 1973

Westminster School

After lunch I strolled round in the sunshine to watch fencing, judo and fives. A column of black smoke rises over Whitehall and we hear that a bomb has exploded. Another bomb outside Scotland Yard has been dismantled and there are rumours of other bombs in Central London.* The boys go about their exercise with little concern though one or two run excitedly to the entrance to Dean's Yard. They want to collect bits of debris, as we collected pieces of shrapnel as children during the war. Later a housemaster tells me that a boarder returned to his house carrying a piece of exploded car and was sent round to Scotland Yard to hand it in.

John Rae

Monday, 26 March 1973

First meeting of the National Theatre's dauntingly named Protocol Committee – members from the NT Board, South Bank Board, the GLC, the DES, Uncle Tom Cobley and all bureaucrats. The committee met to consider trivia – like who should be allowed to strike a medal to commemorate the opening of the NT, or promote some ghastly pot. But we moved on to how you open the new theatre. From the South Bank board came the view that there should be a gala night of a new production with a royal personage, presumably the Queen, there and that Shakespeare would be the best dramatist for the occasion, naturally.

I dropped my spanner into the works. I said I thought the National Theatre stood a good chance of being a scandal. It had cost much and was going to cost more. And it could well look like another pompous institution built for the elite. If we opened grandly with a new production for the Queen, we could have a mass demonstration outside, and slogans daubed all over Denys Lasdun's nice clean concrete. I suggested that the opening of the theatre – as a building – should be

---

* Four car bombs were planted by the IRA on 8 March 1973. Two were defused but the others (near Scotland Yard and the Old Bailey) exploded, killing one person and injuring over 200. Gerry Kelly (Gearóid Ó Ceallaigh), then nineteen, one of nine IRA members convicted of the crimes, later played a key role in the Good Friday Agreement and is currently a junior minister in the Northern Ireland Assembly.

a celebration, not a play; and that the launching of the theatre – as a playhouse – should be spread over the subsequent season.

Peter Hall

Wednesday, 28 March 1973

Alfred Hecht is a very superior framer who lives over his shop in the King's Road. I climbed up the stairs, at the top of which I was astounded to see a superb head of Churchill by Graham Sutherland. This was a non-décor flat, a cream-painted space into which chairs had been placed rather than arranged. The dinner-table was laid with Habitat place mats and napkins and cheap cutlery, the china was plain white and the food was noticeably served by hired hands. But there were superb pictures. A huge Francis Bacon hung behind me, too large for the room, and, in the drawing-room, there was another marvellous Sutherland.

This was an extremely wearing evening, a non-stop flow of hard intellect and hard talk, and a contrary assemblage of guests. To my left sat Jennie Lee, her white hair immaculate, wearing an oatmeal-coloured trouser suit with a blouse in a perfectly dreadful shade of turquoise, and with quite a lot of make-up on when you looked closely. Then there was Michael Foot and his wife. God, what doctrinaire socialists! Indeed Michael Foot began by expressing his dismay that this dinner was not, as he had been led to expect, an International Socialist meeting. After dinner the two of them were unleashed. They harangued us, he raising his voice as though addressing a revolutionary mob. Poor Nin Ryan, the benign American millionairess, one sensed her shudder.

This was an odd sort of evening.

Roy Strong

Tuesday, 5 June 1973
Westminster School

I see three boys who are reported to have been involved in drugs. Two of them asked the third to obtain cannabis, and while the third is surely the more 'professional' all three are equally involved and I rusticate them for three weeks. They are all 14 and must represent the tip of a large problem among the younger boys.

Further enquiries follow as the rustication has the unexpected effect of encouraging some younger boys to talk to their housemasters; it appears that three or four 15-year-olds are said to be hardened professional pushers. If this is true I must pin them down because here the real problem lies.

John Rae

Saturday, 13 October 1973
Saltwood Castle

In my father's study and maudlin on an empty stomach with suspected latent salmonella – result of one mouthful of an appalling 'steak sandwich' at a road-side pub in Preston on the way back from Blackpool conference.

Isn't Blackpool appalling, loathsome … ? Impossible to get even a piece of bread and cheese, or a decent cup of tea; dirt, squalor, shanty-town, broken pavements with pools of water lying in them – on the Promenade, vulgar, common 'primitives' drifting about in groups or standing, loitering, prominently. The conference, not a specially happy one. Bullying of the right by the Heathites (self *again* not called; fifth conference in a row). Heseltine, Peter Walker wouldn't speak to me.

Alan Clark

Tuesday, 11 December 1973

This evening I walk over to the House of Commons where I am a guest at a dinner of the Coningsby Club. Margaret Thatcher, the Conservative secretary of state for education, speaks and answers questions. On independent schools, she says that her reason for defending them is 'more fundamental that Dr Rae's' and explains that citizens should have the right to spend their money as they please as long as the activity is not illegal.

I do not think that is more fundamental than the freedom to run a school independent of the state but I say nothing.

John Rae

Monday, 28 January 1974

Mick McGahey, Vice-President of the National Union of Mineworkers, is in a difficulty because, on the radio tonight, he said 'Many of the troops which may be mobilised are the sons of miners, and if they come to dig coal, we shall appeal to them and explain our case to them.' A perfectly reasonable argument, nothing revolutionary in that. But people are now talking about sedition. I think we're heading for trouble and I am tempted to make a speech in advance which warns that the full moral and criminal responsibility for what might happen will fall on the Prime Minister's head.

Tony Benn

Saturday, 23 February 1974

Today Enoch Powell made his big Birmingham speech – of which I have only heard the briefest reports – where he began to indicate that he would be recommending people who believed in renegotiation (of our Common Market membership) and the sovereignty of Parliament to vote Labour. That is going to be a major issue in this Election. The Common Market has come into its own in the last week. It is the big question because it touches at food prices, at Heath's misunderstanding of the British people and also at the basic question of the freedom of Parliament and the people. Focusing on the Common Market is the main contribution that I have been able to make to Labour Party policy over the last three years.

Tony Benn

Thursday, 28 February 1974
General Election day

We walked together to the polling booth in Great Smith Street. Big crowd of journalists etc. A big lorry pulled out and the lorry driver leaned out and shouted, 'Good luck Harold, my old son.' He was about 25.

[Wilson] sets off to his Huyton constituency at 8.30 pm to tour the polling booths. He has had 20 minutes' sleep and looks and feels much better ... For nearly two hours we tour the constituency, in rain and sleet, very dark, totally lost in miles of council house estates. At first there is almost nobody in the party offices and clubs. All still canvassing. Later there are more people and the reception gets better.

The press follow at a distance but show little interest. The police are polite but do not treat HW especially well. He looks like the local candidate and I sensed that everybody saw him as a loser, finished, who would soon be just an old back-bench MP. At times we walked in the rain, just the two of us, HW and myself, rather lonely figures lost in anonymous wet streets.

Back at the hotel after the polling booths closed the press were gathering in the lobby, but still aloof and obviously not treating him seriously. Fortunately the BBC had sent Michael Charlton, who is nice and polite and serious, and almost the only BBC man who is not out to knock the Labour Party and lick the Tories' arse.

Off to Huyton Labour Club, to tumultuous reception. Everybody singing and chanting. Packed. Woman next to me had tears streaming down her face and was shouting 'I love him, I love him.'

Bernard Donoughue

Sunday, 3 March 1974
Hell Corner Farm, Buckinghamshire

The irony of this election is that the three day week, Ted Heath's gimmick, saved us from potential disaster as with so many people not at work, we had a record early poll. In some stations the poll was already 60 per cent by 6pm. And the immigrants, bless them, whom we had organised brilliantly, turned up trumps.

The result therefore is better than any of us had dared to hope, though stalemate means there is bound to be another Election soon. I told Tom and Jim* as we chewed over the events on Friday morning that I had intended this to be my last Election, but Jim said that, with another Election coming before long, they just would not release me. So here we go for a bumpy ride. Everyone was astonished when Heath did not resign immediately: he has got a bad press over it.

[Harold told me] 'Don't go too far away during the next few days.'†

Barbara Castle

---

*Tom Driberg and Jim Callaghan.
† Barbara Castle was appointed Secretary of State for the Social Services, and chose Jack Straw as her special adviser.

Wednesday, 6 March 1974

10 Downing St

Terrible lunch. We all go upstairs to the small dining room. We discuss the Central Policy Review Staff [the Downing Street 'Think Tank'] and appointments.

Suddenly Marcia* blows up. Already upset because we were eating whitebait. She says she hates them looking at her from the plate. The PM solemnly announced that they were whitebait from the Home for Blind Whitebait, so she need not worry. I added they were also volunteers.

Broke the tension for a while, but then she blew up over Harold and me having a polite and friendly conversation together ...

She stalked out. HW followed, his meal unfinished.

Bernard Donoughue

Thursday, 14 March 1974

This is only our third Cabinet but public expenditure is already rearing its ugly head. Denis [Healey] had put in a memo saying the economic situation the country faced was possibly the worst we had ever faced in peacetime. Unless something was done inflation this year would be over 15 per cent and the balance of payments deficit would jump to £400 million.

There would have to be increases in the prices of nationalised industries; defence should be cut by £250 million and prestige projects reviewed; in his view Concorde should be cancelled. In the meantime he asked Cabinet to accept that for 1974–5 there should be no increase in public expenditure ...

Wedgie came in first about his beloved Concorde. He could not have been more disingenuous. All he asked was that we should cash in on the previous governments refusal to disclose the facts and that he should be allowed to make an early statement revealing those facts ... Wedgie has lived to fight another day.

On defence (how history reverses the roles!) Denis was all for our

---

* Marcia Williams, Harold Wilson's formidable political secretary and head of his political office, later elevated (by Wilson) to the House of Lords as Baroness Falkender.

completing the immediate withdrawal East of Suez, while Roy Mason was full of the difficulties.

Barbara Castle

Monday, 25 March 1974

Twenty years ago Labour dogma was that we must have beautiful municipal theatres and a beautiful National Theatre; that is why the Greater London Council gave the site. The new dogma is that you don't need buildings, that when nine or ten people are gathered together in a space in Brixton or Fulham or Poplar, there is art. It is all balls.

Peter Hall

Friday, 29 March 1974

If I survive I think I am going to find my feet in this job. It is a big 'if' with the papers full of my family planning announcement, gleefully seized on by the *Mirror* as 'Barbara's free love.' My friend, Tom Wood, who took me back to Blackburn, told me the Catholic bishop of Salford is already on my tail. But I never had a moment's hesitation that the family planning service must be free.

Barbara Castle

Easter Holiday, 12–21 April 1974

On Easter Monday I phoned the Prime Minister in the Scillies from the red public phone box at Thorn's Corner, Wickhambrook ... putting coins in the box. He had been out walking and had slept in the sun.

Discussed Eric Heffer who, as a minister, had broken collective responsibility by attacking the government over sending warships to Chile ...

Some reflections on HW after our first session in Downing Street:

He never takes exercise. Spends his days in No 10 and in the Commons. In the car from one to the other. Never seems to feel a desire to walk in St James's Park – or go to Regent Street to look in shops. A totally insulated life. Spent in five rooms – Cabinet Room, Marcia's room, his study and, in the Commons, his room and the Chamber itself.

And his knowledge of the outside world is derived almost wholly from the newspapers. They are reality for him. This is why he reads them so avidly and gets so hurt by them.

Bernard Donoughue

Thursday, 9 May 1974

Some forty members of the Fringe – or as they now call themselves, the Alternative Theatre – visited the South Bank and came afterwards to the NT offices so that we could talk about how they could play from time to time on the South Bank ...

Groups with exotic names, like The Bubble and The John Bull Tyre Repair Outfit, took me on happily. Actually it was quite moving and very English. There was a desire to make contact, yet a desire to keep the difference. And it is impossible for them to like an institution swallowing millions of pounds, when a few hundred can mean the life and death of their own enterprises. I would be the same.

I believe the hand I have extended to the Fringe will almost certainly get badly bitten, bruised and shat upon. But it is a gesture which had to be made. Otherwise I will be running a greedy institution which is out of touch.

Yet I think of Jean-Louis Barrault in Paris in 1968. He made the Odeon, of which he was director, available to the rioting students, so that they could hold their political meetings there and have somewhere to sleep. They repaid him, finally, by breaking up his theatre, destroying his wardrobe, and spurning him as a weak and tolerant liberal. The government responded by sacking him.

Peter Hall

Monday, 20 May 1974

10 Downing Street

Later discussed Ireland, where a state of emergency was declared yesterday in reaction to the Ulster Protestants' strike against the proposed setting up of the Council of All Ireland.

Agreed we needed a small contingencies committee on Northern Ireland – to consider 'the unmentionable' – British withdrawal from Northern Ireland. [Harold Wilson] said that what was not tolerable was British troops being shot by both sides. But we also discussed drawing new boundaries between the north and the Republic. We also saw it as 'the crunch'. He said law and order had gone. Ted Heath's political solution of the Sunningdale conference was about to collapse – if that went there was nothing but 'the unmentionable'.

Bernard Donoughue

Tuesday, 28 May 1974

I know only too well the ghastliness of administration. At the V & A it is MOUNTAINOUS! So much time goes on the unions, staff delegations, pay claims, warders' conditions, works programmes, frantic appeals for money, terrifying cliff-hanging negotiations with the Treasury etc. And now, of course, as one thought, one occupies a central position concerning anything happening in England about the Arts and especially all things of historic interest …

The threatened Wealth and Inheritance Taxes if applied to historic house owners will see … the end of a thousand years of English history and culture, as pell-mell the contents are unloaded into the saleroom, the houses handed over to the Government or demolished. I can't tell you the horrors looming unless one fights and intrigues at every level behind the scenes.

Letter to Jan van Dorsten from Roy Strong

Wednesday, 29 May 1974

Merlyn Rees, the Northern Ireland Secretary, came in at noon and told us that the Protestant workers' strike was over. The Protestants have won. They have succeeded in destroying the experiment with Catholic participation in the power-sharing Executive. His position is that he is pleased the new power-sharing Executive established after Sunningdale has resigned, because it frees his hands to take direct action. And he thinks the Protestants have become very fascistic.

Bernard Donoughue

Tuesday, 4 June 1974

The visiting Bulgarian Minister of Trade had given me as a parting gift a little Bulgarian calculating machine, a tiny hand-held one in beautiful yellow, which had a memory. It was sent away to be debugged in case it had a recording device in it and the technicians had been enormously impressed by the quality of its circuitry which they said was the best they had seen among American, German and Japanese examples. They were very puzzled by how the Bulgarians could have got hold of such marvellous technology!

A group of Scottish Labour MPs came to see me at the House about the workers' newspaper cooperative in Glasgow (the *Scottish Daily News*). They were absolutely persuaded that the workers were serious people who ought to be supported.

Tony Benn

June 1974
Berlin Wall

I have just got back from a short visit to the Nico Hendersons.* After two days in Bonn staying in the pretty, white icing-sugar Residency, we flew to West Berlin and Ann Fleming and I were taken on a tour of the Wall. It was an experience that was dreadfully disturbing.

The wall itself is depressing enough, a slovenly made slice of foul concrete, too high to scale, with greasy curved top to prevent fleeing hands from getting a hold. Those who take a poor chance on their lives by trying to free themselves from life under the Soviets, have to contend with barbed wire, border guards high in their dreadful turrets, and, worse, guns that go off automatically at a vibration; land mines, potholes and terrible Alsatian dogs that are meagrely fed so that they remain savage ... Bomb rubble from the Armageddon of the last war was still there; a few distant traffic signals were working, but there was no traffic to be seen, poverty everywhere, hardly any public transport and a foul stench of cheap petrol filled the nostrils.

The hunting down of escapees or smuggling of any sort is unbelievably thorough, yet in spite of this there are still those who have the nerve, or imagination to overcome *all* difficulties.

Cecil Beaton

Thursday, 11 July 1974

The BMA doctors meeting in Hull have excelled themselves. The *Daily Telegraph* and others carry the headline: 'Doctors jeer at Castle's cash

---

* Nicholas Henderson, British ambassador to West Germany, 1972–5.

transfusion.' As Wedgie said to me 'Could there really be any other group in the country that would jeer at £47 million?' How I am going to cope with that bunch of mavericks ... I don't know. And David [Owen] has worried me by suggesting that he is working on the idea of allowing consultants to continue to work full-time in the NHS and do private work outside the NHS hospitals. I will never put up with that: it would be a direct incentive to build up a private service outside the NHS.

Barbara Castle

Saturday, 3 August 1974
Fairford, Bristol

To Fairford for the Concorde test flight, where we met the chief test pilot, Brian Trubshaw.

At 1.40 about sixty of us climbed into the Concorde and the great plan rumbled to the take-off point.

Some of the shop stewards (from BAC in Bristol) had never flown before, even one of them who had been in the aircraft industry for thirty-seven years. Another had gone to confession last night and another had made his will. Some of them had been up during the war, but not since. It was astonishing that in the aircraft industry, nobody had thought of asking them to fly. I insisted on taking them all up this time.

The whole plane shook. You could see the front portion just wobbling. Then this roaring take-off. We reached Mach 1 as we went supersonic, at about 7–800 miles per hour. It rose to 2.02, which was something like 1800 nautical mph. Absolutely no sensation in the plane at all. Somebody made a three-penny bit stand up on his table in front of him. We just behaved like people on a coach trip to Weston-Super-Mare or Southend.

It was an unforgettable day. I feel very pleased to have nursed that plane through its final crisis before its entry into service.

Tony Benn

Thursday, 15 August 1974

London airport is now the most congested, time-wasteful and farci-cally inefficient in the world – especially by comparison with the new de Gaulle airport in Paris, where all is uncluttered hush and one moves smoothly and uninterruptedly on sliding platforms from arrival at the drum-shaped terminal to the door of the aircraft. London, meanwhile, has evolved a method of embarkation that entails no fewer than five queues. (Six if you are foolish enough to want a cup of airport coffee, courtesy of Charles Forte, despot and bane of British catering ...) Queue #1 is the checking-in counter where baggage is weighed. You then pass to Queue #2 – passport inspection, and from this to Queue #3, where hand luggage is searched for explosives. The most otiose queue follows – #4, at the entrance to a waiting room near the aircraft where we line up to receive the numbered tickets indicating the location of our seats. We next sit in the waiting room until a man summons us, number by number, to Queue #5 which gains admittance to the plane itself. It is worth noting that Queue #4 exists solely to provide an excuse for Queue #5. How the British love micro-regimentation!

Kenneth Tynan

Thursday, 10 October 1974

The second election this year. [Since February 1974] the Labour Government actually have held back rising prices, they have kept mortgage rates down, they've cut VAT, they've introduced fairer legislation on the sharing of North Sea oil revenues and, on the international front, they have been a strongly heard voice in Washington and in the Common Market, and they have actually produced the 'social contract' which seems more than just another economic formula for trying to save the British economy (again) – it is an attempt to use and build on a sense of corporate responsibility among the working classes, which men like Sir Keith Joseph would deny they ever had.

Michael Palin

Friday, 18 October 1974
Westminster School

Talk to the whole school, warning them that if anyone is caught smoking dope in a local café, he will be at risk of expulsion.

This afternoon to two of the school's local community visits, the old people's home in Vauxhall Bridge Road and the day centre for the handicapped in Warwick Row. In both, Westminster boys and girls seem to be giving practical, unpatronising help and to have formed good relationships. Too good, I wonder, in one case? A young scholar has taken an old man from Bethnal Green under his wing; he brings the old man a bottle of Cyprus sherry every week which the man consumes in large gulps.

John Rae

Monday, 21 October 1974

My first major show, *The Destruction of the Country House*, opened amidst salvoes. It is one's first major statement made amidst a blaze of controversy and press and media coverage, a real challenge to those who wish to destroy everything England has created in the last 500 years. They queue to go into the [V & A] at weekends ... The weather has been foul, matching the economic and political situation.

I live in dread of vast slashes to museum spending and facing 1975 with no money, the exhibition schedule in ruins, and the new Oriental wing stopped. The post is now on strike in WC1 ... The Bakerloo and Circle Underground lines are so bad that they might just as well not exist. Sugar and salt are unobtainable.

Roy Strong

Friday, 22 November 1974

I walked through St James's Park and got to Number 10 at 10.30. Harold began by announcing that owing to the bombing in Birmingham last night,* he wouldn't play much part in the discussion but he hoped to look in and out. In fact he disappeared altogether.

The bombing story is absolutely dominant with anger rising, a petrol bomb thrown into a Catholic church, some factories in Birmingham refusing to work with Irish workers. The damage done to Irish people here, even though they may be Protestants, is terrible, every one a victim of the same awful process of escalating violence.

Tony Benn

---

*The bombing of two pubs in Birmingham killed twenty-one people. The Provisional IRA was suspected of carrying out the bombings, although they denied responsibility. The incident resulted in the Prevention of Terrorism Act 1974 being passed within days.

Monday, 2 December 1974

Up early so that I could visit Mother in hospital on my way to the office. She has had to have a clot in her leg removed. She lay crooning in her bed and greeted me: 'It's my Barbara.' Then she sang to me in a high voice all the songs she said Dad had sung to her. When I whispered to her, embarrassed, 'You will wake everyone up,' she retorted, 'They are not asleep and they like my singing.'

The other patients in the ward assured me it was so. 'Sometimes we join in. She's marvellous.'

Barbara Castle

Thursday, 16 January 1975
Cabinet

Finally, the Channel Tunnel. I am relieved that Tony Crosland [Environment Secretary] has decided we can't go ahead. This is not only anti-Common Market prejudice. It is a kind of earthly feeling that an island is an island and should not be violated. Certainly I am convinced that the building of a tunnel would do something profound to the national attitude – and not certainly for the better. There is too much facile access being built into the modern world.

From his diplomatic experience Jim [Callaghan] warned us that we should always 'as far as possible avoid getting into the position of being *demandeur* with the French: they will screw you to the limit.' I thought this was a very revealing comment from someone who is now working hard to get us into Europe.

The theory is that the project can be reopened in five to ten years' time, but I don't think Tony is fooled by this.

Barbara Castle

Wednesday, 5 February 1975

The papers are full of Margaret Thatcher.* She has lent herself with grace and charm to every piece of photographer's gimmickry, but don't we all when the prize is big enough? What interests me now is how blooming she looks – she has never been prettier. I am interested because I understand this phenomenon. She may have been up late on

---

* She had announced her candidature for the leadership of the Conservative Party.

the Finance Bill Committee; she is beset by enemies and has to watch every gesture and word. But she sails through it all looking her best. I understand why. She is in love: in love with power, success – and with herself.

Barbara Castle

Tuesday, 11 February 1975

Everyone agog at the news that Margaret Thatcher has been elected Tory leader with a huge majority. Surely no working man or woman north of the Wash is ever going to vote for her? I feel a lurch to the right by the Tories, and a corresponding lurch to the left by Labour.

To Buckingham Palace for the Queen's reception for the media, at least I suppose that's what we are. Newspaper editors; television controllers; journalists and commentators; Heath looking like a tanned waxwork; Wilson; Macmillan a revered side-show, an undoubted star; a few actors (Guinness, Ustinov, Finney); and all the chaps like me – John Tooley, George Christie, and Trevor Nunn. And Morecambe and Wise.

It was two and a half hours of tramping round the great reception rooms, eating bits of Lyons pate, drinking over-sweet warm white wine, everyone looking at everyone else, and that atmosphere of jocular ruthlessness which characterises the establishment on its nights out.

As we were presented the Queen asked me when the National Theatre would open. I said I didn't know. The Duke asked me when the National Theatre would open. I said I didn't know. The Queen Mother asked me when the National Theatre would open. I said I didn't know. The Prince of Wales asked me when the National Theatre would open. I said I didn't know. At least they all knew I was running the National Theatre.

Home at 2 am with very aching feet. Who'd be a courtier?

Peter Hall

Monday, 3 March 1975

We had another crowded agenda for the ministerial lunch. The troops were delighted when I said I intended to have a blitz on NHS spectacles and suggested I should see Marcus Sieff to ask his advice on how

I could get a top designer to design new frames which we could then have mass-produced.*

The Department's instinctive reaction was that private industry should make the beautiful things and that the NHS the ugly ones. I said I was determined to change all that.

Barbara Castle

Saturday, 15 March 1975

Paris

Took taxi to ... David Hockney's studio. This is in a little courtyard called Cour en Robson where Bonnard lived.

David said he greatly preferred Paris to London, that London was dull and lifeless, nothing was open after midnight, in order to enjoy yourself there you had to spend a great deal of money at expensive nightclubs, there were no cafes etc. And the worst of London was that no one protested. If he came back he would protest.

Stephen Spender

A group of highly motivated Cabinet members had worked hard to persuade the Labour government to hold a referendum on the Common Market (by now called the European Community). Since Britain had already signed up to the EC, a referendum would have to be on whether the British people wanted to stay in or leave. On 17 March 1975 the Cabinet met and itself voted 16 to 7 for recommending staying in the Common Market, but the principle of a referendum had been accepted; a group of Ministers including Tony Benn, Michael Foot, Barbara Castle, Peter Shore and Eric Heffer (the 'dissenting ministers') launched their campaign to persuade the electorate to vote to leave. The referendum was to be held on 5 June 1975. Harold Wilson was extremely angry at the actions of this group.

Wednesday, 19 March 1975

A gloomy scene met me as I entered Harold's room. Harold was sitting in his chair obviously in a shattered state. Mike [Michael Foot] sat at one end of the table opposite him; Jim at the other, head in hands. 'Have a drink,' said Harold morosely and as I helped myself he added, 'I

---

* Sir Marcus Sieff was chairman of Marks & Spencer.

was very insulting to Barbara [on the phone] just now and I apologise. I withdraw what I said.' I went over and kissed him affectionately on the forehead. 'And I am sorry if I upset you, but I can't withdraw,' I replied. 'Don't I get a kiss?' said Jim gloomily. 'God knows I need it.' So I kissed him too and sat down next to him.

'I can't understand why Barbara is so chirpy,' he almost groaned.

'Because I don't think the situation is tragic,' I replied.

Barbara Castle

Friday, 11 April 1975
Manchester Free Trade Hall

I was astonished at the size of the anti-Market rally in Manchester. They came pouring into the Hall, nearly two thousand strong. Everyone spoke well except me. I felt curiously listless. Perhaps it was jet lag, but I think it was also that I cannot get attuned to the oversimplified extremism of the anti-Market case. Peter [Shore] was impressive and well received, but Wedgie, with a more fluent flow of rhetoric than I have ever heard from him, was the hero of the hour. There was a more revivalist atmosphere than the movement has known for years.

Barbara Castle

Saturday, 17 May 1975
Barlinnie Prison Special Unit

This morning I lay in quite late before getting up to go outside and work in the sun as the day was beautiful.

I really got into the carving of this latest [sculpture] enjoying it immensely. I lost myself completely with the feeling, for the first time, of knowing the tools. I spent the whole day at it working patiently and very relaxed. When I parted from it at five o'clock I placed it so that, when in my cell that night, I could look out my window at it.

Jimmy Boyle

Wednesday, 21 May 1975

Westminster School

See Dick Taverne* who is interested in his 15 year old daughter coming to the School next year. She is at Pimlico Comprehensive where – according to her father – she is bored by the lack of stimulus and intellectual challenge. Then I see the father of a boy who is due to come in September. Father tells me that his son is one of the most promising cricketers Surrey has seen for many a year. I warm to father who is unpretentious and very proud of his son. I hope the boy passes the entrance exam. Heaven knows we could do with a good cricketer.

John Rae

Tuesday, 27 May 1975

London

What is to be done about the terrible decline of the country – the total absence of leadership and inspiration in the Conservative Party? In 1939 at least we had Fighter Command and the Navy, and Winston around. Now we have nothing. My windows here are filthy, dirtier even than at Saltwood. *US News and World Report* quite right – whole thing tatty, bad-tempered, lazy, in collapse. Yet of course there is no crisis; everyone flush with money. When will the recovery come? And how?

Yet even as I write this, I feel – too slack, too easygoing. In the train the other evening I thought perhaps I should go the whole way, stand as a National Front candidate, a switch if the Plymouth Conservative Association kicks me out. Or is the thought that I am 'waiting for the call' a concealment of my natural laziness?

Alan Clark

Monday, 2 June 1975

Referendum Day is Thursday. ('Do you think the UK should stay in the European Community?')

I am still undecided ... Either to stay in Europe and keep up with

---

* Dick Taverne had been Labour MP for Lincoln, but in 1972 clashed with his local party over his pro-EC views and resigned his seat. In the ensuing by-election in 1973 he stood successfully as an Independent, but lost the seat to Labour in the October 1974 election. He later joined the Social Democratic Party and is a Liberal Democrat life peer.

the fast pace of material progress which undoubtedly has made France and Germany quite attractive places to live in, or have the confidence to break from the incentive and the protection of Europe and become a one country independent free trader, as in the good old days.

For once a major politic-economic issue in Britain has not been debated on purely class lines. Tories mix with Labour, socialists with Monday Clubbers, unionists and bosses on pro and anti platforms. Only the implacable revolutionaries, who see the Common Market as a purely and quite reprehensibly capitalist device, seem to have unity in the ranks ... I will probably vote 'No' as a vote against the smugness and complacency of the over-subscribed 'Yes' campaign.

Michael Palin

Tuesday, 3 June 1975

Oxford Union debate: 'This House says Yes to Europe'

I sat down to the thinnest applause of the evening ... I knew I had been a flop, but my only feeling was one of relief that I had survived at all.

The most remarkable phenomenon of the evening was Heath. The audience was all his and he responded to it with a genuineness which was the most impressive thing I have ever seen from him. He stood there, speaking simply, strongly and without a note. They gave him a standing ovation at the end, and he deserved it for the best example I have ever seen of The Man Who Came Back. Then mercifully, we were able to escape to the President's room for drinks and the slow stain of the misery of failure began to come through into my soul. Everyone was congratulating Heath and I did too.

Peter [Shore] and I drove back to London and I just wanted to die. I don't mind being beaten – except by myself.

Barbara Castle

Thursday, 5 June 1975

Referendum Day

Melissa and I walked to St Peter's church hall, Portobello Road, where we cast our votes in the Common Market referendum – the first time Melissa had voted.

Back to Bristol where Caroline met me and we drove round in a lorry for four hours with the Loudspeaker shouting 'No to the

Common Market.' The ITN ten o'clock news predicted a 69 per cent Yes vote and a 29 per cent No vote.

I rang Frances (my political adviser). 'O well, people are sick of elections, they are glad it is settled. Harold has scored a tremendous triumph but it's over and done with now. The left has played its trump card and been soundly defeated. This is the moment really to fade out.'

Tony Benn

Wednesday, 2 July 1975
Prime Minister's Birthday Party for the Queen

This is the great diplomatic event of the year, at which Cabinet ministers are expected to help Jim [Callaghan] out as co-hosts, and we had all been allowed to pair by the Whips, even though we were in the middle of a three-line whip on the Industry Bill.

I wanted to go because the dinner was at Hampton Court Palace, which I haven't seen since I was a child and even then I never penetrated inside.

Hampton Court was everything I had hoped; the meal was good and I enjoyed quarrelling with my Luxembourg neighbour about the European Community as I looked up at the high ceiling in the dining hall. 'I do hope they play the Post Gallop,' he said as the band rattled on in the Minstrels' Gallery. 'I have never heard anything like it.' And so they did. We then all trooped through the Tudor courtyard to the garden, with its long avenues and beautifully kempt laws, to hear the Marines play The Retreat as they marched and wheeled in perfect formation on a perfect summer evening. I was interested to watch the diverse diplomats – the one in front of me looked like Haile Selassie – studying the whole performance with rapt attention, while Ted and I tapped our feet approvingly to the tunes, unashamedly patriotic. 'This is one of the reasons I am anti-Market,' I whispered naughtily to my neighbour, as he applauded the Englishness of it all. I love my home and country with a fierce protectiveness.

Barbara Castle

Saturday, 19 July 1975

Went shopping with Melissa and we walked up Kensington High Street. We went into Biba's store which is closing – the end of a dream.

You can see why it failed because it was the final fling for the excrescences of Sixties fashion, now all gone bust.

Tony Benn

Tuesday, 22 July 1975

I heard today that the problem of what we would do with the oil off the Falkland islands has been settled by the Foreign Office. They have insisted that we agree to discuss with Argentina joint exploration of the South Atlantic, and this is intended to get us off the hook.

Tony Benn

Tuesday, 5 August 1975

At Social Services Committee we made further progress with David Owen's pet campaign against smoking. He is very touched that, smoker though I am, I should humour him on this.

I sat next to Harold for [Prime Minister's] Questions. This gave me a full view of Margaret, who slipped into her place as demurely tight-lipped as ever and glossy with her best suburban grooming: fresh flowered summer frock and every wave of her hair in place. How does she keep her hair so unchangeably immaculate? It all adds to the feeling of unreality about her political leadership. Somehow that also is too bandbox. She never risks anything: just sits there listening to Harold with a carefully modulated look of disapproval on her face, then produces one regulation intervention per Question time. When she is ready for this great act she starts to lean forward slightly and an atmosphere of 'wait for it' builds up behind her. When finally she rises our chaps cheer ironically. She ignores them and fires her shaft. It never completely misses but is never (or very, very rarely) deadly. The lads behind her cheer lustily. Once again their tame bird has laid her egg.

Barbara Castle

Tuesday, 12 August 1975
Barlinnie Prison Special Unit

This morning I felt terrible and went to get my chisels and begin a new piece. I started work before nine o'clock and worked straight through till four. The anger in me is really bad and I kept thinking of sculptors from the past wondering if they worked with such torment. I took an untouched piece of stone and nearly completed the sculpture by the time I stopped. I didn't have the remotest idea what I was going to do when I started and it's turned out great. There is no way that the feeling of working while angry can be measured but I am very tired and weary and have to get out of this fucking place or I will go crazy. Prison is killing me.

Jimmy Boyle

Wednesday, 10 September 1975
Chequers

The Devolution discussion began at about 10.20 am in the usual big room, with paintings of fat and bewigged gentry looking down at the long table around which sat some 20 members of the Cabinet … Joe, myself and two private secretaries from No. 10 sitting along one wall.

Every so often the meeting dissolved into grumblings of doubt about the whole exercise. But always Willie Ross [the Scottish Secretary] stepped in to say it was too late. He had warned them years ago and they would not listen or support him. Now they must live with it.

HW was chairing the meeting remarkably firmly and well considering that he was totally bored with the whole question. He privately admitted that he had not read all the papers, and was thinking more of the *Daily Mail* than of the British constitution.

We resumed just after 3. Callaghan, Benn and Rees had gone. The ministers zipped through the rest of the agenda but at the end the proceedings deteriorated into dreadful squabbling. Healey went on and on, saying that the Cabinet had never agreed to devolution. He interrupted HW in a most boorish way. Crosland objected to this. Jenkins obviously was embarrassed by Healey's crude style but agreed with his argument. Ross was booming away at the end of the table that it was too late to object, devolution was a fact of life. HW was trying without success to restore order. For 20 minutes it was like a monkeys' tea party.

It broke up at around 4 pm with Willie Ross booming on about the need to devolve agriculture to Scotland while ministers rushed desperately to the door and down the stairs. The black Rovers streamed up to the back door and swept off down the drive, out of the grounds and back to London. A tremendous sense of power and movement, but a terrible waste of cars and petrol.

Bernard Donoughue

Saturday, 13 September 1975
Westminster School

To watch football practice. This evening I am disturbed to read a series of articles in the *Times Educational Supplement* arguing that as Britain is now multi-cultural schools should no longer pass on a mono-cultural tradition. What nonsense. If the history and literature of the country are watered down to suit ethnic minorities, the United Kingdom will be little more than a geographical expression. Happily, Westminster does not have to take any notice of this misguided idea. A good argument for keeping independent schools – they can ignore the fads and fashions of educationalists.

John Rae

Friday, 26 September 1975
Labour Party National Executive Committee

Everyone has been predicting terrible rows at this year's Conference. Certainly there have been floods of resolutions denouncing the Government's economic policy and expenditure cuts and demanding massive increases in expenditure on this and that. But there were few signs of dissension in the NEC meeting this morning. On the Finance Committee report, we were faced by a resolution of Shirley's [Williams] saying that in view of the Party's acute financial difficulties, Ministers should 'consider' meeting the whole of their expenses at conference this year and the trade union boys should ask their unions to meet their expenses. This led to an involved argument from which it emerged that some union rules would make this difficult. Eventually it was left that Cabinet ministers only should 'consider' this.

I felt aggrieved by two things (1) Why keep picking on Cabinet ministers as though we were Croesuses? It should be done on ability to pay and I bet Mik's [Ian Mikado's] income is bigger than mine. (2) I wish it hadn't been sprung on us at the last minute. If I'd known I would have to find £110 or so for Conference, I would have told Ted we couldn't afford Corfu as well.

Barbara Castle

Wednesday, 22 October 1975

I went down to address the new all-party Heritage Group in the House, about ten of them in all.

They seemed a dim lot; the Chairman, Ted Graham, is MP for Edmonton. From the moment you see him you know he probably wouldn't be able to tell a Rembrandt from a Picasso. The moving force is a Tory MP, Patrick Cormack, amiable, owl-like. Sir David Renton, an old Tory country gent, enunciated attitudes enough to drive one very far Left. Alan Beith, the young Liberal, ex-University of Newcastle lecturer in politics, showed a flicker at thirty-two. Really I wondered what use it had all been. They are such fringe people with no real influence up the line. I gave them the usual mix with a strong plea to keep art museums out of politics. It was depressing and the food was filthy.

Roy Strong

Monday, 3 November 1975
Scotland

Arrived at Aberdeen at 8.30 for the landing of the first oil from the Forties Field.

The first thing I noticed was that the workers who actually bring the oil ashore were kept behind a wire fence and just allowed to wave at us as we drove by.

We were given a cup of coffee as we waited for the Queen to arrive.

Eventually we were taken out on the dais to watch the Queen's Rolls Royce approaching. Out came the Queen in a green dress, followed by the Duke of Edinburgh and Andrew.

Behind another fence were about 500 Aberdonians waving Union Jacks and the Queen and the Duke walked in front of them as if they were animals in a zoo.

To be frank, the day was a complete waste of time and money and when you see the Queen in action, everything else is just absorbed into the frozen hierarchy. All the old bigwigs are brought out into the open as if they were somehow responsible for a great industrial achievement, while the workers are presented as natives and barbarians who can be greeted but have to be kept at a distance. It is a disgrace that a Labour Government should allow this to continue. I also felt that this great Scottish occasion was just an opportunity for the London establishment to come up and lord it over the Scots.

Tony Benn

Tuesday, 4 November 1975

I spoke to the PM when he arrived from Chequers. He was very gloomy about Chrysler and said that he had little to offer. Talks were still going on but it was clear that the Americans would not put in any more money after the end of the month. They even offered us the plant for nothing.

They pointed out that since taking over French Chrysler, they had not lost a single day's work through disputes; in the same period they had not had a single day without disputes in the UK.

The PM went in late to the OPD Cabinet committee to discuss arms sales to Egypt. I went back to my room to read a stream of papers on industrial bankruptcies, import controls, and the bleak economic outlook.

Bernard Donoughue

Thursday, 6 November 1975

I learned that Harold Pinter was incensed when I said on TV a few weeks ago that the English theatre was preoccupied with the minor emotional crises of the urban middle class and never opened its eyes to analyse society as a whole or the world outside England. I named *No Man's Land, Otherwise Engaged* [Simon Gray] and the Ayckbourn Trilogy as examples of the kind of thing I meant, and summed up the plot of the Pinter play as a rich middle-class writer has a wary confrontation with a poor middle-class writer.

Peter Hall

Tuesday, 2 December 1975

David Owen, who though a junior minister is effectively the Minister of Health, came in at 12.20 pm to collect me for lunch and we went out to Chez Victor, which is still one of the best little French restaurants in London. We discussed the doctors' dispute which is coming to a crisis. He said that Barbara Castle thinks of nothing but the pay beds issue – she neglects the rest of the Health Service and Social Security. She is following the dictates of the unions involved. Since *In Place of Strife* she has decided never again to get out of step with the unions. Now she is in danger of destroying the Health Service and does not seem to be aware or care. David also spoke loyally in her defence but admits she is the biggest obstacle to a settlement.

Bernard Donoughue

Thursday, 4 December 1975

When we came to Foreign Affairs and the EEC I said, 'Can I ask one question about passports? On television I saw a picture of our blue British passport disappearing and a purple European Community passport being substituted. That really hit me in the guts. It is quite unnecessary. Everybody knows that Britain is in the Common Market. You could put European Community on the back of the existing passport, you could put on page 3, "This man is a European whether he likes it or not". But we have got to be careful: like metrication and decimalisation, this really strikes at our national identity and I don't like it.'

Harold Wilson said 'I don't need a lecture on Kipling.'

I said, 'Well Harold, if you can talk to the Commission and keep the common touch, I shan't worry.' Everybody laughed but it is a serious concern.

Tony Benn

Tuesday, 16 December 1975

A long schedule of meetings over, I found it was 7 pm and I was already late for the Transport House Christmas party ...

At 8.30 ... empty glass in one hand, empty plate in the other, forgetting that I had my bifocals still on my nose ... I tried to negotiate the curving fan-shaped steps in the half dark I suddenly felt a violent shock. I was flat on my face, hands down, shin-bone in agony, my spectacles spread-eagled in front of me.

It was Shirley [Williams] and some unknown gentleman from

Transport House who dragged me to the car. They got me to the House and somehow to my room. Shirley took charge of me. She was everything one would expect of her: kind, gentle and competent as she fed me hot drinks and found blankets. 'I'll get the whips to find a doctor,' she said. 'Who would you prefer?' 'David,' I said, 'or Maurice Miller.'

It seemed ages afterwards as I lay with my throbbing leg, that there was a stir at the door ... 'Here is a doctor,' said a whip. I then found to my horror that the one they had produced was my political 'shadow', the smiling sepulchre, Gerry Vaughan.*

But of course I had to submit. Gerry examined my leg with intense anxiety, finally pronouncing that it was a very bad fall *indeed*, adding something that I found profoundly contemptible. 'If it were anyone but you, Barbara, I would have sent you for an immediate x-ray.' I knew what he meant: that, with emergency departments shut down by industrial action in a number of hospitals, his wretched profession was waiting to play medical politics with my personal pain. I hissed at him: 'I would not go for an x-ray if I were dying.'

Barbara Castle

Tuesday, 6 January 1976

The terrible sectarian killings have brought the crisis to a head. HW sent for Merlyn Rees who was in Belfast seeing the politicians and told him to come back here to a meeting this afternoon. I said there would be renewed pressure to move Merlyn (whom HW offered to move last summer but he refused). And perhaps he should go. He looks very tired. The basic question to Merlyn is where does he want the Irish situation to be in five years. I am not sure that he has time to look beyond today's latest killing in Crossmaglen.

At 3.30 we had the meeting on Ireland. Merlyn Rees reported in his usual breathless way, full of colourful detail and marvellous anecdotes.

The PM then said he wanted a military initiative, even an over-response, to stress that we are doing something.

Merlyn was not too happy with this. He said it was only a question of 30 Provisionals and 30 Protestant UVF in Armagh doing all the killing. A big army was irrelevant to that.

---

* David Owen was a doctor, as well as being Barbara Castle's Minister of Health; Maurice Miller was a Labour MP and a General Practitioner. Gerard Vaughan was Conservative MP for Reading, and a consultant at Guy's Hospital, London. He was Shadow Secretary of State for Health.

Roy Mason as Defence Minister was in favour of a stronger military presence. He asked to despatch the 'Spearhead' Battalion straight away – the instruction was sent from the Cabinet Room.

They then discussed [the PM's] plan to involve the Tories tomorrow, but Whitelaw and not Thatcher. The PM sent for a railway timetable to discover the time of the earliest train Whitelaw could catch from Carlisle – he had to be telephoned there, after Thatcher has left England, but in time [for him] to catch an early train to London. One of HW's objectives was to freeze out Airey Neave, the official Tory spokesman on Ireland, since HW suspects him of wanting to break the bipartisan approach and bring the Ulster Unionists back into the Tory fold.

Bernard Donoughue

Monday, 26 January 1976

The newspapers are still reporting the repercussions of Mrs Thatcher's attack on the Russians last week, and their retaliation, describing her as the Iron Lady or Iron Maiden, has absolutely delighted the Tory Party.

Tony Benn

Sunday, 1 February 1976

Our prop men want a 50% increase because they're moving from the Old Vic to the South Bank; they're doing the same job but it is in a different environment. We've said no. So our friendly NATTKE* steward, Kon Fredericks, has got the whole stage staff to agree that while they will continue to work they will not, during this fit-up period in the new theatre, touch any of the new machinery until the management make a more realistic offer. They know that now we're nearly open, we're vulnerable.

Peter Hall

---

*The National Association of Theatrical Television and Kine Employees, now part of Broadcasting and Entertainment Trades Alliance.

Monday, 2 February 1976

The papers are full of Jeremy Thorpe, who is in real trouble over this man Scott, who has claimed a sexual relationship with him: it looks as though he's on his way out.

Tony Benn

Tuesday, 2 March 1976

Crosland presented his Transport paper very sensibly. It recommends a switch from rail to road, the opposite of the manifesto, and it is packed with concessions to the railway unions. Most people were worried by parts of the paper – especially the massive increases in fares involved.

Later ... Briefing for Questions went very slowly. [The PM's] whisky was 'off' and he sent for another bottle which took ages to come. He said, 'If they don't hurry up, I shall answer Questions cold sober, which will create a record.'

In Questions he was brilliant, demolishing the Tories and Eric Heffer, Dennis Skinner and various other enemies of the Labour government with a series of sharp thrusts. I felt he was settling old scores, enjoying himself in the last few days.*

Bernard Donoughue

Wednesday, 3 March 1976

George Brown has resigned from the Labour Party. Last night he was clearly incapable. Today the *Guardian* and the *Mail* honourably carry pictures of him, prostrate in the gutter after his broadcast.

The Times excelled itself, [in an article] which included the incredible phrase 'George Brown drunk is a better man than the Prime Minister sober.' I should think even Harold's enemies would be ashamed of it. When I remember what Harold put up with from George for all those years.

Barbara Castle

---

* Wilson had confided to a very few people that he intended to resign in March, and his announcement at Cabinet later in the month took almost everyone by complete surprise.

Tuesday, 16 March 1976

I went to Cabinet at 11. Harold said, 'Before we come to the business, I want to make a statement.' Then he read us eight pages, in which he said that he had irrevocably decided that he was going to resign the premiership and would stay just long enough for the Labour Party to elect a new leader. People were stunned but, in a curious way, without emotion. Harold is not a man who arouses affection in most people.

Nobody knew it was coming [but] there was still a remarkable sort of lack of reaction.

Jim Callaghan who found it hard to conceal his excitement said, 'Harold we shall never be able to thank you for your services to the Movement.'

I left Downing Street about 1. By then there was a huge crowd of people, hundreds of television cameras.

Tony Benn

Tuesday, 16 March 1976

Barbara Castle's room, House of Commons

Mike [Foot] called in too, to tell me he would stand [for the Leadership]. I asked him if Wedgie was standing and he havered a bit. Obviously, he said, it would be better if Wedgie didn't stand, but he wanted to talk to him and tell him he didn't want to get in his way. 'I'll talk to Wedgie myself,' I replied and went at once to Wedgie's room. I found him closeted with Joe Ashton and Joe's wife.

I felt a bit constrained, but said bravely to Wedgie, 'The future is with you, but not at this moment. This election is a forceps delivery.' Looking a bit haggard, he seemed to agree. Joe was passionate. This election was not about personalities, but about policies. Dennis Skinner was right he insisted: every candidate for the leadership should be made to set out the policies for which he stood. The important thing, I suggested was to stop Jim. 'Don't worry,' said Joe grimly. 'The "stop Jim" movement is already under way: from the Right as well as the Left.'

Barbara Castle

Thursday, 18 March 1976

Cabinet and we discussed the Falkland Islands; a paper from Jim pointing out that there were thirty-seven marines there and 2000 islanders and the Argentinians were being very difficult. There was possibly some oil there and we couldn't hold the islands against an attack. He had two suggestions one of which was to ... let sovereignty pass to the Argentinians and lease the islands back and develop the oil jointly.

Tony Benn

Tuesday, 30 March 1976

The results of the second ballot were Jim Callaghan 141, Michael Foot 133, Denis Healey 38. I must say the fact that Denis got only one more vote in the second ballot than I got in the first gave me great pleasure; he was utterly rejected really. It looks as if Jim is going to make it, but there are still uncertainties one way and the other.

At 10.15 I went and voted for Michael Foot in the final ballot.

Tony Benn

Wednesday, 7 April 1976

I went to the Minister for Education's office for the presentation of a medal. The Minister, Fred Mulley, is a north-country slob, coarse of feature, not very bright but affectionate and good in his handling of the occasion. The office was still largely with Mrs Thatcher's décor, suburban hairdresser style: doors with panels of beading laid over and painted gold, and with a white carpet! The Permanent Secretary, Sir William Pile, was very funny about her, how she had slaved to learn French privately for her great visit to Geneva, got into the hotel and tried to order a drink, collapsing back into her hopeless school-girl French. His most revealing moment with her, he said, was when [during a sex scandal] she had steeled herself up one day, when travelling in the back of a car with him, to ask, 'Did men really pay that kind of money for that sort of thing?' She lives in a world apart, unaware how most of the population lives. He said that her law degree wasn't much, her command of facts terrific within a set area but beyond that nothing. Her knowledge of history was nil.

Roy Strong

Monday, 12 April 1976

I had a message to go over to see Jim Callaghan.

'You have great ability,' said Jim. 'I think you could be one of the greatest leaders this country has ever had but I am not sure that you are not aiming to go out and be the darling of the left. Well I can be a very hard man and I shall call you in one day if it goes wrong, and maybe I shall sack you.'*

Jim is handling me skilfully because I am somebody who needs to be at least thought of as not destructive, if not appreciated. I assured him, 'I am not sitting waiting for the revolution to march on London, I live in the naïve hope that one day you will accept the policies that I advocate.'

'When they make sense, I will,' he replied.

I saw Harold tonight wandering round the House and he has absolutely shrunk; it shows that office is something that builds up a man only if he is somebody in his own right. And Wilson isn't.

Tony Benn

Thursday, 29 April 1976

To Winchester for an unpublicised meeting of eight major public schools: Eton, Winchester, Westminster, Harrow, Rugby, Charterhouse, Shrewsbury and Marlborough. We dine in the warden's lodgings and before and after dinner we talk about the threats to the future of our schools at a time of rising fees, falling numbers and political hostility. We agree that whatever happens, we eight will act in concert. The unspoken agenda is that our schools must survive even if other independent schools go to the wall.

John Rae

---

*Tony Benn was retained as Energy Secretary in the Cabinet after James Callaghan's election as Leader of the Labour Party, but Barbara Castle, the Health and Social Security Secretary, was removed.

Saturday, 1 May 1976

At 1415 I drove with Lilibet and Philip in their car, followed by Court Officials in another car, to Wembley.

I was very keen to go to the Cup Final this year because for the first time in history our own local home team, the Saints of Southampton, were in the final against that formidable team, Manchester United. The betting odds were 6 to 1 in favour of Manchester United, but on the way I kept on saying I was undaunted in my backing of Southampton and reminded Philip how often when one is playing with a low-handicap team against a high-handicap team in an open tournament, the low-handicap team could surprise the high-handicap team who then got rattled and the low-handicap team won.

The world now knows that that is exactly what happened; within the last 7 or 8 minutes of the game Southampton shot the one and only goal. The whole place went mad but the Royal Box sat rather glumly there, so I stood up myself and cheered and waved and shouted. I gathered later that this did not pass unnoticed by the Southampton supporters! ... It was a nice clean game too, with hardly any violence afterwards such as has recently been disgracing these big soccer matches.

Louis Mountbatten

Wednesday, 11 August 1976
National Theatre

Our stage staff have refused to work in the Olivier while being on call for the Lyttleton. So this afternoon we had to take the issue to ACAS. News came tonight that they [ACAS] had ruled in our favour and instructed the men to return to work in the Olivier for fourteen days while we sorted out a new agreement.

Peter Hall

Friday, 13 August 1976

A day that lived up to its reputation. We were due for our first technical rehearsal of *Tamburlaine* tonight, but Simon [technical administrator] came to see me to say the stage staff had refused the ACAS ruling and voted against working in the Olivier while they were on call for the Lyttleton. In the Olivier nobody but the stage management and production team was there. Kon Fredericks was lurking about under the stage to make sure we didn't rehearse even a cue.

I am heart-broken, but we must stand up to the wreckers among them now, or the theatre will not be a place in which to work for the future. If *Tamburlaine* has to go to the wall, it must.

Peter Hall

Thursday, 26 August 1976

At about 5 pm I went up to the conference room and signed the new NATTKE agreement ... Among our 17 shop stewards there was one anti, one abstention (Kon) and the rest were finally for it. And the agreement apart from a conciliation clause is exactly the same as one that was thrown out seven weeks ago.

The men were asked if they would give us a dress rehearsal of *Tamburlaine* although the new agreement doesn't come into force until Monday. They refused. The company were furious.

Peter Hall

Tuesday, 31 August 1976
Barlinnie Prison Special Unit

Teddy Taylor* came in ... He is a small balding man who was quite apprehensive though trying not to show it. He offered us all a cigarette and then I took him round ...

We all sat in the meeting room and had a long debate on the Unit and he was all for what we were doing but should do it without publicity ... he was so full of contradictions that it was difficult to accept. He mentioned all his mates and friends who have just come out of prison, some of whom are working for him in the Conservative Party – locally. Then he would say prison nowadays is a soft option and on the other hand that it must be terrible to be locked up with no privacy ...

---

*Teddy Taylor was Conservative MP for Glasgow Cathcart until 1979 (MP for Rochford and Southend East, 1980–2005) and also Conservative spokesman on Scottish Affairs, in which capacity he was presumably visiting the Scottish prison.

He thinks the experiment is going very well and thinks it should continue. This will be on the radio tomorrow morning.

Jimmy Boyle

Monday, 6 September 1976

Genuinely excited and keen to get back to the House. Ladbroke apparently giving evens on a coalition by 1st Jan. I must lay against that. Tories all chattering and yearning about an early election. Personally I don't see it. Why? How can it come about? PMs call elections when they think they are going to win, not in order to commit hari kari. But the gossip and jockeying will be fun.

Alan Clark

Thursday, 9 September 1976

First Cabinet since the summer recess. Tony Crosland (Foreign Secretary) said, 'I expect you have heard, Chairman Mao is dead.' In fact I hadn't heard it on the news. 'I don't suppose there's much point in my trying to assess Mao Tse Tung's role in the world,' said Tony and he just passed over the event. I did feel that Mao merited a moment of reflection in the British Cabinet. In my opinion he will undoubtedly be regarded as one of the greatest – if not the greatest – figures of the 20th century: a school teacher who transformed China, released it from civil war and foreign attack, and constructed a new society there ... he certainly towers above any other 20th century figure.

Tony Benn

Tuesday, 5 October 1976

Now the Government cuts for the V & A have really started to bite with a savagery ... as Director I face the worst crisis since 1939. It is ghastly. I have to lose ninety-four staff out of seven hundred and at every level at an even percentage. I nearly go mad because the Keepers simply have not the practical administrative sense that I have, and their proposals, so tragically well meant, are pure fairyland. To meet what is asked by the Government I am going to have to do something which will set the institution back a hundred and thirty years. I must amputate. The last weeks have been agony, but I have reached my BIG DECISION. Now to find the way forward to do it.

Everywhere here in Britain is so gloomy. I keep looking for GOOD NEWS – WHERE IS IT? The main theme is can we or can we not survive until the 1980s without a collapse of society as we know it.

One is confused, bewildered, despairing.

Roy Strong

Friday, 29 October 1976

Up at 6.30 and Caroline and I flew to a little airport and were driven to Selby for the opening of the new coal mine. There was the Lord Lieutenant, the Duchess of Kent and the High Sheriff of the county.

Joe Gormley [president of the National Union of Mineworkers] was called to speak and he had a few notes and he began in a measured way and then somehow forgot that he wasn't at a pithead meeting and started to talk about productivity and the role of the miners.

Lunch was hilarious. The Duchess sat next to me and Joe leaned across and asked, 'What's your name, love?'

She said 'Katharine.'

'I'm Joe.' Then he held up his glass and said 'If you can't be good, be careful.'

Tony Benn

Friday, 17 December 1976

The truth of the matter over the savage cuts imposed on the V & A is that months ago Fred Mulley, then Secretary of State for Education, did not lift a finger. Jack Donaldson [Minister for the Arts] admitted that nothing could be done. Shirley Williams said that the figures were unalterable. This only shows to me the utter wretchedness of Civil Servants. We were just written off months ago without anyone taking any notice at all of the appalling implications. It means the end of the Regional Services. The letters of protest from places as far as Aberdeen and Portsmouth have made no difference at all, nor lobbying MPs, the Lords, the Standing Commission, nor the Henry Moore–David Hockney petition. 1977 is to be a year of misery as one inflicts the cuts.

Roy Strong

Tuesday, 28 December 1976

It has been a very remarkable year really in the aftermath of the Referendum when the Labour Party was in a terrible state of depression and the Labour government appeared to be going forward with its own right-wing policy unchallenged.

I must think about Europe. I think we should call for major reforms in the Treaty of Rome, committing us to a democratic socialist association of states which will bring about a fundamental and irreversible shift in the balance of wealth and power in favour of the working people of Europe and their families; [and] it should aim at dismantling all the federal parts so that it becomes an open association with none of the present centralisation and bureaucracy.

Tony Benn

Wednesday, 19 January 1977

British Embassy, Paris

At 7 in came the butler and sub-butler with the silver salver and silver teapot and China tea and lemon, scrambled egg, crispy bacon, toast and marmalade.

We flew off to Brussels and to the international press centre ... the journalists who had arrived by 10.45 were drinking at the bar.

We went off from there for a lunch with the Belgians, given by Sir David Muirhead, our Ambassador to the Brussels government, who lives in another of these great fancy houses, with a butler, sub-butler, a log fire and God knows what. I found the Belgians terribly funny, by which I mean they laugh at my jokes.

The truth is that everyone who works at Brussels, be they Ministers, bureaucrats, representatives of the delegations or the press, have just got used to the fraud of it all, the muddle, the confusion and the obscurity.

Tony Benn

Sunday, 6 February 1977

Saltwood Castle

Watched Enoch on TV – quite by chance. Jane spotted that he had already been on for fifteen minutes. Quite wonderful. His clarity of speech and thought, his administrative experience, his living and incomparable patriotism and they ignore him.

Alan Clark

Monday, 14 February 1977
Westminster School

Isaiah Berlin talks to the John Locke Society about 'The Russian obsession with patterns in history'. It is a wonderful talk lifting the spirit by its humanity, range and sheer intellectual brilliance. He draws a crowded meeting and holds them for 50 minutes non-stop. Over lunch in College Hall, scholars do their best to quiz him and it is good to hear them. To put boys and girls in touch with a great mind and to give them the opportunity to test their fledgling intellect on his is an essential part of learning, but in how many schools, in how many universities for that matter, is this possible?

Peter Newsam, the chief education officer of the Inner London Education Authority, comes round from County Hall for a talk. We have met once or twice at those discussions about getting more able boys and girls to do engineering. We mull over the possibility of persuading the government to set up an English version of the Massachusetts Institute of Technology.

John Rae

During March 1977 the Labour government entered a pact with the Liberal Party (the Lib–Lab pact). It was an expedient measure to deal with the government's lack of an overall majority in Parliament and lasted until September 1978 by which time unemployment and inflation were falling. Despite perceptions, the number of industrial stoppages was considerably lower by 1978 – under four years of the Wilson/Callaghan premiership – than in the four years of Edward Heath's premiership. Election fever was strong during 1977 and 1978 but Callaghan decided to carry on until the last possible moment – May 1979. In January of that year, he returned from Strategic Arms Limitation Talks held in Guadeloupe to a media scrum asking him about the 'crisis' in Britain: coincidentally, during the first week of January, lorry drivers (including oil tanker drivers) began a strike, which closed petrol stations across Britain.

Thursday, 26 May 1977

At 9.30 we had the Cabinet committee which deals with Common Market issues and pig-meat was on the agenda. The Commission had appealed to the European Court to rule out of order the pig-meat subsidy that John Silkin (Agriculture minister) had agreed and the court had ordered that this subsidy cease forthwith. Foreign Office advice was that forthwith meant *at once*.

I asked whether this was the first time a European Court decision had been taken against the British Government and I was told it was. Then I asked what would be the effect of this on pig producers in the UK. John Silkin said it would mean in effect the destruction of our industry, the mass slaughtering of pigs and the abandonment of our processing plant in favour of the Danes. All in the name of free competition! That was an absolute turning point.

Tony Benn

Friday, 27 May 1977

Some of the notices of *State of Revolution* are very good and some just mild. But the real revolution this morning was down at the theatre. The workshops, the stage staff and some others came out on strike and began picketing. It is in a way a replay of last summer, but it's also very different. If the plumber had been wrongfully dismissed, there are proper means of arbitration to decide whether or not he should be reinstated; what we're talking about now is rule of law ...

I was in the theatre for fifteen hours negotiating, discussing and wondering. The day was a series of cliff-hangers. Could I return to Glyndbourne where it was my final *Don Giovanni* dress rehearsal? The hours ticked by and in the end, of course, I didn't – the first time this has ever happened to me.

We fought to save tonight's performance of *State of Revolution* but we couldn't.

Peter Hall

Wednesday, 22 June 1977

At the House this evening Audrey Wise told me all about the strike of the women workers at Grunwick.* She had been down there supporting the strike and she saw a policeman pulling a girl's hair, so she put her hand on the policeman's arm. He immediately released the girl and said to Audrey 'You'll do love,' and bundled her into a Black Maria.

I should mention that the fighting this week on the picket line has been on a massive scale. The police have been behaving abominably, plucking people from out of the crowd.

Tony Benn

Thursday, 27 October 1977

Dine at the Garrick this evening as the guest of the Pooh Trustees. A. A. Milne was a scholar at Westminster between the wars and left the school one quarter of his royalties, currently bringing us about £40,000 a year. I am here to represent the school at this occasional blend of good fare and whimsy. A worn teddy bear is on the centre of the table and in his speech, the chairman of the trustees addresses the bear as 'Pooh'.

John Rae

Monday, 14 November 1977

On my way to work this morning it made me sad to see the firemen picketing outside the fire station just behind the Army and Navy store in Victoria. These men of such courage, who lose a man a fortnight in fires and are paid below the national average income, are now being put in the dock.

But the ones who appeared on television today, the first day of the strike, came over very well. They were asked about their consciences

---

* Audrey Wise was MP for Coventry South West. There had been a long-running dispute over pay and conditions and trade union recognition at Grunwick Film Processing Laboratories, in north-west London. The workforce comprised mainly Asian women workers. Over 500 arrests were made between 1976 and 1978.

and they replied, 'We have got consciences but a conscience can't pay the mortgage.'

I don't think the government is going to win on this.

Tony Benn

Wednesday, 28 December 1977

I rang the manager of The Clash, a political punk rock group, because there had been a suggestion from the BBC Community Programme Unit, that I have a four-minute discussion with the group. I have grave doubts, given what the media would make of it, and he agreed with me that four minutes was not enough for a serious discussion. But what he said was interesting. The Clash are apparently very popular with working class youngsters, who don't find anything in our popular culture that meets their needs or reflects their feelings. The group were not really concerned with being commercial and refused a lot of television. They are popular in Sweden, France and Yugoslavia.

Tony Benn

The end of 1977

This has been a strange year, one of problems and mirages, of pageantry and nostalgia, of the stirrings of radical discontent. How enormously complex the broad perspective seems. The middle and the professional classes have had their incomes and their values seemingly flung to the wall. The virtues of talent, hard work, and reward are in disrespect. Taxation is crippling. Any money made in excess of my salary is taxed at the rate of 87 pence in the pound.

And yet we end the year seemingly on a more even keel, North Sea oil promising untold millions and the stock market rising fast but we are still faced with unemployment, vast cuts and strikes. The Wealth Tax rides again, hitting anyone whose property or income exceeds £100,000 ... a house, a cottage, some shares, a couple of pictures, and you are there. The levelling would be achieved but farewell to houses, gardens, collections, patronage – or perhaps not – perhaps the tax will mean spend, spend, spend.

Roy Strong

Monday, 6 March 1978

Home Policy Committee

We agreed in principle that the Labour Party should commit itself to opposing blood sports; we will also look at factory farming, the protection of the environment, vivisection and cruelty to animals.

Tony Benn

Friday, 28 April 1978

Westminster School

After Latin prayers, spend much of the day trying to find out what substance (a good word) there is in this drug rumour.

As news of my enquiry spreads, a master looks in to say that when he was at a dinner party at the Reform Club, a fellow guest said he would never send a son to Westminster because it had been infiltrated by the drug culture. What nonsense! And yet it depresses me. I have spent seven years trying to dispel the druggy and permissive clouds that hung over Westminster's reputation and I will not let them return now. Another master asks whether I realise that some of the rumour-mongering about Westminster's drugs is encouraged by rival schools and especially headmistresses who are losing girls to our sixth form. The competition for pupils can sometimes be a dirty one.

John Rae

Friday, 26 May 1978

Callaghan is personally very popular at the moment and Thatcher is not. I think anyone with any information of substance must realise that Jim's good news basket is a very small one and all the signs are that the present drop in inflation (now down to 7.8 per cent) and unemployment figures cannot be maintained.

Still, I'm better disposed to letting the present Labour government run my country for me than any other group – apart, perhaps, from Pan's People – and I feel better governed (in a moral, rather than material sense) than at any time for many years.

Michael Palin

Friday, 9 June 1978

A visit to Windscale

Windscale was originally an ordnance factory called Sellafield before the war, and after the war it was used to develop our nuclear weapons programme and its name was changed to Windscale. John Hill [chairman of the Atomic Energy Authority] who was present today, reminded me that he worked there in 1950.

We toured the oxide storage ponds, and I must say they are very mysterious, these indoor swimming pools with their dark green water. They are lit up underneath and you can dimly see these fuel elements that are used in nuclear power stations, vaguely threatening, though the water is apparently a complete shield against any radioactivity that gets out.

From a roof we had an immensely impressive view of the site. I remembered John Hill telling me last year that in the early days they didn't really understand what they were handling and the whole site was soaked in radioactive toxic wastes.

I comment on this because when you see this vast complex you are struck on the one hand by the skill and scientific knowledge of the people who run it and on the other by the exceptional vulnerability of such a complicated system. Nobody can truthfully say that this whole project can be handed over to future generations to look after safely when they've no idea whether future generations will be faced with invasion, earthquakes, floods, strikes or plagues. It is a tremendously risky thing to do and the duration of the risk, 10,000 or 15,000 years, is enormous.

Tony Benn

Wednesday, 19 July 1978

All day at the Tory party's Council of the Arts. The conference didn't achieve anything of course, but how could it? It's perfectly clear what the arts want: not, as here, endless wranglings over policy – just more money.

I saw Margaret Thatcher there in true blue, blond hair glinting, with that rapt attentive expression of hers. And it crossed my thoughts that the chief attribute of a political leader now is that he or she must be able to go anywhere and not be out of place. Uncle Jim would be alright down a coal mine, in a factory, in a school, in a hospital, on the lawns of Buckingham Palace, or in a street barbecue in Brixton. Margaret Thatcher wouldn't. I doubt if she'll win.

Peter Hall

Friday, 4 August 1978

Jeremy Thorpe was arrested today along with three others, and taken to Minehead police station, where they were charged with conspiracy to murder Norman Scott. They were released on bail of £5,000 each, put up by Eric Lubbock [Liberal MP for Orpington].

All the rumours that Thorpe is implicated have turned out to be correct. It is the most tragic story. Here is a well-connected, brilliant, amusing man who won North Devon from the Tories in 1959, became leader of the Liberal Party when he was in his thirties and who in February 1974 carried the Party to its greatest electoral achievement since the war. And he has had this terrible anxiety on his mind, being blackmailed by this male model. Inexpressibly sad.

Tony Benn

Tuesday, 3 October 1978

To *Evita* this evening at the Prince Edward Theatre. It can only be a huge hit because it has three hit tunes. It elevates the appalling Evita, who we love because she's a star, but hate because there's the trendy, radically-correct Che Guevara on the sidelines telling us what a monster she is. And what has he to do with it anyway? He's just as big a monster as she is, just as big a star, corrupted by power.

There's no vitality in the piece. It's the cult of the kitsch again, inert, calculating, camp, and morally questionable. I felt out of step with popular taste, which really worries me ...

Peter Hall

Wednesday, 1 November 1978

To Oxford to dine in Worcester College with the Briggs.* A talk with Richard Cobb, remarkable writer on French eighteenth and nineteenth-century history, before dinner. I was much struck by the change in

---

*Asa and Susan Briggs. Lord Briggs was Provost of Worcester College.

the undergraduates (perhaps Worcester is traditionally exceptional in this respect) who had an extremely conventional appearance, now looking much more like undergraduates of the thirties than those of the sixties. But they are much less political, or if political more right wing, than then. The proportion from independent schools is rising quite substantially, owing I fear to the end of the grammar schools and the comprehensive schools not mostly trying for Oxford.

Roy Jenkins

Wednesday, 1 November 1978

This evening the stage staff walked out. The management had met with the NATTKE shop stewards in the afternoon and told them the maximum increase – with all the productivity savings going to the men – the Department of Employment would allow us. The stewards indicated they would recommend it to the shop floor, but the shop floor would have none of it. They walked out. So tonight we were forced to cancel full houses in all three auditoriums.

Bill Gaskill came to see me ... He asked what would happen about today's strike which he considers monstrous. All the men, he said, should be sacked for unprofessional behaviour. He also said roundly that he didn't believe in unions. I enjoyed this from the socialist who has just directed the classic of English working class union life [*The Ragged Trousered Philanthropists*]. No that's not quite fair. He hates unions *now*. And he's bloody right.

Peter Hall

Thursday, 23 November 1978

Lunch with Bernard Levin.

Much talk about the imminent closure of *The Times* and the *Sunday Times* ... I asked him what he thought Uncle Jim was doing in Downing Street. 'Hiding under the table,' said Levin.

Peter Hall

Sunday, 17 December 1978

Worked at home this morning and in the afternoon Lissie [Benn's daughter] and I sat and watched the end of *The Railway Children* and I had a good weep.

I must say the more I think about the political situation the more it looks as if the whole atmosphere is clouding over. I can see a series of disputes starting in the early part of the year. The oil-tankers' dispute could drag on and then we go into a spring with a deepening world recession as a result of the impending oil price rises.

Tony Benn

Wednesday, 21 February 1979

Locals say that the cold has far exceeded their memories of the celebrated '47 winter and, in our case, the water-pipes actually froze.

The tanker drivers went on strike with consequences for getting any petrol. The lorry drivers went on strike which resulted, locally, in the police being brought into a supermarket to break up the scramble by women for food. The railways have been on and off striking throughout this period, something which mercifully has not affected us. At the moment the National Union of Public Employees is on and off striking too – hospital porters, ambulancemen, school porters, dustmen, mortuary workers, etc. In the streets of London the rubbish is piled here and there, spilling out from its bags all over the place. Leicester Square is one large dump and every restaurant is approached through rubbish.

Neither political party seems to present any remedy ...

Roy Strong

Friday, 2 March 1979

Today the results of the devolution referenda were announced. The Welsh voted about 4 to 1 against devolution and the Scots 32 per cent in favour of the Assembly and 30.8 per cent against. So the Yes vote was well below the requirement of 40 per cent of the electorate. Now the Government's life is at risk.

Tony Benn

Sunday, 18 March 1979

Had a call from Bill Burroughs to say there had been a terrible mining disaster in the Golborne Colliery near Wigan. He arranged for an RAF plane to fly me up. We waited with the Mining Inspectorate people and rescue teams and others till Sid Vincent of the NUM arrived. Three men had been killed and eight badly burned. It was really very distressing. I asked if I should go to the hospital but I was told the relatives were too upset. That's the third big colliery disaster I have been to as Energy Secretary.

Tony Benn

Sunday, 1 April 1979

Hilary gave me for my birthday (on Tuesday) a long stick with a mirror and torch attached so that I could look under my car for bombs. Joshua had given me exactly the same thing. So touching.*

Tony Benn

Sunday, 15 April 1979

Saltwood Castle

Tortoises all woke up, tipped their box over and were released [into the garden] ... Filled with loathing of the electorate. Those filthy [train] carriages on the trip down yesterday which annoyed Jane so much, is the nation completely rotten? Yes, and has been since 1916. In the war we were saved by the middle classes who flew the Spitfires and manned the cruisers and frigates.

Alan Clark

Thursday, 3 May 1979

It wasn't at all difficult this morning to vote Tory. In fact it positively felt good: wanting change ... and we have to have change.

The election was fascinating television tonight as always. I shall

---

* Airey Neave, Conservative MP for Abingdon and shadow spokesman on Northern Ireland, was killed by a bomb which blew up his car as he was leaving the House of Commons underground car park on 30 March 1979. The Provisional IRA and the Irish National Liberation Army initially claimed responsibility.

not forget Thorpe's tragic, clown's face as it was announced he'd lost his seat. He should never have stood: no man could survive those allegations.

Peter Hall

Thursday, 3 May 1979
Barlinnie Prison Special Unit

This morning I lay awake listening to the results of the General Election. I was delighted to see Teddy Taylor being thrown out but bitterly disappointed to see Margaret Thatcher getting in. It all makes for terrible times ahead for the poor and needy.

Jimmy Boyle

Friday, 4 May 1979
Brussels

In the afternoon I heard the totally unexpected and dreadful news of Shirley Williams's defeat, and then went home for a sleep before the Beaumarchais' arrived to stay at about 8 o'clock. Late night telephone conversations with Shirley and Bill Rodgers.

Roy Jenkins

Monday, 7 May 1979
Saltwood Castle

Mrs Thatcher (or Mrs Carrington, as Papa amusingly – muddledly – called her) has announced her Cabinet and I'm not in, anywhere.

Alan Clark

Tuesday, 15 May 1979

We are now in a state of post-election euphoria. As one predicted, there is a complete *renversement*. At the Conservative arts election conference I got someone to get up and ask Norman St John Stevas if he would give us the resources to open the V & A again on Fridays if they got in. This produced a commendable diatribe against the Labour Government's treatment of the Museum and a pledge to reopen us. So here we are back in business again. Norman is in the Cabinet, Chancellor of the Duchy of Lancaster, Leader of the House (less onerous as they have a working majority) and Minister with responsibility for the Arts.

The V & A is to reopen and Regional Services is to be put back, so we will be reinstating everything that was dismantled from 1976–8.

Roy Strong

Sunday, 20 May 1979
London

Jennifer and I went to Lew Grade's great Euro Gala at Drury Lane. We had Dickie Mountbatten and Ted Heath in the box with us, Mountbatten boisterously friendly as usual, Ted reasonably friendly to me though basically in a very grumpy mood, partly because he had had this snarl-up with Mrs Thatcher over her incredibly foolishly sending him a written offer of the Washington Embassy. A delicate sounding might have been one thing, a formal written offer was ludicrous. I sympathised with him but got into slight difficulty, knowing that Nicko Henderson had been decided on a week or so before, and nearly telling him that I knew ...

Roy Jenkins

Thursday, 7 June 1979

Euro-election day. No one seems to be taking any notice, but I am moved by it. I remember Europe tearing itself to pieces. Now we are voting to live together democratically. That must be good. Why is nobody interested? Sheer, bloody indifference. For there are no real issues, though most people believe vaguely that it's bad for their pocket. Also, there aren't any stars. Barbara Castle is about the only person anyone's heard of who is seeking a seat.

Peter Hall

Monday, 27 August 1979

Today the Provisional IRA took 'credit' for blowing up Lord Mountbatten's yacht, killing Mountbatten, his fourteen year old grandson and another boy and wounding four others. Two hours later they killed fourteen soldiers in an ambush.

The Mountbatten thing makes me feel almost physically sick.*

Michael Palin

Tuesday, 11 September 1979

Went up to Corby by train for a demonstration by steelworkers. Corby was always a one-industry town. Now the plant, at least the iron and steel-making part, is under threat of closure.

I couldn't tell them but the Labour Cabinet had decided in February this year (three months before the General Election) to support the closure of Corby. These guys are now faced with the possibility of 30 per cent male unemployment and they have called in the Labour Party to help them fight. An awful irony. I felt tremendously guilty.

Tony Benn

Thursday, 15 November 1979

The House got stuck into one of those days which follow long periods of torpor and ennui that conform to Fred Hoyle's theory of the concat-enation of the Universe. For we had more or less simultaneously, the Chancellor's announcement of a 17 per cent bank rate, i.e. 21 per cent overdrafts and a clutch of publicity-seeking Labour MPs each trying to beat the other to the draw ... raising the matter of Blunt's treachery. This was a lucky break for Geoffrey [Howe] because the whole Blunt affair diverted attention from the really alarming manner in which our economy seems to be conducted.

Alan Clark

Monday, 19 November 1979

Started work on the new Python movie. A bright, crisp morning. Cycled to the meeting.

[We had] a general chat about the world. The Anthony Blunt spy

---

* Earl Mountbatten and members of his family were on a fishing trip in waters near his home Classiebawn Castle in County Sligo. The explosion killed Mountbatten, his grandson Nicholas, a local boy Paul Maxwell and Lady Brabourne, who died a day later. In the other incident mentioned by Michael Palin, eighteen soldiers in an army convoy were killed at Warrenpoint, South Down, near the border with the Irish Republic.

story is top news at the moment.* America is about to indulge in its own maudlin fascination with power and privilege now that Ted Kennedy is running officially for President. We in beleaguered England, continually battered by stories of our imminent economic collapse, at least have one of our own scandals to keep us happy.

Have *we* not become as established as the Establishment we seek to kick? Are we not really licensed satirists? Keepers of the Queen's Silly Things, enjoying the same privileges as the Keeper of the Queen's Pictures who has been revealed to have been a very naughty boy – but will be given the full protection of a Cambridge man in an English Establishment that is still Oxbridge controlled?

Michael Palin

Tuesday, 27 November 1979
Westminster School

The Oxford and Cambridge entrance exams are under way and I am glad to see that the history papers are straightforward. This morning I drive to west London to talk to a hall full of sixth formers drawn from four comprehensive schools. It is not a success. I have been asked to talk about values in a changing society but as soon as I start talking some of the girls are reduced to giggles (by my accent?) and some boys talk among themselves. I struggle on, acutely aware of not making contact, but in a discussion that follows the gigglers and the talkers are not short of interesting opinions, so much so that a shouting match develops between a group of white boys who hold unexpectedly right-wing views and a group of black girls who appear to be both more intelligent and more mature.

As I walk away from the meeting I see 'NF' painted on the wall, beneath which someone has written 'No Future.'

John Rae

---

* Palin's footnote: 'Blunt, son of a bishop, Professor of Art History at London University, Surveyor of the Queen's Pictures, had been found to be spying for the Soviets for many years. Though he had been unmasked in 1963, he had been allowed to retain all his posts to avoid scandal tainting the Royal Family.'

Tuesday, 27 November 1979

House of Commons

I was talking to Tony Royle [Conservative MP for Richmond], eminently sensible, never seen him in a flap (ex-SAS I think). But he can be very forthright, no words minced. 'Look at the people around her,' he said. 'Carrington – hates her. Prior – hates her; Gilmour – hates her; Heseltine – hates her; Walker – loathes her, makes no secret of it ... The only people committed to Margaret are Angus Maude, John Biffen and Keith Joseph and the last two are so tortured intellectually as to cast doubt on their stability in a crisis.'

I paraphrase his analysis, but it brought home to one how precarious her position is and what a disaster was the assassination of Airey Neave whose subtlety and insight would have helped to outmanoeuvre these quislings.

Alan Clark

Saturday, 1 December 1979

East Hendred, Oxfordshire

To Didcot to pick up Bill Rodgers ... brought him back to East Hendred, where we arrived at exactly the same time as Shirley Williams from London. I talked with them an hour before lunch and went over the position. There was a fairly good identity of view though both of them, Shirley perhaps a little more than Bill – were anxious to say that it was always possible, though not likely, that things would go sufficiently well in the Labour Party that they would want to stay with it; but they were quite willing to contemplate all other possibilities. Bill in particular struck me as being emotionally committed to a break. Shirley has always been in a sense more intellectually open to it than Bill, but has not yet passed over that watershed that he did some time at the end of November.

They both thought that if Healey were elected leader of the party, Callaghan going in perhaps a year's time, that would be a period of setback [for the future Social Democrats]. There would be a tendency for people to rally to a new, tougher [Labour] leader and give him a chance ... But who can say what will happen?

Roy Jenkins

Friday, 28 December–Monday, 31 December 1979

We dine with David and Patsy Puttnam. David's film *Chariots of Fire* is finished and has been chosen both for the Royal Film Performance and as a British entry for the Cannes Film Festival. Harold Wilson is also a guest. He has recovered from an operation but still looks weak and suffers from short-term memory loss. He cannot remember where the lavatory is and twice heads for the front door before being caught and steered upstairs. But his grasp of historical detail is as extraordinary as ever. Out of the blue he gives me detailed information about the six Westminster boys who became Prime Minister, and when I tell him that one of the best things he did when Prime Minister was to appoint Edward Carpenter the dean of Westminster, he can recall every stage of his battle with the Church of England establishment.

John Rae

Thursday, 3 January 1980
Hilltop, Rutland

The year – and the decade – begins badly with the Soviet invasion of Afghanistan. Imperialist aggression is unacceptable at any time, but when one has actually been to the country concerned (I went through Afghanistan on my way to Pakistan in 1960) there is a feeling of personal affront.

In the end, it may be that, given the appalling terrain, the Russian invasion will prove to be their Vietnam.

Giles Radice

Saturday, 19 January 1980
Chester-le-Street constituency

The GMC [General Management Committee] is interesting ... the Militants are in full strength.

After a few remarks about local affairs I attack the Tories and then turn to Afghanistan.

[I say] that there is substantial evidence that the Militants are in breach of the party constitution. They have a distinctive revolutionary programme; they are a party within a party, with 50 full time organisers to the Labour Party's 70; and they have international contacts. I say that I don't want a witch-hunt but I think we ought to know the facts. The response is good – I feel that the message is going home. The Militants don't dare come back. I also scotch any talk of centre or third parties.

Giles Radice

Wednesday, 6 February 1980

I had a message from the BBC asking if I would join in a discussion on monetarism and government intervention, following the showing of six half-hour talks by Milton Friedman, the American monetarist economist. I would be in discussion with the deputy governor of the Bank of England, Roy Jenkins, and Peter Jay chairing.

I rang up the producer and said that six programmes was more than all the party politicals put together during an election. I had never known the BBC give so much time to this particular religion.

I told her I was prepared to do half an hour with Friedman, but I would not be a token left-winger with three monetarists.

Tony Benn

Tuesday, 26 February 1980

Not having any appetite I decided to go and listen to the Prime Minister being interviewed by Robin Day. She was wonderful and very glamorous looking, though slightly spoilt the effect with over-much ocular grimacing ...

But goodness, she is *so* beautiful; made up to the nines of course for the television programme, but still quite bewitching, as Eva Peron must have been.

Alan Clark

Wednesday, 28 May 1980

It was a rather *piano* Royal Academy Dinner. Hugh Casson, however, just seventy, was looking spryer than ever, Princess Margaret was in transparent virgin white and Mrs Thatcher in black and white. There was the usual gathering of the Establishment and the art mafia. Many more of the men than usual were wearing dinner jackets rather than white tie. The food was filthy and the speeches very dull. Princess

Margaret's speech was written by Hugh Leggatt via Norman [St John Stevas's] office (he wasn't there as he'd gone to see the Pope!) and Mrs Thatcher's I guess was compiled by Robin Coke. The latter asked before dinner whether I would like to meet the Prime Minister ...

I seized my chance and stood my ground saying that the poor V & A mustn't be sacrificed yet again because of Civil Service cuts. She sailed on, saying that she had given the Arts masses of money. I said to her that that wasn't the point.

During her after dinner speech extolling her munificence in terms of cash for the Arts, she interjected, 'In spite of what Dr Roy Strong says,' and gestured down the table towards me. I wanted to sink through the floor but afterwards she came up to me and rather sweetly put her arm through mine and said, 'What is the problem?' and we talked. That I thought rather marvellous of her and I told her exactly what our problem was.

Royal Academy dinners are strange, increasingly run-down occasions that you can set a stopwatch by. Everyone fled early. The designers Zandra Rhodes and Jean Muir at least added zip, Zandra with two eyebrows for a change and Jean impeccable in a little immaculate black number with sequins.

Roy Strong

Friday, 30 May 1980

Frances Morrell rang to tell me about the Rank and File Mobilising Committee, which is working to get together the Campaign for Labour Party Democracy, the Labour Coordinating Committee, the Institute for Workers' Control, the Independent Labour Publications and the Socialist Campaign for a Labour Victory, to agree on a programme of party democracy.

In the evening we had a party, a sort of new left gathering with Frances, Ken Livingstone of the GLC, Victor Schonfield, Audrey Wise, Tom Litterick, Chris Mullin, James Curran (a lecturer) and his wife Margaret, George Osgerby, Dick Clements and Biddy, Geoff Bish, Dawn Primarolo, Jon Lansman, Peter Hain and others. These are the people who ... when the time comes, will be the people who organise the Benn (leadership) election campaign.

Tony Benn

Tuesday, 10 June 1980

The gossip in the PLP is all about the chaotic state of the party. The one day Party conference (which took place while we were in Spain) has stirred things up. Tony Benn has attacked Callaghan on incomes policy. Callaghan has ticked off Tony Benn. John Silkin has lent his support to coming out of the Common Market (trying to outflank Benn). Bill, David and Shirley then issue a statement saying that they will have no part of it. Peter Shore, in turn, gives them a rocket. Meanwhile Roy Jenkins makes a speech to the (press) lobby virtually promising to launch a centre party.*

Giles Radice

Wednesday, 1 October 1980
Labour Party Conference, Blackpool

The Common Market motion was moved brilliantly by Clive Jenkins, talking about food mountains. He said, 'We have had a marvellous barley harvest. Next year we're having harvest festival in a hangar at Heathrow.' Peter [Shore] got in with a Churchillian-type speech.

By 5 million to 2 million we voted to withdraw from the Common Market. That is sensational.

Tony Benn

Friday, 3 October–Sunday, 5 October 1980
Hilltop, Rutland

I am exhausted after Blackpool but Hilltop begins to work its usual magic. Saturday is my 44th birthday. I take stock. A very bad year for the centre-right of the party. We have been beaten convincingly by Benn's coalition of left-wingers, Trots and the Transport and General Workers' Union (TGWU) and the Public Employees Unions (NUPE). The only good thing is that we have now reached crisis point. We have our backs to the wall and the only thing we can do is fight.

Giles Radice

---

* Bill Rodgers, David Owen, Roy Jenkins and Shirley Williams, who were all pro-European, planned to challenge the Labour Party with a new Social Democratic movement. Peter Shore was one of Labour's leading anti-Common Market campaigners.

Friday, 31 October 1980

I voted on Wednesday for Michael Foot as Leader of the Labour Party.

To Bristol to the Wills tobacco factory to meet the shop stewards. The president of the Tobacco Workers' Union was also present. Their joint complaint was that I had approved a resolution calling for the banning of cigarette advertising and they were angry with me, but it was really that they were terrified that the cigarette industry was running down, that Imperial Tobacco might be pulling out of Bristol ...

There are about 35,000 people in Bristol who derive their income from cigarette manufacture.

Tony Benn

Tuesday, 4 November 1980

Dinner with the Haymans at their home. David Sainsbury,* whom we like a lot, is there.

We watch the first results come in from the US presidential election, a landslide for Ronald Reagan. Reagan and Foot, two 70-year-olds (Foot will be 70 by the next election). Ghastly.

Giles Radice

Tuesday, 25 November 1980

Yesterday the Chancellor [Geoffrey Howe] made a 'statement on economic policy' (generally hailed by the press as a 'package' with all the uncomfortable evocation of that word). Very unsatisfactory. He gabbled through an unintelligible Treasury brief couched in their most obscure jargon, then came to the point. Only £1 billion further cuts in public expenditure – of which £200 million was to come from Defence – in other words £800 million was coming from all other sectors combined. So the shortfall had to come from revenue, in the form of increased 'contributions' under National Insurance. The net

---

* Martin and Helene Hayman were neighbours of the Radices. Helene Hayman was a Labour MP, 1974–9, and went on to become the first Lord Speaker of the House of Lords. David Sainsbury became chairman of Sainsbury's supermarket. A Labour supporter, he joined the SDP before returning to Labour in 1996, becoming a Labour minister in the Lords.

effect is that the workers are going to get less in the right-hand column of their payslips, while the so-called Social Wage* remains intact.

This is precisely contrary to the theme in which our campaign was presented and a rejection of the endorsement we received from the electorate last year.

I see that George Morton [Labour MP for Manchester Moss Side] pleaded guilty to an act of gross indecency in a gents in Manchester and was fined £25. Simultaneously his constituency chairman announced that he had complete confidence in him and that it was a 'private matter'. God alive, I would only have to be seen with a blonde on the front seat and the Plymouth Association would demand an instant vote of no confidence.

Alan Clark

Wednesday, 10 December 1980

Went to housewarming …

I saw a familiar and much photographed face, and it was Dr David Owen. He surprised me by talking very frankly about his wish to see a social democrat party established. He said he thought the prospects for this would begin to come clear in January or February. I asked him whether he thought the third party should declare itself then. He seemed to think nothing should happen openly for a year at the end of which the impossibility of the Thatcher or Foot alternatives would become evident. I said I thought that the National government of 1931 was – fifty years later – a precedent which made it extremely difficult to think of any alternative coalition. He said, 'No, I'm not thinking in terms of a Government of all the talents – Heath, Callaghan, Shirley – that kind of thing. I'm thinking of a social democratic party.'

The idea seems to be to wait a year then declare themselves, then fight the next election as a third party.

Stephen Spender

Friday, 12 December 1980

The Prime Minister yesterday was in South Wales where there was a big demonstration with 1200 police on duty and fifty-five arrests. An egg hit her car.

*Services provided by the state including health and education.

The country is ready now for major unrest.

Tony Benn

Tuesday, 13 January 1981

I returned to the House and went into the Smoking Room. Julian Amery [Conservative MP for Aldershot] was holding court in the corner table between the bar and the fireplace. He was in good form ...

'Now Alan, we are just agreeing that we are all hand-to-heart behind the Prime Minister in her economic policies but the trouble is we don't know what these are, can you tell us?'

This is not a good sign, this kind of irreverence from senior and respected Privy Counsellors on the Right of the Party, and later that evening in the Lobby poor Nick Budgen told me how terribly depressed he was ... We agreed that both Geoffrey Howe and Leon Brittan had not a political principle between them and that they would soon get the ship round on its new course.

Alan Clark

Saturday, 24 January 1981

Elizabeth motored me to the Wembley Conference Centre for the Labour Party special conference.

The MPs and peers [were] in the gallery [so] the debate seemed to have even less relevance than usual to the crucial decisions, that these were being cobbled up somewhere else by half a dozen trade union bosses.*

The flavour of the Conference was more assertively proletarian even than usual. Many, perhaps half, of the delegates could not have passed as working class at any time in their adult lives. Yet whenever the proletarian note was struck, it was the winner.

Lord Longford

---

*This special Labour Party Conference at Wembley adopted an 'electoral college' to elect the Leader, comprising 40 per cent weighting for the trade unions, 30 per cent for the Parliamentary Labour Party and 30 per cent for the constituencies.

Monday, 26 January 1981

Roy Jenkins, Shirley Williams, David Owen and Bill Rodgers were splashed all over the front pages with their 'Limehouse Declaration' so-called because it was made from David Owen's house in east London.

Thirteen MPs are supporting the Council for Social Democracy.* If there is going to be a new political party, which the Gang of Four claim, that is important news. But the Left are holding their hand and I think that is right. I don't think it is sensible for us to attack the Social Democrats at the moment; let them come out with their own policies and then we shall raise whether [individuals serving on Labour Party bodies] can be allowed to plan a new party while remaining in the Labour Party.

Tony Benn

Monday, 26 January 1981

Made an intervention today, though not as intemperate as I had originally intended, criticising Keith Joseph personally, and the principle, for meekly paying up another £1bn to British Leyland.† The Lady was sitting in the Chamber and I do not know whether such an intervention increased or diminished my chances of favour, but at least I had warned her about it the previous week. I used the world 'insouciance' which may have been a mistake as some of the Opposition laughed and as it was a serious moment one did not want it to be devalued.

At the Home Affairs Committee Nick Budgen coolly and clearly criticised the Home Office failure to apply objective standards in determining Nationality in the new Bill which is to start tomorrow – 'presumably because they are fearful of offending fashionable opinion.' What a splendid, fearless and thoroughly valuable chap he is; no wonder Willie [Whitelaw] loathes him so much.

Alan Clark

---

*The Council for Social Democracy paved the way for a proper political party, the Social Democratic Party.
† Contrary to the Thatcher government's economic instincts, more taxpayers' money was used in an attempt to improve the fortunes of the nationalised automobile manufacturer.

Thursday, 12 February 1981

Michael Foot addressed the Labour peers.

I asked him about the Party attitude to the Atlantic Pact. He answered with even more elusiveness than usual. 'The Party has recently passed resolutions in favour of unilateral disarmament, multilateral disarmament, and the Atlantic Alliance … You may say that my answer is confused but this is a confused situation.' He went on to warn us against excessive certainties and finished with a denunciation of President Reagan.

Lord Longford

Thursday, 19 February 1981

Meeting at the House of Lords to discuss a proposed Private Member's Bill to strengthen the laws against pornography.

[The Bill] to deal with the limited area of indecent display is likely to pass into law. We debated at length whether to tack onto the Bill a provision to make *all* pornography illegal. When I had to leave the meeting this seemed unlikely as [it was] liable to damage the prospects of the limited measure.

In the evening I distributed prizes at the Prendergast School at Lewisham. The school, with nearly six hundred girls, is in the process of changing from grammar to comprehensive and has a high academic reputation which the young, vital and very pretty headmistress has no intention of allowing to decline.

I distributed a number of prizes to black girls and asked the headmistress why they seemed to be specially applauded. Did the other girls feel sorry for them? No, I was told, it's because they are such good athletes. I am not an observant person but I had noticed their long, graceful limbs.

Lord Longford

Tuesday, 3 March 1981

I have a great sense of relief at the resignation of twelve Labour MPs and I think nine Labour peers including the Gang of Four [from the Party].*

---

*The group, including Shirley Williams, Roy Jenkins, Bill Rodgers and David Owen,

Mrs Thatcher was giving a speech in a church about Christian values and monetarism when some young people got up and shouted 'Jobs not bombs!' They were Young Communists and, of course, that was all she needed. She said in her most pious way 'Now you know what I am fighting against.' It will have given the Communist Party a tremendous boost. They were very courageous, well-scrubbed decent kids.

Tony Benn

Thursday, 5 March 1981

I asked a Supplementary [Question] of the Home Secretary today. A lot of anti-NF stuff was being bandied about apropos of Willie [Whitelaw's] decision to ban their march next week. That lazy, greasy, slob John Hunt [MP for Ravensbourne] stuck in a question about right-wing publications. 'What about the black ones,' I interjected. The Speaker very splendidly called me ... when, by rights, he should have moved on to the next question. This is what I said:

'Can my right hon. Friend think of anything more overtly racist and criminal, or a clearer demonstration of a breakdown in public order, than the behaviour of the young blacks in the march through Southwark on Monday, when they broke into and damaged shops, terrorised the white population and shouted objectionable slogans about the monarchy to try to provoke the police? ...'

This was quite a dodgy opening and the fun lay in seeing if one could stand up for the whole passage.

' ... Will he not recognise that he has to be seen as being completely even-handed or else he will simply add to the very discontent that gives rise to the organisations that Labour Members find so objectionable.'

I hope [the Lady] enjoyed it. I am completely bomb-happy with Willie now. He has done enormous damage to the Tory Party over the years with his obsessional regard for the *Guardian* vote.

Alan Clark

joined the new Social Democratic Party with its 'collective' leadership.

Saturday, 28 March 1981

On the train to London with Denis Healey

He confirms my impression that David Owen has been the driving force in the emergence of the Social Democrats ...

I ask him if he would join the Social Democrats if he were 25 – and he reminds me that he was a Communist at university. He says that he never liked Roy Jenkins – he could never understand all that social grandeur, though he says that Roy has the capacity to attract the fierce loyalty of small groups of individuals and could make brilliant speeches in the House.

Walking up the train corridor to get something to eat, Denis is instantly recognised by everybody. He plays shamelessly on Mike Yarwood's impersonation of him and on his black bushy eyebrows. He is really a tremendous asset to the Labour Party whom we have very short-sightedly discarded in favour of the 'old waffler'.

Giles Radice

Saturday, 11 April 1981

Last night the news came through that Bobby Sands had won the by-election at Fermanagh [and] South Tyrone.*

People are entitled to call Sands a terrorist but whether he lives or dies no one can call him a villain, a label well-adapted to many members of the IRA and the UDA. I find some consolation in the fact that people will be forced to think a little harder instead of averting their gaze, but however hard one looks a solution still seems far off.

Lord Longford

Friday, 8 May–Sunday, 10 May 1981

Hilltop, Rutland

The left have engineered a coup in London – Ken Livingstone takes over as leader [of the Greater London Council], despite Andrew McIntosh having led Labour to victory. What a bastard.

Giles Radice

---

* Sands was a member of the Provisional IRA, and was elected to Parliament as Anti H-Block candidate whilst on hunger strike in the Maze prison, Northern Ireland. He died of starvation less than a month later.

Tuesday, 19 May 1981

A cousin of Elizabeth's who is happy to style herself a lesbian, had asked me to address her group, a flourishing affair with at least three hundred members. My subject was 'Outcasts' on which I have spoken and indeed preached to general audiences. I myself have been described as 'the outcasts' outcast' so I suppose that I have a certain standing in the discussion. I told them that when writing a book on St Francis of Assisi I had selected homosexuals, male and female, as an important category of outcasts. I knew more about male homosexuals than lesbian. I was told by my best friend in my House at Eton that 75 per cent of the boys had had homosexual experience. I said I hadn't noticed it, to which he replied, 'That's because you are somewhat unobservant and also rather repressed.'

Lord Longford

Friday, 10 July 1981

End of term, Westminster School

[In the] garden after dinner guests, governors, colleagues, senior boys and girls and scholars enjoy a drink and a quiet talk. There are rumours of riots in Brixton and some in the garden say they can see the sky across the river is lighter as though buildings are on fire. It is only the following day when I am writing this journal that I am fully aware of the contrast. While young Westminster boys and girls are being congratulated on their Latin and Greek epigrams, their contemporaries south of the river were throwing petrol bombs at the police and looting local shops.

John Rae

Wednesday, 29 July 1981

Sat and watched the royal wedding on TV. There were perhaps two million people out in London and this tremendous ceremonial display was watched throughout the world by 750 million people – without any doubt the biggest television audience that had ever seen anything. The image presented to the world was of a Britain as socially advanced as France before the French revolution!

We've got to fight like anything to recover the position that we had even in 1945.

Tony Benn

Thursday, 20 August 1981

Visited Broadmoor yesterday.

Three quarters of the patients at Broadmoor are schizophrenics, including the two whom I was seeing later. Dr Udwin [the acting superintendent] views it as positively harmful to suggest that they ought to be released more rapidly than at present. For many of them a hospital is the only tolerable answer. He applied his remarks, which were supported by several colleagues present, not just to special hospitals but to mental hospitals generally. I reminded him that in the last twenty five years the numbers of the mentally ill in hospitals had been more than halved. Did he regard this as a mistake? He said, 'Yes, as regards two thirds of them.' He was in fact extremely sceptical about the whole idea of community care, however much effort was put into it.

Lord Longford

Saturday, 12 September 1981

Much heralded debate between Healey, Benn and Silkin, the three candidates for the deputy leadership.*

The audience, or quite a section of it, mostly young, were quite unpleasant to Denis Healey. Robert Carvel, doyen of political commentators, found their attitude the most unattractive feature of the conference ... Benn put on a superlative performance. He sedulously refrained from anything that could be called 'personalities'. He remained cold, calm and collected throughout whilst stirring up fire and turmoil. Every answer he gave was perfectly adjusted to the requirements of the majority of the audience. One recalls what Prince Bulow once said, 'Real politicians are animated by two motives only – love of country and love of power.'

Speaking generally, the trouble about the Healeyites is that a desire

---

* Denis Healey, Tony Benn and John Silkin: Denis Healey (the incumbent deputy leader) won the contest by the narrowest of margins; he remained deputy leader under Michael Foot until 1983.

for distribution of wealth in favour of the poor is not conspicuous among them. If the moderates are ever to achieve any momentum of argument, men like Roy Hattersley and Peter Shore must be called upon to provide a radical inspiration sadly lacking at present.

Lord Longford

Friday, 23 October 1981

I receive a letter from Shirley Williams asking me to speak at a meeting on education in Crosby where she is standing for the SDP in a by-election. She is trying to overturn a 19,000 Tory majority and obviously hopes I might be able to counter those who accuse her of destroying the grammar schools. I would like to do it.

John Rae

Wednesday, 4 November 1981

The day of the opening of *The Splendours of the Gonzaga*. The lead up to this, above all its inauguration by the Prince and Princess of Wales, endowed the whole occasion with an air of high expectancy. This was a tiring week with the battle for the V & A's finance and staff for 1982–3 and the Rayner Scrutiny* going on at the same time.

The Princess looked sensational, her dress cut straight across revealing the by now famous shoulders, but with a triple choker of pearls fastened with a diamond clip around her neck in the manner of Queen Alexandra. She has a clear complexion and lustrous blue eyes. Tonight she seemed a large girl in a billowing white dress full-skirted to the ground with a broad blue ribbon at the waist.

How can I describe her? Well, after the event, I would categorise her as Eliza Doolittle at the embassy ball. Beautiful, in a way like a young colt, immensely well-meaning, unformed, a typical product of an upper-class girls' school. But she has so much to learn, which she will, unless she gets bored with it and it all sours. At the moment she has not learned the royal technique of asking questions. Nervous certainly, so I placed myself next to her and, as I promised Edward Adeane [the Prince's Private Secretary], kept an eye on her the whole

---

* Derek Rayner was joint managing director of Marks & Spencer, brought in by Margaret Thatcher to advise on government efficiency – one in a long line of past and future attempts to reform the Civil Service.

time. Her accent is really rather awful considering that she is an earl's daughter. Not an upper-class drawl at all but rather tuneless and, dare I say it, a bit common, as though it were the fashion to learn to talk down. That is what I meant by Eliza at the ball.

He, in sharp contrast, is now immensely developed. Now thinner than ever not only physically but his hair as well. But he is incredibly easy and so much more assured and mature. Dignity, yes, but with a wonderful sense of humour and a great warmth of personality (which she has too). On the other hand I did not think that he looked after her enough.

Roy Strong

Tuesday, 10 November 1981

Debate on North Sea oil.

Mother and Stephen [Benn's eldest son] came to listen. I had determined that I would clearly get into Hansard the full range of Labour party policy: that we would renationalise without compensation; that we would take BP into 100 per cent ownership; that we would move toward 100 per cent ownership of oil; that we would use the revenues and other money for the alternative economic strategy, industry and the public services; that we would have planned trade and public ownership; that we would withdraw from the Common Market, and so on.

When I made my speech the House was packed and it went down like a bomb. When I came to renationalisation without compensation, Lawson [the Energy Secretary] got up and asked me to clarify it, which I did. But when I sat down Michael Foot was absolutely fuming.

Tony Benn

Thursday, 26 November 1981

Everything is dreadfully depressing. Clearly the SDP are going to win Crosby. How fickle and spastic the electorate are. How gullible, to be duped by someone as scatty and shallow as Shirley Williams. And in today's papers there is the Scarman Report* with its ritual 'we are all guilty' and its call for positive discrimination (i.e. discrimination on

---

* Lord Scarman led the inquiry following the Brixton race riots earlier in the year. There had also been riots in Bristol the same year.

the grounds of colour *against* white people and in favour of black). In other words where a white person is better qualified and more suitable they should nonetheless be rejected in favour of a black person – 'in the interests of racial harmony' as the DPP put it when he withdrew the prosecution from the fourteen defendants in the Bristol Riot trial.

Alan Clark

Sunday, 13 December 1981

Jon Snow has just rung up from Rome. He has been sent there by ITN to cope with the Polish crisis. Shocking that I hadn't realised how grave the situation has become.* The papers didn't say much about it this morning. Jon was going to give me lunch tomorrow having just got back from El Salvador. I hope that he will be back by Wednesday evening when the Order of Christian Unity are presenting him with their 'Valiant for Truth' award, by no means the first television award to come his way. Funnily enough, when he was coordinator of New Horizon† I never credited him, in spite of all his nervous energy, with this extraordinary physical stamina, which he has shown in every continent. How wrong I was.

Lord Longford

Wednesday, 23 December 1981

Today we went to Jock Massareene's‡ party (black tie) for not local – as ours – but county nobs. Icy cold, the Hall of Chilham, standard medieval conditions as Jock had broken the central heating that morning and a huge oak tree blazed in the eight-foot fireplace, scorching those who stood near it, while those guests who stood at receding radii from twenty to sixty feet shivered and could see the steam from their breath as they spoke.

Guests, mainly worthy and rich rather than smart ...

Bill Deedes and I had a long chat. We agreed that the miners' strike was the key battle ground on which a spectacular victory could

---

*The Polish crisis of 1980–81 was an anti-Soviet social movement centred around Solidarity, the first non-communist trade union association in the Soviet bloc.
† New Horizon was a charity set up by Lord Longford for young people in need. Jon Snow worked for the charity after leaving university, and is now its Chairman.
‡ Viscount Massareene and Ferrard was a friend with whom Alan Clark shared an interest in animal welfare, a longstanding cause of Clark's.

turn the tide of public opinion in favour of the Government. The Lady must *not* give up on this.* Unpopular though she is at the moment, she could not be loathed as much as Arthur Scargill.

Alan Clark

Thursday, 31 December 1981

Even on the most limited assumptions about the significance of Britain today in the world scene, the triumphant emergence of the SDP must be for any British observer the sensation of the year. No one who has read this diary will be unaware that a year ago I had no conception of how successful they would have proved by this time.

Of course the conditions have been perfect for them. By any possible standard 1981 has been a rotten year for Britain economically speaking. In spite of Mrs Thatcher's gallant trumpetings, there is no sign of much improvement. If anything the Labour Party has had a worse year than the Conservatives, worse even than I would have forecast a year ago ... The conflict between Right and Left, personal and ideological, is sharper than ever. A new split has developed lately between 'soft left' and 'hard left' with Michael Foot associated with the 'soft left' or so it seems.

An eminent man once told Tennyson that he hoped to leave the world a better place than he found it. 'And I,' said Tennyson, 'seek a new vision of God.' Faint but pursuing, I continue to aspire to both ideals.

Lord Longford

Monday, 8 February 1982

The first big set piece of this session – the second reading of the Employment Bill ... Norman Tebbit is appallingly partisan and makes it clear that he is totally anti-union.

The decision of the Social Democrat [MPs] to support the Tebbit bill may be a turning point. They show themselves to be indecisive

---

*In the 1981 strike, the government settled with the miners but in 1984 it was prepared to fight. In 1974 Nicholas Ridley, a junior minister in the Conservative government, had drafted a report, the 'Ridley Plan', recommending how a government could defeat a strike in a nationalised industry. The plan was implemented in readiness for a future miners' strike which came in 1984.

(some vote for the bill, some against and some abstain) and reactionary. It is very sad that I should now be so estranged from my erstwhile closest political allies.

Giles Radice

Monday, 22 February 1982

The night of our annual dinner with the Home Secretary in a private room at the Garrick.

I think he is a little frightened of me; he seldom catches my eye, but when he does there is sometimes a watery, pleading look in his expression. The trouble is each regards the other as a traitor to his class.

He [Willie Whitelaw] soon became jolly. He told with much bellowing and groaning, of his experiences last week at St Aldate's Church in Oxford where, booked over a year in advance, he turned up for one of those lay preaching, question and answer sessions in the pulpit. To his great alarm he found that the Church was filled to bursting and the atmosphere evangelical in the highest degree. He described how the entire congregation *mimed* the words of each hymn, raising both hands to heaven at such words as 'arise' etc. A man in the congregation had turned to him and said 'I found God here on Wednesday of last week, do you think you will today?' 'I, er, don't know,' bellowed Willie, miserably looking round.

Alan Clark

Tuesday, 2 March 1982

Norman Atkinson [Labour MP] told me that Rupert Murdoch had had lunch with Mrs Thatcher no less than three times last week. He had heard from Ian Gow, Mrs Thatcher's PPS, and Norman had the impression that the Tories were panic-stricken that *The Times* might come out for the SDP.

Tony Benn

Monday, 22 March 1982

A bunch of Argentinians are horsing around in South Georgia.* The thing started as an operation to remove 'scrap' (by what right do they go in there and remove 'scrap' anyway?) but they have now apparently hoisted the Argentine flag. I don't like this. If we don't throw them out, preferably by shedding blood at the same time, they will try their hand in the Falklands.

Before dinner we had a kind of ad hoc meeting of the '92' at the far end of the Smoking Room.

We are all of the same mind. We are the Henty boys – 'Deeds that built the Empire', all that. But I am not sure how much support we can mobilise in the Party. 'Defence' to most colleagues only means The Cold War. They no longer think imperially. I was saying, surely Margaret must sympathise? Nick Budgen sliced in – 'Don't bet on that Alan, she is governed only by what the Americans want. At heart she is just a vulgar, middle-class Reaganite.'

Alan Clark

Thursday, 25 March 1982

Met Graham Allen, Bob Cryer and Willy McKelvey [Labour MPs] and for forty minutes we cried in each other's beer, because after Hillhead, we are very depressed.† The Party isn't doing well, the Left has lost impetus, and the Right hasn't grasped it because they haven't anything to offer, but they are benefiting from the defeat of the Labour Party.

Tony Benn

Friday, 2 April 1982

I was due to go to Plymouth this morning. But when I looked in at Dean's Yard to collect my correspondence for signing in the train the whole room seemed to know that the Falkland Islands had been invaded. Delighted to cancel ... I got back at Sandling [station] at six

---

* South Georgia is a British overseas territory in the middle of the South Atlantic, about 850 miles south-east of the Falkland Islands.
† The by-election in Glasgow Hillhead had been won by Roy Jenkins for the Social Democratic Party.

o'clock. 'We've lost the Falklands' I told Jane. 'It's all over. We're a Third World country no good for anything.'

Alan Clark

Saturday, 3 April 1982
Emergency session of House of Commons

At backbench meeting after the debate Carrington [Foreign Secretary] especially weak. There could be trouble about the government surviving if there is a censure debate next week. All depends on how credible our armada turns out to be in rescuing the Falkland Islands. It has all the making of a heroic tragedy. Watch this space to see whether the PM is Iron Lady or made of aluminium netting. John Nott [Defence Secretary] and Carrington in deep trouble. Words like 'steaming' suddenly in fashion, as in 'Falkland Islands 24 days "steaming" from Portsmouth'.

Michael Spicer

Wednesday, 7 April 1982

The second Falklands debate, immediately following a PLP meeting on the Falklands. At the PLP Tony Benn speaks passionately against sending a task force, but the meeting agrees to give conditional support to the government.

I am called immediately after Tony. I agree with Tony that it will be difficult to mount an effective military operation 8,000 miles away but, in view of such blatant aggression by a military dictatorship, there has to be a tough response.

Meanwhile, we can expect a lot of shuttle diplomacy by the Americans and the UN as the task force steams bravely down to the Falklands – one doesn't know whether to laugh or cry or just sing a Gilbert and Sullivan song!

Giles Radice

Wednesday, 7 April 1982

People who should know better are striding up and down the Smoking Room Corridor telling anyone whom they can apprehend that the *Invincible* is sailing without her radar operative; that many of her weapons systems have already been moved; that the Sea Harrier cannot land on deck in a rough sea; that many of the ships in the Task Force have defective power trains etc. etc.

It is monstrous that senior Tories should be behaving in this way. It is only on such occasions as this that the implacable hatred in which certain established figures hold the Prime Minister can be detected. They oppose Government policy whatever it is – they would oppose free campari-sodas for the middle classes if they thought The Lady was in favour. They are within an ace, they think, of bringing her Government down. If by some miracle the expedition succeeds they know, and dread, that she will be established forever as a national hero.

Alan Clark

Friday, 23 April 1982

To Croydon for the funeral of Terry Parry, the General Secretary of the Fire Brigades' Union, a very popular man. A fireman picked me up and took me to the entrance of the crematorium and the fire brigade was out in force as Terry's body was carried on a fire engine covered with flowers and a union jack. All the Labour Movement's leaders were there. The service which was conducted by Bruce Kent was really moving. Bruce said he had never known Terry, but Terry had requested that he conduct the service. Jack Jones made an excellent speech, Len Murray a good one.*

A friend sang 'The Impossible Dream' and I am afraid I sat there with tears rolling down my cheeks. Afterwards I was invited to go in the coach to Crystal Palace Football Club for a little party.

Tony Benn

Tuesday, 4 May 1982

To the House and heard Thatcher at Prime Minister's Questions. Tam Dalyell scored a direct hit by asking. 'Did the Prime Minister herself personally and explicitly authorise the firing of the torpedoes on the *General Belgrano?*' Thatcher said yes, in effect she had the Task Force under political control … I think they're beginning to worry

---

* Bruce Kent, former Roman Catholic priest, and General Secretary of CND; Jack Jones, former General Secretary of the Transport and General Workers Union; Len Murray, General Secretary of the TUC.

in the Cabinet because of the public disgust at the loss of life on the Belgrano.*

Tony Benn

Wednesday, 5 May 1982

The war between Britain and Argentina is beginning to result in high casualties ...

The thought of two right-wing leaders in Britain and Argentina clinging to their political lives by sending people to be killed is nauseating. Equally, to see the saturation coverage the media is spouting on a KILL, KILL, KILL basis is nauseating. At this moment of writing I have the vivid image of young boys in their teens now reduced to dead bodies and thrown about by the heaving seas with no future left ...

I don't want to be told through the lifeless monotone of a Ministry of Defence spokesman who sits there devoid of all emotion, sombre in his account of the affair, all of which is calculated to reduce public reaction. I want to lower myself into the freezing cold water and feel the reality of these young lives; dying so we are told in a cause of principle.

Jimmy Boyle

Tuesday, 11 May 1982
Westminster School

A lovely fresh summer day. Most of the morning is taken up with interviewing scholarship candidates. It is difficult to assess these bright young 13 year olds and I have found over the years that the interview is no guide at all to the boys' performance in the scholarship papers. The parents reflect Westminster's changing clientele – more millionaires, fewer academics.

John Rae

---

* An Argentinian light cruiser sunk by the submarine HMS *Conqueror*. The circumstances were controversial because of her position at the time of sinking outside the British total exclusion zone around the Falklands. Three hundred and twenty-three men died. The Labour MP Tam Dalyell ruthlessly pursued Prime Minister Thatcher on the circumstances of the sinking and wrote a book on the subject soon after (*Thatcher's Torpedo: The Sinking of the 'Belgrano'*, 1983).

Tuesday, 1 June 1982
Saltwood Castle, Kent

Last night I left Saltwood at 2 in the morning to be driven up to the ABC studios for a night chat show coast-to-coast on the Falklands ... I have long since lost count of the number of appearances I have made on the Falklands – three times on *Walden* alone, since the 'crisis' started.

And *what* a crisis! When I think of the state of utter depression when I got out of the train at Sandling on 2 April – on trial, complete and utter humiliation; I even contemplated emigrating. Now not only have we redeemed everything that was at stake then, but one has advanced immeasurably in self-esteem and in the status accorded to us by the whole world.

And I *did* play my part in this ... I was almost immediately recognised by the media – the 'leader of the war party' (Alan Watkins).

Alan Clark

Tuesday, 15 June 1982

I went to the House to hear the Prime Minister's statement announcing the surrender. Michael Foot congratulated her and her forces; somehow it was odious and excessive. I was called and asked if the PM would publish all the documents and the cost in terms of life, equipment and money of a tragic and unnecessary war. The Tories erupted in anger because this was Jingo day.

Tony Benn

Monday, 26 July 1982

The day of the Falkland Islands Service at St Paul's.

I had an excellent place, under the dome, and there in front of me, still hunched and grey, just as he had been on that Monday 5th April, at Rab's memorial service, was Richard Luce.* 'What's going through your mind,' I asked him. He answered candidly, 'I am shattered, absolutely shattered.'

I squirmed and turned in my seat, staring shamelessly. Soon

---

* Luce, a Foreign Office Minister, resigned immediately after the Argentinian invasion, as did the Foreign Secretary, Lord Carrington.

I realised that the block behind me was filling up with next of kin. Many of them were Para families and, very touchingly, they all wore something red – the red of the Red Beret – about their clothing. The girls wore ribbons or cardigans, the fathers handkerchiefs, and so on. Only two rows behind me sat three adorable winklers, two little boys and a girl, who were dressed in red jerseys with metal parachute badges, looking enormous, pinned on their chest. With the exception of some of the very young children, who were excited and jolly, most of the relatives looked deeply unhappy.

Afterwards, the crocodile moved its way slowly down the aisle, starting from the top. I was on the civilian side, passing row after row of next of kin. Anxiously I scanned their faces, but the only emotion I could see was anguish, sheer anguish.

Alan Clark

Chapter Eight

1982–1990
Civil War

As Giles Radice observed, the Soviet invasion of Afghanistan had started the 1980s badly. The decade ended with the Iraqi invasion of Kuwait. On a visit to Abu Dhabi as Defence Minister in August 1990, Alan Clark wrote: 'If the ruling families [of the Gulf] start to pack up and emigrate to their lodges at Newmarket or Longchamps ... we've had it.' The long-term effects of these wars on foreign and defence policy were considerable, but after the Falklands War of 1982, the politics of the decade were generally inward-looking.

Margaret Thatcher led the Conservatives to a second electoral victory in 1983 and a third in 1987. During the same period the Liberal and Labour Parties were undergoing substantial – and historic – change. Paddy Ashdown became Leader of the newly formed Social and Liberal Democrats in July 1988, shortly after, in Ashdown's words, it had sunk 'disastrously in the polls and became the subject of ridicule.' The new party was a marriage between the Social Democratic Party (SDP), and the remains of the Liberal Party. David Owen of the SDP, who took over from Roy Jenkins (leader 1982–3), would not accept the new party and together with a few Liberals refused to join. The bad feeling led Paddy Ashdown to wonder in his diaries if the great Liberal Party that began with Gladstone would end with Ashdown.

Neil Kinnock won the Labour Party leadership in October 1983 and set in train a process of much-contested modernisation which would be completed by a future leader, not yet elected to Parliament.

Two major domestic conflicts, also with long-term ramifications,

broke out in 1984 and 1985: the first being the Conservative government versus the NUM; the second, News International against the
print unions. The *News of the World* columnist and ex-politician
Woodrow Wyatt, who as a Labour MP had served in Attlee's government, became self-appointed confidante to Margaret Thatcher and
the Murdochs (not to mention the Queen Mother), and fortunately
confided all to his diaries.

'In danger of becoming a devotee,' Michael Spicer was the Prime
Minister's parliamentary aide between the Falklands victory and the
General Election of '83; Edwina Currie, outspoken as a Conservative
MP and perceptive as a diarist, considered her chances of becoming
party leader; and Gyles Brandreth, poised to become a Conservative
candidate in 1990, notes that Margaret Thatcher 'has eaten every
single one' of the Cabinet of 1979.

Saturday, 25 September 1982

Compared to last year, when the Left was riding high with successes
everywhere, this year the Left is very much tail-between-legs. We did
unleash a violent backlash from the Right supported by the media and
the general secretaries, and although the Party is pretty solid on policy
it doesn't want divisions, so we are caught by the constraint of unity
– whereas they, being on the warpath, are not, and are demanding the
expulsion of the Left. It's very unpleasant but I shall just let it ride over
me; at this stage we have to accept that the Right have won and there
isn't much we can do about it.

Tony Benn

Wednesday, 13 October 1982

Plymouth City Council have been bothering me about their proposals
to get Cattedown classified as an Enterprise Zone. God, how boring
local government matters are! Like so many other tasks, the most
notable and glaringly being my tax returns, I simply cannot bring
myself to take action. But today, convulsively, I did so. I have to
attend the quarterly meeting of the Executive Council in Plymouth
and I know that it makes good feeling, and compensates for those
very long periods when Janet Fookes [the MP for Plymouth Drake]
is daily reported for her assiduous peering at cracked pavements and

bent dustbin lids and I am not mentioned at all. So I ... spoke to the City Planning Office, rang the *Western Daily Herald* ... and sent a letter to Heseltine formally supporting their case.

Alan Clark

Thursday, 14 October 1982

This evening to Camden Town Hall to join a meeting on education organised by the National Union of Teachers. A panel of eight, including myself and Neil Kinnock, answer questions from the floor. The first questions are all aimed at me. How can I justify working in the 'commercial sector' with 'privileged children'? I reply that in a free society the state should never have a monopoly of education. They are not won over of course, because they have absorbed the left-wing ideology in which what used to be called the public schools are the root of all evils in society. Then they go for Neil Kinnock who in defending himself overdoes the populist Welsh wizard act. When he realises this is not going well, he switches from fine generalisations to unnecessary detail, citing clauses and sub-clauses in previous education acts as though detail was bound to triumph where rhetoric failed.

John Rae

Monday, 15 November 1982

Drove to Newbury magistrates' court for the trial of eleven women from Greenham Common, who were charged with action likely to cause a breach of the peace for standing in a sentry hut a few yards inside the perimeter fence on 27 August. They've been campaigning outside now for a year, first in huts, which were destroyed, then in tents and sleeping bags.

The court was packed and there was applause as the women came in.

The prosecution had been brought under the 1361 Justices of the Peace Act.

Tony Benn

Tuesday, 21 December 1982

Westminster

Lunch with Hattersley at his home in Gayfere Street ... We review the scene. Clearly Michael Foot has, for the moment, survived the tremendous swing of Labour parliamentary opinion against him. I remind those present that if Michael went just before the election then Denis Healey would get his job, as the sitting Deputy Leader. I also say that Kinnock is Hattersley's real rival in the leadership contest after the [next General] election. We agree that Hattersley should have a talk with Healey and that we should do our best to get Hattersely a stronger union base.

We all know that, with Foot as Leader, we cannot win an election.

Giles Radice

Tuesday, 8 February 1983

My blast on unemployment is the first letter in today's *Times*. On Saturday there was a nasty leader with the insensitive headline 'The nonsense of numbers' which claimed that the British economy is performing better than most others and that the record 3 million unemployed is of only marginal significance and hides many who are not workers.

This is my concluding sentence: 'No civilised society can accept mass unemployment and I am shocked that you should seek to persuade us otherwise.'

The Conservatives are clearly hoping that the vast majority who are in jobs will ignore what is happening to the minority and vote the Tories back again.

Giles Radice

Friday, 11 March 1983

Woodbridge

Up at 6.30. Bang on PM's door at 7.00 and carry her bags to the car. Set out for East Anglia at 8.10.

The PM was in cracking good form when we arrived at Felixstowe Docks – the most flourishing private port in the land. Mrs Thatcher spotted the crane immediately; when told it was one of the tallest cranes in Europe, she became hell bent on climbing it – at least to the first level.

Leaving aside the fact that she would not meet a single voter on either the way up or down, forgetting for a moment the sheer physical hazard of climbing the vertical iron ladder, the immediate worry for her staff was that she was wearing a tight blue skirt and black stockings, with the world's press awaiting at the bottom of the ladder. My job, when her determination to ascend became irresistible, was to put myself between the Prime Minister and every one of the fifty or so camera and TV lenses waiting to record the obvious images for immediate and lucrative distribution around the globe …

To my knowledge no one quite got the picture they were looking for – so much so that one late arrival asked her to do it again.

By the time we got back to Chequers I felt I had earned the bottle of malt whisky which someone had given her and which she generously passed on to me.

Michael Spicer

Sunday, 15 May 1983
Saltwood Castle

Before closing, I should record my last speech in the last adjournment of the old House, knocking poor dear Tam [Dalyell] around as he ploughed on with his batty arguments about the *Belgrano*. So what does it matter when it was hit? We could have sunk it if it'd been tied up on the quayside in a neutral port and everyone would have been delighted. Tam is too innocent to see this.

Halfway through Tristan [Garel-Jones] came sidling up, sat down on the bench and offered me an even £100 that I would be in the next government. He always knows everything, but I took the bet all the same.

Alan Clark

Thursday, 9 June 1983

General Election

The day of catastrophe ... Labour losses come through thick and fast. Joan Lestor is out at Slough, Benn goes at Bristol* and, to my very great sadness, Phillip Whitehead loses Derby North.

Meanwhile the Alliance† with the best third-party performance since the 1920s, piles up seconds throughout the South of England but clearly hasn't broken through. All the SDP Northern MPs, except Ian Wrigglesworth, lose their seats, as does Shirley Williams.

In the end I get a majority of over 13,000 but it is only 51% of the vote ...

After drowning my sorrows in whisky with my helpers, Lisanne [Radice] and I and Adam and Heti drive back to Springwell at 4 in an exceptionally beautiful dawn – Mrs Thatcher's dawn.

Giles Radice

Monday, 13 June 1983

Michael Marland, the head of North Westminster Comprehensive School, telephones. I was due to speak tomorrow to his parents and staff about the state schools and independent schools working together but after last week's general election the NUT members on his staff met and passed a resolution saying that it would be an insult for me to visit their school and that they propose to picket the meeting. Michael apologises but says he will have to cancel the meeting. So much for free speech.

John Rae

Wednesday, 15 June 1983

Department of Employment

[My new Private Secretary, Jenny Easterbrook] makes plain her feelings on several counts (without expressing them): one, that I am

---

*Tony Benn's Bristol South East constituency was redrawn and won by the Conservatives. He was later asked by Chesterfield Labour Party to stand in the 1984 by-election there and returned to the Commons on 1 March 1984.

†The SDP and the Liberal Party formed an electoral Alliance in 1983 to share out constituencies between them; the parties jointly won 26 per cent of the votes and twenty-three seats (six SDP and seventeen Liberals).

an uncouth chauvinist lout; two, that it is a complete mystery why I have been made a Minister; three, that my tenure in this post is likely to be a matter of weeks rather than months.

The Enterprise Allowance Scheme, the Job Release Scheme, the Community Scheme. Convoluted and obscure even at their inception, they have since been picked over and 'modified' by civil servants as to be incomprehensible.

Alan Clark

Thursday, 16 June 1983

George Robertson, Donald Dewar and I have a very gloomy conversation in Donald's room. Is Kinnock capable of winning a general election? Donald sees him as a decent and undoubtedly charismatic man but essentially shallow with a tendency to 'windbaggery'. If we are landed with Kinnock we may lose yet another election. Will Labour ever recover?

Giles Radice

Tuesday, 5 July 1983
Department of Employment

Norman Tebbit is truly formidable. He radiates menace, but without being overtly aggressive.

I have just come from a meeting on 'Special Employment Measures' (these tacky schemes to get people off the Register). My own mind is a maelstrom of nit-picking details, eligibility rules, small print of a kind that civil servants relish – not least because they can browbeat Ministers as a team, with one bespectacled *Guardian* reader in sole charge of each 'Scheme' and thus in complete command of its detailed provisions.

But the moment Norman came in he took complete control. Admittedly the Secretary of State is always right. Rule Number One of Whitehall. Even if he's as thick as a plank ...

Norman's own position is particularly strong as he is known to be a favourite of the Lady, of whom they are all completely terrified.

Alan Clark

Sunday, 2 October 1983

Labour Party Conference, Brighton

The evening is spent in relieved celebration. We have a victory supper at which Roy [Hattersley] gives us all Sheffield penknives. Then Lisanne and I go on to Hat's party at the Old Ship. What does it all mean? Well, certainly a new generation at the helm anxious to use modern publicity techniques. Neil and Glenys go on to the platform after the Kinnock victory – Neil sports the socialist red rose. Then Neil makes a good 'impromptu' speech and pictures are taken of him and Roy with hands clasped aloft. All good media stuff.

Giles Radice

Monday, 27 February 1984

Denis Healey makes a brilliant attack on the government in the House over the Government Communications Headquarters (GCHQ) scandal. Mrs Thatcher has decided to bribe and threaten employees there to give up their trade union rights. Denis makes fun of her, calling her 'the great she-elephant that must be obeyed, the Catherine the Great of Finchley'. She doesn't like it – and the Tories know the government has gone way too far over the issue. The beginning of the Tory slide?

Giles Radice

Tuesday, 3 April 1984

Last night, at last, the closing stage of the Trade Union Bill, Report, on the floor of the House. For Tom King's speech the PM came in ...

She has very small feet and attractive – not bony – ankles in the 1940 style ... [her] foot twisted and turned *the entire time* although her eyes were closed and her head nodded at intervals. The back of her hair is perfect, almost identical to previous days. It can't be a full wig as the front is clearly her own. But I suspect it is a 'chignon'.

She's on the ball about everything in spite of all her worries – the miners, the 'machinery of Govt', Carol (a sad distant piece in today's papers), Mark (must be a source of anxiety).

Alan Clark

Wednesday, 11 April 1984

Leicester

There was a demo by the unemployed. Uglyish mood, they tried to 'rock the car' (the one thing of which civil servants are absolutely terrified). Police useless as always, like Hindus defending a trainload of Muslims.

'I must speak to them.'

'No, no, Minister please don't try. Minister, you must not get out of the car. Please, Minister.'

Wretched people, they were angry but taken aback by my actually dismounting to listen. Some SWP yobs tried to get a chant going but the others really wanted to air their grievances. One man, quite articulate, looked dreadfully thin and ill. He had a nice brindle greyhound on a leash but it looked miserable too.

It's foul, such waste. Uncomfortable, I thought what [Nicholas] Soames and I can spend between us on a single meal at Wiltons.

Alan Clark

Thursday, 19 April 1984

I loved the Lady Torte de Shell more than many, many human beings. She was feminine and capricious, offhand and then suddenly passionately maternal. She arrived over the fields eight years ago and decided that this was her home. Every morning she climbed up the wisteria and through the bedroom window to love me; a lick and a purr and a contented mound of fur encircled my head. She was 'my cat' although she loved Julia and would go to sleep in her arms after asking to be let in under the coverlet.

Oh, the tragedy of losing that little creature, the agony of every last day with the vet, the injections, the trays of food and milk, the tears shed over her as we knew she could not live … How we cried the cry of the bereaved.

Roy Strong

Saturday, 28 April–Sunday, 29 April 1984

I should report a conversation I had on Thursday evening with Neil Kinnock. He is deeply depressed by the way Scargill has conducted the [miners'] dispute and says that he is behaving 'like a fascist.' I try and cheer him up by saying that it was inevitable that we should meet choppy waters after the calm of the last few months. His problem is that, though he knows how damaging Scargill is, he does not dare speak out against him.

Giles Radice

Saturday, 5 May 1984
Chesterfield

It looks as though the miners cannot beat the government.* However with 85 per cent of the pits out, coal stocks must be shrinking like anything, and the steel industry is beginning to be affected. The mines won't budge, and it is a very long strike, already longer than the 1926 strike. The TUC has got to back them because, to put it bluntly, if the miners are beaten, the Government will ride all over everybody and workers couldn't stand up to it again so the miners *mustn't* be beaten.

Tony Benn

Thursday, 24 May 1984

Princess Michael of Kent came to the Prince's Trust sponsored concert at the V & A. She is always sharp and wildly indiscreet. What she said, however, didn't surprise me, which was the catastrophe of the Princess of Wales; droves of the household were leaving and then there was the terrible mother Mrs Shand Kydd, who was a baleful influence. Poor Prince Charles, who had bought Highgrove to be near his former girlfriend. Nothing was happy. Diana was hard. There was no pulling together, no common objectives, and it was a misery for him. How long can it last? And Diana has become a media queen which only makes it worse ...

'Being rude to servants is the lowest thing you can do and she does it.' She then listed off the members of the private entourage who had gone. No one knows this. The Prince is left increasingly isolated. The

---

* On the day that Tony Benn was elected as MP for Chesterfield the miners' strike began. Chesterfield in Derbyshire was a mining town and Benn became very involved in the year-long strike. Giles Radice's constituency in Durham was also badly affected.

Queen is withdrawn. Not that the Kent family sounded that much united.

Roy Strong

Thursday, 31 May 1984

Over the last few days there have been terrible scenes outside the Orgreave Coke Depot in South Yorkshire, where 7,000 pickets have been attacked by mounted and foot police with riot shields and helmets. It looks like a civil war. You see the police charging with big staves and police dogs chasing miners across fields, then miners respond by throwing stones and trying to drag a telegraph pole across a road; there are burning buildings and roadblocks.

Tony Benn

Thursday, 6 September 1984

Good meeting about setting up a Chester-le-Street Enterprise Agency with councillors and an official from the DTI. It really looks as though it might go ahead. At least we will have done something concrete about unemployment.

Further advice centres at South Moor and Burnopfield (I have held six in three days) before going south. General messages on the miners' strike is that, if it wasn't for the work of the support groups, the miners' families would be in a very bad way indeed. I doubt if they can hold out much longer. How I wish we could solve the dispute.

Giles Radice

Friday, 12 October 1984
Saltwood Castle

Before breakfast, when I returned with the dogs, Jane told me there had been a huge bomb at Brighton, the hotel had been all but demolished. They had 'got' Tebbit, Wakeham, Tony Berry, various dignitaries.* The whole of the hotel façade blown away. Keith Joseph (indestructible) wandered about in a burgundy coloured dressing gown, bleating.

*Five people were killed: Eric Taylor, Jeanne Shattock, Muriel Maclean, Roberta Wakeham and Anthony Berry, MP. Margaret Tebbit was permanently paralysed.

Mrs T had been saved by good fortune (von Stauffenberg's briefcase!) as she was in the bathroom. Had she been in the bedroom she would be dead.

But what a coup for the Paddys.

Alan Clark

Monday, 19 November 1984

In the Commons a statement was made about the Animal Liberation Front, who claimed to have poisoned Mars bars with rat poison as a result of which the Mars Corporation had taken their chocolate out of the shops. The ALF said Mars were funding experiments on animals. Well, there was shock-horror from all sides of the House. The only person who spoke up and said the government had been slow to deal with animal welfare was Dale Campbell-Savours ... Everyone else just poured contempt on the ALF and said the RSPCA was being undermined by this sort of irresponsible behaviour.

Tony Benn

Wednesday, 5 December 1984
Westminster School

I have invited two striking miners from Yorkshire to talk to the John Locke Society. One is 51, the other 18.

They put the case for the strike robustly and convincingly but their answers to questions about violence and intimidation are less convincing. The older man comes across as the quintessential Yorkshireman – tough, warm, unsophisticated and shrewd. What is the value of this session for the boys and girls? They are able to see the striking miners as individuals, not as a generalised ogre. And they can recognise that the miners are not foreigners from an alien land. These miners and their families have lived and mined in Yorkshire for generations. They are more truly British than many of those in the south-east, certainly more so than some of the pupils here.

This evening Daphne and I are guests ... at the National Theatre, followed by dinner. It is a large party of between 30 and 40 made up of cabinet ministers, aristocracy, media personalities and so on. I enjoy it, while feeling faintly ill at ease because of the contrast with this morning's meeting with the striking miners. Do we all inhabit the same country?

John Rae

Monday, 28 January 1985

From the opposition front bench I denounce Keith [Joseph's] ludicrous bill on corporal punishment. Nearly two years ago the European Court of Human Rights upheld the rights of parents who oppose corporal punishment. Instead of simply abolishing corporal punishment, Keith has vainly attempted to square the circle (between the Court's decision and his own party's prejudice in favour of beating) by establishing an 'opt out' for the children of parents who oppose corporal punishment. This would have the effect of introducing two systems of discipline in schools. No wonder that most educational authorities and teachers' organisations have called the proposed legislation unworkable. In my speech I call the bill a 'nonsense' and predict the early abolition of corporal punishment.

Giles Radice

Thursday, 10 April 1985
Hilltop, Rutland

The miners' dispute is over. The poor miners, including my own lot at Sacriston, have lost everything, while Scargillism is in retreat. Paradoxically the main gainer is probably the Labour Party and not Mrs Thatcher. The government's triumphalist attitude, the unpopular budget and the new focus on Labour's parliamentary leadership has undoubtedly benefited us.

Giles Radice

Tuesday, 13 August 1985

I am so *bored* by my work. It spreads right across and affects everything so that I am beginning to feel stale, and déjà vu, with all aspects of public life. At the Cavalry Club last week Ian [Gow] and I had our ritual 'round-up' lunch. But even that was not the same. We gossiped. But Ian's contributions did not have that electric quality which used to run through them in the days when he had come straight from the Lady's presence.* He is peevish, and fussed about Ireland.

I said, don't. Ireland is a ghastly subject. Intractable, insoluble. For centuries it has blighted English domestic politics, wrecked the careers of good men.

Ian said the pressure to concede everything to Dublin (and thus expose the decent Loyalists in Ulster to the full force of IRA terrorism) is coming from the Foreign Office, who are themselves reacting to pressure from Washington. One must never forget that the Irish vote in Washington is bigger than it is in Eire. We agreed that the Foreign Office now exists solely to buy off foreign disapproval by dipping into the till marked British Interests.

Alan Clark

Monday, 7 October–Tuesday, 8 October 1985

Shadow Cabinet strategy 'away day' at Rottingdean in Sussex. It is notable for the discussion on defence which Neil promised in June – however we don't make any progress. Healey, Labour's leading defence expert for nearly forty years, opens by repeating the powerful strategic and political case against unilateral decommissioning of Polaris that he made at the Shadow Cabinet in June. There is an awkward pause. It is clear that Neil does not want to engage in an argument. He merely replies that unilateral disarmament is Labour Party policy.

Curiously, the rest of the Shadow Cabinet, most of whom are against unilateralism, remain almost silent. This is not because they are cowards. It is rather that they do not wish to see their young leader, who has spoken so bravely at Bournemouth,† make a fool of himself by talking nonsense in front of them.

Giles Radice

---

* Ian Gow was replaced as Margaret Thatcher's PPS by Michael Alison in 1983. For two months Gow was a minister in the Conservative Government, but resigned over the Anglo-Irish Agreement in November 1985.
† From the Annual Conference platform a week earlier, Neil Kinnock denounced the Trotskyist group within the Labour Party, known as Militant, for its activities on Liverpool Council where its members had a majority.

Monday, 14 October 1985

To King's, Canterbury for a meeting of Eton Group headmasters. 'A' Level results are exchanged. Westminster is by far the best by a comfortable margin leaving St Paul's well behind, though London dinner tables insist on believing that St Paul's has the better academic record. The loudest laugh of the evening comes when someone says that their school doctor is worried about AIDS being spread by the music department because musicians are prone to homosexuality. The disease could be passed on via the mouthpiece of the trumpet. Now why should this provoke such an explosion of laughter?

John Rae

Sunday, 1 December 1985

Rang Margaret. She was put out by the Church's report [*Faith in the City*, on urban deprivation] but I told her not to bother as it was clearly a somewhat left-wing stereotyped committee that had composed it and it was bound to contain nothing of value but would automatically blame the government.

'They seem to be more interested in Mammon than in God,' I said. 'They think you can just solve everything by chucking money at it.'

'Yes,' she said. 'There's nothing about self-help or doing anything for yourself in the report.'

I told her that her interview two Sundays ago with Brian Walden was one of the best I had seen her do, though he laboured the question whether she really cared about unemployment rather too heavily ... I also told her that she looked pretty. 'Not bad for sixty,' she replied.

Woodrow Wyatt

Tuesday, 17 December 1985
Department of Employment

I have made various visits, mainly it seems to workshops for the disabled, to please officials and to give the illusion of activity. But all that has happened is that I am that much older and iller, and I have been kept from the company of my loved ones. I have done nothing for my country, and would guess that (for example) there are more people out of work today than there were a month ago.

Alan Clark

Thursday, 9 January 1986

I was on the phone gossiping to Peter Morrison at his office in the DTI when Judith tiptoed in and put a piece of paper under my nose. 'Michael Heseltine has resigned.'

I whooped and gave him the news, but at that very moment his Private Office had done the same ...

Peter said 'Well this could mean some interesting changes', and we both hung up in order to take more soundings.

David* recounted to me the scene. Michael appears to have done it semi-spastically, *not* the *grand geste*. When he slammed his brief shut and walked out a lot of people just thought he'd been a bit rude, and then gone out to the loo. But the photographers were all waiting in Downing Street, so he must have tipped them off in advance.

Alan Clark

Saturday, 18 January 1986

Rupert [Murdoch] in high spirits. Rang about 9.00 a.m. to say he'd been up till 2.45 a.m. overseeing the printing of the extra section of the *Sunday Times* at Tower Hamlets.

A great new plant with maximum security.† He said the police were ready in case there were pickets and they had riot shields stored in the warehouse nearby and every now and again a police helicopter came over to see there was no trouble.

So far he has got away with it brilliantly.

[He] is nervous for such a powerful man about how he should

---

* David Young had been brought into government from industry by Margaret Thatcher and put in the Lords; he was appointed Secretary of State for Employment in September 1985, and there were suggestions that he was her preferred successor. Michael Heseltine had resigned suddenly as Defence Secretary over the future of Westland helicopters in Somerset, preferring a European consortium to take it over: Mrs Thatcher favoured an American solution.

† During his dispute with the Fleet Street printing unions, Rupert Murdoch had secretly imported American printing equipment and installed it at his News International printing works in Wapping.

speak to Mrs Thatcher whom he has met once or twice before with me at lunch or dinner. I said tell her exactly what you think, as you told me, about her not getting a grip on the Westland affair much earlier.

Woodrow Wyatt

Wednesday, 22 January 1986
Central Hall, Westminster

At 4.30 pm I go to the Hall at the invitation of the All London Parents' Action Group. They have asked me to a rally which they assure me is non-political and aimed at settling the long-running teachers' dispute with the government. I should have realised that this was the lions' den and far from being non-political, and that a public school head-master was bound to have a rough ride. So I do not attempt to please them. Teachers should not be paid a professional salary, I tell them, unless they act professionally in terms of accepting assessment and contracts. Cries of 'Rubbish!' I then add that the crisis in education is not the responsibility of the government but a long term problem of government and teacher attitudes. More cries of 'Rubbish!', which I find stimulating.

Return … to the housemasters' meeting and a discussion on this year's Oxbridge results. We have 72 firm places, a figure that would not have pleased my previous audience. It is the highest ever at Westminster.

John Rae

Monday, 27 January 1986

Every seat in the House had been booked with a prayer card, and they were all up the gangways. For a few seconds, Kinnock had her cornered [over the Westland affair]. But then he had an attack of wind, gave her time to recover.

A brilliant performance, shameless and brave. We are out of the wood.

Alan Clark

Wednesday, 29 January 1986

To National Coal Board for lunch with Mr Ian MacGregor. I was met by
the chauffeur who took us to Nottingham where we had the meeting
with the executive board of the NCB in my campaign to get the working
miners better treated after the strike.

Though he is due to retire from the Coal Board in August he says
he is willing to go on or to do anything which *she* would like him to
do. I think he intended for me to give that message to her. I congratulated him on how brilliantly he had turned the Coal Board around and
apparently he is due to be making an operating profit before long. In
five years he said the NCB or coal will be ready for privatisation.

He says there is one advantage in a nationalised industry. You can
plan way ahead into the future because you are being subsidised by
the public.

He thought very soon now steel could be privatised. It was going
the right way. But he was worried about those who run the unions.

I said, 'The battle is between the old reactionaries and the modern
approach. The modernising element of the TUC will realise that
no-strike agreements, higher pay and modern technology are in the
best interest of their members and the other semi-Communist ones
are the true conservatives who cannot change their ideology – and
in any case want their power by getting their posts in undemocratic
ways.'

Woodrow Wyatt

Thursday, 6 March 1986
Department of Trade and Industry

Last night Tristan [Garel-Jones] called me out of the lobby and said
that the FCO were already making trouble. 'Uh?' A report had gone in
saying that I was 'anti-European'. It can only have been that fucking
Ambassador in Luxembourg [in February] … Tristan nodded gloomily.
Once a report is in, it's in. That's why, if you're really ambitious, you
have to be cagey.

Alan Clark

Tuesday, 17 March 1987

My first visitors at 9 am were Alan Plater, the playwright, Mick Jackson and Sally Hibbin, who are turning Chris Mullin's book *A Very British Coup* into a three part television series. They wanted to ask me what situation would face an incoming radical Prime Minister, what his relations would be with the security services, the Bank of England, and so on.

In a way Chris's book has been a bit overtaken by events. First of all, the likelihood of a leftwing Labour leader is absolutely minimal ...

Tony Benn

Monday, 24 March 1986

The Party's Campaign Strategy Committee, where four men and a woman from something called the Shadow Agency made a presentation.

They flashed onto a screen quotes which were supposed to be typical of Labour voters, for example: IT'S NICE TO HAVE A SOCIAL CONSCIENCE BUT IT'S YOUR FAMILY THAT COUNTS.

What we were being told, quite frankly, was what you can read every day in the *Sun*, the *Mail*, the *Daily Express* and the *Telegraph*. It was an absolute waste of money.

Labour was associated with the poor, the unemployed, the old, the sick, the disabled, pacifists, immigrants, minorities and the unions, and this was deeply worrying. The Tories were seen to have the interests of everyone at heart including the rich. Labour was seen as yesterday's party.

I came out feeling physically sick.

Tony Benn

Wednesday, 21 May 1986

Kenneth Baker is appointed Secretary of State for Education. This is a shrewd move by Mrs Thatcher. When I am asked on the *Today* programme who ought to be Secretary of State for Education – Nicholas Ridley or Kenneth Baker – I reply that Kenneth Baker would be much the better choice, because he is not an ideological right-winger like Ridley and he is likely to be better at getting things done. Jack Straw, who covets my job [Shadow Education] tells me that my answer is quite wrong. I should have said: 'What we need is a new government

– a Labour government and a Labour Secretary of State for Education.' Yes, Jack, that would have been the political answer, but occasionally, just occasionally, politicians are required to give a straight-forward reply to a serious question.

Baker will be a formidable Secretary of State to shadow. He is intelligent, very shrewd politically, a first-class communicator, and, unlike Keith (Joseph), very much a rising star, spoken of as a possible successor to Mrs Thatcher.

Giles Radice

Friday, 23 May 1986

New York

Dinner with Rupert, Anna and Liz [Murdoch].

Rupert is off to London this morning to deal with the Wapping situation. He thinks he may have something which will work. He has been having secret discussions with Brenda Dean* and she has been waiting for the right moment to put his proposals to her members.

Before going to the restaurant we drink champagne at Rupert's *New York Post* office from which he conducts most of his American affairs. He shows us a picture of a fabulous house overlooking Los Angeles which he is buying for about £5 million or thereabouts, including the furniture and the *objets d'art*.

Woodrow Wyatt

Tuesday, 30 September 1986

Neil Kinnock's speech lasted interminably … the standing ovation lasted for six minutes; Glenys Kinnock was brought down from the balcony and he kissed her and waved, and then she went back. The whole thing was like a Nuremberg rally, phoney to a degree.

Tony Benn

---

* Brenda Dean was General Secretary of the SOGAT (Society of Graphical and Allied Trades) union during the 'Wapping' News International dispute.

Thursday, 6 November 1986

A Chinook helicopter carrying workers back from the Piper Alpha oil rig in the North Sea crashes off the Shetland Islands. All forty-five passengers and crew are killed. It is the worst civilian helicopter accident ever recorded. As minister for aviation my instructions are to ensure that everything possible is done to retrieve the bodies and to enable friends and relatives to identify them with as much dignity as possible ... The island is shrouded in thick fog; because of this our pilot is forced to make several attempts at landing before he finds a temporary gap in the mist.

[After ensuring the large hangar housing the corpses is secure] through the Ministry of Defence (I) order a Royal Navy vessel to break off its participation in a nearby NATO exercise and join the search for those who have perished but who have not yet been found.

Michael Spicer

Wednesday, 11 February 1987

To Greenwich for a by-election press conference. I find that Labour has a disastrous candidate, Deirdre Wood. She is a typical London leftie and she and her friends sit around the committee rooms like tricoteuses during the French Revolution. We are certain to lose, especially as the SDP have a most attractive candidate, Rosie Barnes, who is bound to appeal to the Greenwich middle classes. It will give the [SDP–Liberal] Alliance the boost they have been looking for.

Giles Radice

Wednesday, 18 March 1987

I went to see the Duchess of York at Buckingham Palace. There she was in a small office with a secretary lady-in-waiting on the top floor in the old nursery suite. This had all arisen because she had heard from Bill Heseltine [the Queen's Private Secretary] that I was to do a television series on royal gardens and she saw a book in it. So did I, so that was soon settled. She is strikingly refreshing, direct and intelligent, a huge bonus I would have thought. No beauty at all, but good Sloane Street features with large eyes. Her mission, she said, was to be Youth and the Arts, especially in the North of England, but, she added, the invitations never came. I said that I would do what I could to help. I said that it was a shame no member of the Royal Family had a house in the north, to which she replied that the Civil List wouldn't pay for it. She was, she announced, York Enterprises and there is no doubt that they must make a living and she will be the one to do it.

Roy Strong

Tuesday, 14 April 1987

Department of Trade and Industry

I am blighted by the Foreign Office at present. Earlier today a creepy official, who is 'in charge' (heaven help us) of South America, came over to brief me ahead of my trip to Chile. All crap about Human Rights. Not one word about the UK interest; how we saw the balance, prospects, pitfalls, opportunities in the Hemisphere.

I'm Minister for Trade, for Christ's sake, what's the point of keeping up an expensive mission in Santiago if they can't even tell me what to push? When I questioned him he was evasive on all policy matters other than his own tenacious *Guardian*esque obsession.

'Aha but,' soft-spokenly he gloated, 'Community policy is, we are but one in twelve,' etc.

What does he mean? There is no exclusive 'Community competence' in foreign affairs (yet!). I don't think that there is even a Foreign Affairs Commissioner, is there? This man is exactly the kind of mole who is working away, eighteen hours a day, to extinguish the British national identity.

Alan Clark

Sunday, 24 May 1987

Chester-le-Street constituency

A surprisingly promising first week both for Labour and for me personally. On Tuesday Labour's manifesto *Britain Will Win* is launched with much professional razzmatazz by Neil and Roy, with the Shadow Cabinet looking admiringly on. Michael White cheekily writes in the *Guardian* that, with Neil and Roy walking together down the aisle dressed in blue suits, and with red roses in their buttonholes, it looks like a 'gay wedding.' Then on Thursday there is the stunning party political broadcast by Hugh Hudson (of *Chariots of Fire* fame) focusing exclusively on Neil Kinnock. With the help of music from Brahms and

Beethoven, it portrays Neil as an eloquent courageous and decent man (he is all those things) who, despite his inexperience, is capable of running the country – according to Denis Healey, Neil, like Gorbachev, has 'steel teeth'.

Giles Radice

Tuesday, 28 July 1987

On the Tuesday we went in delegation to look at Saltaire Mill, Bradford, with the possibility of establishing it as a South Asian Arts and Crafts centre. The whole project of decentralising the V & A goes back through my directorship.

After Robert [Skelton] became Keeper of the Indian Collections I gave him a brief to start thinking about the ethnic minorities in the UK. The Bradford link then began to develop. Exhibitions like *Petals from a Lotus, India Hats, et al*, went there, but now the idea is to establish a permanent outstation.

Roy Strong

Sunday, 2 August 1987

Hilltop

What is so depressing about our defeat in June is that despite Neil's energetic campaign, we failed to gain more than four percentage points. Mrs Thatcher won a smashing victory and managed to keep her share of the poll at nearly 43% – by any standards a magnificent political achievement after eight years in government.

We may have won on the community issues – health, education and jobs – but completely failed to convince the electors that we could run the economy better than the Tories. Indeed the many electors who have done well out of the Tories – those who have benefited from increased earnings and tax cuts, who now own their council houses and have bought shares in privatised companies – were terrified that Labour would 'ruin it.' Of course defence and the 'loony left' issue continue to be negative factors as well.

Lisanne strongly favours me leaving politics, in part because of the weekend constituency work and the absurdly late parliamentary hours, but of course she wants to leave the decision to me.

I should mention a meeting I had a few days after the Shadow

Cabinet election with my young Durham neighbour, Tony Blair, whom I much admire. I have heard him speak a number of times in my constituency and in the Commons, and he really is impressive. He comes across as fluent, intelligent and sincere – not at all the normal party politician. And he has a most attractive personality. I am sure he has big leadership potential.

Giles Radice

Wednesday, 9 September 1987

The SDP vanished in a puff of smoke last week … [Robert] Maclennan (new leader!) just about symbolised the whole sweet-natured, narrow, naïve and indecisive set-up. Roy Jenkins wanted them to join the Liberals after a decent interval, Owen wanted (and still wants) his own party. They are a shower. It is sad really – they split the Labour vote nicely in '83, and '87 was thus much harder to fight. And there is room for a non-socialist anti-Tory party …

John Prescott on TV tonight explaining that no, they knew it was unrealistic to take back shares without compensation* but that 'compensation' will be the shares' original price; and Alan Tuffin (of the UCW) pointing out that nine million shareholders will vote against that won't they?

Edwina Currie

Sunday, 27 September 1987

Someone with his eye firmly on the leadership is John Moore, who made a strong speech on social security and getting away from the welfare state.

There are only three groups/benefits Moore can tackle: pensioners (but they paid, and there are ten million of them), child benefit (but the Tory ladies like it) and the disabled (he hasn't encountered them yet. Just watch!)

[Charles Murray's book *Losing Ground*] is fascinating and

---

*John Prescott, the Labour Member for Hull, was referring to the privatisation of British Gas by the Conservative government the previous year and of British Telecommunications in 1984 (water and electricity were to follow) and how a future Labour government would compensate shareholders when the utilities were taken back into public ownership. The need for compensation did not arise under the next Labour government which retained the privatised companies.

devastatingly accurate in its view of why more welfare makes things worse, particularly in its destruction of the status rewards of being respectable, law-abiding etc.

Edwina Currie

Sunday, 4 October 1987
Saltwood Castle

Vilely depressed after a bad night. (Tom kept us awake fidgeting and flapping his ears and when I finally staggered down to the yard with him at two a.m. he disappeared for three quarters of an hour ratting and at intervals barking shrilly behind the log pile.)

The papers are full of Heseltine 'to be the star of the Conference', etc. How can he be if he hasn't got a perch? ... Why is it always the bad eggs who seem to get to the top in politics?

Alan Clark

Friday, 16 October 1987
Chester-le-Street

A freak storm strikes southern England in the early hours of Friday morning. The wind reaches 100 mph and as the storm crosses southern England it leaves a trail of damaged houses, uprooted trees and even deaths in its wake.

At 1 pm I take the first available train north. I find that the wind has turned right, into the North Sea so my constituents have at least been spared this disaster. In the club (after my Chester-le-Street surgery) I find my party workers not particularly sympathetic towards the South's difficulties. Secretly they may even feel a certain pleasure that the rich South has at last had to suffer.

Giles Radice

Saturday, 21 November 1987

Nuneham Court, Oxford

Weekend discussion of future privatised structure of the electricity industry. Assortment of civil servants, financial and legal advisers. Chaired by Cecil Parkinson.*

7 pm Permanent Secretary, Cecil P and I meet in Cecil's room. Permanent Sec says that Lord Marshall† and entire board will resign if CEGB is broken up and real competition is introduced. Trade unions will back them ...

I say it is outrageous that the government is being blackmailed in this way by a nationalised industry. I certainly cannot go along with a decision to bow to this, especially as during the day's conference it was agreed with all our technical advisers that it would be perfectly feasible (and desirable) to inject competition into the industry.

CP says he recollects that at our meeting at Chequers the PM said of Lord Marshall on a couple of occasions that 'he might be right'.

Michael Spicer

Sunday, 29 November 1987

Lunch at Number 10 on Monday [with nine other ministers]. Mostly she went on about the NHS and how we are going to have to reform it quicker than expected in this Parliament. She did not specify what she had in mind but she's wide open to the ideas of people like John Redwood and David Willetts (blond prat) all young fit, wealthy and ignorant, and, where they're not wealthy yet, at least trying to forget their poor past. Some of the ideas are inconsistent, e.g. why not pay hospitals per operation and then they'll have to be efficient. But, Prime Minister, I ventured, we do that with dentists now; it does not guarantee efficiency, it discourages prevention and it conflicts with the cash limit controls. I think she's after a 'cash follows the patient' idea; certainly you could use a voucher system for a few limited things, but God help the bureaucracy if we did it on a grand scale.

Edwina Currie

---

* Cecil Parkinson was Secretary of State for Energy; Michael Spicer was his minister responsible for privatising the electricity industry.
† Walter Marshall, Chairman of the Central Electricity Generating Board (CEGB) and of National Power; ennobled by Margaret Thatcher for his role in keeping electricity running during the miners' strike.

Friday, 8 January 1988

Department of Trade and Industry

Sometimes I think all I want to do is stay here long enough to get my fur legislation on the statute book. I was looking through some papers that have come in this morning. Horrific illustrations. Worst was a great circular crater, some 16 feet in diameter, dug out of the frozen earth, (for all around was snow) by a poor badger, just using one hand, as he went round and round and round; caught by a steel jaw on the other leg, chained to a post in the centre, trying (for how long must it have taken him?) to escape, he dug that great pit. Until finally he just lay down and died.

Alan Clark

Sunday, 7 February 1988

The press are speculating that it's a new winter of discontent. After years of decline the unions are picking up membership again. Obviously as unemployment declines – and in some parts of the country and in some trades there isn't any employment – they want more money. Thatcherites to a man, the working classes: lots couldn't give a damn about the old and sick. Just watch the howls if the Chancellor increases the tax on fags.

Edwina Currie

Tuesday, 15 March 1988

Took a party of students from Chesterfield College of Technology and the Arts around the House of Commons. Their lecturer told me with some embarrassment that politics and economics had now been transformed into business studies. He said they had businessmen in to talk about businesses. I asked, 'What about trade unions?'

'We have to tell the students that trade unions are about human resources and their relationship with employers is discussed in that context.'

Nine years after Thatcher came to power we have a new wave of people coming through the system for whom capitalism is not only absolutely normal but the only thing they are taught about.

Tony Benn

Saturday, 26 March 1988

At my local party's AGH I attack the Benn–Heffer leadership bid as 'incredible'. I say that it is as if Brezhnev and Chernenko were attempting a comeback in the age of Gorbachev and glasnost [openness]. In practice it will be not only a diversion but also an opportunity for the leadership to stake out the contours of a new revisionist Labour Party.*

Giles Radice

Sunday, 3 April 1988

I seem to have been in the press endlessly in recent weeks ...

A *This Week* programme, with Margaret Jay† doing her socialist best to discredit the whole of private medicine. I gave a short interview arguing that we don't regard it as so outrageous to have a private market in food, clothing, pensions, so why not health? And half our old people have their own property and own it outright, and might want to use it to realise the asset etc.

All the press picked up was 'Remortgage your house, old dears, and you can buy your ops.'

Then we had 'Don't screw around', an interview in *Family Circle* [which was about] women's health in which I said cervical cancer has a sexually transmitted element, don't screw around and don't smoke (based on sound medical advice as usual). So they are all umpty about strong language. Michelle, the plump young Liverpool girl who works in the Department's Private Office, can't figure out what the fuss is about, that's how they talk at home.

Edwina Currie

Friday, 15 April 1988
Rumania

Bucharest is incredibly grotty and rundown. Giant, flooded pot-holes; battered, rusty trolley buses ... disgorging crowds of sullen, shabby (but overweight) lumpenproletariat. Ceausescu is bulldozing great

---

* Tony Benn and Eric Heffer stood for the leadership and deputy leadership against Neil Kinnock and Roy Hattersley. The results were announced at the Labour Party Conference in October 1988.

† Margaret Jay was a television producer and presenter, and daughter of James Callaghan.

swathes of the old town in order to impose a Haussmann-like pattern of squares and boulevards.

Alan Clark

Tuesday, 14 June 1988
Department of Trade and Industry

I have devoted enormous energy and time to this measure (the Fur Labelling Order), and it is a purely personal triumph – over lawyers, ambassadors, senior civil servants in several Departments including my own; eskimos, furriers, 'small shopkeepers' – they have all been in and alternately (sometimes simultaneously) threatened and cajoled. But yesterday, sinisterly, Charles [Powell] rang from Number Ten to say that the PM would 'like a word' on the subject, could I come to her room after Questions.

[Her PPS Archie Hamilton] was there on an upright chair. The PM and I sat opposite each other on those yellow damask sofas in the 'L' of the room.

'Alan, how are you?'

I ignored this. I said, 'I'm so sorry that you should be getting all this trouble from the Canadians.'*

'Oh it's not really *trouble*. I think there's more to it.'

This was going to be very difficult. She had a letter from [Brian] Mulroney (PM of Canada); from Resource International (I remember being warned about the clout they carried); she was going to address the Canadian Parliament. As the Prime Minister developed her case she, as it were, auto-fed her own indignation. It was a prototypical example of an argument with a woman – no rational sequence, associative, lateral thinking, jumping the rails the whole time.

[She asked] 'Why not labelling of battery hens, of veal who never see daylight, of fish which had a hook in their mouth – what about foxes? Do you hunt?'

'Certainly not. Nor do I allow it on my land. As for veal, I'm a vegetarian.'

'What about your shoes?'

---

* Alan Clark had negotiated the measure whereby fur from Canada which had been obtained by trapping the animal would be labelled as such. Clark's hope was that this would eventually lead to people refusing to buy fur products. Charles Powell had told Clark that the Prime Minister would be visiting Canada, and that objections there to even the minor controls proposed on fur trapping would damage the visit.

I ignored this the first time. The second time I said, 'I don't think you would want your Ministers to wear plastic shoes.'

CP and Hamilton smiled together. She did *not*.

Too far gone in indignation now, she just said something about the feet breathing better in leather.

'It's not like you, Alan. It's so unlike you to respond to pressure.'

'I'm not "responding" to pressure. I'm *generating* it. I believe in it.'

Off we went again. Her sheer energy and the speed with which she moves around the ring make her a very difficult opponent. There was talk of wolves around the house.

'How would you like that?'

'I'd love it.'

Her argument, if such a confused, inconsequential but ardent gabbling can be dignified by that Aristotelian term, was 'it's-all-very-well-for-suburban-bourgeoisie-to-inflict-this-legislation-but-what-about-the-noble-savage?'

I was prepared to respond on a philosophical plane. I said something about it being 'the first step.' This was a mistake.

She grittily repeated the phrase to herself several times, half under her breath, '– the first step?'

'In enlarging man's sense of responsibility towards the animal kingdom.'

She shifted ground again. Didn't like labelling orders, weren't we trying to move away from all that? ... I realised I'd lost. The meeting, schedule for fifteen minutes, went on for forty-five. About three quarters of the way through I said, 'Well if that's what you want I will obey you.'

Later I said, 'When you go to Canada don't have anything to do with the "Humane Trapping Committee". It's a put-up job, you'll just make a fool of yourself. They'll think they've conned you.'

She grunted assent.

I snarled, 'I wouldn't do it for anyone else', and went out of the door.

Alan Clark

Thursday, 30 June 1988

Politically this has been a disastrous month for Labour. It has been all to do with our leader ... Neil had appeared to be trying to shift our defence policy to a more sensible position. [But in a] disastrous interview in the *Independent* on 21 June [he] goes back to his previous unilateralist position. At a stroke he revives our unpopular policy, appears to give in to the biggest union [the TGWU] and raises considerable doubts about his leadership capabilities.

Giles Radice

Wednesday, 14 September 1988
Department of Trade and Industry

I have a bundle of interesting papers to read this evening. The Lady is going to make a speech at Bruges on the occasion of some Euro-anniversary or other. The Eurocreeps have written for her a really loathsome text, *wallowing* in rejection of our own national identity, which has come up to me for comment in the trade context. They even managed to delete a ritual obeisance to Churchill, his ideals, all that and substituted the name of *Schuman*. Really!

Alan Clark

Monday, 26 September 1988
Social and Liberal Democrats Conference, Blackpool

Breakfast, then a number of interviews and the start of the Conference proper. The debate on the name [of the party] was tense and difficult. The speeches were extremely good, with Shirley [Williams] making a two-minute intervention which swung the day. I was surprised when 'The Democrats' won by a clear margin – 650 to 500. But people remain very cross.

The worst aspect was the press outside, who simply refused to believe that we would not break up over the issue ... more trouble to come on this.

Paddy Ashdown

Friday, 7 October 1988

The MMR* launch went very well and the children were just *lovely*! Some of the nicest photos ever taken of me in the press the next day.

---

*The controversial triple vaccination of children against measles, mumps and rubella was launched nationally by the Health Minister, Edwina Currie.

W C Fields was wrong – you should always be photographed with children and animals – as the PM has found, hugging calves during elections campaigns and a koala bear on her recent visit to Australia.

I have slowly begun to realise, and somewhat unwillingly, that I will have a crack at the leadership as soon as I can. Partly because I am in touch with real people, partly because I can offer some leadership and view of the future. I look at rivals like David Mellor and I like me better. In between I need to gain as much experience as possible in government … If you get promoted too fast like John Moore it shows, so I'm not in haste.

Neil Kinnock won his leadership contest [against Tony Benn] with ease at the Labour Party conference this week but having handed him the chalice they poisoned it good and proper, by refusing to change their unilateralist stance on defence.

Edwina Currie

Thursday, 8 December 1988

Following the horrific news of the earthquake in Armenia, the response of sympathy and understanding is amazing, with the Soviet Embassy in London open for gifts and messages.

Gorbachev's unilateral announcement of cuts to half a million troops has put Russian diplomacy right at the top, has ended the Cold War at a stroke and may bring hope to millions.*

Tony Benn

Sunday, 11 December 1988

We have been worried for some time about a rising tide of food poisoning, mainly associated with salmonella from chickens. It is appalling to think that most of the carcasses on sale in this country are infected by this bug, but it is killed by cooking, and only poor handling (e.g. allowing a defrosted chicken to drip over cooked food) will cause any problem. By November we were getting reports of virulent

---

*Gorbachev, the head of state of the then Soviet Union, made his announcement – which included withdrawal of armed forces from Hungary, Czechoslovakia and East Germany – to the UN General Assembly. At almost the same time an earthquake struck the Soviet state of Armenia, killing *c*.25,000 people, which curtailed his visit. Gorbachev formally asked the US for humanitarian help.

infection from cooked eggs, e.g. in lemon meringue pie, scotch eggs, or egg sandwiches. I've just seen papers circulated to Cabinet ... which linked eggs to twenty eight deaths. 'Egg infection has the potential to be fatal,' it says blandly.

Edwina Currie

Wednesday, 21 December 1988

I've enjoyed the last few days being with the kids.* I've enjoyed not having to do sodding (Red) boxes, or adjournment debates late in to the night. I've enjoyed not dining with boring old farts in the Commons, or listening to delegations led by smarmy MPs, who then say something different in the lobby later than night.

Most of all, I can make some money. I'll try for a couple of director-ships; that is the easy money.

Edwina Currie

Tuesday, 17 January 1989

I've had it. The Lady no longer knows my name. David [Young] pinches all the good 'initiatives' and I'm left with nothing. Who am I? Other Ministers of State are high profile. Waldegrave, Patten (both), Mellor (although everyone loathes him), Portillo.

It has been conveyed to me that, after being so prominent, a period of obscurity and 'good behaviour' would be prudent and beneficial. Show I was 'serious', etc.

Alan Clark

Sunday, 29 January 1989

In the evening Caroline and I went to a Socialist Conference fund-raising party in Highgate. About 150 people turned up including Salman Rushdie, who made a little speech about the burning by

---

* Currie's resignation was inevitable (she was a minister in the Health Department) once she suggested that 'most of the egg production' in Britain was contaminated with salmonella, causing a crisis in the industry.

Muslims of his new book *Satanic Verses*, which he autographed and auctioned at the party.*

Tony Benn

Sunday, 12 February 1989

Spoke to Margaret at about 4.00 pm. We discussed Leon Brittan who has gone as a Commissioner to Europe. Immediately he has made a speech saying that we must join the European Monetary System at once. 'They go native as soon as they get there. It's too extraordinary,' she said.

I mentioned that Rupert is attracted by her idea of doing a series of speeches and then linking them together and expanding them into a book.

She said, 'How is it getting on, that Sky Television of his?'

Of course she loves the whole idea because it whittles down the influence of the BBC. It makes the area of choice more open, and it is more difficult for people of left-wing persuasion to mount steady drip drip campaigns against her.

Woodrow Wyatt

Friday, 7 April 1989

At 9.30 pm, to the Guildhall to a reception for Gorbachev ...

About 300 present and all the full pageantry of the Guildhall. Gorbachev is smaller than I thought, but possesses an extraordinary sense of calm and power. He has an almost permanent enigmatic smile playing about his face. A man who appears totally in control of himself and of events. His speech was startling in only one aspect – it had been heavily touted as proposing new initiatives, but it didn't.

He summed up the position on perestroika in the Soviet Union and then listed the kind of things they had done to cut the arms race. The implication was, 'We've gone this far, now it's up to you.'

Mrs Thatcher gave a speech in which her voice was much better modulated than I had heard previously. But it was clearly out of kilter with what Gorbachev said. She commented on things which he was

---

* After the publication of *Satanic Verses*, the Iranian leader Ayatollah Khomeini issued a 'fatwa' calling for Salman Rushdie's execution (for insulting Islam) and he had to go into hiding.

expected to say, but didn't. Gorbachev probably changed his speech at the last moment. For the first time I sensed some menace in what Gorbachev said. He may well be worried that he cannot keep his own internal problems in check unless the West gives him more in recognition of how far he has moved.

Paddy Ashdown

Wednesday, 31 May 1989

Derbyshire

Interest rates are up to an awful 14.5 per cent.

[Ministry of Agriculture, Fisheries and Food] have at last banned using cow brains for human consumption. The BSE scare is worrying and we've had quite a lot of cattle sick round here; the farmers are genuinely upset.

Edwina Currie

Saturday, 3 June 1989

After a day's campaigning in Newcastle [for the European Parliament elections] I finally got back to the London flat and turned on the TV to receive the horrifying news of a massacre in progress in Tiananmen Square. Dozens reported killed. But by the sound of heavy machine-guns firing into massed crowds and the swirl of armour through pedestrian-filled streets, I think the figure is more likely to be in the thousands.

Paddy Ashdown

Tuesday, 13 June 1989

Dinner at the Connaught with just Rupert and Anna [Murdoch] and ourselves.

We both gave poor Rupert the going over. I said about privacy, 'Is it really necessary to do a thing in the *News of the World* whereby the wretched [Bobby] Robson, who was the manager of the English football team, was pilloried by some woman he had had an affair with, who told it all to the *News of the World* with vivid detail?'

So Rupert said, 'He shouldn't have done it.' I said, 'No, but people do that, you know very well. I know *you* don't because you are very straight-laced.' At which point Anna said 'I would be after him with a knife if I found him straying.' She looked as though she meant it.

Woodrow Wyatt

Thursday, 15 June 1989

Alan Walters is back in this country and is going to dinners and lunches spreading dissension – as the PM's official adviser! – saying Nigel [Lawson] is all wrong.

Walters is often right but is unbelievably tactless and that makes it harder for Nigel to back down. On television last Sunday he refused to and was quite firm and therefore implied criticism of Walters and the PM, so there has been uproar all week.

Edwina Currie

Tuesday, 11 July 1989

A disturbing lunch with Sir Robert Haslam, Chairman of British Coal.

On the whole, I had always thought that nuclear power was the safest and the cleanest, least polluting energy one could have and that is why I have been advocating it.

Now there is a new factor. The consumer of electricity is going to have to pay all the costs of decommissioning ancient nuclear power stations ... None of them has ever been decommissioned before so no one knows what will happen.

We are at a very late stage. The Electricity (privatisation) Bill has gone through its final stages.

I must speak to Parkinson and get some satisfactory answers from him both on the cheapness of nuclear power and how we are going to eliminate its side effects over the centuries when nuclear power stations are decommissioned.

Woodrow Wyatt

Monday, 17 July 1989

I went to a strange dinner ... I can't remember before being in a room with so many megalomaniacs. There was Conrad Black saying how powerful he was and how he was going to outdo Northcliffe. There was James Hanson saying he was a creative business man and the best in the country; and he was buying Consolidated Goldfields because he had mining interests at heart and it is similar to what he does making brick. There was Charles Forte preening himself when Hanson said he owned more hotels than anyone else in the world. There was Michael Heseltine who thinks he ought to be Prime Minister and his ambition pops out of his dyslexic eyes.

Woodrow Wyatt

Saturday, 26 August 1989

The key political happening of August 1989, as in the August of 1981, has been events in Poland – this time, the election of the first non-Communist Prime Minister of Poland since the war – indeed the first non-Communist Prime Minister in Eastern Europe since the Iron Curtain came down. Whether a Solidarity led government even under such a principled and charming man as Tadeusz Mazowiecki can solve Poland's immense problems is another matter.

Giles Radice

Friday, 13 October 1989

In the afternoon I watched Mrs Thatcher making her speech [at the Conservative Conference]. She was magnificent.

They went on cheering for ten minutes or more and Willie Whitelaw (in the chair) couldn't stop them. He rang a bell but still they went on shouting. 'Ten more years, ten more years, ten more years,' and they sang as well 'Happy birthday to you.'

She said she had worked until three in the morning on that speech, polishing it and getting it right. She had also put it on the autocue and rehearsed it several times.

Woodrow Wyatt

Thursday, 26 October 1989

Well, she blew it. She really blew it this time: oh dear. Nigel Lawson resigned this afternoon; John Major appointed Chancellor of the Exchequer, all that done by 6.15 pm. Then Alan Walters announces from Washington that he's going too; Nigel's letter mentions Walters's continued presence as the reason for his resignation. By 7.30 pm

Douglas Hurd is Foreign Secretary and David Waddington Home Secretary.

The Chamber pottering through some boring legislation erupts with a huge roar as the announcement is made on a point of order ... Labour MPs dancing in the gangways and singing 'The Red Flag.' Ours standing around dumbfounded and conversing in whispers.

Edwina Currie

Friday, 9 November 1989

The Times has a leader today ... saying we have ceased to be a radical government. I think Simon Jenkins [the editor] is right. And now we hear that there will probably be a challenge to the PM. It's all falling apart, with not much hope of redemption because Major* (a) has got us into the ERM at too high an exchange rate, (b) has not cut public expenditure, (c) is keeping income rates too high.

Michael Spicer

Friday, 10 November 1989

Out of the blue, and quite amazingly, the Berlin Wall is being removed. The Brandenburg Gate was opened yesterday, and today bulldozers and cranes went in and began hammering holes in the wall and thousands of East Germans are coming over into the West. But in reality it is causing enormous anxieties in NATO because the whole defence argument has changed, while the Labour Party continues to call for three Trident submarines as a first priority.

Tony Benn

Saturday, 9 December 1989

A quiet evening in front of the television. It is clear that Mrs Thatcher has been completely isolated in Brussels, just as I suspected she might. But goodness! They are clever. She came waddling back to Britain saying that she was still in the centre of Europe. It's completely untrue of course. But if they say it often enough people will believe them.

*John Major had gone from being Foreign Secretary in July 1989 to Chancellor of the Exchequer in October 1989.

Meanwhile the *Daily Telegraph* opinion poll today shows us [the Liberal Democrats] up to 9 per cent – slowly, slowly making our way back.

Paddy Ashdown

Thursday, 21 December 1989
Ministry of Defence

I have finished my paper, boldly entitled it 'The 1990 Defence Review' and lodged it with Charles [Powell] at Number 10 ...

My paper is succinct and radical. And I have followed the two guiding principles in such matters – keep it short (5 pages and an annexe) and get it in first ahead of any other(s) that may compete for attention. (One thing I have learned in Whitehall is the need to be first 'on the table' and take pole position against which all else is judged.)

Alan Clark

Monday, 8 January 1990

To my amazement I came sixth in the Radio 4 'Woman of the Year' poll. My appeal seems to have enduring quality. PM top of course; (2) Kate Adie; (3) Princess of Wales; (4) Princess Anne; (5) Mother Teresa; (6) 'EC' (7) Raisa Gorbachev.

Edwina Currie

Tuesday, 23 January 1990
European Commission, Brussels

At 3 o'clock, David Williamson, Secretary General of the Commission and Delors' right hand man.* He is bouncing with energy and full of ideas. I was impressed.

He told us that Delors' policy on Europe was what he called 'progressive structural dynamic destabilisation' (I can just hear it in French). What this amounts to is deliberately introducing items on to the European agenda as 'problems.' Each problem, once solved,

---

*Jacques Delors, President of the European Commission.

opens up another problem. Thus he makes progress from economic to monetary union to democratic union and eventually to political union. He never admits his ultimate destination but merely sets the process in train (not a bad strategy for moving a political party, either).

This is more far sighted than I had previously been prepared to concede of Delors.

Paddy Ashdown

Sunday, 11 February 1990

Had phone call telling me that Mandela would be released today and asking me to go to Trafalgar Square at 12.30. There were hundreds of people gathered there and the organisers were, of course, the City of London Anti-Apartheid Group who had been picketing outside South Africa House in the Square non-stop for 1,395 days. There was a tremendous sense of excitement, people were singing and waving their arms and kissing and hugging. Somebody had draped on Nelson's column a banner with the words 'Nelson Mandela's column'.

A really great day. On television live from Cape Town was Mandela, tall, distinguished and with a strong voice, walking out of prison and reaffirming the need for the armed struggle.

Tony Benn

Tuesday, 20 February 1990

I dined at the Cavalry Club with Ian Gow.

He is deeply apprehensive of the future, said that no government had ever been so consistently (over six months) behind in the polls at this level and at this stage – halfway, he said – in the electoral cycle, and gone on to win ... Ian said that all the indicators were bad and that inflation would be 8.5 per cent in November. (He's a terrible old Jeremiah about the inflation rate.)

'Personally I wonder if it matters all that much. It's a million per cent, or whatever, in Brazil and you can still get taxis and delicious meals. Sex doesn't stop.'

Usually when I make remarks of this kind, which are Boswellian, to draw him out, Ian smiles with what is called 'a faraway look.' But he was serious, earnest.

'Evidently you do not appreciate the significance of the month of November.'

Of course! The leadership election.

Ian elaborated. There is a real risk of a challenge, and this time a serious one.

Alan Clark

Tuesday, 27 March 1990

To County Hall for the last meeting of the Inner London Education Authority.* It was really rather moving to think that there had been a London education authority for over 100 years, that my grandfather had been a founder member in 1889 and that my son, Stephen, was a member as it ended.

Tony Benn

Wednesday, 28 March 1990

Heseltine is quite openly spoken about as the heir-presumptive and preens himself in public. How has all this been allowed to come about? The Community Charge has got on everyone's nerves of course, and generated the most oppressive volume of correspondence. Persistent deficits in the polls of a nearly insuperable order rattle people. But I am inclined to think that the Party in the House has just got sick of her. She hasn't promoted her 'own' people much. Her constituency in this place depends solely on her proven ability to win General Elections. But now this is in jeopardy she has no real Praetorian Guard to fall back on.

In the meantime all the Wets and Blue Chips and general Heathite wankers, who seem ineradicable in this bloody Party, stew around and pine for her to drop dead.

I could be faced with the ultimate hideosity of being stuck at MOD during a Heseltine 'reconstruction'.

Oh dear how quickly everything can change.

Alan Clark

---

* The ILEA was abolished by the Conservative Government; the Greater London Council and other Metropolitan County Councils were abolished earlier, in 1986.

Saturday, 31 March 1990

Went to see Rupert at 5.30 to talk about Sky Television.

When I got to Piccadilly the traffic was not moving. I crossed the road and found myself among a number of scruffy-looking people but not unduly violent in appearance or manner. Some were carrying anti-poll tax placards. They looked stupid and bovine and had no doubt come up to enjoy themselves in the free buses provided ... When I got to Rupert's flat I found Anna there alone. She had been sunbathing and sleeping on her balcony. Then Rupert rang to say he was going to be late because he couldn't get through the traffic from Wapping.

Rupert eventually arrived. On television were scenes of utmost violence in Trafalgar Square by the poll tax demonstrators. About three and a half thousand, either from the Socialist Workers' Party or from various brands of anarchists and militants, had come to make trouble. Looting of shops had begun ... smashing windows and goodness knows what else.

We talked a long time about how to combat the attempts of BSB to make Rupert divest himself of all but twenty per cent of ownership of Sky Television on the grounds that he controls thirty six per cent of the newspaper circulation in the country.

Rupert needs to get about two and a half million with the ability to watch Sky before it turns the corner and begins to make profit. I am beginning to think he may succeed.

Woodrow Wyatt

Tuesday, 1 May 1990

In the Tea Room I had a chat with [Michael] Fallon, a nice cool Whip. I complained to him about this rotten, irrelevant unnecessary legislation which clogs our time. Firearms; Football Supporters; War Crimes; *Supermarket Trollies (Local Recovery Powers) Restricted Amendment* ... etc. ad nauseam. Compounded with the abject failure to sort out rioters at Strangeways prison it was all accumulating evidence of a government in decline.

This morning I was on the roof of the old War Office building, looking round at Whitehall. The Admiralty opposite, the Cabinet Office, the Treasury, the Foreign Office. How well it was all planned.

How confident. We ran the empire and the world with the same number of civil servants as presently exist in one department.

Alan Clark

Sunday, 3 June 1990

Somerset

The news broke today that the SDP has finally and formally folded.

The end of a very important week. The key message to get across to the public is not that the SDP has folded but that the rifts in our own ranks have been healed, with most of them joining us. But it's difficult not to feel slightly triumphant, particularly since everybody once said Owen was bound to win.

I listened to the one o'clock news. Owen sounded statesmanlike but very bitter. He sought, even at the last moment, to dismiss us completely and encouraged his members to join either the Tories or Labour.

During the day I spoke to Roy Jenkins and Shirley Williams, both of whom said they would issue statements supporting us.

Paddy Ashdown

Thursday, 14 June 1990

Ah, I feel so sad. Yesterday at dawn Iliescu* sent in the police and troops to clear the demonstrators from University Square. Four hundred people arrested, but of course instantly replaced by thousands more from the university. More troops, Molotov cocktails, determined efforts by the rioters to take over the television station and set it on fire, and at least four people dead, hundreds injured, firing into crowd.

Most Romanians aren't interested in communism or non-communism: only in more basic matters like keeping body and soul together. But Iliescu has been monumentally stupid, preferring to lose all credibility in the West for a bit of peace and quiet on his doorstep.

Edwina Currie

---

* Ion Iliescu was President of Romania. He had been a prominent figure in the successful revolution against the communist regime during the previous year.

Wednesday, 27 June 1990

Cecil Parkinson understandably irritated because Energy Select Committee has gone for him for 'bungling' nuclear power in privatisation of electricity. This is hitting the headlines but very unfair. Privatisation brought out the cost of nuclear.

Michael Spicer

Saturday, 14 July 1990

Hilltop

Nicholas Ridley, buccaneering, outspoken, chain-smoking and anti-European is forced to resign. He gives this foolish interview in the *Spectator* to its editor Dominic Lawson, in which he expresses some astonishingly anti-German sentiments. He accuses the Germans of being 'so uppity' and says that Hitler was preferable to Kohl because you could 'fight back'.

The Ridley affair shows that a lot of Thatcherites are not really reconciled to Europe. Of course, if it is really the case that the new united Germany is a political threat to Europe, you have to devise a European framework that will tie in Germany.

Giles Radice

Tuesday, 17 July 1990

I went to listen to Margaret, the first time she was answering Questions since the Ridley affair ...

She was in total command. Her resilience is amazing and her skill at dealing with questions is fantastic.

I wrote in the *News of the World*, that handing Ridley over to the baying mob would weaken her authority. I fear this may be true. This was very much echoed at dinner last night (with Jonathan Aitken, John Redwood et al) when a number of them said she is now a prisoner of Hurd, Major and Howe.

Woodrow Wyatt

Monday, 30 July 1990

En route to the Ministry of Defence

When I got to the [station] barrier Julian was waiting, looking anxious.

'Minister, I have some very bad news.'

For a split second I feared it must be Andrew.* But something in his eyes was missing (the look of fear, I suppose, and embarrassment that I might actually *break down*). 'Ian Gow has been killed by a car bomb.'

'How spiteful of them,' was all I could say. But I thought particularly of the poor Lady. She wept at the first casualties of the Falklands. I wonder if she did today? Because Ian loved her, I mean in every sense but the physical. And then in the end, as lovers do (particularly that kind) he got on her nerves and she was off-hand with him.

My closest friend, by far, in politics.

He was *insouciant* about death. In the garden of his tiny little house, south of the river, he would point up at the tower blocks which loomed to the east.

'The Paddys are up there,' he would say, in good humour, 'with their telescopes.'

Now they've got her two closest confidantes. Airey and Ian. I suppose I should be apprehensive that they might come for me.

Alan Clark

Friday, 3 August 1990

Serious news today of the Iraqi invasion of Kuwait. Alliances are being built up; the Americans and Russians issued a statement, Thatcher is going to America, Bush warned that Saudi Arabia mustn't be attacked because Baghdad can't be allowed to control two-thirds of the world's oil supplies. We could be hovering on the edge of a Third World War and the only comforting thing you can say about it is that the Cold War is over and the superpowers are not fighting this war by proxy.

King Hussain of Jordan, who is a great friend of Britain, but is also a friend of the Baghdad government, has been to Iraq.

Tony Benn

---

* Alan Clark's younger son Andrew was an officer in the Life Guards, serving in Oman.

Saturday, 18 August 1990

Abu Dhabi

The palace of the Amir is surely the most extravagant building in which I have ever trod.

When we get down to business, it is soon plain that these 'Ruling Families' [of the United Arab Emirates*] are more than a little apprehensive. Iraq, more than any other, is the country of the mob ... The assistance they (the Emirates) hope for is of a specialist kind. Each, in their different way, has asked for a strong detachment, preferably with light armour as well, to protect them, personally. Because of course if things really start to disintegrate they couldn't even trust their own bodyguard.

Nor is this a request that should be treated lightly. If the ruling families start to pack up and emigrate to their lodges at Newmarket or Longchamps or, worse, to patch up some 'Arab solution' deal individually with Saddam, as that oily little runt Hussein, King of Jordan, is openly recommending, then we've had it.

Later at Riyadh, Saudi Arabia

There are F16s here wingtip to wingtip and more transport aircraft than I have seen since Wideawake on Ascension Island in 1982. Once a military build-up passes a certain stage battle becomes almost inevitable.

Alan Clark

Wednesday, 12 September 1990

3 pm meeting in the Cabinet room with PM and Chris Patten to discuss our long-term ideas on housing. PM remarkably bouncy considering what must be on her mind re the Middle East. She explains that council housing has been the bane of this country and we must get rid of it. Patten clearly doesn't agree but keeps his peace. I do agree with her. (As always, it's her enemies she has promoted so I am in a weak position to support) ...

At the end Chris Patten has to leave meeting to catch a train to his constituency (the meeting had overrun by half an hour; went on for

*The United Arab Emirates comprised Abu Dhabi, Dubai, Fujairah, Ras al Khaimah, Sharjah, Ajman and Umm al-Quwain, each of which has a hereditary ruling family.

one and a half hours). I found myself almost alone with her and said, 'We mustn't be despondent. Housing is basically a great success. The French are very envious with what we have done for home ownership.'

She said almost quietly, 'I know but it still depresses me that we have not done more to throw off the dependency culture.'

I said, 'We're getting there.'

She repeated this and smiled. She is an extraordinary woman, at sixty-something looking more dynamic and attractive than ever. All this in the midst of the Gulf crisis.

Michael Spicer

Thursday, 11 October 1990

On Friday morning the Countryside Commission announced that the new Midland Forest is to stretch from Charnwood and Needwood across South Derbyshire to north west Leicestershire. We are to have £100 million of new trees ... Great chunks of South Derbyshire will become green belt, and designated for English deciduous forest. Land values will jump. I can't quite believe it yet – but what good news for us; Swadlincote and Gresley and Newhall to be surrounded by Forest!

Then almost to wrap it up on Sunday we had a service at Gresley church to unveil a stained glass window paid for by the UDM [Union of Democratic Mineworkers], in honour of the miners of South Derbyshire. A lovely service with Gresley male voice choir singing their hearts out – it brought a lump – and Daw Mill Colliery Band in the background.

On Friday evening John Major announced our entry into the ERM* as of Monday and a 1 per cent cut in interest rates.

Edwina Currie

Thursday, 18 October–Friday, 19 October 1990
Eastbourne by-election

The BBC exit poll for Eastbourne was announced on *Newsnight* – it showed us, unbelievably, 1–5 per cent in the lead. The BBC were clearly very worried about its accuracy ... We waited on tenterhooks.

---

*The Exchange Rate Mechanism: an attempt by the members of the European Community to reduce exchange rate variability and achieve monetary stability in preparation for monetary union and the introduction of a single European currency.

Chris Rennard became more and more confident as we approached midnight. Finally at 12.30 he rang me with the result. We'd won fifty-one per cent for us, and a 4,500 majority.

Friday: We arrived at Eastbourne to find a forest of cameras and David Bellotti (the new MP) looking a bit sheepish. I shepherded him through the usual photo sessions etc ...

Into the Television South studios to do a down-the-line interview with ITN. Ken Baker had said 'The parrot has twitched.' To which I replied, 'Some twitch. Maggie has been bitten hard by this one and we intend to bite again' – a little over macho perhaps.*

Paddy Ashdown

Tuesday, 30 October 1990

In the House, Mrs Thatcher runs amok. Her Rome summit statement is cautious, even moderate, but in her reply she goes berserk. Half the Tory MPs love it, the rest are deeply disturbed by her. She practically declares war on Brussels – thus far and no further – and very nearly calls an immediate general election on the defence of the pound, parliament and national sovereignty.

I was called very late ... say that she is living in cloud cuckoo land if she thinks that the voters will support UK relegation to the second division. I see that I have registered a hit when Mrs Thatcher rants and raves, asking why I bother to stand for parliament if I am such an enthusiastic supporter of a single currency.

Giles Radice

Friday, 2 November 1990

Geoffrey Howe has resigned in protest over Mrs T's attitude to Europe. 'I can no longer serve your government with honour.' There's a wonderful picture in *The Times* of the Thatcher Cabinet in 1979. Eleven years later and there's not one of them left. She's eaten every single

---

* The by-election was created by the murder of Ian Gow, who had a majority of almost 17,000 votes in 1987. Chris Rennard was the Liberal Democrats' director of campaigns; Ken Baker was the Conservative Cabinet minister. Margaret Thatcher had mocked the Lib Dems' new bird emblem as a 'dead parrot', viz the *Monty Python* sketch.

one … By way of tribute at the Caprice at lunch with Colin Moynihan, I chose steak tartare.

Gyles Brandreth

Sunday, 4 November 1990

The papers are very bad. Tory Party falling apart, the death blow, that kind of thing …

I don't think she realises what a jam she's in. It's the Bunker syndrome. Everybody round you is clicking their heels. The saluting sentries have highly polished boots and beautifully creased uniforms. But out there at the Front it's all disintegrating. The soldiers are starving in tatters and makeshift bandages. Whole units are mutinous and in flight.

Alan Clark

Monday, 5 November 1990

'Thatcher moves to fight off Heseltine threat' was today's headline. This I did not discuss this afternoon when I had my brief encounter with Sir Thomas Arnold MP.* We exchanged pleasantries and then I came to the point. Sir Tom turned to gaze out of the window. 'Officially, the list is *closed*. It's all done and dusted,' he said. 'But you never know …' He turned back to the desk and flashed a crinkly smile. 'Here are the forms. If you care to fill them in and let me have them back we'll take it from there.' He opened his diary. 'Let's meet again on, say, 19 December at 6.30 pm. Will that suit?' It won't suit at all but I said, 'Yes, yes of course, thank you, thank you so much.'

Gyles Brandreth

Tuesday, 13 November 1990
House of Commons

I forced my way along the Minister of State's bench, stopping two places short of Janet [Fookes] who always sits massively, in the camera-hogging spot just behind the PM.

---

* Brandreth was seeking a parliamentary seat – and was directed to see Thomas Arnold, a vice-chairman of the Conservative Party.

From the moment he rose to his feet Geoffrey got into it. He was personally wounding – to a far greater extent than mere policy differences could justify. Elspeth's hand [his wife's] in every line.

The Labour benches loved it. Grinning from ear to ear they 'Oooh'd' and 'Aaah'd' dead on cue. At one point he illustrated his sense of betrayal with some cricketing analogy, being 'sent in to bat for Britain … only to find before the game the bats have been broken by the team captain.' Everyone gasped …

Geoffrey ended his speech with an ominous, and strange, sentence: 'I have done what I believe to be right for my Party and for my country.' (They all say that.) 'The time has come for others to consider *their own response* to the tragic conflict of loyalties with which I myself have wrestled for perhaps too long.'

Alan Clark

Tuesday, 20 November 1990
Upper Committee Corridor, House of Commons

I wanted to see what was happening in the first ballot for the Tory leadership – Michael Heseltine versus Margaret Thatcher.

It is quite a historic event. By secret ballot, Tory MPs have the power to remove as Leader of their party a Prime Minister who has been elected three times by the British people.

When I got there the whole corridor was packed from the upper waiting hall right down to the far end, with hundreds of people. I had my radio with an earpiece and the aerial sticking up, I must have looked like a man from outer space. I stood on a bench so that I could see everyone – Tory, Labour and Liberal MPs, clerks, secretaries, journalists – a sea of faces. There was a bit of scuffling further up and then all of a sudden, through the crowd, came a number of journalists who ran by so quickly I could hardly recognise any of them. The crowd opened like the Red Sea.

It wasn't for some time that I heard the results. Margaret Thatcher had got 204 and Heseltine 152. It was four short of outright victory for her on the first ballot. Almost immediately I heard her on my radio from Paris (where she is attending the Conference on Security and Cooperation in Europe) announcing that she was going to fight in the second ballot.

Tony Benn

Thursday, 22 November 1990

Very early this morning the phone rang. It was Tristan [Garel-Jones].
'She's going.'

There will be an official announcement immediately after a short
Cabinet, first thing. Then the race will be on. Apparently Douglas
Hurd *and* John Major are going to stand. I said I thought it was
crazy. Heseltine will go through between them. I could sense Tristan
shrugging. 'There you go.'

Alan Clark

Thursday, 22 November 1990

Glasgow

To Glasgow to campaign in the Paisley by-election. On arrival I received
a message to ring the office urgently ... Thatcher had resigned ten
minutes ago!

On the way back to London the aircraft was buzzing with the
Prime Minister's resignation – some people shocked, most very happy.

At PMQs Kinnock who had been carping most of the morning
asked a statesmanlike question, commenting on her record. Me ditto.
She was in gracious mood but well in control of herself. What an iron
will she has.

Then into the No Confidence debate initiated by Kinnock.
Kinnock's speech was not good. It started well but then was rather
torpedoed by Jim Wallace [Liberal Democrat MP] who asked him to
answer simply on the European single currency. He waffled uncontrol-
lably. Lawson came in with a question which completely floored him.
The rest of his speech was lost. Her speech, however, was magnificent
– completely in command of the situation, really enjoying herself and
fast on her feet. The Tories must be feeling they have lost their greatest
asset. They have murdered Caesar and will, I imagine, soon be looking
around for a Brutus.

Paddy Ashdown

Chapter Nine

1990–1997
The Lady across the Water

When Margaret Thatcher stepped down as Prime Minister on 22 November 1990 she predicted the Conservatives would win a fourth general election. On 9 April 1992, John Major her successor duly did so, having removed the first agent of her nemesis, namely the poll tax. He had not removed the second: the European incubus, or, to be more precise, the Maastricht Treaty and the looming prospect of a single European currency. It was, arguably, the biggest crisis in the Conservative Party for 150 years in the view of Michael Spicer, a leading 'rebel'. Other rebels, including Christopher Gill, were suspended from the parliamentary party over Europe. They describe the Kafkaesque progress of the Maastricht Treaty's passage through Parliament. 'The lady across the water,' sighed one MP, 'we miss her so!'

The Iraqi invasion of Kuwait in August 1990 provoked the first Gulf War. The UN-sanctioned force of mainly American and British troops won the battle but failed to press home the victory. In the US, the neo-conservative Project for the New American Century was conceived.

John Major's government grappled with the outbreak of rivalries and violence in a part of Europe that since the Second World War most people had been happy to forget – the Balkans. In June 1991 Paddy Ashdown, the future UN High Representative for Bosnia and Herzegovina, confided to his diaries that he 'didn't even know where all the countries were'.

Alec Guinness, surveying the political and cultural landscape asked 'Oh, Sceptre'd Isle set in the polluted sea, where are we heading?'

Meanwhile the defeated Neil Kinnock had handed on the reform of the Labour Party to John Smith, his successor. Had Smith survived, how might the future Labour Party have looked? After a short but intense struggle with Gordon Brown, Tony Blair took over as party leader. Blair and his fellow modernisers, especially Peter Mandelson, gave new impetus to the modernisation process. They looked back at the internecine strife of the 1980s and concluded that to have a chance of re-election the Labour Party would have to avoid division over policy and organisation, concentrate power in its leadership and abandon any pretence of socialism. New Labour, the Third Way and the Stakeholder Economy had arrived.

Giles Radice witnessed the transition. Chris Mullin, another Labour MP from the north of England, began his diary the day John Smith died and, nor far away in Northumberland, a miner's son, Jimmy Wilson, described how the inexorable decline in the mining industry had affected his family.

In 1995, 'mammal, father, artist, musician' Brian Eno kept a personal diary; coincidentally it was the year the troubles in Bosnia developed, in which Eno became closely involved. Over the course of three years, Lord Longford wrote a 'Prison Diary' – as visitor rather than inmate; and fragments of a diary by Alan Bennett from 1995 to 2004 record the ridiculous and the sublime in England either side of the new century.

Despite political emphasis on being British, the word began to lose what meaning it once had. Devolution of power to Wales and Scotland, membership of (as it now came to be called) the European *Union*, and large-scale immigration from across the globe* all undermined the significance of, and the long-term prospects for a United Kingdom of Great Britain and Northern Ireland.

Tuesday, 27 November 1990

I spent a long time at Shepperton making the Birds Eye Waffle commercial: eight hours to shoot thirty seconds. In the real world Mrs Thatcher is now backing John Major. I'm backing Douglas Hurd. In the

---

*Commonwealth immigration between 1961 and 1991, for example, had increased fivefold.

world of Birds Eye Waffles, no-one seems the least bit interested in who our next Prime Minister is going to be.

Gyles Brandreth

Tuesday, 27 November 1990

What will Major be like as PM? He has risen swiftly, almost without trace. He has few definite views, except his support for a so-called 'classless society'. His voice is a boring monotone. Lisanne thinks, however, that he has a nice smile and will appeal to women voters.

In the evening, just after the result is announced [we visit] the Jenkinses' house in Clapham: Peter Jenkins, Polly Toynbee, James Naughtie and other BBC and independent journalists are present. John Birt, BBC supremo, is also there with his wife. Much muttering about the inadequacy of Neil. The trouble with journalists is that they have helped to get rid of one leader and would now like to have a go at another.

Giles Radice

Wednesday, 16 January 1991
Gulf War Day 1

An awful sense of gloom pervades. War could be declared at any second. It all depends on the military now.

The Parliamentary Party meeting was chiefly on the Gulf situation. Everybody agrees with the line, except Simon Hughes,* who agonised in his usual Jesuitical way about the peace movement in the Party having no spokesman in Parliament and that he should do it. We listened patiently. You can always trust Simon to take out his conscience and wash it clean of all stains.

Home at 11.00 and *Newsnight*. War seems only a few days away. With this in my head I tumbled into bed at 11.50 and turned on the radio to discover that it had started fifteen minutes ago. I leapt out of bed, called Alan [Leaman] who had already got the news, and dictated an early comment. I did a quick round of television and radio

---

* Simon Hughes was the Liberal Democrat MP for Southwark and Bermondsey.

interviews until about 2.30 saying we must support the Government and hope for a quick victory with minimal casualties.

Paddy Ashdown

Thursday, 24 January 1991

I find it strange, as a woman, this war.

It's certainly the biggest logistics exercise since the Normandy landings, and the fire power is just staggering – explosives with one and a half times the power of the Hiroshima bomb were dropped in the *first sortie* ... So I find it, secretly, very exciting and can't get enough of it. There's something powerful and emotive about this war which helps me understand why men enjoy it.

Edwina Currie

Thursday, 28 February 1991

The Gulf War is over. Too soon I think. Bush has ordered a ceasefire. Now a long and messy interlude with Saddam stalling and dodging and quite likely to start shooting again. The Foreign Office has no idea what it wants. Never seems to have given any thought to the post-war pattern, the western military presence, commitments – OBJECTIVES. I could write a scintillating picture on this but I'm exhausted and my morale is at zero.

An article in *The Times* by Robin Oakley – a man who always ignores me – about the leaderless Right. No one mentions my name. How quickly this can happen!

Alan Clark

Tuesday, 12 March 1991

Panic before the dinner party. Mrs [Conrad] Black could not come.

Annunziata Asquith was tried but she had to go to a Benjamin Britten opera ... We then tried Robin Day to ask if he had got somebody he could bring with him which he duly did.

There were some attacks made ... on Robert Maxwell. Everybody agreed that he was a crook, including the Airlies, but in some ways likeable.

Conrad said he couldn't possibly do any deal with him, he was so dishonest and devious and wriggled out of things.

I like Conrad more and more. I had thought he was overweening at one time but he is becoming less bombastic and aggressive the more confident he gets, as is often the way. I think I must mention to Major to give him a peerage. That would bind him very strongly because I think he has loyalty in his make-up quite keenly.

Woodrow Wyatt

Sunday, 12 May 1991
Wembley

To Wembley with Kate [Ashdown's daughter] for the Simple Truth concert in aid of the Kurds of Iraq. Everyone gathered in the VIP lounge including Mary Archer, who is much prettier than she appears on television. He was there too, poncing about and generally being obnoxious.

Kate was in great form. Although plunged into the company of some pretty dizzy names (Marmaduke Hussey, Michael Checkland, Princess Diana etc.) she was totally unawed by them and chatted away as though she had known them all her life. I was very proud of her.

Diana left at 9.00 and Kinnock shortly afterwards. We stayed until about 10.15 so Kate could hear her favourite, the Gypsy Kings (awful noise). We then left through the back of the stage, where Kate had a chat with someone called Chris de Burgh, who was obviously terribly exciting but of whom I had never heard.

Paddy Ashdown

Saturday, 29 June 1991

I have fixed to do TVAM tomorrow on the dreadful complexities of the growing crisis in Yugoslavia. Tim Razzall* had to show me maps as I didn't even know where all the countries were. We spent an hour or so over a couple of whiskies talking about Yugoslavia and what I would say the following morning.

Paddy Ashdown

---

*Tim Razzall, Treasurer of the Liberal Democrats, later Lord Razzall.

Sunday, 4 August 1991

Gelston, Lincolnshire

I am hard at work trying to finish my Europe book.

I am now trying to write the chapter that shows why the British are slowly becoming more European. As I sit in our orchard I can see at least five churches. I reflect that, if I was sitting on a hill in Burgundy, Umbria or Bavaria, I would be able to see a similar number. We are part of the same Christian culture as the continental mainland. Also consider Labour's astonishing conversion on Europe, much influenced by Jacques Delors and his vision of Social Europe.

Giles Radice

Monday, 19 August 1991

On holiday in Italy

I listen to the wireless from England as I swim. Then momentous news came. An emergency committee of eight had put Gorbachev under house arrest and taken control because the country was slipping into an ungovernable state. The Communist hardliners were established and the clock was to be put back and never forward again.

I went past Norman [Lamont's] window on my way to breakfast, he was just waking up, and I shouted 'Gorbachev's gone. He is in prison. Now what about your defence policies?'

Woodrow Wyatt

Wednesday, 6 November 1991

It may not be suicide. It could be an accident. Or murder. Was he an agent for Mossad? He was a monster. And a crook. I know: I sat in reception at Maxwell House for hours on end, saying, 'I'm not leaving without a cheque in my hand,' and meaning it – and getting it – after months and months and months of waiting. Maverick, money-maker, MP, rogue, he really was August Melmotte in *The Way We Live Now*.

Neil Kinnock is completely over the top 'This is truly tragic news.' That he [Maxwell] was ever taken seriously by the Labour Party is amazing. It was pitiful when Peter Jay* allowed himself to become his poodle-cum-*chef-de-cabinet*.

---

*Peter Jay was Chief of Staff to Robert Maxwell at Mirror Group Newspapers, 1986–9.

I must write to [his wife] Anne, but I'm not sure what to say.

Gyles Brandreth

Wednesday, 11 December 1991
Westminster

Go on to Channel 4 early morning news programme to denounce John Major's negotiations at Maastricht. He says, 'Game, set and match for Britain.' I ask 'How can that be when you have had to have not one but two "opt outs"?' I am genuinely astounded that Major has been prepared to let the eleven other members go ahead with a European Social Chapter without Britain.*

In the Commons, Major is welcomed by the Tories as though he is a triumphant hero … he may have united the Tories but at the cost of weakening Britain's European position.

Giles Radice

Sunday, 2 February 1992
Chester

Yesterday I met the Foreign Secretary [Douglas Hurd] for the first time. I was impressed. I liked him too: he seemed civilised, cool, amused. Conservative Central Office told us we could have him in Chester for just 45 minutes. The photographers had us crouching on the banks of the Dee feeding the swans. That was the shot they wanted and that was the shot they were determined to get. The swans were rather reluctant to play ball however, which meant the Foreign Secretary and I had to spend a good fifteen minutes waddling on our haunches at the water's edge. Said Mr Hurd with a wan smile, 'I don't think Mr Gladstone did a lot of this, do you?'

Before the Hurd visit I had an interesting lunch with the leading house-builder in these parts. He wants chunks of the green belt released for development.

---

* John Major had negotiated an opt-out from the Social Chapter provisions on employment law in the Maastricht Treaty. The long-drawn-out divisions over the Chapter and the Treaty itself (which replaced the European Community with the European Union) led to a vote of confidence in the Government. The Treaty was passed in Britain in 1993; by now the EU comprised the original six Member States plus Denmark, Ireland, the UK, Greece, Spain and Portugal. Greenland left in 1985.

Over lunch I sat on the fence, but I may need to come off.

Gyles Brandreth

Tuesday, 3 March 1992

Told Ken Baker that I thought they could do a very good election ploy by announcing the internment of the terrorists in Northern Ireland again and also by announcing that we are going to have identity cards which everybody else in Europe does.

This would stop not only terrorists getting in and out so easily but it would also stop the flood of illegal immigrants pretending to be political refugees.

He disagreed about the internment. He thinks that if you did introduce it, it would simply make southern Ireland a safe haven. But he is attracted by the idea of the identity card.

Woodrow Wyatt

Monday, 16 March 1992

John Smith's shadow budget has to be good news.* The pundits are saying it'll cost middle managers £1500 a year. That's exactly what we need. The Conservative voters who have been crucified by the recession (and I've met quite a few and they're angry) will vote elsewhere this time, but the Tories who are simply wavering (they've been bruised, they're fearful of negative equity, they're worried about redundancy, but they've still got a house and a job), they could come back to us at the last minute, clinging on to nurse for fear of something worse.

Gyles Brandreth

Friday, 20 March 1992

Sir Leon Brittan, the Competition Commissioner at Brussels, came to lunch. So did Chips Keswick, Chairman of Hambros.

Leon is brimming full of cleverness, shrewdness and intelligence. I always liked him though we fell out for a period when he was trying

---

* Smith's shadow budget proposed an increase in the top rate of income tax from 40p to 50p, a policy that allowed the Conservatives in the run up to the General Election to cast the Labour Party as a high tax party.

to push us into a political federation of Europe and shove on top of us a single currency and a single European bank.

On that subject Chips said there was still a chance for London to have that bank. Leon said 'I think that we have missed the boat now. It will probably go to Amsterdam because people don't want it to go to Germany. Of course if you had been willing to join the single currency and had been willing to accept the European bank, it very likely would have gone to London.'*

Woodrow Wyatt

Tuesday, 31 March 1992

Chester

Mr Major brought his soap box to Chester this morning and it was a triumph.

There was excitement, a sense of occasion in the air. As the minutes passed and word went round the city centre more and more people thronged the square. The police reckoned there were 2,000 at least by the time the battle bus arrived. The door opened, we all roared and the Prime Minister with a grin and wave plunged into the throng. It was amazing. The crush was incredible.

We were surrounded by police, TV crews, cameramen and at the Prime Minister's right hand throughout was Norman Fowler.

As we pushed forward, with supporters and shoppers and gawpers pressing towards us, leaning out to touch the Major anorak, reaching out to shake the great man's hand, Norman Fowler kept up a running commentary: 'The soap box is just to the right, John. Look towards the balcony now, see the camera, now wave. And now to the left, there's some girls at the window, another wave. That's it, good, good. It's going well. Nearly there.' Major then clambered on to the soap box and made a proper speech – ten minutes and more – all straightforward stuff, no great rhetoric but somehow phenomenal. Here was the Prime Minister of the United Kingdom on a soap box in the rain, telling two thousand of the people of Chester what he wanted to do for his country. It worked a treat. There was some jokey heckling, which he handled nicely.

Gyles Brandreth

---

*The European Central Bank went to Frankfurt in Germany.

Tuesday, 7 April 1992

Chester

To Blacon, and the worst of the high-rise blocks. They are squalid and soulless, the public parts filthy, the walls covered with mindless graffiti. The Right to Buy has made no impact here. When doors were opened every flat looked equally unloved, unkempt – and then you'd find one belonging to an elderly person, who opened the door a crack, and then opened it wide and you could see how house proud they were and sense how they must hate living where they do, with the neighbours they have to endure. And if and when I become a Member of Parliament, will I be able to make any impact on all that?

Gyles Brandreth

Thursday, 9 April–Friday, 10 April 1992

General Election

As I left [Yeovil] for London at about 2.30 a.m. it became clear that we were having a bad night. We lost … Kincardine and … Eastbourne, but gained North Devon and North Cornwall. Elsewhere we missed, although we did shorten the distance between us and the Tories in a number of seats in the south and west. But by 2 o'clock, the stunning news was that Major had a majority and Labour had lost. A terrible night for Labour. I saw Kinnock on television and he looked broken.

The fact is that we have more MPs, even though our vote has declined.

Paddy Ashdown

Monday, 13 April 1992

Gelston, Lincolnshire

Neil Kinnock resigns. Denis Healey calls him 'Labour's Gorbachev'. His tragedy is that, despite all he has done to make Labour electable again, he has never been trusted by the electorate. Despite that, I think he would have made a good Prime Minister and I write a note to tell him so.

I am still dumbfounded by the extent of Labour's defeat – only 35% to the Tories 42%.

Was it John Smith's tax plans coupled with the Tory lies which scuttled us? Or was it more profound, Peter Jenkins's 'structural' reasons? Can Labour ever win?

Giles Radice

Tuesday, 28 April 1992

Withdrawal symptoms only flare periodically but a lot of suppression is going on. So in subconscious it festers. I dream of reviving Commons privileges, Tea Room, reference library and so on which I wake and realise are closed to me forever.

I am 'put out' by my friends ignoring me. Especially wounded by Richard [Ryder]. I did think that he was a friend, and I a confidant of his. I am filled too with distaste and resentment at all the new Conservative MPs and some of the new Ministerial choices.

I suppose, if I were to get my peerage promptly I could still 'catch up', swoop into the Tea Room, mob around. But notification for the Dissolution Honours has passed, and so – almost – has that for the Birthday.*

Alan Clark

Monday, 18 May 1992

The Tea Room talk is of Thatcher's speech in the Hague. We need to watch out: the Germans are coming and the EC is 'scurrying to build a megastate.' It seems somewhat over-alarmist to me but Bill Cash and co evidently agree with her every word. 'The lady across the water,' sighed Nick Budgen, 'we miss her so!'†

Gyles Brandreth

---

*Alan Clark, having given up his Plymouth seat in 1992, did not receive a peerage, but did succeed in 'reviving his Commons privileges' by re-entering the House in 1997 as MP for Kensington and Chelsea.

† Bill Cash and Nicholas Budgen were both Conservative MPs opposed to the European Union; Gyles Brandreth, reporting from the House of Commons Tea Room, was now Conservative MP for the City of Chester.

Wednesday, 3 June 1992

Westminster

A narrow majority of Danes (48,000) reject Maastricht in a referendum. Political Europe is stunned! The antis everywhere are cockahoop. In the Commons, Major makes a statement saying that the government is still committed to the Maastricht treaty but that debate on the Bill will be delayed until the situation is clearer. Peter Shore says it is a great day for democracy, Benn says how about a referendum in the UK. Only Heath says stands firm.

Giles Radice

Wednesday, 3 June 1992

House of Commons

I came in expecting an all-night sitting but further consideration of the Maastricht Bill is now postponed, instead we had a rather briefer debate on the Rio Earth Summit. I sat through all five and a half hours of it (in a largely deserted Chamber) in order to make a seven minute contribution.

There are 651 MPS but right now – registering concern for the future of the planet – there are just a dozen of us.

Gyles Brandreth

Tuesday, 7 July 1992

I am worried that the oncoming economic depression will be much deeper than most people think and could seriously unfix the whole political and economic system. I don't want us to get out of the ERM [the Exchange Rate Mechanism] – indeed I think that would be a disaster – but it may well turn out to be less a disaster than the alternative. I just hope my sense of foreboding is wrong.

Politics seems completely up in the air at the moment. Nobody knows which way to go. It's like when the birds stop singing and the air goes still just before the thunderstorm breaks. Or that moment of stillness at slack water before the tide starts moving in the opposite direction.

Paddy Ashdown

Wednesday, 16 September 1992

Chester-le-Street

As I drive into Newcastle for lunch at BBC North headquarters it becomes clear that the government has a major currency crisis on its hands. Interest rates have gone up by 2 % to 12% but sterling is still on the ERM floor. All day I follow the crisis on the car radio as I go from meeting to surgeries. Interest rates are subsequently raised by a further 3% to 15% all to no avail. At 7.30 pm Lamont finally announces that the UK has been driven out of the ERM – and the pound is floating ...

Typically the yuppies in the City celebrate bringing sterling down in champagne.

Giles Radice

Thursday, 15 October 1992

An enormous public outcry against the government's decision to close thirty one pits, putting 30,000 miners out of a job at the bottom of a recession. Heseltine and the PM appear shocked by the reaction – shows how out of touch they are. *Tory* MPs rush on TV to denounce the government.

Giles Radice

Wednesday, 9 December 1992

Alex Allan [John Major's Private Secretary] came over and showed me the Prime Minister's statement which announced that the Prince and Princess of Wales were about to separate.

The statement was very simple, claiming there was no constitutional issue. I am not so sure.

Major is describing the purely legal position. But it seems inconceivable that Diana could be Queen now, or that there would not be a problem about the alternative Court that Diana is likely to set up. She will have no private life and any man who visits her (or any woman who visits Prince Charles) is bound to be under public scrutiny. This is just a gradual way of stepping into divorce. The constitutional implications of that would be very considerable. Perhaps even the disestablishment of the Church (hurray).

Paddy Ashdown

Friday, 1 January 1993

A thousand beacons blazed across the European Community at midnight to usher in the single market: one Europe of 340 million people. Mr Major (somewhat startlingly) sees 1993 as 'the year of charity and helping your neighbour'. This makes me a little ashamed to confess that I see 1993 as the year of looking after Number One!

Gyles Brandreth

Thursday, 21 January 1993

I have just come down from the committee corridor here, with colleagues from the National Heritage Select Committee we have been taking evidence from Kelvin MacKenzie, bovver boy editor of the *Sun* ...*

This is the mother of parliaments. Gerald [Kaufman, the chairman] is one of Her Majesty's Privy Councillors. When witnesses appear before us we expect a touch of deference, a bit of forelock-tugging, a certain becoming modesty. We don't expect what we got just now: a cocky, Jack-the-lad, bruiser, joker champion of the working man. He came on strong and he walked off triumphant.

We were lambs to the slaughter – and in large part it was our own fault. We hadn't prepared a considered line of argument. We hadn't done our homework. Complacency and laziness lead inevitably to humiliation.

Gyles Brandreth

During 1993 Paddy Ashdown took time 'outside Westminster' to visit several areas of Britain, staying for days at a time with families whose lives and work he followed and recorded in a journal.

---

* In 1990 an inquiry into the conduct of the press had been undertaken by Sir David Calcutt QC; it recommended the continuation of self-regulation of the press. The Press Complaints Commission was also established. The National Heritage Select Committee was reviewing progress since Calcutt's inquiry.

Monday, 1 March–Wednesday, 3 March 1993
Cornwall, aboard the trawler Silver Harvester

With the nets safely streaming astern of the *Silver Harvester* and making their way back to the sea bed, we turn our attention to the fish now lying in a muddy heap on the deck. The pile we have drawn up from the sea bed includes old boots, rocks, shells, star fish, rubbish ditched from previous ships in passage and, of course the fish that give the *Silver Harvester* its living. The job now is to sort them out. In the midships of the boat are two sets of four baskets into which the fish are thrown. One is for round fish (cod, hake, whiting and pout). The second is for flat fish (lemon and megrim sole, plaice, brill, dabs and turbot). The third is for monkfish, some three or four feet long ... The last basket is for sole, dark and muddy green as the sea bottom, which are our most prized and valuable catch. There are also separate baskets in the midship areas for octopuses, squid, scallops and gurnards which are red, spikey and used for cat food.

When we have sorted the takeable fish into baskets I open a small metal trap door in the sides of the guard rail and using a combination of high pressure sea water hose and an implement like an overgrown squeegee mob, push what is left back out to the sea.

By my calculation I push over the side a weight of fish equal to that we have put into the baskets. But they are all too small, of a kind that we are not allowed to take. All these fish will die because their swim bladders will have been burst by the release of pressure as they are drawn to the surface from the sea bottom. But the laws passed by Parliament in the name of conservation say that, whether they die or not, the *Silver Harvester* cannot bring them to shore for human consumption. They must be left at sea to be food for the gulls or to rot on the sea bottom and pollute it.

But now they will have to cope with a fresh problem; the new Sea Fish Conservation Bill which we have just passed through Parliament. Mike [Hosking, the owner] believes this piece of legislation will prove dangerous, unworkable and extremely damaging to the British and Cornish fishing industry. Under the new regulations French fishermen will have the right to lift more fish out of Cornish waters than Cornish fishermen take. The French quota for cod, for instance, is 13,380 tons in the box which includes the Cornish coast, whereas Britain's quota is 1,450 tons ...

Paddy Ashdown

Thursday, 1 April 1993

BBC Question Time

I think I did OK. No obvious gaffes. I played it straight down the line.

(I think I also blotted my copybook by asking one of the production team what sort of rate David Dimbleby is on. I had to sign a piece of paper accepting a fee of £50. That's their standard apparently. I said, 'It's monstrous, you get four guests on the show for a total of £200. This is BBC prime time. We should be paid properly. What's Mr Dimbleby on – a thousand, two thousand? Look, I'll do it for a quarter of whatever he's getting.' They were not amused. They take themselves – and Mr Dimbleby – very seriously.)

Gyles Brandreth

Monday, 10 May 1993

Number 10 for lunch. There were ten of us in the small panelled dining room on the first floor.

My suggestion that John Smith's lamentable performance last Thursday might prove to be the beginning of the end for him prompted the PM to reveal that he has 'a finger tip feeling' that John Smith won't be leader of the Labour Party at the next election. 'It's just a finger tip thing, a pricking of my thumbs. I'm not sure why, but I just don't believe John'll make it.'

'Who do you think it will be?'

'John Prescott or Bryan Gould.'

Later Convivial drinks in John McGregor's room to mark the successful conclusion of the Railways Bill. We have privatised the railways.

'Will it work?' I asked, innocently.

John gave his Mr Pickwick's laugh. 'It had better.'

Gyles Brandreth

Wednesday, 9 June 1993

Heard Norman Lamont's devastating resignation speech in which he said that the Tories were 'in office without power' which is the title of one of my volumes of Diaries. He also talked about sound bites and public relations which is also one of my themes. I must say it was a very effective speech and did an awful lot of damage to Major, who spoke later and didn't do very well.

It was a beautiful hot evening. It is so rare in Britain to be able to sit out into the night.

Tony Benn

Monday, 21 June–Tuesday, 22 June 1993
Toyota car factory, Derby

I ask Bryan Jackson, a director of Toyota, who is now showing me around and who has spent a life time in the car industry, how many people would have worked in such a press and weld shop ten years ago. 'A very great deal more,' is his laconic reply. (In this shop, assembling 200 car bodies a day, there are 160 robots and fewer than 20 people.)

Toyota, now among the top three of the world's leading car manufacturers by volume, invested £700 million in this Derby car manufacturing factory and a further £140 million in an engine manufacturing plant in North Wales to feed it.

I have come here not to marvel at automation, but to learn about the new working practices, management style and production techniques which many believe Britain will have to adopt if we are going to rebuild our manufacturing industries again.

Bryan tells me that, after recruiting their workforce, they sent many to Japan for training at Toyota's main factory … many had brought back the Japanese practice of doing exercises before work.

This has caused some suspicion and amusement amongst the wider population of Derby.

Paddy Ashdown

Tuesday, 22 June 1993

Michael [Heseltine] has had a heart attack in Venice. The pictures of him being carried off to hospital, his spindly legs exposed to the world, were certainly an invasion of his privacy. Interestingly the Tea Room reaction has been one of shock rather than sympathy, concern for the Government's dwindling majority rather than concern for Michael's health. People here admire him, respect him. They don't appear to love – or even like – him very much.

By uncanny coincidence, Heseltine's henchman, Colonel Mates, the man who led Heseltine's campaign to oust Thatcher in 1990 is also swinging in the wind. He's hanging on (just) but he's doomed.*

It turns out that the Party accepted £440,000 from Nadir, so now we're all tarred with the same brush.

Gyles Brandreth

Tuesday, 20 July–Thursday, 22 July 1993

Debate on the Maastricht Treaty

I worked at home and turned my mind to the court case where Lord Justice Watkins and Mr Justice Auld agreed to accept an application by Lord Rees-Mogg, backed by Sir James Goldsmith, to declare the Maastricht Treaty illegal. I spoke to the Clerk of the House about this because it seemed to me to be a breach of the Bill of Rights, and he said, 'Yes, I agree.'

Of course, I'm against Maastricht and Rees-Mogg's trying to kill Maastricht, but that's not the way to do it.

Wednesday Went to see the Speaker at 11 and she was tremendously supportive. I had a phone call later from her saying, 'I am going to make a statement and you can reply.'

So I drafted a speech and took it to the Speaker's Office and the Clerk's Office.

At 3.30 the Speaker made her statement which was very good. I then made a statement almost as long, which was very well received, and the House really responded because I was defending Parliament against the courts.

Thursday Mass coverage of the Speaker's ruling. *The Times* and *Telegraph* had it on their front page.

I'm not optimistic [about the Commons rejecting the Treaty] but I say this two and a half hours before the vote.

Went into the House at the very end and of course it was absolutely packed. The Speaker's Gallery was full, the Serjeant at Arms gallery was full, the Public Gallery was full.

The first vote – on the Labour amendment to include the Social Chapter – took place; the lobby was crowded and the Speaker was

---

* Michael Mates resigned as Minister of State at the Northern Ireland Office over his links to the businessman Asil Nadir, who was found guilty of false accounting and theft.

there. The place was tremendously tense with excitement, the Press Gallery was jammed with people standing.

As the rumours spread, Richard Ryder, the Tory Chief Whip, came in and nodded at the Prime Minister, and the Prime Minister smiled so we thought we'd lost ...

Finally at about quarter past ten the tellers lined up and the word went round: 'It's a tie.' 317 for the Labour amendment calling for the social chapter to be included and 317 against. So the Speaker got up and read a statement and declared that, in accordance with precedent, she would cast her vote [against] and 'the Noes have it.'

So then there was a division on the Government motion itself ... and the Ulster Unionists went in with the Government. This is what proportional representation would mean if you had a little National Front group: they would be selling their support for all sorts of things.

Then we waited again with great tension and excitement.

Ray Powell was the chief teller and he said, 'Madame Speaker, the Ayes to the right were 316, the Noes to the left were 324.'

So both motions were defeated and we are back where we were.

I must admit I waved my order paper, a thing I've never done before in my life but I was so excited.

Major got up. He had prepared a statement. 'I'm going to put down a motion of confidence in our policy on the Social Chapter and if that is defeated there will be a general election.'

Tony Benn

Friday, 23 July 1993

The House meets at 0930.

After the front bench speeches at the beginning of the debate are concluded the Fresh Start Group* convenes to take stock. In the light of the outcome of yesterday's cliff-hanger, there is no stomach for opposing the vote of confidence and in any case, with the Ulster Unionists bought off, the prospect of defeating the Government is at best tenuous. There is also an uncomfortable and somewhat

---

*The Fresh Start Group were a grouping of Conservative MPs who campaigned vigorously against the Maastricht Treaty and were united by Euro-scepticism (or 'Euro-realism') to a greater or lesser degree. Their number included John Biffen, Michael Spicer, Bill Cash, Roger Knapman, James Cran, Nicholas Budgen, Richard Shepherd, Christopher Gill, Iain Duncan Smith, Teresa Gorman, Teddy Taylor, Tony Marlow, Nicholas Winterton and Toby Jessel.

embarrassing fact that each and every one of us was elected barely twelve months ago in the Conservative cause. The fact that the Government is now supporting policies which are entirely alien to its Conservative roots and traditions is something which the rank and file Party members have yet to understand. It is therefore with heavy hearts that we choose to do the decent thing and live to fight another day ...

The Government motion is carried by 339 votes to 299.

When in the fullness of time the people do realise what has been done in their name their retribution will be decisive and maybe, as far as the Conservative Party is concerned, terminal.

Christopher Gill

Friday, 30 July 1993

We have lost Christchurch to the Liberals. Robert Adley's majority of 23,000 has been transformed into a Lib Dem majority of 16,400 – a swing against us of 35%, the biggest anti-government swing since the war.

Gyles Brandreth

Friday, 6 August 1993

The news from the Balkans continues to be absolutely tragic. You've got Paddy Ashdown and Clinton and other people demanding the bombing of Serb forces or Serbia, and the United Nations commander there warning against it because, he says, if you bomb Serbia they will attack our forces and, of course, we'll be involved in the combat.

You have to be prepared to put a huge army in and occupy the whole of the former Yugoslavia and impose a settlement. This is one of the difficulties.

Tony Benn

Wednesday, 29 September 1993

High conference drama! John Smith, who was on the brink of a highly damaging defeat this morning, wins a narrow but decisive victory this afternoon. John opens the debate in an undemonstrative but firm way and ends his speech by repeating how important it is for Labour to modernise itself. The leader of the AUEW [the Engineering Workers],

Bill Jordan, makes the best speech – Labour must show that John Smith, not Bill Morris, nor John Edmonds,* 'leads the Labour Party'. Morris and Edmonds make the 'dinosaur' speeches.

John Smith has the bright idea of asking John Prescott to wind up. Prescott is incoherently eloquent. Most of his speech is a diatribe against the modernisers, but he ends strongly by saying that John Smith has put his head on the block and he deserves the support of Conference.

Giles Radice

Friday, 8 October 1993

Conservative Party Conference, Blackpool

'Let me tell you what I believe … It is time to return to the old core values. Time to get back to basics. To self-discipline and respect for the law. To consideration for others. To accepting responsibility for yourself and your family, and not shuffling it off on the State. Madam President, I believe that what this country needs is not less Conservatism. It is more Conservatism … It is time to return to our roots.'

It went down wonderfully well. He (Major) did it wonderfully well. I watched it, cocooned inside the Channel 4 commentary box, surrounded by professional cynics, but even they had to concede he'd touched a chord with the faithful. They don't adore him as they adored Thatcher, but they love him and they share his nostalgic longing for Miss Marple's England.

Gyles Brandreth

Saturday, 9 October 1993

It has been said that if a Labour conference makes you wonder why you are a member of the Labour Party, a Tory conference supplies you with the answer.

Michael Howard's nasty conference speech on law and order and his unpleasant attack on one-parent families, Peter Lilley's extraordinary diatribe against so-called 'foreign' scroungers and the faces of

---

* Bill Morris was General Secretary of the Transport and General Workers' Union; John Edmonds, General Secretary of the GMB (General, Municipal, Boilermakers and Allied Trade Union).

the Conservative delegates are almost sufficient an argument in themselves for voting for the Labour Party.

Giles Radice

November 1993
Wearmouth Colliery

[On my father's feet] were black, steel-toe capped safety boots. He was wearing orange overalls, the same type that had adorned our washing line every week for as long as I could remember. He had thick, black rubber protection pads on both knees. Around the belt on his waist was a self-rescuer, a miner's lamp and a black battery ... a cable led from the battery on his waist to a light attached to the front of the helmet ...

Before entering the hole into unknown territory we put gloves on and crawled on our hands and knees. My father and I went in last.

The tunnel was very narrow and the roof was only four feet high so standing was impossible ... The only light came from our cap lamps and there were puddles of water everywhere. To the right of us I saw a raised metal track and a gap of five feet, and there it was, a massive wall of coal.

My father ... said, 'This is an historic moment for me. *My* Dad did this with me when I was 15 and his dad before him. Switch your light off.' I obeyed him and we were plunged into darkness. I held my hand up in front of my eyes and I couldn't see anything at all. It was a very poignant moment and I felt as if a thread of continuity had been broken in my family for ever as I would never experience this again, certainly not with *my* offspring.

We switched our lights back on as we heard a rumbling noise in the distance. I could make out lights and figures coming towards us as the noise got louder and louder. Soon the noise was deafening, like a constant crashing of rocks together and I saw the shearer for the first time. It was a magnificent sight I thought. The shearer was a huge cylinder with spikes all around, spinning fast and advancing towards me. I pinned myself against the wall ... I watched the shearer cut through the coal like a knife through butter, the coal falling effortlessly onto a belt behind ... the miners following the shearer were bare chested or only wearing vests. I was glad that I was wearing knee pads as sharp rocks protruded from the floor. Now I knew how my father's legs had blue scars on them, like veins in a Stilton cheese ... caused by the coal dust getting into cuts ...

My father shouted 'Before the shearer comes back we have to move the roof supports forward and let the rock fall in. If we don't, the pressure on the face by the millions of tons of rock and water above us will squash us like ants.'

Jimmy Wilson

Monday, 15 November 1993

The truth is there's too much legislation, inadequately prepared, pushed through in too great haste. There was a good piece on all this by Anthony King (of Essex University) last week. He noted that on John Patten's last Education Bill there were 278 government amendments introduced during the Commons committee stage, 78 more on Report, 258 more during the Lords committee stage, 296 more on Report and 71 at Third Reading. King reckons this mania for legislation began with Thatcher. Action, revolution, change, never let up, never stop. 'I tinker, therefore I am.'

Gyles Brandreth

Wednesday, 1 December 1993

I gathered up my things from the office and dashed home ... for the Blair dinner.*

I found Blair engaging, very intelligent and constructive. There is very little between his thinking and mine. We have come to the same analysis from different directions. He seems utterly committed to ensuring that the Labour Party does modernise its approach and rethink its ideas, and sees nothing inconsistent between an approach which is based on these lines and socialism in its modern guise. I told him that I too was committed to the reshaping of the centre but that I was not interested in Lib/Lab electoral pacts. I was interested in creating a pluralist system of politics, not in preserving the present structure in a new configuration. Blair agreed to go away and talk to Brown and Mandelson. He is suggesting a further dinner at his house

---

* Blair was at this time Shadow Secretary for Employment; John Smith was leader of the Labour Party.

in January. Mandelson may come to this and I may think it right to invite someone from our side – probably Charles Kennedy.

Paddy Ashdown

Saturday, 8 January 1994

A belated New Year tour d'horizon written on the train from Newcastle to London ...

Despite the ratification of the Maastricht Treaty, there is a pervasive feeling that the élan has, for the moment gone out of the European idea. The destruction of a tight ERM in late August at the hands of the markets has put paid to the idea of a single European currency, at least for the short term. And all the Euro-enthusiastic leaders are under pressure – Delors, Kohl, Mitterrand. Meanwhile the massacres in Bosnia are a terrible reproach to European pretensions – and of course to NATO as well.

There are [other] grounds for cautious optimism – the PLO and Israel have signed a preliminary agreement and are still talking; there will be 'free' elections in South Africa; and the Major-Reynolds peace initiative in Northern Ireland has not yet foundered.

Giles Radice

Monday, 14 February 1994

Last week's tragedy* is followed by this week's farce – or, as it turns out, this week's light romantic comedy. Hartley Booth, Mrs T's soft-lipped, wouldn't-say-boo-to-a-goose successor in Finchley, has resigned as Douglas Hogg's PPS following the revelation of his infatuation with a 22-year-old art college model turned political researcher. Apparently there was no affair, merely a tendresse.

Graham Riddick (admiring the newspaper photograph of the fair Emily): 'I'd have given her one, wouldn't you?'

Bob Hughes: 'Hartley Booth is a gentleman.'

John Sykes: 'He's a wanker.'

The Tea Room is not taking this latest calamity very seriously.†

---

* The death of Stephen Milligan, MP for Eastleigh, Gyles Brandreth's close friend.
† Conservative MPs Douglas Hogg, Graham Riddick, Bob Hughes and John Sykes.

Michele [Brandreth] is joining me for a Valentine Day supper in the Churchill Room.

Gyles Brandreth

Wednesday, 30 March 1994

I go to a supper that the American Minister is throwing ... for MPs involved in the Euro debate. Listening to the passionate speeches from my Tory colleagues among whom the antis, including the voluble Bill Cash, predominate, I begin to wonder whether the question of Europe will actually break the Tories. The antis are so determined that they are unlikely ever to compromise. Is Europe an issue that, like the Corn Laws, will lead to a split on the right of British politics or at least make the Tory Party impossible to lead?

Giles Radice

Monday, 11 April 1994

Teresa Gorman rings to say we must build up a right-wing candidate against Major. I don't know whether she has herself in mind after a spoof article in *The Times* last week by Matthew Parris naming her as the Duchess of Billericay. She would certainly have PMT licked and takes all the right kind of hormone treatment on which she recently lectured in Scandinavia.

Michael Spicer

Sunday, 8 May 1994

Here we go again. Poor Michael Brown [Tory MP and whip] has been outed by the *News of the World*. They are bastards. And he is a fool. He took a young man on a Caribbean holiday. There's some dispute about the boy's age, but he's certainly under twenty one – and the eighteen-plus legislation doesn't come onto the statute book before the autumn.

You've got to pity the poor PM too. As Michele says, 'That's Back to Basics gone to buggery.' (My wife is very funny.)

Gyles Brandreth

Thursday, 12 May 1994

John Smith is dead. Carol Roberton at the *Sunderland Echo* broke the news. A massive heart attack, she said. He had been rushed to Bart's Hospital. No announcement yet, but obituary material coming through on the wire. After I put the phone down I turned on the television just as the surgeon at Bart's was announcing his death.

Chris Mullin

Wednesday, 18 May 1994

Ken Livingstone (an amusing cove, easy, friendly, pleasantly absurd) is going to stand in the Labour leadership race, but won't declare until after John Smith's funeral on Friday. Blair is way out front. *We* want Beckett or Prescott, of course. Brown might be best for *them* long-term: he's the one I find most approachable, most human, and he still seems blessed with a touch of socialist zeal. However they seem to be setting their hearts on the Young Conservative ...

Gyles Brandreth

Sunday, 12 June 1994
European Election results

The papers are having a full-scale love affair with Blair.

Labour's vote up right across the country, sweeping out the Tories and holding up too high for us to win the seats we had targeted in the South.

On the wretched David Dimbleby results programme, which was, as usual, heavily weighted against us, Charles Kennedy got very touchy with Peter Kellner and Peter Snow. Snow brought back the bloody swingometer, which even denies our existence!

In the end we left, quietly satisfied by the two seats in the South West but disappointed by our narrow failures.

Paddy Ashdown

Wednesday, 13 July 1994

Queen Elizabeth Conference Centre, Westminster

Mo Mowlam's media conference.* There was a lot of crap about information superhighways and the wonders of optical-fibre networks all designed to intimidate us into doing away with regulation and allowing the market to let rip. A dreary man from BT told us that it was already possible to transmit the entire contents of the *Encyclopedia Britannica* round the world in less than half a second and that optical fibre made possible a simultaneous two-way conversation between every man, woman and child on the planet. A fat lot of use if you are starving.†

Chris Mullin

Thursday, 11 August 1994

Flassan, Provence, on holiday with the Blairs

By now, he [Blair] had also let me know, and sworn me to secrecy, that he was minded to have a review of the constitution and scrap Clause 4. I have never felt any great ideological attachment to Clause 4 one way or the other. If it made people happy, fine, but it didn't actually set out what the party was about today. It wasn't the politics or the ideology that appealed. It was the boldness. People had talked about it for years. Here was a new leader telling me that he was thinking about doing it in his first conference speech as leader. Bold. I said I hope you do, because it's bold. I will, he said. And he had a real glint in his eye.

He knew that in terms of the political substance, it didn't really mean that much. But as a symbol, as a vehicle to communicate change, and his determination to modernise the party, it was brilliant.

Alastair Campbell

Thursday, 1 September 1994

The news is that the IRA have declared a 'ceasefire'. If this can be made to last, if we can inch our way towards some sort of constitutional settlement, this will be the PM's greatest achievement. For over a quarter of a century there has been bloodshed and terror within the

---

* Mowlam was Shadow National Heritage Secretary, and had organised a conference with key industry figures to debate Labour policy towards the media.
† Ethiopia was in the throes of a serious famine, which troubled Chris Mullin.

United Kingdom. Over three thousand have died, tens of thousands have been wounded ... and now it's stopping.

Gyles Brandreth

Monday, 12 September 1994

At 7 o'clock to Rupert Murdoch's cocktail party. What a gathering! And what a flat! All brightly coloured walls, chromium plated knobs and rather garish modern pictures. There was a lady harpist in the foyer as we came in. She played well, but looked ridiculous.

Then upstairs. The whole of the Murdoch empire was there. And some interesting others as well: Tony and Cherie Blair, Michael Howard and Ken Clarke. Also there Anthony Lester and Richard Branson, Arnie Weinstock, Woodrow Wyatt, Mo Mowlam.

Later I heard that John Major had been invited but had demanded to see the guest list. To which Murdoch said 'Stuff him, this is my party not his' – so he didn't come.

Paddy Ashdown

Monday, 26 September 1994

Strasbourg

A little Euro junket organised by Jack Cunningham. We arrived about two and went immediately to the European Parliament – a monstrous carbuncle of steel, concrete and glass, grafted onto a magnificent medieval city. Our party consists of about twenty MPs, including several good friends. Object of exercise: to familiarise ourselves with the EC and meet our Euro colleagues. About time I learned about the EC since, like it or not, it is destined to play an even greater role in our lives. I am astoundingly ignorant about Europe. This is the first time I have set foot in France for twenty years.

Everything about the European Parliament seems ludicrous. The committees meet three weeks a month in Brussels and in the fourth week the entire circus moves to Strasbourg for the plenary session. Every month tons of papers are transported back and forth in a long convoy of pantechnicons, trailed by hundreds of officials. Outside every MEP's room is a steel trunk into which the members pack their papers for transport back to Brussels or vice versa. The Parliament has virtually no power over the executive. Commissioners make statements, but cannot usually be cross-examined. Obtaining an answer to a written question can take weeks.

Chris Mullin

Saturday, 8 October 1994

At the end of Conference they played 'The Red Flag' in jazztime and people waved Union Jacks, just like demonstrators for the Queen. Another Mandelson gimmick. Just turns your stomach.

There's a semi-fascist element in the Labour Party at the moment, a 'hand over to international capitalism, wave your little Union Jack' tendency.

Tony Benn

Tuesday, 1 November 1994

The entire day has had a weird Alice in Wonderland feel to it. We [the Conservatives] want to conduct the enquiry into 'cash for questions' in private, simply publishing the report at the end. Labour say the hearings should be held in public. Tony Benn (the Mad Hatter) is defying the Speaker (the Cook? The Duchess?) taking his little tape recorder into the sessions and producing his own minutes for distribution to the press. Tony Newton (the White Rabbit) is scurrying hither and yon trying to keep everybody happy and falling between all the stools.

It's exactly 4.00 am and the division bell is going.

Gyles Brandreth

Thursday, 17 November 1994
Westminster

I meet Tony Blair. He has moved back to Neil Kinnock's old office. He is in ebullient form, excited by the Clause 4 campaign. He says that Labour is going to be very pro-European. He is revealing about Robin Cook and his treachery over Clause 4 at Conference. He says that he told Robin that he expected his support. 'Your problem, Robin, is that nobody trusts you,' he told him, 'otherwise you would be sitting in my seat.'

Giles Radice

Thursday, 15 December 1994

I chatted to Tessa Jowell, one of the brightest of the new London MPs and a keen Blairista. She said that most of Tony's supporters had voted for him because they believed he was a winner, and if he turned out not to be, his support would swiftly melt away. We talked about education. She said Tony's decision to send his son to an opted-out school eight miles from home was not controversial among most of her electorate. Education in parts of Southwark was in a state of collapse. Dulwich, her constituency, is full of private schools and most of the middle classes have long since evacuated their children. She wants to see inner city schools providing breakfast for the poorest children and homework clubs for those whose home environment doesn't enable them to do homework. She also wants to see independent schools encouraged to open their facilities to local state schools ...

Chris Mullin

Tuesday, 3 January 1995

We pray for peace throughout the world but I can't help rejoicing at the way the Chechen fighters are picking off invading Russian troops and knocking out their armoured vehicles. And yet the pity of it all: the Russians we see on the screen look like bewildered schoolboys, the Chechens alert and dedicated young men.

Alec Guinness

Tuesday, 10 January 1995

I had my postponed meeting with Hayden Phillips to discuss Honours.* Hayden of course didn't want the meeting to happen in the first place. Indeed after he'd ushered me to a corner of his office and tea had been

---

* Hayden Phillips was Permanent Secretary at the Department of National Heritage; Gyles Brandreth was at the meeting as PPS to Stephen Dorrell, National Heritage Secretary.

served and the door securely closed, he murmured, 'This meeting isn't taking place, you understand.' 'Of course,' I murmured back.

I think Hayden does take it seriously. He enjoys the power of patronage. He also likes playing at being conspiratorial. For much of the meeting he held his notes close to his chest – literally – and when I mentioned a name he would glance slyly down at his papers and then purr at me. 'Mmm – something for Alan Bates? Mmm, yes, I think we can help you there.' He played a funny cat and mouse game with a document which he flashed in front of me, then half-showed me, then pulled away from me, then gave me, murmuring silkily 'I shouldn't, I really shouldn't ... but why not?' I presume he had intended to give me the paper – 'Honours In Confidence' – all along, but by going through the little arabesque he heightened the drama and made me feel I was getting more out of him than I actually was.

Gyles Brandreth

Wednesday, 18 January 1995
New York

I love this National Debt clock on 6th Avenue clicking up $10,000 a second. What a great piece of public art! I'd love to make clocks like that for everything – good news and bad: increase in world population, deaths due to wars, deaths due to Aids, growth in number of cars, forested acreage of the world etc., etc. And then a whole range of other displays, showing changing demographics such as age distribution in the population. A whole area made of information.

Brian Eno

Sunday, 29 January 1995
Evening Standard *Film Awards*

Sat next to Nicola Pagett, which was a comfort. The vast banqueting room was jammed full and hot. Richard Harris, at same table, wore a sort of piratical evening suit and had his hair in a fetching little pony-tail. He made a funny speech. Diana Rigg, looking stunning in black, made a charming but over-the-top citation about me. People were up and down and up and down to receive trophies for *Four Weddings and a Funeral*. The trophy is very handsome – a silvered version of Picca-dilly's Eros. It could prove a lethal weapon for dealing with burglars if you could summon the strength to lift it. And if you dared, the legal consequences of defending your own person and property. Will 1995 be the year of Universal Suing? Policemen, I read, are resorting to the courts because of the state of their nerves after the horrid things they have seen at football matches; and a lot of soldiers want compensation because they have discovered that war is beastly. Oh, Sceptred Isle set in the polluted sea, where are we heading?

Alec Guinness

Monday, 20 February 1995

The PM was on a roll tonight, exhilarated by the triumph of the London–Dublin framework document. There's going to be a Northern Ireland Assembly (with PR); a North/South body with members from both the Assembly and the Irish parliament; an end to the Irish constitutional claim to NI and changes to our legislation to give the people of NI the option of staying part of the UK or voting for a united Ireland. Paisley is ranting that Major has 'sold out the Union' ... but in the Chamber and the Tea Room it went down well.

[Later at Number 10 for a reception for the London arts community] he was at his absolute best: there was energy, easy charm, a sense of purpose. He stood in front of the fireplace on a little footstool and gave a gem of a speech. He talked about the artists who have made Downing Street what it is – he talked about the craftsmen, the furniture makers, the painters. He thanked and celebrated the artists in the room, buttered them up like nobody's business.

I wheeled Hugh Grant over to meet Norma and the light flirtation (on both sides) was charming to behold.

Under cover of the framework document we've slipped out an announcement on prescription charges. They're going up by 50p to £5.25.

Gyles Brandreth

Friday, 3 March 1995

The flight over Egypt was interesting and ended dramatically with us very close to the pyramids – actually my best view. Then from Cairo on to London, devouring newspapers senselessly ... Stepped right back into the British class system with the awful 'cocky' driver who called me 'sir' (which I don't like) in a really nasty, sarcastic way (subtext: 'Sir? You? What a fucking laugh!') which I hate even more.

Home, pulling out the spoils of war, kids climbing all over me.

Brian Eno

Saturday, 4 March 1995

Skegness

Arrived in time to hear most, if not all, of Tony Blair's speech. He was standing at the rostrum smiling, talking about the need to project our values in a new way, and so on.

Paddy Ashdown would have agreed with all of it; the delegates clapped and applauded and gave Blair a little standing ovation.

I walked to the station, icy cold. Skegness station is just like a cattle shed. I had to get a train from there to Grantham; then I had to wait for an hour in Grantham, pretty well, to get a train to Peterborough; and then I had to wait for fifty minutes in Peterborough to get a train to King's Cross. All in all it took me about five hours to get home.

I thought it was a complete waste of time in a way, except for its value as an observation of the Labour Party at this particular period. The Labour Party is unquestionably in a time of transition. The leaders never believed in Clause 4 but there was a sort of place for socialists. There isn't any more – young people come in who don't know anything about socialism; we don't talk about socialism; we just prattle on about values and fairness and equality, without any substance at all.

Tony Benn

Wednesday, 8 March 1995

First appointment is to speak to a bunch of City 'compliance' officers (whose job it is to see that their firms keep to the regulatory rules). They think that the Tory regulatory framework has been a failure but are apprehensive about what a Labour government would do. Briefed by our front bench I say that we would get rid of self-regulation because it has failed, as the pensions mis-selling, the Lloyds fiasco and now the collapse of Baring's demonstrate.*

Giles Radice

---

* Lloyds of London, the insurance market, went through 'the most traumatic period

Sunday, 26 March 1995

A forty-mile section of the Antarctic ice cap has detached itself and is floating free. Evidence of global warming? Scientists are estimating that, if the entire ice cap were to melt, the seas would rise by between 120 and 300 feet. Of course it will take several generations, but that is not a long time in the history of the world. By the end of Sarah's life [Mullin's older daughter] the process could be well under way, unless we wake up in time, but I don't think we will. One half of the human race is entertaining itself to death and the other half is clinging to life by its fingertips. Only a catastrophe which hits Europe or North America will make any difference – and by then it will be too late.

Chris Mullin

Friday, 7 April 1995

Rewatched mind-shifting programme about lesbian motherhood – a subject about which I've thought little and then probably with a slight, under-the breath 'YUK.'

I now feel that possibly the only people who shouldn't be questioned closely about their intentions when having children are lesbian couples. It made it clear to me that the biggest source of confusion in the whole gender topic is the assumption that the biological fact of one's body (whether you're physically 'male' or 'female') is 'hard-wiring', whereas it has a very complex connection with your behavioural and psychological style ...

In the documentary, people kept popping up to say that they considered children needed a man around to create the right sexual balance. This is clearly absurd. When has there ever been the 'right' sexual balance? Would we know it if we saw it? Some of those lesbians looked like they'd make much better fathers than a lot of guys I know.

Instead of thinking of people as male or female, think of a multi-axial field of possibilities running between these two poles. Then look at people as disposed throughout it – and capable of shifting when mood and circumstances require. Encourage exploration. Encourage new hybrids.

Brian Eno

in its history' in the 1980s; there was a spate of revelations of personal pension plans being missold to savers; and the private bank, Barings, collapsed in 1995 when a trader in Singapore, Nick Leeson, lost the bank £827 million.

Monday, 10 April 1995

The courts have ruled that local authorities have no power to ban the export of live animals, on the grounds that it is a legal trade and they don't want mob rule. Really the language of judges and the protection of profit are disgraceful. Old ladies in woolly hats who go out there because they believe that cruelty to animals is wrong, are described as a mob and all the courts are doing is protecting profits. Utterly revolting but there was a marvellous interview (on television) with Nancy Phipps, whose daughter Jill had been killed at Coventry airport on February 1st by a truck, saying that nothing would stop them.*

Tony Benn

Friday, 5 May 1995

I take the train down to London to attend a meeting of a group of experts from St Antony's College, Oxford (on Russia, Eastern Europe, and Germany) with Tony Blair. Sensibly, Tony gets us to go to his house in Islington. We sit on the sunny patio and go through our paces.

Tim Garton Ash, who is much more impressive as a presenter of these issues than the others, says the key issue in Eastern Europe is entry to the EU. He reminds us that there is 'no social base for democracy' and membership would underwrite it there. He argues that Britain has a common interest with Germany in enlargement.

I reflect on the way back to the North-East for a presentation and signing of my book at the Durham University bookshop, what an enormous burden is being placed on Tony's young and inexperienced shoulders.

Giles Radice

Wednesday, 10 May 1995

Liberal Democrats' Parliamentary Party Meeting, Westminster

The PPM was the worst I have ever experienced. Those who promised to back the proposal† didn't, despite the fact that they had all received

---

* Jill Phipps, thirty-one, was a long-term campaigner for animal rights; she was run down by a lorry which was transporting live calves to Baginton airport, Coventry, to be flown abroad.
† The proposal was to abandon equidistance between the Conservative and Labour parties and prepare for cooperation with a Labour government. Ashdown had been

a brilliant and supportive minute drafted by Chris Rennard [Director of Campaigns]. Alan Beith said if we abandoned equidistance it would be misunderstood. Malcolm Bruce agreed. Don Foster was helpful but stressed no pacts, no mergers. Bob Maclennan hardly said anything. Liz Lynne said it was appalling ... Simon Hughes entered the debate in a thoroughly confusing way and lost everybody after half a minute.

The whole thing then spun steadily out of control. I had to send a message out to Jane half way through saying we'd have to cancel our attendance at tonight's Guildhall dinner for the 200th anniversary of the Red Cross, for which she had come in all dressed up.

At 7.45 pm the meeting broke up in disarray. I went out, weak-kneed with despair.

Paddy Ashdown

Monday, 12 June 1995

Mrs T is rocking the boat. The Baroness has been on the radio telling us how much she admires Mr Blair, how she's 'absolutely against' the single currency, how she's glad Major is going more sceptic, how what we really need is more Thatcherism – 'we must get back to Conservative policies.'

Gyles Brandreth

Thursday, 22 June 1995

As I take my seat aboard the Paddington/Worcester train a man leans over from a seat on the opposite side of the gangway to ask me if my name is Christopher Gill. He is Sebastian Hamilton [a reporter] and when I ask him where he's going he tells me he is going to our meeting in Malvern.* Mildly interested to know why the *Sunday Times* consider our meeting worth reporting he tells me that it is because his editor is fascinated to know whether the public meetings we are holding in different parts of the country are the beginning of a revival of this rather old-fashioned mode of political campaigning ...

having secret talks for some time with Tony Blair and leading Labour figures, and visiting his local parties throughout the country, to reach this position.
* Six of eight Conservative MPs who had lost the Whip due to their opposition to the Maastricht Treaty ('the Whipless ones') were addressing a public meeting that night in Malvern on the European question.

Realising that my five colleagues (Richard Body, Nick Budgen, Tony Marlow, Richard Shepherd and Teddy Taylor) must be in a different part of the train I move to another carriage which is where, an hour or so later, Sebastian finds us chatting, completely oblivious of the news he now imparts. 'Major has resigned.' [As leader of the Conservatives.]

The news is staggering – it is barely credible – but Sebastian, who has the benefit of a mobile phone, assures us that it is only too true.

Inside the Winter Gardens (Malvern) an audience of close on a thousand people welcome us with rapturous applause. The atmosphere is electric. Suddenly this long-scheduled meeting is in the cockpit of national politics and the sensation that history is being made as we speak is inescapable.

Christopher Gill

Friday, 23 June 1995

The media seem to have gathered round the national parish pump to discuss the challenge to the Prime Minister and Mr Hurd's resignation [to campaign for the leadership], and to speculate on Messrs Portillo, Lamont and Redwood. Barely a word about Sarajevo.

Alec Guinness

Monday, 26 June 1995

Redwood is the challenger. I've just witnessed his extraordinary press conference. JR was quite impressive in his funny Daddy Woodentop way, but his supporters – ye gods! I've a feeling they may have kyboshed his campaign before it's even started. It wasn't what they said: it was how they looked – Teresa (Gorman) to the right of him in a hideous day-glo green and (Tony) Marlow to the left in a ludicrous striped blazer. Every picture tells a story: this one said, 'Here's a truly barmy army.'

He has some more credible backers as well – Lamont and Edward Leigh were on parade – and in the Tea Room suddenly everybody is much more tight-lipped.

Gyles Brandreth

Monday, 3 July 1995

Members' Dining Room, House of Commons

My heart sank. Making small talk with the PM is never easy.

Silence fell. He looked at his plate. I burbled stupidly. He was monosyllabic. I burbled some more. Silence fell again. I thought, 'Poor sod, this could be his last night as Prime Minister and he's spending it with me, *like this!*' And then a gallant knight rode to the rescue. In came the Rt Hon Peter Brooke, CH, and sat down beside me. He looked across at the PM and said he had just finished reading an article about a certain Surrey cricketer whose heyday was in the 1930s. The name meant nothing to me, but the PM brightened at once. Peter continued, describing some particularly memorable match from the glorious summer of '37 and within a minute the pall that had engulfed the table lifted and Peter and the PM talked cricket – talked 1930s cricket! – in extraordinary, animated, fascinated, happy detail.

Gyles Brandreth

Wednesday, 12 July 1995

A statement from Foreign Secretary Malcolm Rifkind about the cata-strophic situation in Bosnia. Dreadful, mealy-mouthed stuff. He spoke as if both sides were to blame. Fifty years after the defeat of fascism, ethnic cleansers are on the brink of triumph in Europe and no-one wants to lift a finger. My view is the same as it always has been: overwhelming force. If it had been used at the outset we wouldn't be in this mess now.

The Lord Chancellor, Lord Mackay, came to the select committee to talk about judicial appointments. An impressive man. Thoughtful, softly spoken, courteous and radiating integrity. His great strength is that he was brought in from outside the English legal system – and the Tory Party – in an attempt to bust the mighty vested interests. He hasn't entirely succeeded, but not for want of trying. One of Thatch-er's better appointments.

Chris Mullin

Saturday, 5 August 1995

Yes Europe has failed … a lot of the British Left – the people you'd expect to sympathise with Bosnia – actually back the Serbs, because Serbia is a traditional ally of Russia, because Serbia was anti-fascist (i.e. anti-Croat) in WW2 and because certain parts of the left think that any friend of America (which Bosnia has been) must be an enemy of the left – so, ridiculously, that translates into support for Serbia. As a result of all this, Blair has said nothing whatsoever that would reveal even the beginning of a policy line on this. He's so anxious to get elected he can't say anything about anything – and doesn't.

Letter to Stewart Brand from Brian Eno

Tuesday, 5 September 1995

All day (9–7) working on finishing *Help* record*... Tapes appearing from everywhere, me trying to keep some mental track of it. Everything that comes in sounds good: no duds.

Planes and helicopters and couriers standing by. We have to reach the planes with the tapes – which are being sent to Hamburg, Blackburn and somewhere in Holland – or else the records, CDs and cassettes will not be pressed in time for a Saturday release, which means it'll be held over till next week – when Blur are releasing. So Blur will get the number one spot – which we would like, thank you. Enjoyable panic, but I went into Hitler mode in the last few minutes.

Brian Eno

Wednesday, 11 October 1995
Conservative Party Conference, Blackpool

The talk of the town is Portillo's effort yesterday. It was clearly as crude as they come – awful mock heroics, cheap Brussels-bashing, wrapping himself in the Union Jack – but the activists stood and cheered and roared for more. He was shameless.

Don't mess with Britain – don't mess with Portillo. Having paraded Nelson, Wellington and Churchill as his heroes/role models, he coasted to his climax on the coat-tails of the SAS. 'Who dares wins!' The PM [John Major] was on the platform so he had no alternative

---

* *The Help* album was recorded and released to raise money for the charity War Child, started by film-makers Bill Leeson and David Wilson, for children caught up in the Bosnian (and other) wars; musicians on the album included Oasis, Blur, Radiohead, Orbital, the Stone Roses and Portishead. Anthea and Brian Eno were early supporters.

but to lead the ovation – and I presume No 10 cleared the speech in advance.

Gyles Brandreth

Friday, 13 October 1995

Any Questions [on Radio 4]: what a mealy-mouthed bunch. Oh for someone to say, 'Actually I'm not in the least patriotic – in fact, I feel more loyalty to Cuba than to England. Also I think taking drugs is a marvellous eye-opener, pornography is a fun method of self-enlightenment, and I would like to see religions taxed heavily' (all in a horsey, upper-class 'Camilla' voice).

Brian Eno

Thursday, 2 November 1995

In the evening to South Africa House, to the showing of Trevor Baylis's wind-up radio. Baroness Chalker gave a very confident and endearing speech. I looked at that little radio and thought about the potential it has, and thought 'Bugger – if I'd done only one thing in my life that was as clear and simple and useful as that.' But the good news is that the simple ideas haven't all been used up.

Brian Eno

Monday, 6 November 1995

An extraordinary photograph, taken by the Hubble space telescope, has appeared in the papers over the weekend. It shows wide columns of gas and dust six million million miles high giving birth, we are told, to new stars. Two current catch-phrases come to mind – 'How do they *do* that?' and, 'I don't *believe* it!'

> When sorrows come, they come not single spies,
> But in battalions.

On Saturday evening Matthew* was viciously struck on the back of his head. He was taken to hospital for x-ray; reports are OK.

---

* Alec Guinness's son.

Rabin has been assassinated in Tel Aviv.

A police horse has been stabbed in the head by a football hooligan.

Alec Guinness

Friday, 24 November 1995

Yesterday I found myself at short notice taking part in the Radio 4 *Moral Maze* programme. The subject was with special reference to the case of Frederick and Rosemary West. He committed suicide some time ago but she has just been convicted of ten murders.

As I sat and listened outside to the three previous speakers being interrogated I found myself very critical (we all were) of the panel. It was like a viva being conducted by four soi-disant dons interrupting each other and the interviewees incessantly. When my turn came I was determined to make my two heartfelt points: (1) we must hate the sin and love the sinner; and (2) Jesus Christ came to seek and to save those who were lost.

One of the panel, an academic of some kind, began quoting the gospel against me. I asked him snappily, 'Are you a Christian?' and when he said he wasn't, derided him unkindly. I was surprised to be told that, although this programme comes under the auspices of the religious affairs department, God is not usually mentioned.

Lord Longford

Friday, 12 January 1996

Lady Thatcher looked radiantly aggressive on the box making a speech about One Nation and No Nation. I admit I don't quite understand what it all means: or why owning your own home, if you are one of the lucky ones, makes you a One Nation person. Disraeli, we are told, talked of Two Nations – rich and poor – but now I read he never got round to One Nation. On good authority we have been informed that the poor will be with us always. Obviously it is our duty to try to help all we can (without becoming Mrs Jellybys) – but I could do without advertising slogans and 'sound bites.'

Alec Guinness

Tuesday, 16 January 1996

All the little Blairites are rushing around talking about a stakeholder economy as though they have been familiar with the concept all their lives, whereas in truth none of them had ever heard of it before Tony made his speech in Singapore last week.* Ken Purchase [Labour MP] said to me, 'If stakeholding is such a good idea, why have we had nothing to say about the destruction of "mutuality" in the building societies? – surely the very essence of stakeholding.' Quite so. The reason is, of course, because the societies are handing out big dollops of money to their members in exchange for their acquiescence and we dare not offend the middle classes by uttering home truths about greed and short-termism.

Chris Mullin

Tuesday, 23 January 1996

Prime Minister's Questions was absolutely hilarious. Kenneth Baker began by asking John Major whether he didn't agree that the decision by Harriet Harman to send her child to a grammar school showed that she must be a stakeholder at heart. Major agreed. Then Blair got up and said, 'You can't use an eleven year old child to undo the damage done by the Government.' So Major said, 'Well all I am doing is being tough on hypocrisy and tough on the causes of hypocrisy,' which was a mockery of Blair's famous phrase that Labour would be tough on crime and the causes of crime.

Then another Tory got up and said, 'Shouldn't the Prime Minister congratulate the head of St Olave's School on attracting children from fifteen miles and two boroughs away.'

The Tories just collapsed in laughter and the Labour Party was incensed with anger – left, right and centre. I don't think Harriet has any idea what has happened.

Tony Benn

---

* A declaration of New Labour's economic positioning following the scrapping of Clause IV. Blair called for an economy 'run for the many, not for the few ... in which opportunity is available to all, advancement is through merit, and from which no group or class is set apart or excluded.'

Thursday, 1 February 1996

Pale sunshine all day: quite a lot of frost.

Most MPs are putting out feelers for more pay; a few suggest that double their present salaries would be acceptable. Rather a lot, I think, for so much yah-booing. Could not a scheme be devised whereby MPs were paid for by those who voted for them but not, of course, by those who opposed their election? It would make for an interesting disparity of rewards. A letter in today's *Telegraph* points out that the US House of Representatives has only 435 members for a country with about five times our population. Perhaps we could get along quite well with only 300 representatives. Now *there* would be an economy.

Last night we watched, aghast, a TV programme about American mothers training their tiny-tot little girls in the arts of seduction for a glitzy appearance at the Southern Charm Pageant in Atlanta, Georgia. As rabid 'stage mothers' they made our own appalling breed of ambitious mums seem only partially insane.

Alec Guinness

Friday, 2 February 1996
Somerset

A little before 4 a.m. the telephone rang. Jane went to take it. I could hear from the sound of her voice that something was wrong and leapt out of bed. Jane said 'They have got our car!' It was Steph from next door saying that our car was on fire. She had rung the fire brigade.

I immediately rang the police, dressed and dashed out, locking the door behind me and telling Jane under no circumstances to come out into the road. Almost immediately I met Steve [Radley, our other neighbour] running out of his house. We rushed round to ... find the car well and truly ablaze.*

The police took statements while Jane made tea for the firemen – all thirteen of them. Then Steve came out with some more tea and flapjacks. It became quite a midnight party.

---

*In November 1995 Paddy Ashdown had been investigating violent attacks on ethnic restaurants in Yeovil (his constituency), perpetrated by known local criminals one of whom threatened Ashdown with a knife while he was walking through the town. His car was also vandalised. As a precaution, the car had been parked in his neighbours' garage (the Baileys) with their cars, where it was set alight. Ashdown and Steve Radley had to move these cars while his car and the garage were blazing away.

I am now scared to death of the house being fire-bombed with Jane inside. I rang the burglar alarm people to order a new security light and some smoke alarms, and then permanently closed off our letter box as the police said there was a danger of petrol being poured through it.

Paddy Ashdown

Monday, 26 February 1996

I was wrong last week about the snowdrops making a poor showing this year. In the last two days they have put in tardy, rather scattered appearances; far from spectacular but a happy reassurance that spring will come.

A suicide bomb in Jerusalem has killed twenty five people. Here the IRA has indicated that it is to step up its terrorist attacks and no warnings are to be given. The contempt one feels outstrips any apprehensions. In Dublin, Belfast, New York and London yesterday there were massive peace rallies, which is a comfort …

There is a photograph in the paper of a flock of alpaca being reared near Pulborough. They look lovely and not as daunting as llamas. I want one for my birthday but I fear the idea will be frowned upon. Only as a pet, of course, and perhaps as a pullover.

Alec Guinness

Sunday, 3 March 1996
City of Chester

I had a two and a half hour surgery. I had to keep shifting in my chair and jabbing my fingernails into the palm of my hand to stay awake.

It was the usual mixture: housing, Child Support Agency, difficult neighbours, 'the school won't do anything for Darren – they think he's thick but he's got dyslexia.' The only diversion was to have two transvestites on the trot – except they were both so pathetic.

The only bit of light-relief on the radar screen is moon-faced Ron Davies, Shadow Secretary of State for Wales, who has marked St David's Day with a delightfully loopy attack on Prince Charles. Ron says that a man who talks to vegetables, kills animals for pleasure and betrays his wife isn't fit to be king.

Gyles Brandreth

Wednesday, 6 March 1996

Jung Chang, author of *Wild Swans*, and her husband Jon Halliday came
to dinner. They are working on a biography of Mao and Jon is going to
Vietnam in search of people who had dealings with him, which is why
he contacted me.* The Mao project will take three years and they are
interviewing everyone who has ever met him including Heath, Bush
and Kissinger. Jon said Kissinger was trying to distance himself from
his earlier enthusiasm for Mao. Although banned in China *Wild Swans*
has opened a lot of doors ...

We talked about political heroes. Jon reckons that Chou En-lai is
the greatest political figure of the century. Jung is understandably wary
of heroes, given her experience of China, but she suggested Vaclav
Havel and Gandhi. Mandela we all agreed on. Jon suggested the Dalai
Lama, who certainly has my vote. I suggested Ho Chi Minh and Pope
John XXIII, both of whom remained humble to the end of their lives.

History we agreed will be kind to Gorbachev, but he, of course, is
seriously flawed by his neglect of the home front.

Chris Mullin

Friday, 15 March 1996

We all mourn bitterly the horror of Dunblane. Mr Major and Mr Blair
went up there together to express the national distress and the Queen,
they say, will follow. No Moderator, no Archbishop, can give explanation or comfort however well intentioned their consoling words.

The gloom spread through a day which, starting cold, and dim,
managed to provide some hazy sunshine by noon, and the warmth of
the afternoon produced little clouds of dizzily whirling midges.

Alec Guinness

Wednesday, 20 March 1996

I was home by nine. Supper in the kitchen with M [Michele Brandreth]
and Jo [Lumley]. Pasta and peppers of course. M doesn't eat meat and
Jo's virtually a vegan. They think we've known about the dangers of

---

*Chris Mullin had been in Vietnam as a journalist in the 1970s and 1980s; he met his
wife there.

BSE for years and we've been keeping quiet because we don't want to upset the farmers.*

Gyles Brandreth

Wednesday, 27 March 1996

Our beef is now banned around the world. The British beef market has collapsed – and no one in government – least of all the Agriculture Minister – seems to have a clear idea what to do.

According to Roger Knapman last week we were considering slaughtering all 11 million cattle in the country; this week it's four million. We're saying 'beef is safe' but, because nobody believes us, we're going to have to slaughter half the cattle in the kingdom at a cost to the taxpayer of something around £6 billion! ... It's beyond belief.

Gyles Brandreth

Tuesday, 9 April 1996

France

I am reading Roy Jenkins's *Gladstone*. I never realised what turmoil there was in the 1840s and 1850s. Full of parties dissolving and people defecting from one side to another.

It took four decades for the old political structures to dissolve and the new shape of politics to emerge with the Tory and Liberal national parties. I have become convinced that the same thing is happening now.

I have for some time thought that the current shape of party politics in Britain cannot contain all the different forces that are contained within it. So one of the historic roles of the Liberal Democrats, and of my leadership of the Party, is to use this opportunity and my relationship with Blair to start the process of creating a completely new shape for our politics. There is after all no reason why the Labour Party, any more than the Tory Party, should remain the same forever.

If as it appears, I have more in common with Blair than he has

---

*The outbreak of Bovine Spongiform Encephalopathy (BSE or 'Mad Cow Disease') amongst British cattle caused a major public health panic and saw British beef exports to the EU banned for ten years; it was believed to have been caused by contaminated bone and meat supplements in cattle food.

with his left wing surely the logical thing is for us to create a new, powerful alternative force which would be unified around a broadly liberal agenda.

And the sooner we do that, the sooner we will stimulate the break-up of the Tories into pro-European, one-nation Tories like Kenneth Clarke, and the anti-European xenophobes who have taken control of the party under Major.

Paddy Ashdown

Saturday, 11 May 1996

This afternoon we watched the Manchester United and Liverpool confrontation at Wembley. It all seemed rather even paced, good tempered, and [Eric] Cantona scored the only goal – for Man. Utd. I am no aficionado of the game but it seemed to me there was a touch of genius in the sheer direction and power of Cantona's goal – which was made from quite a distance. I hope the hooligan who abused him last year is squirming somewhere on a bar stool. And now it appears that a Liverpudlian fan spat at Cantona when he received the trophy.

Alec Guinness

Saturday, 18 May 1996
Manchester City Hall

National Policy Forum. In a very surly frame of mind. How I resent giving up a weekend to listen to hours of claptrap. 'Dad, why are you always going to meetings?' asked Sarah. Why indeed?

Gordon Brown was much in evidence, exuding artificial bonhomie. What a contrast to Blair who is so relaxed, confident and above all capable of listening. Gordon is constantly wringing his hands and unable to sit or stand still for longer than a sound bite. He made an unscheduled address to the plenary session in an attempt to damp down the outrage at his review of child benefits,* but he was received without enthusiasm. There was the usual talk of tough choices ... Someone asked if we couldn't consider some other tough choices, such

---

* Brown proposed to remove child benefit for the over-sixteens from better-off families and replace it with an Education Maintenance Allowance to encourage young people to stay in education.

as progressive taxation? There is no doubt that Gordon – and Tony (who is obviously in this up to his neck) – have blundered. All that assiduous wooing of the middle classes squandered in a single act of foolishness.

At the workshop on foreign affairs I suggested that we say something about our alleged commitment to amend the Treaty of Rome to have farm animals treated as sentient beings rather than agricultural products. It beats me why we never make more of this ...

Chris Mullin

Friday, 31 May 1996
Chichester, Sussex

The city has streets and streets of immaculate seventeenth and eigh-teenth-century houses, particularly round Pallant House; they're manicured and swept clean and at night are as empty as a stage set. It's quiet too except (and this is a feature of English county towns) in the distance one suddenly hears whooping and shouting and the sound of running feet as young drunks somewhere make their presence felt and kick out against this oppressive idyll.

Alan Bennett

Tuesday, 11 June 1996
Brixton Road

A man came to give the boiler its annual check-up. A former employee of British Gas, he was a victim of privatisation. He now worked for a sub-contractor. No holiday pay. No sick pay. He was paid only by the job. If no one was at home, he got nothing. I asked what training the new masters provided. None. There was still a plentiful supply of employees trained by the public sector. What would happen when they ran out? Who knows? He said that the billing people were all temps, employed only two months out of three. No job security. No pensions. No nothing.

In fairness he did say there had been a lot of abuses under public ownership ... there was a saying among the Islington [public sector] workforce, he said: 'One week's work, six months' sick pay.' That's one thing we never face up to on the left.

Chris Mullin

Saturday, 17 August 1996

[Story breaking in the *Daily Telegraph*] that Michael Howard's new (and in my view undesirable) ID cards were carrying the EU flag. I have tried to stress that Michael Howard is fighting to include the Union Jack.

Michael Spicer

Friday, 27 September 1996

I rang Shirley [Williams] at about four in the afternoon ... Shirley doesn't have a very high opinion of Blair. She had previously, but it has diminished. She thinks he is a fixer and she doesn't know what he stands for. I assured her that it wasn't a burning ambition of mine to be a Cabinet minister. And she should know that.

It was my burning ambition however to deliver the Party to a stronger position and, if the opportunity arose, into government. I want to increase, perhaps to double, the number of MPs we have. I would much prefer to have over forty MPs in the next parliament and not be in Cabinet than, let's say, thirty and be in.

She replied, 'Position is much stronger if being in government is not a burning ambition for you. Most people want to be in government terribly, but then realise how powerless they are when they get there.'

Paddy Ashdown

Tuesday, 1 October 1996
Labour Party Conference, Blackpool

Tony's speech in the afternoon, to which I listen in a packed Winter Gardens, is a success. There are longeurs, especially at the end, and unfortunate phrases such as 'only a thousand days to prepare for a thousand years.' How can you prepare for a thousand years? And referring to a 'thousand years' carries with it dangerous Hitlerian associations. And what on earth does 'Labour's coming home' mean? Yes, I know about England's European Cup song.

But Blair shows that Labour really does have an alternative agenda – education, social cohesion and community, political and democratic reform, and cooperation in Europe.

Two sentences are memorable: 'Ask me my three main priorities for government, and I tell you: education, education and education' and 'We are back as the people's party; and that's why the people are coming back to us.'

Giles Radice

Thursday, 7 November 1996

Whitemoor Prison, Cambridgeshire

To Whitemoor High Security prison near March in Cambridgeshire: March, that fogbound halt where I used to change en route from Leeds to Cambridge forty-five years ago. That station has gone now and the prison is built over what once were the marshalling yards, the ground too saturated in mineral waste for much else. Not that this makes it very different from the surrounding countryside, as that's pretty thoroughly polluted too, all hedges gone, the soil soused in fertiliser, a real Fison's Fen ...

From a distance the prison might be an out-of-town shopping mall, Texas Homecare, Do it All and Toys 'R' Us. There's a creche at the gate and a visitors' centre, as it might be for Fountains Abbey or Stonehenge.

While the prisoners are brought down I wait in a little common room with one or two instructors and interested parties: a blind boy who teaches maths; Anne Hunt who has been seconded from UEA; and another teacher who has come over from Blundeston Prison near Lowestoft to hear the talk. Which is actually no talk at all, as the prisoners rather than be lectured at prefer to ask questions. There are about two dozen, mostly in their twenties and thirties, the most interested and articulate a Glasgow boy with a deep scar on his left cheek, who did *Talking Heads** as an A-level set book last year and is counted one of their successes.

The predominant feeling is one of waste, that these men have

---

* *Talking Heads* was an award-winning series of individual monologues written by Alan Bennett for the BBC, featuring actors Maggie Smith, Julie Walters, Patricia Routledge, Eileen Atkins, Penelope Wilton, David Haig, Thora Hird, Stephanie Cole and Alan Bennett himself.

been locked up and nothing is being done with them. With resources stretched to breaking point, these classes are the next target in the event of further cuts. And this is the other impression one comes away with: the universal hatred and contempt for Michael Howard – prisoners, warders, teachers, everybody one speaks to complaining how he has stripped away from the service all those amenities which alleviate the lives of everyone cooped up here, warders and prisoners alike. Indeed one gets the feeling that the only thing that is holding the prison service together and making it for the moment work is this shared hatred for Michael Howard.

Alan Bennett

Tuesday, 26 November 1996

At 8.15 am, with half a dozen others, I boarded a coach at the Members' entrance and set off for BBC Television Centre. Here John Birt and his senior managers – of whom there were many – briefed us. The BBC, far from sticking at what it is good at, has ambitious plans to expand into commercial activity and use the proceeds to subsidise the core business. 'We intend to be a pioneer of the digital age,' was how Birt put it. Murdoch and the licence fee were their chief concerns. 'We're not indulging in hyperbole,' he said. 'We believe we are at a critical moment.' Murdoch had taken extraordinary risks with an untried technology and he had won. He had tied up rights on soccer and movies for years to come. He had a subscription base of four to five million. It was not worth anyone else's while to invest in a set-top box because no one else had the 'drivers' – soccer and movies rights – to make it saleable. Therefore everyone was going to have to use his system and it was vital that it be properly regulated, particularly the electronic programme guide. Otherwise, how will the consumer find other services in a world where the dominant player controls access? Birt added, 'Every member of the government now regrets that Murdoch was allowed to get into that position.'

Chris Mullin

John Major's premiership had lasted six and a half years: the election victory in April 1992 had been an unexpected bonus for the Conservatives and Major's government continued for a full five years. The General Election of 1997 was therefore set for 1 May. Alan Clark had stepped down from his Plymouth seat in 1992, much to the disappointment of his diary readership, and almost immediately regretted it; in 1997 he decided to seek the Tory candidature of one of the safest seats in the country, Kensington and Chelsea, resuming his diary of political life. Suffering bouts of illness almost from the start, Alan Clark sadly did not survive the Parliament.

In January 1997 the election campaign, under the Party leaders Tony Blair, William Hague and Paddy Ashdown, was underway, Ashdown having held numerous discussions with Tony Blair since December 1993 about the Liberal Democrats' role in a Labour government.

Wednesday, 1 January 1997

Somerset

During the morning I completed the new version of the Partnership Agreement ['Partnership for Britain's Future'] and spoke to Archy [Kirkwood]. Donald Dewar* is off in the Cotswolds living like a hermit in a cottage. He has taken a suitcase full of books with him. Apparently this is his dream way to spend the New Year. What a strange man.

Paddy Ashdown

Sunday, 19 January 1997

Today there was big coverage about a woman called Nicola Horlick, a pension fund manager with Morgan Grenfell earning £1 million a year, who has been sacked. She has got PR people and lawyers working for her and she flew to Germany to see Deutsche Bank, who own Morgan Grenfell. Thousands of miners, steel-workers and car-worker are sacked, but her dismissal gets major coverage. She is claiming £1 million compensation and then, blow me down, today in the *Sunday Express* there was a headline: 'I want to be a Labour MP now,' says Nicola Horlick.

Mandelson is a friend of hers.

Tony Benn

---

* Archy Kirkwood, the Liberal Democrats' Chief Whip, and Donald Dewar, Labour's Chief Whip, were privy to the secret discussions between Ashdown and Blair about a potential Lib–Lab arrangement after the General Election.

Thursday, 30 January 1997

Jack Straw, Shadow Home Secretary, addressed the Labour peers. The audience was courteous but I would think sceptical. I put a question in this way: 'When I visit prisons, as I do once or twice a week, I am always asked by staff and prisoners, "Will things be better under Labour?" May I have an answer from Jack, with whom we all sympathise in this tragic dilemma?'

I was referring of course to the clash between traditional Labour support for penal reform and a desperate competition for votes with the Conservatives. Of course we are all longing to win the election. Jack talked away in reply, but he reminded me of the Irish orator who wound up a speech by saying, 'Mind you, I've said nothing.'

Lord Longford

Monday, 3 February 1997

Today we launched our tearful lion poster as part of our Euro-sceptic tilt – and Robin Cook has helped considerably with his timely suggestion that we'll be part of the EMU by 2002, come what may.

Gyles Brandreth

Sunday, 9 February 1997
Saltwood Castle

I am sitting at the kitchen table; outside is dark and misty. Around me are spread all the constituency engagements, and the active election planning ... the old warhorse smells powder! Bogus of course, because hard to lose this one. In the night I worried if I might be assassinated during the campaign? I don't want to be paralysed, as politicians often seem to be after such attempts.

Alan Clark

Friday, 21 February 1997

To the High Court, just in time to see the three men falsely convicted of murdering Carl Bridgewater walk free. The crowd blocked the Strand. A lot of old friends turned up including three of the Birmingham Six, Paddy Hill, Bill Power and Gerry Hunter.

I had heard that the men were in bad shape but they put on a pretty good show. They said they weren't bitter, just angry. They said some nice things about Ann Whelan, the mother of one of them, who is the real hero of the hour. I have only a walk on part in this one.* The day belongs to Ann, the solicitor Jim Nichol and Paul Foot.

Chris Mullin

Wednesday, 5 March 1997

Nick Budgen gets a very dusty answer at PMQs on 4 March when he raises the question of immigration. When at [today's] '22 Committee† the question is posed as to whether or not the Government are prepared to make immigration an election issue the Chairman moves the business swiftly on without the least attempt or opportunity to discuss what is, after all, a very serious political issue. Marcus Fox's notion that the interests of the Conservative Party are best served by sweeping all controversial subjects under the carpet is profoundly mistaken but the assumption must be that this is what the top brass want. Mercifully the Stalinist mentality which pervades the '22 Committee is not at all evident at the smaller special interest group meetings which continue to provide fora for frank exchanges and meaningful discussions.

Christopher Gill

Thursday, 6 March 1997

Launch our Euro-movement '97 campaign. This is timed for the lull before the election and is designed to counteract the propaganda of the sceptics by setting out the benefits of British membership of the EU. Of course, we have very limited resources – only a quarter of a million compared with Sir James Goldsmith's £24 million with which he is financing his Referendum Party.

Giles Radice

---

* The Birmingham Six and Carl Bridgewater convictions were two of several high-profile cases of miscarriages of justice in which Chris Mullin campaigned to free the innocent men. Carl Bridgewater was a newspaper boy who had been shot when he disturbed burglars at a farmhouse in Staffordshire. The case was covered extensively by investigative journalist Paul Foot.
† The 1922 Committee – the body of Conservative backbench MPs, chaired by Sir Marcus Fox and subsequently Michael Spicer.

Wednesday, 23 April 1997

Newbury

[Visited a school with David Rendel] We were met by a large crowd of Newbury By-pass protestors* and Green Party activists, many dressed in animal costumes, demonstrating outside the school gate.

When we came to leave, Special Branch said I was to jump into the car and drive out through the protestors, so they didn't block the bus. I said, no, I would go out and have a little debate with them.

The usual jeering when I went out, but I said 'Let's go off into a corner, away from the road, and you can make your points to me.' So we did surrounded by press and cameras.

I spotted somebody dressed up in what I thought was a badger's outfit. So I said, 'I would like to hear from this badger first.' The lady dressed as a badger complained, 'I am not a badger, I am a dormouse.'

I apologised profusely for the misunderstanding but said I had been reliably informed she was a badger; why was she masquerading as a dormouse? She said, 'No I am a dormouse and we dormice are feeling very sad and lonely, as are all our friends the rats, the voles, and the bats.'

'Well,' I said, 'I would like to hear from some more animals on this. Are there any other members of the animal kingdom who would like to join the debate?'

I spotted a cow. 'Now, this cow no doubt wishes to make a point.'

The two people in the cow costume waddled forward and said something to the cameras – to a fit of hysteria from the press.

But the Greens took it all terribly seriously. It all made for fine entertainment on the evening news.

Paddy Ashdown

---

* Constituency won by David Rendel for the Lib Dems in 1993; the proposed Newbury bypass was a major environmental issue fought mainly by young 'eco-warriors', who unsuccessfully challenged the bulldozers and chainsaws.

Thursday, 24 April 1997

Labour press officer quote of the day (quote of the campaign perhaps): 'Later today Tony Blair will be spontaneous. Tomorrow he will be passionate.'

Gyles Brandreth

Chapter Ten

1997–2007
'Ultimately he blew it'

New Labour, new diaries. With the election of the Labour government on 1 May 1997 a crop of young diarists – from spin doctors to ballet dancers – anticipated the transformation of Britain under Tony Blair and New Labour. Alastair Campbell, Tony Blair's master of communications, wrote a breathless account of events in and around 10 Downing Street. Lance Price, for a time his deputy, also kept a diary. Starting on the day of the election, for twenty months Deborah Bull, the principal ballerina with The Royal Ballet, kept a diary which, uniquely, combined dancing and politics. Oona King, newly elected Labour MP for Bethnal Green and Bow in east London, gives us a blow-by-blow account as she steps into 'the boxing ring'. And Piers Morgan's editorship at the *News of the World* and the *Daily Mirror* coincided with 'a scandalous decade' (from 1994 to 2004), which he scrupulously records. Lord Longford in his *Prison Diary* ponders 'crime and the causes of crime'.

Tony Benn, after his voluntary departure from the Commons in 2001 continues the diary he had started forty years earlier. Chris Mullin records anticipating a Prime Ministerial summons that took some time to materialise. Alan Bennett confides his thoughts on Diana, mad-cow disease and the impending Iraq war.

The movement to ban hunting with dogs, which had been led by Tony Banks, Michael Foster and a handful of MPs from all parties before 1997, dragged on for seven years.* Meantime the European Union continued to grow in extent and power; there was a humanitarian disaster in Kosovo; the twin towers of New York were attacked and destroyed; the Afghan War began; and the United States and Britain went to war with Saddam Hussein. Despite these international distractions the New Labour government's programme of reform and spending in the public services, notably in education and health, went ahead.

Thursday, 1 May 1997
General Election Day

By 10 pm I was struggling to keep my eyes open after two strenuous shows in fifteen hours and precious little sleep between them. Sensing that something momentous was going on and eager to be there as it happened, I did my best to keep pace with the *Newsnight* swing-o-meter. But election coverage is difficult to follow at the best of times, and the political analysts weren't helping a bit. Nor did it help that my eyelids were getting heavier by the minute, and for about half an hour I fought to stay awake in the belief that with just a bit more concentration I would surely figure out what was going on.

By midnight I was out for the count, and Blair, so it seemed, was in.

Deborah Bull

Wednesday, 7 May 1997
Westminster

The big news of today is the meeting of the new PLP – 418 strong – in the Church of England's grand assembly hall. An extraordinary scene with MPs in serried ranks, including those from such unlikely places as Hove, Hastings and Wimbledon. After a short speech from John Prescott, Tony Blair emerges from a door like a young Kennedy, smiles and waves for the cameras, and makes a stern and moving address to his large army. As he starts a bleeper goes off – very new Labour. Tony

---

*The hunting ban was a manifesto commitment, as were other undertakings which animal welfare groups hoped to see implemented after making contributions to the Labour Party election campaign.

says that 'the weight of history is upon our shoulders'. Rejecting Sir Hartley Shawcross's 1945 dictum, 'We are the masters now,' Tony's dictum for a less triumphalist age is 'We are not the masters. The people are the masters. We are the people's servants.'

He also reminds us that 'It was New Labour wot won it ... we ran for office as New Labour. We govern as New Labour.'

Then there is discipline ... You are here not 'to enjoy the trappings of power but to do a job and uphold the highest standards in public life' – all splendidly sober stuff.

Giles Radice

Wednesday, 18 June 1997

Today was the first reading of my Private Member's Bill. The Private Member's Bill is Parliament's equivalent of the national lottery ... If your number comes up you get a chance to change the law of the land.

I won the lottery when my name came up last month ... Was flooded with ideas for legislation from virtually every lobby group in the country.

My Bill helps people like my GMB (union) members who lost their employment rights when their jobs were contracted out by local authorities.

If a hospital contracts out its cleaning staff at bargain-basement rates, it has only to consider the money it saves. It doesn't have to consider the quality of the service, i.e. are the wards filthy or clean?

(The government whips) said they would support it if I could get the CBI and the TUC and the Tory front bench to support it too. Thanks a mil. Why not ask me to get the Israelis and Palestinians to issue a joint peace statement instead? ... But I'm giving it a go.

Oona King

Thursday, 19 June 1997
Conservative leadership election

The day of decision for the Tories – I run across [Kenneth] Clarke in Westminster Hall and wish him good luck. I ask him whether the deal with Redwood will muzzle the pro-Europeans. 'Not at all,' says Clarke with his usual breezy confidence.

At 5.15 the Tory result is announced – Hague 92, Clarke 70. The

'Molotov–Ribbentrop' pact has failed … So William Hague is the new Tory leader. He seems much older than 36 with his bald head and his measured Yorkshire voice.

Giles Radice

Friday, 4 July 1997

The Americans have landed a computer-driven vehicle on Mars. It made a flawless landing after a journey of 308 million miles. Mind-boggling.

Chris Mullin

Saturday, 2 August 1997
Cincinnati, USA

Rang my brother Dave in London, who read me the list of all the peers who have been appointed, which included Michael Levy, who organised Tony Blair's blind fund, raised £1 million for Blair's office.

Tony Benn

Sunday, 31 August 1997
London

I was awoken at 4 am by the telephone. It was Torje in Toronto. He had just returned from dinner and turned on CNN. 'I thought you'd want to know; there's been a car crash in Paris. They're saying that Dodi Al Fayed is dead, and Princess Diana is injured.' In my semi-conscious state I turned on the television. For about half an hour I watched the coverage, saw the wreckage of the Mercedes in that Paris tunnel and wondered at Diana's luck, to have survived what must have been an enormous impact.* My God! Eventually I dozed back to sleep and the television turned itself off.

Deborah Bull

---

* First confused reports of the car crash in a Paris underpass suggested that Princess Diana had survived. Her friend Dodi Al Fayed (son of businessman Mohammed Al Fayed) and the driver died at the scene but the Princess and her bodyguard were cut from the wreckage and rushed to hospital. Only the bodyguard survived.

Thursday, 4 September 1997

'God created a blond angel and called her Diana.' This is one of the cards on the flowers outside Kensington Palace that the BBC chooses to zoom in on. It purports to be from a child, though whether one is supposed to be touched by it or (as is my inclination) to throw up isn't plain.

HMQ to address the nation tomorrow. I'm only surprised Her Majesty hasn't had to submit to a phone-in.

Alan Bennett

Saturday, 6 September 1997

I watched mainly on TV but then went upstairs to watch [the funeral procession] come across Horseguards, then out to Whitehall as it came past Downing Street and there was more noise than I expected. There was a good mood in the crowd and several moments I found particularly moving. The card from the kids. I thought Elton John was tremendous. TB's reading was OK. The main event though for me was Charles Spencer's tribute, in which he directed barbs both at the press and the royal family. TB was sure the attack on the press would be the main thing ... He asked me to speak to GB and Peter, which I did. They were more relaxed. GB felt, rightly in my view, that Spencer's attacks on the royals would be far more newsworthy.*

Alastair Campbell

Tuesday, 16 September 1997

On Sunday, two days ago, the Greenham Common fence was knocked down at the airbase – the Americans have gone. When they were there, insofar as they were mentioned at all, the women were always referred to as witches and lesbians and trouble-makers and crypto-communists. I thought to myself, 'That is another victory from the bottom up that is never recognised.'

Tony Benn

*TB = Tony Blair; GB = Gordon Brown; Peter = Peter Mandelson.

Saturday, 27 September 1997

Saltwood Castle

This morning the news (leaked) that Hague was going to dispense with hereditary peerages (i.e. adopt Blair's 'reforms'). For me this is the last straw – already. Coming on top of message to Gay Pride, Notting Hill carnival (aren't there any worthwhile causes he could send a message to?). It's got him marked. Give him a good bit more rope, though.

Alan Clark

Tuesday, 30 September 1997

Labour Party Conference, Brighton

Blair's speech electrified the audience. He gave his 'not the biggest, but the best' rhetoric the full Tony, all raised fists and slightly evangelical delivery. I can see Blair doing one of those US preacher-style tours one day – the ones that end with 'I have sinned – now give me your cash, O believers.'

Later we had lunch with him and Cherie, our annual *Mirror* conference tradition. It was all going quite well until the issue came up of Blair's pay rise or lack of it. The *Mirror* had run a campaign to stop him and the Cabinet awarding themselves big salary hikes, and they had eventually backed down.

'It's alright for you,' Cherie said. 'But we have had to give up our house in Islington and we can't make any investments. The pay rise would just bring the Cabinet in line with jobs of similar importance.'

That may be true, I said 'but I don't think the average *Mirror* reader expects their first Labour Prime Minister in eighteen years to be filling his boots quite so quickly.'

Cherie scowled at me.

Piers Morgan

Friday, 3 October 1997

Unexpectedly, Lord Gowrie has resigned his post as Chairman of the Arts Council ... the rumours abound and speculation runs high. Gowrie is without doubt a Tory man through and through. Although an appointment such as this should be apolitical, it has long been feared that he and the Labour administration would not see eye to eye.

It seems that Gowrie's departure may mark the end of an era in the arts. The government has hinted that there is no reason why the post of Arts Council chairman should remain 'non-executive', a euphemism for unpaid. Stand aside what [*Times* journalist] Valerie Grove calls the 'languid well-connected patron of the arts'. Make way for the business manager who, with his market surveys and eye on the balance sheet, will make sure that the 'people's money is spent on the people's priorities', to quote Tony Blair. Clear the stages of *Giselle* and *Swan Lake*, and make way for a new production starring Anthea Turner and a lot of coloured balls.

Deborah Bull

Thursday, 6 November 1997

The government is becoming accident prone. First the botch up over the hunting bill. Now cigarette advertising. Tessa Jowell announced yesterday that Formula One racing was to be exempt from the much-heralded ban on cigarette advertising. The decision seems to have come from Downing Street after a visit by a powerful lobby of motor racers. As if that wasn't bad enough, we learn this morning that Tessa's husband had some sort of commercial relationship with the Formula One team.* Not that Tessa is at fault. She apparently declared the possible conflict of interest months ago.

Chris Mullin

Thursday, 20 November 1997

Breakfast at 8 am at Goldman Sachs with the millionaire economist Gavyn Davies (the Treasury Select Committee's adviser). He tells me that he is the best paid economist in the Western world. He is worried about the Far East crash, especially about its impact on Japan – says that our economy is still overheated and there may well not be a 'soft' landing.

---

* Formula One's president, Bernie Ecclestone, had made a £1 million donation to the Labour Party, which secured an exemption from a ban on cigarette advertising at Formula One's motor racing events. It emerged that David Mills, the husband of MP Tessa Jowell (Public Health Minister at the time), had a business relationship with Ecclestone. It was the first allegation of 'sleaze' – which had bedevilled the Conservatives' last years – to tarnish the recently elected Labour government.

Referring to economists, he says they should be humble considering how many times they get things wrong.

Giles Radice

Wednesday, 10 December 1997

(Monday) I went to the Privy Council dinner – Royal Gallery ... presided by Prince of Wales and including various – Cranborne, Ancram, Tom King and – God alive, how did he get one? – Atkins, R.* Copious and excellent wines.

The Queen is transformed, no longer the wicked stepmother with her frumpish and ill-natured features that have been permanently in place since Mrs T. rescued the 1992 election. As I said at the time, the whole Royal family delighted at the elimination of Diana, and has now settled back comfortably into their favourite role – preservation of their own perks and privileges at the expense, whenever necessary, of other individuals and institutions. The Empire, the Church, the Law, the hereditary principle, the Lords, even a yacht, and now there are droves of faithful servants who are being dismissed in droves as they modernise Sandringham and Balmoral.

Alan Clark

Thursday, 11 December 1997

I was part of history today in a very weird and rather uncomfortable way. Blair had asked me to go and see him at No 10 for a chat along with some of my political team before everyone disappears for the festive season.

When we arrived we were taken in – very unusually – through a back door.

'What's going on?' I asked. 'Look down the corridor,' came the cryptic reply.

And so I did and there were Martin McGuinness and Gerry Adams making the first official visit by Sinn Fein to Downing Street ... waiting with Blair to go out for their historic handshake. It was an amazing moment. And reminded me once again of Blair's real achievement in

---

* Sir Robert Atkins, Conservative MP from 1979 to 1997, was made a member of the Privy Council in 1995.

Northern Ireland. He has worked so hard to get to this point, rarely getting the credit he deserves ...

Ten minutes later, Blair was back in his office, striding towards me to shake my hand. 'Erm, got any rubber gloves, Prime Minister?'

He laughed. 'God those two are nothing. Some of the other world leaders I've had here recently, from some of the African states for instance, make them look like choirboys.'

Piers Morgan

Tuesday, 3 February 1998

Paris with the Treasury Select Committee

The high spots are the meeting with two key EMU players – Dominique Strauss-Kahn in the morning and Jean-Claude Trichet in the evening. Strauss-Kahn, the new Socialist Finance Minister, is a bit like Gordon Brown – powerful, energetic and highly intelligent. If anybody is going to make the French government coherent, it will be him ... He says he is keen to have Britain in the Euro but we cannot be members of the Euro committee unless we join [the currency].

Trichet, the Governor of the Bank of France, has come back specifically from Frankfurt to meet us.

He wants us to join as soon as possible but says that, according to the treaty, the UK should be two years in the ERM to show that our currency is stable.

Giles Radice

Saturday, 14 February 1998

On Thursday I went down to Croydon, to the Fairfield Hall, to hear one of my nephews and my niece in the Bromley Borough Schools' Prom. Last year they sang *Captain Noah and his Floating Zoo*, a Joseph Horowitz composition ... [and] they boasted none other than the eighty-something-year-old Mr Horowitz himself at the piano.

The Bromley Borough Schools' Prom should be required viewing for Education Minister David Blunkett and his cabinet colleagues. No one in the Fairfield Hall on Thursday could possibly doubt the importance of musical (and artistic) education and the benefits it brings to children above and beyond the ability to simply 'strum a tune.'

Last night, at the opposite extreme of individual artistry, I saw the penultimate West End performance of Antony Sher in *Cyrano*.

Sher gave a searing performance – something to be treasured.

Deborah Bull

Tuesday, 17 February 1998

I went in for Robin Cook's speech on Iraq. He made a good case. There is no doubt that Saddam has the ingredients (some of which we sold him) for making all sorts of unpleasant weapons and within a year or two he may have a delivery system. Nor do I need to be convinced that Saddam is a monster and that his overthrow is desirable. I just can't see how bombing his infrastructure will help. What are we going to do for an encore when he pops up afterwards and says 'Ha, Ha, I'm still here'?

I agonised all evening about how to vote. This time round there is no One True Path. Just about everyone is uneasy. I wobbled back and forth all evening. In the end when the bell went I simply stayed in my room and didn't vote. Not a very heroic posture.

Chris Mullin

Friday, 6 March 1998

Went in early this morning for the debate on the Wild Mammals (Hunting with Dogs) Bill. All the Tories turned up in force. The whole thing was occupied with Heseltine, Hogg, Nicholas Winterton and all the fox hunters talking the Bill out. I thought, 'What a bloody fraud!' Here is the Labour Party saying they promised a free vote on hunting with the clear implication that if the House wanted a Bill they would find time for the Bill to go through.

And the Chief Whip has outlined the problems that this will cause in the Lords – there is not enough room in the Lords' timetable for a controversial bill in this session ... So really, many people who voted Labour, and the animal-welfare people who put £1 million into the campaign, have been betrayed.

I had a word with Tony Banks in the Lobby and he is as sick as a dog.

Tony Benn

Monday, 23 March 1998

To the Park Lane Hilton to hear Mandelson talk about the Dome. His claims for the Dome are preposterous – 'the global focus for the new millennium'; 'consumerism and community in equal measure'; 'a great shared national experience'. He speaks mainly in bromides and clichés, but despite the PR hype, he has a certain self confidence and bravura.

Giles Radice

Tuesday, 24 March 1998

Murdoch came up at the Parliamentary Committee. The papers are full of stories alleging that the Main Man* has been ringing up the Italian Prime Minister on Murdoch's behalf. I asked (1) who initiated the call to [Romano] Prodi? and (2) what is our relationship with Murdoch? The Man was visibly irritated. 'I don't reveal the details of private conversations,' he said testily. I replied that I just want to know who initiated it. He seemed to say it was Prodi, adding, 'The story in today's *Telegraph* is a load of balls.' Then he relaxed and said, 'My relationship with Murdoch is no different from that with any other newspaper proprietor. I love them all equally.' He added forcefully, 'I have never discussed media policy with Murdoch.'

Jean [Corston] raised hunting, saying it had become an issue of trust. The Man smiled wearily. 'I do understand the strength of feeling,' he said not very convincingly. The longer this goes on, the more convinced I am that the problem is Mandelson and his friends in high places. Jean approached me in the Tea Room afterwards and reported that Nick Brown (the Chief Whip) had told her that the advice from the Palace is that the Royals are not merely opposed, they won't have it. Won't they, indeed? I thought Mandelson was supposed to be trying to brush up the Prince of Wales's image. If so, the most useful advice he could give his new-found friend is not to side with the Unspeakable.

Chris Mullin

---

* Chris Mullin invariably referred to Prime Minister Tony Blair as 'The Man' or the 'Main Man'.

Wednesday, 25 March 1998

With The Royal Ballet in Germany

The opening night of *Sleeping Beauty* in Frankfurt and I am writing this between appearances as the Fairy of Passion in the Prologue and the Bluebird in Act Three.

[Today] we lost yet another Chief Executive. Mary Allen, after a short seven months in office, has resigned. Amazing. All in all she was with us almost twice as long as Genista McIntosh who took over from Jeremy Isaacs last January and resigned in May.

Once again we have lost our rudder in a fierce and ongoing storm, and I guess a small but select bunch of MPs have pulled on their dancing shoes to dance, yet again, on the grave of the Opera House.*

Deborah Bull

Monday, 6 April 1998

Set off to visit my friend Father Fred in Wandsworth, with paedophiles very much on my mind. The word has suddenly become all too popular, or rather unpopular. It is used in all sorts of misleading ways. One extreme are serial child killers. At the other, like the much-loved Catholic priest who was suspended for a time from his parish for fondling a seventeen year old boy twenty five years earlier.

Matthew Parris has done a useful job in *The Times* in protesting against the lynch-mob hysteria. But much clarification is necessary before any wise measures can be adopted.

Lord Longford

Thursday, 21 May 1998

In the afternoon I went to Millbank Tower [Labour Party Headquarters]. Tom Sawyer the General Secretary of the Party, was very friendly ... we walked round this open plan office with about 150 people there working on computers. He pointed in a general direction and said, 'That's the marketing department; that's the finance department; that's the constitutional department; those are the policy people.'

---

*The Select Committee on Culture, Media and Sport (formerly National Heritage), chaired by Gerald Kaufman, produced some very critical reports on the running of the Royal Opera House (home to The Royal Ballet).

I got the feeling that it was an organisation of an entirely managerial character, with a lot of young people in their shirt sleeves; it might have been a bank, an insurance company, Tory Central Office – it might have been anywhere. There were posters everywhere, pictures of Blair, New Britain, New Labour, No Increase in Taxation, all over the place; it was really weird.

As I was walking back to my car, I saw a very old lady with a walking stick accompanied by a young black nurse. And as I stopped at the car she said to me, 'Tony!' And I looked at her and her face was familiar, though she was very old. She's eighty four now – it was Rosamund John, the actress.*

So I stood and talked to her for quite a while about her films *Green for Danger*, and *The Way to the Stars*. She was very touched I think and very gentle and sweet and at the end I said, 'May I give you a kiss – something I've always wanted to do.'

Then she said, 'I must go now, I must go on walking.'

I said to the nurse, 'She's a very, very famous actress.' The nurse had no idea.

Tony Benn

Thursday, 25 June 1998

There was a Policy Unit lunch today on Europe. Quite clear there is no coherent strategy. Roger Liddle [Adviser on Europe] hugely in favour of the single currency but many sceptics around the table. One idea is to have a Europe minister who reports directly to the Prime Minister. General feeling that TB won't want the next election fought on the single currency but I said that [Blair] having acknowledged that the referendum would be shortly after the election, that was all but inevitable.

Lance Price

July 1998

The government's early indications that they might be on the verge of doing something positive for the arts bore fruit this month with the announcement of the outcome of their annual spending review. Culture Secretary Chris Smith has secured an extra £290 million for

---

* Rosamund John was married to John Silkin, Labour MP for Deptford. She died in October the same year.

his department and much of it will be passed on to the arts, with just a few strings attached. Nice work …

But there's no such thing as a free lunch and all this largesse comes with a price tag. In return, Chris Smith wants improved access and increased educational activities. Joy of joys! This is like handing me a brown envelope stuffed with used notes* and saying, 'You'll have to spend it in Harvey Nichols, though.' Nothing would make me happier and, Mr Smith, nothing will make us arts people happier.

Deborah Bull

Wednesday, 1 July 1998

The master strategists at Millbank, many of whom have never knocked on a door in their lives, are dreaming up more pointless activity to take our minds off mischief. Everyone had been sent a glossy brochure, crammed with useless inserts, to help celebrate the fiftieth anniversary of the NHS. Among them a list of so-called campaigning ideas. Sample:

- Have a photo-op outside a local hospital with a large syringe with the words 'Labour's £2 billion cash injection for the NHS' written on it. Your regional press officer has a four-foot model syringe that can be used for this picture.
- Arrange a photo-opportunity with a long serving local NHS worker who is celebrating their own fiftieth birthday this year.
- Arrange to spend a morning on a normal working day with an ambulance crew. Invite the media, but get your own photographer anyway so you can do a retrospective press release.

And so on … It is as though our masters have set up a vast play scheme to keep us amused while they get on, unhindered, with the serious business of government.

Chris Mullin

Friday, 24 July 1998

It's announced this morning that the three hundred or so soldiers shot for cowardice during the First World War are not to be pardoned, though in a speech later described as 'deeply felt' the Armed Forces

---

* A reference to the 'Cash for Questions' scandal in which a few Conservative MPs had been caught offering to ask parliamentary questions in return for payment.

Minister, Dr Reid, says that their names can now be inscribed on war memorials and that they will be pardoned in our hearts etc. The official reason they cannot be pardoned is that there is now (as there no doubt was then) little evidence as to who were genuinely cowards, poor wretches, and who were innocent and that it would never do to pardon the guilty with the innocent. Why not? If among three hundred there was one who was innocent (and there were many more) then his innocence should procure the pardon of them all. Or so Simone Weil would have said. But Simone Weil doesn't have much clout in the Ministry of Defence ... I write to Frank Dobson, my MP, saying, intemperately, that John Reid is more of a coward than many of the men who were executed.

Alan Bennett

Saturday, 22 August 1998

Clinton launched air strikes against Afghanistan and Sudan ['terrorist targets'] on Thursday night. TB gave immediate support but Robin Cook refused to go on the *Today* programme to defend it, saying there might be collateral damage and it could be difficult ...

Discussions about proportional representation etc. Paddy Ashdown has been in touch with TB in France to talk about proportional representation with a view to keeping the Tories out for a very long time.

Maybe TB is just stringing Paddy along with no intention of going as far as he [Paddy] wants. But it does sound as if a pretty detailed strategy has already been agreed.

Lance Price

Friday, 4 September 1998
Chester-le-Street

To the north for my constituency dinner for Mo Mowlam. Mo arrives at the Riverside ground surrounded by security police, in a state of complete exhaustion. I have to help her up the stairs and she only revives after a Mars bar and a double whisky. It is not surprising that she is exhausted. This week she had all-night emergency legislation and a visit by Clinton and Blair to Omagh to see the aftermath of the appalling destruction by the IRA.* I asked about Clinton's pre-Starr Report mood. 'Bad,' says Mo. 'And Hillary?' 'Even worse.'

I tell the dinner guests that Mo is deservedly the most popular politician in the UK because of her great contribution to peace in Northern Ireland. Mo explains in her speech that she could not have done it without Clinton and Aherne, and she might have added Tony Blair.

At the end she is so tired that I almost have to carry her out to her car. She really is a star.

Giles Radice

Sunday, 27 September 1998
Labour Party Conference, Blackpool

An Asian man from the north-west came up to me today asking if I could advise him on getting a peerage. He said, 'I know Jack Straw.' He'd written to the Prime Minister asking for a peerage and made the point that he was a very active member of CND. Somebody said to me that the trouble with this Conference is that there are too many people on the make. There was a guy who worked for Leonard Cheshire Homes and said that he was leaving Conference early because he was disgusted by all the people who were there to get something.

Tony Benn

Wednesday, 11 November 1998
House of Commons

Oona King to go to the Prime Minister's office immediately. Fucking hell, I thought, what have I done now? A message like that could only be bad.

I knocked on the open door and entered the first of two antechambers. Two people I didn't recognise were sitting at a desk, next to a whirring photocopier.

'They're waiting for you, please go in.'

I knocked peremptorily before pushing the door open, and closing it behind me. Inside were three people who ran the court of Tony, if not the country.

---

*The Real IRA detonated a car bomb in the town of Omagh, County Tyrone, Northern Ireland, on Saturday afternoon, 15 August, killing twenty-nine people and injuring hundreds.

Alastair Campbell sat leaning against a desk to the left. Sally Morgan was sitting at a desk directly ahead. Anji Hunter leaned against a sideboard on the right.* Next to Anji, the door to the main office was ajar, and Tony was sitting at his desk poring over papers in his red Prime Minister's folder, evidently preparing for PMQs which would start in twenty minutes. He looked up and nodded in my direction before returning to work.

'Ah Oona, thanks for coming,' said Alastair jovially.

'No problem, what can I do?'

'We need your help with something,' continued Alastair.

'Always willing to help,' I said, with a bright smile and sinking heart.

'We need you to pen an article.' I breathed a sigh of relief. Maybe it wouldn't be so bad.

'About?'

'Ken Livingstone.'

'Ken?'

'Yeah, Ken.'

'Why?'

'Well, as you know, he's trying to undermine the Labour Party, and we have to ensure he doesn't succeed.'

It was worse than I thought.

'What sort of article?'

'An article saying he can't be trusted ...'

I simply believed that Ken had the right, like any other member of the Labour Party, to put himself forward. It was a democratic process and we shouldn't undermine it. If he won and got selected – well, tough, that was democracy ...

'Thing is,' I said, trying to force a smile, 'I don't go in for personal attacks. It's not my style. And the other thing is, I don't agree with this strategy. We're alienating everyone, and Ken's going to win. Surely that's not what you want.'

This irritated all of them, and they each proceeded to tell me just how much Ken couldn't be trusted, and what a danger he was to the party.

'Look,' said Sally finally in exasperated tones, 'he's out to destroy the Labour Party, and we have to respond.'

---

* Both members of Tony Blair's political office: Anji Hunter was Director of Government Relations, 1997–2001, a post which Sally Morgan assumed for a few years.

'But you see Sally, I don't agree that he's out to destroy the Labour Party. He just has a different point of view.'

'Bollocks!' Sally slammed the desk with her fist, and I jumped involuntarily. She had a knack for the bad cop role …

'Look,' said Alastair in a final, take-it-or-leave-it voice, 'this is a direct request from the Prime Minister. Is your answer yes or no?'

I instinctively looked towards Tony's door to see whether he was listening …

'If you need an answer right this second …'

'Yes we do.'

'Well then … I know it's the end of my political career, but the answer is no.'

Alastair fired back without a moment's hesitation. 'It's not the end of your political career, Oona. Just the next five years. You can go now.'

Oona King

Friday, 20 November 1998
Sunderland South

To a primary school in one of the more prosperous parts of the constituency to talk to a group of nine and ten year olds. I had gone prepared to talk about the environment, animal welfare and various other issues they had tipped me off about, but all they wanted to discuss was teenage gangs. It was amazing. One after another they told tales of bullying or violence at the hands of local yobs. One girl said she had been singled out for not wearing Reeboks. Another because she had been seen coming out of the library carrying books – *books,* for heaven's sake. It was shocking the extent to which violence or the threat of it plays a part in their lives … Even the teachers were surprised.

Chris Mullin

Friday, 11 December 1998

Although the Tories talk tough on immigration, they left a backlog of 70,000 cases. I spoke to a civil servant who told me they were working flat out to clear the backlog. This civil servant also told me that they write letters to people saying the Home Secretary has 'seen the correspondence.' Apparently they wheel thousands of letters past his desk on a trolley. They trudge about with wheelbarrows full of letters, like bureaucratic gardeners. When the Home Secretary gives the wheel-barrow a once over, they can truthfully state that he has seen the correspondence. Or was that a joke? The apocryphal and the mundane blend together at the Home Office like absinthe. It blows your mind. When I visited the headquarters of the Immigration and Nationality directorate in Croydon, they took us into rooms the size of football pitches and showed us acres of correspondence.

Oona King

Wednesday, 16 December 1998

There were air raids in Baghdad just before ten.* I went off to *Newsnight* and there were Menzies Campbell and Michael Howard, and it was treated as a sort of spectacle – over to Baghdad to see the fires burning. I got very angry and I said, 'Look, people are being killed as we are talking, and we are discussing it as if it is a spectator sport' – it quite shook the panel. Then after one or two exchanges they tried to take my microphone from me and I said, 'I'm not leaving the studio,' so the discussion continued. I was unbelievably angry.

Tony Benn

Saturday, 2 January 1999
Gelston, Lincolnshire

Yesterday the single European currency, which many commentators in Britain said would never happen, went ahead but without the UK. It is arguably the biggest event on the European continent since the establishment of the Common Market in 1957 and, as usual, Britain is on the sidelines. We are likely to feel the impact of our self-imposed exclusion both economically and politically during 1999. The sooner we decide to go in the better. The coming of the euro and slowdown in the UK economy will be the big issues in British politics. Whether the global financial crisis, which was halted by the Fed, is really over is an open question. Obviously if things get worse internationally, that will

---

*The earlier war with Iraq over Kuwait in 1991 rumbled on throughout the 1990s. Saddam Hussein consistently refused to comply with UN Security Council resolutions on weapons inspections in his country and in September 1998 the US (under President Clinton) passed the Iraq Liberation Act; four days of bombing followed in December.

have an impact on the UK economy. Hopefully we can escape without too sharp a downturn.

Giles Radice

Thursday, 21 January 1999

To the Home Office to see Gareth Williams, one of the unsung heroes of this government.

A couple of civil servants from the Prison Department gave a little presentation on the work they were doing to encourage prisoners to face up to their offending behaviour.

I asked why prisoners were allowed to paper their cells with degrading pictures of women when we were supposed to be encouraging them to treat women with respect. The men from Prisons hummed and hawed about censorship and where lines should be drawn … There was a bright, attractive young blonde woman present whom I at first assumed to be the minute-taker but she turned out to be a governor-grade prison officer who had recently joined Gareth's office from Feltham Young Offenders' Institution. Gareth asked her opinion and she said she had just drawn up a censorship policy at Feltham. Gareth asked her to consider a policy for the entire prison estate.

Chris Mullin

January 1999

Gone are the days when young people could be beaten – metaphorically – into submission. Legislation enhancing children's rights, in particular the Children's Act of 1989, has put an end to that. And beyond that, we're living in a world where individuality, not conformity, is prized. Young people (and, by definition, young dancers) are encouraged to have a voice and to use it. Yet if the very essence of a corps de ballet is the unquestioning commitment and uniform approach of a mass of young people, then we're heading towards a dilemma. The post-Thatcherite generation is anything but unquestioning and uniform.

Deborah Bull

Tuesday, 26 January 1999

London

In the evening an intriguing dinner at the French Embassy. The new ambassador, Daniel Bernard, had gathered together a heterogeneous collection of guests. They include Sir John Birt and Lady Birt, Mr and Mrs Richard Branson, the Arsenal manager Arsene Wenger, Terence Conran and partner, the Kuwaiti ambassador and his wife, Alastair Campbell and his partner, and Peter Mandelson. Lisanne [Radice] is seated next to the Ambassador and Richard Branson.

Peter is courageous to have come and he behaves with dignity.* I introduce Arsene Wenger, who also has many problems with the press, to him. Wenger who has a thin intelligent face says he was never more than an ordinary footballer but he is a first-class manager. 'Managing a football team is like being a conjuror, you have so many balls to keep in the air – footballers, the board, the agents, the press, the fans,' he explains. A bit like T. Blair?

Giles Radice

Wednesday, 10 February 1999

Parliamentary Committee

When we had finished going round the table, The Man said, a propos of nothing, 'Shall I say a word about genetically modified food?' He was, he said, keen to ensure that we didn't overreact by launching into what he called 'populist mode'. There were all sorts of genetic modifications that we wouldn't wish to discourage. We wanted strict regulation and clear labelling, but we mustn't be stampeded into rejecting genetic modification out of hand. He added that it was a big industry and there were a lot of jobs at stake.

I didn't think anything of it at the time, but soon after we emerged from the meeting, I ran into Alan Simpson,[†] who said there were rumours that Bill Clinton had been leaning on The Man at the behest of Monsanto, which has already bought its way into the American political system and is no doubt burrowing away at ours. Jean Corston

---

*A month before, Peter Mandelson had resigned as a Minister after failing to declare a loan from Geoffrey Robinson, who had become Paymaster General in 1997 (a post he held until January 1999 when he also resigned on account of the loan to Mandelson). Giles Radice commented that it was 'hardly a hanging matter'.

[†] Alan Simpson was Labour MP for Nottingham South and a keen environmentalist.

later asked Ian Gibson,* who knows a lot about genetic modification, how many jobs were involved in this country. 'Very few,' he replied. Curiouser and curiouser.

Chris Mullin

Thursday, 18 February 1999

10 Downing Street

Crazy week dominated by genetically modified food.

The main allegations are that we are rushing ahead too fast with GM food research and allowing 'Frankenstein foods' to be sold without being sure the technology is safe. It's being claimed on extremely dubious grounds that GM foods could cause cancer, kill babies, turn vegetarians and the rest of us into cannibals, while GM crops will help wipe out other forms of life and contaminate non-GM crops. At the same time it is said the government is too close to the GM industry, too gung-ho about its potential, and that David Sainsbury, the science minister, has a conflict of interest because of his links to the family firm of supermarkets and his known enthusiasm for biotechnology in the past.

The week started with TB in a very feisty mood. He both alarmed and depressed David Miliband, whom I like and admire greatly, by suggesting that we should change direction on both health and education – allowing some treatments like varicose veins and cataracts to be taken out of the NHS and into private treatment. On education he was talking about closing down the Local Education Authorities altogether ... the idea is that it's time to think the unthinkable ...

Lance Price

Wednesday, 24 February 1999

Jack Straw rang at lunchtime to tip me off about his statement on the Stephen Lawrence Inquiry.† He was scathing about the Met: 'Incompetence on a grand scale. Makes your hair stand on end. You wonder what we pay these guys for.' Paul Condon will be staying but it is clear

---

* Labour MPs for Bristol East and for Norwich respectively.

† As Chairman of the Home Affairs Committee, Chris Mullin would be entitled to be kept closely informed on Home Office policy; the inquiry was into the misconduct of the initial police investigation into Stephen Lawrence's murder in April 1993.

that he has survived only by the skin of his teeth and on condition he eats a big helping of humble pie.

Chris Mullin

Wednesday, 17 March 1999

A long session with a Home Office minister about the chaos at the Immigration and Nationality Department. The papers have been full of horror stories about lost documents and queues which start forming before dawn. He says the problem started under the Tories, who signed up to a contract for a new computer system which hasn't yet been delivered. The deadline has been extended, but even now it is still far from clear that the company concerned will deliver.

He added that about 80 per cent of public service computer contracts have gone wrong. This one has all the makings of a disaster, but it might still, just, work out. He wants [my Home Affairs Committee] to hold off from launching an enquiry until after the summer recess, by which time the outcome should be clear.

Chris Mullin

Saturday, 3 April 1999

The evening news shows Macedonia police beating back refugees. A huge convoy of misery stretches back ten miles into Kosovo. Exhausted desperate people pleading for help. The very old and the very young are beginning to die. What somehow makes it worse is that they look so like us. They have trainers and baby carriers and even cars. The Man was on TV this evening guaranteeing that they will return home one day. An empty promise.

Chris Mullin

Sunday, 4 April 1999

I am hugely depressed about Kosovo. Those loathsome, verminous gypsies; and the poor brave Serbs. The whole crisis is media-driven. Editors have no idea of or respect for the truth. They are concerned simply with scooping their rivals and/or pre-empting counter-scoops. But an orthodoxy of public indignation is built up, stoked up you could say, and the politicians have to respond ...

I have spoken in the Commons debate, written in the *Observer*, been several times on television – but no one is interested.

Alan Clark

Friday, 16 April 1999
Bethnal Green and Bow

My constituency surgery this afternoon started at 2.30 pm and lasted six hours. As usual I saw loads of desperate people suffering the utmost misery. For the first time, I felt I couldn't face writing all those letters which might have no effect at all. I looked at the woman across the desk, alone, petrified, disabled with lupus, clutching her crutches, tears smeared across her cheeks. Drowning but not crushed. No family, no friends, no money. Anthea's only inheritance was a National Insurance number. Unlike Anthea, the socially included will never know their National Insurance number by heart. She was only twenty-one. How did she get here?

Oona King

Friday, 21 May 1999
Saltwood Castle

Talked this morning to 'Dr Thomas Stuttaford' (no, actually, I did) whom Jane brilliantly spotted as writing on depression. He v splendid, quick and almost reassuring. Said I could be dosed (there is a school of doctors who think in these terms) remedially with Serotonin. 'Replenishes' (sic) the brain. I don't hugely like the sound of this.

Max [a tame jackdaw] is around, flies down benignly; a very different kind of presence. I give him didgys from the Early Morning Tea tin.

Alan Clark

Wednesday, 9 June 1999

In the evening I chaired a meeting on Agent Orange for the Britain–Vietnam Association. About twenty-five people attended, including a man from Monsanto, one of the companies which used to make the stuff. We were addressed by Hugh Warwick an ecologist, and then watched a video showing the horrendous birth defects that are alleged to have resulted [from the US spraying crops with defoliant in the Vietnam War] … the victims were mainly poor peasants living in utter poverty.

The war in Kosovo seems to be over. The Serbs finally put their thumbprints on a timetable for withdrawal at around nine o'clock this evening.

The first contingent of troops under General Mike Jackson is expected to go in tomorrow.

Chris Mullin

Monday, 14 June 1999

Westminster

Go on the *Today* programme to comment on Labour's appalling results in the European parliamentary elections. We end up with 29 seats to the Tories' 36. I say that our campaign was 'abysmal' and that we had no strategy or organisation. We provided no reason at all for our voters to turn out. By contrast, Hague, though making no converts, was able to mobilise his Euro-sceptic Tory vote. The result is not only bad for Labour but also for pro-Europeans …

But how are we to turn public opinion if [Blair and Brown] continue to keep their heads down?

Giles Radice

Wednesday, 14 July 1999

Gordon Brown addressed the party meeting. Never has a Labour Chancellor had such a good story to tell and Gordon made the most of it. Unemployment at a twenty year low; inflation down to 1960s levels, oodles of money being pumped into the public sector. And, coming shortly, the Working Families Tax Credit which will make the lowest paid families up to £60 a week better off.

These days Gordon exudes an aura of competence and self-confidence which, in opposition, he lacked. At last, a Labour Chancellor who is not at the mercy of events.

Chris Mullin

Friday, 6 August 1999

Visited Jonathan Aitken at Stanford Hill Prison. It is a good twelve miles from the station [and] my ever more valued friend Andrew met me at Maidstone.

Jonathan is studying for his theological degree with the possibility of becoming a clergyman. He wakes at five every morning and spends the next two hours in prayer and Bible reading. So we all had a good religious confabulation.

Jonathan told us he has a prayer partner, a Roman Catholic. Although he is an Anglican, Jonathan recently became godfather to his prayer partner's baby. At the end Jonathan delivered a wonderful prayer and I did my best in turn.

He certainly has an electric quality similar to Tony Blair.

Lord Longford

Friday, 10 September 1999

I have been granted the pre-conference interview with the Leader of the Opposition. (Perhaps no one else wanted it?) I went to see him at Central Office in Smith Square.

I had a good hour with William [Hague], but I came away with nothing. Seb (who sat in attendance at the interview with the glossy-lipped Amanda Platell)* claims his boss is 'the most qualified man who ever wanted to be Prime Minister'. Denis Healey says he's a twerp. I reckon the Whitelaw maxim may be nearer the mark. William is 38, a considerable achiever, likeable, clear-headed, quick-witted, rational, reasonable, intelligent, articulate, thoughtful, shrewd. But something's missing. I was impressed, I wasn't moved. I was charmed but not inspired. In theatrical terms, he is a first-class leading man; he knows the lines, he won't bump into the furniture, he'll never miss a performance. But he isn't a star in the way Blair is. He won't be Prime Minister. (Foreign Secretary perhaps, twenty years from now, in our next administration.)

Gyles Brandreth

---

* Sebastian Coe was Chief of Staff to William Hague; Amanda Platell was Hague's press secretary. Gyles Brandreth was defeated in Chester in 1997 and returned to journalism and other professions.

Saturday, 11 September 1999

Last weekend, in an *Observer* interview, TB called for a new 'moral purpose' in Britain. It was totally vacuous and was made up just to give us a good story after two twelve year old girls were found to have got themselves pregnant. But it worked and gave us a good talking point for several days until Alan Clark's death.*

Lance Price

Tuesday, 14 September 1999

Lunch with the British Airports Authority top brass, who included Des Wilson, founder of the homeless charity Shelter. It was preceded by a briefing which revealed that demand for air services is growing at an astonishing rate, especially in the south-east which accounts for about 80 per cent of traffic (although none of them want an airport in their backyard, of course). By 2015, even assuming that terminal five is built at Heathrow, all the main airports will be choked to capacity with no prospect of further expansion. Until now it seems to have been a case of Predict and Provide. Exactly the mess we have got ourselves into with the motor car. Sooner or later politicians are going to have to pluck up the courage to call a halt. Needless to say the airport fraternity won't be satisfied until they have concreted over every blade of grass. Des Wilson (once a great radical, now a corporate fat cat) seemed to think that the right to cheap holidays took precedence over all other considerations. He bleated about all the business we would lose. So be it. One day we shall have to go back to being peasants. There are times when I think it can't come soon enough.

Chris Mullin

Monday, 27 September–Wednesday, 29 September 1999
Labour Party Conference, Bournemouth

[Gordon Brown] promises 'Socialism, credible and radical', ending child poverty and getting rid of unemployment. And he ends by saying that 'We have only just begun.' He gets a rapturous standing ovation.

Tuesday is Tony Blair's turn – he makes a good speech which he

---

* Alan Clark died on 5 September 1999 from a brain tumour.

spoils by going over the top at the end. He says that the old-style class war is over but the struggle for new-style equality – giving everyone an opportunity – has only just begun.

But the finale is over the top: 'And now at last, party and nation are joined in the same cause for the same purpose: to set our people free.' Who needs bishops when you have got Tony Blair?

Giles Radice

Thursday, 14 October 1999
Ministerial visit to Liverpool

Our first call was the Housing Action Trust set up by the Tories to take over a huge slice of Liverpool's worst public housing which the city council was incapable of managing. Most of the Trust's 67 tower blocks are in the process of being demolished and replaced with good quality low rise. It was given a huge sum of money – £260 million – and told to get on with it. Needless to say there was a lot of squealing from Derek Hatton and friends,* but from what I saw it's a great success. I can't remember what Old Labour's line on Housing Action Trusts was, but I bet we were opposed. Something else the Tories were right about.

Liverpool City Council, now run by Liberals, has seen the light and is getting out of housing management. We visited two other estates. One which had been handed over to a housing association and transformed and one which was just about to be. On one we witnessed two large black dogs attacking a villainous looking youth while the owner, another obvious villain, was trying to get them under control. Afterwards the villain who had been attacked beat one of the dogs soundly with a belt. I was later told that the dogs were Neapolitans, which are said to be fiercer than Rottweilers. The villain apparently owned six. As one of my hosts remarked, 'You can't accuse us of stage-managing your visit.'

Chris Mullin

---

* Derek Hatton had been deputy leader of Liverpool City Council in the 1980s and a supporter of the Militant tendency, which many in the Labour Party blamed for Liverpool's troubles; Militant members were gradually expelled from the Labour Party after 1983.

Tuesday, 19 October 1999

Philip Gould analysed our problem very clearly. We don't know what we are. Gordon wants us to be a radical, progressive government but thinks we should keep our heads down on Europe. Peter [Mandelson] thinks we are a quasi-Conservative Party but that we should stick our necks out on Europe. Philip didn't say this, but I think TB either can't make up his mind or wants to be both at the same time.

Lance Price

Tuesday, 30 November 1999

A historic day. At about 11.00 the Commons vote through the order returning powers to Stormont. The peace process is at last beginning to roll, thanks to the patience of George Mitchell* and the courage of David Trimble. David Trimble has faced down the hardline Ulster Unionists and received their backing of his party for setting up the Northern Ireland Executive. Now it is up to Sinn Fein and the IRA to deliver on decommissioning.

Giles Radice

Friday, 31 December 1999

Millennium Eve. We queued for hours. The police and London Underground apologised for any inconvenience caused by the unexpectedly large crowds. How could the crowds be unexpected? It was the Millennium. Although the police knew 10,000 people would be travelling to the Dome via Stratford Station, they only brought *one* X-ray machine.

Oona King

Saturday, 1 January 2000

A new century. My grandchildren, who I hope to survive long enough to meet, will live into the twenty second century. What kind of world will they inherit? The planet is in a worse state now than at any time in my life. Beyond fortress Europe and North America much of the world is in meltdown. In Africa there are countries where all civilised

---

* George J. Mitchell, a former US Senator, was appointed US Special Envoy for Northern Ireland by the Clinton administration.

life has collapsed. Afghanistan has returned to barbarism. The Balkans are in turmoil and even as I write the Russians are bombing Chechnya into the stone age. Already refugees from the chaos are placing strains on the political and social fabric of the developed world that may in due course become unbearable. We should not imagine as we sit smug behind our increasingly fortified frontiers that our civilisation can survive unscathed.

Our main problem of course, is not other people's wars. It is that we have invented an economic system which is consuming the resources of the planet as if there were no tomorrow – and there might not be unless we change our ways. In the United States, the home of the world's most voracious consumers, there is no sign at all that the political process is capable of persuading – or indeed has any desire to persuade – citizens to adopt a sustainable lifestyle. All over the democratic world, politicians increasingly follow rather than lead. And even if an ecological disaster were to occur (perhaps it has already begun) the price will be paid by those least responsible and least capable of protecting themselves. Indeed the consumers of the developed world may not even notice. To crown it all, the emerging economies of Asia are falling over themselves to emulate the mistakes that we have made. Indeed they insist that it is their right to do so.

Maybe, just maybe, this will be the century in which we learn to reduce, reuse and recycle our waste, develop benign sources of food and energy and stop burning up the ozone layer. Maybe Europe will lead the way and others will follow. Who knows, there ought to be money to be made out of going green, in which case capitalism will enjoy a new lease of life.

Or maybe it is too late.

Chris Mullin

Monday, 12 January 2000

At 3.30 we had a statement by Jack Straw explaining why he was going to let Pinochet go.* I got in a question comparing the wars against Iraq and Yugoslavia, when innocent people were killed and it was justified

* General Augusto Pinochet had been visiting London for medical treatment in 1998 when he was detained under an international arrest warrant for crimes against humanity, committed during his period of office in Chile as President, 1973–90. Four thousand Chileans were murdered or disappeared. Home Secretary Jack Straw ultimately allowed his release on medical grounds and he returned to Chile.

on humanitarian grounds, with the release of a torturer on humanitarian grounds. The 'ethical foreign policy' is finished. I was the only person who spoke against it.

Tony Benn

Sunday, 21 January 2000

Tennis at Queen's with Ann [Spicer] and Malcolm Pearson. Malcolm still flirting with UKIP. Nigel Farage rings him to say for £2 million he will call off candidates in some seats, including mine. I tell him (again) – don't touch them.*

Michael Spicer

Thursday, 3 February 2000

Gordon is still diddling around. We discovered via the *Telegraph*, that he's planning a tour of 'heartland' areas. He's also doing a speech on Britishness, trying to argue that despite devolution etc., being British still means something. It also helps portray New Labour as 'patriotic' and defends us a bit from the European arguments we'll face at the election.

Lance Price

Friday, 31 March 2000

How about this for a piece of new Labour claptrap?

> Dear Chris
> I am writing to give you advance notice that Sunderland is one of the local authority areas we have identified to be part of an enlarged Excellence in Cities (EIC) programme ... I don't have to tell you what good news this is ... In the next few weeks we shall be asking schools and authorities to form partnerships to develop EIC plans. These will create new patterns of provision – Beacon and Specialist schools; small Education Action Zones;

---

* Nigel Farage was UK Independence Party MEP for South East England, later leader of UKIP; Malcolm Pearson was a Conservative peer who later joined UKIP and was briefly its leader in 2009.

school-based city learning centres; learning mentors and enriched opportunities for gifted and talented children.

Best wishes
David Blunkett

Goodness knows what all this means, although I am sure it is all terribly worthy. No wonder the teachers are so bewildered.

Chris Mullin

Tuesday, 2 May 2000

There was a statement today by Jack Straw about the demonstration in London yesterday, which I should have reported. At the TUC May Day demonstration 15,000 people marched on Trafalgar Square (there was not a word on the BBC about that). The news concentrated on two or three incidents that occurred in the anti-capitalist demonstration. First of all, the statue of Churchill in Parliament Square was daubed and someone put a slice of turf on Churchill's head so that it looked like a Mohican haircut; and then the Cenotaph was daubed with graffiti. And somebody smashed McDonald's in Victoria Street. Of course that's what the television cameras were waiting for – and they just covered it and covered it.

The BBC is not remotely interested in an argument abut globalisation or capitalism; they're only interested in trouble, and of course that means that if you want coverage you make trouble.

Tony Benn

Thursday, 18 May 2000
On the train from Oxford

Ed Balls is on the train.

He congratulates me on my pamphlet on the euro and says that the decision on entry will be made in the new parliament. I get the impression from Ed Balls that for Gordon Brown winning a third term (and thus ensuring his premiership) is more important than entering the euro, so Gordon will be extremely cautious about joining.

Giles Radice

Wednesday, 24 May 2000

Linger over dinner in the Members' dining room with John Major. I say to him at one point, 'Historians will puzzle over where you really stood on Maastricht.' He smiles and makes no audible response. I suppose that is how he became Prime Minister in the first place.

Michael Spicer

Monday, 17 July 2000

The Murdoch press has got hold of a memorandum, dated April 29, written by The Man himself which is, to put it mildly, embarrassing. For a man whose greatest strength is his ability to think long term it is remarkably shallow and short term. There is an air of panic running through it. He focuses on five issues – the Martin case,* asylum, crime, defence and the family. 'These things add up to a sense that the Government – and this even applies to me – are somehow out of touch with gut British instincts.' He goes on to call for 'eye-catching initiatives'. Example: 'Locking up street muggers … something tough with immediate bite.' (No doubt this is the origin of Jack Straw's nasty little bill, to mete out rough justice to football hooligans, that is currently keeping us up half the night.) Needless to say the Tories and the media are having great fun. It is another spectacular own goal.

Chris Mullin

Tuesday, 12 September 2000

Astonishingly, we are now in the middle of a national crisis. Panic buying has led to most petrol stations (operating on a 'just in time' basis) rapidly running dry. People are saying, 'What are the government doing about it?' Tony Blair, who has cancelled all his engagements, says that he will not give in to blackmail (it is not clear what the blockaders are asking for – a special deal for hauliers? A cut in our stiff fuel taxes? Help for farmers?)† and that, having consulted the oil

---

* Farmer Tony Martin had shot a burglar who had entered his home and was charged with murder: it raised a very passionate public debate on victims' rights of self-defence against criminals.

† The blockade of oil depots was undertaken by various groups including lorry drivers, hauliers and countryside campaigners such as Farmers for Action.

companies, things will be beginning to get back to normal in 'twenty four hours.' This last commitment seems a hostage to fortune ...

Giles Radice

Wednesday, 20 September 2000

Lord Melchett, the executive director of Greenpeace, and the Greenpeace demonstrators were released after being acquitted in court or criminal damage against a genetically modified crop, which they said might pollute neighbouring fields.

Even the media is beginning to notice the fact that politics is now the politics of the streets. That's where all political ideas begin and they end up in Parliament, so there's nothing very strange about it.

Tony Benn

Tuesday, 26 September 2000

Labour Party Conference, Brighton

Possibly my last as an MP.

Labour conferences have changed greatly. Today, they are big business with visitors, the media and lobbyists of one sort or another greatly outnumbering the delegates. They're now much more showcases for party leaders than party conferences where policy is decided. They are usually far less dramatic than they were when party members were at each others' throats. But at least they help rather than hinder the party's standing with the voters.

Looking much older than the fresh-faced young Lochinvar who first spoke to Conference as leader in 1994, Blair begins by admitting mistakes on the Dome and the paltry 75p [old age] pensions' increase. On the Dome, he says: 'If I had my time again I would have listened to those who said that governments shouldn't try to run big visitor attractions.' On the fuel crisis he says that he is listening. But he is also listening about underfunding in the NHS and education. 'The test of leadership in politics is not how eloquently you say Yes. It's how you explain why you're saying No ...' Lots of cheers.

Giles Radice

Thursday, 5 October 2000

A wonderful day. The Yugoslavs liberate themselves from Milosevic.

As in Poland, Czechoslovakia, Romania and East Germany, the people have won. What has happened in Belgrade today completes the democratic revolution in Europe begun in Poland in 1989. The storming of the Parliament in Belgrade joins the unforgettable image – the day the Berlin Wall came down, the great crowds in Wenceslas Square in Prague, the savagery in the streets of Bucharest. A great day for Serbia and for Europe!

Giles Radice

Friday, 6 October 2000

Blair's made a big speech in Poland in which he says the European Union must be a superpower but not a super-state, which is a typical spin doctor's phrase. What the hell does it mean? A superpower has nuclear weapons. Is Europe going to have nuclear weapons?

He wants to enlarge the EU within four years to include Eastern Europe, and that will no doubt mean Serbia. It's quite obvious that a development is in progress that will obliterate democracy.

Tony Benn

Tuesday, 24 October–Friday, 27 October 2000
Treasury Select Committee visit to the USA

The next day at Washington we are received by Alan Greenspan. Received is the right word, as Greenspan has become an almost mythical presence.

We note that Greenspan has, perhaps unwisely, abandoned some of the central banker's inherent caution. He has now joined Abby Cohen as one of the believers in the American 'productivity' miracle. Further growth, high asset and stock prices are justified by a basic technological shift. Of course he points out that the fundamentals of economics have not changed and says that there could even be a pronounced downturn. Whether the US upsurge proves in the end to be soundly based or more likely a South Sea bubble, Greenspan remains for now a colossus before whom either George W Bush or Al Gore will have to abase himself.

Giles Radice

Saturday, 4 November 2000

The doctors saw Caroline today and helped to relieve her pain.*

I realised what an international world we live in. Beatrice, who comes in the morning as a district nurse, is from Nigeria, and there's another nurse from Australia. Irene Chan is a Malaysian Chinese. When Caroline went in last time to Hospital, George Lee, the surgeon, was himself a Chinese from Singapore. His boss, the consultant, is Mr Patel, who's an Indian. We've had carers from the Philippines, from St Vincent, from Kenya, from Hungary. We are part of a world community.

Tony Benn

Wednesday, 8 November 2000

I went to bed last night after early exit polls predicted that Al Gore had won Florida – and therefore the presidency. I woke up this morning to the horrific news that Florida swung the other way and George W Bush is President. The news is so bad, so abominable that nothing can make it better. I feel truly sickened. The leader of the free world is a moron, and the future of the world hangs in the balance.

Oona King

Thursday, 21 December 2000
Department of Employment, Transport and the Regions

Today I saved the taxpayer £1.5 million. Officials came to me with a plan for yet more research into the effect of aircraft noise on sleep. 'What's the point?' I asked. 'Whatever the conclusions, you are still going to tell me that nothing can be done about night flights.' I refused to authorise any more research. They weren't at all happy and no doubt as soon as I am out of the door, they will put it under the nose

---

* Caroline Benn was suffering from cancer and Tony Benn had decided to give up his seat at the forthcoming General Election (2001) to care for her. She died on 22 November 2000.

of whoever succeeds me. Nevertheless, I felt for once that I had done something useful.

Also, I finally managed to wring out of officials in the Aviation Division details of the number of airline employees who have passes to the Department. I obviously touched a raw nerve because I had to ask half a dozen times over a period of several weeks. The answer is that, between them, British Airways, Virgin and British Midland have ten passes and the charter airlines have another four. I'm not sure there is anything very wicked about it, but the fact that merely asking the question proves so upsetting for officials makes me wonder.

Chris Mullin

Tuesday, 9 January 2001

Crashed [the new car] on the way home. I can't explain how distressing it was ... the first time I drove it. I never crashed the banger once in eight years.

Tiberio was standing with the light on in the bedroom looking out, and he'd been waiting for me three hours. I had such a bad feeling. He calmly told me he wanted to leave me, because he'd had enough of waiting for me all night, of me never being home because I was at the House of Commons, because I was married to the constituency not to him. I said, 'What, you're going to leave me because I crashed the car? I'm really sorry I crashed the car but give me a break.'

'No,' he said, 'this is how I felt during the whole holiday, this is how I've felt for the past year.'

It boils down to this: he doesn't see me, he doesn't have a life with me, and he wants a partner who is a partner, not a ghost. He is going to find out if his office can move him to Italy, and if that happens we should separate.

Westminster isn't life. Some sad people make it their life entirely. But it's not. There's nothing there, beyond the chandeliers and the bars and the men in tights. It's not somewhere you want to live, and that's the worst thing about this job; you're *forced* to live there. It's a posh boarding school with crap food.

Oona King

Wednesday, 17 January 2001

House of Commons

[I] tell Gordon Brown about my decision (to stand down). Gordon is very charming, as he can be in private, but would clearly prefer me to stay.

He is fascinated by my Crosland, Jenkins and Healey book (*Friends and Rivals*), obviously seeing its relevance to the Blair–Brown relationship. 'Despite all the difficulties you and Tony are bound together by hoops of steel.' Gordon doesn't contradict me, though he says it is 'complicated'. Half-jokingly I threaten to write a book about Tony and Gordon. 'We are not going to end in failure, like your heroes,' predicts Gordon.

Today is also the day of the Hunting Bill. I am a very 'reluctant abolitionist.' I think hunting is barbaric but I remain worried by the liberty issue. The abolitionist position gets a large majority, though it will be blocked in the Lords. So ends a traumatic day. I have two strong whiskies with Charles Clarke in the Smoking Room.

Giles Radice

Tuesday, 6 February 2001

To a meeting addressed by a retired American admiral called Gene Carroll; he'd come over specially to help with the campaign against the proposed US National Missile Defense System ('Star Wars'). The Admiral said that the Star Wars programme was unnecessary and costly. There was no enemy; it was easy to deliver weapons to the United States, and you could attack New York using a Panamanian ship with a bomb in the hold. He said that the American policy was now 'layered defence' – that is to say, defence at every level – and that laser weapons could be in permanent orbit, which could shoot down other missiles and satellites and could pinpoint and destroy Earth targets; if this happened the United States would totally dominate space and indeed would dominate the world.

He did also say that fear of China was a dominant consideration. 'There is no enemy facing the United States but fear of China is a real fear.' There were huge profits to be made by Boeing, Lockheed and Raytheon and that was really what it was about.

Tony Benn

Sunday, 20 May 2001

Going into Settle this morning we pass a lorry at Austwick loaded with the carcasses of slaughtered sheep* and find the main car park now given over to vehicles, bulldozers and all the paraphernalia of this dreadful travelling circus. Though for the soldiers and the slaughtermen the work must now be just a wearisome routine, cars still slow to watch the mound of carcasses slither down the ramps and it's hard not to think it's but a step from this to the more terrible slaughters that go on in Eastern Europe.

Alan Bennett

Thursday, 31 May 2001

To Doxford International, to visit One2One, a mobile telephone call centre, employing 1,200 people. Doxford is a big success. Altogether 7,500 people are employed there, mainly in jobs that didn't exist ten years ago, some in industries that didn't exist – mobile phones for example. Their fathers and grandfathers worked in shipyards and coal mines and they have graduated to computer screens. For all the sneers that call centres attract from metropolitan journalists, I doubt whether a single one of those employed there would trade his computer for the coalface.

I was shown around by a tall, Hispanic-looking man who appeared to come from another planet. His opening words were, 'What do you hope to get out of the next half hour?' He spoke a language with which I am unfamiliar using words like 'skill-sets' and 'functionality'; his workers were divided into 'communities.' Overhead a banner proclaimed that this or that community had won this month's award for 'A monopoly of Excellence.'

Chris Mullin

---

*Foot and mouth disease swept through herds of sheep and cattle across the country during 2001: ten million animals were killed to halt the disease.

Thursday, 7 June 2001

Worcestershire West

Polling night is, in the words of the young, 'really scary'. Torbay falls early on to Liberals with a swing of 8 per cent and Guildford goes later with a swing of 4.5 pr cent; these swings would have ended me …

Ann and I arrive at [my count] shaking a bit. Wonderful surprise to find Edward there [the Spicers' son]; he has come out of the blue to give support in the event that disaster strikes. As it happens, get a pro-Tory swing of 2.5 per cent rather against the national trend, especially to Liberals.

Michael Spicer

Thursday, 19 July 2001

Home on the 20.00. I sat with David Davis* as far as Doncaster. We discussed the Tory leadership election. He thinks Iain Duncan Smith will win easily. Clarke, he says, would be absolutely untenable given his views on Europe. Portillo, he says, would have lost anyway. 'No one trusts him.'

He is confident that we will make a mess of reforming the NHS. What's needed, he says, is a mixed economy with some hospitals handed over completely to the private sector, and we will never dare do that.

Chris Mullin

Tuesday, 4 September 2001

There are mass redundancies in the electronics industry – Marconi, Hewlett Packard, Compaq – all over the world. I've never wanted to believe there was a slump coming because, although socialists are supposed to welcome the collapse of capitalism, I know perfectly well it ends up with right-wing politics, and indeed already the argument over the asylum-seekers is getting more and more bitter. David Blunkett is complaining to the French that they are setting up another refugee camp near the Channel Tunnel and Eurostar. We are recruiting

---

* David Davis was Conservative MP for Haltemprice and Howden, Yorkshire: once seen as a potential Conservative leader.

teachers from Eastern Europe to fill the gap in our schools ... It is becoming like a jungle. I am getting discouraged.

There's a new Education White Paper out today, which calls for more religious schools. Religious schools, at a time when all that is going on in Northern Ireland is absolutely mad!

Tony Benn

Tuesday, 11 September 2001

Convalescing in Newick, East Sussex

Two engineers arrived this morning to install ONdigital for me in time for the match [Arsenal v Real Mallorca].

I lay on the sofa as Grande [grandmother] prepared a nice pizza for lunch.

Just after two the *Mirror* newsdesk called and said the World Trade Center had been hit by a plane. I switched to Sky and saw a small plume of smoke coming out of one of the twin towers. Just seemed like a tragic accident. 'Keep an eye on it, but it looks like a light aircraft to me, which is a tragedy but not a huge story over here.'

I carried on watching and about twenty minutes later the presenter Kay Burley said we were watching footage of the plane actually hitting the tower, from Fox News.

Only we weren't. She very quickly realised this was *live* and we had seen a second plane hit the *other* tower. 'We saw it – we saw it! That was a big plane, this isn't an accident, it can't be.'

I looked back at the screen. A huge ball of flame was coming out of the second tower, and Sky were already speculating about terrorism.

Dad came in to see how I was ... We both watched in horror.

Then one of the ONdigital engineers asked if he could switch channels to test the football output.

'No, no, can't you see – the twin towers have been hit. Thousands of people work in there.'

Grande arrived with my pizza. 'Sorry, I've got to go,' I said and hobbled slowly upstairs to find a suit.

Piers Morgan

Tuesday, 11 September 2001

Driving up the M40 Jessica, my secretary, rings to tell me about the terrorist attacks in America.

Drive straight to Central Office. Mood is hardening to postpone everything [the Conservative Party leadership election]. I am moving to this view as the ghastliness of the whole business unfolds. It's Pearl Harbour without a known enemy ...

Talk to Hague, then to Clarke and Duncan Smith; we reach an agreement that Hague will make low-key announcement of a 24-hour delay in the count. I put out a message on the pager to colleagues.

Michael Spicer

Thursday, 13 September 2001
London

TB's worry was that GWB [George Bush] would turn inwards ... He felt now was the time to bind in as much international support as possible. He felt a big military hit combined with a big international effort of support and long-term agenda for terrorism was the way to go ... TB was quite troubled afterwards [following a phone call with Bush], said we had to think of a way of getting to the US for a face-to-face meeting. He said he needed to see him in a room, and look in his eyes, not do all this on phone calls with 15 people listening in. TB went through his assessment of the US plan – ultimatum to yield up OBL [Osama bin Laden] and then let outside body move in to get rid of camps. Alternatively, hit OBL straight away, possibly going for the Taliban. And the next step is to look to other countries, including Iraq, and other countries not even linked to OBL. He said their instinct was to resolve the WMD question quickly. We need to consider what such a strategy would be and what part we would play in it ... Geoff [Hoon, Defence Secretary] said [Donald] Rumsfeld had been looking for reasons to hit Iraq. They definitely wanted regime change and that was the channel of advice Bush has been getting since the election. Jack [Straw] said they would be mad to do Iraq without justification because they will lose world opinion. TB said 'My job is to try to steer them in a sensible path.' He said we had to separate these two missions. He said their line of argument will be that it does not matter whether you did the Trade Centre, if you are in the business of terrorism, then we are going to put you out of business. It's possible to be sympathetic to that but the political consequences are all too obvious.

Alastair Campbell

Monday, 24 September 2001

Several of today's papers carry a picture of about twenty westernised Arab youngsters, boys and girls, in front of a pink Cadillac. Everyone looks happy and relaxed. Ringed, in the middle row, is a thin young man in a green skinny rib jumper and flared purple trousers. He is happy, too. This is Osama bin Laden and some of his many brothers and sisters, on holiday in Sweden, 30 years ago. In those far off days, before the earth changed places with the sky. Before everything went so terribly, terribly wrong.

Chris Mullin

Wednesday, 26 September 2001

Tower Hamlets

People are saying the whole world will come to a standstill; the airline industry will shut down, the tourist industry will collapse, an industry relying on travel – a key component of globalisation – will fall apart. September 11th will trigger a depression like that of the 1930s. The days of milk and honey are over. I don't think they were ever here. But September 11th marks a change: because of this new terrorism there is now the prospect of arbitrary death for a minuscule number of people in the West. Before, arbitrary death was mainly inflicted upon vast numbers of poor people in developing countries.

Oona King

Thursday, 4 October 2001

Recall of Parliament

Everyone knows that we were being recalled to discuss a military assault on the Taliban to close down the use of Afghanistan as a base for world terror.

There was no doubt today that [the House's] mood was one of overwhelming resolve to take necessary action against Al-Qaida ... The very Members who would normally have reservations about military action are also those who are most respectful of international cooperation. Today they found it impossible flatly to resist military action, given the impressive global coalition that has been assembled against the Taliban and the clear mandate of the United Nations.

Robin Cook

Friday, 26 October 2001
Livingston, Scotland

A day in the constituency. The only tricky bit of the day was the visit to my local mosque. You are always left at a psychological disadvantage on these visits. First they take your shoes away, which leaves those of us from another culture feeling vulnerable. Then you have to remain standing because there is not a chair in sight across the wide expanse of the mosque carpet. Finally you are entirely surrounded by a circle of the community elders, each of whom can count on total solidarity from everyone else encircling you.

As always there was good humour in the discussion ... For all that, they were unanimously against the military action in Afghanistan. The fundamental problem is that it is not perceived as a targeted campaign against terrorists or the Taliban, but a war against the people of Afghanistan.

Robin Cook

Tuesday, 13 November 2001
Home Affairs Select Committee in Manchester

A morning visiting drugs projects. Everywhere we asked people what they would do and most, but by no means all, replied that they would move towards decriminalising, starting with heroin. One of the most vehement was a police superintendent, another a Methodist minister. Decriminalisation, of course, would bring its own problems. One woman said, 'I worry that we shall become as complacent towards drugs as we are towards alcohol.' GPs will not be keen to have addicts shooting up in their surgeries. There would also be a problem with leakage – prescribed drugs finding their way into the black market. We talked to a couple of addicts, one of whom had just come back from Germany, where he said they have 'shooting galleries'. Safe houses where heroin can be injected in private and needles properly disposed of, instead of being left around in streets.

Chris Mullin

Wednesday, 14 November 2001

Kabul has fallen, along with Jalalabad and Herat. Our new friends in the Northern Alliance are rolling up the map with hardly a shot being fired. The Man made a statement. He did it very well. There was no triumphalism although he must be mightily relieved. No one expected this. A week ago there was talk on all sides that the war would last all winter and now it could be over in a matter of days.

Chris Mullin

Saturday, 1 December 2001

Got a taxi to the Albert Hall for the Bootleg Beatles. Stephen [Benn] had got tickets for the whole family, bless his old heart. He's so efficient! It was a fabulous performance, and it has been a huge success … the audience stood up and cheered and waved their hands – a lot of middle-aged people, I was probably one of the very oldest people there. There were also a lot of young people, who seemed to enjoy it just as much.

Just before I go to bed – there's been a huge suicide bomb in Jerusalem, 130 people injured or killed, and this violence goes on and on and on, on both sides, and the argument that the other side only understands force is what the Americans are saying about the Al Qaeda, what the Islamic Jihad say about the Israelis, and at some stage, you do really have to think of some other way of solving problems.

Tony Benn

Tuesday, 15 January 2002

To the Wilson Room in Portcullis House to hear Jack Straw, who had just come from talking to Colin Powell about America's treatment of the Taliban prisoners.* 'I told Powell, "This isn't doing America any good." He understands.'

---

* Once prisoners (or enemy combatants) from the Afghan War and others implicated

580

Afterwards I remarked to Jack that, although political realities dictated that we had to be nice to him we should never lose sight of the fact that George Bush and the Republican Party represented – I was going to say, 'some of the meanest, greediest, most selfish people on the planet', but Jack finished the sentence for me: 'a bunch of bastards.'

Chris Mullin

Wednesday, 13 February 2002

Had a terrible problem with my electricity supply. London Electricity came to cut me off saying I'd transferred to npower. I said I hadn't. I rang npower, but they didn't know anything about it. I rang London Electricity, they gave me a reference number. I rang npower again, they said it was a mistake. I rang London Electricity back, and they said this happens two or three times a day in London. What an outrage it is!

Tony Benn

Tuesday, 19 February 2002
Sunderland

In the company of management I toured the Dewhirst Menswear factories at Hendon and Pennywell. Row after row of women in yellow smocks sitting at machines which ingeniously cut, stitch, press and iron in accordance with instructions from a computer. The end result of which is six thousand Marks & Spencer suits a week. The problem, which no amount of scientific organisation can avert, is that the same skills are available in Morocco for a fifth of the price and in China for, who knows – a tenth? Now M&S has bowed to the inevitable. Result: a question mark hangs over the entire Dewhirst operation. 'We are staring at a black hole,' said John Haley, the managing director. They are desperately trying to diversify. The only practical option is America, where there is a market for volume menswear. The only

in the 9/11 attacks began to arrive at a special American prison at Guantánamo Bay, Cuba, a debate began on their status and their future prosecution, and the applicability of the Geneva Conventions on War to the men. Donald Rumsfeld stated that al-Qaeda and Taliban members were not entitled to prisoner of war status. Colin Powell was at that time Secretary of State in the US government.

problem is that the home of free trade imposes a 23 percent tariff on textile imports from the UK. So much for the special relationship.

Chris Mullin

Wednesday, 27 February 2002

I scrambled to catch the Eurostar to a meeting of the PES [Party of European Socialists] and steamed into two growing storm clouds for Britain over the Channel. The first arises from the Blair–Berlusconi summit in Rome which has provoked uproar in the Italian left and their close sympathisers in the Mediterranean countries. It doesn't help that Berlusconi hailed this as a new 'Anglo-Italian axis' ... It is preposterous to sign a joint declaration celebrating liberalisation of the economy with a man who has just hobbled the courts in case they imagine that liberalisation and the rule of law applies to his companies.

The other problem rests in deep anxiety about what George Bush intends to do around the world, and that problem will increase as he gets on with it. There is particular concern tonight about the possibility that he will take action against Iraq. I share the deep concerns about how quickly the United States has moved from building a global coalition against terror, to reverting to a unilateralist foreign policy.

Robin Cook

Saturday, 30 March 2002

My 37th birthday and I was looking forward to spending a night's entertainment in the fleshpots of London when a phone call came through [from the *Mirror*] mid-afternoon saying the Queen Mother had died. I wish I could say my first reaction was to bow my head and pay silent tribute to Her Majesty for all she'd done for this country in her amazing life, before racing to the newsroom.

But all I could think was that she had died on a Saturday. Every single royal who has died in my lifetime – Diana, Margaret and now the Queen Mother – died on a Saturday. Which means a third beautifully crafted supplement disappearing into the bin. The number of hours that go into these things can't be overstated – thousands over the years, constantly updating and revising. All gone, because the Sundays have enough time to do their own, that they too will have carefully worked on for decades.

A sad day though; she was a wonderful old bird. 'Never explain, never complain and never speak in public,' she used to say. And that's how she got away with a constant £4 million overdraft and extravagant lunch parties every day, yet still the public loved her.

Piers Morgan

Tuesday, 16 April 2002

Good '1992' dinner. Everyone very supportive of Liam Fox view of NHS: must break up state monopoly and give purchasing power to consumer. Sit next to the doughty Ann Winterton. She is determined that we are going to press for renegotiation of the Treaty of Rome re fisheries. We must support her.

Michael Spicer

Wednesday, 1 May 2002

Andrew MacKinlay dropped a little bombshell at this afternoon's meeting of the parliamentary committee. Apparently, under the Freedom of Information Act, by January 2005 Members' expenses will be subject to public scrutiny, retrospectively. Goodness knows what mayhem that will cause. 'We are in a jam,' said Robin Cook [Leader of the House]. 'Few members have yet tumbled to the juggernaut heading their way.'

Chris Mullin

Tuesday, 16 July 2002
Daily Mirror

Gordon Brown made a tremendous pre-Budget speech yesterday that many believed signalled the start of his charge to Number 10. At the same time a brilliant picture of a large elephant tossing a baby elephant with its trunk came in. So I splashed on that picture with an inset of Brown towering over Blair in the Commons and the headline PACK YOUR TRUNK TONY, I'M IN CHARGE. It was only when I looked at it this morning that I realised it was a ridiculous page that didn't work on any level at all, other than in my weird little mind. It's embarrassing.

Rebekah married Ross Kemp last month in Las Vegas and it's their wedding party tomorrow night. He's an amusing guy, much brighter and more amusing than Grant Mitchell.*

Piers Morgan

Wednesday, 24 July 2002

The stock market has been plunging all day. 'Spare a thought for those of us who were told we had to sell our house and put the proceeds into equities,' remarked The Man as we assembled for the parliamentary committee this afternoon. He said it with feeling. As well he might. He has been well and truly shafted. Equities have plummeted, house prices have soared. That one disastrous piece of official advice has probably lost him more in five years than he's earned as prime minister.

My views on new airports sparked a spirited exchange.† I said, 'During my 18 undistinguished months as Aviation minister I learned two things about the aviation industry. One, that its demands are insatiable. Two, that successive governments have always given way.' I continued, 'There is nothing wrong with expanding regional airports, providing we insist that they are accessible by public transport, but as far as London and the South East is concerned, isn't it time we made a stand?'

There were no takers. The Man said something about bigger and better airports being essential for the health of the economy. Doug Hoyle said that the second runway had made a big difference in Manchester. Tony Lloyd said that airports in the regions benefited from investment in the south-east.

Liz Symons said, 'As Minister for Trade, I'm quite worried about what Chris has said.'

'Have you been on the cannabis again, Chris?' inquired JP [John Prescott] to general hilarity.

'I can see I won't be allowed anywhere near the transport department again,' I said.

Chris Mullin

---

* Rebekah Wade, editor of the *News of the World*, married the actor Ross Kemp (who played the part of Grant Mitchell in TV soap opera *EastEnders*). They divorced in 2009 and she married Charlie Brooks.

† A statement on the future of aviation in Britain had been made to the Commons the day before.

Thursday, 15 August 2002

Post still high despite it being the holiday period. People write all the year round these days. Tories still getting consistently bad press ... Battle between so-called modernisers ('mods'), whose mantra seems to focus on more women candidates and to welcome minority groups, and the 'rockers' who say what we want is a re-establishment of our identity/principles – choice, small state, decentralisation of decisions and appropriate policies (health insurance, low taxes etc.).

Michael Spicer

Tuesday, 3 September 2002

Blair gave a press conference at Sedgefield at 2.30, lasting for an hour and a half, in which, not to put too fine a point upon it, he said he had the evidence and – well, he declared war on Iraq on behalf of Britain in support of America. Totally riddled with error, and he was standing there smirking and smiling. You'd think he'd just done something very clever. But there's no doubt whatever that there will be a war, probably in the New Year.

The war plans are now well advanced.

Tony Benn

Monday, 21 October 2002

Conservative board meeting. Everyone says how wonderful the Conference was and we must have more self-flagellation. Bumped into Eric Forth afterwards: he seems to think a leadership challenge may be on the way.

Michael Spicer

Friday, 6 December 2002

According to the *Daily Mail*, Cherie Blair is dabbling in the occult and cannot decide whether to have tea or coffee in the morning without consulting a medium in Dorking called Sylvia. Mrs Blair surrounds herself with gurus and mystics. It seems you cannot move in No 10 before tripping over crystals and astrological charts.

Marigold said, 'It's good to know that someone of the New Age is married to the most powerful person in Britain.'

Adrian Mole

Wednesday, 29 January 2003

Blair now at odds with his party on four issues: Iraq, firemen's strike, House of Lords Reform (he wants wholly appointed), university top-up fees. His backbenchers almost in total revolt. Meet the charming Alan Simpson in the lobby. He says Blair has become a frightening megalo-maniac. I wonder if we are heading for a national government with the Labour left in opposition. The trouble is the Tory Party is smaller than the government's majority.

Michael Spicer

Tuesday, 11 February 2003

Do you know, the House of Commons adjourned tonight at 5:30! So, on the eve of war, Tam Dalyell having been unable yesterday to get an emergency debate on it, the House goes away, and on Thursday, in two days' time, the House is rising for a week's holiday. I'm not exagger-ating, I think the House of Commons is taking its own life while the balance of its mind is disturbed. It is incredible! But Blair's popularity has dropped now to the same level as that of Iain Duncan Smith.* Blairites will disappear once they realise Blair can't win the election for them – we'll see.

Tony Benn

Saturday, 15 February 2003

R and I go down to Leicester Square at noon, the tube as crowded as the rush hour, then walk up Charing Cross Road to where the anti-war march is streaming across Cambridge Circus. There seems no structure to it, ahead of us some SWP banners but marching, or rather strolling, beside them the Surrey Heath Liberal Democrats. Scattered among the

---

* Iain Duncan Smith ('IDS'), the MP for Chingford and Wood Green, became leader of the Conservative Party in September 2001, just after 9/11, after William Hague stepped down. At this stage Duncan Smith's leadership of his party was in question.

more seasoned marchers are many unlikely figures, two women in front of us in fur hats and bootees looking as if they're just off to the WI. I'm an unlikely figure too, of course, as the last march I went to was in 1956 and that was an accident: I was standing in Broad Street Oxford watching the Suez demonstration go by when a friend pulled me in.

Today it's bitterly cold, particularly since the march keeps stopping or is stopped by the police, who seem bored they've got so little to do, the mood of the march overwhelmingly friendly and domestic and hardly political at all.

On the TV news the police estimate the numbers at 750,000, the organisers at two million, the true figure presumably somewhere in between.

Alan Bennett

Saturday, 15 March 2003

I got up in the middle of the night to fly to Belgrade for the funeral of Zoran Djindjic.*

After the service we adjourned to one of the ugly rectangular boxes which Tito built to house his government. Over the tray of vodka I got the chance to catch up with old colleagues from my days as Foreign Secretary, many of whom had already read in their national press speculation that I might resign. Joschka Fischer [German Foreign Minister] wanted to know how Britain had got into this cul-de-sac and I found that I could not give him an explanation that satisfied even myself. He underlined the degree of opposition to military action by observing to me that 'you and I are not pacifists'. Indeed we are not and we worked together closely on behalf of Britain and Germany during the Kosovo campaign, but neither of us can support this one.

Robin Cook

Friday, 28 March 2003

The Americans – or was it us? – have bombed another market in Baghdad, this time killing at least 50 people and maiming hundreds of others. The evening television news is full of weeping, screaming,

---

* Zoran Djindjic, the reformist Prime Minister of Serbia, was assassinated; he had acquired many enemies during the complex disintegration of former Yugoslavia who saw him as a 'traitor' to Serbia.

angry Iraqis. As usual official spokesmen are lying or obfuscating. Cambodia, Iraq (last time round), Kosovo, Afghanistan, it's always the same. They never own up. I am so glad I voted against this lousy, rotten war.

Chris Mullin

Sunday, 6 April 2003

All of Rupert Murdoch's 175 papers are in favour of the war, though he always claims that his editors are independent and decide for themselves. I wonder whether the Rupert Murdoch Professorship at Oxford maintains the same fiction.* I know I'm a bore on the subject and thought to be an unworldly fool but so long as it bears his name this grubby appointment is a continuing stain on the reputation of the university that solicited it.

Alan Bennett

Wednesday, 9 April 2003
Rafah, Gaza

Right now I am on duty ... my third night at Dr Samir's ...

I have had my head filled with so much propaganda and yet I know that in situations like this half-truths can build on each other exponentially to create a massive wrong conclusion. People believe what they want to ...

Things have gone to shit in Palestine, that is for certain. People die all the time and life is cheap, but why? Some is justified, but the line for me is when I see Israeli troops inflict unnecessary pain. Bulldozing houses and injuring children in assassinations provoke a huge, burning anger inside me. But there is always the 'What if?' ...

When it comes down to it, I have seen no direct actions in major violations of the Geneva convention. Hype can so easily make you lose sight of that fact.

Tom Hurndall†

---

*A News International Endowment funds several posts at Oxford, including the Rupert Murdoch Professorship of Language and Communication.
†Tom Hurndall was a twenty-one-year-old student photojournalist covering the 'human shields' in Iraq, and the International Solidarity Movement. He had gone to Rafah, a Palestinian town on the border of the Gaza strip with Egypt; the Israeli army

Monday, 19 May 2003

Valery Giscard d'Estaing, the former President of France, who is chairing the great forum on the new European Constitution, came to Number 10 today, and the Government is determined not to give us a referendum on it. The *Daily Mail* wants it, *The Times* wants it, the *Sun* wants it, and the Tories want it. Andrew Marr was very candid as he stood outside Number 10 Downing Street. He said the Government don't want it because they think they'd lose it. But the fundamentally undemocratic nature of Blair is coming out bit by bit.

Tony Benn

Friday, 30 May 2003

Watched the Seven o'clock News, and I must say there were some sensational news stories: 2,400 people have been sacked by a company by text message. The workforce haven't received their pay and there is no redundancy money.

Then the Chief Executive of HSBC's subsidiary in America, Household International, was paid £35 million by the directors, and it was upheld by institutional shareholders at the shareholders' meeting, against the votes of individual shareholders.

Another news item was that a British soldier in Iraq had sent photographs to be developed in a photo shop in Birmingham, and the guy who developed these was so shocked at seeing an Iraqi soldier gagged and bound, and hanging in a net from a hook in a forklift truck, that he reported it to the police.

Tony Benn

Wednesday, 4 June 2003

In the corridor behind the Speaker's chair, I came across Alan Milburn and we had a little *sotto voce* conversation about the current state of play. He shares my view that the situation is dangerous. 'Some of our colleagues have decided they want regime change here.' He thinks Clare [Short] might run as a stalking horse for Gordon. 'We need to have

had a strong presence there and Tom was shot in the head by an Israeli sniper on 11 April 2003 while trying to rescue two children from gunfire. He died nine months later. A year after his death an Israeli soldier was sentenced to eight years for Tom's manslaughter.

a grown up conversation with the unions. Tony must tread carefully and not just say, as he has in the past, fuck them.' He added, 'We'd be mad to get rid of the most successful prime minister for years.' He went away saying he was going discreetly to check the party's standing orders to see how many MPs would be needed to endorse a challenge.

Chris Mullin

Sunday, 6 July 2003

Top of the news this evening is that the new Bishop of Reading, who's just been appointed suffragan bishop by the Bishop of Oxford, has asked permission to withdraw. He has to ask the Queen's permission, because she's already appointed him. The reason is, quite frankly, that the African members of the Lambeth Conference would have withdrawn from the Anglican communion worldwide if a gay bishop had been consecrated. They could quite happily live with war and bloodshed, but not with homosexuality, and it shows how terribly vulnerable the church is, because these African churches have become very evangelical and fundamentalist, and for them, gay relations are just worse than killing people.

Tony Benn

Friday, 18 July 2003

I was lying in bed watching TV when they suddenly flashed up that Dr David Kelly, the Iraq expert, who was exposed last week as the source of Andrew Gilligan's claim that the Government 'sexed up' their Iraq war dossier, had gone missing.

I felt the hairs on my back shooting up. Was he dead? Had he killed himself, or been killed? … I raced into the office. That was about as dramatic as politics could ever get.

At 11 am a body was found. And at 2 pm it was confirmed as Kelly's. He had almost certainly killed himself …

Blair looked terrible when he disembarked [off a flight from Japan]. He knows how serious this is.

Piers Morgan

The death of Dr David Kelly brought more obloquy down on the Government's

*head for its Iraq war policy. Much of the Kelly row centred on two govern-
ment documents: the first was published in September 2002, the second in
February 2003. The second of the two was dubbed the 'Dodgy Dossier'*
because of the amount of plagiarised and unattributed material it contained.
The BBC journalist Andrew Gilligan reported on high-level scepticism about
this dossier without revealing any of his informants. But eventually Dr
David Kelly, a former UN weapons inspector in Iraq and MOD expert on
biological warfare, was named as a source. He took his life after intensive
media coverage and speculation and a campaign directed at undermining his
authority as an expert on Saddam Hussein's weapons programme.*

Friday, 26 September 2003

IDS has apparently called for Blair's resignation but no mention of this
in the press – extraordinary. It really does look as if they want to ignore
IDS whatever he does.

Michael Spicer

Tuesday, 7 October 2003

M from Washington called in. He says that contrary to what I was
told yesterday at Vauxhall Cross [headquarters of SIS/MI6] many
of the Iraqi scientists are talking, they are all singing the same tune
and believed to be telling the truth. Namely that Saddam disposed of
his remaining chemical and biological weapons after his sons-in-law
defected and has had nothing for the last seven years.

Chris Mullin

Friday, 24 October 2003

Got up at six. Concorde's last day. I'm going off in just over a couple
of hours to Heathrow for the last flight.

One took off from New York and one from Edinburgh. We were
due to take off at about 2.15.

I was on the very front row of the plane, next to Lord Macfar-
lane. The air hostesses were very charming, and asked us to sign their
programmes. I wandered up and down the plane with my video camera.

---

* *Iraq: its Infrastructure of Concealment, Deception and Intimidation.*

I asked one of the hostesses to take the camera into the cockpit, which they did. They wouldn't let me in while we were flying. I got a picture of the controls showing Mach II and Speed 1,350 miles an hour at 50,000 feet and temperature of minus 53 degrees, and all that. We went supersonic very briefly, and then we slowly came in. We landed about two minutes past four back at Heathrow.

Having flown in it 33 years ago, at the very beginning, I felt the pilot, John Cochrane, and I had flown over a longer span than anybody else.

We came in first, and the Concorde from Edinburgh came in second, and the Concorde from New York came in third.

We were unloaded third, and I went into a hospitality tent, and there was Colin Marshall, the Chairman of British Airways, who came up. David Frost was there of course. It was a very moving day, and I made a little comment about the people who'd designed and built it – that's what I care about. Of course, typical of Britain, the people who really did the work weren't included ... but still, I mustn't gripe about it, because I did enjoy it very much.

Tony Benn

Thursday, 30 October 2003

Denis Thatcher's memorial service. Beautiful music in the Guards' Chapel. Margaret in tears as she walks down the aisle with her grandson. Afterwards at marquee reception in Wellington Barracks. Michael and Sandra Howard move about like the unanointed King and Queen. (He declares later in the afternoon.) David Davis, who has surrendered unconditionally to Howard, looks like a PoW (all the stuffing out of him).*

Michael Spicer

Sunday, 25 January 2004

Colin Powell, the American Secretary of State, has said he doubts whether weapons of mass destruction will ever be found, whereas Blair says he's certain they will be. It did make me wonder whether

---

* Iain Duncan Smith was 'deposed' after a sufficient number of Conservative MPs (as laid down in Party rules) wrote privately to the Chairman of the 1922 Committee (Michael Spicer) withdrawing their support from his leadership. It marked the end of the Euro-sceptic or Euro-realist ascendancy in the parliamentary party.

we could argue that the Prime Minister claims he's speaking the truth, and searches are being made to find out if there is any truth in the Prime Minister, and so far, no evidence has been found.

Tony Benn

Wednesday, 28 January 2004
Daily Mirror

Hutton's cleared everyone in the Government of doing anything wrong at all and blamed it all on the BBC.* I think it's a complete stinking whitewash. But Alastair Campbell immediately appeared to address the nation from some fancy Government building and started banging on about being completely exonerated – and effectively calling for BBC bosses, Greg Dyke and Gavyn Davies to resign. It was a shocking performance, totally lacking in grace or dignity. Alastair's conveniently forgotten that if he hadn't gone to war with the BBC in the first place, then none of this would have happened and David Kelly would almost certainly still be alive. Fact.

I hoped nobody from the BBC would resign, but Davies has quickly fallen on his sword. And Dyke's rumoured to be 'considering his position.' We have done a thunderous attack on Hutton and the Government, and urge the BBC to stand firm. But I fear the worst here.

Piers Morgan

Wednesday, 11 February 2004

The Chinese cockle-pickers who died in Morecambe Bay, in an incoming tide, had apparently paid £20,000 to be smuggled into Britain, and were earning a pound for every thousand cockles they picked. The gang masters got a hundred pounds. One tragic guy had rung all the way home to his wife in China on his mobile phone, stuck in the mud, 'I think I'm going to die. The water's up to my neck. There's nothing I can do about it.' Oh God, talk about the exploitation of capitalism!

Tony Benn

* Lord Hutton, a judge, was appointed in August 2003 to investigate the circumstances of Dr David Kelly's death. His findings took many people by surprise, attacking BBC standards, vindicating the government and exonerating Alastair Campbell.

Friday, 5 March 2004

On the London Underground

I sat down opposite a Bengali Muslim wearing a tunic, hat (i.e. I keep my head covered, I am a holy man) and sporting a trademark mosque-style beard. Even though I've criticised in Parliament the War on Terror becoming a War on Men with Beards, I find that I am now more wary of men with beards. I treat people how I find them but I find that many of the obviously religious men (with beards, hats and tunics) seem to be hostile towards me.

There could be many reasons for this, ranging from the war in Iraq ... to my Jewish background, to the fact that I've campaigned for gay rights, to mere paranoia on my part. This particular man, in his mid twenties, fixed me with a hard and unyielding glare. Our eyes locked, without warmth or recognition and I immediately went into every Londoner's standard 'Do not look or talk to me while I am on the tube,' mode. He did the same ...

The tube arrives at Mile End, and it floats through my mind that I hope the man with the beard doesn't get off with me.

'Excuse me?' He's looking straight at me.

'Yes?' My natural reaction is always to smile. But not to him. I'm waiting to see what he wants.

'You've left your bag,' he says.

Oona King

Saturday, 20 March 2004

Nicholas Hytner* has shown the script of *The History Boys* to one of his former teachers at Manchester Grammar School, who says that teaching these days is so circumscribed that many traditional tools of the trade are now impermissible. Sarcasm, for instance, is out, pupils are never touched and there are often viewing panels in the doors.

Alan Bennett

---

*Nicholas Hytner was the artistic director of the National Theatre, and director of *The History Boys* by Bennett.

Saturday, 15 May 2004

The papers this morning were all about Piers Morgan's dismissal [from the *Daily Mirror*]. It is interesting that the four casualties of the war have not been the ministers responsible for the war, but Gavyn Davis (the Chairman of the BBC), Greg Dyke, (Director General of the BBC), Andrew Gilligan, (journalist for the BBC), who was absolutely right, and now Piers Morgan. It may be the media is now frightened about the way the Government treats them. I think it is quite right to be suspicious of the media, but in this particular case the media are right and the Government's wrong. They say Piers Morgan published hoax pictures, but then, Blair took us to war with false information about weapons of mass destruction.

Tony Benn

Sunday, 13 June 2004

Bethnal Green and Bow

Back in Whitechapel by midday to visit tenants in a block of flats. Terrible antisocial behaviour problems. The usual – heroin and the detritus it leaves behind: foil, plastic bottles, condoms, urine, shit, vandalised property, break-ins, fear. The tenants understandably want me to walk up the stairs to look at the mess. I do, but by now I think my right ovary is about to pop.*

I need to go to hospital. Just as we're leaving a young woman arrives to tell me about her recent burglary. Then somebody else wants to show me the broken exit-door lock. Finally leave, ring the hospital and they tell me to come in for a scan. I keep saying, 'I know there's something wrong.'

Oona King

Monday, 19 July 2004

Meeting with Michael Howard in his room ... I say, 'Parliamentary party restive and anxious. We need to recapture *Sun* readers of the Thatcher (and Disraeli!) years and from whom [we] were totally disconnected at the by-elections. We must reconnect with the patriotic working class, who have left up their crosses of St George on their

---

* Oona King was having IVF treatment at the time.

semi-detached houses and white vans [after the World Cup]. Policies on immigration, Europe, crime, need to be toughened up.' As the son of an immigrant, MH is in a good position to do something about this.

Michael Spicer

Wednesday, 8 September 2004

A Plaid Cymru MP, Adam Price, has put down a motion to impeach Blair over the war. He looked up obsolete parliamentary techniques, and found one that hasn't been used since Lord Palmerston in 1830, and discovered if you did table a motion for impeachment, it had to be debated. Whether the Tories will vote for it, I don't know, but they might. Labour MPs dare not, at risk of expulsion ... my own advice is not to do it. I think it's a mistake because, first of all, MPs would be voting for something they had already voted on, the war, so it would be overwhelmingly defeated, and that would allow Blair to say he's had a vote of confidence.

Tony Benn

Thursday, 28 October 2004

Spending time with George Galloway is like dipping your toe in a bloodbath. He says 'Oona King' as many times as possible in the same breath as 'George Bush'. George Bush and Oona King, Oona King and George Bush. Both of them are at war with Islam. Again and again and again and again.

'The US and Britain, two of the most powerful countries in the world,' said George Galloway, 'with Oona King's approval have massacred far more civilians than Osama bin Laden killed in New York and Washington on 9 /11 ...'

I suppose I should take a leaf out of Galloway's book and sue him for saying that I 'approve massacres'. Instead I point out [on a radio station] that he sipped tea with Saddam Hussein, exchanged niceties with a butcher.

Three times in a row Galloway responds 'You be careful you don't libel me now.' He's great at suing people but he can't sue me for quoting him. Can he?

Oona King

Tuesday, 9 November 2004

Had dinner with the Browns and various political chums of theirs including Harriet Harman, Margaret Hodge and Sue Nye.

Gordon is a strange Jekyll and Hyde character. Over dinners like this one, he's relaxed, chatty, gossipy and extremely charming. Then I watch him on TV and he turns into one of the Thunderbirds, speaking in a relentless high-speed monotone, performing one of the worst stage smirks I've ever seen when he thinks he should lighten up a bit and generally coming across as a dour, stiff Scots bloke who looks after our money. Which is a perfect image for Chancellor but hopeless if you want to make the move to Prime Minister.

His 'people' are all from the same mould. Ed Balls is quite fun away from a screen and so is Alistair Darling. But put them on *Newsnight* and it's like an undertaker's taken over the airwaves to announce mass euthanasia programmes for anyone who laughs in public.

Piers Morgan

Saturday, 13 November 2004

Boris Johnson was sacked by Michael Howard tonight* after more stories of his alleged nocturnal activities hit the papers …

The whole Boris the Buffoon act makes me laugh. The guy is incredibly clever and knows exactly what he is doing. Boris worked out long ago that the public are suckers for that dithering, bumbling, upper-class twit stuff, so he gives them exactly what they want, and they lap it up.

Underneath the phoney bluster is a keen political brain calculating a path to power.

Piers Morgan

Thursday, 18 November 2004

I had the great pleasure of seeing the Speaker, Michael Martin, getting up and announcing that the Hunting Bill would be passed by the Parliament Act. I mean, it couldn't be a more interesting end, and it's

---

*Boris Johnson was the MP for Henley, Conservative arts spokesman and editor of the *Spectator*. He was elected Mayor of London in May 2008 and re-elected in May 2012.

entirely the Prime Minister's fault. If he'd dealt with it seven years ago, it would all have been over by now, but he left it and left it and left it, and the only time he ever voted was not to ban hunting, but for an amendment that would *regulate* hunting. So it's all his fault, and it has enormously angered Labour MPs.

Tony Banks has had a big success.

Tony Benn

Saturday, 1 January 2005
Paris

Last night, New Year's Eve, Tiberio and I celebrated our thirteenth anniversary. But you can't celebrate with a global catastrophe unfolding in the background. Tsunami.

The first reports on Boxing Day said that 10,000 people had died. The next day it was 25,000, then 30,000, then 40,000, 100,000 and as of yesterday 150,000. With such a high number it's almost impossible to register the individual human loss. It was caused by a huge underground earthquake with its epicentre in Indonesia. It was so powerful that it tilted the world on its side, coasts in some areas moved twenty metres in a second and giant waves swept everything before them – humans, hospitals, coastlines, hotels, villages. At least 80,000 Indonesians have been killed. Eighty thousand. Apparently Britain was hit by a tsunami in 5,000 BC. Suddenly Noah's Ark jumps from myth to reality.

Oona King

Saturday, 15 January 2005

Gerry Doherty, the new left wing General Secretary of the Transport Salaried Staffs' Association, came to address the Campaign Group of MPs. I like him so much. He told us: 'We're hoping to shift the union to the left, but I have to be pragmatic.' He said that the railway system is in a state of collapse, no railway building occurs now in Britain, and when you think we built the first railways, and built them all over the world, it is another example of de-industrialisation. He said the public subsidy is an absolute disgrace. I asked whether a European Union Directive made it impossible for us to renationalise the railways. 'Well,' he said, 'that may be so, but the French take no notice of it.'

He said that the railway operators own nothing; they just operate. They don't own the track, they don't own the stations, they don't own the rolling stock, they don't own anything; and what we must do, among other things, he said, is to keep up the campaign for railway nationalisation and restore the building of railway engines and railway rolling stock in Britain. I agree with that – it was wonderful.

Tony Benn

Monday, 24 January 2005

A bad night, pains behind my eyes and at the back of my head. Set out for London stuffed with paracetamol. From the train I rang Sunderland Council's chief executive, about the plastic bags in the trees; they are all over the city.

At the House I ran into Tam Dalyell who said, 'Chris, what are we going to do about Iraq?'

'I think we are stuck. What would you do?' I replied.

'Declare victory and end the occupation.'

'What do you think would happen, if we did?'

'I think there would then be a period of calm.' He quoted one of his Iraqi contacts in support of the proposition.

'How many refugees do you think there would be?'

He cited his Iraqi contact again, 'No more than a 1,000 of those who have collaborated with occupation.'

A very optimistic scenario but, who knows, it may come to that eventually.

Chris Mullin

Tuesday, 1 February 2005

Tower Hamlets, East London (Bethnal Green and Bow constituency)

Most of the Bengali women I meet today are on very low incomes, living with families of up to twelve people in two or three-bedroom flats with serious damp problems, leading to health problems and family breakdown. I outline what the Government is doing to help the poorest. New money for housing, new money to help parents through the Sure Start programme, a new health centre on the Ocean [housing estate], new money to tackle drug addiction, a new childcare centre, new money for babies, new money for this, new money for that. 'But what about our heating bills? The Government doesn't pay for them.' I had mentioned the extra money given to pensioners this year for their winter fuel payments.

'No, you're right, the Government can't pay for everyone's heating bills.' I was starting to get exasperated. We're under attack from middle England for being too preoccupied with the poorest, and yet when I speak to low income families, they're just as angry we haven't given more.

'We're trying our best. In Bangladesh the government doesn't pay for *anything*. Here we pay for a lot.'

In fact if we were in Bangladesh we might be doing a bit better – the birth rate in Dhaka is lower than in Tower Hamlets!

Oona King

Monday, 21 March 2005

[TV agent] John Webber invited me to a glittering Board of Deputies dinner tonight, one of the biggest nights in the Jewish society calendar. Tony Blair was the guest speaker, so this would be the first time I had been in the same room as him since the book came out.* I arrived early and immediately bumped into Victor Blank [chairman of Trinity Mirror] who was as charming as ever. Admittedly he helped sack me when the heat got too close to his own chair, but I hold no grudge against him.

He introduced me to Gerald Ronson, the business tycoon who has fought his way back from the Guinness Four disgrace. Before I could exchange pleasantries, Ronson started berating me for being too anti-Israeli [when I was editor] on the *Mirror*. He was all red-faced and spluttering, as if he was my boss bollocking me for stealing paperclips. 'We always tried to be impartial, Mr Ronson,' I said firmly but he was having none of it and carried on venting his spleen until I gave up defending myself and walked away.

Piers Morgan

---

*The first of two volumes of diaries, *The Insider: The Private Diaries of a Scandalous Decade* by Piers Morgan.

Friday, 8 April 2005

I was going to get on with work, but I watched the Pope's funeral [Pope John Paul II] on television. Every possible comment that could have been made has been made on the television since he died nearly a week ago, but the funeral did reveal a number of things. First of all, it showed the enormous power of religion in the world. Bush went over, Chirac, Schroeder, representatives from Saudi Arabia, the Russian Orthodox Church – a tremendous gathering of people – Blair of course, Prince Charles, of all people, representing Britain. Mugabe was there; Prince Charles shook hands with Mugabe, possibly by mistake.*

Also, the Pope himself: he was an actor really, a very skilful communicator. His attitude to birth control led to the thousands and thousands, millions perhaps, of people being born with AIDS, who could have been protected if their fathers had used condoms. His attitude to women, outrageous. He's been given credit for having destroyed Communism, but I think Gorbachev had much more to do with the transformation of the Soviet Union than the Pope.

Tony Benn

Saturday, 9 April 2005

Sunderland

To the Stadium of Light to see Sunderland beaten 2–1 by Reading. If we get back into the Premiership – and it looks as though we might – we will be smashed out of sight.

Charles married Camilla [Parker Bowles] this afternoon. The Queen looked remarkably cheerful as they emerged from St George's chapel. As one of the commentators remarked, no doubt she was thinking, 'Thank Gawd, that's over.'

Chris Mullin

---

* Prince Charles claimed to have been 'taken by surprise' when Robert Mugabe leaned over to greet him. Zimbabwe, of which Robert Mugabe is President, had been suspended from the Commonwealth in 1992 and Mugabe then withdrew from the Commonwealth.

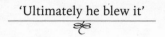

Wednesday, 4 May 2005

Eve of General Election

This is the strangest Election of my life. It's like three managing directors competing for the job of running Tesco. I thought it was totally boring and totally unprincipled. But maybe the Liberals will do well, maybe Michael Howard will do better than he thinks ... I wouldn't like tonight to predict anything.

Tony Benn

Thursday, 5 May 2005

General Election day and I spent most of it convincing myself not to vote, in protest at Blair's Iraq folly. In the end I did cast my name for Labour because of the persuasive 'Vote Tony, get Gordon' arguments. The Tories are still all over the place, Charles Kennedy and his Lib Dems just seem a vacuous bunch of mediocre clods and Labour have undeniably done an OK job domestically. Not a great one, just an OK one. It's just a tragedy that Blair has let himself, and us, be sucked into the horrific position of being America's poodle.

Piers Morgan

Sunday, 8 May 2005

Speak to Michael Howard on the phone. He will stay until the Party conference.

I tell him his legacy will be to have plugged the leaking Conservative ship (provided a semblance of unity) and to have set it sailing again.

Michael Spicer

Sunday, 29 May 2005

France has rejected the European Union constitution, fifty-five to forty-five percent. It's really exciting! It's the first democratic response to the bureaucracy of the new Europe, and the scandal is that the German

Parliament didn't allow the German people to have a referendum, so this is very important. It will put Blair in a difficulty – will there be a referendum here? We don't know. The Dutch are going to vote on Wednesday,* and then there are the Danes coming along. It brought out so clearly what the whole thing was about – whether you want a capitalist Europe working in a globalised economy on a free-market basis run by bureaucrats, or whether you want a democratic Europe. It's a very, very big issue with huge implications. I felt so cheerful, I can't tell you!

Tony Benn

Thursday, 7 July 2005

Olympic euphoria was short-lived. Bombs have gone off all over London, on underground trains at Aldgate, Kings Cross and Edgware Road and on the top deck of a bus at Tavistock Square.

I arrived at Hampstead underground just after nine to find a jam-packed train, doors-open, sitting in the station. At this stage there was no inkling of what had happened. Then a London Underground employee in a blue blazer came and announced that the station was being evacuated due to 'a power surge'. Several people ranted. In particular a well-dressed man who said he was from Greece (as if the Greeks have anything to teach us about the smooth-running of public services) and a red-headed yob who demanded to know how he was going to get to work in Knightsbridge. The Underground man, an Asian, kept his cool admirably.

Outside, still no clue as to what was happening, I walked down the hill and boarded a 24 bus which meandered for about a mile before being turned back at the far end of Camden High Street. Someone said something about a bomb. I got off and started walking. Gradually the traffic dried up. Euston Road was sealed. Police were letting through only ambulances and other emergency vehicles in the direction of King's Cross. Wailing sirens everywhere. I crossed into Tottenham Court Road. People were clustered round shop windows displaying television sets which were showing scenes of chaos just a few hundred yards away ...

By the time I reached the House it was clear that we had a

---

*They rejected the new constitution by 63 to 37 per cent. Tony Blair announced shortly after that there would not now be a British referendum on the EU Constitution.

catastrophe on our hands ... It was announced that The Man was on his way back from the G8 at Gleneagles to chair COBRA (the cabinet committee in charge of emergencies).

Chris Mullin

Thursday, 21 July 2005

Dramatic day. I was interviewed by Cherie Blair at No 10 on the subject of prime ministers' wives for a TV film.

At the end, she leaned forward and asked me whether I would like to have been a prime minister's wife. I burst out laughing. 'What, Harold for PM!'

The bubble coming out of my head read: 'My husband would like to indict your husband as a war criminal, so that's what he would do as prime minister.'

Antonia Pinter

Monday, 10 October 2005

[Then] to Committee Room 14 to hear The Man address the parliamentary party. Better than his conference speech. Brimming with energy and self-confidence; not a note in sight; still less any suggestion that he is contemplating retirement ...

Dave Clelland asked why the government was encouraging private medicine: 'I'm all for choice, but we said we were going to make the NHS so efficient that the private sector will be irrelevant. Now we are encouraging it. Why?' The Man gave no quarter. 'It's the only basis on which we are going to expand.' He added, 'We have expanded the public sector by 600,000 people so when I hear some of our trade union colleagues say, "you are destroying the public sector", I go, "Huh?"'

Chris Mullin

Monday, 7 November 2005

The French riots have now spread all over Europe, and it's obviously a really serious situation. Modernisation means cutting the welfare state and adopting neo-conservative, liberal economic policies, and that hurts people, and many of them are of course low-paid immigrants. Modernising the poor out of existence just won't work, and it will be interesting to see whether the Establishment realises it in time and makes concessions or turns to repression.

Tony Benn

Wednesday, 30 November 2005

My computer crashed today. It went berserk, the screen said it was in "safe mode" and wouldn't do anything. I was suicidal – I can't tell you! I realised that the hard disk contained all my documents going back to 1997; I couldn't recover anything, couldn't print anything, couldn't work on my lecture to the British Library for Monday. It was like a bereavement. I was just desperate. So I rang [my son] Josh. He came over and copied all the things from the hard disk onto floppies so that I would always be able to find them. He also transferred them all on to my laptop so that I can find them there. He installed Word Perfect on my laptop.* Then he changed the setting on my crashed computer so it goes straight to Word Perfect instead of going through Microsoft Word, and it all came right. I mean the guy is an absolute genius. The most precious thing you can do for anybody is to give them your time and your expertise. I was so touched.

Tony Benn

Tuesday, 6 December 2005

Day of the announcement.

David Davis is preparing himself for his concession speech, which he is to make after I have given the results and before David Cameron makes his speech. I hear that he plans to end this with, 'I now give you the next leader of the Conservative Party.' I say, 'That is meant to be my job.' David Davis insists that he will do it himself and that Cameron wants it. I say, 'Maybe we should both do it,' and leave the room. A moment later I come back and say, 'That's a bit silly. You can do it.' Outside I tell Michael Salter (excellent Central Office man who is running the show) what I have decided. He must have told George Osborne, who rushes up to me and says, 'There has been no agreement about this with David Davis. As returning officer *you* should introduce DC.' It is now five minutes before the announcement, scheduled for

---

*Tony Benn remained wedded to the WordPerfect programme long after Microsoft Word had replaced it on most PCs.

3pm. I say, 'I have no wish to quarrel with David Davis at this moment. I am quite happy to leave the stage after I have given the result.' George Osborne consults his PR man (Steve Hilton) who agrees that a handshake between DD and DC and a warm departure from DD would be a good thing. We agree the change of plan and move down the back stairs with Michael Howard, David Davis, David Cameron and me for the event which is the biggest show in town …

Michael Spicer

Friday, 20 January 2006

The tabloids are gunning for Ruth Kelly.* '150 PAEDOS IN YOUR SCHOOLS,' rages this morning's *Sun*. No wonder we are becoming a nation of paranoids and hypochondriacs.

Chris Mullin

Wednesday, 25 January 2006

George Galloway won his appeal against the *Daily Telegraph*.† If they had won, he would have been bankrupted and out of Parliament, so that was really good news. Also, he was booted out of *Big Brother*,‡ which is probably the best thing that ever happened to him. Everybody's making fun of him for dressing up as a cat and supping milk from an actress's hand and looking ridiculous, but when you come to think of it, he hasn't lied to Parliament, he hasn't sent soldiers to their death, he hasn't authorised the rendition of people through British airports to be tortured. So I rang up his office and congratulated them on his victory in the courts.

Tony Benn

---

* Ruth Kelly was appointed Secretary of State for Education and Skills in December 2004, following David Blunkett's resignation.
† Galloway had sued for libel over claims by the *Telegraph* that he had benefited financially from Iraq's 'oil-for-food' programme imposed on Iraq after the war.
‡ *Big Brother*: a reality television programme in which 'celebrities' subjected themselves to twenty-four-hour-a-day TV surveillance in a shared house, and were successively voted out by the audience. Peter Bazalgette, the force behind it and other highly successful television formats, was knighted for services to broadcasting in 2012.

Monday, 6 February 2006

Hosted a meeting in an upstairs committee room for a party of Afghan farmers, for whom I helped the Senlis Council obtain visas.* They were hard, lean men whose sunken cheeks and unsmiling eyes reflected harsh lives. They had between eight and eleven children apiece, save for one who had lost all his to war and famine. The purpose of the meeting, a last minute affair, was to tell us what it was like being on the receiving end of the 'war on drugs'. Everyone in Afghanistan, they said, grew opium. It wasn't possible to survive without doing so. Two said their crops had been aerially sprayed and that the sprayers made no distinction between wheat, fruit, vegetables and poppies. Result: hunger. One said that children in his village had died after eating poisoned fruit. Someone asked how much of the billions in foreign aid had reached them and their families: a kilo and a half of fertiliser, they said.

Chris Mullin

Thursday, 16 March 2006

The big news is these enormous loans to the Labour Party before the general election that were never declared, not even reported to the Treasurer of the Labour Party Jack Dromey, who is Harriet Harman's husband. Nobody knows how many there were, who the lenders were, what the money was used for, whether they've been repaid, whether there was interest, who paid the interest, and indeed how many of the people who lent the money got honours.

Other news today, the Prince of Wales has won a case against the *Daily Mail*, who published his diary of his trip to Hong Kong when the handover occurred, saying that the Chinese leaders were like a lot of waxwork models, which wasn't very tactful.

Tony Benn

---

*Senlis Council (now called the International Council on Security and Development) is an organisation active in Afghanistan that has campaigned publicly against the unsuccessful (and disastrous) poppy eradication policy, in favour of allowing the trade to be licensed for medical use.

Tuesday, 9 May 2006

I walked over to Number 10 Downing Street for the presentation of a letter to Blair, a covering letter, to 1,800 signatures, from American physicists headed up by five Nobel Laureates, warning of the danger of a nuclear attack on Iran. This was a letter drawing the Prime Minister's attention to the warning. The organiser of the Campaign against Sanctions and Military Intervention in Iran is Professor Abbas Edalat, who is the founder of the society, of the campaign, who teaches somewhere in London.

General Sir Hugh Beach, who was Deputy Commander-in-Chief of Land Forces, a distinguished gentleman, very tall, neatly dressed, with an umbrella, was there. For a retired Army General to come out against an attack on Iran, I thought was interesting.

Anyway we went, a few of us, up to 10 Downing Street; the usual business – we banged on the door, Abbas handed in the letter. He thought we might be invited in, but they don't do that. Outside, there were a lot of journalists, permanently camped opposite No 10, so Abbas and I went and made a statement.

Tony Benn

Thursday, 25 May 2006

Prison Reform Trust meeting

Everyone in despair at the current feeding frenzy, which is making impossible rational discussion of penal or asylum policy. It's not helped by John Reid going around saying the Home Office is dysfunctional. Meanwhile the prisons are full to bursting. At the present rate of sentencing it will only be a matter of weeks before a new crisis looms. Later I did an interview with Radio 4 re the asylum frenzy to say that we had all gone barmy.

Chris Mullin

Wednesday, 19 July 2006

Blair's made a statement that Israel should have another week to finish the bombing of Lebanon and deal with Hezbollah. When you also take on board the fact that in an exchange between Bush and Blair, picked up on a microphone, Blair offered to go to the Middle East before

Condoleezza Rice, to do the sort of preliminary work for her, I mean he's a disaster. We don't have a foreign policy.

Tony Benn

Thursday, 28 September 2006

Question Time in Manchester. I've been looking forward to this ever since they asked me. Jack Straw and I have unfinished business.

I boarded the train to find that Ken Clarke and Baroness Jenny Tonge were sitting with me.

Within fifteen minutes they were both fast asleep. Ken, comfortably portly and glowing with ruddy health, woke as we pulled into Manchester.

We reached the studio and were taken to the makeshift green room where the usual array of alcoholic temptations lay in wait. I resisted. This is not the kind of TV programme you want to try and wing while fuelled with Chablis.

The seating plan sorted ... we all had a rather entertaining chat about politics, life and the universe ... The subject moved onto the government's obsession with our diet. 'It's bloody nonsense,' growled Ken, lying back in his chair with his large pot belly proudly on display. 'When I was young we lived on chips and sweets and it never did us any harm at all. Labour want to stop us smoking, drinking and eating. They are the ultimate nanny state.'

'Perhaps you should launch the pro-obesity party, Ken,' I suggested.

'Not a bad idea,' he laughed. 'I just want to spend the rest of my life eating good food, drinking fine wine, smoking great cigars and enjoying myself. What is wrong with that?'

The show's editor arrived. 'Ok, we're ready for you.'

Everyone began clearing throats and straightening ties. The fifth panellist was Lance Price. A former Blair spin doctor.

The show started in a pedestrian fashion, but kicked off when a young woman in the audience launched into an extraordinary attack on most of the panel, branding Straw a 'total disgrace'.

Finally she targeted me: 'And as for you Piers Morgan, you should be absolutely ashamed of yourself ... You are single-handedly responsible for dumbing down this country,' she shouted, really getting into her stride. 'You should be ashamed of yourself.'

'I think you're labouring under the misapprehension that I'm still editing the *Mirror*,' I said. 'But unfortunately I was cruelly removed from that job more than two years ago ... however if you'd like me to take responsibility for the government then I happily will. I apologise unreservedly for Iraq, Afghanistan ...'

The audience roared with laughter. Even the mad woman smiled ... This was the chance to finally pin [Straw] to the floor. He was after all Foreign Secretary at the time.

I went toe to toe with him, lambasting him for the biggest cock-up in modern military history, haranguing him for not resigning, scoffing at his pathetic attempts to justify what happened and generally abusing him.

The audience, as always when Iraq comes up, were united in their fury against him too and with Ken Clarke – who'd opposed the war from the start – joining in the fray, it rapidly descended into a gladiatorial bearpit, with Straw as the helpless young slave being torn to pieces in front of the baying crowd.

He began to physically shrink back into his seat, panic in his eyes ... he was getting well and truly buried.

Piers Morgan

Sunday, 12 November 2006

Nick Griffin of the BNP has been acquitted of incitement to racial hatred because all he did was attack Muslims. Now it appears that Lord Falconer wants the law changed so that you can't attack a religion – well, that would be an infringement of free speech.

Tony Benn

Monday, 4 December 2006

The Man announced, to no one's surprise, that we intend to update Trident, at a cost of between £15 and £20 billion (excluding maintenance). The case for doing so is threadbare (even he admitted it was an 'on balance' decision) and has more to do with 'punching our weight' than military necessity. Some rumbling at this evening's meeting of the parliamentary party, but mainly from Usual Suspects. Margaret Beckett, once a CND supporter, went out of her way to say that she had now changed her mind. The government can afford to be relaxed about a rebellion because it knows it has the support of the Tories.

Chris Mullin

Tuesday, 13 March 2007

There was a wonderful Greenpeace demonstration on a crane right next to the Houses of Parliament. Some activists climbed up it some time last night or early this morning and hung a huge banner which said 'Tony ♥ WMD.' I talked to the police, and they said, 'Well, if we climbed up there, there might have been an accident either to us or to them, so we just left it.' But with the Trident debate tomorrow, it was very amusing.

Tony Benn

Friday, 11 May 2007

A vast industry has grown up analysing The Man's place in history.*

What do I think? That at his best he was courageous, far-sighted, brilliant, idealistic, personally attractive, but that his undoubted achievements are eclipsed by one massive folly: that he tied us umbilically to the worst American president of my lifetime with consequences that were not merely disastrous, but catastrophic. The Man was touched by greatness, but ultimately he blew it.

Chris Mullin

---

*Tony Blair had announced from his Sedgefield constituency that he was standing down as Prime Minister in June 2007.

Postscript

2007–2010
Killing the Goose with the Golden Eggs

The political diary may well have reached its natural end. A new technology has turned the centuries-old concept on its head: the blog, the Twitter and the thread. An essentially reflective private activity has been replaced with instant communication, shared with hundreds of thousands of people. Radical bloggers such as Guido Fawkes and Iain Dale have joined free-thinking, traditional diarists like Tony Benn, Chris Mullin and Michael Spicer in the twenty-first century, without even having to sit in Parliament. And they may prove to be more influential.

In the autumn of 2007, Gordon Brown, successor to Tony Blair, chose not to hold an election. For the next three years a tsunami of crises, including the home-grown MPs 'expenses scandal', overwhelmed political life.

Historian David Marquand commented in September 2008 when the first waves hit Britain, that 'the age of abundance will pass whatever we do ... The choice lies between a gradual controlled but still painful transition to a new age of austerity and an infinitely more painful and destructive transition at a somewhat later date ... The first option is patently the right one yet it involves a transformation of the moral economy – a revolution of mentalities as radical as the reformation or the implosion of communism – of which there is as yet no sign.'

Friday, 14 December 2007

Former Spanish PM Felipe Gonzalez has taken on the mantle of EU Wise Man from Giscard D'Estaing – two less wise men I can hardly imagine, but I digress – and will lead a group of Ten 'Sages' in a so-called Reflection Group whose task will be to assess the next stage of development of the EU. They will report within three years ... The thing is, we all know what it will conclude – that we need ever more integration and this can only be achieved with the release of more national vetoes ... blah ... pooling sovereignty ... blah. And so the whole charade goes on. And it's us poor buggers who suffer from a continual erosion of our hard won democratic rights.

Iain Dale

Wednesday, 18 June 2008

Ask PM: 'Why are there always so many strikes at the end of a Labour government?' *Evening Standard* says I brought the House down.

What was good about the question: it was short (fourteen words) and did not allow PM to think up an evasive answer; strikes should be lower under Labour; 'always' refers back to the Winter of Discontent; 'end' implies Labour will lose next General Election.

Michael Spicer

Friday, 11 July 2008
Sunderland

The head teacher of a local, and much improved, secondary school called in to complain that his school has appeared on a list of schools allegedly threatened with closure if they don't reach 30 per cent A–C grades, including English and Maths. This just seven months after receiving a letter from schools minister, Jim Knight, congratulating the school on being 'amongst the top performing' based on added value. The letter goes on: 'Please pass my thanks and congratulations to your pupils, staff and governors for all their hard work and success ...' Should we laugh or cry?

Chris Mullin

Wednesday, 24 September 2008

The big news, and it is enormous news, is that Bush has put before Congress a policy involving a $700 billion bailout of the financial institutions in order to restore confidence in the banking system. Apparently, the law that's now before Congress, which they've got to decide upon by Friday, exempts any rules made under this legislation from public review or reference to the courts, so democracy has been suspended for the purpose of this operation, and many Republicans don't like it. I heard it described as 'American socialism', 'financial socialism'.

Obama* has been more cautious about it, but [John] McCain has said he's suspending his [Presidential candidature] campaign to go back to Washington to advise on what should be done. A lot of the Democrats and others are saying the whole cost of this will be paid for by the American taxpayers. I think it said it would cost the average American taxpayer $5,000 or something of that kind. There's absolutely no accountability! So, it does raise the question, if you're going to buy the banks, which is what the American Government are doing, why don't you just own the banks and get the profit as they recover? But if this isn't sorted out, there will be a total crisis of confidence in the American economy, and that will spread to the world economy as well.

I looked up what Clem Attlee said in 1945 (I think it was in our Election Manifesto) that the great inter-war slumps were not acts of God; they were the sure and certain result of too much power in the hands of too few men who felt no responsibility – I'm just summarising the argument.

Tony Benn

Monday, 6 October 2008

Parliament back. Stock Exchange collapses (7.9 per cent). We are in the middle of a financial crisis which is set to turn into an economic crisis.

5 pm Together with the Chief Whip I chair an emergency meeting of the parliamentary party which George Osborne addresses. He manages to sell the strategy of cooperating with the government in

---

* Barack Obama was the Democratic presidential candidate: his father was a black Kenyan and his mother a white American.

the eye of the storm. There is an underlying concern about this ...
especially if it leads to our assisting in the wholesale nationalisation of British banks. Capitalism is seen to have failed and the left
is on the attack. We must be careful not to give them (the socialists) cover, especially at the point when the real economy is about
to turn.

Michael Spicer

Monday, 13 October 2008

'A global problem which required a global solution,' says Gordon
Brown, trying to make out that he has been the instigator of the
so-called global solution. What he doesn't tell you, of course, is that
Britain and America are the only two countries which have been hit in
such a devastating way. There's a reason for that. With Brown as chancellor Britain let its finances get out of control and encouraged a debt
boom, the like of which we had never seen before. Countries which
managed their finances more conservatively have had fewer problems.
Any rescue packages they are having to impose are largely due to the
collapse in world markets because of what has happened in America
and Britain, rather than in their own countries.

The Conservatives must not let Brown off the hook. He set up the
current regulatory system and must be held responsible for it. It has
failed and he is the man to blame. He was told over and over again
the tripartite system was not working, yet took no notice whatsoever.
It's all very well to blame bankers for taking short term risks – but the
regulatory system which Brown was responsible for not only allowed
them to do so but positively encouraged such behaviour. The warnings
were there, but Brown ignored them.

There is little doubt that today marks a landmark in Britain's
economic and political history. The long term political consequences
are impossible to determine yet. Labour apologists (and to some
extent parts of the media) are trying to spin this as the day Gordon
Brown discovered his vision for Britain.

Iain Dale

Monday, 13 October 2008

I did a short interview for BBC World Service on the financial crisis, and of course, the big news today, announced during the day, is that the Government has nationalised the Royal Bank of Scotland and taken a 40% stake in HBOS, and in Lloyds Bank, and Barclays have managed without Government money. If I imagined, a year or two ago, that a Labour Government, including Peter Mandelson, would have nationalised the banks, I think I would have merited mental treatment ...

Tony Benn

Sunday, 7 December 2008

Spent the afternoon reading Nigel Lawson's sceptical look at global warming, *An Appeal to Reason*. Beautifully written, scrupulously footnoted. His thesis is that (a) the evidence is ambivalent; (b) if global warming is happening, there are beneficial as well as adverse impacts; (c) the proposed cure – drastic cuts in carbon emissions – is worse than the alleged disease and anyway impossible to implement since the biggest emitters will never co-operate; and (d) that adaptation rather than mitigation is the way forward. Much food for thought. Without doubt a case to be answered.

Chris Mullin

Tuesday, 20 January 2009

Barack Obama, a man whose father might once have been refused service in a Washington restaurant on the grounds that his skin was the wrong colour, was today sworn in as the 44th president of the United States. The event was witnessed by vast, cheering crowds stretching from the steps of the Capitol, away down the Mall as far as the eye could see. Even here, as the hour drew near, the excitement was palpable. All over the building Members, Tory and Labour alike, security guards and Tea Room staff, clustered around TV sets to bear witness. Some nice moments. The shining little Obama girls bursting with pride for their dad, the smaller of the two giving him the thumbs up. And the sweetest moment of all when George and Laura Bush were seen off the premises, escorted by the Obamas to the helicopter that whisked them away on the first leg of their journey home to Texas. You have to hand it to old George W, though. He has behaved with great dignity throughout the handover, which can't have been easy given how keen everyone was to see the back of him. Where the Obama presidency will lead remains to be seen. Expectations are so high they cannot possibly be fulfilled. But it was a moment to savour.

Chris Mullin

Sunday, 15 February 2009

The world news is so grim. The Israelis are now making really serious threats to Iran.

The Afghan War is absolutely unwinnable, and the Russians are offering to help the Americans because they lost 15,000 troops in Afghanistan, and that means America cannot win. The method they're using, of air-power to bomb villages, is creating an enormous number of civilian casualties, which is making Karzai's* position impossible. It's a horrible, horrible world, at the moment, until there's some return of hope.

Tony Benn

Wednesday, 13 May 2009
MPs' expenses scandal

A bidding war has broken out between the main parties to see who can display the most repentance. Cameron (who has himself repaid the cost of having his wisteria trimmed – Tory excesses are so much more elegant than ours) is leading the field with an ultimatum to eight of his Shadow Cabinet that they repay the cost of maintaining their tennis courts, swimming pools, moats etc – or else … On our side Hazel Blears (who surely will not survive the coming reshuffle) has agreed that she will, after all, be paying capital gains on one of her several former residences and tonight an ever so 'umble Phil Hope, announced he would be repaying a staggering £40,000 – the record so far.

Chris Mullin

---

* Hamid Karzai, American-backed President of Afghanistan since December 2004.

Thursday, 21 May 2009

Another colleague rings – can't stand being treated like a crook. Intends to resign and fight a by-election. I advise against this. The whole thing is a catastrophe of massive proportions.

Michael Spicer

Friday, 23 October 2009

Someone in an earlier thread [blog] reckoned that most BNP voters are ex-Conservatives. Oh how I laughed. Funny, I hadn't realised that Blackburn, Burnley, Rotherham, Dewsbury, Dagenham and Barking had ever been Conservative constituencies. I don't know if any academic work has been done in this area, but at a guess, I'd say that 80% of BNP voters are ex-Labour voters. That may not always have been the case, but I'd bet a Pound to a penny it is now.

Far left Fascist parties like the BNP invariably do well under left wing governments which fail left of centre voters. Le Pen rose to prominence in France under Mitterrand. The National Front in this country gained traction under Labour in the late 1970s, and now the BNP is on the rise here again.

Iain Dale

Tuesday, 3 November 2009

'Cameron reneges on EU Treaty vote pledge,' says the main headline in today's *Telegraph* over a report that the Tories are about to abandon – surprise, surprise – their 'cast iron' promise to hold a referendum on the Lisbon Treaty. All very pleasing. Europe remains the fault line running through the Tory party. They just can't shake it off. One has only to toss the word 'Lisbon' across the chamber and the grey pinstripes rise like a lot of Pavlov's dogs. The only other thing that gets them all going is mention of Margaret Thatcher.

Chris Mullin

Sunday, 20 December 2009

The *Mail on Sunday*'s lead story this morning concerns a teacher who has been sacked for offering comfort to the parent of a sick child by offering to pray for her. The teacher specialised in teaching children too ill to attend school. The parent made a complaint and the teacher was sacked by her managers.

Let's, for a moment, swap the religion of the teacher. Does anyone seriously imagine the teacher would have been sacked if she had been a Muslim, and offered prayers for the child? Of course not. And rightly so.

What a warped society we have become when a parent makes a vexatious complaint like this, and when the teacher, who clearly meant no harm, is then told by her employer that sharing her faith could be interpreted as 'bullying'.

Iain Dale

Thursday, 25 March 2010

Our slide in the polls goes on. *Evening Standard* claim we will no longer be the largest party. At the start of the year we were twenty six points ahead.

Michael Spicer

Sunday, 18 April 2010

Clegg mania grows steadily more ludicrous.* Today a poll suggesting he is the most popular leader since Winston Churchill. I have been acquainted with each of the last five Liberal or Lib Dem leaders and he is by far the shallowest.

Chris Mullin

In the 6 May 2010 General Election there were 307 Conservative, 258 Labour, 57 Liberal Democrat and 28 other MPs elected. Labour and the Lib Dems combined would give them a slim majority over the Conservatives. The Conservatives and Lib Dems combined would give them a comfortable majority over Labour and all other MPs ...

---

*The General Election was called for 6 May and a series of televised 'debates' with the three leaders – David Cameron, Gordon Brown and Nick Clegg – favoured Clegg in the run-up to the election.

Saturday, 8 May 2010

A pause while we wait to see who the Lib Dems will appoint to government. Everyone being nice to them. Cameron talking of 'a big, open and comprehensive deal'. Gordon, meanwhile, is insisting that it is his constitutional duty to remain in office until the mist clears.

Chris Mullin

Monday, 10 May 2010

Gordon announces his resignation. As with his Budgets, however, a careful reading of the small print reveals that, subject to the mercy of the Liberal Democrats, he is actually contemplating another five months in office, until a new Labour leader is elected. Suddenly the political landscape is transformed. Nick Clegg announces that talks with the Tories are at an end and that he could, after all, work with Labour. Much talk on our side of 'a coalition of the progressive majority'. The Tories, mightily upset, are talking bitterly of 'a coalition of losers'.

Chris Mullin

Tuesday, 11 May 2010

By late afternoon it is clear that Nick Clegg is back talking to the Tories again. At which point Gordon threw in the towel.

Chris Mullin

Wednesday, 12 May 2010

I may be basking in the warm afterglow of yesterday, but the press conference taking place at the moment is going incredibly well. Cameron and Clegg seem totally at ease with each other. Their body language is very good and yet the hacks still ask the same tired old questions. Boring, boring, boring. If all journalists want to do is ask smart-arse questions about some apparent disagreement on policy which took place five years ago, Cameron and Clegg may well decide such press conferences are a complete and utter waste of their time.

Iain Dale

The 'Con–Lib' government which materialised in May 2010 was a mirror image of the last 'Lib–Con' coalition of 1918.

The Diarists

Leo Amery (1873–1955)

Amery started his political life as a Liberal Unionist, opposed to free trade and a supporter of imperial preference and of the development of the Empire into independent nations. He was Secretary of State for the Colonies 1924–9, spent the 1930s out of government, developing the case against appeasement, and was Secretary of State for India under Churchill 1940–45. His detailed two-volume diaries embrace a span of fifty years, of which the 'wilderness years' in the 1930s are particularly interesting.

The Empire at Bay: The Leo Amery Diaries 1929–1945, edited by John Barnes and David Nicholson (Hutchinson, 1988)

Paddy Ashdown (1941–)

The former leader of the Liberal Democrats kept extensive diaries at a critical turning point for the Liberal Party, and also found time to make a tour of Britain's towns and industries outside Westminster (as did J. B. Priestley sixty years earlier) in 1993. He had his eye always on the bigger international picture and campaigned for military action in Yugoslavia during the violent break-up of that state, becoming in time the UN's 'High Representative' in Bosnia and Herzegovina. The diaries and journal capture the essence of the tumultuous 1990s.

The Ashdown Diaries, Volume One 1988–1997; *Volume Two 1997–1999* (Allen Lane, 2000, 2001); *Beyond Westminster: Finding Hope in Britain* (Simon & Schuster, 1994)

Cecil Beaton (1904–80)

Many of the entries in Cecil Beaton's *Diaries* are really highly polished and honed essays. His subjects range from the work of Coastal Command during the war to the Queen Mother visiting the theatre, and his photographer's eye notices the smallest, most telling details.

The Years Between, Diaries 1939–44; *The Happy Years, Diaries 1944–48*; *The Strenuous Years, Diaries 1948–55*; *The Restless Years, Diaries 1955–63*; *The Parting Years, Diaries 1963–74* (Weidenfeld & Nicolson, 1965–78)

Tony Benn (1925–)

The diary habit began when Tony Benn was fifteen and continued with very few breaks for seventy years. He was elected an MP in 1950 and thus his political diaries embrace Labour Prime Ministers from Clement Attlee to Gordon Brown. As a government minister Tony Benn had a significant influence on post and telecommunications, industry and the energy sector; and as a party policy-maker, on the Labour movement in the 1970s and 1980s – all of which was committed in Hansard-like detail first to paper and subsequently to a tape-recorder.

Years of Hope 1940–1962; *Out of the Wilderness 1963–67*; *Office Without Power 1968–72*; *Against the Tide 1973–76*; *Conflicts of Interest 1977–80*; *The End of an Era 1980–1990*; *Free at Last! 1991–2001*; *More Time for Politics 2001–2007* (Hutchinson, 1987–2007); and *A Blaze of Autumn Sunshine: The Last Diaries 2007–2010* (forthcoming, 2013); all edited by Ruth Winstone

Alan Bennett (1934–)

Eight years' collection of diaries – from 1996 to 2004 – are included in *Untold Stories*. 'On a personal level [they] are pretty uninformative, not to say cagey,' writes Alan Bennett. Be that as it may, as an observer of the English scene, from the death of Princess Diana to the bill to ban hunting, Bennett is invaluable.

Untold Stories (Profile/Faber and Faber, 2005)

Violet Bonham Carter (1887–1969)

The Liberal torch was carried by Lady Violet Bonham Carter for a large part of the twentieth century; she was the only daughter of Liberal Prime Minister H. H. Asquith and his first wife, and mother-in-law of

Liberal leader, Jo Grimond. (Her daughter, Laura, married Grimond.) The diaries from 1914 to 1969 are, however, much more than the story of the survival of the 'Asquithite' Liberals. They chart a close and emotional relationship with Churchill, Violet's efforts on behalf of her remarkable family, and her knowledge of international affairs. Her later years were spent campaigning in the House of Lords (as Lady Bonham-Carter).

Champion Redoubtable: The diaries and letters of Violet Bonham Carter, 1914–1945 (Weidenfeld & Nicolson, 1998); *Daring to Hope: The Diaries and Letters of Violet Bonham Carter, 1946–1969* (Weidenfeld & Nicolson, 2000), both edited by Mark Pottle

Jimmy Boyle (1944–)

No experiments, reforms or liberal Home Secretaries have effectively solved the dilemma of the cost, waste and counter-productive nature of the British system of punishment. Jimmy Boyle, a long-term prisoner, was moved to the Special Unit of Barlinnie Prison in Scotland, which was run on unconventional lines and where he was allowed to work as a sculptor. *The Pain of Confinement* is his diary of prison-life, of his interest in events outside the prison walls, and of how art helped him keep his sanity.

The Pain of Confinement (Canongate, 1984)

Gyles Brandreth (1948–)

The multi-talented Brandreth's first volume of entertaining and self-parodying diaries detailed the progress of his short parliamentary career as a Conservative MP and whip. The 1990s were a turbulent decade for the Tories and Brandreth's diary filled the void left by Alan Clark who decided to leave the Commons in 1992. The second, unexpected volume, *Something Sensational to Read in the Train*, charts Brandreth's pre-parliamentary life beginning with his school audition for *Murder in the Cathedral* and revealing his part in Lord Longford's Pornography Commission.

Breaking the Code, Westminster Diaries (Weidenfeld & Nicolson, 1999); *Something Sensational to Read in the Train: The Diary of a Lifetime* (John Murray, 2009)

Vera Brittain (1893–1970)

The *Chronicle of Youth* made Vera Brittain's reputation as a pre-eminent diarist of the First World War; her less well-known *Chronicle of Friendship* and *Diary 1939–45* are the work of a mature, successful and world-weary writer trying to make sense of the politically confused and complex 1930s and the second world war of her lifetime.

Chronicle of Friendship 1932–1939, edited by Alan Bishop (Gollancz, 1986); *Wartime Chronicle, Diary 1939–45*, edited by Alan Bishop and Y. Aleksandra Bennett (Gollancz, 1989)

Benjamin Britten (1913–76)

The youthful idealism and activism of Benjamin Britten are reflected in the composer's early diaries and letters, written against a background of looming international events which led Britten and Peter Pears to leave England for a short spell to live in America. Highly evocative, like Vera Brittain's diaries, of the pessimism of the 1930s felt by many on the left, they are also an engaging picture of childhood in rural Suffolk.

Journeying Boy: The Diaries of the Young Benjamin Britten 1928–1938, edited by John Evans (Faber, 2009); *Letters from a Life: Selected Letters and Diaries of Benjamin Britten, Vol. 1, 1923–39* and *Vol. 2, 1939–45*, edited by Donald Mitchell and Philip Reed (Faber, 1991)

Alan Brooke (Field Marshal Lord Alanbrooke) (1883–1963)

'The man at Churchill's elbow (and sometimes his throat).' The epic and masterful complete diaries of General Alan Brooke did not pull any punches when describing some of the military colleagues and Allied leaders he encountered. In 1939 he was General Officer Commanding Southern Command, becoming Chief of the Imperial General Staff at the end of 1941 and forming a vital partnership with Churchill for the rest of the war. During the war years he maintained his lifelong interest in ornithology.

Field Marshal Lord Alanbrooke: War Diaries 1939–45, edited by Alex Danchev and Daniel Todman (Weidenfeld & Nicolson, 2001)

Robert Bruce Lockhart (1887–1970)

Bruce Lockhart's adventurous life as a journalist and author, spy, diplomat and footballer was captured in a number of biographical works; his diaries for the 1920s and 1930s are somewhat tame in comparison.

The Diaries of Sir Robert Bruce Lockhart, Vol. 1, 1915–1938, edited by Kenneth Young (Macmillan, 1973)

Deborah Bull (1963–)

Deborah Bull wrote a diary for a year, and in it combined her adventures as a ballet dancer at the top of her profession with highly developed political instincts. Starting with the election of Labour, 1997–8 was a very eventful year for Deborah Bull and The Royal Ballet and the diaries uniquely bring the two worlds together.

Dancing Away: A Covent Garden Diary (Methuen, 1998)

Alexander Cadogan (1884–1968)

The conflict at the Foreign Office between the two senior civil servants, Cadogan and Robert Vansittart, was a sub-plot of the political drama occurring immediately before the Second World War; however, from 1938 when Vansittart was appointed 'Chief Diplomatic Adviser' to the Government (i.e. removed from the top Foreign Office job), Cadogan was in charge as Permanent Under-Secretary. His published diaries start with a dramatic and emotional account of the events of 1938 and continue in detail to August 1945, ending, 'There are terrible times ahead of any government in this country.'

The Diaries of Sir Alexander Cadogan, OM, 1938–1945, edited by David Dilks (Cassell, 1971)

Alastair Campbell (1957–)

Campbell is one of the most enigmatic of modern diarists. A long-standing Labour supporter, principled and highly motivated, hard-working and loyal to Tony Blair, he is also known to be ruthless. The diaries are a highly detailed record of life at the centre of the Labour maelstrom for ten years, but they belie the complexity of Campbell's character.

The Blair Years: Extracts from the Alastair Campbell Diaries (Hutchinson, 2007)

Barbara Castle (1910–2002)

Politically, Barbara Castle was quite as tough as her co-diarists in the 1964–70 and 1974–76 Wilson Cabinets, but she gave greater vent to her personal feelings in her diary – and there were plenty of disappointments and frustrations during those years. Not least were two epic and time-consuming and ultimately unsuccessful battles – with the trade union establishment over *In Place of Strife* and the consultants over the issue of private beds in NHS hospitals.

The Castle Diaries 1964–1976 (Weidenfeld & Nicolson, 1980)

Henry 'Chips' Channon (1897–1958)

The notorious diaries are of interest principally for their portrayal of the excesses of the very wealthy in 1930s London. Channon was an admirer of the Prince of Wales and Wallis Simpson, and details the close social connections between his set and their German counterparts. He was on the 'appeasement' wing of the Conservative Party, and was PPS to Rab Butler from 1936 to 1940. He and his wife, Honor Guinness, were both wealthy (he through his American family). They separated soon after their son Paul was born. Channon's hidden homosexual life can be inferred from his writing. He was MP for Southend, which had been represented by members of his wife's family and which his son, Paul, in time also represented.

'Chips': The Diaries of Sir Henry Channon, edited by Robert Rhodes James (Weidenfeld & Nicolson, 1967)

Walter Citrine (1887–1983)

Citrine was an electrician from Wallasey, Merseyside, and quickly established himself as a brilliant trade union organiser and became General Secretary of the TUC from 1924 to 1944. Thanks to his diary for the mid-1920s, the miners' strike and the traumatic General Strike are described from the perspective of the TUC in dramatic detail. He ensured that the Trades Union Congress exerted its influence over the Labour Party and he was instrumental in removing Ramsay MacDonald from the Labour Party in 1931.

Robert Taylor, 'Citrine's Unexpurgated Diaries, 1925–26. The Mining Crisis and the National Strike', *Historical Studies in Industrial Relations*, No. 20, 2005

Alan Clark (1928–99)

Clark's published diaries start in 1972 and end after his death in 1999, poignantly completed by his wife Jane. Alan Clark was his own editor of the first volume (during which he was a minister in Margaret Thatcher's government), and he did not sanitise them. They reflect his passions in life – Jane, vintage cars, other women, the Conservative Party, the Army, England, animals; in each case his personal feelings and his political instincts are interrelated to a degree rarely found in political diaries. Two further volumes were edited by Ion Trewin and published posthumously.

Diaries. In Power: 1983–1992 (Weidenfeld & Nicolson, 1993); *Diaries. Into Politics: 1972–82*, edited by Ion Trewin (Weidenfeld & Nicolson, 2000); *The Last Diaries. In and Out of the Wilderness: 1992–99*, edited by Ion Trewin (Weidenfeld & Nicolson, 2002)

Peter Clarney (dates unknown)

Peter Clarney was a Yorkshire miner who wrote a diary for the first months of the miners' strike of 1972, when Arthur Scargill's 'Flying Pickets' were employed. It is a pity he did not keep it for longer, because what there is gives unusual detail and texture to the miners' battle.

The unpublished diary is filed with the TUC Collections at the London Metropolitan University Library.

John 'Jock' Colville (1915–87)

John Colville was a Third Secretary in the Diplomatic Service, aged only twenty-four, when he was assigned to the Ministry of Economic Warfare in September 1939. 'I was given an empty desk and nothing whatever to do.' He went on to become a Private Secretary, briefly to Prime Minister Neville Chamberlain, and then to Churchill, getting to know the Churchill family and becoming a trustee and executor of his former boss. After the war he became Princess Elizabeth's Private Secretary before rejoining Churchill for the 1951–5 Conservative government. The diaries contain delightfully sceptical cameos of the 'great men' with whom he rubbed shoulders.

The Fringes of Power: Downing Street Diaries 1939–1955 (Hodder & Stoughton, 1985)

Robin Cook (1946–2005)

The Point of Departure is a day-by-day account of events leading up to Cook's resignation as Leader of the House of Commons in 2003 over his Government's invasion of Iraq. Cook had been Foreign Secretary and was a potential leader of the Party but as Blair told him in 1994 'Your problem, Robin, is that nobody trusts you. Otherwise you would be sitting in my seat.'

The Point of Departure: Diaries from the Front Bench (Simon & Schuster, 2003)

Alfred Duff Cooper (1890–1954)

The Conservative MP Duff Cooper held a number of posts between 1934 and 1947, including Secretary of State for War, First Lord of the Admiralty, and Ambassador to the Free French, then to France. He was outspoken in Cabinet against Neville Chamberlain's policy towards Germany and resigned over the Munich Agreement in 1938. His marriage to the actress Diana Manners appeared to be volatile and he made no secret in his diary of his many affairs and louche lifestyle. Duff Cooper was made Viscount Norwich in 1952.

The Duff Cooper Diaries 1915–51, edited by John Julius Norwich (Weidenfeld & Nicolson, 2005)

Noël Coward (1899–1973)

Coward's diaries began in 1941, as he embarked on his wartime concert tours in Britain (which he found irksome), and continued to the end of 1969, thus encompassing huge cultural changes (*Waiting for Godot* was 'pretentious gibberish'). During this time he moved out of and back into theatre fashion. He was knighted in 1969.

The Noël Coward Diaries, edited by Graham Payn and Sheridan Morley (Weidenfeld & Nicolson, 1982)

Richard Crossman (1907–74)

Crossman died in 1974 before his diaries were published. But the subsequent proliferation of political diaries owes a great deal to him because of the ground-breaking posthumous legal struggle with the country's top civil servants to establish the right to publish Cabinet discussions. He began a diary in 1951, and continued it throughout the 'wilderness years' and while in government from 1964 to 1970. The *Backbench Diaries* of political life in the 1950s is just as illuminating as the Cabinet diaries. 'His intellectual eminence – some would say arrogance,' his friend and biographer Tam Dalyell wrote '– left a powerful legacy.' Janet Morgan's unravelling and editing of Crossman's work and her commentary, notes and biographical entries set the standard of editorship inimitably high.

The Diaries of a Cabinet Minister: Vol. 1, Minister of Housing and Local Government 1964–66; Vol. 2, Lord President of the Council and Leader of the House of Commons 1966–68; Vol. 3, Secretary of State for Social Services 1968–70 (all Hamish Hamilton and Jonathan Cape, 1975, 1976, 1977); *The Backbench Diaries of Richard Crossman 1951–64* (Hamish Hamilton and Jonathan Cape, 1981). All edited by Janet Morgan.

Edwina Currie (1946–)

The five years covered by Edwina Currie's diaries were vital ones in the recent history of the Conservatives and for her personally. She doesn't pull any punches and, looking at the talent available, considered running for the Party leadership herself.

Edwina Currie, Diaries 1987–1992 (Little, Brown, 2002)

Iain Dale (1962–)

From outside the House of Commons, Iain Dale exerts a disproportionate influence in British politics, as a publisher, blogger and radio journalist. His is the only 'blog' used, given the shortage of Conservative diarists in the first decade of the twenty-first century. He has managed to voice the concerns of the right of the Party in public when its parliamentary representation appeared to have gone quiet.

Iain Dale's Diary (iaindale.blogspot.com/)

Hugh Dalton (1887–1962)

Dalton became the short-lived Labour MP for Peckham, South London, in 1924, and moved to Bishop Auckland (which his wife Ruth had previously represented) in 1929; he remained there for the rest of his parliamentary career. Clever, but overbearing and not popular with colleagues, he reached the office of Chancellor of the Exchequer in

1945, which ended prematurely due to a minor (by today's standard) Budget leak. Thereafter he encouraged the careers of his protégés, particularly Hugh Gaitskell. The diaries are useful in the huge span of Labour history which they cover, revelling in the personal rivalries (long before Blair–Brown) in the Party particularly after the 1945 election. It was a shock when Dalton's editor, Ben Pimlott, who had produced an award-winning biography of the almost-forgotten Dalton in 1985, died of leukaemia in 2004 aged fifty-nine.

The Political Diary of Hugh Dalton 1918–40 and 1945–60, edited by Ben Pimlott (Jonathan Cape, 1986)

Audrey Deacon (1918–2012)

Most of the action in Audrey Deacon's diary takes place in and around Plymouth where she was recruited and trained in cipher work and attached to the Commander-in-Chief. The constant fear of bombardment in that city is mixed with the tragic death of her newly-wed husband, a Second Lieutenant in the Sixth Airborne Division.

Diary of a Wren, 1940–1945 (The Memoir Club, 2001)

Bernard Donoughue (1934–)

Donoughue was a clever young economist teaching at the LSE when he was attached to Harold Wilson for the General Election of 1974, and went on to work for Prime Minister Wilson and his successor James Callaghan. Coincidentally, Donoughue and Marcia Williams, whom he was to meet and clash with at No. 10, were educated in Northampton at the same time. The diaries give a highly personal, entertaining and revealing account of his life as an adviser in the 1970s.

Downing Street Diary: With Harold Wilson in No. 10 (Jonathan Cape, 2005)

Blanche 'Baffy' Dugdale (1890–1948)

These unusual diaries by the niece of Arthur Balfour describe the day-to-day progress and the single-minded determination of a group of Zionists in England to establish a Jewish state in the Middle East. The diaries start in 1936, and continue throughout and beyond the Second World War, when the idea of a state of Israel became a fact, with all the ramifications for the second half of the twentieth century.

Baffy: the Diaries of Blanche Dugdale, 1936–1947 (Vallentine Mitchell & Co., 1973)

Brian Eno (1948–)

This is Eno's description of himself from his diaries: 'I am: a mammal, a father, a European, a heterosexual, an artist, a son, an inventor, an Anglo-Saxon, an uncle, a celebrity, a masturbator, a cook, a gardener, an improviser, a husband, a musician, a company director, an employer, a teacher, a wine-lover, a cyclist, a non-driver, a pragmatist, a producer, a writer, a computer user, a Caucasian, an interviewee, a grumbler, a "drifting clarifier".' And once a musician with Roxy Music! His diary for the year 1995 is a reflection of all or most of these attributes – highly personal and truly unique.

A Year with Swollen Appendices: Brian Eno's Diary (Faber and Faber, 1996)

Hugh Gaitskell (1906–63)

Gaitskell's appearance was 'like a certain type of High Church clergyman with a slum parish'; but his ecclesiastical looks belied a liberal approach to private life and a great sense of fun. He was one of the Labour MPs swept into Parliament on the 1945 tide – the Member for Leeds South. His diaries bridge the gap between the euphoria of the 1945 Labour election victory and the inevitable disillusionment with Clem Attlee, whom he replaced as Leader of the Labour Party at the end of 1955. His diaries ceased during the intense pressure of the Suez crisis and were never resumed. He died unexpectedly in 1963, as did John Smith thirty-one years later, leaving the Labour Party to consider what might have been.

Diary of Hugh Gaitskell 1945–1956, edited by Philip Williams (Jonathan Cape, 1983)

Christopher Gill (1936–)

The memoir by Christopher Gill gives a blow-by-blow description of the Conservative rebels' tactics on the Maastricht Treaty between 1992 and 1994, the ramifications of which continued until 1997. The title of the book refers to the removal of the Whip from eight of the rebels; Gill subsequently left the Conservatives and joined the United Kingdom Independence Party.

Whips' Nightmare: Diary of a Maastricht Rebel (Memoir Club, 2003)

Joyce Grenfell (1910–79)

Between January 1944 and March 1945 Joyce Grenfell and her pianist Viola Tunnard travelled between England and North Africa, Iraq, Iran, India and Eastern Arabia for ENSA ('Every Night Something Awful'), putting up with cold rooms, no water, no wardrobes and ENSA inefficiency. Edited by theatre director, James Roose-Evans, the *Wartime Journals* are one of the unexpected treats which I discovered among the 100 volumes on my reading list.

The Time of My Life: Entertaining the Troops – Her Wartime Journals, edited by James Roose-Evans (Hodder and Stoughton, 1989)

Alec Guinness (1914–2000)

The diaries of the great actor Sir Alec Guinness are spare, wry and poignant, as he comes to terms in his eighties with life at the end of the century.

My Name Escapes Me: The Diary of a Retiring Actor (Hamish Hamilton, 1996)

Peter Hall (1930–)

Peter Hall's move from the Royal Shakespeare Company he founded, to the National Theatre while it was still under construction on the South Bank, coincided with one of the most volatile political decades and with the increasing disputes between the worlds of the arts and politics. Given the overwhelming problems described in the riveting *Diaries*, it is a miracle that any play was ever produced there in the mid-1970s.

Peter Hall's Diaries: The Story of a Dramatic Battle, edited by John Goodman (Hamish Hamilton, 1983)

John Horner (1911–97)

Horner became General Secretary of the Fire Brigades Union, aged only twenty-seven, in 1939 and used the wartime conditions to build up the union, recruiting the new 'Auxiliary Fire Service' members, and to transform the fire service itself, fighting for it into the 1950s and 1960s. He was also a Labour MP, 1964–70.

Forged in Fire: The history of the Fire Brigades Union, edited by Victor Bailey (Lawrence and Wishart, 1992)

Tom Hurndall (1981–2003)

A student photojournalist covering the work of the International Solidarity Movement, Tom Hurndall was fatally shot by an Israeli sniper while in Rafah in the Gaza Strip. In his youthful journal he tried to unravel the propaganda and the half-truths of the Israel–Palestine conflict.

The Only House Left Standing: the Middle East Journals of Tom Hurndall (Trolley Books, 2012)

Roy Jenkins (1920–2003)

The most significant entries in the diary kept by Roy Jenkins as President of the European Commission, 1976–80, concern the state of the Labour Party and the emergence back in Britain of the Social Democratic Party, which he was instrumental in founding.

European Diary, 1977–1981 (Collins, 1989)

Thomas Jones (1870–1955)

As Deputy Cabinet Secretary and fellow Welshman, Thomas Jones got to know David Lloyd George well during the latter's premiership. Both spoke Welsh as their first language; and Jones became part of Lloyd George's intimate circle. He went on to become President of the University College of Wales in Aberystwyth.

Whitehall Diary, Vol. 1, 1916–25, edited by Keith Middlemass (Oxford University Press, 1969)

Oona King (1967–)

Possibly one of the hardest working Members of the House of Commons, Oona King, the MP for the Asian-dominated East End constituency of Bethnal Green and Bow, somehow found time to keep a diary from her election in 1997 to her very public defeat in 2005. It is a unique mix of the parliamentary, constituency and personal agonies of an MP who faced a ruthless macho culture.

House Music: The Oona King Diaries (Bloomsbury, 2007)

Alan Lascelles (1887–1981)

The nature of Sir Alan Lascelles' contempt for the Prince of Wales (Edward VIII) and his thoughts on the Abdication Crisis became clear when his private diaries were published in 2006: Lascelles was Assistant Private Secretary to the heir to the throne in the 1920s but left his service in 1928; when he returned to work for George V in 1935 little did he know that the crisis was just around the corner, and that he would end up working with Edward's brother, King George VI, and for a short while Elizabeth II. He was in office during the transition from coalition war government to the Labour administration of 1945.

King's Counsellor: Abdication and War – The Diaries of Sir Alan Lascelles, edited by Duff Hart-Davis (Weidenfeld & Nicolson, 2006)

Nella Last (1890–1968)

The woman who was known only by the description 'housewife' and the number '49' to the Mass Observation project proved to be a highly talented, intelligent and perceptive writer. The daily record of her domestic routine, her WVS work, her sons' prospects, her neighbour's troubles, her husband's moods, written throughout the war and the following years, and sent weekly to the MO office, were discovered and published posthumously. Thanks to her editors, millions of words were reduced to two compelling volumes, *Nella Last's War* and *Nella Last's Peace*. The Last family lived in the shipyard town of Barrow-in-Furness which was continually battered by war-time bombing.

Nella Last's War: A Mother's Diary, 1939–45, edited by Richard Broad and Suzie Fleming (Falling Wall Press, 1981); *Nella Last's Peace: The Post-war Diaries of Housewife, 49,* edited by Patricia and Robert Malcolmson (Profile Books, 2008)

Lord Longford (1905–2001)

Lord Longford's eccentricities are engagingly illustrated in his two books of diaries, in which he is a perceptive judge of people in and outside political life and a well-known proponent of reform of prisons and prisoners.

Diary of a Year (Weidenfeld & Nicolson, 1982); *Lord Longford's Prison Diary*, edited by Peter Stanford (Lion Publishing, 2000)

Harold Macmillan (1894–1986)

It is amazing that Macmillan managed to carry on writing a diary during his premiership from 1957 to 1963, given the many foreign and defence policy issues and other preoccupations of that time. The three volumes demonstrate Macmillan's consensual, paternalistic brand of Conservatism – particularly the years between 1951 and 1954 when he held the housing and local government portfolio – as well as his dry sense of humour and prodigious energy. Alongside his political life he continued an active interest in the family publishing business and read voraciously, describing Sir Walter Scott as his favourite vice. He was MP for Stockton-on-Tees before the war and Bromley from 1945. He married Lady Dorothy Cavendish, daughter of the 9th Duke of Devonshire, who was partly brought up at Chatsworth House, Derbyshire.

War Diaries: Politics and War in the Mediterranean January 1943–May 1945 (Macmillan, 1984); *The Macmillan Diaries: The Cabinet Years, 1950–1957* (Macmillan, 2003) and Vol. II, *Prime Minister and After, 1957–63* (Macmillan, 2011), both edited by Peter Catterall

James Maxton (1885–1946)

Maxton was a school teacher by profession and chairman of the Independent Labour Party (ILP) for two periods in the 1920s and 1930s; he had been a conscientious objector in the First World War, and became a Glasgow Labour MP in 1922. He was a highly effective speaker and parliamentary operator. He is the subject of a biography by Gordon Brown.

David Temple, *The Big Meeting: A history of the Durham Miners' Gala* (TUPS Books/Durham Miners Association, 2011)

Piers Morgan (1965–)

Two diaries published by Piers Morgan embrace show business and politics during his eleven years as a talented and ruthless (and occasionally soft-hearted) young journalist, starting in 1993 at the

Murdoch press, progressing to editorship first of the *News of the World* aged twenty-eight and then to the *Daily Mirror* and beyond after his sacking in 2004 over an Iraq war story.

The Insider: The Private Diaries of a Scandalous Decade (Ebury Press, 2005); *Don't You Know Who I Am?* (Ebury Press, 2007)

Louis Mountbatten (1900–1979)

The published diaries of Louis Mountbatten have been divided into three volumes by his editor Philip Ziegler. From 1920 to 1922, when Lord Louis was a young sub-lieutenant; the war years 1943–46, when as Admiral Lord Louis Mountbatten he was in Supreme Command of the Allied forces in South East Asia; and as Admiral of the Fleet, Earl Mountbatten of Burma, from 1953 until 1979. In the post-war years he was Viceroy of India, First Sea Lord and from 1959 to 1965 Chief of Defence Staff. Mountbatten's war-time military colleague, Field Marshal Alanbrooke did not have a high opinion of him, attributing his SEAC success to 'a number of talented subordinates'.

Mountbatten was a cousin of the Prince of Wales (Edward VIII – both were great-grandsons of Queen Victoria), and the diaries are an incomparable account of aristocratic, naval and public life in the twentieth century.

The Diaries of Lord Louis Mountbatten 1920–1922 (Collins, 1987); *Personal Diary of Admiral the Lord Louis Mountbatten 1943–1946* (Collins, 1988); *From Shore to Shore: The Final Years. The Diaries of Earl Mountbatten of Burma 1953–1979* (Collins, 1989), all edited by Philip Ziegler

Malcolm Muggeridge (1903–90)

'St Mugg' travelled from political idealism back to the Christianity of his youth, and his early diaries are full of soul-searching and unhappiness between flashes of humour and insight. As a correspondent in Moscow, he abhorred the Webbs' naive view of communism in the Soviet Union in the 1930s. Muggeridge was appointed to Lord Longford's enquiry into pornography in 1971 and was described by Gyles Brandreth (an unlikely fellow committee member) as 'broadcaster and sage, looking like a dandified turtle'.

Like It Was: A Selection from the Diaries of Malcolm Muggeridge, edited by John Bright-Holmes (Collins, 1981)

Chris Mullin (1947–)

Chris Mullin had already had a number of works published (including the political thriller *A Very British Coup*, 1982) when he became Labour MP for Sunderland in 1987. His diaries are written with a journalist's craft – and without an axe to grind despite the reputation he had as a left-wing trouble-maker before his election.

A View from the Foothills. The Diaries of Chris Mullin (Profile Books, 2009); *Decline & Fall, Diaries 2005–2010* (Profile Books, 2010); *A Walk-On Part, Diaries 1994–1999* (Profile Books, 2011)

Harold Nicolson (1886–1968)

Many letters and diaries were written by Harold Nicolson throughout a life which embraced several changes of career – from the diplomatic service, to journalism, Parliament (National Labour MP for Leicester West), ministerial life (briefly) and successful authorship. The diaries are endearingly self-deprecatory and candid, with affectionate descriptions of his remarkable family life. The Nicolsons lived at Long Barn in Kent until 1930 and moved thence to Sissinghurst Castle where they devoted much of their time to the gardens.

The Harold Nicolson Diaries 1907–1963, edited by Nigel Nicolson (Weidenfeld & Nicolson, 2004)

Joe Orton (1933–67)

Joe Orton had been writing his diary for a year when he was killed with a hammer by his homosexual partner, who also killed himself. Orton's diaries are preoccupied with detailing his prolific sexual encounters with other men; but they are interesting for the sentiments expressed by the successful young playwright which ran counter to the prevailing liberal orthodoxy of the 1960s.

The Orton Diaries, edited by John Lahr (Methuen, 1986)

George Orwell (1903–50)

Orwell's diaries of the 1930s and 1940s are an eccentric mix of political observations and rural preoccupations: when extracts were published as a 'blog' in 2008, this format perfectly suited them.

Orwell Diaries, edited by Peter Hobley Davison (Harvill Secker, 2009)

Michael Palin (1943–)

A Python's thoughtful account of the Heath years, the Labour government, the election of Margaret Thatcher and the making of *The Life of Brian* (and the ferret trouser sketch).

Diaries 1969–1979: The Python Years (Weidenfeld & Nicolson, 2006)

Frances Partridge (1900–2004)

The 'last of the Bloomsburys', Frances Partridge lived for the whole of the twentieth century, and for much of it she kept personal diaries. Her observations, as a pacifist, on the post-Second World War years and the 'nuclear bomb' generation, demarcate the pro and anti camps in the developing Cold War.

Everything to Lose: Diaries 1945–1960 (Gollancz, 1985)

Lance Price (1958–)

For a few years, Lance Price, a BBC political correspondent, gave up the BBC to work with Alastair Campbell in the Prime Minister's office. His diaries are cool, level-headed and candid about No. 10 and the role of a spin doctor.

The Spin Doctor's Diary: Inside Number 10 with New Labour (Hodder and Stoughton, 2005)

J. B. Priestley (1894–1984)

In 1933, Priestley visited every part of England and *English Journey* was the result. Although not strictly diaries, the essays are contemporary in nature and give a highly evocative picture of the English at leisure and work.

English Journey (Heinemann in association with Gollancz, 1934)

Giles Radice (1936–)

Of the diarists of the second half of the twentieth century, Giles Radice is one of the most informative and enlightening. A committed European, Radice wrote his diaries during a highly eventful historical period as communism collapsed and the European Union expanded and changed its nature. He also described the vicissitudes of the Labour

Party in and outside Parliament; he was Labour MP for Chester-le-Street/North Durham, 1973–2001, and a Select committee chairman.

Diaries 1980–2001, From Political Disaster to Election Triumph (Weidenfeld & Nicolson, 2004)

John Rae (1931–2006)

Rae was the radical headmaster of Westminster School from 1970 until 1986; he tried to change the culture of the famous public school by recruiting girls and trying to establish a closer relationship with the state sector and society outside the school walls. His diaries reveal the extent of the connections between the educational, religious and political elites of London; the hostility of some of his colleagues to his ideas; and the burgeoning problem of drugs – and parental interference – in the school.

The Old Boys' Network: A Headmaster's Diaries 1970–1986 (Short Books, 2009)

John Reith (1889–1971)

The first general manager of the British Broadcasting Company, the Scot John Reith confided his hopes and ambitions to his diaries with frequent reference to his Christian convictions. They partly reveal the troubled man whom John Freeman interviewed in his BBC *Face to Face* programme; and hint at Reith's difficult relations with governments in the 1920s and 1930s, his authoritarianism and the direction in which he wished to take the BBC. He was made a minister in the wartime government but was not successful and, to quote John Colville, 'he loathed Churchill, whom he found insufficiently Puritan'.

The Reith Diaries, edited by Charles Stuart (Collins, 1975)

George Riddell (1865–1935)

The circle of confidantes around Lloyd George included George Riddell, who was a solicitor and newspaper proprietor; and from 1903, managing director of the *News of the World*. He was used by Lloyd George during the First World War and at the Paris peace negotiations to handle relations with the press. Ennobled by Lloyd George, the financial relationship between the two would not have passed a Ministerial Code of Conduct test.

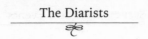

Lord Riddell's Intimate Diary of the Peace Conference and After, 1918–1923 (Gollancz, 1933)

Stephen Spender (1909–95)

The poet began his first Journal on the eve of war, September 1939 ('the hysteria of the public disaster was for me compounded by a private disaster of my own, the breakdown of my first marriage') and was still writing at the start of the 1980s.

Stephen Spender Journals 1939–1983, edited by John Goldsmith (Faber, 1985)

Michael Spicer (1943–)

After serving in Margaret Thatcher's administration, Michael Spicer became a leading opponent of the euro and therefore of the Maastricht Treaty (signed by John Major in 1991); his diaries give a subtle view of the turmoil which preceded and followed its ratification in the House of Commons. His chairmanship of the 1922 Committee (i.e. the Tory backbench MPs) from 2001 put him at the heart of the Party dramas during the years of Tory opposition and readjustment. He retired in 2010; the *Spicer Diaries* may well be the last political diaries as we know them.

The Spicer Diaries (Biteback Books, 2012)

Frances Stevenson (1888–1972)

David Lloyd George did not keep a diary, but fortunately his mistress Frances Stevenson did, giving a highly subjective and vivid account of 'D's' life as Prime Minister of the post-war Coalition, and of his role in the demise of the Liberal Party in the 1920s and 1930s. They shared a house together at Churt, Surrey, though Lloyd George continued to maintain the façade of a happy marriage to his long-suffering wife, Margaret. He and Frances married, after Margaret died (in 1941), in 1943; Frances became the Countess Lloyd-George in 1945. They had a daughter, Jennifer, who died in 2012.

Lloyd George – A Diary, edited by A. J. P. Taylor (Hutchinson, 1971)

Roy Strong (1935–)

The sharp and observant *Diaries* record a volatile period in art and politics when Strong was a young, unconventional director, first of the National Portrait Gallery and then of the Victoria and Albert Museum, where he attempted to bring order to a dysfunctional organisation. The years were at times painful, he wrote. His diaries owe a great deal to Cecil Beaton's influence.

The Roy Strong Diaries 1967–1987 (Weidenfeld & Nicolson, 1997)

Kenneth Tynan (1927–80)

Theatre critic Kenneth Tynan gained notoriety because he used the 'f-word' (in full) on live television and caused uproar; his diaries are an irreverent and sceptical commentary on life in the 1970s. He created a musical *O! Calcutta!*, which included scenes with naked performers. This led Roy Strong to note: 'I have never been so aware how anti-erotic nudity could be.' But it was nevertheless successful.

The Diaries of Kenneth Tynan, edited by John Lahr (Bloomsbury, 2001)

Evelyn Waugh (1903–66)

The irascibility and sense of the absurd are present in Evelyn Waugh's diaries from the very start of his school days, beginning in 1911 at Heath Mount prep school and later at Lancing College.

The Diaries of Evelyn Waugh, edited by Michael Davie (Weidenfeld & Nicolson, 1976)

Beatrice Webb (1858–1943)

Clever and rich, and conscious of her 'social superiority', Beatrice Webb had a great influence on the evolution of the Labour Party into a paternalistic, anti-syndicalist, reforming body. She and Sidney Webb contributed intellectually and practically to a wide range of other public and socialist causes, including higher education, through the London School of Economics and Imperial College, wage and welfare policy, and the Fabian Society. She was a shrewd judge of character and a brilliant analyst of political situations, although her critical judgement was suspended when she and Sidney visited the Soviet Union. Had she married her Liberal suitor, Joseph Chamberlain, instead of Sidney Webb, Labour in the twentieth century might have been quite different.

Beatrice Webb's Diaries 1912–1924 and *1924–1932*, edited by Margaret Cole (Longmans, Green and Co., 1952)

Charles Wilson (Lord Moran) (1882–1977)

Churchill's personal doctor during the war, Charles Wilson was President of the Royal College of Physicians from 1941 until 1950. He accompanied Churchill on most of his overseas visits from December 1941 and continued to advise him throughout the 1950s. He was given a peerage by Churchill in 1943. Beautifully written and with insights on the war years and after, from his unusual and privileged perspective, Moran's diaries caused an outcry on their publication after Churchill's death. Moran excused his revelations, wrote John Colville, 'on the fallacious grounds that Churchill's health affected the outcome of the war. It was President Roosevelt whose powers were failing, not Churchill.'

Winston Churchill: The Struggle for Survival 1940–1965 (Constable, 1966)

Jim Wilson (1951–)

Jim Wilson is a retired Northumberland miner who started his training in 1968 while still a teenager. One of his jobs was to look after the pit ponies in Glebe Colliery.

Ken Smith, *The Great Northern Miners* (Tyne Bridge Publishing, 2008)

Jimmy Wilson (1973–)

Jimmy is the son of Jim Wilson, who took his son down the Wearmouth Colliery in 1993. Jimmy recorded his impressions of the experience – and the end of a family tradition.

Ken Smith, *The Great Northern Miners* (Tyne Bridge Publishing, 2008)

Virginia Woolf (1882–1941)

Virginia Woolf kept diaries from 1915 until her suicide in 1941. One of the most idiosyncratic and original writers of the twentieth century, her diaries are a compelling stream of observations about her neighbours, her servants, her 'set', public figures and her own mental state. She and Leonard founded and ran the Hogarth Press and thus knew many of the budding writers, and their works, in the years between the wars, including T. S. Eliot, D. H. Lawrence and James Joyce – on all of whom she had acute opinions.

The Diary of Virginia Woolf, Vol. 2, 1920–24; Vol. 3, 1925–1930; Vol. 4, 1931–35; Vol. 5, 1936–1941; all edited by Anne Olivier Bell (Harcourt Brace Jovanovich, 1978, 1980, 1982, 1984)

Woodrow Wyatt (1918–97)

Through journalism (including a column for the *News of the World*) and his business interests in horse-racing, Woodrow Wyatt appeared to be on intimate terms with members of the royal family, as well as with Rupert Murdoch and Margaret Thatcher. It is sometimes forgotten that he was also a Labour MP between 1945 and 1970. His journals, written during an eventful period for the Conservative Party and the royal family, are colourful, amusing and revealing, although they may have to be taken with a pinch of salt.

The Journals of Woodrow Wyatt, Vol. 1, 1985–1988; Vol. 2, 1989–1992; Vol. 3, 1992–1997 (Macmillan, 1998, 1999, 2000); all edited by Sarah Curtis

List of plates & photographic acknowledgements

1. Alan 'Tommy' Lascelles (right) with the Prince of Wales, Edward Windsor in the USA, 1924. Photo: Hulton Archive / Getty Images
2. Beatrice Webb, 1926. Photo: Getty Images
3. Virginia Woolf with T. S. Eliot, photograph by Lady Ottoline Morrell, June 1924. Photo: © National Portrait Gallery, London
4. Left to right: Frances Stevenson, Lloyd George, the nanny, Jennifer Stevenson, the Dutch captain of the ship on which they were travelling, early 1930s. Photo by A. J. Sylvester. Photo: By permission of the National Library of Wales (PG3058/15 Llyfr Ffoto LLGC : NLW Photograph Album 1219)
5. Walter Citrine with George Lansbury marching at the National Demonstration on Unemployment, Hyde Park, London, 1933. From *Men & Work: An Autobiography* by Walter Citrine, Hutchinson, 1964
6. Shirley and John Catlin on holiday with their mother, Vera Brittain. Photo: courtesy Shirley Williams
7. Sir John Reith, leaving the Annexe of Westminster Abbey, London, after superintending the broadcast arrangements for the coronation service, 3 May 1937. Photo: P A Photos/AP /Putnam
8. J. B. Priestley at a fund-raising cricket match between authors and actresses, Highgate, London, July 1938. Photo: Topfoto
9. Cecil Beaton with albums. Photo by an anonymous photographer, late 1930s. Photo: © National Portrait Gallery, London
10. Benjamin Britten outside a fisherman's hut, Portland, Maine, September 1940. Photo: Bicknell Photo Service. Image reproduced by courtesy of the Britten-Pears Foundation (www.brittenpears.org) Ref. PH/1/69
11. John 'Jock' Colville with Clementine Churchill at Chequers, 1941. Photo: Private Collection
12. Blanche 'Baffy' Dugdale in Israel, *c.*1944 photo by Liselotte Grschebina. Photo: The Israel Museum, Jerusalem/The Bridgeman Art Library
13. Nella Last with her son, Cliff, 1940. Photo: private collection courtesy of Peter Last

14. Charles Wilson, Lord Moran, with nursing staff, September 1949. Photo: Warburton/Topical Press Agency/Hulton Archive/Getty Images
15. Joyce Grenfell performing to soldiers at the Hans Crescent Red Cross Club, London, January 1944. Photo: David E. Scherman/Time & Life Pictures/Getty Images)
16. Malcolm Muggeridge in Moscow, 1959. Photo: Mirrorpix
17. Prime Minister Harold Macmillan with England captain Ted Dexter (left) and West Indian Test cricket captain Frank Worrell (right) following their lunch at Chequers, September 1963. Photo: Central Press/Hulton Archive/Getty Images
18. Kenneth Tynan, February 1956. Photo: PA Photos
19. Joe Orton, photograph by Lewis Morley, 1965. Photo: Topfoto
20. Jimmy Boyle at work on a sculpture in Barlinnie prison, 1980. Photo: *Daily Record* Archives/Mirrorpix
21. Violet Bonham-Carter and Jo Grimond during a break from the Liberal Party Assembly in Llandudno, September 1962. Photo: AP/PA Photos
22. Barbara Castle, Minister of State for Transport, at the wheel of the *Royal Daffodil II*, March 1967. Photo: Keystone/Hulton Archive/Getty Images
23. Louis Mountbatten with HM Queen Elizabeth II and her corgis watching competitors during the Royal Windsor Horse Show, May 1973. Photo: PA Photos
24. Tony Benn (right) with Minister for Industry Lord Beswick (left) and French Secretary for Transport M. Marcel Cavaille discussing the progress of Concorde, March 1975. Photo: PA Archive/PA Images
25. Sir Peter Hall with the English actor and director Laurence Olivier on the terrace of the National Theatre, London, May 1973. Photo: *Evening Standard*/Getty Images
26. Sir Woodrow Wyatt at the Cheltenham Gold Cup, March 1987. Photo: Topfoto
27. Alan Clark with his wife Jane at their home, Hythe, Kent, June 1994. Photo: John Giles/PA Photos
28. Foreign Secretary Robin Cook (right) reads the form with Channel 4 racing presenter John McCririck, Brighton, September 1997. Photo: Topfoto/Sean Dempsey/PA
29. Deborah Bull performing in 'Concerto', 1998. Photo: © Robbie Jack/Corbis
30. Chris Mullin is re-elected MP for Sunderland South. Photo: *Sunderland Echo*
31. Oona King MP meets potential voters while campaigning at the Columbia Road flower market, London, April 2005. Photo: O. Anderson/AFP/Getty Images

While every effort has been made to contact copyright holders, the publishers will be happy to make good in future editions any errors or omissions brought to their attention.

Acknowledgments

I would particularly like to thank the following for their help and generosity in allowing me to use their work: Giles Radice, Tony Benn, Chris Mullin, Deborah Bull, Gyles Brandreth, Paddy Ashdown, Oona King and Bloomsbury Publishing, Bernard Donoughue, Brian Eno, Christopher Gill, Lord Norwich, Philip Ziegler, Michael Spicer, Jim Wilson.

Two bodies were extremely efficient and took a great deal of trouble in locating and lending books or documents: the TUC Library Collections (at the London Metropolitan University) under the Librarian Christine Coates; and Bideford Library in North Devon (thanks to Devon County Council for preserving its service).

The Britten-Pears Foundation generously granted me use of Benjamin Britten, *Journeying Boy: The diaries of the young Benjamin Britten 1928–38* edited by John Evans, Faber and Faber (2009); *Letters from a Life 1923–39* and *1939–45* edited by Donald Mitchell and Philip Reed, Faber and Faber (1991).

*****

Lord Alanbrooke, *War Diaries of Field Marshal Lord Alanbrooke 1939–45* edited by Alex Danchev and Daniel Todman, Weidenfeld and Nicolson (2001) by permission of David Higham Associates

Leo Amery, *The Empire at Bay: Diaries 1929–45* edited by John Barnes and David Nicholson, Random House (1988) by permission of David Higham Associates

Paddy Ashdown, *Diaries Volume One 1988–97* Allen Lane (2000); *Volume Two 1997–99* Allen Lane (2001); *Beyond Westminster*, Simon & Schuster (1994)

Cecil Beaton, *Diaries: 1939–44 The Years Between; 1944–48 The Happy Years; 1948–55 The Strenuous Years; 1955–63 The Restless Years; 1963–74 The Parting Years.* Weidenfeld and Nicolson (1965, 1972, 1973, 1976, 1978) by kind permission of Rupert Crew Ltd

Tony Benn, *Years of Hope 1940–62* (1994); *Out of the Wilderness 1963–67* (1987); *Office Without Power 1968–72* (1988); *Against the Tide 1973–76* (1989); *Conflicts of Interest 1977–80* (1990); *End of an Era 1980–90* (1992); *Free at Last 1991–2001* (2001); *More Time for Politics 2001–2007* (2007); *The Last Diaries 2007–10* (forthcoming) edited by Ruth Winstone; Hutchinson by kind permission of Tony Benn

Alan Bennett, *Untold Stories* Profile/Faber and Faber (2005)

Violet Bonham Carter, *Champion redoubtable: Diaries and Letters 1914–45* (1998); *Daring to Hope 1946–69* (2000) both edited by Mark Pottle, Weidenfeld and Nicolson. By kind permission of Aitken Alexander Associates on behalf of the Bonham Carter estate

Jimmy Boyle, *The Pain of Confinement: Prison Diaries*, Canongate (1984)

Gyles Brandreth, *Breaking the Code*, Weidenfeld and Nicolson, (1999); *Something sensational to read in the train*, John Murray (2009). By kind permission of Gyles Brandreth

Vera Brittain, *Chronicle of Friendship* 1932–39 (1986); *Vera Brittain's Diary* 1939–45 (1993) edited by Alan Bishop. Victor Gollancz

Robert Bruce Lockhart, *The Diaries of Sir Robert Bruce Lockhart* Volume I, edited by Kenneth Young, Macmillan (1973)

Deborah Bull, *Dancing Away 1997–98*, Methuen (1998) By kind permission of Deborah Bull CBE and Methuen

Alexander Cadogan, *Diaries of Sir Alexander Cadogan 1938–45* edited by David Dilks, Cassell (1971)

Alastair Campbell, *The Blair Years: Extracts from the Alastair Campbell Diaries* Hutchinson (2007). Reprinted by permission of the Random House Group Ltd

Barbara Castle, *The Castle Diaries 1964–76* Macmillan (1980) by permission of David Higham Associates

Henry 'Chips' Channon, *The Diaries of Sir Henry Channon* edited by Robert Rhodes James, Weidenfeld and Nicolson (1967)

Walter Citrine, *The Mining Crisis and the National Strike* Historical Studies in Industrial Relations, 20 (2005)

Alan Clark, *Diaries 1983–1992*, Weidenfeld and Nicolson, (1993) © 1993 Alan Clark; *Into Politics: Diaries 1972–82*, Weidenfeld and Nicolson edited by Ion Trewin (2000) © 2000 The Estate of Alan Clark; *The Last Diaries Diaries: 1992–99*, Weidenfeld and Nicolson edited by Ion Trewin (2002) © 2002 The Estate of Alan Clark. Jane Clark's Journal © 2002 Jane Clark. By kind permission of Weidenfeld and Nicolson, a division of the Orion Publishing Group, London

Peter Clarney, diary manuscript in the TUC Library Collections with thanks to the Librarian of the Collections, London Metropolitan University

John Colville, *The Fringes of Power: Downing Street Diaries 1939–55*, Hodder and Stoughton (1985)

Robin Cook, *Point of Departure*, Simon and Schuster (2003)

Alfred Duff Cooper, *The Duff Cooper Diaries 1915–51* edited by John Julius Norwich, Weidenfeld and Nicolson (2005) by kind permission of Lord Norwich

Noel Coward, *The Noel Coward Diaries* edited by Graham Payn and Sheridan Morley, Weidenfeld and Nicolson (1982) © Graham Payn 1972. By kind permission of Weidenfeld and Nicolson, a division of the Orion Publishing Group, London

Richard Crossman, *Minister of Housing and Local Government 1964–66* (1975); *Lord President of the Council and Leader of the House of Commons 1966–68* (1976); *Secretary of State for Health and Social Security 1968–70* (1977); *Backbench Diaries 1951–64* (1981): all published by Hamish Hamilton and Jonathan Cape and edited by Janet Morgan

Edwina Currie, *Diaries 1987–92* Little, Brown (2002) by kind permission of Little Brown Book Group

Iain Dale *iaindale.blogspot.com* By kind permission of Iain Dale

Hugh Dalton, *Political Diary of Hugh Dalton 1918–40* and *1945–69* edited by Ben Pimlott, Random House (1987) reprinted by permission of the Random House Group Ltd and the London School of Economics and Political Science

Audrey Deacon, *The Diary of a Wren*, The Memoir Club (2001)

Bernard Donoughue, *Downing Street Diary*, Jonathan Cape (2005) reprinted by permission of the Random House Group Ltd

Blanche Dugdale, *Diaries 1936–47*, Valentine Mitchell (1973)

Brian Eno, *A Year with Swollen Appendices: Brian Eno's Diary*, Faber and Faber (1996)

Hugh Gaitskell, *Diary of Hugh Gaitskell 1945–56* edited by Philip Williams, Jonathan Cape (1983)

Acknowledgments

Christopher Gill, *Whip's Nightmare*, The Memoir Club (2003) by kind permission of Christopher Gill

Joyce Grenfell, *The Time of my Life: Entertaining the Troops – her War time Journals* edited by James Roose-Evans, Hodder and Stoughton (1989)

Alec Guinness, *My Name Escapes Me*, Hamish Hamilton (1996) by permission of David Higham Associates

Peter Hall, *The Peter Hall Diaries* Hamish Hamilton (1983) by kind permission of Peter Hall

Viviene Hall, extract from *The Home Front* ed Norman Longmate, Chatto and Windus (1981)

John Horner quoted in *Forged in Fire: The history of the Fire Brigades Union* edited by Victor Bailey, Lawrence and Wishart (1992), with thanks to the FBU

Tom Hurndall, *The Only House Left Standing: The Middle East Journals*, Trolley Books (2012) by kind permission of Anthony and Jocelyn Hurndall and Trolley Books

Roy Jenkins, *European Diary*, Collins (1989)

Thomas Jones, *Whitehall Diary* Vol. 1 1916–25, Vol. 2 1926–30 edited by Keith Middlemass, TUC books (1969) by kind permission of the OUP and TUC Publications

Oona King, *House Music: The Oona King Diaries*, Bloomsbury (2007), © Oona King, courtesy of Bloomsbury Publishing plc

Alan Lascelles, *King's Counsellor – Abdication and War: Diaries of Sir Alan Lascelles* edited by Duff Hart-Davis, Weidenfeld and Nicolson, an imprint of the Orion Publishing Group, London. © The Estate of Sir Alan Lascelles 2006

Nella Last, *Nella Last's War* edited by Richard Broad and Suzie Fleming, Falling Wall Press (1981); *Nella Last's Peace* edited by Patricia and Robert Malcolmson, Profile (2008) Reprinted by permission of Curtis Brown Group, Ltd

Lord Longford, *Diary of a Year* Weidenfeld and Nicolson (1982) and *Prison Diary* Lion Publishing (2000) Reproduced with permission of Curtis Brown, London on behalf of The Estate of Lord Longford © Lord Longford 1982 (*Diary of a Year*) and 2000 (*Prison Diary*)

Harold Macmillan, *War Diaries: The Mediterranean 1943–45* (1984); *The Macmillan Diaries: 1950–57* (2003) edited by Peter Catterall; *The Macmillan Diaries 1957–66* edited by Peter Catterall (2012). All published by Macmillan by kind permission of the Macmillan Trustees

Lord Moran, *Winston Churchill: The Struggle for Survival* 1940–65, Constable (1966)

Piers Morgan, *The Insider: The private diaries of a scandalous decade*, Ebury Press (2005) Reprinted by permission of The Random House Group Ltd

Piers Morgan, *Don't you know who I am?* Ebury Press (2007) Reprinted by permission of The Random House Group Ltd

Louis Mountbatten, *Diaries of Lord Louis Mountbatten 1920–22* (1987); *Personal Diary of Admiral the Lord Louis Mountbatten 1943–46* (1988); *From Shore to Shore: The Final Years 1953–79* (1989) all edited by Philip Ziegler, Collins

Chris Mullin, *A View from the Foothills 1999–2005* (2009); *Decline and Fall 2005–2010* (2010); *A Walk on Part 1994–1999* (2011) all edited by Ruth Winstone, by permission of Chris Mullin and Profile Books

Malcolm Muggeridge, *Like it Was: A selection from the diaries of Malcolm Muggeridge* edited by John Bright-Holmes, Collins (1981)

Harold Nicolson, *Diaries and Letters 1907–64* edited by Nigel Nicolson, Weidenfeld and Nicolson (2004) By kind permission of the Nicolson family

Joe Orton, *The Joe Orton Diaries* edited by John Lahr, Methuen (1986)

George Orwell, *Diaries* edited by Peter Hobley Davison, Harvill Secker (2009) Reprinted by permission of the Random House Group Ltd

Peter Pain quoted in *Forged in Fire: The history of the Fire Brigades Union* edited by Victor Bailey, Lawrence and Wishart (1992) by kind permission of the FBU

Michael Palin, *Diaries 1969–79: The Python Years*, Weidenfeld and Nicolson (2006) © Michael Palin 2006. By permission of Weidenfeld and Nicolson, a division of the Orion Publishing Group, London

Frances Partridge, *Everything to Lose: Diaries 1945–60*, Gollancz (1985) by permission of Rogers Coleridge and White

Lance Price, *A Spin Doctor's Diary* Hodder and Stoughton (2005)

J. B. Priestley, *English Journey* Heinemann in association with Gollancz (1934) Reprinted by permission of United Agents on behalf of The Estate of J. B. Priestley

Giles Radice, *Diaries 1980–2001*, Weidenfeld and Nicolson (2004) by kind permission of the Orion Publishig Group, London © 2004 Giles Radice

John Rae, *Old Boys' Network*, Short Books (2009)

John Reith, *The Reith Diaries* edited by Charles Stuart, Collins (1975)

George Riddell, *Lord Riddell's Intimate Diaries of the Peace Conference 1918–23*, Gollancz (1933)

Stephen Spender, *Journals 1939–83* edited by John Goldsmith, Faber and Faber (1985)

Michael Spicer, *The Spicer Diaries*, Biteback Books (2012) by kind permission of Lord Spicer and Biteback Books

Frances Stevenson, *Lloyd George – A Diary* edited by AJP Taylor, Random House by permission of David Higham Associates (1971)

Roy Strong, *The Roy Strong Diaries 1967–1968*, Weidenfeld and Nicolson (1997) © 1997 Roy Strong. Reproduced by permission of Felicity Bryan Literary Agency and the author

David Temple, *The Big Meeting: A History of the Durham Miners*, TUPS Books in association with the Durham Miners' Association (2011). With thanks for the Ramsay MacDonald and James Maxton extracts, by kind permission of David Temple and TUPS Books

Beverley Tinson, *The Gresford Letters: Aftermath of a disaster*, Avid Publications, (2009)

Kenneth Tynan, *Diaries* edited by John Lahr, Bloomsbury (2001) courtesy of Bloomsbury Publishing plc

Evelyn Waugh, *Diaries of Evelyn Waugh* edited by Michael Davie, Weidenfeld and Nicolson (1976) an imprint of the Orion Publishing Group, London © The Estate of Evelyn Waugh 1976

Beatrice Webb, *Diaries 1912–24* and *1924–32* edited by Margaret Cole, Longmans Green and Co (1952, 1956) by permission of Little, Brown Book Group and the London School of Economic and Political Science

Charles Wilson *see* Lord Moran

Jim and Jim Wilson, quoted in Ken and Jean Smith, *Great Northern Miners*, Tyne Bridge Publishing (2008) by kind permission of Ken Smith and Jim Wilson

The Duke of Windsor, *A King's Story: The Memoir of HRH the Duke of Windsor*, Cassell (1951). Extracts of letter from 'Bertie' (later George VI) to 'David' (later Edward VIII)

Virginia Woolf, *The Diary of Virginia Woolf* Vols 2–5 edited by Ann Olivier Bell, published by Hogarth Press (1978, 1980, 1982, 1984) Quentin Bell and Angelica Garnett; reprinted by permission of the Random House Group Ltd; and by kind permission of Houghton Mifflin Harcourt Publishing Company; and with thanks to the Society of Authors, as the Literary Representative of the Estate of Virginia Woolf

Woodrow Wyatt, *Journals of Woodrow Wyatt* Vol. 1 1985–88, Vol. 2 1989–92, Vol. 3 1992–97, all edited by Sarah Curtis, Macmillan (1998, 1999, 2000). By permission of Pan Macmillan, London © Woodrow Wyatt 1998, 1999, 2000

Index

Index

Index